D1379414

Enhanced Cognitive–Behavioral Therapy for Couples

Enhanced Cognitive–Behavioral Therapy for Couples

A CONTEXTUAL APPROACH

Norman B. Epstein and
Donald H. Baucom

American Psychological Association
Washington, DC

Samford University Library

Copyright © 2002 by the American Psychological Association. All rights reserved. Except as permitted under the United States Copyright Act of 1976, no part of this publication may be reproduced or distributed in any form or by any means, or stored in a database or retrieval system, without the prior written permission of the publisher.

Published by
American Psychological Association
750 First Street, NE
Washington, DC 20002
www.apa.org

To order
APA Order Department
P.O. Box 92984
Washington, DC 20090-2984
Tel: (800) 374-2721, Direct: (202) 336-5510
Fax: (202) 336-5502,
TDD/TTY: (202) 336-6123
Online: www.apa.org/books/
Email: order@apa.org

In the U.K., Europe, Africa, and the
   Middle East, copies may be ordered from
American Psychological Association
3 Henrietta Street
Covent Garden, London
WC2E 8LU England

Typeset in Goudy by AlphaWebTech, Mechanicsville, MD

Printer: Port City Press, Baltimore, MD
Cover designer: Naylor Design, Washington, DC
Technical/Production Editor: Jen Powers

The opinions and statements published are the responsibility of the authors, and such opinions and statements do not necessarily represent the policies of the American Psychological Association.

Library of Congress Cataloging-in-Publication Data

Epstein, Norman, 1947-
   Enhanced cognitive-behavioral therapy for couples : a contextual approach / Norman B. Epstein and Donald H. Baucom.
      p. cm.
   Includes bibliographical references and index.
   ISBN 1-55798-912-5 (hardcover : alk. paper)
   1. Marital psychotherapy. 2. Cognitive therapy. I. Baucom, Donald H. II. Title.
   RC488.5 .E66 2002
   616.89'156—dc21   2002001967

British Library Cataloguing-in-Publication Data
A CIP record is available from the British Library.

Printed in the United States of America
First Edition

RC
488.5
.E66
2002

This book is dedicated with love to our wives,
Carolyn Epstein and Linda Baucom
and to our children
Meredith and Christine Epstein
and Brian, Jennifer, and Anna Baucom

CONTENTS

PREFACE

We are delighted to present this book as a product of two decades of our collaboration in developing cognitive–behavioral theory, research, and clinical practice for couples' relationships. The title reflects our emphasis on enhancing the traditional conceptual model and methods of cognitive–behavioral couples therapy (CBCT) by increasing our attention to the characteristics of the two people who have chosen to form a relationship, the interaction patterns that the couple develops to meet individual and relationship needs, and influences of the couple's physical and interpersonal environment. Our enhanced model also involves a developmental perspective on the inevitable adjustments a couple must make over time as the partners and their life circumstances change. Throughout the book, we have attempted to present theoretical and research support for adopting this multilevel, developmental context for understanding and treating relationship problems. Our attention to individual, couple, and environmental factors affecting a couple's relationship significantly increases the ways in which cognitive–behavioral approaches can be useful to therapists with psychodynamic, family systems, experiential, and other theoretical orientations. In this way, we hope to contribute to the current worldwide movement toward integrative approaches to psychotherapy.

One important test of a model is whether it is consistent with personal experience. For us, the components of our enhanced model of relationship functioning closely parallel the development of our own collaborative relationship over the past two decades. As the empirical findings indicate, one key factor in the success of a relationship is a base of similarity in the two individuals' characteristics—basic values or worldview, interests, experiences, and so forth. When we discovered each other's work through our publications and presentations at meetings of the Association for Advancement of Behavior Therapy, we were both struck by similarities in our theoretical views, educational backgrounds, and research interests. Although both of us had developed primary interests in developing assessment and treatment methods to modify distressed couples' behavioral interactions, each of us had a strong background in individual personality theory and research, beginning with our respective graduate educations at University of California at Los Angeles and the University of North Carolina at Chapel Hill. Consequently, as we pondered over research findings suggesting the limited effectiveness of a strictly behavioral approach to treating couples, we turned to characteristics of the individual partners for some answers.

Initially we focused on identifying types of cognition (selective perception, attributions, expectancies, assumptions, and standards) that influence the quality of couples' relationships, and we collaborated on research to develop measures of these variables. For the first decade of our working together, the research that one or both of us had conducted in the areas of cognitive complexity, empathy, gender role beliefs, personality styles, depression, and anxiety was not explicitly woven into our cognitive–behavioral approach to assessing and treating couples. Although our first coauthored book *Cognitive–Behavioral Marital Therapy* (Baucom & Epstein, 1990) was well received by the field, both of us felt that it still fell short of conveying the full sense of the ways in which we sought to understand the unique characteristics of each couple we treated. Given our shared individual characteristic of "thoroughness," the book provided what some have described as encyclopedic descriptions of behavioral, cognitive, and affective factors in relationship distress, as well as methods for assessment and intervention.

However, the basic question of what led some couples but not others to think, feel, and behave in particular problematic ways remained largely unanswered. When we discussed this issue, we discovered that in clinical practice each of us was guided more by our background in the study of individual differences than our publications might suggest. As we made plans for this new book, we were committed to developing a broader cognitive–behavioral model that integrates our understanding of the characteristics that the two partners bring to their relationship. On the one hand, the couple is faced with adapting to demands that each individual's characteristics place on their relationship, for example, meeting each person's differing need for intimacy. In this book we describe ways that therapists can help couples adapt better to individual differences that have been challenging for them.

On the other hand, each partner brings personal resources that can be of great value to the couple as partners experience life together. In terms of our own working relationship, beyond our similarities each of us has brought unique areas of knowledge, clinical experience, and so forth, to our collaboration, and we have learned much from each other over the years. At this point, it is difficult to differentiate the individual ideas that each of us contributed to the end products of the conceptual model and clinical methods that we present in this volume. For that reason, we decided the order of authorship for our first book by a coin toss, resulting in Don being first author, and as agreed, Norm is first author of this second book. Because we cannot remember which ideas were whose, we are glad to take mutual credit for all of them.

The second major focus of our enhanced cognitive–behavioral model, the couple's dyadic patterns, builds on the strong theoretical and empirical bases of behavioral couples therapy that have always been a foundation of our work. The patterns that a couple has developed through efforts to meet each person's needs, as well as those of the couple as a unit, can be sources of stress or of strength. In terms of our own collaboration, we have worked together since the early 1980s, and we consider ourselves to have a successful relationship. Maintaining a mutually satisfying relationship of any type requires flexibility, good communication and problem-solving skills, commitment, and a sense of humor. For example, early in our planning for this book we realized that our ability to develop the complex conceptual model that integrates (a) individual, dyadic, and environmental levels of analysis; (b) behavior, cognition, and affect; (c) developmental processes; and (d) concepts of adaptation to life demands required extended face-to-face meetings, in addition to frequent e-mail and telephone discussions. We located the geographical midpoint between our homes, Chester, Virginia, and scheduled frequent meetings there on weekends and during breaks in our academic schedules. On several occasions during these meetings, just when we thought that we had crystallized our enhanced cognitive–behavioral conceptual model, one of us would interject a comment with the theme, "Uh oh. But what about …," and we both would temporarily feel deflated and overwhelmed. However, some humor and a well-deserved break to watch some basketball or football generally allowed us to regroup and take a fresh look at our conceptualization. Writing a book together, like other major demands in life, requires that two people know not only how to work hard together but also how to adapt and reduce stress. We found our most creative discussions to involve a synergistic process in which we continuously play off each other's ideas. We also have pushed each other to maintain the long process of creating this book, particularly during extended weekends of working on our respective notebook computers in hotel rooms when we would much prefer being at home with our families.

Our enhanced model also reflects the growth of cognitive–behavioral conceptualizations to take into account the important roles that a couple's physical and interpersonal environments play in their life together. In this book we describe ways in which a couple must adapt to demands in their environment and also how the environment can be a source of important resources, such as social support from extended family, friends, social agencies, and so on. Our ability to develop an enhanced cognitive–behavioral model and methods for assessing and treating couples likewise has been facilitated by our turning to resources in our personal and professional environments. As noted earlier, we have expanded the context of our model by integrating knowledge concerning individual difference variables, systems theory, family stress and coping theory, and developmental models. During the past two decades, a growing body of research findings that we review in this book has demonstrated the efficacy of a number of approaches to couples therapy, such as insight-oriented and emotionally focused therapies. Rather than perceiving this evidence as threatening to the status of CBCT, we examine the results and try to determine their implications for expanding our model. Indeed, our model has been broadened to integrate important components of insight-oriented couples therapy (especially the focus on prior relationship experiences, prior trauma, and relatively stable personality styles) and emotionally focused couples therapy (elevating the role of affect in our model to a level of parity with behavioral and cognitive processes). The current openness of cognitive–behavioral researchers and therapists toward consideration of individual differences (personality styles, needs, psychopathology) provides a supportive context for our current work. Clearly, the field and our own thinking have experienced considerable developmental change, and we are excited to contribute to growth of the field through the publication of this book.

At a more immediate level, our ability to sustain the work necessary to develop this book has been facilitated by our working in supportive and stimulating settings. We are very fortunate to be a part of an extremely bright, creative, fun-loving family of couple researchers from around the world. Much of the time it is hard to distinguish whether we are working together or just playing; it is a unique intellectual environment that we wish all scholars could experience. Over the years we have learned a great deal from our colleagues in the Department of Family Studies at the University of Maryland, College Park, and the Department of Psychology at the University of North Carolina at Chapel Hill. Interacting with colleagues with a variety of theoretical approaches to understanding individuals and the relationships they form has challenged our thinking and has encouraged us to integrate individual, dyadic, and environmental systems levels into our conceptual model. Furthermore, the ethnic and cultural diversity of our colleagues, students, and clients, as well as opportunities we have had to collaborate with international colleagues, has increased our understanding of broad cultural and societal factors that affect couples' functioning and that must be considered when deciding how best to help a particular distressed couple resolve their concerns.

Finally, the supportive and loving environments of our two families have been crucial in our ability to maintain our energy and focus over the years that it took to move from the initial conception of the project to the day when we could answer "Yes!" to their periodic teasing question, "Is that book about finished yet?" Life includes many challenges, and this book certainly has been one for us. At times we were unsure that we would survive it, but it truly has helped us grow, as individuals and as a team. We learned a great deal by writing it, and we hope that you, the reader, will find it to be valuable in your research, teaching, and clinical work.

ACKNOWLEDGMENTS

Although this book is the direct product of our work as individuals and as a team, it has come to fruition because of many levels of support that we have received from people in our personal and professional lives. The enhanced cognitive–behavioral model that guides our work emphasizes the multiple levels of resources in people's lives, and we are very grateful that the model has described our circumstances so well. We would like to acknowledge the wealth of support that we have experienced throughout the long process of conceiving and completing what we agree is the most ambitious project that each of us has undertaken in our careers. We also have decided that any attempt to provide a list of specific individuals who have influenced our work would inevitably be inadequate and would risk omitting some people who should be identified. Consequently, for the most part we describe categories of people who have enriched and supported our work.

First, we want to thank the editors at APA books for encouraging us to undertake this substantial project and for their support and flexibility as we revised sections of the book in the course of clarifying our model and determining the best way to present it. Margaret Schlegel began the process with us, validating our belief that we had meaningful new contributions for the field, and Susan Reynolds and Ed Meidenbauer were instrumental in helping us shape the book into its final form. Jennifer Powers made the production process proceed more quickly and smoothly than we ever could have imagined.

Throughout the writing process, we did extensive and repeated editing of each other's chapters. In addition, we benefited from the expertise of skilled, dedicated, knowledgeable people in our lives who understand relationships and who can edit on a professional level. We are truly grateful to Don's wife, Linda Baucom, who copyedited the entire manuscript more than once over a number of years. Many thanks also to Susan Stanton, one of Don's doctoral students, who provided invaluable comments and editing. Their input contributed significantly toward making our organization logical and our writing style more "user friendly."

Our work has been influenced in immeasurable ways by being part of a national and international network of scholars whose work is focused on various aspects of couple and family relationships. In particular, we want to acknowledge our colleagues in the couples research special interest group of the Association for Advancement of Behavior Therapy (AABT), who continue to produce cutting-edge work on theory, research, and clinical practice, in an atmosphere of warm collegiality and collaboration. The AABT couples' SIG is our professional family, where we can count on thoughtful, expert feedback on our ideas, as well as opportunities to learn from individuals who are advancing knowledge on the assessment, treatment, and prevention of relationship dysfunction. A large percentage of the citations to the professional literature in this book involve the work of these colleagues who have contributed so much to our field.

In our more immediate day-to-day professional environments, both of us have been very fortunate to work in academic departments comprised of stimulating, collaborative, supportive colleagues, from whom we have learned a great deal over the years regarding theory, empirical research, and clinical practice. For Norm, the Department of Family Studies at the University of Maryland, and for Don, the Psychology Department at the University of North Carolina at Chapel Hill have provided settings in which we have been encouraged and supported in developing our personal scholarship. Our colleagues freely share their expertise and contribute to making these departments our academic homes. Their ongoing support has been invaluable in our developing and completing this book.

Each of us has been enriched and stretched by working with bright, motivated graduate and undergraduate students who challenge us to examine carefully our theoretical concepts, research methodology, and clinical methods. In particular, those graduate students in our research labs who have collaborated with us on couples research projects and students in our couples therapy courses have helped us refine our thinking about factors affecting intimate relationships, as well as appropriate ways of assessing and intervening with relationship problems. As we wrote this book, we gave it a "trial run" in our couples therapy classes and research labs and were highly encouraged by the positive feedback our students provided. In part the book is our way of giving something back to them—the end product of many years of developing our model and methods and testing them in the research lab and classroom, as well as in clinical practice.

Ultimately the value of our work depends on its relevance for the couples who seek assistance for some of the most personal concerns in their lives. Each of us has had an active part-time clinical practice for decades, and our ways of conceptualizing and intervening with relationship problems have been shaped significantly by getting to know the couples who sought our help. We have felt honored by the trust that they have put in us and impressed by the courage that they have demonstrated in engaging in the often difficult process of couples therapy. Although our enhanced cognitive-behavioral model certainly has been influenced by research findings from our own and others' studies, we have learned immeasurably from observing the limitations that our concepts and methods have had as we have applied them with our clients. We want to express our appreciation to our clients, who over the years have helped us understand the intricacies of living in a long-term intimate relationship and adjusting to both the normative and unpredictable challenges that life brings. If the pages of this book reflect any depth of understanding of couples' subjective personal experiences and interpersonal processes, it is a result of the many hours that we have spent sharing in our clients' lives.

Our greatest resource throughout the course of this project and our adult lives has been our families. We want to express our deepest love and appreciation to our wives, Carolyn Epstein and Linda Baucom, and our children, Meredith Epstein, Christine Epstein, Brian Baucom, Jennifer Baucom, and Anna Baucom, for their steady encouragement, loving support and, last but certainly not least, patience. To undertake and complete a challenging task is rewarding for its own sake, but the experience means so much more if it fits within the fabric of your life. You, our families, are our fabric, and we feel blessed.

I

THEORETICAL AND EMPIRICAL FOUNDATIONS

INTRODUCTION: THEORETICAL
AND EMPIRICAL FOUNDATIONS

This book presents an enhanced cognitive–behavioral model and approach to understanding and treating problems in couples' relationships as well as for building on couples' existing strengths. In this first section we describe the components of the enhanced cognitive–behavioral model and provide empirical support for their importance in couple relationships. We also provide the theoretical and empirical foundation for the clinical assessment and intervention strategies and methods that we detail in Part II.

The enhanced model includes the major foci on behavioral, cognitive, and affective factors that have been prominent in prior approaches, but it adds emphases on (a) broad patterns and core themes in intimate relationships, (b) personal characteristics of the two individuals who comprise the couple, (c) the couple's interactions with their interpersonal and physical environment, and (d) developmental changes in the partners and relationship to which the couple must adapt. In addition, the enhanced model places emotion on an equal footing with behavior and cognition, in contrast to the secondary role that it traditionally has played in cognitive–behavioral approaches. Finally, cognitive–behavioral couples therapy has had a tendency to focus on problematic aspects of couples' relationships, a characteristic it has shared with most theoretical approaches to understanding and treating couples' concerns. Our enhanced model is consistent with recent trends toward recognizing and increasing positive characteristics of close relationships, including strengths, resources, and resiliency.

Chapter 1 provides an overview of the enhanced cognitive-behavioral model. First, the importance of attending to both discrete relationship events and broader or "macro level" patterns and themes is described. Second, the impacts on the relationship of the individual partners' characteristics, including motives or needs, psychopathology, and unresolved issues from past personal experiences, are noted. Third, the importance of elevating partners' emotional experiences to equal status with their behavior and cognitions in clinical assessment and intervention is stressed. Fourth, we describe the role of positive experiences in determining relationship adjustment and satisfaction and explain how our approach attends to a couple's strengths as well as their problems. Fifth, we incorporate aspects of systems theory in emphasizing the reciprocal relationship between the couple and their interpersonal and physical environment (for example, in-law relationships and job demands). The chapter presents a model of couple functioning that places the dyad in a broad context, which includes levels of influence ranging from each individual's personal characteristics, to their dyadic interactions, to their relations with various levels of their environment. The model includes a core assumption that in a well functioning relationship there is a balance between stability and change, and there is potential for growth for each partner as well as for the dyad. Couple therapy is intended to enhance not only the quality of the couple's relationship, but also the fulfillment of each individual's needs.

In chapter 2 we review the state of knowledge concerning positive and negative behavioral factors in couple relationships. We review research findings supporting the importance of both positive and negative behavior in couple relationships, and we illustrate how an individual's behavior may be directed toward one of the members of the couple, the couple as a unit, or the external environment. We distinguish between communication behaviors and noncommunication behaviors. *Communication behaviors* involve expressing one's own and listening to the partner's thoughts and feelings as well as engaging in systematic decision-making or problem-solving steps as a couple. *Noncommunication behaviors* include a wide range of instrumental and affectionate acts, such as working on household chores and doing favors for the other person, which may convey positive or negative messages but are not explicitly intended to convey information, as communication behaviors are. We also review findings concerning gender differences in couple behavioral patterns.

Concerning positive behavior, we discuss issues such as factors that interfere with individuals' expression of their needs to their partners, the characteristics of intimate interactions, couples' relationship-enhancing involvements with their environment, the balancing of instrumental role behaviors, forms of social support that partners may provide for each other, decision-making or problem-solving skills, the impact of family developmental stages on couples' interactions, the link between microlevel behaviors and macrolevel patterns, differences between partners in preferred positive behaviors, and cultural factors that may influence the types of behavior members of a couple are likely to value and exhibit.

In the chapter we review types and functions of negative behaviors directed toward the self, partner, relationship, or environment as well as destructive impacts that such acts have on the individuals and couple. We also describe partners' common responses to each other's negativity. Implications of research findings for creating a balance between positive and negative behavior, particularly over the course of the couple's relationship, are considered.

In chapter 3 we provide an overview of important cognitive and emotional factors that influence the quality of couples' relationships. The forms of cognition we describe are responses to specific events (selective attention, attributions, and expectancies) and broad relationship beliefs (assumptions and standards). Theoretical and empirical literature on these forms of cognition is summarized, as is evidence for individuals' automatic processing of life events, beyond conscious awareness. Implications for clinical assessment and intervention with relationship cognitions are discussed.

Chapter 3 also is intended to elevate the significance of couples' emotions within a cognitive–behavioral perspective. Among positive emotions, we focus on major categories of happy–joyful and close–warm feelings as well as levels of emotional activation involving energy–vigor and relaxation–calm. Concerning couples' negative emotions, we describe the key roles of depression, anxiety, and anger as well as contempt and fatigue. We note the impacts on the couple relationship of each person's transitory positive and negative emotional states versus relatively stable emotional traits, and we review factors in each person's past, the couple's history, and the current quality of the relationship that influence the degrees to which the person experiences and expresses emotions. Finally, we discuss empirical knowledge about the impact of emotions on partners' cognitive and behavioral functioning and consider implications of this knowledge for clinical assessment and intervention.

In chapter 4 we focus on characteristics of individual partners that affect the individual, the couple, and the couple's interactions with their environment. These characteristics include needs or motives, personality styles, clinical and subclinical levels of psychopathology, and unresolved issues from the person's past relationship experiences. We describe the origins, characteristics, and forms of motives as well as empirical findings concerning the impact of partners' motives on the couple's relationship. Major types of motives involving approach are those that are communally oriented (emphasizing connections to others) and those that are individually oriented (emphasizing autonomous functioning, achievement, and control). Other motives involve avoidance of pain or emotional discomfort. In this chapter we discuss gender differences in motives, issues of balancing potentially conflicting motives both within individuals and between partners, and developmental changes that affect couples' conflicts over motives.

In chapter 4 we also review evidence for individual personality styles and temperament (e.g., extraversion, conscientiousness) that may have positive or negative effects on the quality of a couple's relationship. In addition, we review clinical psychopathological disorders, subclinical levels of symptoms, and individuals' long-standing unresolved issues from their prior life experiences that may affect the couple's relationship and that in turn may be affected by the quality of partners' interactions. We illustrate such influences through the example of an individual's depression within the couple context. Potential obstacles to improvement in a partner's psychopathology are discussed; for example, improvement might disrupt patterns that have become familiar and comfortable to a couple.

In chapter 5 we focus on behavioral interactions between partners and between the couple and aspects of their environment. We describe both macrolevel patterns of interaction and the microlevel acts that comprise them. Our enhanced cognitive–behavioral approach pays increased attention to macrolevel patterns and their functions in maintaining stability in a relationship and in facilitating needed changes. We describe evidence concerning particular types of macrolevel patterns that meet partners' communally and individually oriented needs (e.g., rituals, boundary-setting patterns, social support, power–control).

A couple's interactions with their interpersonal and physical environment can have positive and negative impacts on their relationship. In chapter 5 we describe negative effects that environmental demands can have on a couple's ability to meet each other's needs as well as positive resources that the environment can offer the couple for fulfilling their individual and joint needs. We describe various ways that environmental demands may affect a couple's interactions, such as interfering with valued rituals or overwhelming the partners with demands that compete with their ability to fulfill their needs for intimacy with each other, achieving shared life goals, and so on. In contrast, we describe how couples can turn to their environment—such as extended family, religious organizations, and community agencies—for resources. Factors that affect the degree to which couples are willing to use available environmental resources are discussed.

Finally, in chapter 6 we present an adaptation model of relationship functioning, which is a core element of our enhanced cognitive–behavioral approach. We draw on existing models of individual and family stress and coping to emphasize the dynamic, evolving nature of an intimate relationship. A couple is continually faced with adapting to characteristics of the individual partners, the couple as a dyad, and their environment, and these demands may change over time. Whether demands are positive or negative experiences, they place pressure on the couple to respond, and the couple's ability to respond appropriately will affect the quality of their relationship. On the one hand, a couple may experience what we label *primary distress* as a result of individual, dyadic, or environmental demands that interfere with fulfillment of their basic needs for intimacy, autonomy, achievement, and so on. On the other hand, if the couple's attempts to resolve such concerns involve maladaptive patterns, such as mutual verbal attacks or cycles of demand–withdraw behavior, the couple will experience *secondary distress* associated with these dysfunctional solutions to sources of their primary distress.

In chapter 6 we describe several dimensions of demands (e.g., normative vs. non-normative, volitional vs. nonvolitional) and their impacts on the couple. We also detail major types of adaptation strategies, resources on which the couple can draw to cope with demands, vulnerabilities of the individuals and couple that may interfere with coping, and cognitions that may affect a couple's responses to life demands and their use of available resources. Finally, we consider risk factors for a couple developing a crisis state involving disorganized functioning and severe distress when their adaptive strategies fail, as well as the role of the therapist in crisis intervention.

1

INTRODUCTION

In this book we seek to build on the previous cognitive–behavioral models that we and other writers have put forth (Baucom & Epstein, 1990). This expanded cognitive–behavioral model includes a balanced perspective and integration of discrete events and broader relationship themes. We address what each partner as an individual brings to the relationship, the couple's interactive processes, and the role of the environment in couples' functioning. The important role of emotion in relationship functioning is emphasized, and the disproportionate prior emphasis on negatives is balanced by a fuller consideration of the role of positive emotions in healthy, intimate relationships.

Two people fall in love, make a mutual lifetime commitment, and begin to build a life together. Despite their positive feelings toward each other, their attempts to bring pleasure and meaning into each other's life, and the good wishes of families and friends, approximately 50% of couples in the United States who marry end their relationships in divorce (Cherlin, 1992). Furthermore, for about half of the couples who divorce, the relationship will end within the first 2–3 years of marriage. In essence, these marriages have just begun before one or both persons start to question their desire to be with the other (Napier, 1988). Even among community couples who continue their marriages, our surveys suggest that approximately 20% of them appear to be distressed (Baucom, Epstein, Rankin, & Burnett, 1996). These statistics do not include the many couples who enter committed relationships without marrying, only then to end the relationship in distress. At the same time, numerous couples do sustain their relationships and thrive. They either lead lives somehow free of significant complications, or manage to endure major crises, overcoming familial, economic, and sociocultural hardships while experiencing a meaningful, caring relationship that grows with time. How can we understand the various paths and outcomes that these couples experience?

There are clearly no simple answers, and we will not attempt to provide full explanations for these different life courses. However, the field of intimate relationships has experienced a significant growth in theory, basic and applied research, and clinical intervention that has increased our understanding of intimate relationships such as marriage. The development of sophisticated therapeutic interventions for couples based on sound empirical evidence has led to a recognition of couples therapy as a distinct form of mental health treatment, sought out by the public and increasingly supported by health insurance companies.

It is not surprising that various theoreticians, researchers, and clinicians have emphasized certain factors or phenomena in their discussions of committed relationships, highlighting some variables and minimizing others. Although a selective emphasis on certain phenomena is essential to provide coherence and to avoid creating an overwhelmingly complex theory, such a focused view means that other potentially important aspects of couples' lives are de-emphasized in each theoretical model. For example, our own theoretical approach—cognitive–behavioral couples therapy—has been established as an empirically supported intervention for assisting distressed couples (Baucom, Shoham, Mueser, Daiuto, & Stickle, 1998). Even so, it has focused on certain phenomena in intimate relationships while de-emphasizing other important aspects. During the years since we first published descriptions of our cognitive–behavioral approach (e.g., Baucom & Epstein, 1990; Epstein & Baucom, 1989), we have expanded our conceptual model and range of clinical methods. Our goal in this volume is to describe an expanded cognitive–behavioral approach to couples' relationships that provides a broader conceptual perspective and addresses other important areas of couples' lives that have not received adequate attention in the cognitive–behavioral literature.

First, although cognitive–behavioral approaches to couples' relationships have provided useful information about specific behaviors and interactions that have been the targets of therapy (e.g., George does not talk with Jane much at dinner), it has largely neglected the broader patterns and core themes in intimate relationships, such as differences in needs for intimacy (a need for close contact, mutual disclosure, and other forms of sharing in another person's world). We will present a conceptual model that integrates this traditional focus on discrete, detailed behavior within the context of broader relationship patterns.

Second, cognitive–behavioral perspectives have focused on couples' interactive processes, the ways that partners communicate with each other and respond behaviorally to each other. We concur with Karney and Bradbury's (1995) contention that, in addition to the dyad's interactive processes, it is important to attend to (a) the two unique individuals and all that each person brings to the relationship and (b) the context or environment within which the relationship exists, including, for example, demands of children and work, relationships with extended family, the physical health of the partners, and the nation's economy (see Figure 1.1). Therefore, we will discuss the uniqueness of each individual and how that individual's characteristics affect the couple's relationship. This discussion will include a consideration of individual differences among psychologically healthy and well-adjusted partners as well as the role of individual psychopathology in couples' functioning.

Moreover, the environment exerts a significant impact on all couples and, in many instances, external and environmental stressors are major factors in understanding couples' current functioning. The loss of a job, a hostile work environment, or a family's move to an unfamiliar location all place major demands and stress on a couple. Both major stressors and the accumulation of minor stressors can influence a couple's relationship. Therefore, we give a broader consideration to the role of stressors and their impact on a couple's relationship (McCubbin & Patterson, 1983). In doing so we draw heavily from the stress and coping literature.

Third, as the term suggests, cognitive–behavioral approaches have emphasized the roles of behavior and cognitions in relationships. Emotions have not been ignored but have been given somewhat secondary status, being viewed as the result of the partners' behaviors and cognitions. Consequently, by changing behavior and cognitions, the partners' feelings toward each other could be altered. Mate selection in Western cultures is based largely on love, affection, and other positive sentiments, and a major reason for ending relationships is deterioration in those subjective emotions. Consequently, we believe that it is essential to elevate the role of emotions in a discussion of couples' functioning (Johnson & Greenberg, 1994b).

Fourth, cognitive–behaviorists have long differentiated between the positive and negative valences of specific behaviors and cognitions. However, even here there has been a differential emphasis on positive and negative relationship phenomena. As we discuss in subsequent chapters, strong evidence supports the centrality of negative cognitions and behaviors in understanding relationship distress. This evidence has led clinicians and researchers who work from a cognitive–behavioral perspective to give primary emphasis to alleviating negatives, with less emphasis and fewer interventions designed to maximize positives in the couple's relationship. We believe

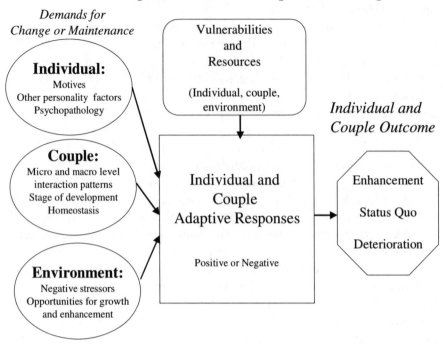

An Adaptation Model of Couple Functioning

Demands for Change or Maintenance

Individual:
Motives
Other personality factors
Psychopathology

Couple:
Micro and macro level
interaction patterns
Stage of development
Homeostasis

Environment:
Negative stressors
Opportunities for growth
and enhancement

Vulnerabilities
and
Resources

(Individual, couple,
environment)

Individual and
Couple
Adaptive Responses

Positive or Negative

*Individual and
Couple Outcome*

Enhancement

Status Quo

Deterioration

Figure 1.1. An adaptation model of couples' functioning.

that for couples to derive maximum fulfillment from their relationships an equal emphasis must be given to the roles of positive behavior, cognitions, and emotions in relationship functioning.

DISCRETE BEHAVIORS AND RELATIONSHIP THEMES

Cognitive–behavioral therapy (CBT) typically focuses on particular, independent incidents, or "micro" behaviors. We propose extending our understanding of these discrete behaviors to clarify how these events form "macro" patterns across the relationship. In chapter 2 we explore the balance between specific behaviors, as previously investigated in cognitive–behavioral approaches, and overall themes in couples' behaviors.

In attempting to understand a couple's relationship it is important to address both (a) discrete relationship events and specific areas of concern and strength and (b) the ways in which these discrete events recur, change over time, and fit with other areas of concern and strength to give meaning to the relationship. These repetitive aspects of relationships and the patterns they form are a critical part of relationship distress and operate at two different levels. First, individual partners and couples have a tendency to repeat the same, or nearly identical, behavior across time. Thus, a husband's pattern of behavior might involve walking into the house every night after work, calling "hello" to family members, and immediately attending to the mail that is on the kitchen counter. At a dyadic level, two partners may consistently respond to disagreements by repeatedly interrupting each other as they express their opinions.

Second, the two individuals involved in this recurring behavioral pattern each experience it in some internal way, often with the two partners having different subjective experiences; that is, when each person experiences these repetitive behavioral patterns that individual often has thoughts and emotions about these events. Thus, a wife may notice her husband's behavioral pattern of focusing on the mail rather than the family when he comes home at night, and she may perceive that it fits with other behaviors, such as his frequent silences during dinner. The wife's internal experiences may begin to become organized around major relationship themes, such as her view of her husband as detached or her feeling that their relationship is distant. Focusing on each of these behaviors separately (mail reading and silence at meals) without understanding how they are interpreted by the wife as parts of a broader theme could easily lead a clinician to make inappropriate or inefficient interventions.

This dual attention to (a) discrete relationship events and specific areas of concern (what we call *microbehaviors*) and (b) the long-term behavioral patterns and relationship themes that evolve (what we call *macropatterns*) requires an expansion of the cognitive–behavioral model we described previously (Baucom & Epstein, 1990). Although there have been exceptions (e.g., Christensen & Heavey, 1990; Jacobson, 1983), cognitive–behavioral approaches to exploring committed relationships generally have emphasized detailed analyses of specific relational events or microbehaviors without commensurate attention to couples' long-term, macrobehavioral patterns and the couple's experiences of relationship themes. Couples who present for therapy often can provide a long list of detailed concerns about their relationships, including a range of specific behaviors that displease them. In many instances, these specific complaints fall into meaningful patterns. The therapist's awareness of the patterns provides insight into the couple's functioning and can lead to the development of a thoughtful treatment plan. As we discuss in chapter 4, on the basis of the typical motivations that people have for entering into intimate relationships, distressed couples are likely to be responding to issues concerning several common relationship themes.

Consistent with this discussion, a guiding principle of this volume is that to understand and assist couples adequately one must focus on both discrete events and specific areas of concern, along with broader behavioral patterns and relationship themes. Many of the cognitive–behavioral interventions that we and others have previously studied continue to be important (cf. Baucom & Epstein, 1990; Jacobson & Margolin, 1979; Stuart, 1980). However, we believe that existing interventions can be more effective if they are used within the context of understanding the broader patterns and themes that characterize couples' relationships.

THE COUPLE AND THE INDIVIDUAL IN RELATIONSHIP FUNCTIONING

Although traditional cognitive–behavioral marital therapy has concentrated on couples' interactions such as communication skills and information processing, we suggest supplementing these approaches with an examination of individuals' characteristics that affect the relationship. In doing so, therapists address not only how a couple interacts but also why they interact in such a manner. As we discuss in chapter 4, an individual's needs, personality, and psychopathology are key components in relationship functioning.

Once a clinician has noted the major behavioral patterns and relationship themes that describe a given couple, he or she is faced with the task of trying to understand why the couple has developed this pattern of behavior, the partners' individual ways of interpreting the relationship, and their emotional responses. To a large degree, early behavioral models of relationship distress (Jacobson & Margolin, 1979) viewed couples' relationship behavior as resulting from normal learning experiences. Partners were viewed as behaving maladaptively either because they had learned to do so or because they lacked the skills to behave appropriately. For example, on the basis of detailed, microanalytic approaches, behaviorists documented communication differences between distressed and nondistressed couples and concluded that distressed couples generally have a skill deficit in communicating (Notarius & Markman, 1993; Weiss & Heyman, 1997). Consequently, it was thought that if distressed couples could be taught appropriate communication skills, then they would communicate differently, and their relationships would improve.

However, the results of behavioral marital therapy outcome studies have demonstrated that in many instances increases in communication skills have not resulted in commensurate improvement in marital adjustment (Halford, Sanders, & Behrens, 1993; Iverson & Baucom, 1990). Also, when behavioral marital therapy has been compared with other theoretical approaches that do not teach behavioral skills, the various interventions typically have been equally efficacious in alleviating marital distress (Baucom, Epstein, & Gordon, 2000; Baucom et al., 1998). Thus, learning behavioral skills is not sufficient for all distressed couples, and some couples benefit from interventions that do not emphasize behavioral skills training.

Recognizing that a strictly behavioral skills deficit model was too restrictive, researchers broadened behavioral models over time into cognitive–

behavioral models of couples' functioning (Baucom & Epstein, 1990). A primary emphasis of these models was placed on taking into account ways in which partners experience their relationships in subjective ways, clarifying the nature of possible cognitive distortions, and helping the individuals reassess their thinking. Cognitive–behavioral approaches have assumed that once the individual processes information about the relationship differently, important emotional changes can be made. For example, if a wife interprets her husband's behavior in a more benevolent way, then she is likely to feel more positively toward him. Again, this perspective assumes that once the partners develop more productive ways of thinking about their relationship, they will use them.

Although there appear to be many instances in which behavioral skills deficits and faulty information processing contribute to a couple's relationship difficulties, a skills deficit model apparently is too limited to account fully for the great variety of processes contributing to difficulties among couples who present with relationship discord. In essence, noting the behavioral excesses and deficits and the distorted cognitions provides an important glimpse of the topography of relationship distress. However, such descriptions do not explain *why* partners behave and interpret each other's behaviors in these maladaptive ways. Proposing that they "don't know any better" and merely need to learn an effective way of approaching a relationship has been a reasonable hypothesis, but we believe that there is adequate empirical evidence at this point to indicate that such an explanatory model is sometimes helpful but often too restrictive.

MOTIVES AND NEEDS IN INTIMATE RELATIONSHIPS

How, then, can one understand a couple's behavior and internal experience as these relate to previously investigated behavioral skills deficits and information-processing errors? We propose that adults seek to meet a variety of important human motives and needs, both communal and individual, within the context of their intimate relationships. Different individuals vary in the strength of these motives and needs, and they use a variety of strategies for meeting them. McClelland (1987) defined a *motive* (which he tended to equate with a need or a drive) as "a learned, affectively charged anticipatory goal state aroused by various cues" that "activates the organism to learn the instrumental responses necessary to bring about the goal state" (p. 132). For example, some individuals appear to be motivated to create a great deal of closeness and intimacy to experience their couple relationship as rewarding and fulfilling. On the other hand, other individuals seem to need less closeness and in fact become uncomfortable and experience a violation of their personal space when a partner seeks to increase emotional closeness. In essence, each partner probably has some range of closeness and intimacy with the other person that he or she finds rewarding. If a person feels too distant from a partner, that individual has several options. He or she can engage in a variety of adaptive or maladaptive strategies to respond to the lack of fulfillment: attempt to create a greater sense of closeness, lash out to express frustration or discontent, withdraw to avoid further frustration, or attempt to accept the situation as it is. This motivation for intimacy is only one example of what we view as communal or relationship-focused motives, which we discuss in this book.

In addition to communal needs for closeness and intimacy, all people have a variety of motives or needs related to individual functioning that affect their relationships in important ways. For example, some individuals have a strong motivation to achieve in the outside world. Such needs and motives can be adaptive for both the individual and the couple but, if not handled appropriately, such strivings can come into conflict with one or both persons' communal needs. We propose that many of the behaviors of distressed couples result from unmet human needs or from maladaptive strategies that partners use in their attempts to meet those needs. As a consequence of our research, we have found that helping couples identify and negotiate the fulfillment of communal and individual needs and the motives of both persons is an essential focus of couples therapy.

Much prior theory and research on needs and motives, derived largely from personality trait theory, might appear to be contradictory to cognitive–behavioral conceptualizations of relationship functioning. However, to propose that an individual has a strong need for intimacy with a partner does not imply that such a need is invariant across time or situations. Instead, it suggests that an individual has a general tendency to desire closeness with a partner. At the same time, this need might be accentuated when the two individuals have had little time together in recent weeks; similarly, this need for closeness might either increase or decrease over the life span of the relationship.

In their recent elaboration of behavioral principles in integrative couples therapy, Jacobson and Christensen (1996) noted the importance of acceptance for successful relationship functioning. One of the most challenging questions deriving from this perspective is, "What should be accepted, and where should there be attempts to promote change?" We believe that one of the most central aspects of acceptance involves a recognition of and understanding that the two partners are different people who may vary considerably in what they need and desire from the relationship. As Lashonda[1] articulated to her husband,

---

[1]We introduce a variety of couples to the reader throughout the book using fictitious first names. All case examples are based on our clinical experience, but background information and details of the cases have been changed to ensure confidentiality.

I know that you need a lot of closeness and intimacy, but I'm just not that way. I never have been, and I don't think I ever will be. It's not that I don't love you; I do. I just don't need the same things from our relationship that you do.

This couple might experience significant difficulty in addressing these differences between the partners. However, being aware of their different needs can be quite important in altering their cognitions, understanding their emotional responses, and formulating behavioral strategies to meet their needs. To integrate the many contributions from cognitive–behavioral conceptualizations of couples' relationships with an understanding of human motives and needs, we draw from a variety of theoretical orientations, such as emotionally focused therapy (Greenberg & Johnson, 1988; Johnson & Greenberg, 1995) and insight-oriented marital therapy (Snyder & Wills, 1989).

PSYCHOPATHOLOGY AND INTIMATE RELATIONSHIPS

The preceding discussion focuses on normal variations in individual differences that can influence relationships (e.g., some partners desire a great deal of closeness; some have a strong need for control). In addition, individual psychological distress or psychopathology is an important factor in intimate relationships. In their review of longitudinal research in marriage, Karney and Bradbury (1995) concluded that neuroticism or negative affectivity in one individual is one of the most consistent predictors of relationship difficulties over time. The dynamics of relationship functioning and individual psychological distress appear to operate in a reciprocal fashion. For example, in their discussion of the relationship between depression and marital distress, Gotlib and Beach (1995) demonstrated how marital distress can lead to an increase in many negative behaviors (e.g., increased aggressive behavior, denigration and criticism, and disruption of routines) and a decrease in positive behaviors for the partners (e.g., decreases in self-esteem support, spousal dependability, and intimacy). For many people, this increase in negatives and decrease in positives can precipitate an episode of clinical depression. Conversely, depression often involves several symptoms that can place stress on a relationship, such as decreased motivation, difficulty meeting daily responsibilities, a self-focused perspective on life, decreased sexual drive, irritability, and a decreased sense of humor (Beach, 2000). Although this example focuses on depression, similar descriptions can be provided about the interrelations between marital distress and several other clinical disorders (Snyder & Whisman, in press).

In some instances, the clinician will conclude that a major factor in the couple's difficulties is one person's long-term alcoholism, anxiety disorder, or other disorder. Often the couple has little idea of how to be of assistance to the individual or how to protect the relationship from the stress associated with the disorder. Several empirically supported interventions have recently been developed that use a couple- or family-based format for addressing individual psychopathology and relationship distress (see Baucom et al., 1998, for a review of the empirical status of these interventions). Later in this book we discuss these "intimate relationships" between individual psychological disturbance and relationship distress, providing guidelines for how the clinician can approach these complex clinical issues.

EMOTIONS IN INTIMATE RELATIONSHIPS

Although not originally considered a major focus of CBT, emotions and the importance of specifically addressing them have been recognized recently by clinicians and researchers. The utility of addressing emotions in distressed couples typically has focused on the reduction of negative emotions. We urge therapists to consider also helping couples examine the role of positive emotions in their relationship. In chapter 3 we discuss the role of emotions and cognitions, paying particular attention to the balance between positive and negative emotions that we believe is necessary for optimal relationship functioning.

An increased emphasis on individual psychopathology and normal variations in human needs and motives implies an increased importance of emotions in couples' functioning. This importance might be obvious in considering psychopathology; however, emotions also are central in a consideration of motives and needs. As noted earlier, McClelland's (1987) definition of a motive involves a learned, affectively charged anticipatory goal state. Often strong, negative emotions result when important needs are not being addressed in a relationship. Frustration, anger, and hurt are likely to develop when a partner does not satisfy certain needs that are important to the other individual. If one person has been unable to have an important need met in his or her intimate relationship with a partner, then simply directing that need to another relationship might not be successful. Consequently, if a wife has a strong motivation for closeness with her husband, but he is unresponsive to her requests or is uncomfortable with closeness, then suggesting that she develop close relationships with female friends might not satisfy her need. Motives and needs occur within a context and are not necessarily easily focused elsewhere. As Frances lamented,

> I don't want to be close to other people; I want to be close to you. You're my husband. It's not like I can rent a movie to pick me up when I'm feeling down. It needs to come from you.

Our model elevates the role of emotions to a level consistent with behavior and cognitions in conceptualizing relationship functioning, integrating an understanding of emotional responses with the various factors just described.

Within the context of attempting to understand and explore emotions in couples' relationships, we believe that it is essential to increase our attention to positive emotions (along with positive behavior and cognitions) and to show how to help couples experience positive feelings toward each other and their relationship. For many years, behavioral marital therapists have noted that positive and negative behaviors do not always operate oppositely of each other. That is, because a husband stops insulting his wife, he may not automatically begin saying affirming things to her: A decrease in his negative behavior does not necessarily lead to an increase in positive behavior. Because negative behavior is so destructive to relationship functioning, cognitive–behavioral couples therapy has placed a great deal of emphasis on decreasing negatives. Unfortunately, much less emphasis has been placed on increasing positive behavior, positive cognitions, and positive emotions. We believe this relative focus on negatives within cognitive–behavioral couples therapy significantly contributes to the finding that only about 50% of couples receiving cognitive–behavioral couples therapy appear to be happy in their relationships at the end of treatment (Baucom et al., 1998). Many couples seek more from life than not being distressed, including contentment, joy, happiness, security, fulfillment, and peace; in this volume we attempt to broaden this emphasis on positives.

It is fortunate that researchers have recently begun to conduct empirical investigations of the importance of positive behaviors among couples. For example, Cutrona and her colleagues (Cutrona, 1996b; Cutrona, Cohen, & Igram, 1990; Cutrona, Hessling, & Suhr, 1997; Cutrona & Suhr, 1994; Cutrona, Suhr, & MacFarlane, 1990) and Bradbury and his colleagues (Bradbury & Pasch, in press; Pasch & Bradbury, 1993, 1998; Pasch, Bradbury, & Davila, 1997; Pasch, Bradbury, & Sullivan, 1997) have demonstrated the important and beneficial effects of partners' provision of support to each other at times when they experience stress in their personal lives. Osgbarby and Halford (1995) described the importance of couples focusing on the positive experiences they have had as a couple, such as reminiscing together about positive events from their past. We believe that not all positives are created equally; some behaviors are more central than others to relationship success, and they are likely to involve important themes, motives, and needs. For example, if one person needs considerable autonomy, then a meaningful gesture from a partner might be an agreement that the partner will care for the children one evening a week while the other goes to the gym to work out alone.

This emphasis on positives need not focus solely on the two partners or the relationship. As we noted earlier, it is important to consider the couple within the context of their environment. We propose that the fullest, most rewarding relationship is one in which the needs of the individuals, the couple as a unit, and their interaction with the environment are all considered. Thus, we discuss how couples can contribute positively to their own relationship by contributing to the community beyond themselves as a couple. Giving time and energy to a community cause (e.g., environmental protection, animal welfare, a religious organization) can help a couple reaffirm their values and sense of purpose in life beyond themselves.

THE RECIPROCAL RELATIONSHIP BETWEEN THE COUPLE AND THEIR ENVIRONMENT

Traditional cognitive–behavioral couples therapy has focused on the negative interactions between the partners. We incorporate systems theory in examining the influence of the environment in producing stressors. In chapter 5 we discuss how couples' vulnerabilities and resources influence their responses to both internal and external stressors. In chapter 6 we use a stress-and-coping model to consider how couples adapt to normative and atypical stressors in the context of the stage of their relationship.

Not only do couples have an opportunity to influence their environment, but they also are affected by forces outside themselves. Many couples experience difficulty either when small environmental stressors build or when major stressors occur and the couple cannot find ways to respond appropriately (Boss, 1988). For example, financial difficulties can occur unexpectedly when a company downsizes, or spouses can find themselves suddenly needing to respond to an elderly parent who has become ill. Such forces push a couple to adapt, and there is much to be learned from the stress-and-coping literature about couples' responses to such events. It is important to understand that the couple is a system and that the partners are part of several other systems, such as immediate family, extended family, and local community. Therefore, characteristics of systems and how systems respond to stress are integral to understanding the couple's response to ever-changing internal and external environments. As a consequence of this, we address how external and internal stressors impinge on a couple's functioning and how the couple's vulnerabilities and resources interact with their environment to influence their relationship at a given point in time.

In addition to atypical, unanticipated stressors most couples will experience several rather predictable stressors as a result of being in their particular stage of life and phase of the family or couple life cycle (Carter & McGoldrick, 1999). Thus, it also is important for the therapist not only to understand a given point in time in the couple's relationship but also to develop a long-term perspective on the couple. The demands on the couple and the focus of the couple are likely to change over time, often in a somewhat predictable fashion. Ask couples how their lives changed with the birth of a first child, and they will report some changes that are predictable as a function of being parents of young children. In general, parents of young children go out less, focus significant energy on raising children with less emphasis on the couple per se, and often are too tired for sex and many other potentially pleasurable activities (Belsky, 1990). When children reach adolescence, the challenges and rewards change: Partners spend considerable time discussing appropriate limits as the children's desire for autonomy increases, and the couple has more time for themselves (one couple discussed in amazement having the opportunity to take a walk on the beach alone as a couple for the first time in 14 years). Thus, these different stages and phases of life place different demands on the couple. Many couples function well until they face a transition or enter into a new phase of family life. Either they do not recognize the need to change how they function, or they recognize the need to change but are unsuccessful in doing so. We discuss later the demands on couples at different phases of the life cycle as normal developmental stressors that most couples will confront.

A CONCEPTUALIZATION OF INTIMATE RELATIONSHIPS AND COUPLES THERAPY

The goal of our enhanced therapy is to provide a broad perspective from which therapists can help couples understand their current situation and work toward an optimal but realistic relationship. In addition to focusing on how individuals think, act, and feel in a relationship, we believe enhanced cognitive–behavioral couples therapy should attempt to identify individuals' needs and personal goals at the same time as it improves how individuals function as a team. We also recommend that therapists help the couple to assess the role that external demands play in their interactions. Finally, placing couples at a particular developmental stage in their relationships should assist couples in determining the desired balance between short-term sacrifices and long-term goals. In chapters 8–14 we provide intervention strategies based on various aspects of couples' functioning described in the first six chapters.

In the preceding discussion, we described many of the factors that we consider in attempting to understand couples' relationships and design effective interventions. To synthesize these various pieces and develop effective interventions, we believe that clinicians, researchers, and theoreticians must rely on a philosophy of couples' relationships that operates either implicitly or explicitly in their work with couples. Therefore, before beginning a more in-depth discussion of important factors in intimate relationships and clinical intervention, we make explicit some of our philosophical perspectives on intimate relationships that incorporate the factors mentioned earlier. These perspectives are influenced by empirical findings, clinical experience, and theory.

We believe that in a healthy, intimate relationship both partners as individuals and the couple as a unit have a sense of efficacy and control over the relationship. Often when couples seek couples therapy they are dispirited, feel helpless or lost, and lack understanding of how to change the relationship. For couples to feel in control of their lives and their relationship, they need to understand themselves as individuals and as a couple. They also need to be aware of how various aspects of the environment affect their relationship. When couples seek treatment, they have typically come to view one or both people and the relationship in rather distorted and negative ways, such as viewing each other's behaviors as intentionally hurtful. The partners' negative perspectives contribute to hurt and angry feelings, along with hostile and/or destructive behavior toward each other. Consequently, a major goal of therapy is to increase the couple's sense of efficacy by helping them to understand and experience their current situation (including each individual, the couple as a unit, and the environment) in a more realistic and well-balanced manner.

For couples to achieve realistic views of the factors that are influencing their relationships, it is critical for the therapist to create a safe environment within which the individuals will feel free to explore all relevant factors. Given that most couples seeking treatment have experienced a significant amount of hurt, they come to treatment feeling defensive and respond in ways to protect themselves. If each person is going to assess his or her own contributions to relationship difficulties, then both persons must experience that they can do so without fear of being attacked or having self-disclosures used against them at a later time.

As suggested earlier, we believe that a healthy, intimate relationship is one in which both individuals continue to grow and develop as unique persons and in which the individuals work together well as a couple. Our research findings indicate that individuals are more satisfied with their relationships if they perceive that their partners contribute to their sense of personal growth and autonomy as well as to the welfare of the couple unit (Rankin-Esquer, Burnett, Baucom, & Epstein, 1997). Thus, it is important for the couples therapist to help each person identify what he or she needs both on a daily basis and in the long term to meet personal goals and be happy. The relationship itself can provide each individual with opportunities for continued growth.

Often both members of a couple and their therapist focus on whether each partner likes and respects the other; however, it is equally important for each individual to like and respect him- or herself within the context of the relationship. Each individual should be challenged to evaluate who he or she wishes to be in an intimate relationship and to determine ways to achieve that identity. Such an identity involves the ways that the person wants to be able to think, feel, and behave within the relationship. For example, Luke stated, "I walk around feeling angry so much of the time, and I don't want to be an angry person." Individuals in distressed relationships usually do not like or enjoy their own behavioral, cognitive, and affective responses within the relationship, or those of their partners. Few people find it gratifying to attack or say hurtful things to other people, yet they often do so within distressed relationships. Most people like to see themselves as caring, thoughtful, giving individuals. We believe that in an optimal intimate relationship each individual is able to say, "I really like and care about you. I also like the kind of person *I* am in this relationship. I like what this relationship brings out in me; I'm a better person because of being in this relationship." That is why it is important to explore concepts such as altruism in intimate relationships. For many people, giving without expecting something in return is an important part of their self-concept and whom they wish to be.

One common factor that interferes with continued personal growth and self-actualization within intimate relationships is that many individuals enter relationships with significant unresolved personal issues, such as the effects of traumatic experiences in previous relationships. Not only are such unresolved issues and psychological problems difficult for the individual who experiences them, but also such individual difficulties are predictive of relationship problems (Karney & Bradbury, 1995). For these individuals, adult intimate relationships can provide opportunities for new experiences, for behaving differently with current partners and having their needs met in appropriate ways. Thus, couples therapy can provide an opportunity for individuals to make important and sometimes fundamental changes in the ways they relate to other adults. Effective couples therapy must address growth and self-actualization within the healthy, optimal range of individual functioning as well as attending to long-standing individual difficulties and psychological distress.

In healthy, intimate relationships such as marriage, the couple also must function well as a team or a unit. There is a massive amount of research data that indicate that happier couples communicate more effectively than distressed couples and are more effective at resolving relationship problems and handling day-to-day tasks and at coparenting as a team. Consequently, it is understandable and appropriate that researchers and clinicians have focused on couples' interactive processes. At times, couples' maladaptive interactions result from skill deficits, such as not knowing how to solve problems effectively. On other occasions, negative interaction patterns are the result of a gradual trajectory that has developed over a long period. Distressed couples who have been married for several years frequently complain that they are spending less time together and devote less energy to communicating with each other. Often this gradual shift has occurred with the birth of children, increasing professional commitments, and so forth. Neither person decided to spend less time with the other, but gradually the relationship has eroded; a form of "relationship drift" has occurred. Consequently, it is important for couples to examine their relationship from a longitudinal perspective to understand how various demands at different points in the family life cycle have affected their current functioning. Often, couples have allowed the demands of day-to-day life to shape the nature of their current relationship. Instead, we believe that it is important for couples to be explicit and proactive in deciding what they want what their relationship to be, and then to build their life around this vision. Doing so requires a realistic assessment of environmental demands and stressors along with a variety of factors that impinge on the couple.

When a couple takes a longitudinal perspective on their relationship, they may need to make decisions that involve temporary sacrifice for one or both persons. For example, a couple might decide that while they have young children, one of them will stay at home with the children and not work outside of the home. This decision can involve a financial sacrifice for both people as well as a professional sacrifice for the individual who stays at home. Consequently, the couples therapist must help the couple define a healthy sense of balance, taking into account the needs of each individual, the couple, and other family members, and demands and opportunities in the environment. All of this must be accomplished while viewing the current situation as a particular point in a lengthy family developmental life cycle that will produce different circumstances in the future.

This emphasis on achieving balance within the context of a particular point in the family life cycle has implications for understanding healthy, intimate relationships. For example, several investigators have concluded that spouses become less happy with their marriages after the birth of children (Belsky, 1990). Often such results are interpreted to mean that children are bad for marriages. We believe, however, that many criteria are important in assessing happiness within a healthy, adaptive, long-term relationship. Few people would describe being happy in terms of getting up in the middle of the night with a sick child, suffering long-term sleep deprivation, and having less time and energy to devote to a partner whom one loves. At the same time, having children can be deeply gratifying and fulfill a long-term desire for the couple, such that the partners are willing to endure the hardships of parenting to fulfill their wish to nurture children. Individuals and couples frequently must make temporary sacrifices and forego momentary happiness to fulfill long-term goals. The therapist can assist the couple in evaluating how well they are adapting to normative stressors such as the demands of parenting. In addition, the therapist can help the couple evaluate whether they have made plans to alter their relationship appropriately as they enter different developmental phases of their relationship (e.g., "We will structure our schedule around your on-call schedule while you are in medical residency training, but when the training is finished, we need to re-evaluate how we spend our time").

Understanding healthy individual differences and vulnerabilities, unresolved personal issues, psychopathology, what the couple or family needs as a unit, and sources of external stress and support can assist a couple in making good decisions. These decisions often involve one or both persons agreeing to make certain behavioral changes. At other times, couples come to understand that behavior change is not needed, preferable, or possible. As the couple gains a new understanding of the situation through cognitive restructuring and emotional change, they are at times able to accept certain aspects of their relationship that previously were troubling (Jacobson & Christensen, 1996). On other occasions, they conclude that continuing their relationship is not the healthiest solution for one or both of them. If the couple has made significant efforts to address relationship concerns and has evaluated their relationship reasonably, then we believe that divorce or termination of the relationship can be viewed as a reasonable and adaptive resolution from a mental health perspective. However, such a solution typically involves significant pain and difficulty for one or both persons, along with other family members, such as children. We have worked with many couples over the years who likely would be happier and have a greater opportunity for personal fulfillment if they terminated their relationship. Given that divorce affects a number of people, the decision often is complex, because what is optimal for one person might be destructive for other persons involved in the situation. In the intervention section (chapters 8–14) of this book we discuss the role of the couples therapist in helping couples make this difficult decision. At the same time, we believe that divorce has become much too commonplace in Western cultures, particularly the United States, and this book is devoted largely to helping couples make their relationships work.

SUMMARY

In this chapter we have provided an overview of our enhanced cognitive–behavioral model of relationship functioning. This approach incorporates new empirical findings, seeks linkages among various theoretical perspectives, and attempts to redress imbalances in earlier cognitive–behavioral models of relationships.

- The enhanced cognitive–behavioral model of couples' relationships presented in this book examines characteristics of the couple's relationship, the individual, and the external environment.
- In addition to reviewing the field's knowledge about specific "micro" behaviors and their associated cognitions and emotions, we discuss in chapters 2 and 3 how these specific behaviors, cognitions, and emotions form broader "macro" patterns and themes important to the conceptualization of couples' functioning.
- We give new emphasis to the importance of positives and emotion in couples' relationships, described most prominently in chapter 3.

- In chapter 4 we address the role of individual differences, including variations in needs and motives, personality characteristics, and individual psychopathology in relationship functioning.
- The enhanced cognitive–behavioral model makes use of contributions from various theoretical orientations. In chapter 5 we incorporate a systems perspective when looking at the couple's reciprocal relationship with their environment; in chapter 6 we use a stress-and-coping model to assess the couple's current functioning within the context of normative and unexpected stresses at given stages of the life cycle.
- The intervention section of this book, chapters 8–14, grows out of the conceptualization of the previous chapters. Thus, intervention strategies take into account individuals' psychological functioning, the couples' interactive process, and the couples' reciprocal relationship with their environment.
- Although the interventions we describe in this book appear more complex than those in traditional CBT, we believe many cognitive–behavioral couples therapists have been considering these factors even though they have not been systematically discussed. We draw on new, empirically validated intervention strategies to make explicit what seems to have been implicit in traditional cognitive–behavioral couples therapy.
- We attempt to provide a broad-based discussion of various factors that clinicians can take into account when assessing a couple; however, the therapist's task is to decide the extent to which the various factors are applicable to each couple's assessment, treatment plan, and intervention strategies.

2

BEHAVIORAL FACTORS IN COUPLES' RELATIONSHIP PROBLEMS

In this chapter we highlight the role of positive and negative behaviors in couples' relationships. These behaviors may be directed toward the partner, self, couple, or environment. By exploring (a) the types of positive and negative behaviors common in couples' relationships, (b) the reasons and patterns for such behaviors, and (c) the impact of behaviors on the individuals and the couple, we provide a framework for understanding the various patterns of couples' behavior. In addition, we address the developmental stages, cultural context, and frequencies of large and small acts of kindness that also can affect the expression of positive behaviors.

When a distressed couple sits for the first time in a clinician's office and begins to describe their relationship, the clinician quickly sees what empirical findings repeatedly demonstrate: Overall, compared to happy couples, distressed partners engage in much less positive behavior and much more negative behavior toward each other (cf. Baucom & Epstein, 1990; Gottman, 1994a; Halford, Kelly, & Markman, 1997; Weiss & Heyman, 1997). Although each couple presents different behavioral excesses and deficits, distressed couples often demonstrate one of three patterns of positive and negative behavior. First, and perhaps this is the stereotype of distressed couples, some couples present as angry, conflicted, and hostile, with an excess of negative behaviors toward each other, along with few positive behaviors. Second, often evidenced among those who have been together for several years, couples complain because the relationship feels somewhat devitalized; that is, there is a deficit of meaningful, rewarding positive behaviors between the two partners. For these couples, often there is not an excess of negative behaviors; there simply is little life in the relationship, with few negatives or positives. Finally, some distressed couples demonstrate a high level of both positive and negative behaviors. These relationships can be experienced as "stormy." The couple vacillates or experiences a blend of both positive and negative behaviors that makes them ambivalent about their relationship. Such couples might have torrid arguments only to experience subsequent periods of reconciliation and tenderness.

Along with other investigators, cognitive–behavioral researchers have devoted considerable energy to detailing the specific microbehaviors and behavioral patterns demonstrated by distressed couples. In doing so, these researchers have studied both communication and noncommunication behaviors. *Communication behaviors* include interactions that involve expressing and listening to each partner's thoughts and emotions as well as seeking possible solutions to specific problems. In contrast, *noncommunication behaviors* include a wide variety of instrumental and affectionate acts (e.g., working on household tasks, doing favors for each other) that partners exchange during daily interactions. Such behaviors certainly can convey either positive or negative messages to their recipients, and research studies have demonstrated associations between rates of pleasing and displeasing partner behaviors and the recipients' levels of relationship satisfaction (Baucom & Epstein, 1990; Weiss & Heyman, 1990a). However, we have labeled them *noncommunication* behaviors to distinguish them from behaviors that are explicitly intended to convey information from one person to another. Both communication and noncommunication behaviors are important in understanding a couple's functioning.

POSITIVE BEHAVIOR IN INTIMATE RELATIONSHIPS

Mounting empirical evidence supports positive behavior as a key to unlocking the secrets of a happy relationship, but psychologists have failed to present a satisfactory theory of positive behavior in close relationships. Although frequent negative behaviors may be the hallmark of distressed couples, positive behaviors appear to elevate couples from the nondistressed range to the optimal range of functioning. Several investigators have asked individuals to report on the presence or absence of specific pleasing and displeasing behaviors from their partners. In general, the findings confirm that happy partners report more pleasing and fewer displeasing behaviors compared to distressed partners (Barnett & Nietzel, 1979; Birchler, Weiss, & Vincent, 1975; Broderick & O'Leary, 1986; Halford & Sanders, 1988; Jacobson, Follette, & McDonald, 1982; Margolin, 1981). In addition, when spouses are asked to record both pleasing and displeasing behaviors on a daily basis and then to rate their marital satisfaction for the same day, their daily ratings of marital satisfaction are correlated with a higher frequency of pleasing and a lower frequency of displeasing behaviors (Christensen & Nies, 1980; Jacobson et al., 1982; Jacobson, Waldron, & Moore, 1980; Margolin, 1981; Wills, Weiss, & Patterson, 1974).

Similarly, when couples are asked to communicate with each other, and their communication is coded with any one of a variety of observational coding systems, the findings generally corroborate the importance of positive communication. Although the findings are not totally consistent, several studies have demonstrated that happy couples exhibit a higher rate of positive communication than do distressed couples when the partners are having a conversation with each other (e.g., Birchler et al., 1975; Revenstorf, Hahlweg, Schindler, & Vogel, 1984; Schaap, 1984). However, the specific positive communications that differentiate happy and distressed couples do not appear to be consistent across various investigations. In a review of the role of positive communication in marital functioning, Osgarby (1998) concluded that, although findings are not consistent across studies, evidence exists for the following differences between satisfied and distressed couples:

> Satisfied couples used more assent (Margolin & Wampold, 1981; Schaap, 1984), approval and caring (Birchler, Clopton, & Adams, 1984; Schaap, 1984), empathy (Birchler et al., 1984), humour, smiling and laughing (Margolin & Wampold, 1981; Revenstorf et al., 1984; Schaap, 1984), positive physical touch (Margolin & Wampold, 1981; Revenstorf et al., 1984) and problem description and solution (Birchler et al., 1984; Margolin & Wampold, 1981; Schaap, 1984). (p. 24)

Although there is clear evidence that positive behaviors are important in couples' functioning, we are somewhat limited in having an articulated theory with supporting empirical evidence to understand these important positive phenomena. To develop a clearer understanding of the role of positive behavior in couples' functioning, it is important for both couples and therapists to have a way of categorizing positive, potentially meaningful behaviors. There is no agreed-on typology of positive behaviors within committed relationships, but there appear to be at least two major categories that are related to marital adjustment. Elsewhere we and our colleagues have referred to these as two major forms of investment, or ways that the partners can give to their relationship (Baucom, Epstein, Daiuto, & Carels, 1996; Baucom, Epstein, Rankin, & Burnett, 1996). First, partners can engage in *expressive* behaviors that signify caring, concern, affection, and love. These behaviors have little to do with the pragmatics of life; instead, they focus on the emotional aspects of a relationship, of helping a partner feel cared about and valued. Second, partners can engage in positive, *instrumental*, or task-oriented acts that help to maintain the relationship. Money must be earned; food must be prepared; a variety of household tasks must be accomplished; decisions must be made. Feeling that they are working together effectively as a team to accomplish the tasks of the couple or family can be important for a couple's sense of "coupleness" and feelings of being respected as individuals. In addition, it is difficult for the couple to continue to progress in an organized manner if these tasks are not completed.

The Focus of Positive Behaviors

Positive and negative behaviors also can differ in their focus: They typically are aimed toward one of the two individuals in the relationship, the couple as a unit, or some aspect of the external environment. To enhance or maintain the relationship, a partner might need to direct his or her efforts in a given way. For example, some individuals are very "other-directed," which can be positive in meeting other people's needs. However, when carried to the extreme, other-directedness can lead to self-neglect, resentment, and depression. Similarly, other persons have become too self-focused and might be encouraged to focus more of their efforts on pleasing their partners and contributing to the well-being of the relationship as a unit. Likewise, some couples find it rewarding and fulfilling to devote time and effort together as a couple to give back to society in some meaningful way.

For heuristic purposes, in this chapter we describe a specific behavior as having a given focus; in reality, however, a single behavior often has multiple impacts. That is, in many instances, a given behavior will affect both partners and the relationship as a whole. For example, when Kendra was feeling ill, Jamal volunteered to come home early to take their daughter to her soccer game, and he stayed to watch the game. His behavior was intended to assist Kendra, but he also felt good about himself as a caring husband. In addition, it gave him a rare opportunity to spend time alone with his daughter and celebrate her athletic prowess. Also, most partner behaviors do not occur in isolation, in a unidirectional fashion. Typically, one person behaves, and the other person responds, with partners mutually influencing each other. If Jamal changes his schedule to help Kendra when she is sick, she is more likely to respond to him in positive, caring ways as well.

This tendency for a positive behavior from one partner to increase the likelihood that the other partner will respond in a positive manner is referred to as *positive reciprocity*. Similarly, the increased likelihood that a negative behavior from one partner will evoke a negative behavior from the other partner is called *negative reciprocity* (Gottman, 1979). Although negative reciprocity exists for both distressed and nondistressed couples, it appears to be a stronger phenomenon for distressed couples. Distressed couples also maintain negative reciprocity for longer sequences of interaction. As distressed couples frequently note, once they begin to argue, the argument takes on a life of its own, and they have difficulty stopping it. The importance of both positive and negative reciprocity in relationships cannot be overstated. A single behavior can have a ripple effect, ultimately affecting the two individuals, the relationship, the outside environment, or some combination of these.

Positive Expressive Behavior

Focusing on the Partner

As noted earlier, positive, expressive behaviors (acts of caring, concern, and affection) can be aimed toward an individual member of the couple, either the partner or the individual engaging in the behavior. Among distressed couples, one person frequently complains that the other individual has decreased or stopped providing caring and loving acts toward him or her. The kinds of behaviors that individuals find to be caring and loving are likely to differ from one person to another. Some individuals value thoughtful acts, such as giving flowers or cards, because they signify that an individual is being remembered. Similarly, some individuals value physical, affectionate behavior as a way of showing care and warmth.

Many partners clarify that they would be happy to engage in caring, thoughtful, loving acts for their mates, but they do not really know what to do. We believe each person is responsible for remaining attentive and finding ways to express caring for the partner. At the same time, having the partner clarify what he or she enjoys or finds meaningful can be helpful. Some individuals experience difficulty asking their partners for what they like, prefer, or need. At least three factors can be at work here. First, one person might believe that it is inappropriate or "pushy" to ask a partner for what he or she wants. Second, many partners clarify that it detracts from the meaning of the actions if they have to *ask* someone to be loving or thoughtful. This sentiment seems to be particularly true if an individual makes a request for a behavior to occur during a specific interaction. Saying "it would really be nice if you brought me some flowers tonight" would probably reduce its meaning for most people, both the giver and receiver. However, partners might be much more amenable to providing general input about preferences to the other person, such as "I really like it when you call during the day. It just makes the day a little brighter." Third, even if the person believes that such a request is appropriate, he or she still might have difficulty expressing those desires, wishes, or needs. In such instances, teaching the couple emotional expressive skills might be important.

Not only is positive, expressive behavior toward a partner important on an ongoing basis, but it might also be particularly important when an individual is experiencing personal distress. Within such a context, these behaviors can be viewed as a form of *social support*; that is, when one person is distressed about life issues outside the relationship, he or she might turn to the partner for support. In their Social Support Behavior Code, Cutrona and her colleagues described 23 different support-intended communications that partners might offer to each other (Cutrona, Suhr, & MacFarlane, 1990). These behaviors fall into five categories:

> emotional support (communicating love, concern, or empathy); esteem support (communicating respect and confidence in abilities); informational support (providing information about the stress itself or advice on how to deal with it); tangible aid (providing or offering to provide goods or services in the stressful situation); and social support network (communicating commonality with or belonging to a group of persons with similar problems or interests). (Cutrona, Hessling, & Suhr, 1997, p. 384)

The first two of these categories, emotional and esteem support, fall within the context of expressive behaviors. Thus, when one person is struggling with a stressful situation, the partner often can be of assistance by expressing concern for the individual, along with demonstrating respect for the person and, where appropriate, confidence in the individual's ability to confront the situation. Individuals might differ regarding the kinds of social support they value, and the forms of support each person prefers also might vary according to the types of situations that he or she is confronting. At times, an individual might want someone to listen and provide emotional support; on other occasions the person might want advice or assistance with household tasks so he or she can devote energy to coping with a very stressful situation.

Focusing on Oneself

Whereas couples and therapists often think of an individual's positive, expressive behaviors as being directed toward a partner, it also is important to recognize the importance of directing such behaviors toward oneself; that is, relationships might well benefit when individuals pamper or do nice things for themselves. Taking care of oneself can be a significant issue for young couples with children. Women with young children frequently devote considerable energy to supporting the needs of the children and their partners. To avoid resentment, rejuvenate themselves, and maintain a sense of self-worth, they also need to treat themselves well—for example, by giving themselves time with friends without the children present. Such efforts are likely to require the cooperation and support of the partner because there are so many competing demands for time and energy.

Focusing on the Couple

Some expressive behaviors might focus on the couple as a unit. One individual might decide to "do something nice for us as a couple," such as

EXHIBIT 2.1
Prager's (1995) Components of Intimate Interactions

1. Share personal information exclusively with partner.
2. Create positive emotional tone between partners.
3. Feel heard or understood by partner.

planning a weekend for the couple to relax and get away from their typical environment. Such a weekend can provide the partners with an opportunity for much-needed time together, and it signals to both partners that they are important and deserve to be pampered on occasion.

In addition to a wide variety of noncommunication expressive behaviors, partners often demonstrate their desire to relate in an emotional realm through their communication with each other. We (Baucom & Epstein, 1990) noted that couples typically communicate with each other for one of two reasons: (a) to share their thoughts and feelings with each other or (b) to reach a decision or resolve a conflict. At times, the expression of thoughts and feelings can be used for the purpose of self-disclosure or to create an experience of closeness between the two partners. As Prager (1995) pointed out, "All conceptions of intimate interactions seem to center on the notion that intimate behavior consists of sharing that which is personal" (pp. 20–21). More specifically, Prager and Buhrmester (1998) demonstrated that intimate interactions typically involve three components (see Exhibit 2.1): (a) sharing of personal information that typically is not disclosed to other people, (b) creating a positive emotional tone between the two partners, and (c) feeling heard or understood by one's partner. Given these findings, it appears that sharing one's thoughts and feelings with a partner does not ensure a sense of closeness. If the other person does not listen or understand, the couple is unlikely to experience the interaction as an intimate encounter. Thus, intimate interactions truly involve a couple-focused, interactive process.

Focusing on the Environment

Finally, caring and thoughtful acts might be directed outside of the couple, toward their environment. For example, Sean and Eric decided to forego giving each other expensive gifts for a holiday; instead, they used a comparable amount of money to purchase a plane ticket for their nephew to visit them over the holidays. When asked why they found this to be meaningful, Eric replied,

> It was a way for us to put our money where our mouth is. Since my sister got divorced and moved away, we rarely get to see my nephew. It was a way to tell him, and to remind us, that we really care about him.

Sean added,

Maybe it's strange, but it actually helped Eric and me feel closer to each other. When we do something together for other people, it makes me feel good about us as a couple. I like to feel like we're good people who do things for other people, not just for ourselves.

As Sean suggests in this example, focusing efforts outside of the relationship and the family in altruistic ways can be important in helping the couple explore and affirm where they fit into a larger societal context. Some couples devote significant energy to environmental causes, religious organizations, or philanthropic societies. Often these efforts involve a combination of expressive and instrumental behaviors. Involvement in these activities can be meaningful to couples because they can clarify what they believe in and value. Moreover, many couples have a strong desire to affiliate with others outside of their own relationship. Therefore, they might be rewarded by activities such as entertaining other couples for the evening or hosting group meetings to get to know other couples.

Positive Instrumental Behavior

The preceding discussion emphasizes the importance of caring and thoughtful expressive behavior in helping a couple develop and maintain the emotional climate within the relationship. In addition, many tasks must be performed, and decisions reached, for the relationship to function adaptively. As Sarah commented, "We really work well together as a team. It's pretty clear who is to do what in our relationship, and we're pretty effective at it."

Such instrumental behaviors can be important for a variety of reasons. First, accomplishing tasks and making decisions are important for the relationship to proceed smoothly. Second, when tasks are not accomplished, or decisions are not made in a satisfactory manner (or both), negative feelings between the partners often result. This negative mood then affects whether partners are likely to engage in a variety of caring and affectionate behaviors. Third, and quite important, is that at times these instrumental behaviors carry meaning to the partners. Thus, mowing the lawn might not only be mowing the lawn; it might signify to one person that the partner is committed to the relationship. As with expressive behaviors, instrumental behaviors can be focused on one's partner, oneself, the couple, or the environment.

Focusing on the Partner

Either through explicit discussion or through a more implicit, evolutionary process within the relationship, partners typically adopt given roles. A significant aspect of these roles involves the tasks or responsibilities that each person assumes. For example, one person might be responsible for paying monthly bills and balancing the checkbook, while the other partner assumes responsibility for buying groceries, preparing meals, and cleaning up after meals. Although it does not seem to be essential that both partners contribute 50% to such tasks for the relationship to proceed smoothly or for the couple to be satisfied, it does seem to be important that there be some sense of equity, that both persons are contributing to the relationship in a reasonable way.

Although there is no research bearing on this issue, it appears that the proportion of the instrumental responsibilities that each individual assumes is not the only relevant factor; rather, the focus of the acts also is important. The couple's relationship is likely to be more rewarding if each person focuses some instrumental behaviors on the partner. For example, one person might pick up the other's laundry or assume responsibility for servicing the other person's automobile. Individuals generally seem to appreciate their partners' doing something for them as individuals. It contributes to a sense of feeling valued. Therefore, even without redistributing the total amount of chores and responsibilities that each person will assume, these tasks can be redistributed such that each person is focusing some time and energy on the partner.

The preceding discussion highlights the importance of focusing instrumental efforts toward one's partner on a day-to-day basis. In addition, each person's willingness to engage in behaviors that facilitate the other's long-term goals and desires appears to be important. For example, one partner might agree to move to a new location and accept a less desirable job to facilitate the other partner's ability to return to school. Although it is unlikely that most couples sit together and develop a five-year plan, it can be helpful for couples to find some way to clarify what each person needs and desires in the long term for individual fulfillment.

Instrumental behaviors can be particularly important as a form of social support when one partner is confronting a significant stressor. As noted earlier, two major categories of social support that Cutrona, Suhr, and MacFarlane (1990) identified during partners' interactions are relatively focal to instrumental social support: tangible aid (providing assistance or services needed during the stressful situation) and informational support (providing information about the stress or offering a suggestion about how to deal with the stress). Failure to receive instrumental support along with emotional support at important times can feel traumatic. As Rachel explained to her husband,

> I don't think I'll ever get over the fact that I had to drive myself and our new baby home from the hospital when she was born. Your feeling that you had too much work to do to see your first child come home is unimaginable to me.

For many people, having a partner to count on during difficult times in life is an extremely important part of a meaningful, rewarding relationship.

Focusing on Oneself

As noted previously, it is important for individuals to do nice things for themselves. Individuals also can engage in task-oriented behaviors focused on themselves. Some individuals focus on the needs of a partner, the relationship, or a profession and fail to attend to their own day-to-day needs. For example, some partners report that they cannot find the time to purchase clothes that they need, respond to correspondence, or eat lunch. In such instances the individual and the couple might have allowed their schedules to drift gradually out of control. In addition, one or both partners may have adopted a personal standard that it is inappropriate or selfish to focus on one's own instrumental needs.

Second, individuals must learn to accomplish tasks for themselves and take appropriate responsibility as adults. Some individuals seem to develop a dependent relationship with their partners in which their partners "take care of them." For example, Gabriela complained to her partner, "You want me to put your dishes away when we finish a meal. You seem to expect me to bring you a beverage or make you a snack when you are just as free as I am." And then come the dreaded words: "I'm not your mother." Having one's partner "spoil" oneself on occasion or take over when assistance is needed can contribute to feelings of well-being within the relationship. However, if these requests for task-oriented assistance are excessive or are not reciprocated, the "giving" partner is likely to feel devalued, unappreciated, or neglected. Such tendencies can be disruptive to the relationship, because the other partner is likely to experience an imbalance in the relationship, with a lack of the positive reciprocity that is a key factor in healthy relationships.

The preceding discussion, in which we addressed instrumental behaviors focused on one's partner, differentiated between smaller, day-to-day actions versus major behavioral acts, such as taking on a second job to support a partner's career aspirations. This same differentiation between day-to-day activities and major goals also applies to focusing on oneself. In many instances, one or both partners devote their efforts to the demands of their current, day-to-day existence, to the exclusion of addressing their long-term goals for themselves and their lives. Many couples seek professional assistance when one or both persons appear to have a midlife crisis. Such crises frequently arise when an individual recognizes that his or her direction in life or the roles that he or she has assumed are not gratifying or rewarding.

In essence, the efforts of both individuals need to strike some balance between meeting the needs of each person and the relationship. In previous cognitive–behavioral formulations a primary emphasis has been placed on how each individual can contribute to the well-being of the relationship. Much less emphasis has been placed on the importance of meeting the individual needs, goals, and desires of the two persons comprising the couple. The balance between individual needs and the needs of the relationship is likely to vary across couples and individuals, as a function of the individuals involved and their cultural backgrounds. For example, in current mainstream American culture there appears to be a significant emphasis on the individual's autonomous functioning; however, in many Eastern cultures there is much greater emphasis on the needs of the group (Hsu, 1985; Stevenson, Chen, & Lee, 1992). People with these latter cultural backgrounds might feel selfish personally and question the credibility of the therapist if major emphasis is placed on meeting individual needs.

Focusing on the Couple

In some instances it might be artificial to differentiate between instrumental, task-oriented behaviors that are focused on an individual versus behaviors that are focused on the couple. For example, assuming household chores as an individual means that one's partner will not be overburdened; it also increases the likelihood that the relationship will function more smoothly. Both persons benefit from dishes being cleaned and garbage being removed.

At least two difficulties appear to arise with regard to these couple- or family-focused instrumental behaviors. First, partners often disagree about the distribution of these tasks and what is considered an equitable distribution, given the additional contributions that both persons make to the relationship. Thus, if one person works full-time outside the home, and the other person does not work outside the home for a paid salary, how are household tasks and chores to be distributed? If both persons work full-time outside the home, how are additional responsibilities to be handled? Even though married women with full-time paid jobs spend significantly less time on household tasks than those who are not employed outside the home, they still spend much more time on such tasks than their husbands do. Couples who have conflicts between work and family roles or an unequal distribution of housework are more likely to experience marital distress (Barling, 1990).

Second, in addition to the distribution of household tasks and other instrumental responsibilities, often one partner complains about having assumed a role that we call *the family manager*. This role involves keeping abreast of the various tasks that have to be accomplished, attending to the needs of different individuals, assessing available resources, and integrating the schedules of different family members. If children are involved, this task often includes knowing who needs to go where on which days, scheduling parent–teacher conferences, making certain that meals are ready when various family members arrive at the end of the day, and so on (Leslie, Anderson, & Branson, 1991). Although having one person in charge might be efficient and beneficial for the overall well-being of the family, difficulty can arise when the person serving as the family manager has never explicitly agreed to assume this role. Instead, the role has evolved without explicit discussion or agreement, often according to who is working outside the home and who is at home or with the children more often. Furthermore, the responsibilities associated with this role appear to falls on women more often than on men regardless of the partners' employment situations (Leslie et al., 1991). As Ashley clarified,

> It's not just the amount of household chores and other tasks that I have. It's also that I'm the one responsible for keeping up with everything. It's exhausting. Richard is willing to "help out" when asked to, but that's not the point. I need for him to take responsibility for seeing what needs to happen.

Ashley voiced what many family managers experience: When one partner assumes the role of family manager, the other partner feels free from having to think about those responsibilities.

Some couples function satisfactorily with a general family manager, but others experience distress. Some couples successfully address this concern by establishing domains within which each person assumes responsibility. For example, one partner might become the family manager for finances and oversee the budget, savings, and investments, whereas the other partner might assume primary responsibility for overseeing the children's schedules.

It can be helpful to differentiate between who actually carries out a given task versus who assumes the managerial role for overseeing that tasks in a given domain are accomplished. The person responsible for overseeing the budget is not necessarily the only individual who writes checks and produces income. Helping couples to differentiate between the roles of family manager versus implementer of a task can be enlightening and helpful. This distinction can help couples to renegotiate who will assume the "managerial" role in a given domain, along with discussing who will carry out which chores and responsibilities.

As implied throughout our discussion of instrumental activities, often partners need to negotiate how various tasks and responsibilities will be accomplished. At times, couples attempt to have goal-directed decision-making or problem-solving conversations addressing such issues. Although not all decision-making or problem-solving interactions focus on instrumental behaviors, many of them do. As Bennun (1985a, 1985b) has demonstrated, behavioral couples therapy that focuses on problem solving is particularly successful for addressing instrumental concerns. Numerous research investigations have consistently found that distressed couples experience significant difficulties when they attempt to make decisions as a couple, particularly in areas of disagreement. More specifically, distressed couples are less likely to engage in positive, cooperative communications during these interactions and are more likely to engage in negative, hurtful communications. For example, Gottman (1994a, 1994b) found that criticism and contempt, along with defensiveness and withdrawal, predict long-term distress and instability.

Broader patterns of interaction during problem-solving conversations also are important. Christensen and his colleagues developed the Communi-

EXHIBIT 2.3
Association Between Stages in Relationships and Positive Behaviors

Courtship	Frequent, varied, positive, expressive behavior
Early years	Substantial decrease in positive behavior due to demands of startup activities; for example, birth of a first child
Middle years	Increase in positive, joint activities, once they rediscover their interests

Transitions may prove to be difficult if couples do not recognize the changes and their effects on the relationship or do not know how to adjust to new stages.

balanced approach to life as they entered a new phase of their committed relationship.

On other occasions the couple is fully aware that their lives have changed in particular ways, but they have not been able to accommodate to those changes. As Ramon noted,

> I know the baby takes a tremendous amount of time and energy. I want and value that, but I still feel neglected. I can't imagine doing this for years to come. We are going to have to find some ways to improve this relationship, or it's going to die. Given how busy and how tired we both are, I just don't see how to do it.

Couples in the early stage of family life likely will need to devote considerable energy to these various startup activities involving the couple, the family, and their careers. Consequently, younger couples might be less likely to devote considerable energy to giving back to society. Couples in their middle years often need to devote less energy to childrearing and therefore might find it more feasible and rewarding to focus on each other or contribute to the community in a variety of ways. Thus, as children leave the home, many couples are likely to become involved in environmental causes, volunteer in the local schools, or assume leadership roles in religious settings. However, some couples have become unfamiliar with spending time together after years of attention to childrearing, jobs, and household tasks. Consequently, they find it awkward and anxiety provoking to begin sharing time and activities in the community and initially may need assistance from a therapist in overcoming inertia and avoidance of each other. As they engage in activities together, their concerns about "having nothing in common" or "having nothing to say to each other" frequently dissipate.

Thus, the amount and focus of positive behavior are likely to be influenced not only by the particular individuals involved in the relationship but also by the demands inherent in the various stages of the family life cycle. Often it is helpful for a couple to recognize the demands of a given stage of life and to discuss actively how they need to adapt their behavior accordingly. As we discuss in Chapter 3, when the role of cognitions in committed relationships is addressed, this understanding can help the couple not only to adapt their behaviors but also to understand why each partner might be be-having in a given way.

Relative Contributions of Frequent, "Minor" Positive Behaviors and Infrequent, "Major" Positive Behaviors

Often when therapists ask partners to think about caring or thoughtful ways that they can behave toward each other, the couple suggests major events or activities, such as "Maybe in a couple of months, we can get away for the weekend. I probably could ask my parents to keep the children for us." Even though such major events can be rewarding, they also may be difficult and expensive to arrange, and therefore are likely to occur infrequently. More-over, focusing their energies on such major events can lead some couples to overlook the importance of engaging in positive, constructive behaviors on a daily basis. At present, no research findings exist that might help us under-stand the relative contributions to healthy relationship functioning of major positive acts versus minor, ongoing positive acts. Our clinical observation suggests that ongoing, minor acts of caring, support, affection, and love, along with ongoing instrumental behaviors that keep the family running smoothly, are of great importance to most couples. These behaviors constitute the fab-ric of the couple's day-to-day existence and contribute to the overall tone of the relationship. Such behaviors might include, for instance, kissing the other person good morning, finding time to have a cup of coffee together during the week, or washing the dinner dishes before going to bed.

Partners comment frequently that small, caring acts are a minor part of their relationships. As noted in Exhibit 2.4, at least three reasons may be operating here. First, many individuals have been raised in families in which such behaviors were not displayed frequently. As a result, caring, thoughtful acts are not a central part of their conceptualization of a committed relation-ship. Often such persons neither think about behaving in caring, expressive ways nor recognize opportunities for such behaviors. Second, many persons acknowledge that they were loving and affectionate early in their relation-ships, but the demands of life have taken precedence over what seem to be "nice" but optional behaviors. Although decreasing these caring, loving be-haviors is likely to result in long-term erosion in the couple's relationship, the partners are unlikely to experience the effects of decreasing these caring behaviors on a day-to-day basis.

Third, some partners comment that small, caring behaviors still occur but no longer have the impact they once had, due perhaps to what Jacobson and Margolin (1979) have referred to as *reinforcement erosion*. More specifi-cally, if a behavior is repeated over a long period, its reinforcing qualities might diminish. Such erosion is likely to be particularly true for acts of car-ing, because one of the qualities of caring behavior is that it suggests the

1. Individuals do not think about relationships in terms of small, positive behaviors or do not recognize chances to demonstrate such behaviors.
2. Early affectionate behaviors give way to demands of life and positive acts decrease.
3. Positive behaviors still occur but lose their impact, either because they become dull and predictable or because they are delivered in a different way.

individual is thinking about the partner and considers him or her special. If the same behavior, such as a good morning kiss, is repeated daily for years, then it might lose its meaning. Instead, such behaviors might be experienced as routine and meaningless without much thought behind them. This common expectation that caring and affectionate behavior will have a spontaneous and novel quality taxes the creativity of many individuals. It is unfortunate that many people seem to have a limited repertoire when they think about how to behave in a caring way toward their partners. Once they go beyond gifts, cards, and a backrub, their list becomes very short. At the same time, some caring behaviors seem to have lost their impact because the individuals now deliver them in a less meaningful way. For example, the good morning kiss that was once delivered with tenderness now has become a quick peck on the lips as one partner rushes out the door.

Even though variety is important in helping to maintain the impact of expressive behaviors, rituals also can be meaningful to the couple. Although it is not clear what circumstances or qualities make individuals experience the repetitive behaviors involved in rituals as meaningful rather than as mechanical and meaningless, there probably are some differentiating characteristics. Rituals can remind the couple of what is important and central to them. Thus, setting Thursday evenings aside as a date night likely reminds the couple that they are a high priority to each other (Gottman, 1999). In addition, this weekly ritual still provides for novelty regarding how the couple chooses to spend the evening together. Also, rituals can provide structure and predictability that can be helpful for couples whose lives are chaotic or for couples who are busy and become easily preoccupied with activities and responsibilities that are not as rewarding. Each individual likely will need to understand the importance of both novelty and rituals in giving meaning to their particular relationship.

In addition to day-to-day positive behaviors, major positive acts are also important in helping to rejuvenate the couple, reawaken tender feelings, and help them end negative interaction cycles. Meaningful, significant gifts can serve a similar function. For example, Dan and Sally had been in marital therapy for some time. Their frequent arguments made both of them feel belittled and devalued. After much effort, they learned to interact with each other in a more positive, supportive way. The focus of therapy then shifted to helping them increase their sense of intimacy. As a symbolic act, Dan had a ring designed for Sally in the shape of an infinity symbol with their two birthstones imbedded in it. Although most couples cannot afford such expensive gifts, they can create special opportunities or give smaller items that are appropriate and meaningful within their lifestyle.

Although there are no data bearing on this issue, small, frequent, day-to-day positive behaviors might have a larger impact on couples' cognitive processing than do less frequent major, positive events that are likely to occur in atypical settings. As we discuss in chapter 3, over time individuals develop personae about their partners or make assumptions about their partners' characteristics. In addition, they make attributions for their partners' behaviors. It would seem likely that frequent, ongoing behaviors have a large impact on an individual's assumptions about the partner and the subsequent attributions or explanations given for a partner's behavior. Thus, if a partner engages in caring, loving behaviors on a frequent basis, the other person is likely to experience the individual as caring and thoughtful. However, if a partner is thoughtful and loving only while on vacation, this behavior can more easily be minimized or explained away: "Of course he was nice. We were on vacation. He didn't have his toys to distract him."

Relative Contributions of Positive Instrumental and Expressive Behaviors in Close Relationships

Both expressive and instrumental positive behaviors can contribute to the well-being of a relationship; however, it appears that various individuals differentially value these two types of behaviors in their committed relationships. Our research on relationship standards indicates that valuing both of these types of behaviors correlates with relationship adjustment (Baucom, Epstein, Daiuto, Carels, et al., 1996; Baucom, Epstein, Rankin, & Burnett, 1996). However, our findings indicate considerable variability among individuals in terms of how they value instrumental versus expressive behaviors. Some partners emphasize pragmatic tasks, such as Emily, who retorted, "Look, I appreciate the card, but it would mean a whole lot more to me if you would clean up the kitchen as we agreed." On the other hand, some individuals place a high premium on expressive acts: "Yes, I did want a new lawnmower, but could you be a little more romantic on our anniversary?" It is not surprising that individuals often engage in behaviors that they themselves value rather than what their partners might value or desire. "Sweetheart, I bought you a new, state-of-the-art computer. I think you'll love it." Unfortunately, some people are not very skilled at perspective taking and understanding what their partners would value in a given context. Therefore, in spite of their true efforts to please the partner, the partner feels unappreciated or unloved.

Individual and Couples' Differences in Positive Behaviors

As should be clear by this point, individual partners and couples vary in the types of specific behaviors that they find to be positive and rewarding. These preferences vary as a function of whether the behaviors are expressive versus instrumental; day-to-day activities versus major events; and whether the behaviors are focused on the individual, the couple, or some aspect of the couple's external environment. There is no "right" way to balance these various foci; instead, each couple must be sensitive to both partners' needs within the context of their current stage of relationship development.

Even if the couple places a major premium on positive couple-focused behaviors, there still are many different ways in which they might spend their time together. For example, some individuals and couples enjoy relaxing together, perhaps reading in the same room or watching a movie. Other couples prefer more active forms of entertainment, such as playing tennis or taking walks together. Still other couples derive joy from working together on household projects, perhaps refinishing furniture or growing a vegetable garden. What is important is for each couple to become aware of the various types of individual, couple, and externally focused activities that they prefer and find fulfilling. Too often, couples allow the busy pace of their lives and their multiple responsibilities to shape their daily activities. We believe that couples should articulate the kinds of activities and experiences that they wish to build into their lives and then proactively create some of these experiences within realistic constraints that they face.

Impact of Cultural and Contextual Factors on Positive Behavior

Many factors influence how an individual or couple will behave in a given setting and how a partner will experience that behavior. One such factor is the couple's culture and subculture. Halford, Hahlweg, and Dunne (1990) compared the communication of German and Australian couples during problem-solving discussions, all coded with the same well-validated behavioral coding system, the KPI (Katergoriensystem fur partnerschaftliche Interaktion [Coding System for Marital/Family Interaction]; Hahlweg, Reisner, et al., 1984). Although some consistencies arose between nationalities in the couples' behaviors (no differences were observed in direct verbal expression and acceptance–agreement or in positive and negative nonverbal behaviors), there were some significant cultural differences in communication. German couples exhibited less use of neutral information (problem descriptions and metacommunication), more critique (criticisms), and more refusals (justifications, disagreements, not listening) compared to Australian couples. In essence, the German couples were more willing to disagree openly with each other without experiencing negative implications for their relationships.

Research on communication in Chinese interpersonal relationships has indicated that the ways in which messages are presented and interpreted (e.g., when it is appropriate to speak, how one expresses politeness) depend heavily on the specific cultural contexts in which the communication occurs (Bond, 1996; Gudykunst & Ting-Toomey, 1988). For example, the principle of *hanxu* emphasizes the value of implicit, indirect communication, in which one does not openly express one's attitudes and emotions, particularly those that are strong or negative (e.g., joy, love, anger, depression). Practicing *hanxu* and sending implicit meta-messages through nonverbal behavior (e.g., hand gestures, smiles, and shrugs) avoids imposing one's feelings on others and thus maintains harmony in relationships. In marital and other close relationships within Chinese culture, love is rarely verbalized but is instead expressed indirectly through caring and altruistic acts (Bond, 1996; Gudykunst & Ting-Toomey, 1988). This traditional principle of Chinese communication stands in stark contrast to the emphasis on direct and open communication of feelings that is emphasized in Western approaches to intimate relationships and couples therapy.

Cultural factors can influence how the couple relates to other people as well. In Indian culture, the family of origin and extended family are central even after an individual is an adult and married. This concept affects one's sense of commitment and loyalty to family concerns. For example, Riva, who was born in the United States into a family from India, married George, also from the United States. As the oldest sister, Riva felt committed to help her family. When her sister began experiencing emotional difficulties, Riva felt responsible to invite the sister to live with her and George. Finding this proposal unacceptable, George stated, "When you get married, you put your partner and your marriage first. You need to cut the strings with your family." Individuals' standards for marriage, family, and individual behavior are influenced by several factors, including culture. Ignoring such factors can lead to an inappropriate conceptualization of the couple and simplistic or detrimental intervention strategies.

Researchers and clinicians must consequently be sensitive to cultural and subcultural differences and the meaning of specific behaviors for a given relationship. Most research on married couples has been conducted with White, middle-class couples in the United States, Europe, and Australia, and the applicability of these research findings to other populations is unclear. Within the United States, there is a dearth of research on behavioral interactions among African American couples. What is clear is that over the past few decades, African Americans have shown a disproportionately large decrease in marriage rates (Rodgers & Thornton, 1985), a disproportionately large increase in divorce and one-parent families, and a low rate of remarriage after divorce (Furstenberg & Spanier, 1984). Clinicians and policymakers must be cautious in assuming that the way to alleviate stress among African American couples is to teach them to behave in ways similar to happy, middle-class White couples. In many instances the clients will need to educate the therapist about their culture and how each individual has been influenced by that culture. Perhaps as dangerous as having no knowledge of the individuals' culture is assuming that because a person comes from a given culture he or she will behave and think in certain ways. Learning from the couple and conducting a careful assessment are critical.

NEGATIVE BEHAVIOR IN INTIMATE RELATIONSHIPS

Negative behavior can be focused on oneself, the partner, the relationship, or the environment, and a single negative behavior may set off a chain of destructive behaviors. The distinction between instrumental and expressive behaviors is not as clear for negative behaviors as for positive. Negative acts take on relationship meaning and, in turn, typically contribute to decreases in partners' satisfaction. In this section we discuss the reasons for, patterns of, and responses behind negative behaviors directed toward the partner as well as how negative behaviors engendered by an individual, the couple, or their surrounding systems may adversely affect the couple's interpersonal relationship.

An excess of negative behaviors typifies many distressed couples. In fact, on the basis of a wide number of investigations exploring both communication and noncommunication behaviors, Weiss and Heyman (1997) concluded that the frequency of negative behaviors tends to have a greater impact on partners' satisfaction with their relationships than do positive behaviors.

The bulk of research on couples' behavior has focused on communication rather than noncommunication behavior. The findings from these studies demonstrate that, as a group, distressed couples almost always can be differentiated from nondistressed couples on the basis of the frequencies of negative communication behaviors, such as criticizing, blaming, putting down, and denying responsibility (see Baucom and Epstein, 1990, for a more thorough review).

Distressed couples not only demonstrate a high frequency of negative behaviors, but they also have an increased tendency to reciprocate each other's negative behaviors. It is interesting that partners often seem to have an awareness of this interrelatedness between the two people's behaviors. Unfortunately, there is a tendency for each individual to see the sequence of negative behaviors as originating with the partner and one's own negative behavior as a response to the partner's negative behavior. Watzlawick, Beavin, and Jackson (1967) referred to this tendency as a *punctuation error*. Each person punctuates the behavioral sequence as beginning with the other's inappropriate behavior and sees his or her own behavior as a justifiable response. "I only responded that way because you had just criticized me"; "Well, the reason I criticized you was because you just made a really tacky comment in front of the neighbors." When partners view their interactions in this way, the therapist must help each person learn to take responsibility for his or her own behavior (Halford, Sanders, & Behrens, 1994) and be willing to terminate the negative sequence of behaviors, even if the other person is responsible for initiating a particular negative interaction. In the intervention section of this book (chapters 8–14), we present strategies for addressing these behaviors.

In the discussion to follow we differentiate among negative behaviors that are focused on oneself, the partner, the relationship, and the external environment. However, because of negative reciprocity, a single negative behavior often initiates a negative sequence of interactions that are destructive in multiple ways. Couples do not typically seek couples therapy unless one person's negative behavior has a strong impact on the other person or the relationship. Negative behaviors that are primarily damaging to the self usually result in a request for individual psychotherapy. Consequently, most of the behaviors we discussed next include negative implications for the partner and the relationship.

Earlier, when discussing positive behaviors, we differentiated between behaviors that are primarily expressive versus instrumental in nature. This distinction appears to be somewhat more difficult to make in regard to negative behaviors. It has been our experience that, within the context of a committed relationship, few negative behaviors are experienced as instrumental only. The behaviors typically affect one's partner and the relationship and take on relationship meaning, giving them expressive qualities. Consider Sally, who preferred to plan many aspects of her life and valued maintaining a precise schedule. James was aware of these characteristics; however, frequently he became involved in experiments in the laboratory and arrived home late. Furious with his repeated lateness, Sally began scolding James if he was more than 5 minutes late. Her goal was to influence James to come home on time so they could proceed with their evening. However, James viewed her scolding as a desire to control him and a lack of trust in him. For James, the scolding held emotional meaning as well. Given the interwoven nature of expressive and instrumental negative behaviors in intimate relationships, we will not discuss them separately; instead, we describe a variety of negative behaviors, pointing out the potential instrumental and emotional aspects inherent in a single behavior.

Negative Behavior That Affects the Partner

Although this is not universally true, one or both partners typically initiate couples therapy when the rate of negative behaviors has become intolerable in the relationship. Why do relationships that began in a caring, loving, supportive manner deteriorate into such negative exchanges? There are no ultimate answers, and different theoretical perspectives offer a wide

EXHIBIT 2.5
Reasons for Negative Behavior Toward the Partner

1. Partners are unaware of the negative impact of their behaviors.
2. Individuals learn negative behaviors as a strategy for promoting behavior change.
   a. To have own needs met.
   b. To end partner's negative behaviors.
3. One partner acts destructively to create distance in the couple.
4. Partner's negative behavior results from individual psychopathology.
5. Negative behaviors spring from frustrated needs and spiral into negative reciprocity, so that the interaction pattern itself causes distress.

range of tentative answers. From a broad, cognitive–behavioral perspective, we propose several reasons for these negative behaviors.

Reasons for Negative Behavior Toward the Partner

As noted in Exhibit 2.5, there are a number of reasons why individuals behave negatively towards their partners. In some instances, partners do not monitor their behaviors carefully and seem to be unaware of the negative impact of such behaviors on the other individual or the relationship (Halford, 2001). When we videotape partners interacting with each other and then share these videotapes with them, many are surprised to see their own behavior. Even after observing these videotapes, however, many of them continue performing negative acts. Perhaps such people still do not monitor their behavior adequately, or they lack the skills to change the behaviors even though they recognize that the behaviors are destructive.

Second, individuals behave negatively toward their partners because they have learned this strategy for promoting behavior change. In some instances, such an approach seems to typify one person's general way of interacting with the world; that is, the person generally is somewhat negative and punitive with others as a way to get what he or she wants. In other instances this behavior appears to be more focal to the current relationship. For example, in many couples, one person learns that he or she is most successful in gaining the other individual's attention by becoming increasingly negative. As Yolanda commented, "I just can't get Roger's attention unless I yell or become nasty with him. I'm generally not that way with other people. I'd much prefer to do it pleasantly, but it doesn't work with him." These negative behavior change strategies often will have one of two foci. First, one person may want the other to address some important needs or preferences. In such instances, he or she may behave negatively as a way of attempting to get those needs met. For example, Tom frequently was frustrated that Lynn spent the evenings preparing for work the next day. Over time, he found that if he became unpleasant and called her a workaholic, then she would spend more time with him. She felt demeaned and unappreciated, and Tom really did not enjoy talking to Lynn in this way. However, they both felt caught in a trap that they did not know how to change. Second, this negative behavior strategy often is intended to terminate the other person's negative behavior. It is as if one partner appears to be saying, "I'm not willing to let you treat me that way. If you're negative with me, you're going to get it back."

A third reason for behaving negatively toward a partner is to create desired distance in the relationship. The person might intend to remain in the relationship but simply desire more distance from the partner. Alternatively, the person may be contemplating terminating the relationship and uses the negative behavior as a way of driving the other individual away or pushing him or her toward ending the relationship, thus not accepting responsibility for the relationship's demise.

Fourth, negative behavior from one individual often is a manifestation of his or her individual psychopathology. For example, some individuals with poor self-esteem attempt to bolster their self-worth by degrading another individual. Kevin, a narcissistic person, invested considerable time and effort attempting to convince both himself and others of his intellect, professional success, and general value to society. He made frequent disparaging remarks about his wife to demonstrate his relative superiority. Similarly, depressed individuals, who often have a generally negative frame of mind, frequently make negative remarks about themselves, their partners, and the world around them.

Sometimes negative behaviors occur independent of any of the reasons just described. Given the strength of negative reciprocity, negatives appear to beget negatives. By the time a couple seeks therapy, often the negatives have begun to play on one other in a complex fashion. Difficulty with communication is one of the most common complaints among distressed couples seeking treatment (Geiss & O'Leary, 1981). In some instances, the negative communication results from couples' becoming frustrated when important relationship needs and preferences are not met over time, thus creating even more frustration and prompting the couple to discuss their concerns in increasingly negative ways. Over time, the negative interactions take on a life of their own, perhaps even unrelated to the original concerns. As partners often note, "At this point, we just fight and argue. Often I don't even know what we are arguing about."

By the time the couple seeks therapy, their highly aversive negative communication itself has become a major problem for them, and it will need to be addressed by the therapist early in the intervention. However, helping the partners to stop attacking each other or defending themselves might not be all that is needed. From a traditional cognitive–behavioral perspective, this behavioral pattern likely would have been conceptualized as a communication skills deficit. In many instances, however, the partners and the therapist find that other important relationship needs can—and must—be addressed once the partners refrain from behaving so negatively toward each other.

Thus, the clinician must be cautious in assuming that decreasing highly salient, negative behaviors will result in long-term relationship satisfaction. Treatment outcome studies using a skills-based, traditional, cognitive–behavioral model are consistent with this caution. Outcome research indicates that only about one third to one half of couples receiving cognitive–behavioral marital therapy are in the nondistressed range on satisfaction measures at the end of treatment (Jacobson et al., 1984). Moreover, Baucom, Sayers, and Sher (1990) and Halford, Sanders, and Behrens (1993) found that the degree of increase in relationship satisfaction has little correlation with increases in communication skills per se. Many couples seem to be seeking more from treatment than decreasing negative exchanges—increasing positives and perhaps having important needs met that are yet unfulfilled, even though the couple is communicating more effectively.

Forms of Negative Behavior Toward the Partner

There are many ways an individual may behave negatively or destructively toward a partner. A great deal of research has examined communication between partners. These investigations have consistently found that higher rates of negative communication and negative reciprocity are correlated with concurrent relationship distress. However, as we discuss shortly, it does not appear that all of what investigators have labeled as negative communication has long-term negative consequences for the relationship. Indeed, couples need to be able to address problematic areas and express when they are upset. It is unrealistic to expect that these interactions will occur in ways that feel positive and constructive at the moment. What, then, is particularly destructive with regard to "negative" communication and interaction? We propose that two sets of empirical findings might hold the key to understanding when negative behaviors and communication have long-term negative consequences.

- Frequent, negative behaviors and interactions bring about a general, continual feeling of negativity in the relationship.
- Particularly malevolent forms of communication, such as criticism, contempt, and hostility, may damage the self-esteem of a partner.

Creating a pervasive negative atmosphere. Frequent, negative behaviors toward the partner and extended sequences of negative interaction and reciprocity likely are destructive to the relationship. Most people simply do not like to live in a negative environment; it sets an overall negative tone for their lives. Thus, frequent negative exchanges and long sequences of negative reciprocity serve as a backdrop for a negative atmosphere in the relationship. Avoidance of a negative atmosphere also is likely to be a factor in the consistent finding of numerous empirical investigations that depressed people elicit many negative responses from other individuals (e.g., Coyne,

1976; Gotlib & Beach, 1995; Gotlib & Robinson, 1982), including a desire to avoid interaction with the depressed person in the future (Coyne, 1976; Howes & Hokanson, 1979). Being around individuals who are depressed tends to be distressing because of the atmosphere that depressed persons create.

Undermining a partner's self-worth. Evidence is mounting from several fields of investigation to suggest that certain types of negative behavior are particularly deleterious, both to the recipient of the behaviors and to the relationship. Gottman (1994a) concluded that contempt and criticism expressed toward the partner have long-term, negative consequences for the relationship. Contempt involves a strong, general dislike; disapproval; and perhaps a desire to harm the other individual. Criticism involves a negative response to specific behaviors or attributes of the individual. Similarly, the expressed-emotion literature demonstrates that individuals with a variety of types of psychopathology are likely to relapse if they live in a family atmosphere that includes a high level of hostility (similar to contempt) and criticism (Butzlaff & Hooley, 1998).

Why are these particular types of communication and behavior destructive to the recipient and to the relationship? Contempt and criticism can strike at the very essence of the individual's sense of self-worth and value. Most people turn to their intimate relationships to feel esteemed, valued, and affirmed. Contempt and criticism detract from an individual's sense of self-esteem and self-worth and create a hostile, unsafe environment where one must be on guard and ready to protect oneself from one's partner. In our terminology, *contempt* and *criticism* destroy the expressive, emotional quality of the relationship.

The preceding discussion points out that many negative communication behaviors are destructive because they undermine the self-esteem and sense of worth of a partner. This pattern of devaluing is not restricted to couples' communication and conversation. Either intentionally or unintentionally, an individual can behave in a variety of ways that make the other person feel devalued, unimportant, or unloved. These behaviors may be as simple as ignoring the individual when he or she comes into the house. Many distressed partners lament that when they arrive home, no one seems to notice. Similarly, during social occasions when other people are present, one person may focus attention and conversation on others, at times ignoring the partner. In essence, there are virtually countless ways in which an individual can interpret a partner's behavior as meaning that the individual is not valued.

Undermining important relationship assumptions. The behaviors just discussed often have a negative impact on the partner because they occur on a repetitive basis. A single incident of being late is unlikely to bring a couple to therapy. In contrast, some other negative behaviors occur less frequently but can have a devastating impact on the partner and the relationship. Many of these behaviors fall within the category that we call *interpersonal traumas*. For example, being struck physically by a partner only once or being humiliated by a partner in front of one's parents on a single occasion can have serious consequences. As has been discussed elsewhere (Gordon & Baucom, 1998c, 1999; Gordon, Baucom, & Snyder, 2000), traumatic events such as physical abuse or extramarital affairs are different from other negative relationship behaviors. These traumatic events take on special meaning, because they involve a violation of important assumptions about the relationship and issues of trust, safety, predictability, control, and ability to count on the other person. As we discuss in chapter 13, these interpersonal traumas require special handling. Often, even if the negative behavior ceases, the injured partner cannot simply move forward with the relationship. After being hit or suffering the consequences of infidelity, the partner and the relationship cannot heal without a great deal of additional processing.

Creating annoyances for the partner. Toward the other end of the continuum from traumatic acts are irritating or troubling behaviors related to a person's individual style or personality that the partner finds difficult to endure. These behaviors might include relatively normal differences in personality; for example, one person might find it difficult to be around a partner who eats food loudly or chews gum vigorously. "I know this sounds silly, but I really can't sit beside him in a movie theater. I feel like he is crunching popcorn right in my ear." An individual who prefers that the house be tidy and orderly may have trouble living with a partner who prefers a "more relaxed living environment." One person who prefers to sleep late may encounter difficulty with a partner who wishes to greet the dawn and begin the day's activities. In these instances, neither person is likely to feel devalued or unimportant, as is the case with hostile and contemptuous statements and behaviors. However, these daily annoyances can become difficult to tolerate because they are contrary to the positive atmosphere and lifestyle that the individuals are attempting to create.

On the other hand, some annoying or destructive negative behaviors appear to be part of an individual's psychopathology. For example, an anxious partner's frequent requests for reassurances about safety can become tiresome. When one individual is depressed and therefore does not accomplish his or her daily responsibilities and tasks, the partner experiences a direct impact. If work paychecks are not deposited in the bank account, both individuals may experience the complication and embarrassment of writing bad checks. Chapter 4 includes a more detailed discussion of the role of individual psychopathology in relationship functioning.

Responses to Negative Behavior Directed Toward the Partner

When one person behaves negatively, the partner has several options regarding how to respond. Two of these options correspond to the fight-or-flight responses seen in a variety of species when the organism is threatened. First, the partner might "fight," or actively reciprocate a negative. Such responses are typical of distressed couples. The couple experiences this escalating negative reciprocity as an argument or fight. Although arguments at the time typically are experienced as unpleasant, this does not mean that they should always be avoided. In a recent study of healthy, long-term marriages, Palmer and Baucom (1998) found considerable variability in the ways that long-term, happy couples approach disagreements. Several couples reported unpleasant arguments, but two factors appeared to mitigate a long-term negative impact. First, although the partners disagreed and at times were loud and unpleasant, their unpleasantness did not include contempt for a partner. Second, the couples had developed some strategy for reconciling or putting the relationship back on track after a negative interaction. At present, we have an incomplete understanding of the impact of disagreements among partners. However, it appears that disagreements that are extremely frequent, continue for a long time, and involve belittling one's partner are likely to be destructive.

As an alternative to striking back at the partner, an individual might withdraw in response to a negative behavior. Christensen and his colleagues have conducted a variety of investigations that consistently demonstrate a demand–withdraw pattern, in which one person attempts to engage the partner and the partner withdraws, as typical of distressed couples (Christensen & Heavey, 1990, 1993; Christensen & Shenk, 1991). Similarly, Gottman (1994a) concluded that defensiveness and "stonewalling" have long-term deleterious consequences for the relationship. Withdrawal might occur for a variety of reasons. Gottman and Levenson (1992) found that men in particular appear to experience high levels of physiological arousal while engaging in a conflictual discussion with their female partners. It appears that because this level of arousal is uncomfortable, they withdraw to return to a more comfortable state. Second, Christensen and Heavey (1990) found that the particular topic under discussion influenced which partner engaged in the demand role and which partner engaged in the withdraw role. Men generally assumed the role of withdrawal more frequently. However, when the couple discussed a behavior change that was important to the male partner, he was more likely to engage with his female partner, who was then more likely to withdraw. Consequently, a person who wants to maintain the status quo is more likely to withdraw or stonewall to retain the current state of affairs. The notion of maintaining the status quo is related to power and control. The less powerful person in the relationship must push for what he or she wants, while the more powerful person might withdraw to maintain control over the relationship in its current state.

As a more adaptive response to either demanding or withdrawing, the partner can respond to a negative behavior by attempting to redirect the interaction in a more positive manner, or at least by not responding negatively, a process that Gottman, Markman, and Notarius (1977) referred to as *editing*. Notarius, Benson, Sloane, and Vanzetti (1989) explored the extent to which distressed and nondistressed spouses responded in a non-negative way to a negative message from the partner. They found that given a negative evaluation of their male partners' antecedent messages, distressed wives were more likely to offer a negative reply than were distressed men, nondistressed women, or nondistressed men. Whereas these findings indicate that distressed wives are particularly unlikely to edit what they view as a negative message from their partners, it is unclear whether this reflects a communication deficit or results from other factors. It might be possible that these wives are responding to husbands who are less cooperative on a daily basis, resulting in greater frustration for wives during the interaction. Similarly, during the conversations their husbands might be reporting on problem situations in a distorted manner, making it difficult for the wives to edit a negative reaction to the husbands' comments. As Vivian (1991) noted, most coding systems ignore the content of what is being discussed and the relationship between the conversation and what occurs outside of the session, thus potentially omitting important information about the couple's interaction.

The interaction cycles just described are not necessarily consistent over the life of a couple's relationship. Partners may adopt a variety of strategies to deal with discord. Over time, if none of the above-mentioned strategies is successful, a couple might adopt the strategy of abandoning attempts to address conflict or even approaching the other person. As Snyder and Regts (1982) found, some distressed couples engage in a high level of conflict, but others are emotionally disengaged from each other. Johnson and Greenberg (1995) warned that it will be extremely difficult to assist couples who have become disengaged and no longer turn to each other to satisfy basic attachment needs.

It also is important to understand that various couples avoid addressing problematic aspects of their relationship for different reasons. Some couples avoid pressing issues because they are emotionally disengaged, no longer feel invested in the relationship, and have decided that it is not worth their effort to discuss issues with the partner. Other avoidant couples, however, are still emotionally engaged with each other yet are uncomfortable with conflict or do not wish to impose their will on their partners. The clinician must differentiate between couples who no longer seem to care about their relationship versus couples who are particularly sensitive to avoiding a negative mood state, wishing for the partner to remain happy and the relationship to be positive at all costs.

Negative Behavior That Affects Oneself

The idea of negative behaviors directed toward oneself may conjure up the image of a pathological, masochistic individual. Although such people do exist, in most instances negative behaviors that either are focused on oneself in a relationship or have negative implications for the self are less dramatic. These negative behaviors can occur in at least three different ways. First, some behaviors would have a negative impact on the individual, regardless of whether he or she was in an intimate relationship. For example, Adam managed a restaurant, and at the end of the evening, he often would have two or three beers before driving home. Once he arrived home, he would drink one or two more beers. This pattern began to interfere with his job performance. In addition, he became withdrawn when drinking this heavily. The couple sought therapy, initiated by Adam's partner, to deal with the distance in their relationship. The therapist noted that Adam's use of alcohol was a significant factor contributing to the relationship distress as well as interfering with Adam's own individual success. In such instances the therapist must consider whether individual intervention for the self-destructive behavior is needed or whether it is more appropriately addressed within the context of couples therapy.

Second, some negative behaviors directed toward oneself result from being part of a relationship per se. For example, some partners believe that they should be self-sacrificing and expect little personal reward from the relationship. Therefore, they fill their lives with chores, meeting the partner's needs, and focusing on children if they are present. Each individual behavior in which the partner engages may be positive and appropriate in isolation; however, the cumulative effect creates a negative environment for the person. The individual can understandably feel overwhelmed and unappreciated; in some instance, the person him- or herself is a significant contributing factor in creating this role in the relationship.

Finally, an individual's behavior can have negative implications for that individual because it results in negative reciprocity from the partner; that is, when the individual behaves in certain ways, the partner might respond in a negative way. In essence, the individual does not behave negatively toward him- or herself but behaves toward the partner in a way that is likely to evoke a negative response. In doing so, the individual might create a negative environment for him- or herself without intending to do so.

Negative Behavior That Affects the Relationship

Many of the negative behaviors just described affect the couple's relationship. Behaviors that influence one's partner and oneself within the relationship eventually also affect the overall relationship. In addition, some behaviors or activities inherently include the two individuals as a couple. Often one person's behavior will significantly affect these couple-focused behaviors. For example, each individual serves as a parent for the couple's children. In addition, parenting often involves working together as a team in raising the children. Often children benefit not only from being parented by two individuals but also by having a common set of expectations from parents who work together effectively. When one individual undercuts the partner's authority with the children, makes inappropriate unilateral decisions regarding the children, or attempts to form an alliance with the children when unhappy with the partner, the parenting alliance falters. This failure is destructive not only for the children but also for the couple's relationship. Amy and Devon had a child with attention deficit disorder (ADD) who experienced significant difficulty both at school and at home. Unfortunately, they had very different perspectives on what would be helpful for the child. Devon believed that they needed to be very strict with him, set clear boundaries, and punish him when he behaved inappropriately. Amy believed that their son was doing the best he could and that he would benefit primarily from being loved and supported. She advocated making few demands on the child and refraining from drawing attention to his failures. The therapist attempted to help the couple see that they could become an effective parenting unit, providing both structure and warmth and no longer undermining their own marital relationship by arguing or making unilateral parenting decisions.

In addition to parenting, a host of other activities require both individuals' participation for the couple to function as a team. Obviously, sexual intimacy is by definition an interpersonal process. Thus, if one partner is disinterested in sexual interaction on an ongoing basis, or if one partner insists on particular types of sexual behavior that the other individual finds uncomfortable, the sexual relationship becomes disrupted. When assessing such difficulties the clinician can be susceptible to a punctuation error, as described earlier. That is, a husband's low desire for sexual interaction might not be the initial cause of the couple's sexual problem. If he has attempted to initiate sexual interaction with his wife on numerous occasions and has felt consistently rebuffed, he might no longer seek out his wife as a source of sexual fulfillment. In many instances, it is impossible to determine the ultimate, initial source of a couple's difficulty. However, for the couple's sexual relationship to proceed in a fulfilling and rewarding manner, both people must contribute positively to the process (Metz & Epstein, in press).

The dual emphasis on couples' functioning and individual functioning often poses a dilemma for the therapist as well as the couple. Partners often experience confusion regarding how to balance individual freedoms and well-being with relationship and couple needs. Returning to the previous example of Amy and Devon, whose child had ADD, the couple was uncertain how to proceed. Devon, who believed that the child should be held accountable for his behavior, understood the importance of developing an effective parenting team and presenting a consistent set of expectations to their child. However, when his individual values for childrearing conflicted with the need for the couple to provide consistent parenting, Devon believed that his own values should have higher priority. As a result, he often made unilateral decisions that contradicted arrangements that Amy had made with the child. Thus, sometimes what a person believes individually can be detrimental to a relationship. In such instances, the therapist can point out this dilemma between individual versus couple needs and help the couple decide where to make a compromise.

Negative Behavior That Affects the Couple's Environment

Sometimes one individual's behavior or the couple's behavior will have a negative impact on a significant aspect of their interpersonal environment. In such instances the couple's own relationship can suffer as well. For example, Susan was humiliated, because when she and Nick were with their friends, he often said or did whatever was on his mind. As she recounted,

> This is hard to believe, but he actually did it. We had a couple over for dinner, and at about 9:30 p.m., Nick announced that he was tired and was going to bed. The rest of us just sat there in stunned silence. I have never been so mortified in my life.

This actual event may seem extreme, but it is one of numerous examples we have heard from individuals who report that they have been embarrassed by the social behavior of their partners.

At times, the behavior is more than embarrassing; it creates significant family rifts. In-law jokes exist because it often is difficult to integrate an individual into another person's family of origin. Each family has its own style of interacting, including the degree to which it is considered appropriate to disagree with and confront one another, along with a whole set of traditions, rituals, and acceptable behaviors. One person may view the behavior of the other's family members as maladaptive. Consider the following example, in which Carla explained to Robert,

> I'm really worried about taking you home to be with my family. The last time we were there, you caused a real problem with my mother. I know she's domineering and likes to have everything a certain way, but that is just the way she is. When you tell her we're not going to do things her way, it just creates more difficulty. I wish you could accept them for who they are and enjoy them when we visit. We're not there for very long. Why can't you just let it go?

Robert clarified why he could not let it go:

> I think it's ridiculous. Your mother bosses everybody around, and everyone just takes it, doing exactly what she says. I'm not going to tolerate that from anyone—your mother or anyone else. If she can't treat me respectfully, we're going to go at it with each other.

In addition to difficulties that result from one person's inappropriate or challenging behavior and interaction with others, difficulties between the couple and the external environment can occur because the two individuals differentially value relating to people and institutions outside of themselves.

Some people are very sociable and seek considerable time interacting with other couples. The other partner may not enjoy such activities and may not put appropriate effort into making needed arrangements. Therefore, one partner might "forget" to arrange a babysitter so that they can get together with another couple, or a partner might "forget" to set the alarm clock so that the family can get up on Sunday morning to attend church. Such oversights might not be clearly intentional, but often they result from a lack of motivation or desire on the part of one person. Negative behaviors that disrupt the couple's interaction with others can lead to personal or relationship dissatisfaction.

BALANCING POSITIVE AND NEGATIVE BEHAVIORS IN COUPLES' RELATIONSHIPS: A COMPLEX PHENOMENON

A large body of research points out that, as a group, couples in distressed relationships engage in more negative and less positive behavior toward each other. In the foregoing discussion we have gone beyond these basic findings to articulate specific ways in which these negative and positive behaviors are experienced within the fabric of couples' lives. It is unfortunate that research investigations to date have not explored the role of positivity and negativity at this level of detail. Yet, on the basis of the findings that do exist, it is tempting to encourage couples to be as maximally positive and as minimally negative as they can be. However, the findings should not necessarily be interpreted in this manner. It might well be that distressed couples engage in more negative behavior and less positive behavior than is optimal. However, it is not necessarily true that couples should seek a relationship that involves only consistent positive behaviors with no negative behaviors. Such a relationship conjures up family sitcom television from the 1950s. Instead, there might be some combination or ratio of positive to negative behavior that is optimal for couples. Of course, not all positive behaviors have the same impact; neither do all negatives. Therefore, it is unlikely that any kind of a reasonable numerical ratio can ever be put forth. Gottman (1999) found that a 5:1 ratio of positive to negative communication behaviors differentiates between stable couples versus those that eventually divorce; however, these findings should not be overgeneralized. They apply only to communication behavior during conversations assessed with Gottman's particular observational coding systems. The findings do not imply any general ratio of positives to negatives for noncommunication behaviors between partners.

In addition, results of longitudinal studies of marriage caution against viewing all current negative exchanges as being detrimental over time. Similarly, not all positive exchanges have constructive, long-term effects on the couple. Moreover, the same investigations suggest that there may be gender differences in how positive and negative behaviors are used within a relationship. Levenson and Gottman (1985) found that more positive affect in wives predicted a *decline* in marital satisfaction 3 years later. Similarly, Gottman and Krokoff (1989) found that wives' positive verbal behavior was positively related to their current marital satisfaction, but wives' positive behavior actually predicted a decline in marital satisfaction over 3 years.

Karney and Bradbury (1997) reported a similar relationship of newlywed wives' positive communication and subsequent changes in marital satisfaction over the first 4 years of marriage. Rather than maintaining separate codes for positive and negative communication, they created a summary variable assessing communication negativity (operationalized as the number of negative communication behaviors minus positive communication behaviors). They found that when wives were more negative prior to marriage, there were less rapid declines in both husbands' and wives' marital satisfaction over the first 4 years of marriage. Thus, three longitudinal studies have demonstrated that wives' being more positive or less negative (or both) actually predicts more distress longitudinally.

However, a different pattern emerges when husbands' communication is considered. Levenson and Gottman (1985) found that more positive affect in the husband predicted greater marital satisfaction 3 years later. Karney and Bradbury (1997) found that more negative (or less positive, or both) newlywed communication by husbands was associated with greater declines in wives' satisfaction. In essence, these findings suggest that among men, more positive and less negative communication does indeed predict positive outcomes for the marriage several years later. Overall, the effects of positive and negative behaviors appear to be in opposite directions for men and women.

These basic research findings are supplemented by treatment outcome investigations. When Baucom and Mehlman (1984) followed couples for 6 months after they had received behavioral marital therapy for discord, they found that couples who showed more positive communication at posttreatment were actually more likely to separate subsequently. Schilling, Baucom, Burnett, Allen, and Ragland (2000) investigated the effects of a weekend-format cognitive–behavioral prevention program (Premarital Relationship Enhancement Program, PREP; Markman, Stanley, & Blumberg, 1994) for couples planning marriage. They found that, as anticipated, the program led to increases in positive communication and decreases in negative communication for both men and women. However, when they followed the couples for up to 5 years, the results were consistent with the longitudinal studies just described. More specifically, men who demonstrated an increase in positive communication and decrease in negative communication after attending PREP were less likely to experience the onset of marital distress several years later. Overall, the women's communication was not as predictive of long-term distress onset as the men's communication, but it was in the opposite direction— that is, women who showed an increase in positive communication after PREP were more likely to experience marital distress several years later.

In integrating the findings from cross-sectional and longitudinal studies, we believe that a picture begins to emerge. In cross-sectional studies of couples, those who generally demonstrate higher rates of positive behaviors and lower rates of negative behaviors are more satisfied with their relationships. However, what is experienced as satisfying at present might be quite different from what is beneficial in the long term. Often couples need to address difficult issues, and during some of these interactions one or both persons' communication and other behaviors are likely to be somewhat negative. However, this negativity might be necessary to resolve issues, or alter one or both persons' behavior. In essence, what is experienced by the partner as negative and coded by an outside rater as negative might at times have beneficial long-term effects.

Equally striking are the findings of many studies demonstrating consistent gender differences across investigations. The results suggest that a relationship benefits longitudinally if the female is more negative, less positive, or both. It is important to remember that these results are relative, not absolute; that is, the relationship might not function optimally if the woman attempts to be extremely positive while expressing very few negative behaviors, or if she does so while being unhappy with the relationship. This set of findings might exist because many women assume the role of initiating conversations about problematic aspects of the relationship. As Christensen and his colleagues demonstrated, women are more likely than men to assume the demand role in couples' interactions. The findings from these investigations converge to suggest that a relationship does not function well over time if the woman does not contribute to this role of pushing the couple to address relationship concerns. If she is willing to behave positively at all costs, then problematic issues might not be addressed. There is no reason to suggest that women alone should assume the role of raising relationship concerns. Rather, the findings may be interpreted as suggesting that women have often assumed this role in our society. Instead of perpetuating this differential role for the two genders, the therapist might serve the couple well by ensuring that both partners assume responsibility for addressing relationship concerns while treating each other with respect, courtesy, and support. In addition, the therapist must address other patterns associated with socialized gender roles when working with same-sex couples; for example, relationships in which two women engage in an excessive degree of relational thinking, or two men simultaneously avoid dealing with relationship issues (L. S. Brown, 1995).

SUMMARY

Cognitive–behavioral approaches to intimate relationships have always stressed the importance of behaviors in understanding distress and satisfaction. This continues to be a strong part of our enhanced model. Understanding the role of behaviors in relationship distress and developing efficacious interventions can be enhanced if the broad categories of positive and negative behaviors are further differentiated as described next.

- Negative behaviors and communication appear to distinguish between distressed and nondistressed couples, whereas positive behaviors may play a role in elevating nondistressed couples into the range of more highly satisfied couples.
- To examine more specific positive behaviors, it is useful to distinguish between *expressive behaviors*, which signify caring, concern, affection, and love, and *instrumental behaviors*, which consist of accomplishing tasks necessary for the maintenance of the relationship. Some behaviors, however, may take on both expressive and instrumental meaning.
- Although it is useful to think about whether a positive or negative behavior focuses on the partner, oneself, the couple, or the environment, a given behavior also may have multiple impacts. *Positive reciprocity* refers to the tendency for a positive behavior from one partner to increase the chances that the other person will respond positively. *Negative reciprocity* is the tendency for one partner's negative behavior to be followed by a negative behavior from the other partner.
- Although many individuals say they do not always know how to express caring and concern for their partners, some ways in which couples demonstrate positive, expressive behaviors are by sharing thoughts and feelings, jointly participating in altruistic activities, or providing social support to a partner during times of distress.
- Partners assume responsibilities to help the relationship proceed smoothly, avoid negative feelings, and demonstrate commitment to the partner and relationship. The division of tasks in the relationship must feel equitable to both partners and provide time for the pursuit of personal goals.
- Positive behaviors may wax and wane depending on the stage of the relationship.
- Ongoing, minor acts of caring and support and instrumental behaviors essential to maintaining the relationship often become infrequent. Major acts of love may be important in helping to rejuvenate a couple or end negative interaction patterns.
- Partners engage in negative behavior because they are unaware of the impact of their behavior; they hope to promote behavior change; they want to create distance; or they are manifesting subclinical or clinical levels of psychopathology, such as low self-esteem or depression. Traumatic negative behaviors affect

the relationship by undermining assumptions about trust, safety, predictability, and control; by irritating the partner; by creating a negative atmosphere that colors all other behavior and communication in the relationship; or by reducing the self-esteem of a partner.

- Partners may respond to negative behavior by withdrawing, striking back, or attempting to redirect the interaction in a more positive manner.
- Addressing negatives in a respectful way is essential for later relationship satisfaction. Conversely, being too positive and avoiding conflict may create current happiness but can lead to dissatisfaction with the relationship in the future.

3

COGNITIVE AND EMOTIONAL FACTORS IN COUPLES' RELATIONSHIPS

Although behaviors may be readily observed and discussed by a couple and a therapist, untangling a couple's various interpretations of and reactions to events in relationships can seem dauntingly complex. By differentiating between the cognitions and emotions in partners' subjective experiences, in this chapter we explore factors that contribute to a couple's beliefs and feelings about their relationship. After describing the types of cognitions and emotions that are most relevant to couples' functioning, we examine how these subjective experiences affect the individuals, their partners, and their relationships.

In the previous chapter we discussed the critical role that behaviors play in intimate relationships. Distressed partners routinely express concern about the other individual's behavior or about the negative interactions between the two of them. In addition, partners have internal, subjective experiences of those behaviors that greatly influence their satisfaction with their relationships. Many therapists have had the experience of sitting in a therapy session with a couple for the first time and wondering whether the two partners were describing the same relationship. Often, partners remember events differently in terms of what actually occurred, interpret the meaning of the events in different ways, and respond with different emotions. Pam and John recounted the trauma of watching their home burn in very different ways. With great sadness, hurt, and anger, Pam described it thus:

> The fire started about 6:00 p.m. I got everyone out of the house and immediately called the fire department. Then I called John's office and told his secretary what happened. I couldn't even get him on the telephone. He didn't come home until about 7:30. John walked right up, ignored all of us, and started speaking to the chief of the fire department about the house, but asking nothing about his family. I have never been so hurt and disappointed in my life.

Not surprisingly, John remembered and described the incident quite differently:

> That simply is not true. I did not refuse to take her telephone call. I had stepped out of the office, and as soon as I returned, my secretary immediately told me what happened. I dropped everything and came straight to the house. When I arrived, I immediately looked for Pam and the children, but I couldn't find them. So I went to the fire chief, and the first thing I asked was if Pam and the children were okay. He assured me that everyone was fine, and he briefed me on what had happened and what they were doing. He told me where he thought my family was, and I immediately came and found them. It was an awful experience, but I can't believe Pam is upset with me about how things happened. I was worried sick. I showed up in the dark; I didn't know if everyone was alive; our house was in flames; and somehow I ended up as the bad guy. There is no way to win.

Such experiences can be etched indelibly in the minds of both people: For Pam, the incident is a prime example of how she can never count on John to be there and a clear sign of how unimportant she is in his life. For John, the incident epitomizes his belief that he can never please Pam and that she sees him as inadequate and inept, no matter what he does.

In this chapter we discuss the internal, subjective experiences that give meaning to and color intimate relationships. For heuristic purposes, we differentiate between the thoughts or cognitions that partners have about their relationships and the emotions that they experience. We believe that many individuals do not clearly differentiate between their thoughts and their feelings; instead, their subjective experience tends to include both elements indiscriminately. For many happy couples this approach works well. However, we find it useful to differentiate between cognitions and emotions, because relationship distress for some partners may result primarily from their ways of thinking about the relationship or interpreting the other person's behavior. For other partners, relationship distress may relate more to difficulties with their emotions, such as poor affect regulation, difficulty controlling their behavior when in a given mood state, or the experience of disabling depression or anxiety. Although this differentiation is useful, we will also show how cognitions and emotions are integrally related and how, at times, they are not clearly distinguishable.

COGNITIONS IN MARRIAGE

The ways in which couples assimilate the information provided by their partners' behaviors are often the results of learned, automatic processes. In this section we explore how couples may selectively attend to aspects of events, draw meaning about the relationship from their partners' behaviors, and approach the relationship with expectancies about how their partners will act in the future. These cognitions about specific events may stem from a set of basic, broader beliefs about themselves, their partners, and their relationships. Finally, we look at how cognitions in relationships may be affected by the extent to which partners think about everyday events in terms of their relationship.

Reactions to Specific Events

Selective Attention

Partners selectively attend to, or idiosyncratically notice, certain aspects of an interaction or an event, and they fail to notice other aspects of an event (A. T. Beck, Rush, Shaw, & Emery, 1979); in more extreme instances, at times partners cannot even agree on whether an event occurred. This selective attention often serves as the basis of complaint from one partner: "Why is it that you seem to notice everything that I do wrong? But when I do something right, it goes right over your head without your even noticing it." Similarly, partners can selectively attend to positive qualities in their mates, often ignoring important destructive behaviors or patterns. For example, Jane pondered whether to tell her best friend Alice that Alice's husband was having an affair. As Jane remarked to her own husband,

> I don't know what to do. It is so obvious to me that Larry is involved with Melissa. Alice just doesn't seem to notice how inappropriate he is when Melissa is around. It's like she's wearing blinders or something. I think she really doesn't want to let herself see it.

Selectively attending either to positive or negative aspects of the relationship while ignoring other important behaviors can lead to distorted experiences of the partner, oneself, or the relationship. Because of selective attention, distressed couples often have low rates of agreement about whether some event actually occurred in their relationship on top of disagreement about what led up to and followed the event. For example, Jacobson and Moore (1981) concluded that spouses generally agree less than 50% of the time about whether specific events occurred in their relationship during the past day.

Through a variety of strategies, therapists from diverse theoretical orientations attempt to help one or both partners develop a more balanced perspective, seeing both the positive and negative behaviors in a realistic manner. It also is important that the therapist and the couple distinguish between negative versus distorted cognitions and perceptual processes. Because one person reports many negative behaviors from a partner does not necessarily mean that the individual is selectively ignoring positive behaviors. In some instances, one person does behave very negatively, with few positive behaviors toward the partner. Frequent criticism by a husband in the absence of positive behavior toward his wife will lead to different interventions than if the wife simply is not noticing her husband's frequent positive behaviors.

Attributions

Once an individual notices certain behaviors or aspects of an interaction, he or she might make inferences to explain the behavior. These attributions, or explanations for relationship events, are important aspects of an individual's subjective experience of the relationship. When Pam and John's house burned, Pam interpreted John's talking to the fire chief as an indication that he valued their property more than he valued her and the children. This interpretation was a major reason that Pam recounted the incident frequently when she and John had an argument. When one person interprets the other's behavior as being malevolently or selfishly motivated, or reflecting a lack of care or concern, it can trigger strong negative emotions and destructive behavior.

Numerous empirical studies indicate that, compared to nondistressed couples, distressed partners tend to blame each other for problems and attribute each other's negative actions to broad and unchangeable traits more than nondistressed partners do. Conversely, distressed individuals are less likely than nondistressed partners to attribute each other's positive actions to traitlike characteristics (Bradbury & Fincham, 1990; Epstein & Baucom, 1993). Holtzworth-Munroe and Jacobson (1985) labeled this attributional bias on the part of unhappy couples as *distress maintaining*. Such interpretations leave little room for optimism that one's partner will behave in a more pleasing manner in other situations or in the future. Epstein (1985) described how the attributions of distressed spouses are similar to those of depressed individuals in that the attributions foster a sense of hopelessness about positive change. Distressed partners tend to view the other person's negative behavior as being due to enduring traits. They then explain and justify their own behavior as a response to their partners' negative traits. "Of course I get upset with you and then finally blow up; who wouldn't? You're so picky and perfectionistic; no one can please you." When distressed individuals notice the other person's positive behaviors, they often explain these positive actions in ways that minimize them. They might attribute the positive behavior to chance, unstable factors, or factors that are outside of the relationship. "She treated me nicely because she felt good about the raise she got at work."

Distressed partners do not attribute relationship problems solely to the personality or traits of the other person. Sometimes their explanations reflect negatively on the relationship itself; that is, they see problems as resulting from the other person having negative intent, wanting to hurt them, or failing to love them: "You did that because you don't care about me and wanted to hurt me" (Fincham, Beach, & Nelson, 1987; Pretzer, Epstein, & Fleming, 1991). When spouses make negative attributions for relationship problems, they also are more likely to have ineffective problem-solving discussions and to behave more negatively toward each other (Bradbury & Fincham, 1992; Miller & Bradbury, 1995). Thus, attributions influence not only how partners feel about their relationship but also how they behave toward each other.

Expectancies

Attributions involve explanations for behaviors that have already occurred. In addition, individuals make predictions about the future. These expectancies involve various predictions about the future status of the relationship or how the partner is likely to behave. Once an individual develops an expectancy, it affects his or her emotions and subsequent behavior. When Barry and Joan came for couples therapy, he pronounced

> I've basically given up. I know that she is never going to listen to me when I am upset about something. So at this point, I have withdrawn; she is correct on that front. I just don't make an effort to talk to her anymore. What's the use? I'm tired of being disappointed.

As is apparent in this example, when one person predicts that the other person or the relationship is unlikely to change, that person might give up hope and be unwilling to make the effort needed to improve the relationship. On the other hand, if that person views the same situation in a more hopeful manner regarding the future and potential for change, such an interpretation can provide the needed motivation to improve the relationship.

Several studies have shown that negative expectancies about the relationship appear to be part of relationship distress (Fincham & Bradbury, 1989; Pretzer et al., 1991; Vanzetti, Notarius, & NeeSmith, 1992). These negative expectancies seem to influence how an individual thinks about specific interactions with the partner as well as the future of the relationship more broadly. Vanzetti et al. (1992) found that, compared to nondistressed partners, distressed individuals predicted that their partners would behave more negatively during specific conversations. Often these negative predictions are borne out, which confirms the partner's belief about the hopelessness of the situation. At times, this series of interactions appears to be part of a self-fulfilling prophecy. Consider Mel, who was convinced that Evelyn did not really care about him and did not want to listen to him and accept his feelings. As a result, he was extremely angry with her: "Why bother telling her anything? She doesn't want to hear anything I say." During therapy sessions he made numerous derogatory statements about her. Typically she defended herself or attacked him in return, prompting him to point out how she had confirmed what he already knew: "See, I knew you wouldn't just listen to me. As soon as I speak, you turn it on me." These types of interactions often lead one or both partners to enter therapy with very negative predictions and many supporting experiences. When such instances occur, the therapist's role is not to automatically challenge any negative statement. In some instances, negative predictions may seem quite valid. In other instances, predicted outcomes might be less certain if the couple can learn to handle the situation differently.

Some positive predictions might be equally destructive. Jeremy had had 12 extramarital affairs in 10 years, the last 3 with the same woman over a 3-year period. On each occasion when Carol discovered the infidelity, Jeremy protested that he would change and never do it again. Each time, Carol believed him and gave their marriage another try. During couples therapy she came to understand his well-ingrained patterns and many of the factors that were driving his behavior. She concluded that these factors were unlikely to change and then faced the difficult decision of whether to continue a relationship with someone she loved but who was likely to be unfaithful to her in the future.

Expectancies do not occur in isolation; often, predictions about the future relate to how the past has been interpreted. That is, expectancies and attributions are integrally related. For example, Pretzer et al. (1991) found that when partners attributed relationship problems more to their own behavior and less to the partner's behavior, personality traits, malicious intent, or lack of love, then these partners were more likely to predict that they would improve their relationship problems in the future.

More broadly, various cognitions—such as selective attention, attributions, and expectancies—are integrally related to each other and to emotions. If one person selectively attends to negative behaviors from the other, then he or she is more likely to view these behaviors as characteristic of the partner. Then the person sees the behavior as unlikely to change (i.e., makes stable attributions), leading to negativistic expectancies for the future of the relationship. Such negative cognitions are likely to spawn negative emotions, ranging from depression to anger to anxiety about the future. Next we turn to a consideration of how these negative emotions influence subsequent thoughts about the partner.

Broad Relationship Beliefs

Assumptions

Assumptions are beliefs that each person holds about the characteristics of individuals and intimate relationships (e.g., assumptions about typical characteristics of males and females). That is, assumptions involve how people think the world and people actually operate (Baucom & Epstein, 1990). For example, each person usually develops an image of the partner—who the person is, how the person behaves, what the person likes and dislikes. These assumptions then can serve as the basis for making attributions about a partner's specific behaviors. Thus, if Bruce views Kelly as considerate, then when she forgets his birthday he might attribute it to her being overwhelmed and distracted by her father's serious illness. Consequently, the basic beliefs that each person develops about the partner and the relationship can influence how specific behaviors or events are experienced.

Several assumptions about one's partner and the relationship appear to be essential for a long-term, intimate relationship to be rewarding. These include the assumptions that one's partner is honest, trustworthy, predictable, committed, and provides safety and support. In fact, negative events are experienced as traumatic when these basic assumptions about the partner or the relationship are disrupted (Gordon & Baucom, 1999). For example, an extramarital affair may be overwhelming, largely because it disrupts the assumptions that the partner is trustworthy, honest, committed, and has the couple's best interest as a top priority. As we discuss in the intervention section (chapters 8–14) of this volume, a significant aspect of helping couples address such traumas is to assist them in developing a new set of assumptions about the partner. When assumptions become disrupted, the person no longer knows how to interpret the other person's behavior or how to behave oneself. "I don't know you; you aren't the person I thought you were. I can't move forward with this relationship until I figure out who you are."

The preceding example demonstrates how confusing it is when one partner's assumptions about the other become disrupted. In addition, by the time that many couples seek therapy, they have evolved a set of clear but very negative assumptions about each other. "He is a self-centered, hostile, mama's boy who throws a fit when everyone's life doesn't revolve around what he wants." With such an image of a partner, it is understandable why marital distress is self-perpetuating. Such a view of a partner will greatly affect the person's attention, attributions, expectancies, emotional responses, and behaviors toward the partner. An essential goal for couples therapists from almost any theoretical orientation will be to help the individual reassess whether such assumptions are valid and reasonable.

Although there is only limited evidence, certain ethnic groups might differ in their assumptions about relationships and the two genders. For example, several investigators have concluded that, in addition to making positive assumptions about their own ethnic group, there is a tendency for African American women as a group to see African American men as less responsible and reliable than they desire (Braithwaite, 1981; Cazenave, 1983; Joseph & Lewis, 1981; Turner & Turner, 1974). Some African American men also seem to hold negative assumptions about African American women. Cazenave (1983) found that middle-class African American men tend to believe that African American women have more opportunities available to them and that the increasing power obtained by African American women has contributed to African American men's lowered sense of control over their lives (Willis, 1990). Although such assumptions might be destructive for intimate relationships, therapists must understand the societal context and experiences that have contributed to such beliefs.

Standards

Whereas assumptions involve an individual's beliefs about how things actually are, standards involve personal beliefs about the characteristics that an intimate relationship and the partners "should" have (Baucom & Epstein, 1990; Baucom, Epstein, Sayers, & Sher, 1989). Partners use standards to evaluate whether each person's behavior is appropriate and acceptable. Individuals might hold standards about how partners should express affection, what they should tell each other and what they should keep to themselves, how often they should be in contact with in-laws, and so forth. At times, these standards might coincide with the person's assumptions about how things actually are; at other times, standards and assumptions are inconsistent with each other. For example, a woman might hold an assumption that men are virtually emotionless but may hold a standard that her husband should be able to experience and express strong, loving feelings for her. Such discrepancies can be a major source of relationship discord.

Standards develop from a variety of sources, including families of origin, popular media, religion, and peers. By living in a family of origin, most people develop a set of beliefs about how people should behave, interact with each other, carry out rituals and holidays, and so on. In many instances the standard evolves from a set of experiences that the individual comes to value without having any explicit discussion with others about how people should behave. On other occasions individuals develop standards or beliefs about relationships based on teachings that are more explicit. Several investigations indicate that more religious people report having happier marriages, for example. When Clayton and Baucom (1998) explored the cognitive and behavioral factors that could help to explain this association, the findings indicated that a common set of standards about relationships is taught by most major world religions. The endorsement of these widely taught standards about relationships (e.g., forgiveness, giving high priority to the relationship) can help to explain the relationship between religiosity and marital satisfaction.

Consistent with these findings, our research generally indicates that married partners are happier in their relationships when they have "relationship-oriented standards." That is, when partners believe that the two people should have a great deal of closeness and sharing, should solve problems in an egalitarian manner, and should be highly invested in giving to the relationship, the partners are happier in their marriages (Baucom, Epstein, Daiuto, & Carels, 1996; Baucom, Epstein, Rankin, & Burnett, 1996). Because the findings are correlational in nature, the cause–effect relationship between marital standards and satisfaction with the relationship is unclear.

In many instances people's standards about intimate relationships are well ingrained, deeply held, and of great importance. Often these standards involve a person's sense of morality. However, the centrality of relationship standards in a person's life cannot be assumed. Instead, the importance of relationship standards in individuals' lives seems to vary in at least three ways:

- the degree to which individuals develop a variety of standards about interpersonal relationships and articulate these standards,
- the degree to which these internal standards influence their behavior, and
- how emotionally upset they become when their standards are not met.

During therapy sessions one member of a couple might clearly describe his or her views on marriage, what each person's roles should be, and how they should treat each other. The other partner might then respond

> Do you really sit around and think about all that stuff? What you are saying makes sense, and I agree with most of it. But to be honest, I almost never spend time thinking about how husbands and wives should treat each other. I just get up, go to work, come home, and try to be a good parent and partner.

It can be frustrating to a couple when one person seems to live in a psychological world, thinking about values and standards, whereas the other person gives little thought to such issues.

Although it is important to avoid stereotyping men and women, several investigations suggest that women spend more time than men contemplating values and standards (Bielby & Bielby, 1989; Leslie, Anderson, & Branson, 1991). In addition, there might be differences in the extent to which men's and women's standards relate to their behavior. Rankin-Esquer, Burnett, Baucom, and Epstein (1997) found that women's behavior was consistent with both their own standards and their partners' standards. Thus, women appeared to be attuned to how both people believed the relationship should operate, and they behaved accordingly. However, men's behavior was not correlated either with their own standards or their partners' standards for marriage. Consequently, even when people are able to articulate their standards, there appears to be variability in the extent to which their relationship standards affect the way they behave.

Researchers also have found that regardless of the particular standards an individual holds, that person is happier with the relationship if those particular standards are being met (Baucom, Epstein, Rankin, & Burnett, 1996). These findings are consistent with our clinical experience that committed relationships do not have to take a particular form. Instead, there likely is a good deal of variability in what partners view as appropriate ways to conduct a relationship. Within reasonable limits, having one's standards met likely contributes to relationship satisfaction, regardless of the particular standards. Consequently, it is important for couples therapists to understand each partner's standards and beliefs about what an intimate relationship should be like and to evaluate whether the relationship is meeting those standards. Unless the standards seem to be inherently destructive to one of the partners, the therapist should be cautious before proposing to the couple that their relationship should operate in a particular manner. Given that the majority of couples therapists are White, middle-class individuals, they must be cautious not to assume that their own standards for relationships are inherently healthy or should be the model for all couples. Not imposing one's own standards is particularly important when working with individuals from different cultures or subcultures who view relationships differently from the therapist.

Most models of committed relationships are similarly based on therapists' knowledge of first marriages. It might be that standards for second and subsequent marriage are quite different or that the same standards have different implications in second marriages. When Allen, Baucom, Burnett, Epstein, and Rankin-Esquer (1996) explored the standards of couples in first and second marriages, they found that people in second and subsequent marriages believe that overall there should be more boundaries, more separateness, and more autonomy in marriage compared to those in first marriages. A closer look showed that this belief was held only in certain domains, however. More particularly, women in second marriages believed that they should have more autonomy regarding finances, children, and friends and family. In essence, these resources often are brought into a second marriage, and these women viewed these areas as more separate. Most important, among second marriages, standards for greater autonomy and boundaries in these areas were not related to marital distress. Thus, believing in greater separateness in areas such as children, friends, and finances is not a negative factor in second marriages. In other domains, such as emotional closeness and intimate communication, people in first and second marriages did not differ in their standards.

Finally, couples' assumptions and standards are associated not only with current relationship distress but also with the development of future distress (Baucom & Ragland, 1998; Halford, Kelly, & Markman, 1997). Epstein and Eidelson developed the Relationship Belief Inventory (Eidelson & Epstein, 1982; Epstein & Eidelson, 1981), which assesses the degree to which members of couples hold several potentially unrealistic beliefs: (a) expression of disagreement is destructive to one's relationship, (b) partners cannot change their relationship, (c) marital problems are due to innate differences between the sexes, (d) partners should be able to mind-read each other's thoughts and emotions, and (e) one must be a perfect sexual partner. The first three of these beliefs are assumptions, and the last two are standards about intimate relationships (Baucom, Epstein, et al., 1989). Research with the Relationship Belief Inventory has indicated that adherence to these standards and assumptions is associated with current and future relationship distress, negative attributions about relationship problems, preference for individual rather than couples therapy, low expectancies for future improvement of relationship problems through therapy, and more negative behaviors directed toward partners during couples' discussions of relationship problems (Baucom & Epstein, 1990; Bradbury & Fincham, 1993; Epstein, Baucom, & Rankin, 1993; Fincham, Bradbury, & Scott, 1990).

Baucom and Ragland (1998) demonstrated the predictive importance of marital standards in a longitudinal study of newlywed couples. In an assessment of couples' standards for marriage and marital adjustment within 6 months after marriage and again 3 years later, they found that during courtship how happy couples were with their relationship was unrelated to whether they felt their standards for marriage were being met by their partners. In essence, many couples seemed to be saying, "Our relationship really doesn't conform to my standards, but that's okay. I'm still very happy with our relationship." However, among women only, if their standards for marriage were not being met during courtship, they were distressed 3 years into the marriage. The findings seem to suggest that although their male partners were not behaving in ways that the women thought that they should during courtship, the women minimized the importance of this discrepancy, perhaps focusing on the excitement of their marriage. However, 3 years later these same women were unhappy; in essence, being married to a man who did not meet their standards had caught up with them. Thus, it appears that individuals in committed relationships should not try to minimize the importance of whether their partners are meeting their relationship standards.

Automatic Cognitive Processing

Research on these major types of cognition has relied on self-report questionnaires, based on the assumption that individuals can accurately report on the content of their own cognitions: "My standards for how much time we should spend together are...." However, people's cognitions not only have particular content, but they also involve the processing of information. People notice certain events and fail to notice others, retrieve memories related to similar incidents from the past, and reach some conclusions about why the event occurred. In some ways, one can think about attributions, expectancies, assumptions, and standards as the outcomes of cognitive processes.

Considerable evidence from basic cognitive science research indicates that much cognitive processing occurs beyond the level of consciousness. When Peggy seems to notice primarily the negative things that Jim does and ignore the positive things, she probably is not consciously deciding to do so. This is simply what she notices and, therefore, it is her reality. Fincham, Garnier, Gano-Phillips, and Osborne (1995) and Osgarby and Halford (1995) used cognitive science methodology to assess memory retrieval processes in distressed versus happy couples. They found that, compared to happy partners, distressed partners demonstrate greater "accessibility" to negative information about their partners and relationships and less accessibility to positive information. More specifically, distressed partners showed shorter response latencies in retrieving negative information about the other person from their memories.[1]

Clinically speaking, this type of finding suggests that often one partner is not just being difficult and deciding to process information about the relationship in a negative way; instead, it seems to be an automatic process. A significant part of couples therapy involves helping couples become aware of several factors in their relationships that appear to have become automatic. On the one hand, therapists help partners become aware of ways in which they cognitively process information about each other and their relationship in a biased manner. On the other hand, therapists work to increase partners' awareness of the behavioral interaction patterns that they display in an apparently automatic way. Taking what has become automatic and bringing it into awareness is an important step in couples therapy. Until partners begin to self-monitor and become aware of a variety of maladaptive behavioral, cognitive, and emotional patterns, these patterns are difficult to change.

Our clinical observations and initial research findings suggest that one important factor in information processing for intimate relationships is the degree to which an individual processes daily interactions in relationship terms. Rankin-Esquer, Baucom, Clayton, Tomcik, and Mullens (1999) referred to this process as *relationship schematic processing*. Authors have used a variety of labels to describe similar constructs that individuals hold about the

---

[1]Cognitive psychologists generally view high accessibility of information as meaning that the information is part of a person's core schemas or concepts about a person or event. Thoughts associated with a schema about a partner are the ones most likely to dominate the person's moment-to-moment thinking about the partner.

characteristics of their intimate relationships: *relational schemas* (e.g., Baldwin, 1992) and *relationship schemas* (Baldwin, Carrell, & Lopez, 1990; Horowitz, 1989) are two examples. Rankin-Esquer et al. (1999) developed a questionnaire in an attempt to assess the degree to which each person routinely processes information in terms of the self in relation to a partner or in relationship terms (*relationship schema*) versus processing information from a perspective focused on one's individual functioning (*individual schema*). They found that women are more likely than men to engage in relationship schematic processing, attending to the impacts of their own behavior on their couple relationship. Regarding individual schematic processing, Rankin-Esquer et al. (1999) found that men were more likely than women to report becoming absorbed in individual activities and remain unaware of other people's behavior. The findings also showed that marital adjustment was related to being aware of both one's own and one's partner's behaviors during an interaction and negatively related to becoming absorbed in individual pursuits and being unaware of the partner's behavior. These findings seem to be consistent with many clinical examples in which one partner becomes quite distressed when the other person becomes absorbed and inattentive to the couple's interaction. As Julie noted,

> At times he is such a space cadet. He gets totally lost in the stratosphere and has no awareness of what is going on around him. Last week at dinner, our daughter knew he wasn't paying attention and she said, "Dad, I've got great news. I flunked my math test today. Isn't that great?" And he actually responded, "That's wonderful, darling." It makes for a great story, but it is horrible to live with.

Sullivan and Baucom (2000) created an observational coding system to assess relationship schematic processing. This coding system evaluates both how often a person demonstrates relationship schematic processing in his or her conversation with a partner and how well the individual seems to process information in relationship terms. That is, some people view almost the entire world in terms of interpersonal interactions (high frequency of relationship schematic processing), but they do not evaluate this information realistically. Some partners complain that the other person gives relationship meaning to everything that occurs even when it seems unlikely to have relationship meaning. As Natasha commented, "Sometimes wanting to go to sleep is just fatigue, and it means nothing about our relationship." Sullivan (1999) found that, among distressed couples, women engaged in more and higher quality relationship schematic processing compared to their male partners. In addition, both men and women were happier in their marriages if their partners engaged in a high quality of relationship schematic processing. On the basis of this same sample of couples who received cognitive–behavioral marital therapy, Baucom (1999) found that the intervention increased the quality of relationship schematic processing for men but not for women. Most important, women were happier with the relationship at the end of treatment to the degree that their male partners increased in their quality of relationship schematic processing. This finding seems to echo the request of many women that they want their male partners to think about and process their relationship in a more sophisticated way.

EMOTIONS IN COUPLES' RELATIONSHIPS

Rather than describing their attributions, standards, and other cognitions about their relationships, many couples concentrate on how they feel about their partners. In this section we focus on the role of emotions in couples' relationships, examining what emotions are most likely to influence couples' functioning, how partners experience their emotions and convey those feelings to their partners, and the ways in which emotions interact with the cognitive processes and behaviors discussed previously.

Emotions are a hallmark of intimate relationships such as marriage. In large part, people select their partners because of how they feel about them. When people fall in love, they experience joy when around the other person and sadness and longing when not with that other individual. Particularly during courtship, these strong emotions can lead to a variety of behaviors and cognitions. Although such intense emotional states usually do not persist for years, strong emotional responses along with accompanying thoughts and behaviors toward the partner and the relationship do persist. In a recent study of couples married 30–60 years, Palmer and Baucom (1998) found that a number of couples reported feeling that they have married that special someone; have great respect, admiration, and love for their partner; and derive their identity in large part from being part of the couple.

At the opposite end of the spectrum, many distressed couples seek treatment when one or both people are deeply unhappy or distraught. As Adrian commented during an early therapy session,

> My own personal happiness has gone down consistently for about the last five years of this marriage. And that isn't typical for me. I've always seen myself as an upbeat, happy person. Either this relationship has to get better, or I have to get out. I'm really miserable.

Other couples complain about the absence of both positive and negative emotional response to the partner:

> Look, this relationship is over. I just don't feel anything. I used to be angry, but even that is gone now. When I look at you, I don't feel anything. And neither you nor I can do anything to bring the feelings back.

Lazarus (1991) summarized what the above couples are experiencing:

> Emotions are complex, patterned, organismic reactions to how we think we are doing in our lifelong efforts to survive and flourish and to achieve

what we wish for ourselves. Emotions are like no other psychosocio-biological construct in that they express the intimate personal meaning of what is happening in our social lives. (p. 6)

Consequently, emotions are central to intimate relationships such as marriage.

Important Emotions in Intimate Relationships

Specific Emotions

There is no agreed-on comprehensive list of human emotions, and it is not our intention to catalogue all emotions that members of a couple may experience. Instead, we are concerned with emotions that are important in intimate, interpersonal relationships. Elsewhere we have differentiated emotions into two broad positive and negative categories (Baucom & Epstein, 1990). For some purposes, this broad differentiation is sufficient, but in other instances, to understand a particular couple, greater differentiation among emotions can be helpful. In Exhibit 3.1 we have grouped positive emotions and negative emotions into several categories. Among the positive emotions, two categories reflect an overall positive state: (a) happy–joyful and (b) close–warm. We have differentiated between these two groups of positive emotions because of their different interpersonal focus (as we discuss later in the chapter, emotion researchers have developed several schemes for grouping emotions). The emotions in the happy–joyful group, such as cheerful, excited, happy, and joyful, describe a general emotional state of a person. These emotions do not explicitly focus on the person's feelings about another individual. On the other hand, the close–warm emotions (e.g., loving, devoted, close, friendly, affectionate, sympathetic) have a more explicit interpersonal focus. It is important to understand whether an individual is feeling positive in general and whether the emotions are focused on the partner.

Two other categories of positive emotions relate to level of activation: (a) energy–vigor and (b) relaxed–calm. In addition, several other specific positive emotions, such as ambitious, do not fit neatly into these categories. In defining these emotions as positive we mean that the person experiencing these emotions is likely to view them in that way. In many instances, when one person expresses or experiences these emotions, the partner and the relationship also are likely to benefit. At times, a wife's energy and liveliness might be exactly what are needed if her husband is discouraged and overwhelmed with responsibilities. Similarly, a husband's relaxed, calm approach might be helpful if his wife feels anxious and confused about their child being out late at night after curfew. However, depending on the situation, expression of such emotions might not always have a positive effect. A wife who remains cheerful when her husband has received devastating news might be experienced by him as unfeeling or unsympathetic.

EXHIBIT 3.1
Common Positive and Negative Emotions in Couple Relationships

Categories of positive emotions	Categories of negative emotions
• Happy–joyful—General emotional state (other examples: cheerful, excited)	• Depressed–sad—General emotional state (other examples: discouraged, gloomy)
• Close–warm—Interpersonal focus (other examples: loving, devoted, friendly)	• Anxiety—General emotional state (other examples: tense, worried, frightened)
• Energy–vigor (other examples: lively, vigorous)	• Anger—General emotional state (other examples: annoyed, furious)
• Relaxed–calm (other examples: peaceful, gentle)	• Contempt—Interpersonal focus beyond mere anger; reflects global, negative view of partner (other examples: criticism, disdain)
• Other positive emotions—ambitious, inspired	• Sense of fatigue (other examples: exhausted, lifeless)
	• Other negative emotions—Jealousy, guilt, shame

Much more has been written and researched about negative emotions in couples' relationships than about positive ones. Although the distinctiveness of the negative emotions that clients experience and report often is unclear, it is helpful to differentiate among depressed feelings, anxious feelings, and angry feelings. From a cognitive perspective, each of these emotions is often linked to a different cognitive experience. Depressed and sad feelings usually result from a sense of loss or the thwarting of some important goal. Anxiety typically is related to an appraisal that something is dangerous, threatening, or unpredictable. Anger more typically is related to a sense of unfairness, injustice, or the violation of one's territory or rights. Knowing that Mark is sad because Ian came home late and disrupted their evening together is quite different from knowing that he is furious because he interprets Ian's lateness as a sign that Ian is self-centered.

In addition to these "big three" negative emotions (depression, anxiety, and anger), other negative emotions occur in intimate relationships. Gottman (1999) proposed that it is important to distinguish between feeling angry and feeling critical and contemptuous. Expressing anger does not predict divorce, but expressing criticism and contempt do. Critical and contemptuous feelings are destructive because of their strong interpersonal focus; they suggest a global, negative sentiment and attitude toward the partner. As such, criticism and contempt likely are best viewed as an emotion–cognition complex including both an emotional and an evaluative component. Although a person's anger also typically has an interpersonal focus, often it is associated with much more specific events or circumstances and does not reflect a global perception of the other individual. Therefore, although researchers, theoreticians, and clinicians often have regarded angry, critical, and contemptuous feelings similarly, it seems important to view critical, contemptuous, and disdainful feelings as separate from angry feelings. A fifth category of negative emotions involves a sense of fatigue. Finally, several other negative emotions, such as jealousy, guilt, and shame, tend to involve a combination of emotions; for example, jealousy tends to be a combination of anger and anxiety.

As with positive emotions, negative emotions not only affect the individual who experiences them; in many instances, they also negatively affect the person's partner or the relationship. As noted earlier, several investigations have demonstrated that after being with a depressed person individuals typically feel negative emotions such as depression. At the same time, depending on the circumstances, negative feelings expressed by one individual will not necessarily engender similar feelings in the partner. Instead, the partner may experience a complementary emotion; that is, when one person is feeling fatigued or depressed, the other person might be motivated to create a more positive atmosphere. Similarly, a person might experience great warmth and tenderness toward the partner after the partner fails. Although such complementary or reciprocal emotions can be appropriate in some instances, at times relationships become destructive when one person feels better as the partner feels worse. If a husband feels better when his wife is frightened of him, for instance, then the relationship likely needs significant assistance.

Although not a comprehensive list, these emotions are likely to have greatest meaning in an interpersonal context: positive emotions related to happiness, closeness–warmth, energy, and calm, and negative emotions related to sadness, anxiety, anger, contempt, and fatigue.

State vs. Trait

In considering emotions on an individual and an interpersonal level, it is helpful to differentiate between (a) the specific emotional state that one partner is experiencing at the moment versus (b) the more general emotional tone that the person experiences in life overall, or the overall sentiment that the person feels toward the partner (Weiss, 1980). Spielberger (1985) made this important and useful distinction in discussing anxiety as both a trait and a state. A particular person might have a general tendency to experience a high level of anxiety across a broad range of situations and over many years (*high trait anxiety*). However, at a given moment, that person might or might not be anxious (*state anxiety*). Similarly, in a consideration of intimacy, Prager (1995) differentiated between an *intimate interaction* that occurs at a given moment and a broader sense of an *intimate relationship*. Although they use different labels, researchers and clinicians from a variety of perspectives have noted the importance of differentiating between an emotional response at a given time or in response to a given situation (often called a *mood*) versus a broad set of feelings about oneself, the world, or an intimate partner and relationship.

This distinction is important, because the overall emotional tone of a couple's relationship likely has a much greater impact on them than a momentary experience or expression of a given emotion. If a wife generally feels warm toward her husband, that is likely to be extremely important in determining the overall quality of their marriage. However, if on a given night she feels distant from him, it might cause minimal long-term disruption to the relationship. Nevertheless, the expression of certain emotions might be quite damaging even if they occur infrequently and do not represent the person's broader feelings about the partner. Distressed partners are notorious for remembering and reminding the other person of some very hurtful emotions that the person expressed on one occasion: "I remember after that huge fight, you said you were disgusted and couldn't stand looking at me any more. The real you came out that night. I know you dislike me and want to end our marriage."

Individual differences. Thus, in addition to specific emotional reactions to particular circumstances, it appears that one can look at a person's emotional experiences on a broader level as well. In fact, there appear to be striking individual differences in the likelihood that a given individual will experience positive or negative emotions. Beach and Fincham (1994) provided a thoughtful analysis of this issue and its applicability to relationship functioning. They noted that investigators who have studied the structure of emotions have developed a variety of models that appear to be closely related to each other. Watson and Tellegen (1985) developed a two-dimensional model of emotion that can be represented as a circumplex with two primary dimensions: positive affectivity and negative affectivity. In addition, the fundamental emotions proposed by Izard (1977) can be ordered within the two-dimensional space of positive and negative affectivity.

With the terms *positive affectivity* and *negative affectivity*, Watson and Tellegen (1985) were not only referring to an individual's response to a specific situation but also proposing that a person has a general tendency to experience particular degrees of these emotions across situations and time. The empirical literature seems to support this notion of consistency in emotional experience over time. Schuerger, Zarrella, and Hotz (1989) concluded from a review of the stability of emotions over different time periods, ranging from less than 1 year to more than 20 years, that positive affectivity has an average stability coefficient of .72 and negative affectivity has an average stability coefficient of .64.

Beach and Fincham (1994) summarized the characteristics of individuals high on positive and negative affectivity. People high on positive affectivity are likely to be adventurous and energetic, experience well-being, and display social dominance (Clark & Watson, 1991). In addition, they may be more responsive to situations that produce positive mood and more interested in achievement, social interaction, and sexual intimacy. On the other hand, people high on negative affectivity are more likely to experience anger, sadness, anxiety, and feelings of rejection—the major negative emotions that we noted earlier. Moreover, they are likely to be more responsive to situations that induce negative emotion (Larsen & Ketelaar, 1991). Beach and Fincham proposed a fourfold typology based on the two dimensions. A person who is high on both positive affectivity and negative affectivity, for instance, has a tendency to approach other people and be dominant but also is easily angered, reactive, and hard to please. They suggested that an individual high on positive affectivity but low on negative affectivity also has a tendency to approach others but generally is calm, dominant, and easily satisfied.

Affectivity and relationships. What are the implications for intimate relationships of these differential levels of positive and negative affectivity? First, one person's overall affectivity will affect his or her day-to-day mood and therefore the people in that individual's environment. People high on positive affectivity and low on negative affectivity are likely to create a more positive overall environment for themselves and their family. Their upbeat, optimistic style will be appealing to most partners. This idea is similar to the notion of "uninfluenced stable steady states" within marriage developed by Cook et al. (1995), based on the concept of homeostasis from general systems theory. By *uninfluenced stable steady states* is meant "what each person brings to the interaction before being influenced by the partner. This is determined both by the history of the relationship and the person's temperament" (Gottman, 1999, p. 34). Consequently, some partners are likely to bring a generally positive mood and positive approach to the interaction, based in part on their overall tendencies toward positive affectivity. Second, a person's affectivity is likely to influence interactions that the individual has with the partner. We conjecture that individuals high on positive affectivity and low on negative affectivity generally bring a positive mood to specific interactions with their partners, are responsive to positive behaviors from the partners, are less responsive to negative behaviors from the partners, and thus contribute to the long-term well-being of the relationship.

In contrast, people with a high level of negative affectivity and a low level of positive affectivity create a generally negative atmosphere within the relationship, are particularly sensitive and reactive to negative behaviors from the partner, are less responsive to positive behaviors, and thus are likely to engage in and possibly escalate negative interaction cycles. Over time, this can contribute to the development of relationship distress. As we have discussed, relationship distress itself seems to evoke many of the same responses (e.g., a focus on the negative, less attention to positives) that typify these people. Therefore, a person in a highly distressed relationship who brings a difficult temperament to the relationship likely will have more difficulty behaving in a positive manner and experiencing a partner's positive behavior. Considerable effort might be needed to induce positive moods in such individuals during couples' interactions. This situation will present a particular challenge to the therapist as well as to the couple. Consequently, it is not surprising that Bradbury and Karney (1993) concluded on the basis of longitudinal studies that neuroticism or negative affectivity predicts future marital distress.

In summary, the individuals' levels of positive and negative affectivity likely influence their relationships by (a) providing a general tone that affects others and contributes to a general family atmosphere and (b) influencing their interactions with their partners and making them differentially sensitive to positive and negative behaviors from their partners. In their longitudinal study of marital stability, Cook et al. (1995) presented findings consistent with both of these ideas. First, couples who remained together had more positive, uninfluenced, stable steady states (i.e., what each person brought to the interaction was more positive) compared to couples who eventually divorced. Second, couples who remained together influenced each other in a positive direction, whereas couples who eventually divorced influenced each other in a negative direction (Gottman, 1999).

Recognizing the existence of some stability in people's affectivity does not mean that a therapist should not hold each partner responsible for his or her moods and behavior because of temperamental factors. Instead, each individual might need to confront certain situations in his or her relationship with a great deal of thought and preparation. For example, Rich acknowledged that most of his current and past friends and family would describe him as a rather irritable individual. In particular, he had a tendency to become angry and verbally attack people when things "did not go right." Unfortunately, his wife and all of their children showed signs of attention deficit disorder, and Rich frequently became enraged with them for making mistakes and not following through on agreements. In couples therapy a major focus was to help him recognize his tendency toward irritability and to develop plans for how he could calm himself and think about expressing his concerns in a way that the family could hear.

Factors That Influence the Experience of Emotions

To understand emotions within intimate relationships, it is helpful to understand what factors affect a person's emotional experience. Several somewhat stable factors develop over time and contribute to a person's current emotional experience. In addition, several factors focal to the present also influence current mood (see Exhibit 3.2).

Distal and Stable Factors That Influence the Experience of Emotions

Personality or individual differences. The preceding discussion of positive and negative affectivity points out that there are long-term, relatively stable differences in the extent to which people experience positive and negative moods. Often these differences are viewed as aspects of personality or tem-

EXHIBIT 3.2
Factors That Influence the Experience of Emotions

Distal and stable factors
Personality
Experiences in earlier relationships
History of the current relationship
Cognitions about emotions
Coping styles
Proximal factors
Current stage of the relationship
Current environment in a person's life
Current interaction with the partner

perament. In addition to differences in positivity versus negativity, there appear to be stable individual differences in the course of experiencing emotions in terms of the magnitude as well as the duration of emotional responses (Stuart, 1980). Some individuals seem to experience a strong level of anger, express it, and then feel ready to move forward. For other people the anger appears to simmer for a longer time. It may take longer before these latter individuals are ready to reconcile with a partner after conflict because the anger, upset, and hurt stay with them longer. Partners frequently learn this about each other and can describe each individual's pattern of emotional experience for different emotions, such as anger, anxiety, excitement, and sexual passion. Many couples are able to adapt to the two partners' patterns of emotional experience in a way that does not further provoke negative mood or conflict between the two persons. Marcus and Rita had developed a strategy that worked well for them. As Marcus described,

> When Rita gets angry, I just give her a wide berth. I stay away from her and try not to say or do anything that will provoke her further. She usually needs to sleep on it overnight, and then when things die down, we can talk about it. Personally, I would rather discuss it right away, but I learned early on in our relationship that that is a disaster for us.

Gender differences might also be at work here. When McCarter and Levenson (1996) exposed men and women to a loud, unexpected sound, they found that men demonstrated a larger cardiovascular response than women did; men also required more time to recover from the cardiovascular arousal than women did. Consequently, when one partner responds that "It just takes me longer to calm down than it takes you," that person might be speaking literally. Helping the couple to recognize and respond adaptively to these individual differences in the frequency, magnitude, and course of emotional experience can help them to negotiate these important individual differences.

Experiences in earlier relationships.   Adults enter intimate relationships having had a variety of relationships throughout life. These experiences not only affect how they think about relationships and behave, but they also influence how individuals respond emotionally within intimate relationships. Many of these experiences began in the family of origin. For example, Hetherington (1972) demonstrated that when their parents divorced, girls were subsequently more likely to become sexually promiscuous when they reached adolescence. One interpretation is that these girls felt abandoned by their fathers, felt insecure, and were attempting to prove to themselves that they were valued and appealing to other males. On the other hand, children who grow up in a stable environment in which parents attend to their needs might develop a perspective that other individuals can be counted on as resources of support and comfort. In adulthood these people are more likely to experience calmness and security in their intimate relationships.

Previous experiences in other romantic relationships also contribute to current emotional experiences in intimate relationships. Thus, if an individual's earlier romantic relationship ended after a partner's unexpected affair, that individual might be quite sensitive to potential rejection and deception in subsequent relationships. The result could be ongoing anxiety in the present relationship, even though it appears to be satisfactory and stable.

Different theoretical perspectives use varying terminology to address these earlier experiences that shape emotional responses within adult intimate relationships. From a cognitive perspective, Young (1990) referred to *cognitive schemas* that develop over long periods of time through multiple relationships and that influence emotional experiences in a person's current intimate relationship. Both basic researchers (Simpson & Rholes, 1998) and therapists (Johnson & Greenberg, 1994b) also rely on attachment theory to explain how these early relationship experiences shape individuals' internal concepts about intimate relationships and affect current emotional reactions to their partners.

History of the current relationship. One of the most important factors affecting the current experience of emotion within a couple's relationship is the history of the relationship itself. As Weiss (1980) explained, an individual typically develops an overall sentiment or global feeling about the partner and the relationship based on a series of interactions over time. Once this sentiment develops, it can greatly influence the person's emotional response to a current interaction. Consider Derek, who reported

> It doesn't really matter what I do now. She is so angry and bitter about our relationship over the past decade that my current behavior has no impact. I can bring her a cup of coffee in bed on Saturday mornings, and she expresses contempt for me. At this point, her feelings toward me are so set, I don't think anything that I do makes a difference.

A major task for the therapist is to help the couple differentiate their current interactions from previous patterns and the resultant sentiment that has developed over time. If couples allow their overall negative sentiment to dominate their experience of current and future interactions, then improving the relationship becomes increasingly difficult.

The importance of an individual's overall sentiment toward the partner can help explain Gottman's (1999) finding that the single best predictor of divorce is the amount of contempt expressed as partners interact with each other. He found that happy, stable couples express essentially no contempt toward each other during conversations. We believe that this is because contempt is much more than the behavioral expression of a temporary mood state; rather, contempt is a more global sentiment that evolves over the history of the relationship and then is expressed at particular moments of distress or conflict. When one partner experiences contempt and has a lack of respect for the other individual, then a decline in relationship quality over time is quite likely. It is important to note that Gottman (1999) also found that the expression of anger per se does not predict relationship decline. This is likely because anger is an immediate emotional response experienced by a wide range of couples, quite different from a sustained sense of contempt for the other person over an extended period.

Cognitions about emotions. People have cognitions about their own and others' emotions. From a variety of sources, ranging from family of origin, religion, friends, and teachers, to mass media, people learn and develop attitudes and beliefs about emotions. Some people are taught that emotional experience is what makes life worth living, and they are encouraged to experience their emotions fully. Other people are taught that emotions are a sign of weakness or immaturity and interfere with making informed, rational decisions. Similarly, some people are taught that specific emotions are either helpful or inappropriate. When Bonnie complained that Fred never let her see when he was feeling down or vulnerable, Fred explained,

> In my family growing up, males didn't feel vulnerable. It was a harsh world that I grew up in, and I was told directly that feeling those emotions got you in trouble. So, I just don't allow myself to feel vulnerable.

In essence, Fred developed a standard that experiencing certain emotions was wrong, along with expectancies that negative consequences would follow if he did experience those emotions.

Individuals are taught standards not only about negative emotions but also about positive emotions toward others. Some people learn that they should experience passion toward their partner on an ongoing basis. When these feelings wane, they begin to worry that their relationship is doomed. Similarly, some individuals are taught that if they are in a committed relationship they should not experience attraction toward individuals other than their partners. These various standards can result in significant internal or interpersonal conflict when such emotions arise.

When one partner does not appear to experience or express certain emotions, the therapist can benefit from exploring that person's beliefs about emotions. An absence of emotional expression might not be a skill deficit, and attempts to initially address the issue with skills training might be unsuccessful. When Alex and Paula's couples therapist concluded that she needed to explore Alex's beliefs about emotions before attempting skills training concerning emotions, Alex explained

> I'm a doctor. I wear the white coat. That means I don't have emotional responses; it is not adaptive. I have to maintain a clear, clinical perspective at all times. I learned that in medical school, and it has been reinforced every day for the last 30 years. I can't walk out the door, come home, and suddenly be emotional. That is impossible. I simply can't work that way.

The therapist recognized the need to explore with Alex why there might be some value in his trying to alter the way that he dealt with emotions. Otherwise, the therapist might find herself in a struggle as she urged Alex to experience emotions when he believed that doing so was maladaptive.

Coping styles to deal with discomfort.   Many people appear to be uncomfortable experiencing emotions. For some individuals the physiological arousal that accompanies emotions is distressing. Gottman (1999) proposed that important gender differences exist regarding physiological activation and response to this activation. He found that men are flooded emotionally by lower levels of negative affect during couples' interaction than are women (Gottman, 1994a, 1994b), apparently because such interactions arouse their sense of danger and need to remain vigilant. In response to this arousal Gottman and Levenson (1988) found that men are more likely than women to withdraw emotionally from negatively arousing interactions. Thus, one response to interactions that arouse uncomfortable emotions is to withdraw from the interaction, either by altering the content or focus of the discussion or by withdrawing behaviorally, such as leaving the room (the response that Gottman, 1999, called *stonewalling*).

In addition to withdrawing, two other behavioral responses to discomfort with the emotional tone of the couple's interaction are (a) engaging the partner, often in a negative manner, or (b) holding one's ground and defending oneself. Both of these strategies can be used to lessen the intensity of the emotional experience, sometimes successfully and at other times unsuccessfully. In terms of engagement, some people appear to become physically abusive of their partners when they are emotionally aroused and feel inadequate to confront the situation in other ways. Baucom, Epstein, Daiuto, Carels, Rankin, and Burnett (1996) found that in a community sample many individuals reported that when the couple experienced marital conflict, the individual felt personally responsible for the difficulty and was emotionally upset. However, that same individual frequently responded by doing something negative or damaging toward the other person. That is, even when a person can acknowledge internally that he or she is responsible for a problem, the response to experiencing a negative mood may be to attack the other individual. Such aggressive behavior may increase the individual's sense of control over the situation and decrease anxiety.

An alternative strategy is to defend oneself behaviorally in an attempt to lessen the impact of a partner's behavior that has created the negative mood state. Gottman (1999) concluded that a typical pattern for couples whose marriages eventually end in divorce is for one person to criticize and for the other individual to become defensive. Behavioral interaction patterns that include withdrawal, defending, and attacking serve a multitude of functions, but finding a way to lessen uncomfortable negative moods may be a major reason for such responses.

In addition to behavioral strategies to lessen uncomfortable moods, people use a variety of internal strategies. Many individuals learn to suppress, discount, or not attend to their emotions. Often the partners of such individuals are distressed by this pattern, because it means that they have little capacity to evoke emotional responses from the other individual. This unresponsiveness contributes to an escalation process in which one person behaves in an increasingly extreme manner to produce an emotional response in the other person. Many distressed partners acknowledge that they use extreme, sometimes outrageous behavior to elicit a response from the other person because this is the only strategy that works. Even though the person who is escalating dislikes the pattern, it is reinforced because the other person eventually responds emotionally.

An alternative strategy for dealing with uncomfortable emotions is to alter the emotion that is experienced. Johnson and Greenberg (1995) differentiated between *primary* and *secondary* emotions: "In this categorization, the primary emotions are viewed as essentially biologically adaptive, orienting the organism to the personal significance of outside events in relation to needs and goals" (p. 126). That is, primary emotions mobilize an individual to respond in accordance with outside events in ways that will help the person achieve his or her goals, such as when fear mobilizes the individual to withdraw as a protection from threats.

On the other hand, secondary emotional responses often result when primary emotional responses have been thwarted. For example, Kyle tried to express his sense of loneliness and isolation when Jesse focused on her work at home rather than spending time with him. Over time, he found that Jesse defended her behavior when he expressed his isolation, so he developed a pattern in which he became angry and attacked her rather than expressing his loneliness. Secondary emotions often are responses to primary emotions. If a husband is frightened that his wife might leave him, but he views fear as unmanly, he might experience and express anger that she is not focusing enough attention on him. From a therapeutic perspective, Johnson and Greenberg argued (1995) that the therapist's role is to attempt to focus on primary emotions and the unmet needs associated with them and to explore secondary emotions only as a means of accessing underlying primary ones.

Christensen, Jacobson, and Babcock (1995) differentiated between *soft* emotions, which imply vulnerability, and *hard* emotions, which portray strength and dominance. Christensen et al. proposed that soft emotions almost always accompany hard emotions, and the emphasis in integrative couples therapy is on helping individuals access and express their more vulnerable emotions to their partners. Although we agree that individuals often focus on hard emotions to the exclusion of soft emotions, both types of emotion can be equally important. For instance, strong emotions related to a need for power and control are just as important for some individuals as emotions evoked by a need to be close. Overall, however, major approaches to couples therapy based on attachment theory and social learning theory agree and emphasize that individuals often avoid experiencing threatening or unacceptable emotions and replace them with less threatening or more acceptable ones. These views also are consistent with a more psychodynamic perspective that emphasizes the ways a person uses various defense mechanisms to avoid unacceptable feelings.

Proximal Factors That Influence the Experiencing of Emotions

Stage of the relationship. Just as individuals experience different stages of personal development, couples experience different stages in the family life cycle. Although theoreticians and researchers propose different stages, almost all models of couple and family development include normative transitions that are related to having children (Carter & McGoldrick, 1999). As Lindahl, Malik, and Bradbury (1997) pointed out, the stages are typically identified by transition points, such as the transition from dating to marriage, then to parenthood, when children become adolescents, to the "empty nest," and finally to retirement. Although each couple is likely to respond differently to the specific stages, each stage ushers in fairly typical needs for adaptation and change. For many couples, courtship before marriage and the early years of marriage often involve significant passion, excitement, and a focus on spending time together. However, after the couple has been married for several years, has assumed increasing economic and social responsibility, and has experienced a decrease in the novelty of the relationship, this overall level of passion and excitement decreases for many couples. Similarly, when parents experience significant anxiety when their first child obtains a driver's license and is away from home without supervision, the couple might experience a broader atmosphere of tension in which they are quick to snap at each other for a variety of behaviors unrelated to adolescent driving.

External environment. The external environment also can serve as a source of stress or support that will significantly affect an individual's current mood. In chapter 5 we discuss in depth the impact of the environment on couples' functioning. At this point it is simply important to recognize that the environment can be a significant factor in the emotions that an individual or couple experiences. Many couples remark that they function well as a couple as long as one of them is doing well individually. However, when both of them experience significant external stressors, such as overload at their jobs at the same time, they have little resilience. Both people are likely to be in negative moods, feel less tolerant of each other's foibles or idiosyncrasies, and more likely to reciprocate negative behavior with a negative behavior. Consequently, many individuals find it helpful to disclose to the other person that they are in a negative mood because of external stressors. This information can help to ensure that the partner does not misinterpret the individual's mood and corresponding behavior as results of events in the relationship, and it can provide an opportunity for the partner to offer support.

Current interaction. An individual's emotional experience also is influenced by current interactions between the two partners. We list this factor last to make a point. In addition to the current interaction, hosts of factors just described influence a person's overall mood and specific emotional response during a given interaction. Unfortunately, partners frequently simplify their perceptions of causality and view their internal and behavioral responses as resulting largely or solely from the other person's current behavior: "Of course I'm furious. You ignored me all evening." Given the multitude of factors that affect a specific emotional response, it is not surprising that therapists often experience confusion when one partner responds to the other's behavior with strong emotions that seem to go beyond what is occurring at the moment.

Factors That Influence the Expression of Emotions

Many of the factors just discussed that influence the experience of emotion also influence the expression of emotion. Obviously, it is difficult to express an emotion if it has not been experienced. In addition to the factors just discussed, several additional factors can influence whether an individual will express an emotion to his or her partner.

Emotional Expression to Meet Personal Needs

The expression of emotions has a strong interpersonal component. One person communicates information to another person about his or her own experiences and the status of their relationship through verbal and nonverbal expressions of emotional states. One function of this communication is that an individual's expression of a given emotion to a partner may help the person achieve personal goals. Consequently, the degree to which the person expresses emotions will be influenced by how successful the communication is in reaching the desired goals. For example, individuals vary greatly in their needs for closeness and intimacy. As Johnson and Greenberg (1995) pointed out, expressing emotions is a major way to regulate attachment and the related sense of security, closeness, and so on. If one partner desires greater closeness, or needs confirmation that the other person cares, expressing tender emotions of love, caring, and warmth is one possible way to elicit those behaviors from the other person. In fact, Prager (1995) concluded that an intimate interaction centers on sharing something that is personal, including vulnerable emotions. Therefore, it is not surprising that people who seek a high level of closeness also emphasize expressing tender emotions to others. Unfortunately, when these verbal expressions are unsuccessful in eliciting reciprocal caring and intimate behavior from the other person, the individual might resort to expressing secondary emotions, such as anger and becoming demanding or coercive. The goal of such expressions of negative emotions still may be to elicit caring behavior from the partner, or it can be to punish the partner for neglecting the person's needs.

Some other individuals seek more distance in their relationship and therefore are less emotionally expressive overall, or they express mainly negative emotions that serve a function of creating more distance.

Beliefs About the Expression of Emotion

Just as individuals have beliefs about experiencing certain emotions, they also have cognitions about expressing emotion. These beliefs about experiencing versus expressing emotions might or might not coincide. For example, some people believe it is appropriate to experience anger but that it is inappropriate to express anger to another person. Fitzpatrick (1988) concurred that openness and self-disclosure are not valued equally by members of all couples. Consistent with this point of view, Glick (1996) found in a community sample of married couples wide variability in couples' beliefs about the appropriateness of expressing emotions and their comfort in doing so. Overall, women viewed expressing emotions as more important than their male partners did, and women were more comfortable expressing their emotions.

There appear to be cultural differences in addition to gender differences regarding beliefs about expressing emotions. As we noted in chapter 2, Halford, Hahlweg, and Dunne (1990) found that German couples were more likely to express disagreement and other negative communications compared to Australian couples. In some Asian cultures strong expression of emotion is considered inappropriate, but in Hispanic cultures strong display of emotions is regarded as more appropriate (Hines, Preto, McGoldrick, Almeida, & Weltman, 1999). Members of multicultural couples might experience difficulty understanding the other person's display or lack of display of emotions, and they might find such displays either upsetting or rewarding.

Skills in Expressing and Regulating Emotions

When an individual does not express emotions to his or her partner, or does so with some difficulty, it is easy to assume that the individual has a skill deficit. The preceding discussion should make clear that a multitude of factors impinge on the expression of emotion. In some instances, however, an individual does appear to have a skill deficit in expressing emotions. This skill deficit can take a variety of forms, but two broad domains are important:

- the inability to label and describe the emotions that one is experiencing, or to relate one's emotions to internal experiences or external circumstances, and
- difficulty in expressing emotions in a modulated manner, with an appropriate level of intensity.

Some individuals appear to experience difficulty in discriminating between different internal emotional experiences beyond identifying their feelings as positive or negative: Many partners have trouble going beyond stating that they are upset. As Sharon responded when urged by her therapist to clarify what she meant by feeling upset, "I don't really know. I'm not very good at these emotions. About the best that I can ever do is to know whether I am upset. But I don't really know if I'm angry, sad, or what."

Other individuals are able to label their emotions, but they have difficulty knowing the basis of their emotional responses; that is, they are unable to relate their emotions to their internal cognitions or to circumstances in the external environment. Seeing these linkages is important because it can help the individual experience a greater sense of control over emotions rather than feeling that emotions arise from nowhere. In addition, it is important for the person's partner to understand what makes the individual happy or distressed. Without such understanding, both partners can feel like slaves to one individual's emotions.

Some individuals experience difficulty expressing their emotions at an appropriate level of intensity. In some cases partners express their feelings in such a muted way that the other individual does not recognize their importance. As Claudia said,

> I would have stopped if I knew my kidding was really hurting you. You said you didn't like it, but you said it so mildly I didn't realize you really wanted me to stop. I don't purposely try to upset you; I just don't know how you feel usually.

At the other end of the spectrum, some individuals exhibit an unwillingness to modulate their expression of strong emotions, believing that this is how emotions should be expressed. Occasionally, however, a strong, unbridled expression of anger and hostility results from poor emotion regulation. Linehan (1993) emphasized the centrality of poor emotion regulation among individuals with borderline personality disorder. However, a significant number of people in distressed relationships have poor emotion regulation without having borderline personality disorder. Rather than experiencing emotions such as anger on a continuum, they appear to experience anger in an all-or-nothing manner such that any experience of anger is at full throttle. When distressed couples seek intervention, it often is difficult to distinguish between a high level of anger that is typical in distressed relationships versus strong anger that reflects poor emotion regulation. Over time, the therapist may recognize that, even with extensive efforts by a couple and improvement in their relationship, one individual consistently expresses extreme anger in situations that seem inappropriate. In these instances, working with one individual on emotion regulation might be critical. Otherwise, couples therapy can take the form of crisis management, in which the therapist must focus on attempting to decrease intense emotion with little opportunity to progress in a reasonable manner toward addressing the couple's difficulties. At present there is almost no research on emotion regulation difficulties within the context of relationship distress, although treatments for partner abuse typically include strategies for addressing such problems (Heyman & Neidig, 1997). It is important to recognize and intervene with emotion regulation difficulties so that the couple and the therapist do not become discouraged by destructive interactions within and outside sessions.

Impact of Emotions on Cognitive Functioning

Discussing emotions in isolation is almost meaningless. As noted earlier, emotions are integrally related to cognitions and behavior. We have discussed how cognitions in general influence emotions (e.g., if a wife attributes her husband's long work hours to his desire to avoid her, then she might feel hurt, unloved, or angry). In addition, we have described how individuals have beliefs about emotions that influence both the experience and expression of emotions. The very notion of expressing emotions implies that there is a behavioral component to emotional functioning. Consequently, it is important to understand the relationships among emotions, cognitions, and behavior.

The most prevalent cognitive model relating behavior, cognitions, and emotions proposes that a behavior occurs, an individual cognitively processes what has occurred and, on the basis of these cognitions, the person responds emotionally (Ellis, 1986). This model views emotions as endpoints resulting from behavior and cognitions. In addition, emotions can influence behaviors and cognitions. For example, Rolls (1990) pointed out that emotions influence both cognitive evaluation and memory. When an individual experiences something as problematic or rewarding, emotions direct attention and thoughts toward that aspect of the environment. Also, converging evidence suggests that different mood states are related to different styles of information processing (e.g., Bless, Hamilton, & Mackie, 1992; Bless, Mackie, & Schwarz, 1992; Isen, 1987; Schaller & Cialdini, 1990; Schwarz, Bless, & Bohner, 1991). Next we describe some of the effects of emotion on cognition.

Emotions and Degree and Specificity of Cognitive Processing

When individuals are in negative moods, they are likely to engage in more analytic, elaborate, and detailed processing of information (e.g., Bless, Hamilton, & Mackie, 1992; Bless, Mackie, & Schwarz, 1992; Isen, 1987; Schaller & Cialdini, 1990; Schwarz et al., 1991). Holtzworth-Munroe and Jacobson (1985) investigated the circumstances under which couples seek attributions or explanations for events that occur within their marriage and concluded that searching for attributions resulted from events that the partners experienced as negative. On the other hand, when in a positive mood, people are likely to exhibit less systematic and analytic processing. According to Rook and Pietromonaco (1987), "Because of differences in adaptive significance, it may be functional for people to be more sensitive to aversive interpersonal experiences than to enjoyable ones, even though this orientation has costs for their emotional lives" (p. 23). In essence, individuals might dwell on negatives in their lives because ending these negative experiences seems central to their well-being or survival.

Emotions and the Quality of Cognitive Processing

Negative emotions may initiate a great deal of cognitive activity, but the quality of information processing is not necessarily enhanced. Gottman (1994a) proposed that negative mood leads to an absorbing state, "one that is difficult to exit once it is entered" (p. 284). During a negative absorbing state a person typically attends to and responds to the negativity. Therefore, a negative mood initiates negative cognitive processing, as described earlier in this chapter, including selectively attending to negative events or qualities of the partner, providing negative attributions, developing negative expectancies for the future, and so forth. When in a negative mood state, the individual focuses in a skewed fashion on the negatives and pays minimal attention to other aspects of the situation that would provide a broader perspective on what has occurred. As Gottman (1994a) noted, the diffuse physiological arousal that accompanies negative emotions such as anger simultaneously limits an individual's access to learning new information (e.g., not recognizing that the partner is making strong efforts to please the individual) and increases the individual's access to ingrained cognitions (e.g., "She doesn't really care about me"). Thus, if an angry person's partner exhibits new, more constructive behavior, then the person's negative mood is likely to interfere with his or her noticing the behavior change.

Emotions and Memory

Emotions also influence the storage and retrieval of information in memory. Although research on mood-congruent memory is controversial and fraught with methodological problems, there is some evidence that people may be more efficient at recalling material when their current moods and the tone of the material to be retrieved are congruent (Blaney, 1986). That is, when a husband is in a bad mood, he is more likely to remember negative events. It appears that when memories are stored, part of the context, including emotions, is stored with the memory. Rolls (1987, 1989, 1990) has hypothesized that memory recall is enhanced when the content reflects a similar mood state because neural activity—or, more specifically, the modified synapses—closely resemble each other in those situations. With regard to intimate relationships, this can serve a positive or destructive function. Satisfied couples appear to experience a relatively high frequency of positive feelings toward each other. These positive moods among happy couples are likely to facilitate positive memories of the relationship (Beach & Fincham, 1994).

For a distressed couple, their frequent negative moods are likely to facilitate the recall of negative memories (Beach & Fincham, 1994). If Rolls's (1990) theory is correct, then a negative mood resulting from a fight with one's partner would trigger other negative memories. Therefore, when a couple is arguing, the likelihood of recalling similar negative memories is enhanced, leading partners to bring out the "laundry list" of complaints once they become embroiled in an argument. Sandra was perplexed by the apparent inconsistencies in Karen's memory:

> I really don't understand. I ask her to bring home a gallon of milk; I put a sticky note on her briefcase, and I leave a voicemail reminder. No milk. But let me forget to pick up smoked turkey when I'm at the grocery, and she suddenly turns into a walking encyclopedia of information. She can tell me every food purchase I've forgotten in the last 5 years: the item, the date, and how much she had to spend for lunch that day as a result.

In fact, the overall sentiment in the relationship can even lead to systematic memory distortion. Osgarby and Halford (1995) conducted an investigation in which happy and distressed couples were asked to record positive and negative interactions as they occurred. One week later, when they were asked to recall these events, happy couples accurately remembered the extent of negative interactions that had occurred, but they overestimated the extent of positive interactions. In contrast, distressed couples underestimated the number of positive events and overestimated the number of negative events.

Conclusions

What does all of this tell us about the role of mood in cognitive processing within intimate relationships? One important finding is that negative mood seems to result in more focused and detailed cognitive processing. Unfortunately, this processing seems to emphasize the negatives without appropriate attention to more positive elements. In many instances, such processing is likely to lead to distorted conclusions about one's partner and the relationship. Second, mood seems to influence memory by facilitating recall for other events that have a similar emotion associated with them. Therefore, distressed couples who experience more negative moods concerning their partners and their relationships are likely to perpetuate this negativity by having greater access to memories for negative events. In contrast, happy couples are likely to have access to more positive memories.

Impact of Emotions on Behavior

Individuals' emotional states influence their behavior within a family context. When Jouriles and Farris (1992) randomly assigned couples who were parents to have a conversation with each other, either about a source of conflict in their marriage or a nonconflictual topic, and then asked each parent to interact with their young sons, they found that the preceding conversation between spouses influenced the subsequent parent–child interaction. On a couple level, Pasch, Bradbury, and Davila (1997) found that when partners were asked to interact with each other and provide support to one person concerning a personal issue unrelated to the couple, the extent to which one partner offered support was affected by that person's mood before the interaction began.

Impact of Negative Emotions on Behavior

As noted earlier, Lazarus (1991) suggested that emotions are critical because they inform a person of how he or she is progressing in his or her attempts to survive and flourish. Survival involves two primary goals: (a) avoiding threat and danger and (b) meeting basic needs. Negative emotions can influence or motivate behavior in helping the individual achieve these two survival goals. Some negative emotions are responses to feeling threatened physically or psychologically, or feeling that important needs and goals are being thwarted. The individual is then motivated to terminate the situation that is the source of the threat. For example, both psychoanalytic and cognitive–behavioral formulations of panic disorder involve the idea that the individual is inappropriately experiencing danger when no danger actually exists or the source of danger is identified incorrectly. In this sense, anxiety serves as an important but at times faulty warning system that survival is threatened, and the individual responds to eliminate the sense of threat.

Destructive behaviors between partners. What does this have to do with marriage and other intimate relationships? One would hope that the partner and the relationship serve primarily as sources of pleasure and fulfillment and help the individual flourish in life. Distressed partners unfortunately often view the other individual as a major source of threat or danger. This sense of threat appears to be critical in the development of relationship discord and dissolution across time. From a series of longitudinal investigations,

Gottman (1999) isolated four types of communication that predict marital distress and divorce: criticism, contempt, defensiveness, and stonewalling.

We believe that two of these four types of communication are particularly caustic because they involve a threat to the psychological well-being or survival of the partner who is receiving the message. "Criticism is any statement that implies that there is something globally wrong with one's partner, something that is probably a lasting aspect of the partner's character" (Gottman, 1999, pp. 41–42). Furthermore, Gottman (1999) found that contempt, "any statement or nonverbal behavior that puts oneself on a higher plane than one's partner" (p. 45), is the single best predictor of divorce. What do the two variables of criticism and contempt have in common that is so detrimental to the couple? In both cases they serve as an assault or attack on the receiver of the message, a belittling put-down, or an attempt to diminish the other individual. To the degree that the critical or contemptuous message is successful, it can destroy the self-esteem and psychological well-being of the receiver, a threat to the psychological survival of the individual.

Gottman (1999) pointed out two additional forms of communication that predict divorce: defensiveness (any attempt to protect oneself from a perceived attack) and stonewalling (a withdrawal from the interaction), which are two basic strategies commonly used to ward off the damaging effects of a partner's criticism and contempt. These strategies might protect the individual, but they are unlikely to benefit the relationship. Defending oneself in many instances merely intensifies the "assault" from the other person, or, over time, the other person might learn not to approach at all: "Why bother? She won't listen; she just defends herself."

Creating negative environments. We believe that criticism and contempt are destructive because they are direct attacks on the recipient's sense of value and worth. In addition, there are other ways that one partner's negative mood affects a couple's relationship. For example, in their review of longitudinal studies of marriage, Bradbury and Karney (1993) found that neuroticism or negative affectivity as a broader personality trait of one individual predicts marital distress. Neuroticism and negative affectivity refer to the tendency for some individuals to experience the world in negative ways, such as being prone to depression or anxiety. It is unclear how such broad, negative tendencies affect the couple relationship, but we propose that it is through two mechanisms discussed earlier in this chapter. First, it is possible that such individuals are more likely to become critical and contemptuous of their partners when they experience difficulties in their relationships.

Second, individuals who have a general tendency to experience the world negatively can have a broad impact on the emotional tone of their environment; that is, they have a tendency to create a negative atmosphere for the people around them. Being around a depressed person induces negative emotions in other individuals and can diminish an individual's important life goal of flourishing and thriving. Ed expressed this sentiment in describing his life with Libby:

> I hate to say this because it will hurt her, but it is so discouraging being around her. She has battled depression her entire adult life, just like her mother did. I don't blame her for it, but it is so hard to be around. I come home from work feeling happy but within a few minutes, I get dragged down. She rarely smiles, doesn't want to do things to have fun, and usually she tells me why my ideas won't work, why they're unrealistic. Well, they aren't unrealistic to me; I didn't grow up this way, and I'm not this way. I think you have to be upbeat and optimistic. I feel like I drag her through life, trying to keep her spirits up. And I fail. I don't want to live in such a depressing environment any longer.

Conclusions. In summary, we believe that one partner's negative mood can have a destructive influence on a relationship in at least two ways. At times, this negativity is directed toward the other individual, with criticism and contempt. When this occurs, the self-esteem and psychological survival of the partner are threatened. The second mechanism does not involve a direct attack on the partner, and thus its impact might be less noticeable in a given interaction. Instead, the individual who typically has a generally negative emotional response to the environment contributes to making the environment of the relationship limited, negativistic, and pessimistic.

Impact of Positive Emotions on Behavior

Just as with negative emotions, positive emotions can influence one's own behavior and, depending on how this positive emotion is expressed, it also can influence the partner's behavior. As noted earlier, when people are in positive moods they generally behave more positively, both with family members and with others. In such instances, positive mood resulting from any source might benefit the relationship. This is one way that a positive, stable environment can affect a couple's functioning.

Positive behaviors between partners. Often an individual's positive moods are experienced in response to or directed toward the partner, the relationship, or the individual's own behavior within the relationship—that is, they occur within the context of the couple's interactions and affect subsequent behavior. Just as negative emotional reciprocity is a characteristic of relationships, so is positive emotional reciprocity. As we noted elsewhere (Baucom & Epstein, 1990), positive reciprocity does not appear to be as robust a phenomenon as negative reciprocity in relationships, at least when it is measured in couples' communication during a conversation in a laboratory setting. There are at least two possible explanations for this finding. First, positive reciprocity might involve a longer time lag; that is, after a wife behaves positively toward her husband, her husband reciprocates, but his positive response occurs later.

Conversely, it could be that, with regard to reciprocity, positive behavior simply does not have the same magnitude of effect on a partner that negative behavior does. As noted earlier, negative emotions often arise in response to feeling threatened, and therefore they channel attention and call for an immediate response to stop the threat. Many positive moods likely do not create a similar sense of urgency. For instance, if a person behaves in a way that helps the other partner feel calm and relaxed, the partner might simply wish to relax and enjoy the pleasant emotional state. After a relaxing backrub from Jackie, Gary felt no strong urge to reciprocate; to the contrary, he wanted to simply lie down and relax. In essence, offering immediate reciprocity might disrupt the positive state that the individual is enjoying.

In addition, immediate positive behavioral reciprocity is unlikely to occur in instances when couples want to focus the positives on one person. Such offers carry the message that one person's needs can be delayed for the well-being of the other individual. Many partners do not like the idea of "owing" the other person for something positive that was given. It is much more appealing to have a view of relationships in which both people are responsive to the other's needs and want to bring the other person joy and pleasure. Thus, positive behaviors are given freely, with no expected immediate reciprocity.

In essence, in healthy relationships partners appear to trust that they both will give to each other in positive ways, and the resulting positive moods are to be enjoyed; that is, a quid pro quo arrangement for exchanging positives seems to typify distressed rather than nondistressed relationships (Gottman, 1999; Murstein, Cerreto, & MacDonald, 1977). Such an understanding that equity exists allows an individual to continue feeling positively toward a partner during the times when the partner is not immediately reciprocating his or her positive behavior.

However, there likely is a limit on positives that individuals will give freely. If over a long period the offering of positives appears to go in one direction only, couples are likely to experience relationship distress. Thus, we do not know whether the lack of a quid pro quo arrangement for exchanging positives creates a satisfactory relationship, or whether satisfactory relationships within which both people give freely to the other in some type of mutually rewarding way have no need for a quid pro quo arrangement. For example, a very giving wife who is married to a husband who rarely gives to her might over time develop a quid pro quo mentality, recognizing that her husband does not give a great deal when left to his own devices. In such an instance, quid pro quo does not create the marital distress but rather evolves from an imbalance in the relationship.

Regardless of the cause–effect relationship between positive reciprocity and happiness in couples' relationships, positive moods that result from a partner's behavior might not lead to immediate reciprocal behavior in healthy relationships. Even though a lack of immediate positive reciprocity can be a sign of a healthy relationship, difficulties can result when positive behavior and positive mood do not elicit the same level of focused, cognitive processing by the members of a couple that a negative mood does. This means that a given positive behavior might be overlooked because it is processed at a somewhat vague level: "I'm aware of what you did; I just wasn't focusing on it." Over time, this can cause one person to feel devalued or taken for granted. Different individuals appear to have different levels of need for explicit statements of acknowledgement or appreciation by their partners. Similarly, different couples appear to develop different patterns of how often they express appreciation and acknowledgment. Some couples respond to almost any positive behavior from the partner with some type of acknowledgement: "Thanks for turning off the light." Other couples who are quite happy in their relationship verbalize appreciation much less often, yet they maintain a sense of positive balance in behavior between the two partners that works well for them. What seems crucial is that both members of a given couple find acceptable the particular level and pattern of reciprocity in their relationship.

Another important factor in determining the impact of positive emotional reciprocity on a couple's relationship satisfaction is the couple's ability to adjust their pattern of exchanges to adapt to changes in their life together. The level of positive reciprocity, how immediate it is, and how explicit it is might need to change as the couple faces new circumstances. When the couple is under stress from sources outside their relationship, or when their own relationship has developed some problems, the partners may need to use more explicit and frequent positive reciprocity so that it will be noticed and appreciated by the other person.

In discussing the effects of negative emotion on behavior we noted that at times the negative emotion resulting from interacting with one family member subsequently affects interactions with other family members. It can be a source of concern when negative emotions color other interactions negatively; however, the "bleeding" of positive emotions into other areas can be constructive. For example, a couple's positive interactions with each other can carry forward into interactions between each partner and their children. Similarly, if one child is involved in positive interactions with the parents, this might influence how that child interacts with siblings. When as couples researchers and therapists we study only the two people interacting, it limits our observations of the interactions that the partners have within their larger family system. If only the couple is present, and a husband behaves positively toward his wife, her only option in that setting is to respond to her husband. However, this does not necessarily occur when the couple is at home with their family. When the husband helps his wife to feel good about herself, their child might be the primary recipient of the mother's positive feelings. The concept of reciprocity suggests that the behavior is exchanged with the original sender, but there also might be more of a "family contagion" in which the positive feelings induced in one person are then directed to a new individual, dyad, or larger subgroup of the family.

Creating positive environments. Just as with negative emotions, positive emotions can affect one's own behavior more broadly. People who are in good moods help to create a positive environment that other people seek, even if their behaviors are not directed toward a given individual. An upbeat, positive emotional tone creates a context in which others feel free to have fun, take chances, be creative, and generally feel safe. One of the greatest compliments we pay to colleagues or students in letters of recommendation sounds like this:

> Mary is the kind of person that you will want as a part of your professional environment. She is upbeat, cheerful, finds the good in almost everything without ignoring problems, and brings a positive energy that creates goodwill, excitement, and enthusiasm for other people around her.

Although no one is expected to be in an upbeat mood all the time, when people can describe their partner and their relationship in similar terms then the couple can greatly benefit from such a rich resource.

Relationship Between Positive and Negative Emotions

Emotions are a critical part of relationships, and they are essential in helping the individual to survive and flourish. Emotions influence attention, the thoroughness of cognitive processing, memory, and one's own and the partner's behavior. In many instances the individual's own goals of psychological and physical survival, meeting fundamental needs, and thriving are consistent with the well-being of the relationship. However, if the individual begins to experience the partner or the relationship as a major source of threat or impediment to meeting important needs, then the individual views his or her own well-being and the well-being of the partner and the relationship as being in conflict. This conflict evokes strong negative emotions in the individual, and his or her subsequent behavior toward the partner might be detrimental to the relationship even though it protects the individual in the short run.

Although positive and negative emotions are similar in some respects, in other ways they might operate differently. In particular, positive emotions might not lead to immediate reciprocity of positive affect, especially in happy relationships. An absence of immediate positive reciprocity can reflect a sense of trust that both persons will be treated well and have their needs addressed over time; however, it creates the risk that one or both persons might feel taken for granted. As Gottman (1999) suggested, a key for couples and therapists is to help couples maintain a balance between positives and negatives exchanged at multiple levels, including emotions. Members of all couples experience negative feelings toward each other, and they behave in response to those negative feelings. It is critical that negative behaviors not be frequent and destructive and that they are offset with a high level of positive emotions and subsequent behaviors.

SUMMARY

In addition to the ways that partners behave toward each other, they have rich internal experiences of their relationships that include both their cognitions and emotions. In this chapter we delineated the various cognitive and emotional factors that help color a person's experience of his or her intimate relationships, noting the interplay between cognitions and emotions.

- Distressed couples respond to their negative emotions about their relationships by noticing the negative aspects of interpersonal situations, assigning a negative explanation for the occurrence of a specific event, and using an event to feed their expectations for more negative interactions with the partner in the future.
- Distressed couples hold more negative, global assumptions about how people and relationships actually function and standards about how they should work.
- Partners' individual levels of positive and negative affectivity influence the general tone of their relationship as well as the interaction with their partners.
- In addition to the current interaction, partners' current emotions may be governed by their personalities; their experiences in past relationships; the history of their current relationship; their standards about how to react to emotionally charged situations; their coping styles of withdrawal, defensiveness, avoidance, suppression, or alteration of emotions; the stage of the relationship; and the external circumstances in their lives.
- Partners show emotions in their attempts to gain a sense of closeness to, distance from, or power over their partners.
- Partners may have difficulty expressing emotions because of a skill deficit in labeling and describing their emotions or in regulating the intensity with which they display emotions.
- The tendency for distressed couples to dwell on negative events in the relationship results from partners' more analytic and detailed processing of information when they are in negative moods. A negative mood also increases the likelihood that they will remember other negative events.

- Criticism and contempt from one partner threatens the other partner's self-esteem, motivating the attacked partner to counterattack (and engage in negative reciprocity), withdraw, or become defensive. Partners often find it easier to leave an attacking relationship than to leave one in which one person's negative outlook on life creates an unpleasant, depressing atmosphere in the relationship.
- Although positive reciprocity does not show the same magnitude of effect as negative reciprocity, an overall sense of trust in the relationship appears to color partners' daily behaviors in a constructive manner.

4

WHY COUPLES ARE THE WAY THEY ARE: INDIVIDUAL INFLUENCES

In previous chapters we have focused on a traditional cognitive–behavioral model of behaviors, cognitions, and emotions that commonly occur in couples' relationships. In this chapter we describe an enhanced cognitive–behavioral model in which we advance a step further in examining patterns of functioning for particular couples. Specifically, we examine characteristics of individual partners that can influence how couples act, think, or feel the way they do. We explore the individual dispositions in motives, personality styles, and psychopathology that each partner may bring to the relationship. Knowledge of individual-difference characteristics can help therapists tailor cognitive–behavioral treatments to the particular needs of each couple.

The traditional cognitive–behavioral model of couples' functioning has focused on describing the types of couples' internal cognitive and affective responses as well as the partners' overt interpersonal behaviors that are associated with relationship distress (Baucom & Epstein, 1990). The model tends to focus on *what* occurs within and between partners during dysfunctional couple interaction rather than *why* it occurs. Why do members of one couple hold particular standards and other cognitions that contribute to distress while members of another couple do not? Why are particular emotions, such as anger, so prevalent in some relationships but not others? Why are some couples' behavioral interactions marked by frequent battles for control while other couples tend to share power in a relatively easy manner?

Because the answers to these questions have important implications for designing an appropriate treatment plan for each couple, we have developed an enhanced cognitive–behavioral model that takes into account several important personal characteristics of individuals that shape their cognitive, affective, and behavioral responses within their relationships. In this chapter we consider partners' motives, personality styles, and forms of psychopathology that may influence the functioning of the couple. In chapter 5 we describe characteristics of couples' dyadic interactions that commonly are interpersonal manifestations of these individual characteristics.

Each person brings a variety of relatively stable individual characteristics to a relationship: motives, personality styles and, in some instances, psychopathology. Consistent with our cognitive–behavioral perspective, we do not view these characteristics as invariant traits that will inevitably produce the same responses from an individual across many situations. Instead, we assume that an individual's motives, personality style, and psychopathology are *tendencies* to think, feel, and behave in particular ways under particular circumstances. Comprising cognitive, affective, and behavioral components, they produce a certain degree of consistency in an individual's responses to life events. As we describe in this chapter, empirical evidence indicates that such individual-difference variables do influence individual and couple functioning; however, the degrees to which partners' dispositional characteristics are likely to affect the couple depend on contextual factors; that is, whether a particular situation "pulls for" particular motives, personality styles, and psychopathological responses.

A focus on relatively stable characteristics of individual partners has traditionally not been a significant part of the behavioral and cognitive–behavioral models of couples' functioning, as it has been in psychodynamic models. Behavioral theorists have tended to emphasize situational factors that elicit or reinforce each person's responses during couples' interactions (Jacobson & Margolin, 1979). Thus, an individual who has positive interactions with friends may behave aversively with his or her partner because the partner's behavior elicits and reinforces the person's aversive responses. Even the literature on relationship belief systems that are assumed to be fairly stable (Baucom & Epstein, 1990; Baucom, Epstein, Rankin, & Burnett, 1996) has emphasized how such beliefs are elicited in particular situations, such as during conflicts between partners.

However, individual-difference variables increasingly are being integrated into cognitive–behavioral theory and research. This trend can be seen in studies on the impact of neuroticism on marital interaction (Karney & Bradbury, 1997), adult attachment styles in marital relationships (Lawrence,

Eldridge, & Christensen, 1998), and stable individual differences in the experience of emotion within couples' relationships (Beach & Fincham, 1994). Gottman (1999) examined couples' marital interactions over a 4-year period, assessed the content of what partners talked about as they attempted to resolve relationship problems, and noted that many couples continued to discuss the same issues year after year. In fact, he concluded that 69% of the time they were talking about "differences in personality or needs that were fundamental to their core definition of self. Only 31% of the discussions involved situationally specific problem-solving" (p. 56). Thus, our enhanced cognitive–behavioral model includes an assumption that each member of a couple brings some dispositional characteristics into the couple relationship. In this chapter we describe the major forms of dispositional motives, personality styles, and psychopathology that can affect relationship functioning and how they can be "translated" into their cognitive, affective, and behavioral components, which can be assessed and modified through cognitive–behavioral methods.

We are devoting substantially more space to a description of motives than to other personality characteristics or to psychopathology because motives have received the least attention in the literature on couples' relationships, particularly within cognitive–behavioral approaches. In this chapter we describe the characteristics of motives and the ways in which they shape the major themes and patterns of couples' interactions and presenting problems. We believe that incorporating motives into a cognitive–behavioral model of couples' functioning is an important step in advancing the practice of couples therapy.

BASIC NEEDS AND MOTIVES IN INTIMATE RELATIONSHIPS

Individuals vary in their motivation to pursue particular goals in their lives and specifically within the context of their couple relationships. Understanding partners' compatible or conflicting motives provides a framework for identifying and addressing key themes that organize individuals' thoughts, emotions, and behaviors toward each other. In this section we examine the development of motives, the types of motives most salient for couples' relationships, gender differences in the experience and expression of motives, and the balance between individually oriented and communally oriented motives.

Characteristics of Motives

Before we describe the major types of motives and illustrate their contributions to relationship problems, it is important to define the characteristics of basic human needs or motives.[1] If these concepts are to be useful to cognitive–behavioral therapists, it is important that we identify their compatibility with the basic constructs in our model. The study of needs, drives, and motives has a long history in the psychological literature, particularly in the areas of personality and learning. Theorists typically have included motives within the broader realm of personality or relatively stable individual differences. As we explain later, motives can be differentiated from other dispositional personality characteristics that also influence close relationships.

Learning theorists such as Thorndike (1911), in accounting for animal learning processes, have described drives such as hunger and pain as innate forces that energize behavior, orient the organism's behavior toward goals, and select responses that produce rewards. In Hull's (1943) learning model, drives were restricted to forces pushing for tension reduction, as when hunger motivates an animal to eat and thereby reduce tension. However, animals and humans also are motivated to act to *increase* certain types of stimulation, as when an individual seeks out interesting and exciting work and leisure activities (McClelland, 1987). N. Miller and Dollard (1941) expanded the concept of drive to include any strong stimulus, innate or learned, that energizes and directs behavior.

Similarly, McClelland (1987) defined a *motive* in terms of learning processes, as a "learned, affectively charged anticipatory state aroused by various cues" (p. 132). McClelland noted that a motive involves a recurrent concern with achieving a particular outcome. In other words, the individual has cognitions concerning achieving the goal, is emotionally aroused in seeking that outcome, and exhibits behavior directed toward achieving the outcome. Because each individual has a different learning history, he or she develops somewhat idiosyncratic ways of behaving to reach a goal. For example, two individuals may have equally strong levels of motivation to experience the pleasure of exercising power over their environments, but each may have learned different ways of exerting power. One person may have learned to exercise power through supervising others in a job setting, whereas the other person may have learned to satisfy the same motivation by making unilateral decisions in personal relationships.

McClelland (1987) noted that as a person develops cognitively and has a variety of life experiences, he or she learns more varied and elaborate strategies for achieving certain goals. A very young child who is motivated to exert control is likely limited to simple manipulation of objects, such as dropping a spoon onto the floor and seeing a parent pick it up. In contrast, an

---

[1]The terms *need, drive,* and *motive* often have been used interchangeably in the literature. However, *need* and *drive* tend to suggest tension reduction, whereas the term *motive* seems more generic and equally applicable to processes that lead an individual to seek greater tension (as in *motivation to explore*). We prefer the generic term *motive,* although we also use the term *need* when necessary to be consistent with usage in the literature.

older child learns more sophisticated ways to influence other people, such as arguing successfully, withdrawing, and achieving success or failure in school. A child whose parents provide him or her with few experiences in ways to exert control may develop a fairly limited schema concerning ways to demonstrate power. In contrast, a child whose parents provide many ways to experience some control in family interactions is likely to have a more complex schema for alternative ways to express power.

Parents can influence a child's motives by explicitly communicating the value of pursuing particular goals (McClelland, 1987). For example, if parents repeatedly emphasize to a child that it is very important to perform well in school, sports, and other activities, then the child may be more likely to develop a strong motivation to achieve. Parents also may communicate implicitly values concerning particular motives, either by modeling behaviors associated with a motive (e.g., working hard to achieve status in one's career) or by expressing different degrees of pleasure or displeasure when the child's behavior is consistent with the parents' values. Of course, sometimes children resist pressure from parents by valuing goals that are the opposite of those emphasized by their parents, such as de-emphasizing motivation for achievement. As an adult, such an individual may become upset whenever his or her spouse invests time and effort toward career advancement.

Many people who seek individual or couples therapy exhibit limited repertoires of behavioral skills for meeting their needs as well as limited awareness of alternative behaviors that might be used to achieve their personal goals (Baucom & Epstein, 1990; D'Zurilla, 1988; Weiss & Heyman, 1990b). Consequently, cognitive–behavioral therapists typically use skills-training procedures to broaden their clients' strategies for achieving outcomes that they desire. Problem-solving skills training in the cognitive–behavioral couples therapy literature emphasizes helping the members of a couple to think about and enact new behaviors they can use to achieve personal goals (e.g., Baucom & Epstein, 1990; Jacobson & Margolin, 1979).

Nevertheless, cognitive–behavioral approaches to problem solving have paid relatively little attention to the identification of the types of motivation underlying couples' difficulties. This information can be valuable in tailoring therapeutic interventions to address each couple's particular needs. For example, knowing that both members of a couple are highly motivated to exercise control can guide a therapist in helping the couple focus on using problem-solving skills in collaborative ways that the partners do not experience as "giving in" or "losing." Thus, McClelland's (1987) view of motives as comprising cognitive schemas, emotional arousal, and behavioral repertoires for meeting particular goals is highly compatible with a cognitive–behavioral approach to understanding and treating relationship problems, and we apply it throughout this book. Motivation concepts add a framework for identifying and addressing key themes that organize individuals' thoughts, emotions, and behavior toward each other.

Motives tend to become aroused in particular relevant situations. For example, an individual who tends to be highly motivated toward achievement may cooperate with a partner in situations that require teamwork for success, such as completing the household chores, as long as he or she does not experience those situations as competitive. However, in situations that involve comparisons of the two partners' levels of achievement (e.g., when discussing their job salaries), the individual might become competitive and aggressive. Beach and Tesser's (1993) research on self-evaluation maintenance (SEM) examined how individuals compare themselves to their partners when both members of the couple are attempting to achieve in the same area or activity. They found that an individual who compares him- or herself unfavorably to a partner's level of success is likely to respond in a competitive manner.

Changing conditions over the course of a couple's relationship also can increase or decrease the degrees to which each person's motives are aroused and expressed. Sometimes an individual has a fairly strong motive but does not express it until the conditions change at a particular time. Consider Tyrone and Laura, who were both very achievement oriented and attracted to each other's desire to be successful and contribute to society. Laura had been raised in a family that also emphasized emotional intimacy and nurturance in their relationships. For the first 5 years of their marriage, both partners were supportive of each other, devoting considerable time and energy to their careers. However, when the couple decided to have children and Laura became pregnant, they began to have discussions about future life goals and how they would divide their time between work and family responsibilities. After the birth of their first child, Laura's motivation for intimacy and nurturing others increased, and she focused her priorities on creating a close-knit family. In contrast, even though Tyrone had strong, loving feelings for their daughter, his overall needs for nurturance and intimacy were less strong than Laura's, and his position as a scientist in a government agency continued to stimulate his desire to achieve. He found it difficult to make choices to spend extended time with Laura and their daughter when he had professional papers to prepare for national and international conferences, which resulted in a significant amount of conflict between him and Laura. The motives that Tyrone and Laura brought to their relationship had not changed over time, but their entry into the child-rearing stage of their relationship decreased the degree of match between the motives that each of them expressed.

The conceptualization of motives as factors influencing couples' relationships is useful to cognitive–behavioral therapists to the extent that one can translate motives into affective, cognitive, and behavioral components that can be addressed in assessment and treatment. McClelland's (1987) definition of a motive refers to the positive or negative emotional aspects of anticipating and attaining goals or of failing to reach them. An individual is likely to feel happy, for instance, when he or she is able to fulfill intimacy needs with a partner or fulfill achievement needs by successfully completing a difficult task. In contrast, the frustration of not meeting such needs can produce negative emotions such as anger, anxiety, and sadness.

McClelland's (1987) definition of a motive also includes the concept of an *anticipatory goal state*, which involves cognitions. The individual holds expectancies or predictions that taking particular actions will produce the goals that he or she is motivated to pursue. For example, Jasmine is strongly motivated to affiliate with other people and has an expectancy that joining social organizations is likely to help her form enjoyable new friendships outside of her marriage. The expectancies involved in motives also may have their roots in broader assumptions that the individual holds about people and close relationships. Sid tends to be motivated to exert power and control in his relationships with people. When he was a child, his mother devoted herself to home and family, sporadically working part-time explicitly for the purpose of helping to pay the bills. Sid had noticed that when there were decisions to be made, his mother typically deferred to his father. Consequently, Sid developed a general assumption that women with lower career aspirations tend to be relatively submissive. Sid was attracted to Alexis in part because she emphasized her intent to focus her efforts on raising a family more than on an outside career. On the basis of his assumption that a woman who is not career oriented tends to be submissive, he expected that he would make most of the major decisions in their marriage. In therapy Sid described his surprise and upset about his wife's "playing hardball" when they negotiated decisions about finances, because her behavior was inconsistent with his assumptions regarding the distribution of power in their relationship.

Regarding the behavioral component of motives, theorists such as McClelland (1987) have described how an individual learns specific instrumental behavioral responses to achieve desired goals. Individuals develop a variety of behaviors for eliciting caring responses from their partners, such as behaving in a caring manner themselves, acting needy, assertively requesting the desired responses, nagging the partner, withdrawing from the partner, or attempting to arouse jealousy in the partner by spending time with other people. Of course, the degree to which the individual uses each of these behaviors depends on cognitive factors as well, such as personal values or standards about the appropriateness of each behavioral strategy. Thus, one spouse might be tempted to exercise his or her desire for power by bullying his or partner but might refrain from doing so because it is inconsistent with that person's personal values.

Types of Motives Relevant to Couples' Relationships

Investigators who have studied motivation have attempted to identify the fewest basic motives that can account for the complexity of human behavior. Some models of human motives have been primarily theoretical, such as H. A. Murray's (1938) list of needs, Maslow's (1954) hierarchy of needs, and Bakan's (1966) two-dimensional model of psychological needs. Others have been based on statistical analyses seeking patterns in empirical data (Cattell, 1957; Prager & Buhrmester, 1998). Results of these factor analytic studies have varied, because they are influenced by the particular set of characteristics that the investigators chose to include (Kagan, 1994).

Our goal in this chapter is to identify major motives or needs that affect relationship functioning. The communally oriented and individually oriented motives that we describe in detail and apply throughout this book appear consistently in the theoretical and empirical literature, although different subsets of each type have been identified by different theorists and researchers. Other motives or needs have been identified and validated in research studies, such as a need for engaging in effortful cognition (Cacioppo, Petty, Feinstein, Jarvis, & Blair, 1996), a need for structure (Schaller, Boyd, Yohannes, & O'Brien, 1995), and a need to evaluate (Jarvis, Blair, & Petty, 1996). Although these other motives or needs can have important effects on individuals' functioning within their intimate relationships, their relevance to therapists' understanding and treatment of couples' relationships does not appear to be as central as communally and individually oriented motives. Thus, we do not elaborate on them.

The communally oriented and individually oriented motives on which we focus involve *approach* responses, in which an individual strives toward positive goals, such as achievement and intimacy. However, there are some other motives that involve *avoidance* of outcomes, such as emotional pain—for example, the motive to avoid rejection by others. These avoidance motives are important because they often lead an individual to avoid a partner and may counteract the individual's pursuit and fulfillment of positive, communally and individually oriented needs. Therefore, after discussing the major types of communally and individually oriented motives we describe representative motives associated with avoidance.

Motives Involving Approach

As just noted, the theoretical and empirical literature suggests two major categories of core motives that affect couples' relationships: (a) *communally oriented motives*, which involve connection with another person, and (b) *individually oriented motives*, which involve autonomous functioning, achievement in the world, and the experience of exercising some control over one's environment.

Researchers, using a variety of methodologies, consistently have generated evidence for these two sets of communally oriented and individually oriented motives in both children and adults (McAdams, Hoffman, Mansfield, & Day, 1996; Prager & Buhrmester, 1998; Reiss & Havercamp, 1998). Communally and individually oriented motives also correspond, respectively, to motives of communion and agency identified by motivation theorists such as Bakan (1966) and McAdams (McAdams, 1985, 1988; McAdams et al., 1996).

Communally oriented motives. In an extensive review of theoretical and empirical literature, Baumeister and Leary (1995) found evidence that people have a basic need to form and maintain strong, stable relationships with others and that the failure to have one's need for "belongingness" met is associated with problems in psychological well-being. Four core communal motives that are central in couple's relationships involve

- *affiliation*: a need to be with people rather than engaging in solitary activities;
- *intimacy*: a need for close contact, mutual disclosure, and other forms of sharing in another person's world;
- *altruism*: a need to take care of other people's needs, even when it involves personal sacrifice; and
- *succorance*: a need to be nurtured by others.

Motivation for *affiliation* affects a variety of behaviors reflecting a preference for interaction with others (e.g., group activities, parties) rather than solitude (Mehrabian, 1994). Members of couples commonly report that one factor that attracted them to their partners was an expectancy that a relationship with the partner would provide for a variety of pleasurable social experiences. As we noted earlier, members of distressed couples commonly report a marked decrease in their positive affiliative experiences with each other over time. Prager (1995) argued that affiliation (which she labeled *cohesiveness* and which includes togetherness, sharing of time, and sharing of activities) is a requirement for intimacy but can exist in the absence of intimacy. Consistent with her position, studies by McAdams and his colleagues (e.g., McAdams, 1980; McAdams & Powers, 1981) support the distinction between the affiliation and intimacy motives, demonstrating that measures of these two communal motives have a low correlation with each other.

In contrast to the central "togetherness" component of affiliation, *intimacy* involves sharing personal information and emotions, mutual understanding, or physical touch and sexuality. Prager (1995) stressed that the key to intimate relating is sharing something deeply personal with the other person, not only spending time with him or her. She suggested that it is unlikely that a person's need for intimacy can be fulfilled by any single intimate interaction with another person, such as one conversation involving mutual self-disclosure of personal feelings. Therefore, for an individual to fulfill his or her need for intimacy, an ongoing intimate relationship is needed. Prager's extensive review of the empirical literature indicated that partners' scores on a variety of intimacy measures correlate positively with measures of relationship satisfaction. Christensen and Shenk (1991) found that incompatibility in partners' intimacy needs contributes to relationship discord.

Sometimes one member of a couple has a strong need for affiliation but not a strong need for intimacy, and this produces confusion for one or both partners. For example, Vince's strong need for affiliation had since childhood led him to have an active social life. He had spent a lot of time with friends, joined clubs, and dated. Tina was attracted by Vince's outgoing style and his interest in spending time with her. She had strong needs for both affiliation and intimacy, and she interpreted Vince's social behavior as evidence that they wanted a similar kind of relationship. Over time, Tina made efforts to increase the level of intimacy in their dating relationship by disclosing more personal information about her feelings, insecurities, and family background and by encouraging Vince to be more self-disclosing to her. She was surprised and distressed when Vince attempted to end such discussions quickly, and she began to complain to him that their relationship was superficial. Tina concluded that Vince was not interested in having a close relationship. When the couple clarified this difference between affiliation and intimacy during therapy, they spent some sessions engaged in problem-solving discussions to determine whether they could find mutually satisfying ways to mesh their needs.

Altruism involves a prosocial motivation to care for other people's needs, even when such efforts involve ignoring or sacrificing one's own. There is considerable empirical evidence indicating that individuals vary in a tendency to behave in unselfish, altruistic ways toward others (e.g., Batson, 1987, 1991; Brehm, 1992; Carlo, Eisenberg, Troyer, Switzer, & Speer, 1991; Penner & Finkelstein, 1998; Reiss & Havercamp, 1998). Brehm (1992) noted two major pathways to altruistic behavior: (a) an observer's *empathic distress* concerning another person's problems and distress and (b) the individual's *emotional attachment* to the other person, which motivates him or her to try to make the other person happy. Both forms of altruism involve cognitions, including understanding of the other person's subjective experiences and prosocial values about helping others, in addition to these emotional aspects.

An individual's capacity for empathy commonly increases naturally during childhood as he or she develops cognitively. In addition, parents and others can help develop a child's empathy and altruism by exposing the child to others' experiences, coaching the child in noticing cues of others' emotional states, and directly teaching the child prosocial values and behaviors (Goldstein & Michaels, 1985). Given the importance of mutual support in couples' relationships (Cutrona, 1996a), therapists need to determine each person's levels of empathy and altruistic motivation toward his or her partner. Some individuals enjoy giving to their partners and bringing their partners joy. If such a person has a partner who has difficulty receiving from others, the person who enjoys being altruistic may feel frustrated in the relationship.

Finally, *succorance* involves an individual's desire to receive caretaking from another person. Attachment theorists (e.g., Bowlby, 1988; Kobak,

Ruckdeschel, & Hazan, 1994) have emphasized the strong, innate, emotional bonds between children and their caregivers as well as the emotional and behavioral reactions that occur when a child's bond with a caregiving figure is threatened. According to attachment theory, children develop internalized "working models" or cognitive schemas concerning the degree of security and dependability that one can expect in relationships with caregiving figures, and these working models have considerable stability as the individual matures, extending into adulthood (W. H. Berman, Marcus, & Berman, 1994; Bowlby, 1989). In fact, empirical findings demonstrate at least a moderate degree of stability in individuals' attachment schemas across situations and ages (Davila & Bradbury, 1996; Davila, Burge, & Hammen, 1997; Rothbard & Shaver, 1994).

Overall, attachment theory has conceptualized the caretaking involved in close bonds in parent–child and adult romantic relationships as natural and basically healthy (W. H. Berman et al., 1994; Kobak et al., 1994). In fact, it is common for individuals who are quite competent in meeting their own needs still to enjoy having their partners take care of them from time to time. The succorance provides a form of connection and closeness between the members of the couple, and it gives the recipient opportunities to be nurtured by the partner. However, theory and research also have identified processes that occur in relationships involving individuals with insecure attachments (see Simpson & Rholes, 1998).

Attachment theorists have described how individuals develop tendencies to behave in particular ways to elicit intimacy and caretaking (succorance) from significant others when it is needed. An individual who has a secure working model of attachment, for example, is likely to express thoughts and emotions directly, telling the other person clearly what the individual needs or desires (Kobak et al., 1994). Thus, a secure person can directly express emotions and concerns to a partner who seems preoccupied with his or her job. The person in need gives the partner an opportunity to provide reassurance and decrease the distance between them. In contrast, attachment theorists predict that an individual with an insecure working model, who does not anticipate reassuring caretaking responses from attachment figures, is more likely to communicate his or her needs in an unclear, indirect manner (e.g., Kobak et al., 1994). He or she may complain about the partner's job rather than state a desire for more time together. Such behavioral strategies for coping with insecure attachment can backfire and alienate the individual's partner.

Whereas a child depends on a parent in a unilateral way for basic physical survival, caregiving between two adults tends to be much more mutual and focused on emotional needs rather than physical ones. Kirkpatrick (1998) described adult "pair-bonding" as characterized more by mutual altruism based on love than by attachment based on anxiety concerning physical survival. Flexibility in partners' roles allows each member of a couple to be the provider of support at some times and the recipient of support at other times. Thus, although the concept of a succorance motive commonly has been taken to connote immature, childlike, and even pathological functioning, we concur with Kirkpatrick's contention that seeking the comfort of being nurtured by a partner can be part of a healthy relationship. In turn, expressing an altruistic motive by providing various kinds of support for one's partner can be part of a healthy connection between two people rather than a sign of pathological "enmeshment" that clinicians may sometimes overdiagnose. In addition, it is important to consider normal cultural variations in motivation for altruism and succorance. For example, Latino families tend to emphasize communal motivation, including mutual support among kin (Hines, Preto, McGoldrick, Almeida, & Weltman, 1999), and this tendency may be misconstrued as overinvolvement by a clinician whose own cultural background emphasizes more autonomous functioning.

These four communally oriented needs commonly coexist in couples, but there is good reason to consider them separately in clinical assessment and treatment. Members of a couple may differ in the relative strengths of their affiliation, intimacy, altruism, and succorance needs. For example, one member of a couple may value intimacy highly but have low needs for succorance and altruism, while the other member has high levels of all three types of motivation. Thus, for the first individual intimacy is independent of mutual nurturing, but for the second individual intimacy is strongly associated with caretaking. Consequently, the second person may be distressed when his or her partner fails to give or accept much caretaking. Helping couples understand the differences among these communally oriented needs is an important step toward assisting them in finding new ways to fulfill each person's needs as much as is realistic in their relationship.

Individually oriented motives. The individually oriented, or *agentic* motives most consistently identified in the theoretical and empirical literature (e.g., Bakan, 1966; McAdams, 1985, 1988; McAdams et al., 1996) are

- *autonomy*: a need to operate freely within one's environment, pursuing one's personal interests and goals independently of other people;
- *power*: a need to exercise influence over and experience impact on one's environment; and
- *achievement*: a need to perform well on tasks, gaining mastery and improved status in one's own or others' eyes.

Autonomy motivation involves an individual's desire to operate relatively independently of other people, even when he or she has chosen to be involved in a significant relationship (Prager, 1995). Some people with strong autonomy needs prefer to make decisions by themselves rather than discussing issues with other people. Such individual problem solvers like to think things through on their own and then inform their partners or others of their decisions. Individuals who have a high need for autonomy also might express a preference for working on tasks alone, suggesting that the couple divide household tasks so each person can do it his or her own way. Some people who are highly motivated toward autonomy also might desire a large amount of solitary time for simply doing whatever they prefer. However, others might value socializing but divide their time among several friendships, each one limited by specific roles that restrict the individual's personal involvement. For example, David has several golfing buddies with whom he has fun on the golf course each Saturday, but he has virtually no other contact with them. David fulfills his need for autonomy by compartmentalizing his relationships with various people, and he has no interest in setting up couple get-togethers for himself and Greta with his golfing buddies and their wives.

When a clinician observes that an individual prefers a high level of autonomous functioning in the context of a couple's relationship, it is important to determine whether this preference is due to a true positive motivation toward autonomy or to a desire to avoid close interaction with the partner. Thus, an individual's preference for autonomous functioning might be due to motivation to avoid affiliation or intimacy, if close contact with a partner is experienced as unpleasant. We discuss motives based on avoidance of distress and pain further after we describe the other individually oriented motives that involve approaching valued goals.

The central goal of the *power* motive is experiencing one's impact on and control over aspects of one's environment, including significant others (McAdams, 1985). Power has been one of the major characteristics studied in research on close relationships (Huston, 1983; Markman & Notarius, 1987). Attempting to determine the strength of an individual's need for power within a relationship by observing how often the individual pressures the partner to comply with his or her preferences can be misleading. Huston (1983) noted that even one "win" may counteract many "losses" in a particular couple's relationship. Clinicians commonly observe such patterns in which the overall balance of power seems to be determined by one partner's dominance in key situations rather than by the outcomes of routine daily decision making. Thus, an individual who has a high need for power may demonstrate it subtly by selectively exerting pressure on a partner.

Similarly, an individual who is motivated to exert control in a relationship may do so through a pattern of withdrawal. Julien, Arellano, and Turgeon (1997) provided a power motivation explanation for men's common withdrawal during problem-solving discussions with their wives. Julien et al. suggested that, given females' commonly superior communication skills, males may perceive that communicating with their partners is unlikely to achieve their personal goal of exerting influence on decision making. Consequently, they may use withdrawal as an effective control strategy in which they block the partner's attempts to discuss and negotiate solutions to problems.

Considerable evidence demonstrates that the distribution of power and control influences the quality of the couple relationship. Gottman (1979) found that couples with dominant husbands (i.e., whose behavior predicted their wives' subsequent behavior, but not vice versa) tended to be distressed, and a variety of studies have shown that relationships characterized by shared control are more satisfying, less conflictual, and less violent than those in which one partner is dominant (Coleman & Straus, 1986; Frieze & McHugh, 1992; Gray-Little, Baucom, & Hamby, 1996; Gray-Little & Burks, 1983). As an important reminder that clinicians must consider cultural differences in relationship patterns, Gray-Little (1982) found that among African American couples both traditional (male-dominated) and egalitarian patterns of power were associated with relationship satisfaction. Overall, when one or both members of a couple have strong power motivation, it is important for a therapist to help them develop a decision-making pattern that both individuals can experience as satisfying and fair.

A negative connotation has commonly been attached to the concept of a person having a motive or need to control. We suggest that it is important to differentiate between being motivated to experience a sense of control and *how* one attempts to achieve control in various life situations, including one's couple relationship. The literature on assertive versus aggressive behavior (e.g., Alberti & Emmons, 1986) has emphasized the positive aspects of being able to exercise influence in relationships but has differentiated constructive from problematic ways of doing so. In some couples one person tends to experience a sense of control by acting in ways that decrease the other person's sense of control. Clinicians need to identify instances in which one or both partners are trying to exert control through inappropriate or destructive means, such as verbal, psychological, or physical abuse.

Finally, the need for *achievement* is based on the goal of performing well on instrumental tasks (McAdams, 1985; McAdams et al., 1996; McClelland, 1987; Winter, 1973). However, the types of activities or tasks involved in people's achievement efforts can vary greatly. Some individuals tend to focus their efforts on achieving success in forming and maintaining a close relationship with a partner. In other words, their motivation is achievement oriented, even though the goals they seek to achieve are communal or relationship oriented. Thus, Amanda grew up in a family where social status was highly valued, and the criteria for social status were education, popularity with friends, and career status. She developed a high level of achievement motivation and worked hard to attain her family's valued goals in all of those areas of life. Amanda put considerable effort into making and maintaining many friendships. Although her communal social behavior was based partly on affiliation motivation, it was based even more on her high level of achievement motivation. In fact, some people described her as a person who "collects friends."

In contrast, other individuals are motivated toward achievement on individually oriented tasks, such as a career or athletic accomplishments. At times, this motivation is expressed through autonomous efforts (e.g., spending long hours at the office), but at other times they may involve an individual's joint efforts with a partner. In the latter case, the individual's desire to achieve can become a significant influence on the relationship with the partner. For instance, Janis and Will had been married 5 years and had no children. They had frequent arguments about how to spend their time at home each evening. Will wanted to relax, spend time with Janis, and just enjoy themselves as a couple after a day of work. Janis had a high level of achievement motivation in many areas of her life, including making their home as attractive and well run as possible. Consequently, for Janis the couple's relationship during their time at home together largely revolved around accomplishing chores. She believed that relaxing and enjoying each other was important but that it should occur only after all of the chores were done. Will interpreted Janis's pressure concerning chores as reflecting a lack of interest in him as a person. Identifying how Janis and Will experienced and expressed their achievement motivation was crucial in the assessment of issues to be addressed in therapy.

Other people have strong achievement motives that are focused on accomplishment in professional arenas. In many instances, the desire and drive toward professional accomplishment are consistent with the individual's view of his or her role as a partner and family member. As Jamie explained,

> A big part of my role is to be successful professionally—not only for me, but also for my family. We need for me to make a fair amount of money, and I also want the children to realize that you have to work hard in life.

However, sometimes a strong individual motive to achieve can become detrimental to a relationship, such as when one person becomes a workaholic and neglects the family or uses work as an excuse to avoid addressing relationship concerns. In addition, many individuals experience role strain as a result of their attempts to perform simultaneously at high levels in work and family roles (Nickols, 1994). Nevertheless, a strong desire to achieve and contribute to the well-being of oneself, the family, and a broader community can be a positive motivation and not necessarily contrary to a successful relationship.

SEM theory (Beach & Tesser, 1993; Tesser, 1988) proposes two opposing processes that can influence individuals' reactions to their partners' achievements:

- *comparison* of oneself with another person's accomplishments, such that one is better, equal to, or worse than the other person, and
- viewing one's value as a *reflection* of another person with whom one identifies and feeling good about oneself when one's partner accomplishes highly valued goals, or bad when the partner fails.

The SEM model suggests that a person who has a high-achieving partner can experience conflicting reactions to the partner's success. On the one hand, comparing oneself with a partner's excellent accomplishments can be threatening to one's evaluation of one's own accomplishments and competence. On the other hand, associating oneself with a partner's positive accomplishments can enhance one's self-evaluation.

Beach and Tesser (1993) noted that an individual's tendency to compare his or her achievements with those of the partner takes on a more meaning when the individual is motivated to achieve in the same area. Consider Calvin, who felt threatened by Meghan's success as an architect because he had personal aspirations to be successful in the same field. In contrast, if the individual has no personal investment in the area in which the partner succeeds, the comparison process is less relevant, and the person can share in the partner's glory through the process of reflection.

Ubiquitous impact of communally and individually oriented motives in couples' relationships. The communally oriented and individually oriented motives that we have described are among the most basic and universal tendencies influencing people in their daily lives. They involve connecting with others and functioning effectively as individuals, two processes that are essential in human survival and growth. Beginning early in life, the vast majority of people are motivated to establish their individual identities and to develop some degree of competent autonomous functioning. They also exhibit motivation to have an impact on their world and strive to achieve goals. At the same time, from early childhood people are motivated to form relationships with others, which can vary considerably in depth and duration. In addition to the pleasures of affiliating with others, individuals commonly seek intimate sharing with at least one other person and report significant gaps in their lives when such relationships are lacking. Relationships with others not only meet affiliation and intimacy needs but also provide opportunities to give and receive caretaking.

Adolescence commonly has been described as a period marked by the child's conflicting motives to maintain bonds with parents and to establish him- or herself as an individual (Prager, 1995). For many people this dilemma of how best to balance connectedness and individual functioning resurfaces when they form significant adult couple relationships. It is our observation, supported by research that we have cited, that when therapists listen for the themes in distressed couples' relationship problems, the themes that frequently emerge involve communally and individually oriented motives. The degree of harmony or conflict in most relationships is likely to be influenced by the matches or mismatches in the partners' motives and how the couple handles these differences. In the intervention section of this book (chapters 8–14) we describe how therapists can help couples identify and resolve problems arising from the relative strengths and the expression of these motives that move partners toward particular goals. Before we describe some of the ways in which these motives can contribute to couples' problems, we turn to a discussion of some other motives that involve the goal of avoiding particular outcomes.

Motives Involving Avoidance of Emotional Pain

Theorists and researchers have identified a variety of human motives that involve avoiding physical or emotional pain rather than approaching a pleasurable communally or individually oriented goal (McClelland, 1987; Reiss & Havercamp, 1998). These motives are self-protective and may involve

- avoidance of physical discomfort, emotional discomfort, or both, associated with intensive work on tasks involved in achievement;
- avoidance of distress associated with a relationship's restrictions on fulfilling individually oriented goals; and
- avoidance of emotional pain associated with rejection by significant others.

Motivation to avoid psychological or emotional discomfort associated with intensive work on achievement tasks can influence a couple's relationship if it leads one or both partners to avoid important tasks concerning their jobs, household management, finances, or childrearing, especially if one person's avoidance creates hardships for the other person. For example, in dividing responsibilities in their relationship, Marcia and Phil agreed that Phil would take care of all banking tasks, including paying their bills. However, Phil experienced considerable anxiety whenever he worked on balancing their checkbook, because doing so made it clear to him that the couple was not saving money for their retirement or their children's education. Given that Phil had a strong achievement motive and often worked overtime at his job to earn more money, seeing the evidence that their expenses often were greater than their monthly income made him feel anxious and frustrated. As is typical when individuals avoid anxiety-provoking situations (Barlow, 1988), this emotional experience was so aversive to Phil that he avoided paying bills and working on the bank statements. Marcia was upset about this, partly because of her concern that important bills might go unpaid and partly because she perceived Phil as not doing his fair share of the tasks as they had agreed.

Motivation to avoid distress associated with a relationship's restrictions on fulfillment of individually oriented goals tends to focus on expectancies that "too much" involvement with a partner will interfere with the fulfillment of one's autonomy, achievement, or power (McClelland, 1987). The actual or anticipated experience of having a partner restrict one's freedom, achievement, or control leads the individual to avoid close involvement. Esther grew up in a family in which her parents were very intrusive and the children had little privacy. As an adult, she valued autonomy and found Larry's frequent questions about her thoughts and feelings aversive. Consequently, she was highly vigilant for signs that Larry was about to "get in my personal space" and quickly avoided contact with him at such times.

Motivation to avoid the distress associated with rejection by significant others has been identified as influencing individuals' tendencies to avoid interactions with intimate partners and others. Mehrabian (1994) investigated sensitivity to rejection as a motive that can counteract an individual's motivation to affiliate with others. The person's tendency to withdraw is based on the aversiveness of either potential or actual negative responses from the other people. Within a couple's relationship, an individual who avoids distress associated with possible rejection may avoid arguments with the partner, inhibit expression of his or her opinions, hesitate to make requests of or impose on the partner, and overreact to minor negative feedback from the partner (Mehrabian, 1994).

These examples of self-protective motivation are meant not to be comprehensive but rather to illustrate how members of a couple may be motivated to avoid particular types of interaction with each other. At times, avoidance motivation can interfere with couples' attempts to fulfill their communally and individually oriented goals within their relationships. Therefore, it is important to consider self-protective motives in clinical assessment of relationship dynamics. Although some degree of self-protective motivation is likely to be adaptive and common in well-adjusted relationships, higher levels have the potential to contribute to demand–withdraw patterns, disengagement, and alienation between partners.

The degree to which an individual is motivated to avoid physically or emotionally stressful situations may depend on his or her ability to tolerate distress. Individual differences in discomfort tolerance may be due to variations in people's emotional reactivity or temperament (Kagan, 1994) or to differences in individuals' experience, skills, and attitudes concerning tolerance of distress. Ellis (e.g., Dryden & Ellis, 1988) described how individuals vary in the degree to which they believe that they are able to tolerate, or should have to tolerate, frustration and other distressing states. Meichenbaum (1985) also addressed individuals' deficits in skills for coping with emotional and physical stress. Similarly, Linehan's (1993) dialectical behavior therapy focuses on helping clients develop their ability to tolerate and manage emotional distress, and Jacobson and Christensen's (1996) integrative couple therapy emphasizes strategies for increasing partners' abilities to accept characteristics of their relationships that they have been unable to tolerate. Thus, cognitive–behavioral therapists increasingly have noted the significant impact that avoidance of discomfort has on individuals' personal adjustment, including their ability to cope with relationship problems. In Part II of this book we describe therapeutic approaches for increasing partners' ability to tolerate distress and for decreasing avoidance patterns.

Gender Differences in Motives

Our clinical observations suggest that there may be a difference in the values that men and women tend to attach to the sharing of power. Specifically, among individuals who are motivated to exercise power, some men are less comfortable sharing power and input regarding decision making than women are. In choosing partners, men with high power motivation may either try to avoid potential mates who would be rivals or they may behave in coercive, competitive ways to overpower their partners. In contrast, women with high power motivation tend to choose spouses who value and use power, with an expectation that they will share power and decision-making influence. In a sense, men with high power motivation appear to value power for themselves, whereas women with high power motivation value power for themselves and their partners.

Relatively little research has been conducted on possible gender differences in communally and individually oriented motives or motives involving avoidance of emotional pain. Although the existing research indicates minimal gender differences in the levels of these motives, there is some evidence that males and females may differ in the ways that they express their motives. For example, no differences have been found between males and females in their overall levels of power motivation assessed in terms of themes in individuals' Thematic Apperception Test stories, but males and females who are high in power motivation appear to choose mates somewhat differently and experience their relationships differently (McAdams, 1985). Men who score high on power motivation tend to marry women who are less likely to pursue careers in subsequent years, and they tend to be less satisfied with their marriages. In contrast, women with higher power motivation tend to marry men who are successful in their careers, and they are more satisfied with their marriages than low-power women are (McAdams, 1984; Winter, McClelland, & Stewart, 1982; Winter, Stewart, & McClelland, 1977). Furthermore, the couple relationships of men (but not women) who score higher in power motivation are more likely to break up (McClelland, Davis, Kalin, & Wanner, 1972; Stewart & Rubin, 1976; Winter, 1973).

Thus, men who are high in power motivation appear to be in a motivational bind, in that they seek out partners who do not threaten their achievement and power goals, but their relatively lower marital satisfaction suggests that their relationships still do not meet some of their basic needs. Our clinical observations suggest that in some of these couples the man becomes ambivalent about his partner's less assertive approach to life, comparing her negatively with women in the workplace who have higher levels of power motivation. In other couples, the woman becomes increasingly ambivalent about her partner's desire to dominate their relationship; even though she initially was attracted by his assertiveness, she is unhappy with his coerciveness.

Concerning intimacy motivation, research has indicated minimal gender differences: Males and females tend to agree on what the characteristics of intimacy are, describing self-disclosure as a key (McAdams, 1988; Prager, 1995; Reis, Senchak, & Solomon, 1985). However, there are some gender differences in the ways that females and males seek intimacy. Women tend to value and engage in mutual self-disclosure in close relationships more than men do, whereas men tend to view sharing activities and interests as means of achieving intimacy more than women do (Prager, 1995; Prager & Buhrmester, 1998). Thus, when Myrna complained that she and Josh lacked the degree of intimacy that she wanted in their relationship, Josh suggested that they could go for hikes in the countryside more often. Myrna replied, "I enjoy hiking, too, but when we're out on a trail we're usually walking single file and not talking much. That doesn't make me feel close to you." In return, Josh noted, "Talking is great, and I talk more with you than with anyone else. But I feel close to you just knowing we are out there doing something together." In couples' relationships these types of gender differences have the potential to create conflict between male and female partners who may value different ways of achieving intimacy.

The research on gender differences in communally and individually oriented motives unfortunately is limited in amount and scope. The results from Thematic Apperception Test studies can be conceptualized within a cognitive–behavioral perspective as possible reflections of individuals' schemas concerning these motives, but there is a clear need for investigations using other methodologies, including self-report questionnaire methods, such as those used by Prager and Buhrmester (1998) to measure partners' satisfaction with how their needs are being met. Also, most of the studies were conducted up to 20 years ago, and it is not clear how more recent changes in gender roles may have affected the gender difference. In addition, the research on motivation in close relationships has been restricted to heterosexual couples, so there is a lack of information about effects of partners' motives in same-sex couples.

Intra- and Interpersonal Balancing of Motives

Communally and individually oriented needs or motives sometimes have been conceptualized as incompatible because the former focus on relating to other people and the latter tend to focus on autonomous pursuits. At times we have heard both professionals and laypeople suggest that meeting affiliation, intimacy, altruism, and succorance needs through relationships with a partner is likely to interfere with the pursuit of individually oriented goals associated with autonomy, achievement, and power needs, and vice versa. On the one hand, each member of a couple could experience internal conflict between his or her communally oriented and individually oriented motives. As Jim put it,

How much do I want to focus on building our relationship, and how much do I want to grow as an individual? I have a limited amount of time and energy, and I feel pulled between our relationship and myself as an individual.

On the other hand, mismatches between the relative strengths of two partners' communally and individually oriented motives may produce conflict between partners.

Although communally and individually oriented motives can be the basis for conflicts both within and between members of a couple, there is evidence that a balance between fulfillment of communally and individually oriented motives may be not only possible but also desirable (Prager & Buhrmester, 1998; Rankin-Esquer, Burnett, Baucom, & Epstein, 1997). Rankin-Esquer et al. (1997) assessed the degree to which members of a sample of community couples perceived that their partners encourage their independence and individuality and the degree to which they perceived that the partners provide closeness. Perceptions of the amounts of autonomy and relatedness provided by their partners were positively correlated, and both were positively associated with the individuals' relationship satisfaction.

These findings indicate that communally and individually oriented motives can coexist without producing problems. However, the findings do not rule out the possibility that a particular individual might have an internal conflict between his or her own communally and individually oriented motives, or that two partners might have a conflict due to differences in their levels of the two types of motives. The degree to which an individual experiences conflict between communally and individually oriented motives depends on how much he or she perceives that the available ways of fulfilling the two types of needs are mutually exclusive versus mutually facilitative.

An individual may perceive that, to fulfill companionship needs, he or she must spend so much time on sharing activities with the partner that insufficient time remains for individual activities that would fulfill autonomy needs. The accuracy of the person's perception that companionship and autonomy activities conflict with each other can depend on several factors. The couple may have insufficient time available for all of the companionship and autonomous activities that they have chosen. This is especially likely to cause difficulty if an activity chosen to fulfill a need is very time consuming. Thus, Vicki was highly motivated to have an intimate relationship with Peter, but she also was focused on her desire to achieve through pursuing a career as a physician. The extensive time and energy commitment to medical studies, internship, and residency left little of her personal resources available for building intimacy with Peter.

Furthermore, the particular communally and individually oriented activities that each partner prefers can determine whether the two types of activities appear to be compatible. Consider Aaron and Scott, who both were content to fulfill their individually oriented needs through their separate careers. However, when it came to communally oriented motivation, Aaron preferred shared activities focused on the outdoors (e.g., hiking, camping), but Scott preferred cultural activities (e.g., museums, concerts), and each had limited interest in the other's preferences. Consequently, although the overall levels of their communally and individually oriented motives were similar, both partners perceived considerable conflict in balancing their communally oriented needs within their relationship.

Finally, an individual may be distressed about a partner's motives if he or she makes negative attributions about the behavior that the person uses to fulfill the motives (Baucom & Epstein, 1990). Jason greatly valued his relationship with Yvonne, who desired a lot of shared time with Jason. However, Jason also was highly motivated to experience power and control, which he expressed through his involvement in local politics. When Jason spent a considerable amount of time (especially during political campaigns) out of the house attending meetings and fundraising events, Yvonne interpreted these activities as meaning that Jason cared little about their relationship. She even feared that perhaps Jason wanted to leave her for someone involved in politics. Yvonne perceived incompatibility between their levels of motivation for intimacy because she attributed Jason's behavior to wanting little closeness with her rather than his desire to experience power through involvement in politics.

On the other hand, members of a couple may be able to facilitate the fulfillment of each other's communally and individually oriented motives within their relationship (Rankin-Esquer et al., 1997). One of the things that attracted Doris and Jerome to each other was their common interest in playing bridge. In playing together, particularly in tournaments, they were able to fulfill simultaneously their desires for affiliation and intimacy as well as their needs to achieve and be successful. A relationship also can serve as a base from which an individual can pursue the fulfillment of his or her own needs independently, as long as such efforts are not threatening to the partner.

Finally, although there are advantages when partners have relatively similar motives, at times this similarity can result in notable gaps in their relationship. Partners who share a strong desire for intimacy but who both lack an achievement orientation might experience financial difficulty because neither of them makes strong efforts to advance professionally.

Developmental Factors That Affect Conflict Over Motives

When two people are initially becoming involved with each other they are likely to focus on the qualities that attract them to each other and to downplay the significance of ways in which they might not meet each other's needs (Goldstine, Larner, Zuckerman, & Goldstine, 1993). They tend to go out of their way to behave in ways that meet each other's needs, and it is easy for them to assume that it will always be that way. Over time, however, the degree of fit between needs and need fulfillment may change, on the basis of personal development in the individual partners, shifts in the couple's interaction pattern, or changes in life circumstances (e.g., children, extended family, job, personal illnesses). Anderson, Dimidjian, and Miller (1995) observed that partners' failure to continue to satisfy each other's needs commonly produces the conflict and distress that motivate midlife couples to seek couples therapy. Furthermore, it is common in midlife for individuals to engage in some "life review" in which they consider their aspirations, the degree to which they have attained their goals, and the finite amount of time they have left to do so.

Some couples experience relationship distress when one of the partners grows and changes over time, such that the relationship no longer meets that person's needs in the way that it once did. Consider Jose, who was several years older than Anna. She had come from a rather neglectful family and felt that no one had ever taken care of her, offered her advice, or "protected" her. Jose was more experienced in the world, and he enjoyed nurturing Anna and being the leader of the family. For many years, Anna found these complementary roles rewarding and fulfilling. With Jose she experienced security, gained confidence in herself, and developed an increasing desire for autonomy within their relationship. Jose was delighted with Anna's personal growth, but he also experienced difficulty with the changes. He no longer felt needed or as important to Anna; if she no longer needed the same level of advice and nurturance that she once had sought, then what was his role? How would he now show her that he cared for her? Anna's continuing personal growth and development meant that the couple would need to learn to relate to each other in new ways. They needed to support Anna's increasing motivation toward autonomy and yet find ways to maintain intimacy and express caring for each other. Jose also was faced with the task of adjusting to the fact that his motivation to nurture (and perhaps control) Anna had to be channeled differently.

Many couples function well in one stage of marriage and similar committed relationships but falter when a new stage places different demands on their relationship. Even when neither person's motives have changed, the demands from the couple's environment change, such as when the couple's first child is born. Carter and McGoldrick (1999) provided an excellent overview of family life cycle stages and their characteristics as well as cultural variations in family norms and patterns, that clinicians need to take into account. The common decline in marital satisfaction during the years when couples are parenting children has been linked to the decreased ability of the partners to satisfy each other's companionship and intimacy needs during this period as well as to major childrearing expenses that limit the couple's financial achievement (Anderson et al., 1995; Belsky, 1990). However, when adolescents eventually are "launched" and the couple reaches the "empty-nest" stage, the couple commonly experiences an increase in relationship satisfaction, associated with opportunities to increase their intimacy and pursue both individual and shared activities that meet their needs (Belsky, 1990; White & Edwards, 1993).

The negative impact of developmental changes is likely to be greater if the couple lacks the flexibility or skills to find new ways to meet their needs (H. I. McCubbin & Patterson, 1983). In addition, sometimes couples are unaware that developmental changes have interfered with the fulfillment of important needs, so they fail to take appropriate corrective action. For example, Lorenzo and Fran both desired and had experienced a great deal of intimacy in their marriage. They were excited about having children together, but after their first child was born they no longer had much time or energy for each other. When they discussed their distress with a couples therapist they described parenthood as exhausting, but they did not seem to have a clear sense of how the changes in their daily life had affected their feelings of intimacy. Both partners assumed that because they cared about each other they should continue to feel intimate no matter what daily stresses they faced.

Implications of Motives for Understanding Couples' Relationships

Motives serve as the basis of many themes and patterns that are observed in couples' interactions. For example, the types of motives we have described commonly contribute to issues involving major dimensions of individuals' personal standards concerning their couple relationships, which we and our colleagues have investigated in previous research (e.g., Baucom, Epstein, Rankin, & Burnett, 1996):

- struggles that some couples have for *control* over decision making;
- approach–avoidance patterns associated with differences in partners' needs for *boundaries* or degrees of autonomy between them; and
- conflicts over differences in partners' levels of *investment* in achieving career success, a higher standard of living, and other goals.

Therapists in clinical practice commonly see couples who experience conflict and distress concerning mismatches or conflicts in the two individuals' motives. For example, relationship problems in which one person has a need for more intimate interaction than the other are well documented in the clinical literature (Jacobson & Christensen, 1996; Johnson, 1996). Therapists also see many couples in which one partner has a much stronger achievement motive than the other and loses respect for the person with less drive. The arousal of individuals' power motives often contributes to conflict between partners, particularly when the partners attribute each other's controlling behaviors to malicious intent. In addition to such communally and individually oriented motives, motives associated with the incentive of avoiding emotional and physical pain have the potential to contribute to demand–withdraw patterns that increasingly have drawn the attention of couples therapists and researchers (Christensen & Heavey, 1993; McClelland, 1987). Thus, understanding partners' motives is an important means of identifying the major themes that organize their subjective experiences and behavioral interactions in their couple relationships.

INDIVIDUAL PERSONALITY STYLES

Partners' differences in personality characteristics may complement each other, thus strengthening the relationship, or they may be at odds with each other and create distress. In this section we discuss how the Big Five and other personality traits—such as organization, emotional reactivity, and coping styles—may affect the individuals, the couple's dyadic interactions, or their interactions with their environment. Examples of beneficial and deleterious effects of personality characteristics are provided. Understanding how individual personality styles color interpersonal functioning offers clues to the patterns governing couples' interactions.

Theorists have recognized that motives are not the only dispositional characteristics that affect people's behavior. Individuals also bring a variety of other relatively stable personality styles to their adult relationships. Personality *styles*, or *traits*, are cognitive, affective, and behavioral patterns of responses that are exhibited with some degree of consistency across various life situations (Buss, 1995; Kagan, 1994). Individuals who tend to focus on details, for instance, are likely to exhibit that tendency in many situations (e.g., reading the written descriptions of paintings in museums, spending much time editing the reports they write at work), compared to less detail-oriented people. Similarly, individuals who tend to be shy because of an inhibited temperament (Kagan, 1994) are likely to self-disclose little in most situations with strangers. In keeping with our multilevel approach to understanding couples' relationships, we consider it important to identify ways in which personality styles and temperament affect the individual partners, the dyad's interactions, and the couple's interactions with their environment.

Variations in personality between members of a couple can be a source of pleasure or stress for the two persons. The possible combinations of two partners' personality styles and how the couple addresses them are almost unlimited. The clinician must remain aware that a variety of personality factors might adversely affect the couple or serve as positive resources for them. Although it would be implausible to provide a complete listing of all the personality factors that might affect a couple's relationship, we next briefly discuss some personality styles that commonly affect couples' functioning.

A variety of personality factors exist, and generally it is not necessary for a clinician to have a fixed, standard checklist of personality dimensions to assess with each couple. However, a parsimonious framework for conceptualizing dimensions of personality that can affect couples' interactions is the set of Big Five personality factors that have gained increasing prominence and empirical support in recent years (Buss, 1995; Costa & McCrae, 1992; Digman, 1989; John & Srivastava, 1999):

1. *Extraversion* (e.g., sociability, warmth, assertiveness, adventurousness)
2. *Agreeableness* (e.g., trust, altruism, compliance, sympathy)
3. *Conscientiousness* (e.g., competence, orderliness, achievement striving, self-discipline)
4. *Neuroticism*, or emotional instability (e.g., anxiety, hostility, depression, impulsiveness)
5. *Openness to Experience* (e.g., curiosity, imagination, varied interests, unconventionality)

Although focusing on the Big Five personality factors can be useful for identifying broad individual tendencies, Paunonen (1998) found that assessing more specific components of each broader trait provided important information for understanding people's interests, attitudes, and behaviors. Paunonen described how a broad characteristic such as conscientiousness actually involves several subcomponents (e.g., orderliness, ambition, and self-discipline), and a particular individual might exhibit different degrees of these subcomponents. Thus, Leslie was pleased that Mark demonstrated some aspects of conscientiousness but was upset that he lacked others. She liked his high levels of ambition and self-discipline because she could count on him to work hard on tasks. However, Mark also exhibited a low level of orderliness, such that his hard work typically was disorganized. Thus, a consideration of only the broader, overarching trait of conscientiousness may cause a clinician to overlook specific traits that contribute to a person's relationship problems.

Regarding the Big Five factor of Extraversion, partners often differ in the level of stimulation and activity that each person experiences as comfortable (Buss, 1995). Considerable evidence indicates that from birth individuals differ in *temperament*—moderately stable physiologically based behavioral and emotional responses that appear to be at least partly genetically determined. Temperament includes an individual's levels of physiological reactivity and subjective comfort with environmental stimulation such as novelty (Kagan, 1994; Strelau, 1985). Differences in temperament affect people's ways of relating to the world, including interpersonal relationships, throughout their lives. In particular, Kagan (1994) distinguished between children and adolescents with an *inhibited* temperament (uncomfortable and reserved in novel, unfamiliar situations) and those with an *uninhibited* temperament (actively engaging unfamiliar situations with positive emotion). Similarly, as adults some people seek a high degree of stimulation, which might be demonstrated through strong desires for novelty, a high level of activity, and learning new things about many areas of life. The partner of such an individual might need much less stimulation or might prefer the stability that comes with a more routine approach to life. This difference in temperament might be reflected in the partners' differing desires, such as their interest in traveling to new places or how frequently they wish to go to parties versus staying at home for a quiet evening.

Kuhl (1994) reviewed research concerning a related personality dimension of action versus state orientation as modes of coping that individuals use in situations that arouse fear and other strong positive and negative emotions. *State orientation* refers to ruminative thinking and inhibited behavior when faced with options. An example of state orientation is continuing to do something boring when one is aware of a more interesting option. On the one hand, behavioral inhibition can be adaptive, because it can protect an individual from negative consequences of behaving impulsively. However, behavioral inhibition also can interfere with an individual's abilities to plan, initiate, and complete beneficial activities. Flora, for example, was frustrated when Lenny failed to work with her on developing better ways to invest their money for retirement and their children's college education. Lenny acknowledged that this goal was important, but he described feeling "frozen" whenever he sat down to think about investments. In contrast, *action orientation* involves the tendency to initiate systematic problem-solving thoughts and behaviors without being urged and directed by others. Results of empirical studies suggest that socialization during childhood contributes to the development of a person's disposition toward a state or an action orientation (Kuhl, 1994). Children whose parents frequently interrupted their activities score higher on a measure of state orientation, suggesting that the interruptions interfered with the children's ability to maintain concentration on the completion of a desired goal.

At times, a couple can profit from differences in these personality styles. One person can provide a source of excitement and new experiences for the other or can be a major force in changing the status quo when the couple is unhappy with it. In turn, one person can teach the other to relax and enjoy the more routine pleasures of life or to avoid impulsive responses that involve risk to their relationship. Thus, Abigail sometimes felt frustrated with the extent to which Michael pored over detailed reports of companies' performances before agreeing to invest the couple's money in particular stocks, but she generally accepted his style because his efforts had been lucrative for them.

In other instances, partners experience significant distress due to temperament and other personality style differences (Jacobson & Christensen, 1996). Over time, for example, one person might find the other to be boring, feeling "Why do I have to keep initiating activities for us? If I didn't make the effort, I think we would just sit here, day in and day out." The less active partner might find the more active one to be "unable to relax and just enjoy herself. She constantly has to be doing something. I think she distracts herself by keeping herself busy all the time." Thus, not only does each person find the other's preferred level of activity and variety uncomfortable, but he or she might also attribute it to undesirable personal characteristics of the partner.

Partners' personality styles can have negative consequences for their individual functioning, how they relate as a dyad, and how they relate as a couple to their environment. Elana tended to be relatively disorganized in her approach to tasks, both at home and in outside settings such as her job. She commonly began one task and then shifted her efforts to other tasks that caught her attention. At an individual level, this characteristic interfered with Elana's productivity, leaving her feeling frustrated with herself. In fact, she described feeling depressed when she looked at all of her unfinished jobs and thought, "I may never finish them." At the couple level, Elana's lack of organization led to arguments with Brad, who tended to be systematic in his work and criticized her for "keeping the house in a state of confusion." He was especially frustrated when they decided to work on a task together, such as cleaning out the garage in preparation for a yard sale. As Brad tried to focus on organizing one part of the task, something would catch Elana's eye, and she would stop working with him. This stylistic difference between partners interfered with their ability to work together and created conflict, which became chronic. Concerning the couple's interactions with their environment, Elana's tendency to move from one activity to another often made the couple late for appointments, including social events, such as friends' parties.

Couples and therapists are faced with examining the advantages and disadvantages of two partners having differences in personality characteristics and with determining what might be done to decrease the negative impact of the disadvantages. Living with someone who approaches life in very different ways than one does is likely to involve effort on a daily basis. These differences need not be damaging to a relationship, but they do mean that the couple must find effective ways to cope with them (Christensen & Jacobson, 2000). In chapter 6 we describe how concepts from stress-and-coping models can be valuable in helping couples adapt effectively to personality differences.

Behaviorally oriented approaches to couples therapy have traditionally paid little attention to motives, temperament, and other individual-difference characteristics. However, the evidence that partners' responses to each other are influenced by normal variations in such dispositional characteristics is compelling (Jacobson & Christensen, 1996) and helps explain why individuals experience aspects of their couple interactions as pleasing or displeasing. Behavioral concepts such as negative reciprocity can account for predictable patterns in couples' interactions; however, they tell little about the reasons *why* the members of one couple are frequently in conflict and engage in vicious negative exchanges while another couple has relatively infrequent and brief arguments. The particular combination of two partners' motives, temperaments, and other personality styles can be sources of compatibility and satisfaction, but they also can be the basis of conflict and distress. Thus, integrating concepts concerning personality styles into our cognitive–behavioral model allows us to better understand the meaning of a couple's interactions. Next we consider another important type of characteristic that some individuals bring to their couple relationships: patterns of dysfunctional affective, cognitive, and behavioral responses.

INDIVIDUAL DYSFUNCTIONS

Symptoms of psychopathology experienced by one partner might require couples intervention because the relationship may serve as a stressor for the disorder, or the psychopathological symptoms may act as a stressor for the relationship, adversely affecting communication and daily interactions. In this section we examine how an individual's psychopathology may affect the fulfillment of both partners' individually and communally oriented needs, activities or daily functioning of the couple, and interactions with other people in the couple's social network. We describe potentially harmful effects of symptoms and discuss how improvement in an individual's symptoms also can be stressful for a couple. Finally, we examine the effects of subclinical characterological traits, such as emotional dysregulation, and long-standing unresolved issues or schemas formed during childhood, prior adult relationships, or traumatic events in the current relationship.

Clinical Disorders and Individual Psychopathology

In addition to normal variations in motives, temperament, and personality styles, members of couples often experience varying degrees of psychopathological symptoms that influence, or are influenced by, the quality of the partners' interactions. There is evidence that the causal link between individual psychopathology and relationship problems can operate in either direction (Halford & Bouma, 1997). Therefore, it is important that the couples therapist determine the degree to which an individual partner's symptoms are linked to causes that transcend the relationship or are direct responses to relationship dysfunction.

It is important, for example, to distinguish between depression as a stressor that can contribute to marital distress versus marital distress as a stressor that can precipitate a depressive episode in an individual who may have a pre-existing vulnerability to depression. Beach and his colleagues (e.g., Beach

& O'Leary, 1992; Beach, Whisman, & O'Leary, 1994) and Jacobson, Dobson, Fruzzetti, Schmaling, and Salusky (1991) found that if an individual's depression appears to be primarily a reaction to marital distress, then the treatment of choice might be marital therapy, and the depression often is alleviated as the marital distress lessens. However, if an individual has a history of depression, if the current depressive episode predates the couple's relationship difficulties, and if the depression occurs in response to events beyond the relationship as well as within it, then it is unlikely that marital therapy alone will be sufficient.

Even when an individual whose depression appears to be associated with factors that are independent of his or her couple relationship benefits from receiving individual therapy, providing additional assistance to the couple still might be important, for two reasons:

- There might be relationship difficulties that are unrelated to the etiology of the individual's depression but that serve as stressors that exacerbate depressive symptoms.
- The couple might not cope well with the person's depression, and the maladaptive response to depression might contribute to relationship distress.

Concerning relationship problems that are unrelated to the etiology of clinical disorders but affect their course, a literature review conducted by Baucom, Shoham, Mueser, Daiuto, and Stickle (1998) indicated that the quality of couple and family interactions can have important effects on the maintenance of, or relapse from, a variety of individual clinical disorders, including depression (Beach, Sandeen, & O'Leary, 1990), anxiety disorders (Craske & Zoellner, 1995), bipolar disorder (Miklowitz & Goldstein, 1997), schizophrenia (Miklowitz, 1995), eating disorders (Root, 1995), alcohol abuse and dependence (McCrady & Epstein, 1995), and sexual dysfunctions and desire disorders (Kaplan, 1983, 1995). Even in the case of disorders such as schizophrenia and bipolar disorder, for which empirical studies have implicated biological vulnerabilities rather than family interactions as etiological factors, research has indicated that stressful family interactions can exacerbate existing symptoms and increase the probability of relapse. Consequently, clinicians who treat couples that include partners with such disorders need to evaluate possible contributions of current couple interaction patterns to the course of individual symptoms.

Concerning problematic responses to a partner's depression, some nondepressed partners believe that the depressed person can just "snap out of it" if he or she tried, and therefore they criticize and cajole the depressed partner (Beach et al., 1990). As Hooley and Teasdale (1989) demonstrated, high levels of criticism appear to worsen the course of depression rather than help the depressed individual. Moreover, a high level of nagging and criticism from the nondepressed partner can contribute to the development of a maladaptive demand–withdraw pattern in the couple's interactions. Even when the nondepressed person's demands are based on frustration rather than hostile intent, the depressed partner is likely to perceive the other person as critical and may withdraw. Demand–withdraw patterns are frustrating for most couples and are highly associated with marital distress (e.g., Christensen, 1988; Christensen & Heavey, 1990; Christensen & Shenk, 1991; Gottman, 1994a).

As Arkowitz, Holliday, and Hutter (1982) and Biglan et al. (1985) have found, people who live with depressed individuals often feel conflicted and uncertain of how to interact with the depressed person. They commonly feel at least somewhat protective of their suffering family member and guilty about causing the person additional distress by pressuring him or her to change. Consequently, their communication to the depressed individual can take forms other than confrontation, at times becoming indirect. Consider Wes, who had repeatedly tried to motivate Shannon to get involved in various activities rather than lying around the house feeling depressed; however, his urging usually led to arguments and Shannon's withdrawal. Wes came to believe that confronting Shannon only made things worse, so he decided to try to keep his feelings of frustration to himself. Unfortunately, he did not express his concerns to Shannon directly and withdrew from her during interactions so that he would not become upset with her, a response that Shannon readily noticed. Intervention with a couple can focus on modifying such response patterns that are increasing their distress.

In turn, as noted earlier, the symptoms of one partner are likely to affect the quality of the couple's relationship. The following are some examples of negative effects that an individual's symptoms might have on the couple's relationship.

Individuals who experience clinical depression often express their negativity about themselves and their life situations in their conversations with their partners, and the negativity may include criticism of the partner (Beach et al., 1990). Other common symptoms of depression, such as suicidal ideation and behavior, withdrawal, decreased sexual desire, insomnia, irritability, and lethargy, are likely to affect couples' interactions and the well-being of the individual's partner as well. One frequent problematic response is that the depressed person's partner takes such symptoms personally, concluding, for instance, that the individual's withdrawal and decreased sexual desire reflect a personal rejection of the partner. Similarly, if the partner attributes the depressed person's lethargy to the person having decreased investment in their relationship, he or she may become angry and critical of the person (Beach et al., 1990).

Other clinical disorders also can have negative impacts on couples' relationships. Miklowitz and Goldstein (1997) described how stressful the symptoms of bipolar disorder (e.g., grandiosity, impulsive spending and decision making, and hyperactivity during manic episodes) can be for spouses and other family members. Similarly, partners and other family members of individuals experiencing panic disorder with agoraphobia commonly are affected by the individual's distress concerning panic and his or her dependence on "safe" others to enter feared situations (Craske & Zoellner, 1995). Partners of alcoholics are faced with various negative impacts of alcohol on the other's functioning (e.g., verbal and physical abuse, emotional withdrawal, employment and financial problems) as well as the social stigma and personal embarrassment of interacting with extended family, friends, neighbors and others (O'Farrell & Rotunda, 1997). Family members of schizophrenic individuals commonly have to cope with chronic symptoms that severely limit the individual's ability to function in interpersonal relationships as well as perform instrumental tasks at home or in the outside world (Falloon, Boyd, & McGill, 1984). Sexual desire disorders and dysfunctions can significantly affect the quality of a couple's sexual relationship and in turn their overall relationship (Kaplan, 1995). A partner's eating disorder symptoms (e.g., body image dissatisfaction, rigid personal rules about eating and exercise patterns, bingeing and purging behaviors) can be distressing and disruptive to the couple's relationship. Thus, it is important for clinicians to determine the frequency and intensity of individual symptoms of psychopathology and their impact on the individual's partner and the couple's interactions. This information is crucial in treatment planning, particularly in decisions concerning individual versus conjoint therapy sessions and the focus of couple sessions.

An Example of Depression

Impact on the individual. An individual's symptoms of depression are likely to interfere with the fulfillment of both partners' communally oriented and individually oriented needs (I. H. Gotlib & Beach, 1995). Symptoms such as withdrawal, irritability, decreased sexual desire, and lethargy decrease the individual's own ability to express communal motivation for affiliation and intimacy. Furthermore, the depressed individual's tendency to be self-focused reduces his or her expression of altruism. Although the individual's need for succorance may increase because of feelings of helplessness that are common in depression, he or she may be a difficult person for the partner to help because of symptoms such as general negativity and irritability. In turn, the individual's depression is likely to disrupt his or her ability to fulfill the partner's communally oriented needs. In addition to having limited opportunities for affiliation and intimacy, the partner of a depressed person commonly will experience frustration in his or her attempts to be altruistic, because those attempts tend to be ineffective in reducing the depression. Finally, the imbalance in functioning that develops in the couple's relationship commonly leaves the nondepressed partner without his or her primary source of succorance because the depressed person is not available to provide caretaking.

Symptoms of depression also can disrupt fulfillment of both partners' individually oriented needs. Lethargy, fatigue, indecision, and self-criticism are likely to interfere with the depressed person's typical desire for achievement, and the powerful sense of helplessness can counteract efforts toward autonomy. In turn, the more time and effort that the nondepressed partner puts into taking care of the depressed person (including taking over tasks that the depressed person is unable to perform), the more his or her own opportunities for fulfilling achievement, power, and autonomy needs will be limited.

In addition to blocking the individual partners' need fulfillment, depression is likely to produce distress by interfering with the expression of other personality characteristics. For example, one of the characteristics that attracted Craig and Felice to each other was their shared preference for a high degree of order in their daily lives. They both liked to keep the house neat and clean and to plan their daily schedules. However, when Craig experienced an episode of major depression, his fatigue and inertia led him to neglect a variety of personal and household tasks, changes that were frustrating to both partners.

Impact on the couple's interaction. An individual disorder such as depression commonly affects aspects of a couple's dyadic interaction. A couple's ability to communicate effectively involves skills for expressing oneself and for listening carefully. Decision making or problem solving requires the couple to coordinate their efforts in defining issues, generating appropriate solutions, enacting the solution, and evaluating the outcome. However, symptoms of depression can interfere with the couple's attempts to communicate in those ways. Thus, Matt's rumination about what he viewed as the hopelessness of his life distracted him from listening to Alicia's messages, and Alicia's mixed feelings about Matt (sympathy and frustration) distracted her from listening to him. Usually, when they tried to discuss an important topic or solve a problem, they digressed into a discussion of how Matt was feeling. Matt's depression also resulted in a substantial decrease in the couple's going out together socially. This change in their social life decreased their marital satisfaction. Alicia's frustration with Matt's depression led her to criticize him for not trying harder to complete tasks and go out socially. In turn, Matt criticized Alicia as being insensitive and uncaring. Before Matt became clinically depressed, the couple had rarely exchanged criticisms, so this pattern represented a significant and upsetting change in their daily interactions.

Impact on the couple's interaction with their environment. An individual disorder such as depression can interfere with a couple's interactions with their environment, including children, extended family, friends, and social institutions such as jobs and schools. As just described, a partner's depression may lead a couple to withdraw from their social network, depriving them of pleasant experiences and sources of social support. Empirical evidence suggests that depression also can have negative effects on parenting (Cummings, Davies, & Campbell, 2000) and, if an individual's depression severely interferes with his or her functioning at work, it may lead to the loss of a job and economic hardship for the couple. If the depressed person tends to be highly self-critical, he or she also may resist support that family and friends offer. In fact, both members of a couple may associate a stigma with one partner's disorder and isolate themselves to avoid others' disapproval.

Because there are countless ways in which psychopathology can influence couples, it is important for clinicians to conduct an assessment of each couple's circumstances. The negative effects of psychopathology will depend on the severity of the symptoms, the degree to which the partners evaluate the symptoms negatively (e.g., as shameful or as evidence of a personal defect), and limitations in the resources such as social support available to the couple. In chapter 6 we further describe this conceptualization of psychopathology as a set of demands with which couples cope with varying degrees of success.

Potential for Mixed Reactions to Improvement in Psychopathological Symptoms

As distressing as symptoms of psychopathology can be for both members of a couple, clinicians need to be aware that improvement in an individual's symptoms can at times be stressful for some couples. Possible causes of negative responses to improvement include (a) that the individual's symptoms had payoffs for the couple and (b) that the improvement disrupts familiar patterns.

Both systems theory and social learning theory suggest that one partner's symptoms may have some payoffs for the members of a couple. Systems theorists speak of the symptoms "serving a function" in the couple's relationship (Nichols & Schwartz, 2001). For example, if the cohesion between partners has been decreasing, and there is increasing danger of the relationship ending, then an individual's depression can provide a new bond in which the nondepressed person becomes a caretaker for the dependent, depressed person. Similarly, Goldstein and Chambless (1978) proposed that the development of panic disorder with agoraphobia can stabilize a distressed relationship. This type of conceptualization is similar to the social learning concept of secondary gain in which the occurrence of symptoms results in positive or negative reinforcement, such as an increase in a partner's nurturing behavior or a decrease in a partner's criticism.

Although empirical evidence suggests that relationship problems are among the most common antecedents of clinical disorders such as depression and panic disorder, the evidence that symptoms serve positive functions for couples has been inconsistent. In laboratory investigations of couples' communication, two studies (Biglan et al., 1985; Nelson & Beach, 1990) found that husbands were less likely to behave aggressively toward their wives after the wives exhibited depressive behavior, an apparent positive consequence for the wives. However, in Schmaling and Jacobson's (1990) study wives' depressive behavior did not suppress husbands' aggressive behavior. In the absence of more substantial information about the effects of depressive and other symptoms on couples' interaction, it is best to be cautious about assuming that symptoms have positive payoffs for couples and that clients may be reluctant to give up such benefits. The bulk of research findings suggest that when one partner experiences psychological symptoms, both members of the couple find the symptoms to be stressful, look forward to their amelioration, and do not exhibit deterioration in their relationships as the psychopathology improves (e.g., Daiuto, Baucom, Epstein, & Dutton, 1998). Nevertheless, the potential for secondary gain exists, and it is important that clinicians look for such patterns when assessing each couple.

Improvement in an individual's symptoms might create stress in a relationship by causing *disruption of patterns that have become familiar to both partners*. In adapting to an individual's psychopathology, the members of a couple commonly develop an interaction pattern that works best for them under the circumstances. Consider the partner of an agoraphobic individual, who often takes on some of the symptomatic individual's roles that require venturing into the outside world, such as shopping. The partner of a depressed person may become the primary decision maker when the depressed individual experiences symptoms such as difficulty with concentration, indecisiveness, fatigue, and self-criticism. Similarly, partners of individuals whose functioning is debilitated by effects of alcohol abuse commonly take over roles and responsibilities normally belonging to the alcoholic. In such cases, the partners may become accustomed to roles that are different from those that they had at an earlier time, or that they would prefer. When the individual's symptoms improve, there is potential for the couple to shift their roles, and they may be pleased at that prospect. However, the change may be anxiety provoking, and the clinician may notice that the partners are avoiding steps toward adjusting their patterns. Consequently, it is important that clinicians help couples anticipate difficulties in adjusting to relationship changes that accompany improvement in the individual's symptoms. Furthermore, clinicians can help couples can devise ways to cope with greater sharing of decision making and more autonomous behavior on the part of the identified patient.

Subclinical Dysfunctional Characterological Traits and Long-Standing Unresolved Issues

In addition to clinical syndromes such as depression or anxiety disorders, problematic individual characteristics of one or both persons often contribute to the couple's difficulties but do not fit formal psychiatric diagnoses. Some people have long-standing personality or characterological attributes that would make it difficult for them to function effectively in many intimate relationships beyond the current one. As we described in chapter 3, some people have significant difficulty regulating their emotions, particularly distress and anger. Linehan (1993) highlighted the centrality of this difficulty among people diagnosed with borderline personality disorder; however, difficulties with emotion regulation appear to be much more common than in this group alone and can represent a subclinical dysfunctional aspect of an individual's temperament. Deficits in emotion regulation become important in intimate relationships, because partners who experience extreme anger and distress are likely to have difficulty addressing concerns in their relationship. Similarly, individuals vary in the degree to which they cope adaptively with the high level of arousal that accompanies that distress. Some individuals respond to their strong emotional arousal with problematic behaviors, such as loud and destructive arguments, self-destructive behavior, and various forms of verbal and physical abuse. These difficulties with emotion regulation need to be understood and taken into account in treatment planning, otherwise the clinician might attempt to address these inappropriate expressions of emotion with routine communication training, only to find that one person becomes so distraught and upset when discussing emotions that the skills training is unsuccessful. More sophisticated intervention strategies to help couples in which one or both members of a couple experience difficulties with emotion regulation are being developed (Gordon & Baucom, 1998a, 1998c; Halford, Sanders, & Behrens, 1994). Similarly, individuals who have anger control problems can be treated with cognitive–behavioral interventions that include regulation of emotion as well as skills for behaving in constructive ways when one does become angry (Deffenbacher, 1996). Interventions for emotion regulation difficulties are described in chapter 11.

Other individuals have major unresolved issues in their lives that involve particular themes and that affect their current relationships. Cognitive theorists tend to focus on core schemas (e.g., Young, 1990), with their roots in childhood, as the source of these themes, whereas psychodynamically oriented theorists would be more likely to view these as unresolved intrapsychic conflicts. Some of these themes involve negative self-perceptions involving one's own worth, adequacy, and so forth, which were shaped during childhood in parent–child and other significant relationships. Many of these negative schemas can result from chronic, nontraumatic family patterns, such as having an emotionally distant caretaking parent. However, childhood traumatic events such as physical abuse, sexual abuse, rancorous parental divorce, and parental death are especially significant risk factors for the development of chronic problems, such as low self-esteem, depression, low trust, deficits in assertiveness, and sexual aversion (Cummings et al., 2000). Self-schemas may be manifested within the individual's adult couple relationship in terms of endless requests for validation and assurance that one is appealing, attractive, intelligent, and lovable. Similarly, core schemas might involve themes about how one anticipates being treated by loved ones, such as fears of abandonment based on early abandonment experiences (Kobak et al., 1994). These schemas need not be manifested as diagnosable psychopathology, but they still can have negative effects on individuals' intimate relationships.

Regarding impacts on a couple's relationship, a schema involving the potential for abandonment might lead the concerned individual to attend selectively to and interpret cues that the partner is contemplating leaving their relationship. Such inferences are likely to elicit a variety of emotional and behavioral responses (e.g., anxiety, anger, clinging behavior) that can create problems between the partners. From an attachment theory perspective, such individuals would be viewed as having an insecure attachment that developed in childhood and now contributes to distress in the couple's relationship (Johnson & Greenberg, 1994a). Although different theoretical approaches use different terms and explanations for the phenomena, most theoretical approaches acknowledge that some people have long-standing, unresolved issues that focus on a particular theme and that can significantly influence their current relationships.

In addition to these long-term thematic concerns that have developed from early in life, individuals have various experiences throughout life, including adulthood, that can significantly influence their subsequent relationships. Adult traumatic events, such as being raped or having a partner engage in an affair, can lead to a variety of responses, such as a lack of trust, difficulty becoming vulnerable to another person, and sexual aversion disorder. These responses to prior trauma can affect how the individual experiences interactions within the current relationship (Calhoun & Resick, 1993; Glass & Wright, 1997; Gordon & Baucom, 1998c, 1999). Moreover, to the extent that a traumatized individual's partner fails to empathize with the person's past and current distress, his or her neutral or negative responses can contribute to conflict in the couple's relationship.

The existence of partners' long-standing unresolved issues or themes, either resulting from childhood experiences or other adult relationships or traumatic events, has important implications for treatment planning regarding the appropriateness of couples versus individual therapy. It is unfortunate that at present there are no empirical findings to help guide these important clinical decisions. It appears that two interrelated factors can be helpful in making the decision of whether couples therapy is an appropriate modality for addressing individual psychopathology: (a) the individual's awareness and insight about the issue and (b) the pervasiveness and severity of the issues.

Partners' levels of awareness of their unresolved issues are likely to influence whether the issues can be handled successfully within a couples therapy context. Individuals who lack such awareness may need the focus of individual therapy to become attuned to problematic personal responses that exist relatively independently of the couple's interactions. Some symptomatic individuals hold their partners responsible for their problems, and individual sessions can help them reduce their defensiveness and take more responsibility for working on the problems. Thus, if a husband can articulate that he realizes that he was abandoned by his alcoholic mother during childhood and cannot help but be concerned that his wife will do the same, then this understanding might make it easier to approach these issues in couples therapy. His insight is likely to help him to differentiate the current relationship from the past one. However, if the person does not seem to understand the issues involved, then individual intervention to clarify the issues and deal with painful emotions associated with these early events is likely to be more productive.

The *pervasiveness and severity of an individual's unresolved issues* also are likely to influence treatment decisions concerning conjoint versus individual therapy. A clinician might decide that couples therapy is the appropriate treatment modality because an individual who is responding to his or her partner in inappropriate ways on the basis of unresolved issues appears to be capable of the new learning experiences that conjoint sessions can provide. Thus, the therapist will have multiple opportunities to demonstrate to both partners that the current relationship differs significantly from past traumatic relationships and that the relationship will ebb and flow over its developmental course. The therapist can help the partners understand that there will be natural variations in degrees of closeness between them and that an individual with an insecure attachment "working model" has relatively little to fear about actually being abandoned (Johnson & Greenberg, 1992).

In contrast, a clinician might determine that one or both partners' schemas resulting from prior trauma and other chronic negative life events produce such pervasive and intense negative responses to each other that they are unlikely to be modified by new types of couples' interactions during conjoint sessions. In such cases the clinician may decide that individual therapy is needed for one or both partners to address these broader thematic issues before the individuals will be ready to experiment with new ways of relating in couples therapy. For example, if the clinician concludes that an individual's mistrust and fear of abandonment are so strong that he or she will not be able to process new experiences in a different light and learn from couples therapy, then individual intervention is likely needed.

SUMMARY

In this chapter we described major forms of characteristics of individual partners that are likely to influence the quality of a couple's relationship and that must be taken into account in clinical assessment and interventions. These include needs or motives, temperament and personality styles, diagnosable and subclinical forms of psychopathology, and unresolved issues from earlier experiences in each person's life. We addressed the following points:

- Communally oriented needs or motives, such as intimacy, affiliation, altruism, and succorance, and individually oriented motives, such as autonomy, power, and achievement, involve normal human strivings. However, the coexistence of certain motives can produce conflict within and between members of a couple.

- Individual partners' temperaments and personality styles (e.g., degree of conscientiousness) may be functional in some aspects of their lives but can produce conflict in their couple relationship.
- Diagnosable and subclinical forms of psychopathology, such as depression, panic disorder, or substance abuse, may influence or result from relationship distress, pointing to the possible benefits of couples therapy for individual psychopathology.
- Unresolved experiences from earlier life events, such as traumas, may negatively affect current couple interactions, although clients often do not mention such events during couples therapy.
- A difference in two people's needs, temperament, psychopathology, or other personality characteristics will not necessarily be harmful if the partners are able to develop ways of interacting that allow them to cope with, or even appreciate, the differences.

5

INTERPERSONAL PROCESSES: PARTNERS' INTERACTIONS WITH EACH OTHER AND THEIR ENVIRONMENT

Whereas in chapter 4 we described characteristics of individuals that affect the functioning of their couple relationships, in this chapter we focus on behavioral interactions between partners and between the couple and their environment. Our enhanced cognitive–behavioral approach builds on the traditional behavioral couples therapy focus on specific microbehaviors by tying them to broad, consistent, and repetitive macrobehavior patterns of couples' interaction. These macrolevel patterns serve the function of providing continuity in the fulfillment of the partners' needs, either by maintaining stability of satisfying behaviors over time or by allowing the couple to adjust their behaviors to adapt to changes in life circumstances and the partners' needs. In addition to the couple's patterns of relating to each other, they also must adapt to demands from aspects of their physical and interpersonal environment. On the other hand, the couple's environment may provide resources that assist them in fulfilling their needs. In this chapter we examine the ways in which a couple's functioning is influenced by the partners' micro- and

145

macrobehavioral interactions with each other as well as by their micro- and macrobehavioral interactions with their environment.

EXPANDING THE FOCUS FROM MICRO- TO MACRO- LEVEL INTERACTIONS AND TO COUPLE EXCHANGES WITH THEIR ENVIRONMENT

As we noted in chapter 2, there is a tradition in cognitive–behavioral therapy of attending to behavioral exchanges between members of a couple (Gottman & Notarius, 2000). Marital distress has been linked to high rates of negative exchanges and low rates of positive exchanges. In chapter 2 we described three problematic responses in which couples may engage when in conflict: (a) attack–counterattack, (b) attack (or demand)–withdraw, and (c) mutual avoidance or withdrawal. Consequently, from earlier approaches (e.g., Azrin, Naster, & Jones, 1973; Stuart, 1969) to more recent ones (e.g., Baucom & Epstein, 1990; Rathus & Sanderson, 1999), assessment and thera- peutic procedures have been designed to target specific distressing and pleas- ing interactions between partners.

However, behavioral analyses of couples' interactions have tended to focus on "micro" behaviors, with relatively little attention to broader "macro" level interaction patterns (Weiss & Heyman, 1990b, 1997). This focus on discrete actions is not surprising, given that behavioral marital therapy was heavily influenced by social exchange theory (Thibaut & Kelley, 1959), ac- cording to which relationship satisfaction is based on the ratio of benefits received to costs incurred. The model emphasizes the frequencies of posi- tives and negatives received, regardless of their specific content or whether the individuals experienced them as parts of broader patterns in their rela- tionship. Early applications of a cognitive mediation model (e.g., Epstein, 1982) noted that individuals' idiosyncratic appraisals of their partners' be- haviors influenced how pleasing or displeasing particular actions were, but this expanded model still tended to focus on interpretations of microbehaviors. For example, clinicians and researchers have paid considerable attention to individuals' attributions about their partners' specific behaviors: "The fact that she didn't call me to tell me she'd be home late tells me that her job is more important to her than I am."

Marital researchers have increasingly attended to repetitive patterns in couples' interactions and their association with relationship distress and dis- solution. In laboratory studies, couples have been asked to hold discussions of topics that are sources of conflict in their relationships, and the research- ers have conducted analyses of the sequences of behaviors exchanged be- tween the partners. These analyses of communication have indicated that distressed couples engage in longer sequences of negative reciprocity than nondistressed couples do; that is, after one person says something negative, the other is likely to do the same, in a pattern of mutual attack (e.g., Revenstorf, Hahlweg, Schindler, & Vogel, 1984). Gottman's (1994a, 1999) research went a step further, identifying "cascade" sequences, in which criticism–defensiveness patterns contribute to the deterioration of a couple's relationship over time. Thus, it is not merely the exchanges of negative behaviors that are destructive, but rather the particular types and patterns of negatives that are exchanged. Gottman (1999) described how deteriorating behavioral interactions between members of a couple are associated with the partners' development of increasingly negative cognitions about each other, particularly negative attributions about each other's traits and intentions. Nevertheless, Gottman's work does not directly identify the distressing meanings that particular micro- and macrobehavior patterns have for the members of a couple, or why some couples develop such patterns but others do not. In this chapter we provide a framework for seeking answers to such questions, based on our model, which considers the partners' motives and other individual characteristics, a developmental perspective, and concepts from systems theory.

Regarding the impact of a couple's external environment, cognitive–behavioral approaches have included relatively little attention to the dyad's micro- or macrolevel interactions with people and events outside their relationship. Systems theorists have described how a couple's relationship is a small social system embedded in layers of larger systems (Nichols & Schwartz, 2001). These systems may include a nuclear family with children, an extended family with each person's family of origin and other relatives, a neighborhood, informal and formal components of the larger community (e.g., schools, religious organizations, job settings, social agencies), and broader societal systems (e.g., law enforcement, the legal system, local and national economic systems). The functioning of a couple's relationship can be influenced in positive or negative ways by factors operating at any of these system levels. For example, extended family can provide many resources for a couple, such as companionship, social support, assistance with instrumental tasks, and financial support. However, they also can create problems, such as engaging in feuds in which the couple becomes involved. An individual's job can fulfill a variety of needs (e.g., financial security, opportunities for achievement), but it can place demands on his or her time and energy that affect the couple's relationship. Given these and many other possible environmental influences, we believe that a cognitive–behavioral approach to couples therapy must consider couple–environment links.

INTERACTIONS BETWEEN MEMBERS OF THE COUPLE

Although individual microbehaviors can elicit positive or negative cognitive, emotional, and behavioral responses from the recipient, the subjective quality of couples' interactions also seems to be due to the ways in which microbehaviors comprise macrolevel patterns. In the first half of this chapter we examine the role of macrolevel patterns in interactions between partners. We begin by cautioning the reader about subjectivity in defining macrobehavior patterns and by stressing the importance of identifying functions that macropatterns serve in maintaining stability or facilitating change in a couple's relationship. Then we turn to a description of major forms of macrobehavior patterns, such as rituals, boundaries, and social support, that address couples' communally and individually oriented needs. Finally, we tie together macrolevel patterns and the microbehaviors that compose them, suggesting that attention to gaps between a couple's interaction patterns and the fulfillment of their needs requires attention to the partners' subjective cognitions about the behaviors as well as the actual microbehaviors that occur.

Subjectivity in the Identification of Macropatterns

Often the members of a couple are aware of their broad patterns, but in some cases they remain unaware until an outsider, such as a therapist, draws attention to the patterns. Sometimes the lack of awareness of a pattern may simply be due to the difficulty of observing one's own behavior accurately at the same time that one is in the midst of interacting with one's partner. In addition, such patterns are—at least to some extent—in the eye of the beholder, and one person observing a couple's interactions may perceive a particular pattern while another person does not. A person's partner might identify a pattern in the person's behavior by perceiving consistency in the ways that the person has behaved in a variety of situations. However, such perceptual processes and inferences are subject to error and bias (e.g., Fiske & Taylor, 1991). Thus, Ray held a general assumption that women try to control male partners, based on his previous experiences in his family of origin and his first serious couple relationship. As a result, he was alert for signs that his current partner, Valerie, was trying to control him. Although Valerie went out of her way to have egalitarian relationships with people, Ray tended to overinterpret things she did as power tactics. On several occasions, Ray became angry with Valerie during therapy sessions when he perceived her as trying to control him, and the therapist helped Ray examine his inferences in light of feedback that Valerie provided about her intentions.

Members of a couple are likely to make inferences about the existence of macropatterns in each other's behavior, and they will respond positively or negatively to the patterns they perceive, because the patterns are relevant to fulfillment of their motives or needs. A crucial issue in clinical assessment is differentiating the degrees to which a perceived macropattern actually exists in the behaviors of the partner versus in the mind of the perceiver. If, indeed, Valerie actually tried to exert control in the couple's interactions so much that the balance of power was skewed, then one of the goals of couples therapy might be to help the partners work toward a more egalitarian relationship. If, however, the problem was more a matter of Ray's interpreting Valerie's behavior as control maneuvers when she was motivated to share power, then more attention might be paid to working on cognitive restructuring with Ray.

It also is important for therapists themselves to be cautious in identifying patterns in couples' interactions, because therapists' perceptions and inferences can be subject to bias as well. There is great diversity among theoretical orientations to couples therapy in the basic assumptions about the causes of dysfunctional relationship functioning, and a therapist's theoretical leaning can lead him or her to notice particular types of patterns in clients' interactions (Nichols & Schwartz, 2001). For example, strategic family therapists commonly emphasize power and control dynamics in family relationships (Madanes, 1991). In contrast, emotionally focused therapists assume that relationship problems develop from difficulties with attachment and intimacy between partners, and they focus on partners' behaviors that are dysfunctional ways of meeting their attachment needs. Thus, clinicians must be aware of the potential for their own subjectivity to influence their assessment of each couple's patterns of interaction.

Stability and Change: Functions of Macropatterns

Systems theory concepts have been used widely in the field of couples and family therapy to account for the broad interaction patterns that maintain a balance between stability and change in a relationship (Nichols & Schwartz, 2001). On the one hand, any relationship's survival requires interaction patterns that maintain *stability*, providing some consistency in meeting the members' needs. Otherwise, the members of a couple would be faced with repeatedly finding and negotiating new ways to fulfill their basic communally oriented and individually oriented needs. For example, one reason why Keith was attracted to Claudia was that she fulfilled his need for intimacy in a variety of ways. She was an excellent listener when he shared his feelings with her, she shared her own feelings with him, and they had a good sexual relationship. However, as Claudia became increasingly busy in her career, she was less available to meet Keith's intimacy needs. Both partners missed the closeness they had enjoyed previously, but they felt incompetent to find ways to maintain intimacy when there was less time available.

A second reason why some couples have difficulty maintaining stability in meeting their needs involves taking positive aspects of their relationships for granted and gradually decreasing the behavior patterns that have been satisfying (Jacobson & Margolin, 1979). As Harold stated, "Sylvia and I just got lazy with our relationship. When it took effort to do the things that made us feel close, we gradually made choices to let things slide." Sometimes couples are consciously aware of the choices they make that involve taking their relationships for granted, but at other times the process of neglect is subtle. When we ask couples to describe the history of their relationship as part of our initial assessment, some couples are surprised at the degree of erosion in their intimacy and report that they had hardly noticed that it was occurring, particularly if they were preoccupied with raising children, meeting their work obligations, and so on. For couples who have a history of more satisfying interaction patterns that have deteriorated over time, an important component of therapy involves helping them see the importance of maintaining stable patterns for fulfilling communal needs.

In addition to macrobehavior patterns that maintain stability in a relationship, a couple also requires interaction patterns that allow them to *adapt to changes* in environmental demands (e.g., the birth of a first child) and developmental change in the partners' needs, preferences, and goals (Carter & McGoldrick, 1999). Thus, in addition to maintaining ways of meeting old needs, the couple must be able to develop ways to meet new needs. An inability to shift into new ways of relating will hamper the couple's coping with change. As Claudia's career developed, she became more motivated to reach a high level of achievement in her work, but the couple's pattern of relating to each other had not included opportunities for her to pursue her individual goals. Both partners felt uncomfortable when Claudia spent significant amounts of time working on her laptop computer at the dining room table, because in the past "at-home time" meant "together time" for them. Now, Keith repeatedly interrupted Claudia while she was working, and Claudia often stopped her work to check on Keith. As is the case with interaction patterns that maintain stability, a couple's deficits in adapting to change may be due to their failure to recognize a need for change or to see change as appropriate. Claudia and Keith both valued Claudia's professional growth and felt guilty even thinking about how her working at home was decreasing their sense of intimacy. When their couples therapist helped them see that devising new patterns to balance intimacy and achievement needs did not imply devaluing Claudia's emphasis on achievement, they were open to engaging in problem solving in that area.

Systems theorists have described the balance between stability and change in a relationship in terms of *homeostasis*, a concept borrowed from the physical sciences. We believe it is useful to analyze a couple's macrobehavioral patterns in terms of homeostatic processes, identifying how they contribute to stability or adaptability in meeting the partners' communally oriented and individually oriented needs as well as the survival of the dyad. At times an assessment will reveal that a couple requires better skills for maintaining stability to meet ongoing personal needs; in other cases, the assessment identifies deficits in a couple's skills for adapting to changes in the partners' needs. As we have described, the partners' cognitions about the need for stability and change in their macrobehavior patterns also influence whether they use their existing skills or are willing to develop new ones.

An additional factor influencing stability and change in couples' relationships to which systems theorists have paid less attention involves individual differences in partners' preferences for maintaining the status quo versus creating new experiences (McClelland, 1987; Schaller, Boyd, Yohannes, & O'Brien, 1995). Some individuals are most comfortable with stability in their lives and attempt to minimize changes in their daily experiences, whereas others find it more pleasant to seek out variety and change, finding stability somewhat boring. Consequently, some individuals will behave in ways intended to maintain interaction patterns over time, but others will attempt to introduce change. At times, these opposing tendencies can put partners into conflict with each other. Thus, Walter often intentionally behaved in unpredictable ways to "keep our relationship interesting," such as unexpectedly bringing home plane tickets for Cara and himself to go on a weekend trip. In contrast, Cara felt most comfortable with familiar routines and carefully considered plans. Walter tried to "loosen Cara up" by initiating new patterns, and Cara tried to "settle Walter down" by pressuring him to sit down and make plans with her. This couple's struggles over variety versus predictability were driven more by their personality characteristics than by more universally opposing tendencies toward stability and change that allow all relationships to survive over time.

Macrobehavior Patterns That Meet Communally Oriented and Individually Oriented Needs

Although one can identify idiosyncratic macropatterns of behavior that meet or fail to meet the communally oriented and individually oriented needs of a particular couple, there are several major types of macropatterns that seem to be especially common and relevant to the satisfaction of partners' needs. The following are descriptions of these types of macropatterns.

Rituals

One type of homeostatic macrobehavior identified in the family therapy literature is family *rituals*, or repetitive behavioral patterns that have become traditions in a couple's or family's life (e.g., Bennett & Wolin, 1990; Imber-Black, 1999). Some rituals occur frequently (e.g., a kiss when partners reunite at the end of each workday, one partner's weekly evening out with friends), whereas others are regularly occurring special occasions (e.g., an anniversary dinner at a special restaurant, returning to a favorite vacation spot each summer). Bennett and Wolin (1990) described how rituals contribute to relationship identity and stability through their repetitive nature and the special meanings that the members attach to participating in the rituals together. In particular, Bennett and Wolin emphasized ways in which these types of rituals contribute to cohesiveness in a relationship. They found that if families with an alcoholic parent were successful in maintaining the behavioral rituals that contributed to family cohesiveness, fewer instances of alcoholism developed among the children as they grew up. Similarly, Gottman (1999) described a variety of "rituals of emotional connection" that are important for intimacy in a relationship. For example, Eve and Tomas celebrated each 6-month anniversary of their first date together by having dinner in the same restaurant where they had that initial date, and they used the occasion to reminisce about the good times they had shared since that time. These forms of rituals meet the individuals' communal needs for affiliation, intimacy, altruism, and succorance through patterns of mutual approach. Our clinical experience suggests that communally oriented rituals not only enhance relationships but also serve as buffers when couples face life stressors. Some partners view the rituals as evidence of a bond between them that can survive difficult times.

Other rituals contribute to the fulfillment of the partners' individually oriented needs. Some couples have a daily routine in which each partner has some time alone to unwind when they both get home from work. Andre went to a gym after work 3 days a week, and he enjoyed working out by himself after a hectic day of dealing with many people at the office. The time alone helped fulfill his autonomy needs, and by the time he got home he felt ready to spend time with Tanya. Tanya also addressed her needs for autonomy by having a "night out with women friends" once each week. Neither partner was upset by the other's individual activities, because they became familiar and predictable rituals and did not involve active withdrawal from each other.

Many types of life events and changes can disrupt rituals that previously satisfied a couple's needs. For example, the birth or adoption of a first child not only brings much joy but also can make it difficult for the partners to share some of their traditional rituals, such as daily walks together after dinner (Belsky & Kelly, 1994). Although good problem solving may help couples maintain some rituals in their entirety or in part (e.g., the couple could take their baby along in a stroller and continue their walks after dinner), other rituals must be sacrificed for a given phase of life. Similarly, rituals that have fulfilled autonomy and achievement needs can be disrupted by life events. For several years, Betty, an attorney, had spent some of her free time taking art classes at a local college. Because most of her time was devoted to meeting others' needs at work or focused on sharing time with her husband Dean at home, Betty used her art classes to fulfill her needs to focus on herself. However, when Dean had a mild heart attack and coronary bypass surgery, Betty shifted into a caretaker role for several months and stopped her art classes. Although she adjusted her schedule willingly, the prolonged periods without an opportunity to focus on herself led to resentment and subsequent guilt for feeling this way.

Another common factor that disrupts a couple's pattern for meeting communally or individually oriented needs occurs when one or both partners experience a developmental change in their needs (Carter & McGoldrick, 1999). In the early years of their relationship Ross and Maureen were attracted to each other partly because Maureen's altruistic tendency to give frequently to Ross complemented his need for succorance or to receive care. They developed a daily ritual of talking together over a glass of wine after the evening's household chores were completed, and Ross typically sought advice and emotional support from Maureen concerning problems with coworkers at his job. Over time, however, Ross's need for succorance lessened as he experienced successes at work and in other areas of his life. His level of motivation for intimacy increased concurrently, and he desired a sense of mutual sharing with Maureen. Thus, he still had strong communally oriented needs, but the type of communal motivation had changed. Maureen was upset when Ross rebuffed her efforts to help him with stressors in his life, and Ross experienced Maureen's "hovering" as interfering with a sense of intimacy between two equals.

Boundary Patterns and Fulfillment of Communally and Individually Oriented Needs

Couples vary in the degree to which the members desire and contribute to clear boundaries between them and around their relationship. Structural family therapists (e.g., Minuchin, 1974; Todd, 1986) propose that a healthy couple relationship requires the existence of a "permeable" boundary between the partners. The characteristics of a *permeable interpersonal boundary* are clear, open communication and access to each other to meet communally oriented needs, balanced with opportunities for autonomous functioning and privacy to meet individually oriented needs. Rankin-Esquer et al. (1997) suggested that the degree of boundary permeability between partners should be conceptualized in terms of two separate dimensions, involving how much the relationship provides for (a) the members' communally oriented needs and (b) the members' individually oriented needs, because satisfied partners are likely to view their relationships as providing for both types of needs. Similarly, couples who have a permeable boundary around the relationship interact with their children, extended family members, friends, and members of social institutions but also have sufficient privacy and autonomy as a dyad to protect the relationship. Clarity of interpersonal boundaries is conceptualized as ranging along a continuum from rigid (minimal interaction occurs across the boundary, with the partners mutually withdrawing) to diffuse (minimal independence between members of a couple, little autonomous functioning of the couple vis-à-vis other people in their lives; Minuchin, 1974; Todd, 1986). Although the rituals that we have described are important patterns that increase or reduce boundaries between partners, other types of behaviors influence boundaries as well. In fact, rituals that address partners' communally oriented and individually oriented needs can be considered a subset of behaviors that define the extent of the boundaries between members of a couple.

Baucom, Epstein, Rankin, and Burnett (1996) identified several types of behavior characteristic of couples who maintain low levels of boundaries between the partners, such as communicating openly about personal thoughts and emotions, sharing time and activities, and sharing similar ideas and values. In addition, common nonverbal approach versus withdrawal behaviors, such as physical proximity, eye contact, and open versus closed posture, can serve to regulate boundaries or closeness–distance between partners. Although these verbal and nonverbal behaviors can lower boundaries and contribute to the fulfillment of partners' communally oriented needs, a relative absence of boundaries between partners can create an enmeshment that interferes with individually oriented needs. A couple with a low level of boundaries between them tends to view themselves as a unit more than as two individuals.

Couples vary in the extent to which they engage in these forms of sharing in each other's world, and the approach behaviors involved in sharing or togetherness may or may not comprise rituals (behaviors that are repeated at predictable or scheduled times and have shared symbolic meaning for the participants). Thus, Glenda and Ryan were both active in outdoor recreation and environmental conservation organizations, and they had met when each joined a hiking club. They viewed their joint participation in those activities as a major part of what defined them as a couple. Whenever one of them thought about being involved in an activity, he or she automatically thought about the other person being involved as well and was sure to suggest it. Thus, their macrobehavior pattern consisted of joint rather than individual involvement in a variety of leisure activities and, for both of them, participating together in those activities was a predictable ritual that defined the closeness in their relationship. Other couples engage in frequent activities together and share their feelings with each other, but in relatively unsystematic ways that neither partner would identify as rituals. We are not aware of any empirical evidence that rituals per se are necessary to fulfill couples' needs, but it is clear that some couples attach significance to such predictable events and are distressed when they are disrupted.

Attachment theorists have described how individuals have negative emotional responses, such as anxiety and anger, when they experience an increase in the boundaries between partners (e.g., Johnson & Greenberg, 1994a). These negative feelings motivate the person to behave in ways to elicit more caretaking (lower boundaries) from the partner. Although there are many instances in which members of a couple are distressed by the existence of too great a boundary between them, for other couples an insufficient boundary between partners interferes with the fulfillment of partners' individually oriented needs.

Several cognitive–behavioral interventions actually have attended to boundary-related issues between partners, for example, increasing distressed couples' pleasurable joint activities as well as improving their skills for expressing and listening to each other's thoughts and emotions (Baucom & Epstein, 1990). However, cognitive–behavioral therapists typically have not conceptualized these interventions as ways of decreasing macrolevel boundaries between partners, as structural therapists would likely do. Neither have these behavioral interventions necessarily taken into account that the two members of a couple may have different responses to such boundary shifts, depending on each person's levels of communally and individually oriented motives. Interventions designed to decrease boundaries are supported by Baucom, Epstein, Rankin, and Burnett's (1996) finding that standards for minimal boundaries are significantly associated with greater marital satisfaction. However, Baucom et al.'s finding was only modest in magnitude, demonstrating that some individuals are most satisfied with minimal boundaries in their relationship, whereas others prefer more distinct boundaries. Baucom et al.'s findings also indicate that regardless of what individuals believe their relationship should be like in terms of boundaries between partners, their relationship satisfaction depends on the degree to which the individuals' standards are met. Consequently, clinicians need to consider the two individuals' needs concerning close interaction and individual functioning.

When therapists work toward a goal of helping distressed couples improve their relationships, it is easy to focus on increasing interactions that fulfill the partners' communal needs while paying less attention to their individually oriented needs. However, structural family therapists such as Minuchin (1974) propose that minimal or diffuse boundaries interfere with the individual development of each person because individual differences (e.g., interests, opinions, talents) are discouraged. Such enmeshed relationships also can hinder the couple's ability to cope with life stressors, because the individuals are blocked from performing separate roles and coordinating their efforts. Research cited earlier (Baucom, Epstein, Rankin, & Burnett, 1996; Rankin-Esquer et al., 1997) indicates that individuals are more satisfied in relationships that also provide for their autonomy and other individually oriented needs.

Marcy and Aidan neglected their individual needs because they emphasized feeling close and setting few boundaries between the two of them. The couple met in their freshman year of college and became inseparable. They shared similar interests, political values, and life goals. Both in school and after graduation, they either spent time with each other or socialized with other couples. Each began a good entry-level job that initially placed only modest demands on their time but also paid a modest salary. Over time, each partner was offered opportunities for promotions and higher salaries in his or her company, but Marcy and Aidan repeatedly turned down the offers because they did not want their work to interfere with their time together.

Their combined income was barely covering their living expenses, and they had been unable to save any money for emergencies, vacations, or special purchases. However, when Marcy talked with Aidan about a promotion she had been offered, he was upset that she would consider a position that clearly would involve much longer work hours, including some weekend meetings and travel. Seeing Aidan upset made Marcy uncomfortable about the impact of the promotion on their close relationship, so she turned it down. Marcy was never offered promotions in her company again, her raises seemed to be smaller than those of her coworkers, and the couple struggled financially. Over time, she began to question her decision and began to feel resentment toward Aidan for "holding her back." This example illustrates the impor-tance of boundaries that balance togetherness with the partners' individually oriented needs and their abilities to function independently. Marcy and Aidan focused so much on togetherness that when financial problems arose, they had limited options for problem solving, given that they had rejected solu-tions that involved autonomous functioning.

Overall, empirical tests of the hypothesized negative effects of enmeshed couple and family relationships have not identified such negative impacts. As we noted earlier, our own research indicates that couples who hold stan-dards for fewer boundaries have more satisfying relationships. However, the measures in our own studies and those of others do not seem to tap the high degree of involvement that clinicians describe as *enmeshed*, so the research results may not capture the problematic effects of the kind of overinvolvement that becomes dysfunctional. In the functional analytic tradition of the cog-nitive–behavioral model, we take the position that, to define a couple as having too few boundaries between them, we must examine the consequences of that macropattern.

Couples' Social Support Patterns and Fulfillment of Needs

As we described in chapter 2, substantial empirical evidence suggests that the social support partners provide for each other has positive effects on each person's own well-being as well as on his or her satisfaction with the relationship (e.g., Beach, Sandeen, & O'Leary, 1990; Carels & Baucom, 1999; Cutrona & Suhr, 1992; Julien & Markman, 1991). Social support interac-tions tend to involve mutual approach between the individual who provides the support and the partner who receives it. At a microbehavior level re-searchers have developed coding systems for categorizing a variety of specific types of supportive acts that members of a couple can exhibit toward each other during a conversation. As noted earlier, the Social Support Behavior Code (Cutrona, Suhr, & MacFarlane, 1990; Suhr, 1990) identifies 32 sup-portive behaviors within seven positive categories, including emotional sup-port, informational support, tangible aid, esteem support, attentiveness, so-cial network support, and tension reduction as well as one category of negative, unsupportive behaviors. Similarly, Pasch and Bradbury's (1998) Social Support Interaction Coding System is used to code a "helper" partner's communication when responding to a "helpee" partner's description of a personal problem. The Social Support Interaction Coding System places specific behaviors into broad categories of positive instrumental, positive emotional, positive other, negative, neutral, and off-task behavior. Examples of positive instrumental supportive behavior are suggesting a specific plan of action, offering a specific type of assistance, and asking the helpee specific questions designed to focus on the problem. Examples of positive emotional supportive behavior are helping the partner clarify feelings, reassuring the partner, expressing affection and caring for the partner, and providing encouraging comments on progress made toward solving the helpee's problem.

Studies have demonstrated that when such behaviors are assessed by trained coders in a laboratory setting, high levels of specific supportive behaviors are associated with couples' current and subsequent levels of relationship satisfaction (Pasch & Bradbury, 1998; Pasch, Bradbury, & Davila, 1997). However, there also is considerable evidence that partners' perceptions of each other's supportiveness are quite subjective and stable (Beach, Fincham, Katz, & Bradbury, 1996; Carels & Baucom, 1999). Overall, research on social support has indicated that the support an individual perceives, rather than the support that is actually available, contributes more to the recipient's well-being and satisfaction. Within couples, an individual's attempts to be supportive to his or her partner will be perceived as supportive to the extent that the recipient appraises it in particular ways. The recipient must view it as appropriate for the other person to be offering support in the particular situation. Direct or indirect offers of support are likely to be appraised as appropriate if the recipient views himself or herself as in need. For example, Arnold was upset when Faye offered to help him plan an anniversary party for his parents, because he felt competent to do it by himself. Moreover, a recipient's reactions to a partner's offers of support also depend on the attributions that the recipient makes about the partner's attitudes and intentions. Arnold also was upset at Faye's offer to help him plan the party because he attributed her repeated offers to her lack of confidence in his ability to plan and carry out a social event. Similarly, a behavior that is attributed to a partner's desire to control is unlikely to be perceived as supportive regardless of the partner's actual intent. Research on marital attributions suggests that if the recipient is making a negative trait attribution about the partner's behavior, the potential for distress is even greater. If Arnold perceives Faye's offers of help to be part of a broader macropattern of lack of respect for him, or as a desire to control their relationship, then he may have a particularly negative response, such as telling her to mind her own business, and the couple may develop a demand–withdraw pattern in which Faye attempts to provide support and Arnold refuses it.

Beach et al. (1996) noted that if an individual has a negative self-concept he or she may discount it or consider it erroneous when a partner attempts to provide emotional support in the form of positive evaluations, because the partner's feedback is inconsistent with the person's self-concept. Carolyn was frustrated because whenever she attempted to support Nate by complimenting him on his strengths and past successes, he generally responded by pointing out his limitations and how he could have done better. Beach et al. (1996) similarly described how individuals who have insecure attachment styles (feel a need for support but are insecure about whether significant others will consistently provide it) may undermine support from their partners by behaving in negative ways. Robin had a strong desire for emotional support from her partner but alienated him by sometimes clinging to him and sometimes criticizing him for not providing as much support as she needed, thereby creating a demand–withdraw pattern in which her pressure led her partner to distance himself from her. Because an individual can have negative biases that decrease his or her perception of the support available from a partner, clinical assessment and intervention must take such helpee characteristics into account.

Differences among individuals' standards about *how* people should help each other can affect individuals' responses when their partners attempt to be supportive. One person may prefer to receive a particular type of support when he or she has a problem, whereas another person may dislike the same type of supportive behavior. Personal preferences for types of support also tend to vary according to the type of problem the person is facing. Lydia worked in a management position in a company and had strong skills for analyzing and solving personnel problems. She personally valued systematic problem solving, and she generally provided logical analyses and suggestions to Rick whenever he told her about problems in his life. However, Rick tended to respond to life stressors with a high level of emotional tension, which he experienced as aversive, so he preferred that Lydia help him become distracted from his problems and relax, perhaps by joking or watching television together. Unfortunately, the couple had a pattern in which Lydia would notice that Rick was tense, encourage him to tell her what the problem was, and then attempt to help him solve the problem through a logical analysis of his options. Rick would become frustrated and attempt to interrupt Lydia's efforts to help. The couple eventually would have an argument and walk away from each other. Lydia felt unappreciated, Rick felt that Lydia would only accept doing things her way, and the couple was unsuccessful in resolving these concerns because their discussions quickly deteriorated into mutual attack followed by mutual withdrawal.

When we work with couples who appear to be mismatched in the kinds of help they prefer and offer each other, we stress that there are natural and normal individual differences in people's preferences for various types of help for personal problems. We note that what one person finds helpful may not help another and that this is not a matter of determining who is right or wrong. We also note that success in providing support to each other depends on communicating clearly each person's preferences, accepting that the other person may prefer different types of support, and trying to provide what one's partner prefers as long as this is not harmful to oneself.

Changes in partners' personal standards about the types of social support that are appropriate can lead to shifts in a couple's pattern of supportive behavior. Once an individual identifies a particular category of support that his or her partner finds helpful and accepts it as appropriate to provide, a therapist can help the couple identify how that type of support can be used in different situations. Thus, it became clear that Margaret experienced esteem support from Jack as very helpful when she faced challenging life problems. The couple's therapist helped them list several forms of esteem support that Margaret found appealing. Margaret stated that she liked it when Jack directly stated his confidence in her abilities and when he reminded her of her past successes with difficult problems. Jack initially believed that this kind of support was superficial, but he came to accept the value of it when Margaret emphasized how good it made her feel. As a result of this intervention, the couple shifted from a pattern of arguments over Jack's misguided attempts to be supportive by giving Margaret advice to a pattern in which Jack offered various forms of esteem support and Margaret expressed her appreciation.

Macrolevel patterns of social support between partners and the microbehaviors that compose them are likely to contribute to relationship satisfaction to the degree that they are consistent with the individuals' communally and individually oriented needs. Providing support to one's partner can fulfill one's motivation to be altruistic and meet the partner's need for succorance. The supportive relationship also may fulfill one or both partners' affiliation and intimacy needs. However, the person who receives support from a partner may experience it as interfering with his or her sense of achievement and autonomy. Consequently, when a clinician observes conflict between partners over support giving, it is important to assess both parties' motives that may be contributing to a mismatch between what one person is giving and what the other wants.

Gender differences can influence both the forms of support that individuals provide to their partners and what the partners experience as helpful and satisfying. Reviews of empirical studies indicate that women tend to provide more support to their partners than men do, but a gender difference is not found consistently (Pasch, Bradbury, & Davila, 1997). Furthermore, claims in popular literature that women tend to provide emotional support and men tend to provide advice and problem solving have not been supported by studies of intimate relationships. Nevertheless, even when no gender difference is found in the overall amount of support provided, there is some evidence of gender differences under particular conditions. For example, Pasch, Bradbury, and Davila (1997) found in a sample of satisfied couples that husbands are less likely to exhibit positive emotional support behavior when their wives are prone to anxiety, depression, and anger, whereas wives are more likely to exhibit positive emotional support when their husbands are high in such negative affectivity. Pasch et al. noted that this gender difference might not be found if a couple's relationship becomes distressed.

Carels and Baucom (1999) found that men and women differentially weight the importance of (a) partners' immediate responses versus (b) distal characteristics of the couple's relationship when experiencing support. More specifically, women's experience of support during the discussion was more highly associated with the supportive quality of their spouses' responses during the present interaction (as judged by independent raters). In contrast, men's experiences of support during the interaction were more highly correlated with their ratings of overall qualities of their marriages, including their overall marital adjustment, positive attributions for the support their wives generally provided, frequencies of supportive and unsupportive interactions in the relationship in general, and overall satisfaction with the degree to which their standards for support were met in their relationships. Thus, men's experiences of support during an interaction were influenced more by their global perceptions and feelings about their relationships than were women's, a process that Weiss (1980) described as *sentiment override*.

It is important not to make overly generalized conclusions about the gender differences in perceived support that have been found in a few studies. However, these findings suggest that clinicians should be aware that gender can contribute to two partners having different experiences of support within their relationship. As we described earlier, there is considerable potential for partners to misunderstand each other's needs for support, so clinicians who are helping members of a couple provide the types of support that each person desires should take gender differences into account.

Macrobehavior Patterns Involving Couple Teamwork vs. Individual Initiative

A couple's ability to adapt to changes and problems in their life together is likely to be influenced by their capacity to coordinate their efforts. Some problems may be solved easily through one person's efforts, but in many cases a joint effort is needed. In two-parent families, for instance, raising children generally requires consistency between the partners' approaches to discipline. Similarly, financial stability tends to require that the partners have similar goals and methods for spending and saving money. However, couples vary in the degree to which the partners adopt a collaborative approach to problem solving versus working as individuals. Couples who tend toward greater collaboration are more likely to initiate conversations with each other about an existing or potential problem and encourage an exchange of ideas. They also are likely to find compromises when they have different approaches to a task or problem so that their efforts will be compatible (Baucom & Epstein, 1990).

In contrast to coordinated mutual approach efforts, members of some couples tend to be individually oriented problem solvers who are more likely to reach solutions without consulting the other person and are less receptive to suggestions from the partner. By withdrawing from each other while making decisions and operating relatively independently, the two individuals might at times interfere with each other's efforts. Thus, Nadiya and Wayne had different childrearing philosophies and methods. They each tended to try to solve their children's behavior problems on their own. Neither partner recognized the validity of the other's approach, so both of them persisted with his or her own approach, hoping to undo what the other had done. As a result, their children did not take either parent's guidance seriously, inciting arguments between Nadiya and Wayne that distracted them from noticing the children's misbehavior.

A variety of factors might influence the degrees to which members of a couple tend to exhibit a macrobehavior pattern of collaboration or one of individual problem solving. First, each person's tendency toward collaboration or individual problem solving will be influenced by the strengths of his or her communally and individually oriented motives. Partners who have high levels of communal motivation seem likely to value interaction patterns that make them feel connected to each other, whereas those who have high levels of autonomy and achievement motivation will more likely prefer to master problems on their own (McAdams, 1988; McClelland, 1987; Prager, 1995). However, as we described in chapter 4, collaborative efforts not only address partners' communally oriented needs but also can contribute to the fulfillment of individually oriented needs. For example, Allison had a high level of achievement motivation, and she worked hard with Trevor to build a successful family business.

Second, differences between partners on other personality characteristics, such as preference for order (Schaller et al., 1995), may lead some individuals to prefer working on their own rather than trying to tolerate the other person's style. Millie and Toby both wanted their house to be neater than it typically was, but they often argued if they tried to set aside a "cleanup day" to work together. Because Millie had much more stringent personal standards for orderliness, she typically monitored Toby's cleaning and criticized his efforts. Toby responded with frustration and anger, often refusing to continue working together. Because the partners had been unsuccessful resolving their differences in this area, Millie often waited until Toby was out of the house and cleaned it her way, producing resentment in both individuals.

Third, members of some couples tend to focus on individual problem solving rather than collaboration because they have had little prior experience with the latter. Sometimes this lack of familiarity with collaboration is based on the individual's experiences in his or her family of origin. Marty was an only child whose parents had both worked full-time from the time he was 5 years old. From the age of 10 he had been a latchkey child, letting himself into the house after school and caring for himself until his parents arrived home from work. He was used to keeping himself busy and making many decisions on his own. In college, he had roommates but tended to keep his own schedule and had few collaborative experiences. After college, he lived alone and dated periodically until he met and fell in love with Gloria. When they moved in together, it was the first time he was truly faced with coordinating his efforts with those of someone else to whom he felt committed. Gloria was frustrated that Marty seemed to make decisions individually and do tasks on his own without consulting her. Consultation and collaboration felt awkward to Marty, because he had learned throughout his life to make decisions individually.

Understanding a couple's tendency to work on tasks and solve problems through a pattern of collaboration or one of individual efforts requires attention to specific microlevel behavioral skills as well as each person's cognitions and emotional responses. For a couple to collaborate, the partners need to have good problem-solving skills and be able to coordinate their efforts in specific situations they face. Coordination between two individuals requires attention to what microbehaviors the other person is enacting, plus effective communication about each person's ideas about ways to accomplish the task. As described earlier, skills for working with other people tend to be learned from an early age, but significant individual differences exist in people's learning histories. A strength of the cognitive–behavioral approach to couples therapy is its focus on teaching clients more effective skills for working together when they have deficits in this area (Baucom & Epstein, 1990; Jacobson & Christensen, 1996; Jacobson & Margolin, 1979). In addition, the cognitive–behavioral approach identifies cognitions and emotional responses that can interfere with couples' collaborative macrobehavior patterns. For example, individuals who lack trust in their partners' intentions or abilities may prefer to solve problems on their own. Furthermore, couples who have a history of failing to solve problems well together may have expectancies of future failure and avoid joint efforts (Pretzer, Epstein, & Fleming, 1991). In terms of emotional responses, the process of negative "sentiment override" (Weiss, 1980) can lead an individual who has generally negative feelings about his or her partner to overlook or discount positive collaborative efforts that the partner makes. Thus, a macropattern of collaborative problem solving is a complex process with behavioral, cognitive, and affective components. Given the importance of collaboration for a couple's success in navigating the varied and changing stresses of life, it is crucial that therapists be prepared to assess and intervene with the factors that interfere with joint efforts.

In spite of our emphasis on the importance of the couple functioning as a unit, it is important to note that at times the most efficient and effective approach to solving a problem is for one partner to work autonomously. It is common that each member of a couple has particular talents and strengths and that one member's abilities may be better suited to solving a particular problem that the couple faces. Mindy had stronger skills than Reese for organizing large amounts of information, so she handled most of their family finances, including decisions about putting funds into savings, extra payments on their mortgage, or other investments. The couple had discussed the possibility of considering those decisions together, but both felt comfortable with Mindy having the primary responsibility in that area. Many other couples divide various role responsibilities between the partners on the basis of their appraisals of each other's interests and abilities. Of course, this role division still requires a certain degree of collaboration and trust between partners, which in some cases is lacking.

Behavioral Patterns Involving Power and Control

As described in chapter 4, empirical evidence suggests that, although there are individual differences, couples who hold standards for, and achieve, an egalitarian sharing of power in their relationships are more satisfied with their relationships (Baucom, Epstein, Rankin, & Burnett, 1996). Researchers have attempted to assess degrees of balance versus imbalance in influence between members of a couple, in terms of microbehaviors (e.g., whether one person's verbal request is followed by the other's compliance) or macrobehaviors (e.g., when partners disagree about possible solutions to a problem, whose initial preference is reflected in the final joint decision; Markman & Notarius, 1987; Weiss & Heyman, 1997).

Concepts from alternative theoretical approaches, as well as an understanding of human motives, help broaden the traditional cognitive–behavioral model of interpersonal power interactions. For example, attachment theory describes how individuals' attempts to control their partners' behavior often are motivated by their insecure attachment, such that they try to coerce their partners into providing caretaking responses (Kobak, Ruckdeschel, & Hazan, 1994). In other words, controlling behaviors may reflect power motivation, or these behaviors might be a person's means of attempting to fulfill other needs, such as succorance or intimacy.

It is important for therapists and their client couples to understand how individuals differ in their desire, often based on their prior life experiences, to control and have power. Individuals may be less upset when they observe their partners attempting to exert power if they are able to view it as an understandable outgrowth of the person's socialization rather than as an indication that the partner has negative intentions toward them; that is, they form a more benign attribution for the partner's behavior (Baucom & Epstein, 1990; Epstein & Baucom, 1993). Consequently, an important therapeutic intervention involves increasing both partners' understanding of the individual's strong motivation for power and control, its possible origins, and its meaning for the couple's relationship. Thus, Justin and Maura's therapist encouraged Justin to describe how his parents strongly encouraged him to compete aggressively against his older brother and peers in sports and how they used a coercive parenting style with him. The therapist's goal was to increase the couple's understanding of factors that have made power such a salient aspect of personal relationships for Justin. The therapist then coached both members of the couple in exploring the attributions that each had made about the causes of Justin's controlling behavior. Maura had tended to make attributions that Justin felt superior to her and wanted to take advantage of her. However, her increased insight, and some sympathy concerning the family pressures that contributed to his motivation for controlling her, helped her to make less blaming attributions when Justin pressured her to comply with his wishes. In fact, she became adept at handling such occurrences with feedback, such as "Justin, are you sure you want to try to control me on this? I'm not trying to compete with you." Justin recognized that his behavior toward Maura conflicted with his personal value regarding equity in marriage; this resulted in increased self-monitoring. On the basis of the couple's modified attributions about Justin's behavior, now neither person blamed him for his controlling behavior, and they both took greater responsibility for trying to behave in ways that would decrease those behaviors.

A second issue for clinical assessment and intervention involves determining whether there are settings in or occasions on which one person's attempts to exert control might be useful and acceptable to a couple, versus settings in which they consider them unacceptable. Justin and Maura concluded that Justin was strongly motivated to be in control at work and that his behavior in work settings had largely produced positive results, such as job advancements. Neither partner had a goal of reducing his expression of control and leadership at work, but both of them considered it desirable for him to reduce its expression in their marriage.

A third therapeutic issue concerning couples' distress over each other's behavior involves determining whether each individual is dissatisfied with the fact that the other person is motivated to exert control or whether he or she is distressed by the particular behaviors that the other uses to exert control. At times, an individual is less concerned about a partner's attempt to exert control per se but is distressed by how the partner expresses it. Thus, therapists can target coercive exchanges of attack behaviors such as criticism, blaming, and verbal threats as well as defensive responses in which an individual refuses to yield and responses in which an individual exerts control by withdrawing.

It is our experience that relationship quality is more likely to improve when (a) the motives and needs that underlie partners' attempts to exert power are understood by both individuals and (b) specific aversive behaviors that compose the couple's macropattern of control interactions are reduced. When both types of change have been achieved, then isolated negative behaviors by one person are less likely to elicit negative responses from his or her partner. The recipient is more likely to make benign attributions for an isolated coercive act, realizing that the partner may not be able to inhibit every expression of a behavioral pattern that he or she developed over the course of many years.

Behavioral Patterns Involving Investment in the Relationship

The traditional cognitive–behavioral model conceptualizes individuals' levels of investment in their couple relationship in terms of the frequencies with which they engage in expressive and instrumental behaviors that are pleasing to their partner. Research indicates that partners who exchange more of such positive approach behaviors are more satisfied with their relationships (Weiss & Heyman, 1990b). In addition, studies of standards we and our colleagues have conducted indicate that the more individuals believe that there should be high levels of mutual affective and instrumental investment in their relationship, the greater their relationship satisfaction is (e.g., Baucom, Epstein, Rankin, & Burnett, 1996). Members of a couple need to understand how well their investment of time and energy addresses each person's standards and their communally and individually oriented needs. Once an individual believes that his or her partner is invested in their relationship, the individual is more likely to discount specific incidents in which the partner fails to carry out positive expressive or instrumental microbehaviors (Cutrona, 1996b). Although reaching this kind of understanding may reduce individuals' overreactions to their partners' microbehaviors, believing the partner is making efforts may not be enough. The degree of change in one person's microbehaviors might not be sufficient to satisfy the other's needs on a consistent basis. In such instances, it must be determined (a) whether one person actually is giving very little to the relationship, (b) whether some key types of investment behavior have been overlooked, or (c) whether the dissatisfied person may have unrealistically high standards for the partner's behavior.

Integration of Micro- and Macrolevel Processes in Couples' Interaction

In traditional cognitive–behavioral couples therapy (CBCT), therapists often help partners identify specific microbehaviors that they would like each other to increase and to structure agreements for each person to enact some of the other's desired behaviors. Therapists sometimes use self-report instruments such as the Areas of Change Scale (Weiss, Hops, & Patterson, 1973) to help partners identify the specific expressive and instrumental behaviors they would most like their partners to increase or decrease. Similarly, therapists identify specific, microbehavioral components of couples' communication that may be increased or decreased to produce more effective or satisfying exchanges (Baucom & Epstein, 1990). For example, an individual's listening skills may be improved by having him or her practice interrupting the partner less often; maintaining more eye contact as the partner speaks;

and providing brief, specific summaries of what the partner seems to be expressing.

Although changes in such behaviors often increase partners' satisfaction with each other, in many cases the impact of the change in a particular microbehavior may be limited. It is a common occurrence that an individual observes that a partner has produced desired change in a microbehavior, but the individual still concludes, "I appreciate it, but she really hasn't changed." Interventions that focus solely on discrete microbehaviors at times have limited success because they are not perceived by the members of the couple as changing the overall macrobehavior patterns that are distressing to them: "Yes, you now kiss me each morning before you leave for work. But it still doesn't seem that you want to be close to me." In such instances, a more systematic effort is needed to identify and modify classes of microbehaviors that compose a distressing macrobehavior pattern, which an individual tends to view as a negative trait within the partner (Baucom & Epstein, 1990).

Consider a relationship in which the wife has a long history of exercising control across many situations in the couple's interactions (e.g., usually getting the last word in discussions; implicitly determining the couple's daily routines, such as bedtime; dominating the outcomes of decision-making discussions). She might agree to comply with her husband's request that they alternate weekly in choosing a leisure activity for the couple to share on Sundays. However, the wife may continue to control the couple's interactions in other specific ways, and the isolated behavior change may be the only way in which the couple attempts to address power issues. The husband might consequently experience little increase in overall relationship satisfaction because he is aware that the basic power distribution in the couple's relationship has not changed and that most of the couple's power interactions still are unbalanced. However, if the agreement to alternate deciding on Sunday activities sets in motion a broader shift in which the couple begins to share power in other contexts, then a macrolevel behavior change has occurred. Unless such broader change is underway, it seems likely that in many cases the individual will fail to experience a substantial or sustained level of satisfaction with the relationship. In our experience it often is helpful to assist a couple in understanding the broader issue involved in the distressing macropattern (e.g., an imbalance in power during decision making) and then to identify specific microbehaviors that can be changed in the service of altering the larger pattern.

For each type of larger macropattern that we have described, several discrete microbehaviors can be identified. For example, carrying out a ritual such as a quiet talk after the children are in bed might involve both partners setting aside individual activities at a particular time, indicating verbally and/or nonverbally that they are ready to talk, perhaps preparing something to eat or drink, sitting down together, and using good expressive and listening skills to discuss their thoughts and feelings. Members of a couple are likely to perceive each other as contributing to such an intimacy ritual to the extent that they see each other enacting these microbehaviors with some consistency.

In addition, subjective cognitive appraisals can affect partners' responses to each other's microbehaviors. Each member of a couple might weight specific behaviors differently in perceiving the other's tendency to seek intimacy. Thus, Emma noticed that Dylan often remarked that they needed to set aside time together after the children were asleep. However, Emma assumed intimacy was not as high a priority for Dylan as for herself after noticing that he disappeared into his study to catch up on work as soon as the children were in bed. Once Emma made the source of her dissatisfaction known, Dylan quickly changed his behavior and joined her after he had said goodnight to the children. Nevertheless, Emma still viewed Dylan as less motivated toward intimacy than herself because he self-disclosed relatively little about his personal feelings when they sat together over a cup of tea or a snack. Dylan had different ways of defining intimacy in terms of particular behaviors. He agreed with Emma that his previous pattern of working in his study did not constitute intimate behavior, but he viewed setting all else aside to sit and talk over tea was "clearly in the ballpark," regardless of whether he was talking about his inner feelings. The essence of the microbehaviors that he considered intimate was that they involved focusing one's full attention on the other person.

Even if two partners understand, value, and respect each other, they may not have found effective ways to accommodate each person's needs through particular microbehaviors. Accommodating each person's motives and responding to each person's preferences can be a challenge, whether the two persons are similar to or different from each other. For example, both persons might greatly value intimacy with their partner but seek couples therapy because they feel distant from each other and their relationship feels devitalized. In this instance the clinician should be attentive to various factors that prevent the couple from establishing broader, macrolevel behavioral patterns that meet their shared goal of being close to each other. Jake and Gretchen were in their fifth year of marriage, and both wanted to feel close to each other, but they also had strong career aspirations. Being at early stages in their careers, they both invested significant energy in their professions, and both endorsed the need to do so. Unfortunately, the amount of time and energy that they were devoting to their professional development significantly interfered with their development of intimacy. In other words, they adequately addressed their individually oriented achievement needs but failed to sufficiently address their needs for closeness. They had not identified ways in which they could enhance their experiences of intimacy without sacrificing progress in their careers. Their problem-solving efforts had been limited to occasional, brief discussions in which they would agree that they did not feel close to each other, and they would quickly decide on one or two behaviors to try, such as going to a movie together. These behaviors often resulted in brief feelings of warmth and closeness, but because they were not parts of a broader macropattern the positive feelings were short lived. As Prager (1995) noted, an intimate relationship tends to be defined by a broad pattern of sharing rather than by individual, intimate interactions between the two people.

At times, when one or both persons experience difficulty having some important needs met in their relationship, this becomes the eventual basis for a couple's decision to end the relationship; that is, they conclude that they "just aren't a good match" for each other. Although this explanation can at times seem like an excuse for not making sufficient effort or compromise, there are instances in which the partners thoughtfully conclude that their differences are so great that the relationship is unlikely to be rewarding to both persons. Barbara and Stan were unusually articulate spouses who presented their views of marriage during the initial assessment. In response to the clinician's question about each person's standards for a marriage, Barbara summarized her beliefs:

> I think the basis of any good relationship is two healthy, independent people. The two people's abilities to function as individuals have to be the top priority. If their needs aren't met, then the relationship is doomed. The relationship works because each person goes off and does their own thing, and then they both have a lot to bring back to the relationship to share with the other person. The individuals have to drive the relationship, not the other way around.

Stan's standards for a marriage were quite different:

> Of course the relationship has to take the individuals into account, but I think the relationship has to be the center of life. It should be what comes first. Marriage is so demanding that if you don't make it your top priority, it won't work. Rather than going out into the world like Barbara suggests and coming back and reporting, I want a mate with whom I can explore the world. I don't want a report. I can get that on the news.

Further inquiry by the therapist revealed that these perspectives on marriage influenced a variety of specific behaviors that each partner desired in almost every aspect of the couple's life together, from what to do on Saturday mornings to how much time to spend at work. The therapist also determined that neither person's attributions about the other's motives were distorted. Eventually Barbara and Stan concluded that although they respected and loved each other in many ways, their approaches to relationships were so different that they should end their marriage. A couples therapist has great responsibility for helping partners understand the roots of their conflicts in the two individuals' personal characteristics, in combination with their micro- and macrobehavior patterns that may interfere with their adaptation to those characteristics. In the end, the members of the couple must decide how much they are willing to accept the existing ways in which their interactions address their needs and how much they are prepared to work on modifying unfulfilling or frustrating patterns.

INTERACTIONS BETWEEN COUPLE AND ENVIRONMENT

The enhanced CBCT model also recognizes that the quality of a couple's relationship is affected not only by the interactions within the dyad but also by the couple's interactions with various aspects of the environment. In this section we turn to a description of positive and negative influences that a couple's environment can have on the functioning of the relationship. We discuss the ways in which macropatterns may be interrupted by demands or stressors in the couple's environment. Conversely, resources in the couple's environment can aid the fulfillment of their communally oriented and individually oriented needs. Finally, we consider some clinical issues in the assessment of demands and resources, such as clients' perceptions, disclosure, or cultural beliefs about what constitutes demands or resources for their relationship.

No couple relationship operates in isolation; rather, ongoing interaction occurs between a couple and a variety of aspects of their interpersonal and physical environment. To understand why a couple is functioning well or is experiencing problems it is crucial to consider the influences of their interactions with their environment. Those influences are bidirectional. On the one hand, environmental factors help or hinder the individual functioning of each partner as well as the couple's interaction patterns. Thus, one person's demanding work schedule may make him or her fatigued and anxious. At the interpersonal level, heavy work demands may decrease the couple's available time for intimacy, such as talking or shared leisure activities. On the other hand, the individuals and couple may fulfill their needs by turning to the environment. For example, a couple may fulfill their needs for intimacy with each other as well as their altruistic needs, by volunteering together at an agency serving homeless families. In the following sections we describe a variety of ways in which a couple's interactions with the environment can strengthen the relationship or place it at risk.

As is the case with interactions between the members of the dyad, one can examine the impacts of specific, *microlevel interactions* between the couple and environment. For example, Burt came into the house so upset about the speeding ticket that he had gotten while driving home that he was very irritable with Elaine and their children, resulting in an argument between the spouses. Although the upset that Burt felt about the ticket "spilled out" into his family relationships, this was not part of a broader macropattern in their life together. When Burt subsequently apologized to Elaine and the children for taking out his frustration on them, the couple were able to discuss the anxiety that he felt about the ticket.

Other interactions between a couple and the environment comprise broader, *macrolevel patterns* that are relatively consistent and involve particular themes. For example, Kristin and Oren each often complained to their own parents about the other person's behavior, thereby breaking down the boundary of privacy around the couple. As we discussed concerning interactions within a couple, individuals may be able to discount or accept isolated negative microlevel interactions with the couple's environment, but macrolevel patterns commonly are more distressing, because the partners tend to interpret them as defining the basic nature of their relationship. Kristin and Oren viewed each other's sharing of complaints with their parents as signs that there was little respect and trust between the two of them.

In this section we describe several important ways in which micro- and macro-interactions between a couple and the environment affect a couple's relationship, including the impact on both partners' communally and individually oriented needs. Some of these interactions involve *demands* from the environment that impinge on the couple, and some involve positive *resources* that the environment provides that can enhance the couple's functioning.

Environmental Sources of Demands on Individuals and Couples

Considerable evidence indicates that couples who are coping with significant life demands, such as work problems, financial problems, parenting issues, and conflicts concerning extended family relationships, are more likely to experience relationship distress and dissolution (Lindahl, Malik, & Bradbury, 1997; Wright, Nelson, & Georgen, 1994). Most commonly, *stressors* or *demands* have been defined as events or transitions that place pressure on an individual, couple, family, or larger social system to adapt or change (Boss, 1988; M. A. McCubbin & McCubbin, 1989). As we describe in detail in chapter 6, one of the major dimensions along which life demands can be classified is whether they are *internal*, having a locus within members of the relationship, or *external*, involving events imposed from outside the relationship. In this section we focus on external demands in the environment and how they affect a couple's relationship.

Indirect and Direct Effects of Environmental Demands on Couples' Functioning

Environmental demands can affect a couple indirectly, through their impact on one of the members, or they may directly alter the dyad's patterns of interaction. Consider Gabe, who spent many hours each week arranging adequate care for his mother, who was in the advanced stages of Alzheimer's disease. His fatigue, depressed mood, and irritability resulting from the demands of being a caretaker contributed to more arguments and less intimacy with his wife Dawn, thus indirectly affecting the dyad. A second couple, Cathy and Evan, were eager to become parents and had been trying to become pregnant for more than a year. They had been motivated to have a baby not only to fulfill their own needs but also because both sets of their parents had been exerting pressure on the couple to give them grandchildren. As they found themselves increasingly uncomfortable being with their parents, whom they had previously viewed as sources of warmth and support, they began to feel isolated with their infertility problems. In addition, the couple had consulted an infertility specialist, and they were in the midst of increasingly intrusive tests, which they felt interfered with their intimacy. Thus, the environmental demands from their parents and from the infertility treatment had direct effects on the couple as a dyad.

This distinction between direct and indirect effects of demands on a couple is important because of its implications for treatment. In instances of indirect effects, where the impact of environmental demands on a couple is mediated by their effects on one of the partners, more effort may be directed at helping that person develop his or her own coping ability. Thus, Gabe and Dawn's therapist spent time focusing on Gabe's ways of coping with the demands of caring for his mother. The therapist encouraged Gabe's increased use of local community resources that were available for caretakers and addressed Gabe's personal standards about seeking help from outsiders. Moreover, the therapist assisted Gabe and Dawn in functioning better as a dyad, such as teaching them to cope more effectively with Gabe's fatigue and moodiness.

As we detail in chapter 6, environmental demands that can have indirect or direct effects on a couple can be based on positive as well as negative life events (Boss, 1988). Job promotions, for example, are likely to be experienced as exciting and fulfilling, potentially contributing to one's desire to achieve. Nevertheless, a promotion might also tax the individual's interpersonal and job skills, placing pressure on him or her to adapt to the new circumstances. As in the case of negative life events, such positive environmental demands may also influence the couple's dyadic functioning indirectly through their effects on the individual (e.g., distraction, anxiety, fatigue), or the demands may directly alter the ways that the partners interact with each other. When Ursula was promoted to the position of director of public relations in her company, it was important that she and Ken frequently attend social events in the community. These generally formal social engagements, which Ken referred to as "command performances," filled the time that the couple previously had available for leisure time together and contributed to their feeling less intimate with each other.

Ways in Which Environmental Demands Affect Relationship Functioning

Environmental demands have negative effects on two partners and their relationship by interfering with the behavioral patterns in a couple's relationship. Demands impinge on the ways that each person's communally oriented and individually oriented needs are met. We now offer some examples of how stressors can affect partners' behaviors and potentially interfere with important needs and desires being met.

First, environmental demands can *disrupt important rituals*, which we described earlier. For example, Sabrina and Joel established a ritual of taking long walks together after dinner in a large park near their home. Their walks not only helped them relax after a busy day but also provided them an opportunity to talk without distractions and feel close to each other. After the birth of their first child, their "couple walks" were supplanted by "family walks" as they took turns trying to soothe the baby, who had difficulty falling asleep. Thus, the demands of caring for the baby disrupted an important ritual that the couple had used to bolster their intimacy.

As described earlier, regardless of whether a couple's interaction patterns constitute repetitive rituals, they commonly comprise broader macropatterns that fulfill particular needs of the two partners. Consequently, environmental demands that disrupt these patterns are likely to interfere with the fulfillment of important individual and couple needs and preferences. Consistent with our earlier discussion, we now describe examples of ways in which environmental demands can alter couples' interactions involving boundaries, investment in the relationship, mutual social support, collaborative versus individual problem solving, autonomy, achievement, and power and control.

Environmental demands can *affect the boundaries* between partners as well as the boundary around a couple that allows them to function with some independence from their environment. As noted earlier, one of the boundaries that a couple must define is the one around their relationship, regulating the degree to which they will interact with, and be influenced by, the environment. Structural family therapists have argued that a crucial task facing a couple is the establishment of their identity as a unit, relatively independent of their families of origin and other people (Minuchin, 1974; Nichols & Schwartz, 2001; Todd, 1986). Couples vary widely in the degree to which they interact with extended family members and others, and some couples have significant conflicts over the partners' different standards about the amount of exchange with other people that they consider appropriate. Boss (1988) used the term *boundary ambiguity* to describe situations in which it is unclear to what degree other people are psychologically and/or physically present within the boundary of a couple's relationship. The boundary around a couple may become ambiguous if outsiders intrude into their relationship, either by attempting to gain information about aspects of the couple's relationship that most people would consider private or through their physical presence.

Many couples have become members of the "sandwich generation," wherein they have become caretakers for their elderly parents while they are still busy raising their own children (Blacker, 1999; Walsh, 1999). These circumstances intrude into a couple's relationship boundary and interfere with their ability to interact with each other in ways that meet their affiliation and intimacy needs. In addition, the partners may feel so "stretched" that they do not feel they are doing an adequate job in taking care of anyone. Consequently, even their desires to be altruistic are frustrated. They are unable to invest sufficient time and energy into their couple relationship or other significant relationships. In addition, the tendency has recently increased for a couple's grown children to return to live with them, for example, when they complete college. The adult children's presence can be experienced as intrusions into the couple's boundary, affecting privacy and other aspects of the couple's interactions.

It is important to note that the involvement of a third party does not necessarily interfere with the fulfillment of the partners' needs. Darryl and Natalie found that adopting a child not only contributed to their sense of altruism and nurturance but also increased their intimacy as a couple. They experienced the time and effort spent together caring for their new child as a meaningful form of sharing with each other. Similarly, some couples fulfill their needs to affiliate, be intimate, and show altruism by becoming involved together in community service activities. In fact, couples who try to set up a strong boundary around their relationship by isolating themselves from involvements with other people may place themselves at risk by cutting off opportunities for social support in the event that they need it.

Issues concerning the boundary around a couple's relationship are not limited to intrusions of other people. They also may occur because of an individual's involvement with a job, hobby, or other activities that exclude the partner. Lucia complained that Isaiah was

> having an affair with his job. His boss keeps giving him new projects and responsibilities. We used to spend evening time together, but now when I walk by and see him working on his computer in our dining room, I feel like throwing the monitor out the window!

Such involvements with other people and activities are likely to raise issues of how invested the individual is in the couple's relationship. As Lucia expressed, "I wish Isaiah would spend as much time and energy with me as he does with the computer." It is important for the therapist to determine the degree to which partners experience each other's interactions with the environment as (a) boundary violations and (b) investment in outside interests.

Although we have focused on intrusions caused by demands that originate in the environment, sometimes it is the members of a couple who initiate the involvements with outsiders, which then result in the violation of their relationship boundary. For example, some forms of intrusion described earlier (e.g., a partner sharing a couple's private information with outsiders) are initiated by the partner rather than by the outsiders. Similarly, some individuals enlist children, extended family members, friends, or therapists as allies in coalitions to bolster their power in conflicts with their partners (Todd,

1986). It is unfortunate that forming alliances with outsiders may interfere with the couple's ability to collaborate with each other to resolve their differences.

Living under dangerous, noisy, or crowded environmental conditions can create stress on a couple by interfering with interaction patterns that involve mutual social support and *investment in the relationship*. For example, couples who are raising families in neighborhoods characterized by crime and violence and who are coping with economic hardship are likely to be concerned about their ability to nurture their children and keep them safe (McKenry & Price, 2000). When physical survival is at stake, these conditions interfere with the partners' patterns of providing social support for each other, given the energy that is required of each person to meet the family's basic physical needs. Furthermore, survival activities can decrease the time that members of a couple have available for individual pursuits. Thus, it is important for a therapist to gain an understanding of environmental conditions that compromise a couple's coping and block the fulfillment of the partners' basic psychological needs.

Environmental demands also can interfere with a couple's *ability to work together collaboratively on tasks*. For example, from the beginning of their relationship, Blaine and Georgia had made significant decisions about their family life together (e.g., large purchases, childrearing and discipline practices). However, when Blaine's job began to require extended travel, he periodically was unavailable for discussions with Georgia about issues that arose unexpectedly. Although neither partner doubted Georgia's competence in making decisions, Blaine's work demands disrupted the couple's collaboration, which had contributed to their sense of sharing and intimacy. The necessity for Georgia to make decisions without Blaine present also threatened Blaine's sense that he had equal control in the couple's relationship.

These examples are not intended to be comprehensive descriptions of the ways environmental demands can interfere with the interaction patterns that couples can use to meet their relationship and individual needs. In a clinical assessment of a distressed couple, it is important to survey various environmental demands in their lives, identify how the demands influence the partners' daily interactions, and determine the degrees to which the fulfillment of their communally and individually oriented needs are affected.

Before we turn to a discussion of ways a couple's environment can provide resources for their relationship, it is important to reiterate that many environmental demands on couples are derived from otherwise positive circumstances. For example, work demands commonly arise from jobs that people seek and enjoy. Consequently, it would be overly simplistic for a therapist to focus on reducing environmental demands. However, in cases where the demands have been sought by the couple, the therapist can explore with them the extent to which they can reduce demands to some degree without sacrificing the activities and overall goals that they have chosen.

Environmental Resources

As noted earlier, a couple's environment also may provide resources for them, including social support, companionship, assistance with instrumental tasks, and financial support (M. A. McCubbin & McCubbin, 1989; McKenry & Price, 2000). For example, extended family, friends, and neighbors can provide babysitting that allows a couple to spend some leisure time alone and feel close to each other. Social relationships with others (e.g., friendships, memberships in organizations) also can reduce pressure on the couple's relationship to meet the partners' social needs in totality. Extended family, friends, and social institutions also can contribute to family rituals. Family and friends commonly share in a couple's celebrations of holidays, birthdays, and anniversaries. Religious organizations such as churches and synagogues hold weekly services and special services on holidays as well as less formal events in which couples and their families participate. Schools and local governments also hold special yearly events (e.g., the Halloween party at the elementary school; the town's Fourth of July festivities) that commonly serve as rituals for couples. Ritual celebrations at all levels of the social systems surrounding a couple provide a sense of stability, meaning, and shared experience for the partners. As we describe in chapter 7, our assessment of a couple includes an inquiry about the types and frequencies of rituals in which they participate as a dyad and each partner's subjective experience of those shared events. This assessment includes information about aspects of the couple's environment that create and support the rituals in which the partners participate.

Extended family, friends, and community organizations such as childcare facilities also contribute to the well-being of each partner as an individual. Such resources can attend to children and allow the couple to pursue their careers. In addition, individuals, religious organizations, and social agencies can be sources of information or provide direct assistance to couples in solving problems and mastering tasks. Stacey and Austin's church periodically sponsored workshops for couples on topics such as coping with difficult people in the workplace and setting realistic personal career goals. For couples caring for children or elderly parents with chronic illnesses and disabilities, community resources can provide respite services that allow the partners to fulfill their job obligations and meet the family's economic needs.

Perceptions and Appraisals of Environmental Demands and Resources

Theory, research, and clinical practice increasingly have focused on how individuals' perceptions and appraisals of demands influence the impact of the demands on well-being (e.g., Lazarus & Folkman, 1984). As we discuss in chapter 6, negative psychological and physiological responses to demands depend on the individual's appraisals of how much threat or danger exists in a demand, and his or her own abilities to cope with the demand. Individuals who perceive demands as exceeding their coping abilities are likely to experience greater tension and stress, regardless of whether the appraisals are accurate. Boss (1988) noted how individual differences and cultural factors affect whether people define particular events as demands. Omar and Julia received a phone call from Julia's younger sister, who told them that she had been abused by her husband and asked if she could stay with them for a while. Although having Julia's sister move in with them was an environmental demand that disrupted the couple's life, they perceived it as the natural thing they should do to help a relative in distress and consequently felt minimally upset about it. Their perception of the demand was shaped in part by their cultural background, in which extended family ties and loyalty were valued above individual functioning and achievement.

Similarly, individuals' subjective appraisals can influence the degree to which they define someone or something in their environment as a resource for meeting their needs. For example, Esther and Jerry had revealed to some of their friends that they were experiencing stress because Jerry's employer was downsizing, and he was likely to be laid off. Jerry was busy trying to apply for other jobs, and Esther was pursuing a possibility for a higher paying position in her company. A couple who had been friends of theirs for a long time repeatedly invited them to go to dinner or movies as a way of relaxing and getting a break from their problems. Although Esther and Jerry appreciated the couple's gesture, they did not view socializing and "playing" as what they needed to do to solve their job and financial problems. Some other couples may have perceived the opportunity to spend leisure time relaxing with friends as a helpful resource, but this couple did not.

Sometimes couples lack knowledge of resources that are available to them. They may have grown up in families in which their parents made little use of outside resources. Some community resources simply are not well publicized, or in some instances a couple may be so focused on coping with daily demands that they have not made inquiries about possible resources. Therapists should not assume that couples are aware of the range of resources available to them; a discussion of potential resources can be educational and beneficial for some clients.

Client Disclosure of Environmental Demands and Resources

Although individuals often tell couples therapists about sources of environmental stress in their lives, it is our experience that many people fail to report such demands if they do not see them as relevant to their relationship problems. Thus, an individual may be experiencing difficulties associated with a job, an ill or dying parent, or conflicts with extended family members but might not share this information with the therapist. Moreover, couples sometimes fail to provide information to therapists about environmental demands because they are embarrassed to reveal the information. For example, Beatrice and Carl had chronic problems with debt but did not share this information with their therapist because they felt that only incompetent people developed debts. When couples fail to appreciate the impact that environmental demands are having on their relationships, they also are likely to overlook environmental resources that may be helpful in resolving their problems. Even when they are aware that certain environmental resources exist, they may refrain from using them because of their beliefs about the appropriateness of seeking such help. Clinicians need to identify any cognitions that might interfere with the couple's use of environmental resources. For example, some individuals hold standards that emphasize self-sufficiency, and such beliefs lead them to reject help from others, at least in certain domains, such as finances. Beliefs about what uses of environmental resources are appropriate often have been passed down from one generation to the next in families, and clinicians must understand the degree to which strong family tradition is influencing the couple's decisions. Such beliefs concerning acceptance of assistance from outsiders can be influenced by cultural values as well as the traditions of an individual family.

McGoldrick, Preto, Hines, and Lee (1991) reviewed differences in help-seeking attitudes and behaviors of families from different ethnic groups, including Irish, Puerto Rican, African American, and Chinese American. McGoldrick et al. argued that within the culture of Irish American families individuals are likely to believe that life problems are issues between themselves and God and that receiving help from outsiders is embarrassing. Chinese families, except for those who are highly acculturated into mainstream Western society, also commonly emphasize self-help and informal social support networks over formal community resources such as mental health services. In contrast, Jewish families tend to be more likely to view therapy and similar forms of assistance as desirable and helpful. In spite of differences in culture among Hispanic individuals from different countries, McGoldrick et al. noted a common emphasis on family commitment and obligation, with reliance on extended family and friends rather than outsiders for support. African American couples and families also tend to value kinship bonds highly, including strong support networks provided through African American churches (Billingsley, 1992), and they tend to be cautious about relying on agencies of the larger society. While cautioning against stereotyping particular groups, McGoldrick et al. stressed that it is important for therapists to be aware that ethnic groups tend to differ systematically in their members' valuation and acceptance of assistance from people outside their immediate or extended families. A clinician's knowledge of potential group differences can serve as a guide for interviewing couples about their personal beliefs and use of environmental resources. Couples are likely to appreciate and benefit from efforts that their therapist makes to understand the cultural context within which they respond to the demands and resources in their environment. Furthermore, discussing with the partners the implications of cultural factors for the relationship problems that they are experiencing provides them with a macrolevel framework for their interaction patterns.

Thus, a couple's environment, from the levels of their nuclear and extended families to community agencies, not only creates various demands on the couple but also provides opportunities for resources to aid the couple in coping with life problems and meeting their individual and couple needs. It is important to determine (a) what environmental resources are realistically available to a couple, (b) the extent to which the individuals are aware of those resources, and (c) what factors are likely to influence the couple's decisions about whether they will use available resources.

SUMMARY

Our enhanced cognitive–behavioral model focuses on both the microlevel behaviors that occur in a couple's interactions and broader macrolevel patterns. In this chapter we described major types of macrolevel patterns and the microlevel acts that compose them.

- Knowledge of communally oriented and individually oriented needs and the broader, macrobehavior patterns that serve those needs should be used as guides for identifying specific, microbehavior changes that are most likely to benefit a couple's relationship.
- Some macrobehavior patterns that can meet individual and communally oriented needs include *rituals*, behaviors with symbolic meaning that the couple repeats on a regular basis; *boundary-defining behaviors*, concerning the degrees of sharing and autonomous behaviors of the partners; *social support behaviors* exchanged by members of the couple; *collaborative versus individual efforts* toward accomplishing tasks and solving problems; behaviors involved in exercising *power and control* within the couple relationship; and behaviors representing each person's *investment* of time and effort in the relationship.
- Macropatterns will be satisfying to the degree that they address both partners' communally oriented and individually oriented needs. Mismatches between behaviors and needs can result from behavioral skill deficits, but they often are at least partly due to the partners' cognitions about each other's behavior.
- A couple must adapt to a variety of environmental demands or stressors that may interfere with larger, macrobehavior patterns, thus preventing the partners from fulfilling their needs.

- A couple's environment also can provide many levels of support for the fulfillment of individual and couple needs and preferences and for adapting to various life demands that interfere with need fulfillment.
- Identifying a couple's environmental demands and resources hinges on addressing the partners' awareness of available resources, their beliefs about the acceptability of using resources, and their cultural views of environmental demands as natural, acceptable experiences versus troubling threats to one's well-being.

6

AN ADAPTATION MODEL OF RELATIONSHIP FUNCTIONING

This chapter furthers the understanding of couples' functioning across time as we examine how partners' adaptations to past and current developmental changes suggest opportunities for intervention. Couple relationships require a balance between the maintenance of roles and the ability to respond to expected or unexpected events in couples' lives, whether the events are positive or negative. The adaptation model we describe in this chapter considers a couple's ability to adjust to hardships, unfulfilled needs, or challenges from positive as well as negative events. Consistent with our enhanced cognitive–behavioral model, we look at adaptation to changes in the individual, couple, and environment in terms of behavioral, cognitive, and affective responses.

In chapter 1 we outlined an enhanced cognitive–behavioral model that takes into account multiple individual, couple, and environmental factors that influence a couple's relationship. Within this model, the clinician identifies the cognitive, affective, and behavioral components of the partners' individual personality characteristics and psychopathology, the dyad's characteristics and interaction patterns, and the couple's ways of relating to the environment. Our model is consistent with recent "ecological" models that focus on the development of couple relationships at the individual, dyadic, and environmental context levels (Larson & Holman, 1994). In chapters 2–5 we have provided detailed descriptions of the individual, couple, and environmental factors that influence the functioning of a couple's relationship.

Descriptions of individual, couple, and environmental characteristics provide a snapshot of a couple's current relationship. However, a relationship is not static; it evolves over time. Consequently any snapshot that one may take of a couple's relationship at one point necessarily will offer a limited view of how it has changed over time and how the couple might adapt to future changes in circumstances. Knowledge of developmental changes is important, both for understanding how an initially satisfying relationship has deteriorated and for helping satisfied couples prevent the development of problems in the future. Many theoretical approaches to couples therapy, including traditional behavioral couples therapy, have tended to downplay history in favor of a focus on current conditions affecting a relationship, even though they have recognized that many couples experience problems when they fail to adapt well to change. As we discuss in this chapter, taking a history of a distressed couple's relationship and merely identifying such deterioration is unlikely to benefit the couple. Our interest in historical information is that we, and our clients, can use it to pinpoint deficits in their adaptation to both unexpected and normative changes and to plan interventions that will lead to better adjustment. Furthermore, by carefully assessing how a couple is currently attempting to adapt to problems they face, we can help them to identify and change strategies that are ineffective or even damaging to their relationship.

Our cognitive–behavioral model must consequently account for ways in which a couple's relationship adapts to current characteristics of the individual members, the dyad, and the environment. It also must describe how couples adapt over time to changing circumstances. A variety of family therapy models based on general systems theory have emphasized that the success of a relationship depends on a balance between two processes noted in chapter 5: (a) the members' ability to maintain a certain degree of *stability* and (b) their ability to *adapt* their relationship in response to forces pressing for change (see Nichols & Schwartz, 2001, for an extensive review). On the one hand, a relationship is unlikely to survive if the members cannot consistently maintain roles and interaction patterns that meet their basic needs. For example, if the members of a couple are so busy coping with competing demands on their time that they fail to spend even a minimal amount of time meeting each other's intimacy needs, then they are likely to experience a significant deterioration in their emotional bond.

On the other hand, systems theorists use the term *morphogenesis* to describe a couple's or family's capacity for adapting to both unexpected and normative developmental changes in their life together (Nichols & Schwartz, 2001). Even though the partners are satisfied and functioning effectively at one point, they subsequently might have difficulty adjusting to changing circumstances and may become distressed. At times, such a shift from relatively "smooth sailing" to difficult times is very disconcerting to a couple who assumed that they would have a well-functioning relationship. A central goal of premarital intervention programs is to prepare couples to adapt constructively to both predictable and unpredictable demands and changes that are likely to occur over the course of their relationships' development (Van Widenfelt, Markman, Guerney, Behrens, & Hosman, 1997).

Our emphasis on couples' adaptation to the demands of life events involving the individuals, the dyad, and their environment is consistent with stress-and-coping theories that have been developed to explain people's adaptive processes. Although the term *stressor* has a negative connotation suggestive of dysfunction, it has been used to denote both positive and negative life events that place demands on individuals and relationships to alter the status quo. Stressors create pressure on an individual or relationship by imposing various hardships or negative impacts (H. I. McCubbin & Patterson, 1983). Stress researchers have noted that people generally think of stressors as negative life events that most individuals would prefer to avoid, but even an event or goal that an individual, couple, or family desires may involve hardships. For example, although both members of a couple may be pleased that one of them has earned a job promotion with a higher salary and greater prestige, the promotion also can serve as a stressor for the individual and the couple through the hardships of increased responsibilities, decreased sleep, and difficulty in finding time together as a couple. Some authors use the term *challenge* rather than *stressor* to describe any positive or negative event or transition that requires adaptive responses (Wills, Blechman, & McNamara, 1996). Although this term is less broadly negative in connotation than *stressor*, we prefer to use the term *demand*, because it includes both positive and negative events and conveys the pressure that is placed on the members of the couple to adapt.

Partners' personal needs tend to involve positive goals that the individuals pursue, and fulfillment of these needs can place various demands on the couple. As we described in chapter 4, some of these needs involve communally oriented goals, such as affiliation and intimacy, and others involve individually oriented goals, such as autonomy, achievement, and power. When the partners' needs are unfulfilled to some degree, the couple is faced with finding ways to maximize the attainment of positives for each person without detracting from the functioning of their relationship. Thus, if one person pursues fulfillment of his or her autonomy needs to the extent that the partners spend minimal time talking with each other, it is likely that their ability to maintain a cohesive relationship will suffer.

Even though the members of a couple may have very positive intentions about fulfilling not only their own but also each other's personal needs, the process of adaptation is likely to include some hardships. For example, if the members of a couple agree that their hectic schedules are interfering with their desire to spend time together and meet their intimacy needs, they may be faced with making sacrifices in their daily lives to find more time alone together. They may fall behind on work projects, spend less leisure time with their children, and turn down appealing social invitations from friends. Similarly, if both members of a couple want to support the fulfillment of one person's achievement needs, they may experience hardships such as spending savings money on additional education for that person.

A couple's adaptation to the demands of the two partners' communally and individually oriented needs also must take into account that these needs may change over time. Sometimes partners' personal needs have gone unfulfilled from the start, but in many cases there has been a deterioration in need fulfillment over time. It is common for these individuals to describe how they had many mutually enjoyable experiences together early in their relationship but that those positive times have decreased over time. These changes might be due to "reinforcement erosion" or habituation (Jacobson & Margolin, 1979) or perhaps follow from a traumatic event, such as an affair. Finally, as we described in chapter 4, developmental changes in each partner's degrees of communally and individually oriented needs can influence what they experience as rewarding from each other. A couple's movement into a new developmental stage in their relationship may influence what needs are most prominent and what types of partner behavior will be rewarding. Thus, intimate and affectionate behaviors may be very important prior to the birth of a child; however, with the increased demands of an infant, instrumental acts, such as helping with child care and household tasks, may be increasingly valued. The developmental changes produce new demands in the form of unmet needs.

When one partner experiences the demands or hardships of a life experience, it usually places a strain not only on the individual but also on the couple's relationship. When an individual develops a debilitating physical illness, experiences psychological symptoms, has an increase in job demands, or has a conflict with a member of his or her family of origin, the demands on the person are likely to affect the quality of interactions with his or her partner (McKenry & Price, 2000). For example, symptoms of clinical depression, such as fatigue, depressed mood, decreased interest in daily activities, diminished concentration, and a sense of worthlessness are likely to interfere with an individual's participation in both leisure activities and instrumental tasks within a relationship (Gotlib & Beach, 1995). In addition, external events involving job demands, friends in need, children's behavior problems, or conflicts among extended family members also can reduce one's time and energy for attending to the maintenance of one's couple relationship.

Furthermore, some characteristics of the couple's relationship itself can place demands on them to adapt. As we described in chapter 4, when partners have potentially conflicting motives, contrasting personality characteristics, or different preferences about aspects of daily living, they are faced with finding ways of resolving their differences. For example, partners who have a basic temperamental difference in their natural activity levels may find it difficult to establish a mutually comfortable daily interaction pattern; she wants to play while he wants to relax.

As we described in chapter 5, when members of a couple have been unsuccessful in meeting their personal needs within their relationship, they may resort to negative strategies, such as criticism and threats. These negative responses themselves then become demands on the relationship. We distinguish between *primary distress*, which partners experience concerning unmet personal needs, and *secondary distress*, which is associated with negative strategies for attempting to meet needs. Cognitive–behavioral couples therapy (CBCT) often focuses initially on decreasing the partners' negative responses to their unmet personal needs. Once these stressful negative responses have been reduced, the couple might still be faced with their unfulfilled needs, and it is not surprising that many couples still are not satisfied with their relationships at this point. The next stage of therapy involves helping the couple use constructive strategies to develop new ways to meet their unfulfilled needs. For example, Nikki was strongly motivated to achieve intimacy in her relationship with Conrad through in-depth conversations about personal feelings, but Conrad showed little interest in such talks. Conrad had grown up in a family in which his parents allowed him little privacy, and he greatly desired autonomy in his relationships with others. Nikki expressed her frustration and tried to induce Conrad to talk to her by criticizing him as being "distant and uncaring." Conrad viewed Nikki's criticism as nagging and tended to respond to it by withdrawing or criticizing her in return. Their couples therapist helped them see that a core problem they faced was finding constructive ways to balance their positive needs for intimacy and autonomy in their relationship and that the first step in doing so was to reduce the negative exchanges that they had developed. As the couple decreased their criticism and withdrawal, they were able to collaborate on problem-solving discussions to devise ways to balance fulfillment of their intimacy and autonomy needs in a more mutually satisfying manner.

AN ADAPTATION MODEL OF COUPLES' RELATIONSHIPS

Departing from a static focus on a couple's characteristics at a particular point in time, we now draw on concepts of stress-and-coping theory to understand the adaptive processes that occur over time in a relationship. We describe the ABC-X family stress-and-coping model conceived by Hill (1949, 1958) as well as elaborations on its basic concepts in H. I. McCubbin and Patterson's (1983) double ABC-X model and Karney and Bradbury's (1995) vulnerability–stress–adaptation model. We emphasize how those models have addressed processes of adaptation to life demands and translate their components into cognitive–behavioral terms. We show how stress-and-coping concepts may address unfulfilled positive needs as well as adaptation to negative life events. After describing the adaptation model, we consider how the characteristics of the demands affect the development of relationship problems. Then we identify a variety of characteristics of individuals, the couple, and aspects of the environment that can function as resources or vulnerabilities for adapting to demands that the couple faces. Finally, we examine cognitions regarding demands and resources as well as the potential for crisis states to develop in couple relationships.

Hill's (1949, 1958) ABC-X family crisis model has been widely applied in research on family responses to stress (McKenry & Price, 2000). Hill noted that life events and the demands or hardships inherent in them (the A *factor*) have the potential to create a crisis state of disorganization (the X *factor*) within a relationship when they overwhelm the couple's or family's adaptive abilities. Hill identified two major classes of factors that influence the extent to which stressor events produce disorganization in the functioning of the members of a relationship. These two types of factors that moderate and potentially buffer the effects of stressors are the family's resources and strengths (the B *factor* in the model) and the meanings or appraisals (the C *factor*, which clearly involves cognition) that the members of the family attach to the stressors and their own coping abilities. M. A. McCubbin and McCubbin (1989) noted that when individuals and families are able to cope effectively with life stressors or demands by using their resources and by appraising the stressors in positive ways, they may experience little subjective distress and resolve the situations with minimal negative impact on their well-being. On the other hand, if family members (a) lack sufficient resources; (b) fail to use their available resources; (c) are limited in their ability to adapt because of the presence of particular vulnerability factors,[1] in contrast to the absence of resources; or (d) cognitively appraise demands in ways that increase their negative responses to them, they may have considerable difficulty adjusting to the life events. The greater the discrepancy between the demands placed on the family members by life events and the family's capabilities for adapting to them, the more subjective distress, disorganization of functioning, and incapacitation the family will experience. In the ABC-X model, a crisis state is said to occur when the couple's adaptive abilities are overwhelmed by the demands of life events.

Our adaptation model of couples' functioning, outlined in chapter 1, parallels the ABC-X model. The demands that a couple experiences based on the characteristics of the two individuals, the couple, and the environment are consistent with the concept of stressors (the A component). How-

---

[1]Vulnerabilities were not included as a separate factor in the original ABC-X model but were added later by M. A. McCubbin and McCubbin (1989).

ever, our model provides a more detailed view of how both positive and negative characteristics of the individual partners, the dyad, and the couple's environment place pressure on the couple to adapt. Effective adaptation can either maintain the status quo or enhance the quality of the couple's relationship. Ineffective or destructive adaptive strategies have the potential to produce deterioration in the relationship's capacity to meet the partners' needs and to be a source of satisfaction in their lives.

Demands That Affect Relationship Functioning

In Hill's (1949, 1958) ABC-X model *stressors* are defined as events or transitions that place demands on an individual, couple, family, or larger social system to adapt or change (Boss, 1988; M. A. McCubbin & McCubbin, 1989). As noted earlier, it is important to distinguish between the events themselves and the amount of subjective distress and disruption in functioning that the event produces in the members of a family. The demands that an event or condition creates depend on the hardships associated with it. For example, for one individual the loss of a valued job may be associated with hardships such as being short on funds to pay bills, having to answer friends' questions about the circumstances of the job loss, and interviewing for a new job. These hardships directly place pressure for adaptation on the individual and couple. In contrast, a different person who has lost a job may experience a decrease in the hardships he or she has experienced that were associated with working for a demanding supervisor. Consequently, the removal of those hardships may balance some of the new hardships involved in finding a new job. As we describe later, individuals' idiosyncratic cognitive appraisals of life events—the C component of the ABC-X model—also influence the degree of hardship experienced. It is important to go beyond an identification of demanding events and to specify the hardships that are most directly taxing a particular couple's ability to adapt. Boss (1988) presented six dimensions for classifying stressors, which influence the hardships that a couple will experience. We briefly describe each of these dimensions (using our preferred term, *demands*) and how they contribute to the hardships with which couples must cope.

Internal vs. External Demands

Boss's (1988) first dimension involves a distinction between *internal demands*, which have a locus within members of the relationship (e.g., a member of a couple gets drunk) and *external demands*, which are events imposed from outside the relationship (e.g., an individual's employer declares bankruptcy). Throughout this book, we refer to demands in the environment outside the couple as *external* and those that occur within either partner or in the interactions between partners as *internal* to the relationship. To be consistent with our focus on individual, dyadic, and environmental factors in relationship functioning, we differentiate between demands that are internal to each individual and those that are dyadic in nature.

A variety of common demands are internal to the individual, such as normal, developmental changes in a person's life. For example, an individual who is approaching a "milestone" birthday (e.g., those that end in zero) may engage in a review and evaluation of his or her life achievements and unfulfilled goals. To the extent that the individual concludes that life has been disappointing or unfulfilling, the impending birthday may become stressful for the person and very likely for his or her couple relationship as well. Also, each partner's unfulfilled communally oriented and individually oriented needs place demands on both the individual and couple to adapt. Similarly, the partners' other personality characteristics, such as temperament (e.g., activity level), can place demands on the individual and couple. Furthermore, an individual's psychological symptoms (e.g., depression, agoraphobia) and unresolved issues (e.g., insecure attachment developed in the family of origin) are likely to create pressure on the couple's interactions. Thus, a variety of characteristics of individual partners, which we reviewed in chapter 4, can create hardships not only for the individuals but also for the couple as a dyad.

Interpersonal demands within a couple's interactions can function at both the micro- and macrobehavioral levels. On a microlevel, if on a particular day Joseph is slow getting ready to leave the house and Jan responds by leaving without him, the couple is likely to experience considerable stress. Similarly, broad macrobehavioral patterns, such as inequitable distribution of power in couples' decision making in a variety of situations, can produce stress when these patterns fail to meet the needs of one or both partners. As described earlier, a couple's aversive interaction pattern in response to partners' unmet needs places demands on the couple. For example, when Ernie's intimacy needs are not met, he tends to become demanding, and Audrey withdraws. In such instances a clinician must address both the demands of the couple's negative interaction pattern and the demands of the individual partners' unfulfilled needs.

As we described in chapter 5, common environmental demands external to a couple's relationship can have their locus within the nuclear family (e.g., a child's oppositional behavior), the extended family (e.g., conflicts or intrusions involving in-laws), the partners' wider social network (e.g., a needy friend), social institutions (e.g., pressure from school officials concerning a child's classroom behavior), and broad societal factors (e.g., discrimination against racial minorities and same-sex couples). In chapter 5 we described how environmental demands can affect a couple either indirectly, through their effects on one partner, or directly, through their influence on the couple's interactions. It is important for clinicians to identify how an external demand interferes with the behavioral patterns that otherwise would meet a couple's needs.

Some couples have come to take for granted certain societal sources of environmental demands so much that they fail to recognize the impact of the hardships on their relationships. For example, even though members of African American couples are likely to be aware of the potential for racial discrimination on a daily basis, they may overlook the ways in which persistent worry about the physical and psychological well-being of their children influences their relationship (Hines, 1999). Members of some same-sex couples may fail to realize how the pressure they feel to conceal their relationships in many public settings (e.g., attending workplace parties as a single person) affects the level of intimacy between them (L. S. Brown, 1995). Therefore, a clinical assessment of a couple's environmental demands must take into account the various social systems in which the couple's relationship occurs.

Normative vs. Non-normative Demands

Boss's (1988) second criterion for categorizing demands differentiates between *normative demands*, which are events that commonly occur during the individual or family life cycle (e.g., birth of a child, retirement), and *non-normative demands*, which are unexpected (e.g., a car accident, death of a child). Family crisis theorists note that the relative predictability of normative demands allows individuals and families opportunities to prepare for them, but the unpredictability of non-normative demands more often leads to shock, confusion, and a sense of helplessness (Figley, 1983). Consequently, a clinician assessing a couple who has recently experienced non-normative demanding events should recognize that the partners' emotional upset and disorganized behavior may, at least to some degree, reflect the immediate impact of the demands, rather than being typical of the couple's way of relating to each other. Because many couples seek therapy only when events have raised their level of distress beyond a tolerable threshold, a therapist must keep in mind that the people sitting in the office during the intake interview may be functioning at a level far below what is typical for them.

Although couples are likely to be aware of non-normative demands because they are unexpected and disconcerting, at times they might fail to focus on normative demands because those seem to be a natural part of life. For example, Terry and Cynthia sought couples therapy because they had begun to have frequent arguments and were becoming increasingly distant from each other. Within the last year they had moved so Terry could attend graduate school, leaving friends and family behind; they had experienced a significant decrease in income along with increased school costs; Cynthia was pregnant and felt miserable; and their only "child," a cat named Silky, was dying. Yet, the couple did not relate their relationship problems to these demands, which they viewed as "just things most people go through."

Individual and relationship life cycles exert pressures for adaptation at particular normative, developmental transition points (Carter & McGoldrick,

1999; Minuchin, 1974). For example, when members of a young couple are in the process of forming their own family, they may experience demands associated with supporting themselves financially. They also may experience demands involving their parents' attempts to intrude into their privacy and decision making as a couple. When a couple become parents they commonly face the physical and psychological demands of taking care of a helpless infant, reduced time together as a couple, and increased expenses. Therefore, the assessment of demands must take into account both normative and non-normative changes that occur in a couple's life together over time.

As we described in chapter 4, in addition to demands that tend to be experienced as negative life events, demands involving the fulfillment of partners' positive communally and individually oriented needs also can be differentiated as normative or non-normative. Thus, when Loretta and Gary's first child was born, both new parents experienced an increase in their motivation to spend time nurturing the baby and focusing on family togetherness. This normative shift, which is experienced by many new parents, placed demands on the couple, because they had to find ways to find time together as a couple while keeping up with their careers. In contrast, Meredith and Cory faced a non-normative stressor when Meredith unexpectedly inherited some money. Meredith felt torn between using the money to pay for a special vacation that the couple had dreamed about for years versus spending it on classes that she knew would be helpful in moving her toward a promotion at work.

Carter and McGoldrick (1999) presented a richly detailed description of normative changes in the family life cycle, including the diversity of traditional and nontraditional family forms in today's society as well as important cultural group variations in life experiences and demands. Familiarity with these variations increases therapists' cultural sensitivity in assessing the demands that their clients have experienced or may experience in the future.

Ambiguous vs. Unambiguous Demands

A third dimension along which to categorize demands differentiates between relatively *ambiguous demands* versus *unambiguous demands* (Boss, 1988). In some instances, the circumstances surrounding a demand may be so ambiguous that individuals may not be sure that the events are occurring or do not focus on them as sources of stress. In contrast, unambiguous demands involve clear information about what is occurring, when, or to whom. For example, as described earlier, an individual may become depressed by an impending birthday that elicits a self-analysis of his or her life's accomplishments. However, neither member of the couple may be aware that the birthday and its associated hardships are the basis of the person's depression. In contrast, the hardships that arise when they learn that their child has a life-threatening illness tend to be much less ambiguous. In some cases, a couple has failed to cope effectively with a demand because they lack adequate resources to do so. However, in other cases a couple may have failed to identify the nature of the demands affecting them and therefore has not made use of available resources that could reduce the stress.

Sometimes couples do not have a clear understanding that their lack of satisfaction with their relationship results from large, macrobehavioral interaction patterns that fail to fulfill their needs. This ambiguity interferes with their ability to make changes in their relationship that would better meet their needs. During their first two couples therapy sessions, Stephanie and Grant both expressed vague, global dissatisfaction with their relationship. Although each person could list several specific changes that they desired in each other's behavior, they could not articulate what it was that they found pleasing or displeasing about particular acts. At the third session, Stephanie said that she felt better about how they were getting along. When the therapist inquired about any specific changes in behavior that seemed to be associated with Stephanie's changed feelings, she replied that she felt closer to Grant when he called her unexpectedly at work and told her that he was thinking about her. The therapist helped the couple identify how this and a few other behaviors that they found pleasing seemed to address their need for intimacy, which had been neglected in recent years. Once the ambiguity was clarified, they were able to plan ways to increase their overall sense of intimacy.

Volitional vs. Nonvolitional Demands

Fourth, Boss (1988) noted that demands can be *volitional* (wanted and sought, such as a chosen job) versus *nonvolitional* (not sought but occurring, such as being fired from a job). Sometimes members of couples have been so focused on positive aspects of a volitional demand (e.g., moving to a different city that had long been the couple's dream) that they fail to anticipate associated hardships. At times, focusing on the positive aspects of the situation can help a couple tolerate the hardships. Thus, Anthony stated,

> We chose to have a baby even though our financial situation wasn't good, because having a family is very important to us. Right now it is hard getting by on one income, but whenever we feel upset, we look at our beautiful child and feel lucky.

Some other individuals seem to avoid focusing on hardships associated with a volitional demand because doing so might produce ambivalent feelings about their decision. For example, a desired move to a new city may result in unhappy adolescent children who had to leave their friends, difficulty finding new doctors with whom the family members are comfortable, and unforeseen problems with a new house. Thus, the experience of moving may have been volitional, but the hardships associated with it were not, and the couple may avoid weighing the advantages against the disadvantages because of their fear that in hindsight their decision may appear unwise.

Volitional and nonvolitional demands can affect the couple differently because of the way they are processed internally. The partners may be confused about how they should think and feel about demanding experiences that were chosen but have resulted in various hardships, some anticipated and some not. One or both partners chose to create the circumstances and therefore might not feel free to complain or request assistance. As Kim stated, "As the old saying goes, 'You made this bed, now lie in it.'" In addition to the individuals' internal conflicts, a volitional demand can lead to conflict between partners if it was chosen in an attempt to meet one person's needs, and it creates difficulties for the other person. "Look, you brought me to this God forsaken place to help your career, so you could at least spend time with me. I really don't know many people here, and those I do know, I could do without."

Nonvolitional demands present different challenges to the couple and the therapist. Although they are likely to result in less blaming or guilt than volitional ones, they are more likely to induce a sense of helplessness, loss of control, or despair for one or both partners. As Arthur remarked, "For years, Marla and I looked forward to retiring and traveling all over the world. Now with her severe arthritis, traveling is very difficult. It seems that our dream has died." As we discuss in more detail in the chapters on therapeutic intervention, it is important to counteract a couple's sense of helplessness in the face of nonvolitional demands by helping them identify areas of their lives over which they still have some control.

Chronic vs. Acute Demands

Fifth, demands can either be *chronic* (e.g., a disease such as diabetes) or *acute* (e.g., a child injured in an automobile accident; Boss, 1988). Sometimes members of couples fail to report chronic demands because the demands have become such a routine part of their lives that the partners do not think of them as relevant to their current relationship problems. Although the chronic nature of a demand may have given a couple ample time to develop coping strategies, it also may have led to a "wearing down" process in which the couple's coping resources have become depleted over time.

As is the case with demands involving negative events, demands associated with positive events also can be acute or chronic. For example, when Meredith inherited a substantial amount of money from a great-aunt, it suddenly opened up an opportunity to leave her job and return to school to pursue an advanced degree. This opportunity produced an increase in her emphasis on achievement, which had been relatively neglected over the past several years as she worked in a "dead-end" job. Cory was surprised by Meredith's motivation to achieve because he had known her only during the time when she had held her current job, and the couple now was faced with adapting to the demand of meeting her increased desire to advance professionally. In contrast, the demands of Ernesto and Rosalie's weekly "dates" to maintain their sense of intimacy were a chronic or stable characteristic of their relationship. Although both partners were aware of their needs and how their dates helped fulfill them, the demands of putting that time aside for the two of them in the midst of their hectic schedules often were challenging.

Because couples often do not have time to prepare for acute demands, their sudden onset is likely to create an initial period of confusion until the partners understand what problems they are facing and what must be done to adapt to them (Figley, 1983). Consequently, even a well-functioning couple may be ineffective in responding to an acute demand.

Cumulative vs. Isolated Demands

Boss's (1988) sixth dimension involves the degree to which demands are *cumulative* (piling up, such that the individuals have not resolved one demand before having to cope with others) versus *isolated*. At times a pile-up of demands can produce a "last-straw" phenomenon in which a couple may have difficulty coping with even a relatively minor demand if it follows other demands that have taxed their coping abilities. As is the case with negative life events, an accumulation of demands associated with fulfillment of positive needs can overwhelm a couple's use of their resources for adapting (M. A. McCubbin & McCubbin, 1989). Greg and Celia fulfilled a long-standing dream of opening their own restaurant and, after a glowing review of the restaurant appeared in the local newspaper, it became so popular that they and their staff were very busy every lunchtime and evening. In the midst of what they considered good fortune, they learned that Celia was pregnant. Even though they previously had tried to have a baby, and they had not been using birth control, at that point they had virtually put parenthood on hold while they worked on starting the restaurant. Consequently, the pregnancy was unplanned. Even though they were excited at the prospect of becoming parents, the combined stresses of the business and impending parenthood placed a major strain on their coping ability.

An individual's adaptation to a pile-up of demands can be influenced by his or her cognitive appraisal of the pile-up (M. A. McCubbin & McCubbin, 1989). For example, an individual may conclude, "My life is nothing but problems. What's the use of trying?" However, if couples experience several demands and experience some success in adapting to them, they may develop increased confidence in their coping abilities. Their appraisal of themselves as "survivors" may contribute to resilience in the face of subsequent demands. Thus, a pile-up of demands can have both advantages and disadvantages, and therapists can help couples become more aware of the "silver lining inside the gray cloud" by helping them identify ways in which prior experiences with demands enhanced their adaptation skills. We discuss such therapeutic strategies in detail in Part II.

Forms of Adapting to Demands

According to the ABC-X model, the members of a couple typically respond to a demand with some form of coping or adaptive strategy. These strategies can include (H. I. McCubbin & Patterson, 1983; M. A. McCubbin & McCubbin, 1989):

- *avoiding* the demand or hardship by denying or ignoring it,
- *eliminating* the demand by actively removing it or changing its meaning so it no longer influences the relationship, and
- *assimilating* the demand by making changes in the relationship to take the demand or hardship into account.

Each of these adaptation strategies can involve cognitive, behavioral, or emotional elements, or a combination of the three. We find it helpful to apply M. A. McCubbin and McCubbin's (1989) concepts of avoiding, eliminating, or assimilating a demand to couples' relationships, because they capture different forms of adaptation. Avoidance seems to be based on an individual's sense that neither the individual nor the demands are likely to change, so the best strategy is to steer clear of the demanding situations. In contrast, elimination strategies appear to involve a sense that one can take actions that will modify the demands, and assimilation strategies involve a sense that one can (or must) change oneself to live with the demands. We are not aware of any research investigating such cognitions that couples may have about the potential for change in demands or in themselves, but it seems important for clinicians to explore client appraisals associated with their choices of adaptation strategies.

As described in chapter 2, the behavioral patterns involved in adapting to demands can involve positive or negative forms of approach, holding one's ground, or withdrawal. Couples' avoidance, elimination, and assimilation adaptation strategies can be described in terms of these types of responses. Behavioral avoidance of a demand involves withdrawing from the situation as much as possible. For example, Andrew avoided the demands of taking care of his newborn child, a responsibility he found intimidating, by staying late at the office and bringing home work that he told Camille he must do. Behavioral patterns for eliminating a demand can include forms of positive or negative approach, including active problem solving or coercive acts. An example of a positive approach response is Camille's assertively telling Andrew that they needed to develop ways of sharing child care that would give each of them rest periods. An example of a negative approach response to a demand is Andrew's screaming at Camille for "pressuring me to do more than I can handle," which led to an escalating argument between the spouses.

Behavioral responses that assimilate a demand by changing the couple's relationship might include positive "backing off" behaviors. Andrew and Camille had a long-standing pattern in which Camille would immediately discuss problems with Andrew when he walked into the house after work. Even though this was not how Andrew preferred to be greeted, he participated in those discussions because he knew that it relieved Camille to be able to share her concerns (e.g., about budgeting for their expenses). Once their therapist helped them identify the demands that Andrew experienced as well as those that Camille experienced as the "sole parent," they agreed that having a child had created an overload for them and that each person needed a lessening of pressure. The partners agreed that discussing problems when they first saw each other in the evening was adding to the stress they both experienced. They decided on a 1-hour "backing-off" period after they greeted each other when Andrew arrived home, when they either would spend time in different parts of the house or would avoid discussing household and childrearing issues. This pattern reduced the demands that Andrew experienced, leading him to improve his child care skills.

Partners' approach, "holding ground," and withdrawal responses to demands can be cognitive as well as behavioral. An individual can actively approach a stressful problem by thinking about possible solutions to it, stubbornly refusing to consider alternative ways of viewing it, or shifting his or her attention away from it entirely. The individual's cognitive adaptation strategies often will parallel his or her behavioral responses, but not always. Steven tended to withdraw from Maggie behaviorally when she wanted to discuss relationship problems with him. However, at a cognitive level, Steven spent a lot of time "approaching" the problems by worrying about them (a fact that was not evident to Maggie, who concluded that Steven did not care about the problems). When a clinician assesses a couple's adaptive responses to demands in their life, it is important to inquire about both the overt behavioral and the internal cognitive and emotional responses.

Any coping strategy is likely to have both advantages and disadvantages, although empirical evidence suggests that particular approaches can be especially problematic. Lazarus and Folkman (1984) described how denial and avoidance (forms of adaptation through withdrawal) can lower emotional distress but interfere with an individual's behavior in ways that can solve problems. In a retrospective study of adult children of alcoholics, Easley and Epstein (1991) found that the use of particular adaptation styles by the family or the individual was associated with adult functioning. Those who reported greater use of passive appraisal among members of their family of origin or who reported that they themselves used escape and avoidance as ways of coping with parental alcoholism had poorer functioning later as adults (as indicated by psychological symptoms, alcohol abuse, or both).

Lazarus and Folkman (1984) noted the importance of differentiating between coping strategies that may reduce stress in the short term but have negative impacts on long-term adaptation. In the early stages of a relationship, a couple may successfully reduce distress by avoiding conflicts about their roles and life goals. In a classic study of couples' interaction styles, Raush,

Barry, Hertel, and Swain (1974) identified maritally satisfied couples who avoided direct discussion of conflictual topics. Thus, there is evidence that withdrawal from the demands of dealing with conflicts can contribute to some harmony in a relationship. However, a couple's avoidance may be ineffective at a later stage of relationship development, as when the birth of a child forces them to add parental roles to their couple roles. A failure to discuss and negotiate the division of child care and household tasks may have worked when there were few such responsibilities, but having a newborn baby at home may result in one or both partners finding the unresolved issues to be distressing. Assessment of a couple's adaptive abilities should include a developmental perspective, tracking the strategies that they have used over time and the adequacy of the match between those strategies and the current demands they experience.

Within our adaptation model of couples' functioning, the potential for distress, disorganization, and dissolution of a couple's relationship increases as the balance between demands and the couple's adaptive abilities shifts toward overwhelming the adaptive capacities. This process is consistent with stress-and-coping models such as the ABC-X model, in which stressors overwhelm coping responses and lead to a crisis state in which normal individual or relationship functioning breaks down (M. A. McCubbin & McCubbin, 1989; McKenry & Price, 2000). At the individual level, the symptoms of a crisis state include a variety of affective, cognitive, physiological, and behavioral changes, such as anxiety, confusion, a sense of helplessness, and withdrawal (Freeman & Dattilio, 1994; Greenstone & Leviton, 1993). At the interpersonal level, the negative effects of ineffective adaptation in couple or family relationships include disruptions of role enactments and deterioration in their communication and coordinated efforts to solve problems as well as an increase in aversive behavior exchanges. The effectiveness of a couple's adaptive strategies in warding off such distress and disorganization depends on the individual, couple, and environmental resources that they have available, as well as vulnerability factors that impede coping efforts and the couple's cognitive appraisals of the demands and resources. Next, we describe resources and vulnerabilities as they are conceptualized within our model as well as in the original ABC-X model and its later elaborations.

Individual, Couple, and Environmental Resources

Consistent with the work of family stress researchers such as H. I. McCubbin and Patterson (1983), our model includes three major categories of resources that may be available to help a couple adapt to demands in their life: (a) the personal resources of each individual member, (b) resources within the couple's relationship, and (c) resources available to the couple from outside their relationship. Each of these three types of resources can be used to help the partners avoid, eliminate, and assimilate demands they face. Because we have described these characteristics of individual partners, the couple relationship, and the dyad's environment in previous chapters, we will not reiterate those in detail at this point. However, we will explain how those characteristics play roles as resources in our adaptation model of couples' functioning.

Individual Resources

Resources of the individual partners include a wide range of inherent and acquired characteristics, such as health, intelligence, problem-solving skills, self-esteem, education, financial savings, job skills, and personality characteristics (e.g., high self-esteem, secure attachment style) that contribute to the individual's resilience. Individual resources also include each partner's cognitions, such as realistic standards that contribute to setting manageable goals as an individual and couple (Baucom & Epstein, 1990). For example, it is easier for partners to achieve a satisfying balance between time spent on work and family activities if they hold realistic standards for their performance in their work and family roles. In addition, skills for monitoring and evaluating the validity of one's own thinking are an important resource for counteracting upsetting cognitive distortions of life experiences (A. T. Beck, Rush, Shaw, & Emery, 1979). Jacobson and Christensen's (1996) model of integrative couples therapy emphasizes how partners' capacity to accept problems and differences between them is a crucial resource for facing circumstances that are very difficult or impossible to change.

Whereas some of a person's resources might have a strong genetic component (e.g., general physical health), other resources are acquired over the course of a lifetime. Some acquired resources are learned (e.g., job skills, interpersonal skills), some are received as gifts from others (e.g., inheritances), and others are earned through effort (e.g., salary). At times clients merely need to apply their existing resources more effectively, but in other instances they need assistance in developing their resources further. Simon and Gina were faced with financial stressors associated with Simon's history of losing jobs or failing to earn promotions. When the therapist determined that Simon's limited skills for organizing his work contributed to his lack of productivity, helping him develop his organizational skills became a key therapeutic goal.

Couples' Resources

Resources within a couple's relationship include characteristics such as joint communication skills for expressiveness and listening, problem-solving skills, and a history of interacting in ways that foster a sense of cohesiveness and mutual social support (Epstein & Schlesinger, 1994). Although communication and problem-solving skills are behaviors characteristic of individuals and can be taught to individual members of couples, it is important to assess each couple's communication and problem solving as dyadic processes as well. Each couple's pattern of communication is an idiosyncratic interaction between the two parties. Therefore, an individual might express feelings, listen empathically, and engage in collaborative problem solving with friends, coworkers, and even with the therapist, but this same person might communicate much more ineffectively or negatively with his or her partner. In fact, this complaint is frequently expressed by distressed partners. For example, Judy stated, "I don't know what's wrong. I can have disagreements and differences of opinion with my coworkers and my friends, and it's no problem. But any time Zach and I disagree, it quickly turns into a big battle." It is important to know whether each partner has demonstrated more constructive and effective communication and problem-solving skills with others, because the therapist then has a sense of whether the couple's problem is a skill deficit at the individual level or a problem when these particular two people interact with each other. If the problem seems to occur specifically between the members of the couple, the therapist needs to determine whether the partners' cognitions (e.g., negative attributions about each other's intentions) and emotions (e.g., anger) lead them to avoid using constructive individual skills as resources with each other.

Another possibility is that the partners have no negative cognitions and emotions that interfere with communicating and solving problems together but are ineffective in working together (Baucom & Epstein, 1990). Lisa and Daniel each were competent and effective problem solvers at their jobs, but when they tried to solve problems at home they had considerable difficulty, because they had different styles of approaching problems. Lisa tended to spend time comparing details of alternative plans before taking action, but Daniel tended to think of an idea that seemed promising and use a trial-and-error approach. Each person's style worked well on its own, but the styles did not mesh well.

Environmental Resources

Finally, environmental resources available to a couple from outside their relationship can include various forms of social support (e.g., emotional support, financial aid, assistance with problem solving, and help with tasks such as child care) from extended family, friends, neighbors, and social agencies, as described in chapter 5. Increasing a couple's access to and use of resources can contribute to coping with demands of unfulfilled positive needs as well as those associated with negative life events.

A systematic clinical assessment should not only identify potential resources that are not yet being tapped by a couple but also evaluate the advantages and disadvantages of the couple's current adaptation strategies. On the one hand, a couple's adaptation to demands may be improved by activating new resources, such as an extended family member's help. On the other hand, if a couple's use of resources contributes to an ineffective adaptive strategy, then a therapist may need to focus on reducing reliance on those resources.

For example, if a couple is experiencing stress because their 10-year-old child has been suspended from school for fighting, extended family members may offer support by inciting the couple to deal with school officials in an aggressive manner. Although a therapist may want to point out the positive side of the cohesiveness within the extended family, he or she also would want to help the couple consider the likely negative consequences of such an adversarial approach as well as the advantages of alternative approaches.

Individual and Couple Vulnerabilities

In contrast to personal and relationship resources, stress researchers have described vulnerabilities as characteristic weaknesses that increase the probability of a negative outcome when people are exposed to risk factors (e.g., Cowan, Cowan, & Schulz, 1996; Karney & Bradbury, 1995; M. A. McCubbin & McCubbin, 1989). A *vulnerability* is a characteristic that increases the negative impact of life demands on the functioning of the individual or relationship. Although Hill's original (1949, 1958) ABC-X family stress-and-coping model did not explicitly include a component of chronic vulnerabilities that a family and its members bring to their efforts to cope with stressors, more recent models include such factors. M. A. McCubbin and McCubbin (1989) proposed the Typology Model of Family Adjustment and Adaptation that elaborated on the ABC-X model by adding a vulnerability factor (V). McCubbin and McCubbin described vulnerable families as having a variety of characteristic negative ways of responding to stressors, such as emotional upset, low respect for each other, blaming others for problems, low levels of mutual understanding, little sense of purpose and meaning in life, a low sense of control over life events, and rigidity about trying new behaviors. McCubbin and McCubbin's conceptualization of family vulnerabilities seems consistent with the definition of vulnerabilities used in the general stress-and-coping literature (e.g., Cowan et al., 1996) in which an inner weakness leaves an individual or relationship more susceptible to negative impacts of stressors. Our own conceptualization of vulnerabilities also extends beyond the absence of positive resources to the existence of characteristics that actively interfere with constructive adaptation to demands.

Individual Vulnerabilities

Vulnerabilities can exist within the individual partners. Several factors can function as individual vulnerabilities and influence the couple's relationship. Among the partners' relatively stable individual vulnerabilities are demographic characteristics (e.g., young age, limited education), personal historical experiences (e.g., abuse in one's family of origin, poor parental marital quality), and relatively stable personality characteristics (Karney & Bradbury, 1995; Larson & Holman, 1994). In terms of traditional psychiatric diagnostic categories, individual difference characteristics can include relatively stable *Diagnostic and Statistical Manual of Mental Disorders* (American Psychiatric Association, 1994) Axis I disorders, Axis II personality disorders, and nondiagnosable traits. As we discussed in chapter 4, psychopathology such as clinical depression can not only create demands to which a couple must adapt but also can reduce individuals' abilities to cope with other life demands. Similarly, Axis II disorders, such as borderline personality disorder, significantly interfere with individual and interpersonal adaptation to demands (Linehan, 1993). Personality characteristics that do not qualify for formal psychiatric diagnoses but have received considerable attention as vulnerability factors in the development of distress in intimate relationships are *insecure attachment styles* (W. H. Berman, Marcus, & Berman, 1994; Kobak, Ruckdeschel, & Hazan, 1994) and *neuroticism* or *negative affectivity*, which is the tendency to be highly reactive in experiencing and expressing distress in many life situations (Jocklin, McGue, & Lykken, 1996; Karney, Bradbury, Fincham, & Sullivan, 1994). Other traitlike vulnerabilities of individual members of a couple can include deficits in self-esteem and other personality and temperament characteristics such as those described in chapter 4.

The individual partners' vulnerabilities can exacerbate the subjective intensity of demands experienced by a couple and interfere with the couple's adaptive responses to situations they are confronting (Karney & Bradbury, 1995). For example, Larson and Holman (1994) noted that, some partners, because of individual personality traits and psychopathology, are likely to perceive relationship events in negative, distorted ways and to overreact to them. Thus, some people have a tendency to react to stressful events with strong negative emotion, increasing their impact. An individual with generalized anxiety disorder, for example, is likely to worry excessively, catastrophize about life demands, and experience symptoms (e.g., a keyed-up feeling, difficulty concentrating, muscle tension) that reduce his or her ability to use effective adaptation strategies. This person's strong emotional reactivity also is likely to interfere with his or her ability to work with a partner to avoid, eliminate, or assimilate life demands.

Unresolved issues from a person's previous relationships (e.g., abuse in the family of origin) can interfere with his or her adaptation to current demands if the current circumstances elicit overlearned dysfunctional responses such as avoidance. Consider Todd, who learned to inhibit expressing his feelings during childhood to avoid being hit by his father. This pattern of inhibited expressiveness continued into adulthood and generalized to his interactions with his wife, Maxine, and the two sought treatment because they felt distant and disconnected.

In addition, an individual's insecure "working model" or schema concerning attachment is conceptualized as a form of vulnerability in the face of relationship demands (Johnson & Greenberg, 1995). When the individual experiences an increased need for emotional support because of an external stressor or observes that his or her partner has become less emotionally available, that person is likely to express emotional distress and cling to or criticize the partner. These negative responses to stressors may lead to even greater distance between the partners and to a decreased ability of the couple to work together in adapting to the demands that the individual and couple face.

Individual vulnerabilities also can include a variety of cognitions and beliefs that one or both partners might have (Epstein & Schlesinger, 1994; Larson & Holman, 1994). Individuals might hold standards that interfere with expressive and listening skills as well as with collaborative problem solving. More specifically, a belief that loving partners should be able to mind-read each other's thoughts and emotions may lead an individual to withhold information, expecting the other person to sense it intuitively. In contrast, an individual who believes that in a close relationship people should share all their thoughts and emotions might disclose negative feelings to the partner in a rather tactless manner that hurts and alienates him or her. As we discussed in chapter 3, a variety of distorted and extreme beliefs can make a couple vulnerable to the impact of life demands when these beliefs interfere with the couple's ability to evaluate and respond to problems in a realistic manner.

Our enhanced cognitive–behavioral model also incorporates vulnerabilities involving individuals' cognitive–affective styles, their relatively stable tendencies to process information in particular ways. Baucom, Sayers, and Duhe (1989) found individual differences among members of couples in their tendency to have a generalized *attributional style*; that is, the degree to which they consistently attribute negative partner behavior to global, stable traits across situations. Individuals who make these types of attributions tend to blame their partners for negative behavior and feel hopeless about their relationship (Holtzworth-Munroe & Jacobson, 1985). Similarly, Weiss's (1980) notion of negative *sentiment override* or a person's global, negative affective response toward a partner can function as a vulnerability factor, because the individual tends to indiscriminately experience the partner's behavior as negative. Thus, negative attributional styles and sentiment override make the individual vulnerable by increasing the likelihood that he or she will be distressed by the partner's behavior.

Couples' Vulnerabilities

Couple-level vulnerabilities can include dyadic adaptive patterns that exacerbate or fail to resolve conflict, such as two partners' tendencies to engage in mutual, reciprocal avoidance of each other or in escalating arguments during periods of conflict (Christensen, 1987, 1988; Cowan et al., 1996). Patterns of reciprocal withdrawal and escalation of negative behavior and emotion become sources of vulnerability when couples lack an ability to interrupt them. Distressed couples are less likely than nondistressed couples to exit sequences of reciprocal negative behavior exchanges during discussions of relationship problems (Gottman, Markman, & Notarius, 1977; Revenstorf, Hahlweg, Schindler, & Vogel, 1984). The repetitiveness of their negative exchanges acts as a vulnerability factor in that it interferes with the partners' ability to solve problems together, thus adding to their distress. Similarly, some couples have a tendency to "feed off" each other's anxiety or depression, with each person perceiving the other's negative verbal and nonverbal expressions as evidence that the demands they face are overwhelming. Neither partner is able to step back and do things to calm the two of them. Consequently, it is crucial that couples develop strategies for getting back on track with constructive interactions after they have had arguments rather than engaging in further conflict or entering a period of icy withdrawal. As Colin described, "After we have a big argument and we both calm down, I go to her and just hold her, and we both know it will be okay. It works for us."

Concurring that conflict is inevitable in close relationships, Wile (1993) emphasized that a couple will be vulnerable to negative effects of conflict if they respond to it in negative ways and lack effective ways to recover from fights. He teaches couples a set of principles designed to help them recover through constructive thinking and communication. These "recovery" principles are similar to cognitive restructuring and behavioral skill-building approaches typically used in CBCT to increase couples' resources for resolving conflicts. Therapeutic approaches such as Wile's and our own are based on an assumption that it is possible to reduce sources of vulnerability in couples' dyadic responses to the demands involved in resolving conflicts between partners. In Part II of this book we describe methods for assessing and modifying couples' dyadic vulnerability factors.

Just as the personal history of each individual may involve unresolved traumatic experiences that act as vulnerabilities, past traumatic events that have occurred between partners can become chronic vulnerabilities. Past infidelity, substance abuse, and psychological or physical abuse commonly have lasting negative effects on the partners' cognitions, emotions, and behaviors toward each other (Glass & Wright, 1997; Gordon & Baucom, 1998c; Heyman & Neidig, 1997; O'Farrell & Rotunda, 1997). As a result, the couple may be less able to adapt to current demands that occur in their relationship. After Jane became aware that Seth had been having an affair, the couple entered couples therapy and made considerable progress in addressing factors that had led Seth to be very unhappy in their relationship. Both partners were committed to making their relationship succeed, and they experienced significant increases in their overall satisfaction as they worked together in therapy. Nevertheless, the couple experienced tension and conflict whenever Seth had an opportunity to engage in independent activities, such as going out to dinner with a group of people from his workplace. Seth felt constrained, both by his own concern about making Jane feel insecure and by Jane's "grilling" him about his social plans. Whenever Jane heard that

Seth had a potential social plan or other independent activity, she experienced anxiety and painful memories of learning about Seth's affair. Because of these responses, the couple was vulnerable to conflict whenever faced with the demand of Seth's need for some autonomy in their relationship.

Cognitions Regarding Demands and Resources

A hallmark of CBCT is its focus on individuals' idiosyncratic cognitions regarding their experiences in their relationships. To a great extent, models of family stress and coping are based on cognitive–behavioral principles. In particular, in the ABC-X family stress-and-coping model the family members' perceptions of events (the C component of the model) play a significant role in whether the family copes effectively with stressors or experiences dysfunction (Boss, 1988). First, each individual appraises the hardships involved in a demand: To what extent does he or she perceive the circumstances as altering the status quo and requiring that the members of the couple adapt? Second, each individual appraises the degree to which there are sufficient resources available to adapt to the demands that the couple is facing. To what degree does the individual believe that the hardships associated with a demand are manageable with available resources? These two types of appraisals are similar to Lazarus and Folkman's (1984) description of *primary appraisal* and *secondary appraisal* of stressors, respectively. Thus, cognitions influence adaptation to demands by affecting how severe the demands seem to each person and how adequate each person believes the available resources are for coping with those demands.

Boss (1988) noted that if the members of a relationship appraise a stressor and available resources in the same way, it can be an advantage, but not if the members share a distorted view of the situation. For example, both members of a couple may be highly distressed because they view their adolescent child's relatively normal oppositional behavior as severely deviant. Similarly, two spouses may attribute their mutual verbal abuse to traits that they are powerless to change: "We're just both strong-willed people who speak our minds; that's who we are." If both members of a couple appraise the danger in an event as catastrophic or uncontrollable, they will confirm each other's negative views and even intensify each other's emotional upset and ineffective coping.

Use of a resource likely depends on cognitive processing involving (a) recognizing that the resource exists, (b) expecting that the resource can be helpful in coping with the demand, and (c) believing that one will be able to access the resource successfully. These cognitions involve outcome expectancies and efficacy expectancies, described by Bandura (1977). On the one hand, an *outcome expectancy* is an individual's prediction that behaving in a particular way is likely to produce a particular consequence. On the other hand, an *efficacy expectancy* is the individual's estimate of the probability that he or she actually is capable of carrying out the behaviors that would lead to that consequence. An individual would need to make both types of predictions before deciding to try a particular approach to solving a problem. Curtis and Becky were experiencing severe financial stress because of limited income and poor budgeting. They were not aware of low-fee money management counseling services in their community. However, making them aware of this resource did not start them toward active problem solving. When the therapist pointed out its availability, Becky and Curtis concluded that such assistance would not be effective in helping them balance their income and expenses (a low outcome expectancy). The therapist also asked them about the possibility of asking a wealthy relative for a temporary loan, but they believed that the relative was unlikely to respond favorably to such a request (a low efficacy expectancy). They also identified getting another part-time job as a way to increase their income, but they did not believe that they had the qualifications to be hired for a position that would provide sufficient income to make the hardships of extended work hours worthwhile (another low efficacy expectancy). Thus, adequate clinical assessment of a couple's resources requires careful consideration of the partners' cognitions about them.

A couple's success in adapting to demands of each other's unfulfilled needs is likely to be influenced by the ways that the partners perceive the demands. An individual might attribute a partner's desire for some autonomy as a reflection of a lack of love for him or her and therefore might be unsympathetic with the partner's efforts to maintain a boundary between them. The negative attribution about the partner's motives can contribute to anger and a desire to punish the partner. Other cognitions that can influence a couple's coping with positive demands are the partners' belief systems. For example, some people feel guilty or embarrassed about receiving positives that fulfill their needs because they hold beliefs that attending to one's own needs is selfish. Ralph experienced mixed feelings about receiving nurturing from Bonita. Although he felt calm and secure when she gave him emotional support, his parents had taught him that people do not respect individuals who depend on others, so he also experienced discomfort from accepting Bonita's caretaking.

A couple's past experiences can influence their cognitions concerning their ability to adapt to a current demand together (Baucom & Epstein, 1990). Past successes in adapting to demands together can help a couple develop self-confidence (i.e., high self-efficacy expectancies) for adapting to future life problems. Conversely, past failures may leave the couple with a generalized expectancy that they are incompetent as a team.

Maladaptation, Disorganized Functioning, and Potential for a Crisis State

A couple's failure to adapt effectively to demands in their life together can lead to chronic negative effects, including dissatisfaction with their relationship. Although chronic distress and dissatisfaction are significant problems in themselves, an imbalance between demands and a couple's adaptive abilities can escalate further, to the point of reaching a crisis state (Karney & Bradbury, 1995; H. I. McCubbin & Patterson, 1983; M. A. McCubbin & McCubbin, 1989). Stress theorists and researchers define a *crisis* as a state of disorganized functioning that results when life demands overwhelm an individual's, couple's, or family's coping efforts. For example, a couple's ability to adapt to financial problems may be overwhelmed if their reliance on their typical resources (e.g., working extra hours to provide more income) has become ineffective. If they also have catastrophic cognitions about the situation, such as believing that they are likely to face foreclosure on their mortgage, they may enter a crisis state. In contrast to life demands, which are *events* that create hardships for the couple, a crisis is a *state* of disequilibrium in which individual and dyadic functioning are disrupted and compromised. In a crisis state, the couple may experience a high level of emotional arousal, impaired cognitive abilities, physiological symptoms, and disorganized behavior (Greenstone & Leviton, 1993).

During a crisis state, individuals who typically function at a high level in their personal and work lives may find themselves unable to concentrate on relatively simple tasks, and they may be distressed by their marked mood fluctuations. At the dyadic level, a couple who has a long history of clear communication and mutually satisfying interactions may find themselves frustrated by misunderstandings and easily irritated by each other's behavior. It is common for partners who are in a crisis state to be very concerned about the implications of their disturbed individual and couples' functioning. Individuals who find themselves anxious or crying easily may fear that they are "having a nervous breakdown" and that they will never function well again. Similarly, members of a couple may fear that their relationship has "fallen apart" and is irreparably damaged. Because many couples seek the help of professionals only when their problems have deteriorated into a crisis state, it is important for therapists to evaluate the contrast between each couple's current and usual functioning. This information is important not only as a benchmark for assessing the couple's potential range of adaptive skills but also for providing the couple some reassuring feedback that the deterioration that they have seen in their functioning might be a temporary aspect of a crisis state.

When in a crisis state, a couple is at risk for resolving their disequilibrium through maladaptive responses, such as substance abuse, physical abuse, taking out ill-advised loans, and separating. However, they also have the potential to develop new means of restoring the balance between demands and their adaptive abilities (McKenry & Price, 2000). Because people who are in a crisis state are experiencing deterioration in their normal functioning, they may be unable to devise new adaptive strategies on their own and may require crisis intervention from an outsider, such as a couples therapist.

A couple whose functioning has deteriorated in the face of severe financial problems because of a member's sudden unemployment could be coached in initiating any of several new strategies to adapt to the demands of unemployment and financial difficulties. They could reduce the number or intensity of hardships they are experiencing by reducing other expenses, to have sufficient funds to make mortgage payments. They could acquire additional resources if the unemployed partner can find a new job, even if it is temporary and less desirable than the old one. They also could manage the subjective emotional arousal and other symptoms of the crisis state by engaging in physical exercise and expressing their emotions to each other in a nonblaming manner. Likewise, they could modify their negative appraisals of the situation by replacing blaming of the self and partner with a more positive focus on both individuals' good intentions and efforts to solve the couple's financial problems. M. A. McCubbin and McCubbin (1989) noted that the process of family adaptation to the overwhelming demands of life stressors during a crisis state involves the members' understanding that they can restore stability and satisfaction to their relationship by modifying their roles, interaction patterns, and ways of coping with their life demands. Effective adaptation during a crisis depends on the degree of pile-up of demands, the resources that can be tapped to eliminate demands or reduce their negative impacts, and cognitions that enhance positive coping. Even if an individual, couple, or family has experienced a crisis, their subsequent use of resources and their cognitions about their situation play crucial roles in determining long-term functioning (M. A. McCubbin & McCubbin, 1989). Thus, although it is preferable for a couple to avoid a crisis state in the first place by drawing on resources, reducing their vulnerabilities, and maintaining constructive cognitions, the development of a crisis can be not only a danger to the couple's viability but also an opportunity for growth.

SUMMARY

Our enhanced cognitive–behavioral model highlights the roles of demands, personal needs, environmental influences, and developmental changes while taking into account cognitive, behavioral, and affective components of individual and dyadic functioning. This application of an adaptation model of relationship functioning broadens the cognitive–behavioral model of couples' relationships and dysfunction, increasing opportunities for clinical intervention.

- The adaptation model of couples' functioning assumes that the degree to which couples adapt to demands in their relationship will determine the quality and stability of the relationship.

- Demands can result from positive or negative characteristics of the individuals, the couple relationship, and the environment.
- Adaptation to unfulfilled needs involves increasing the use of individual, couple, and environmental resources as well as considering dyadic and individual vulnerabilities.
- Couples must identify and modify cognitions regarding demands and their coping resources that have interfered with constructive adaptation.

II

CLINICAL ASSESSMENT
AND INTERVENTION

INTRODUCTION: CLINICAL ASSESSMENT AND INTERVENTION

In Part I we described the components of our enhanced cognitive–behavioral model of couples' functioning, emphasizing characteristics of the individual partners, their couple relationship, and the couple's interactions with their environment. In the following chapters, we describe systematic approaches to assessment and intervention with couples' relationships, focused on the components of the model.

Chapter 7 covers interview, questionnaire, and behavioral observation methods designed to assess behavioral, cognitive, and affective aspects of the individual, couple, and couple–environment components of the model. The assessment procedures described in chapter 7 produce a wealth of information about the individual partners and the couple, including factors influencing the partners' functioning in the past and present. On the basis of the assessment, the therapist determines (a) the demands that the partners have faced individually and as a couple; (b) the individual, couple, and environmental resources that the partners have had available and those that they have used; and (c) individual and couple characteristics that have acted as vulnerability factors. In chapter 7 we also describe how a therapist provides feedback to a couple concerning these factors and collaborates with the partners in setting therapy goals and priorities.

For a therapist to use these assessment data to help a couple, he or she must be able to manage the overall process of therapy, including engaging the couple in therapy, building an alliance with both partners, collaboratively setting treatment goals with the couple based on the results of the assessment, and defining the respective roles of the therapist and couple during and outside sessions. In chapter 8 we focus on these general procedures for conducting couples therapy.

In chapters 9, 10, and 11 we describe major cognitive–behavioral strategies and techniques for intervening with factors that interfere with couples' abilities to adapt to demands in their lives. These techniques address behavioral, cognitive, and emotional aspects of the demands that couples experience, the resources the couple uses to adapt to the demands, and vulnerability factors that interfere with adaptation.

In chapter 9 we provide an overview of two major types of behavioral interventions: (a) a wide variety of *guided behavior changes*, designed to address demands associated with meeting partners' needs, differences in partners' personality styles, an individual's psychopathology, aversive "secondary distress" behavior occurring when individuals' needs are unfulfilled, and so on, and (b) *skills-based interventions*, such as modification of communication, including patterns that partners use to discuss their thoughts and emotions and patterns involved in goal-oriented decision-making conversations. Our consideration of guided behavior changes is much broader than the concept of "behavior exchanges" that has been emphasized previously in the cognitive–behavioral couples therapy (CBCT) literature. Traditional behavior exchange interventions have focused on asking partners to reciprocate behaviors that the other finds pleasing and to decrease reciprocal negative behaviors. In contrast, our adaptation model identifies many types of behavior changes that will benefit couples and that do not involve remediation of skill deficits, and many of these changes do not involve any form of exchange or reciprocity between partners. For example, we have described situations in which the ways that a couple typically interact do not meet the partners' communally oriented and individually oriented needs well and in which a therapist can collaborate with the couple in devising specific behavior changes that will more effectively meet those needs. In chapter 9 we review interventions for structuring such behavior changes.

The second major type of behavioral interventions includes two kinds of communication that couples must be able to use effectively to adapt to demands in their lives. One involves a *couple's discussions* of the partners' thoughts and emotions, and the other involves collaborative *decision-making conversations* focused on finding solutions to issues the couple faces. Cognitive–behavioral couples therapists have traditionally emphasized skills involved in communicating well and have focused on teaching distressed couples specific communication skills that they assumed the couple would continue to use to maintain a satisfying relationship in the future. However, as we note in chapter 9, we often use communication exercises as types of "rehabilitation" procedures that modify existing problematic patterns, and we do not assume that it is necessary for couples to use those communication patterns indefinitely.

In chapter 10 we describe a variety of interventions that can be used to alter partners' distorted or inappropriate (e.g., unrealistic) cognitions about themselves, their couple relationship, or their environment. The technique traditionally most commonly associated with cognitive therapy involves *Socratic questioning*, in which the therapist engages in "collaborative empiricism" (J. S. Beck, 1995). The therapist asks the client a series of questions that evaluate the validity of his or her cognitions by examining available evidence that does or does nor support them. A second approach to cognitive restructuring, *guided discovery*, involves techniques that create new experiences that each partner can use to evaluate his or her thinking about the relationship. In chapter 10 we describe the advantages and disadvantages of using these two approaches in couples therapy and discuss the most appropriate ways to use them. The overall goal of cognitive restructuring within CBCT is to increase the range and flexibility of partners' cognitions regarding their relationships.

In chapter 11 we describe interventions focused on three major aspects of partners' emotional experiences within their relationships. First, some individuals have difficulty being aware of their emotions and thus appear to be underresponsive emotionally to events that occur in their couple relationships. We describe interventions designed to enhance these individuals' experience and expression of their emotions. As we discussed in chapters 3 and 4, other individuals are highly emotionally responsive to events in their lives, and they have difficulty regulating those responses. In chapter 11 we discuss several interventions used to increase clients' ability to regulate their emotions. Finally, members of couples vary in how constructively or destructively they communicate their emotions to each other. Drawing on behavioral interventions detailed in Chapter 9, we describe techniques for facilitating partners' constructive communication about their emotions.

Following the descriptions of major types of intervention techniques in chapters 9, 10, and 11, in chapter 12 we apply behavioral, cognitive, and affective interventions to address couples' difficulties in adapting to demands based on characteristics of the individuals. In chapter 13 we apply these interventions to demands involving the couple, and in chapter 14 we apply these interventions to demands involving the couple's environment. In chapter 14 we also describe ways of enhancing couples' positive involvement with their environment, individually and as a couple, to meet their needs. Finally, in chapter 15 we provide a summary of our model and therapeutic approach.

7

ASSESSMENT

In this chapter we describe the use of interviews, questionnaires, and behavioral observation to assess individual, couple, and environmental factors contributing to partners' concerns regarding their relationship. General goals and guidelines for conducting couples assessments are presented, followed by detailed descriptions of conjoint couple interviews, individual interviews, and the assessment feedback session. Special issues, such as the assessment of partner abuse and substance abuse, also are discussed.

For our enhanced cognitive–behavioral model to be useful in planning interventions, it must serve as a guide for clinical assessment. Our model provides a guide to characteristics of (a) the two individual members of a couple, (b) their dyadic interactions, and (c) their interactions with their environment that are relevant to planning an appropriate treatment. In this chapter we discuss the goals of assessment and the steps that provide the information needed in these three areas. We also describe the major modes of assessment—clinical interviews, questionnaires, and behavioral observations—that can be used to gather information. Finally, we explain how the therapist integrates the information and provides feedback to the couple, leading to collaboration with the couple in setting goals for therapy.

GOALS OF ASSESSMENT

The overall goals of assessment are as follows:

- To identify the problems for which a couple has sought assistance.
- To identify the factors in the couple's life that are influencing the presenting problems.
- To clarify whether couples therapy is appropriate for these clients.
- To identify existing strengths in the couple's relationship, which can be enhanced and used to help the couple resolve problems.

Our assessment focuses on identifying factors that influence the concerns that brought the couple to therapy. On the basis of the adaptation model described in chapter 6, we seek information about demands on the individual and couple that involve characteristics of the two individuals, their dyadic interactions, and influences of their environment. These demands may involve either negative stressors or difficulties in adapting to the partners' normal personality characteristics and positive communally and individually oriented needs. The assessment identifies current factors affecting a couple's functioning, but we also examine the relationship in a developmental context. The histories of the two partners as well as the history of the couple relationship, provide important information about their past experiences that may continue to have negative effects on the couple.

Sometimes one partner may be committed to improving the relationship, but the other wants to work out an amicable separation. Assessing the partners' goals is a crucial early step that has major implications for subsequent interventions. If one or both members intend to end the relationship, the major goal becomes finding constructive ways for the couple to disengage from each other and, if they have children, to reduce stress on them as much as possible.

Even when both partners are committed to improving their relationship, the therapist needs to determine whether conjoint sessions are appropriate or whether one or both partners would benefit from individual therapy for personal issues. These issues might include psychopathology or unresolved issues such as trauma in the family of origin, which affect the individual and do not appear to be caused by the couple relationship.

In addition to assessing the individual, couple, and environmental resources that a couple currently is using, the therapist inquires about resources they have used in the past and others that might be tapped more effectively. It also is important to identify beliefs that block partners from using resources, such as a view that accepting help from others is a sign of personal weakness.

A structured assessment period typically precedes the beginning of treatment. The initial assessment begins with one or two joint interviews, each lasting approximately an hour, with a focus on identifying the couple's concerns, taking a history of their relationship, and obtaining a behavioral sample of their communication. Unless a couple presents with a relatively circumscribed problem and has a relatively uncomplicated relationship history, it is likely that two joint sessions will be required for this initial dyadic assessment. Next, the therapist typically conducts a 1-hour individual interview with each partner, to gather information on his or her personal history and current functioning (occupational, relationships, psychopathology symptoms, etc.). Finally, the therapist has a 1-hour meeting with the couple, to provide them feedback from the assessment and to collaborate with them in setting goals for therapy.

Beyond the initial structured couple and individual interviews, assessment is an ongoing process throughout therapy. Quite often, members of a couple reveal more information about themselves as they become more familiar and comfortable with the therapist. Ongoing assessment of the characteristics of the couple and its two members steadily creates a more complete picture of the factors affecting the quality of the couple's relationship.

STEPS AND METHODS OF ASSESSMENT

The assessment of a couple is conducted in a series of steps:

- The initial identification of presenting problems and the partners' goals in seeking therapy, based on the initial phone contact, possible use of self-report questionnaires, and the presenting problems identified by the couple in the first session.
- A relationship history and assessment of current relationship functioning (including observation of the couple's interaction patterns).
- Individual history and current functioning of each partner.
- The therapist's assessment feedback summary to the couple.

At the conclusion of the initial assessment, the therapist and couple collaborate in setting therapy goals.

SOURCES OF ASSESSMENT DATA: INTERVIEWS, QUESTIONNAIRES, AND BEHAVIORAL OBSERVATION

In clinical practice, we base our assessment of couples' behaviors, cognitions, and emotions on interviews with the couple and each individual, self-report questionnaires, and direct behavioral observation of the partners' interactions. As is typical in couple and family assessment (Snyder, Cavell, Heffer, & Mangrum, 1995), we rely heavily on interviews in our data collection. On the one hand, clinicians need to be cautious about some characteristics of individual and conjoint interviews that may limit the reliability and validity of the information collected. For example, some individuals may be reluctant to reveal particular types of information in the presence of their partners during joint interviews and will more readily report the information on questionnaires or in individual interviews (Snyder et al., 1995). This is especially likely when an individual has been abused by the partner and fears retaliation for revealing the abuse to the therapist (a special issue that we address later in this chapter). Other individuals may be motivated to describe themselves in a positive light during individual and joint interviews and to convince the therapist of the partner's responsibility for relationship problems, thus presenting skewed information. Furthermore, because of "sentiment override" (Weiss, 1980), an individual's negative feelings elicited by the presence of his or her partner in joint interviews may lead the individual to remember and report negative aspects of the couple's relationship and overlook positives. In contrast, some individuals may be more likely to endorse items on structured questionnaires that describe positive characteristics of a partner and relationship, because they are not currently being provoked by the partner's negative responses.

On the other hand, self-report questionnaires can be susceptible to response biases similar to those that affect interviews, such as biased presentations of the self and partner (Snyder et al., 1995). In addition, questionnaires do not allow the clinician to gather information about each partner's idiosyncratic experiences, and individuals may vary widely in their interpretations of structured questionnaire items. In contrast, clinical interviews allow a clinician to ask follow-up questions to clarify partners' responses. Furthermore, joint interviews serve as opportunities to observe a couple's interactions as well as each person's reactions to the ways that the other person describes their relationship to the therapist. In fact, we assume that the two individuals' reports during joint interviews are subjective, reflecting their cognitions about themselves, each other, and their relationship (Epstein, Pretzer, & Fleming, 1987). The joint interview allows the therapist to assess discrepancies in partners' views as well as the couple's emotional (e.g., anger) and behavioral (e.g., criticism) responses to these differences. Thus, the therapist is cautious regarding the reliability and validity of partners' reports during individual and joint interviews, and even turns the limitations of partners' subjective reports to an advantage by observing how the couple deal with each other's cognitions about their relationship. The therapist evaluates the reliability and validity of the individuals' interview responses by noting the degree of consistency from one interview to another in their self-reports about particular aspects of the relationship and by comparing self-reports with the therapist's own observations of the couple's interactions during sessions. For example, the members of a couple may consistently disagree about the level of equity in their decision making, but when they discuss possible solutions to issues during sessions, the therapist may observe that the balance of power is more skewed than one partner portrays it.

Direct sampling of a couple's behavioral interactions also has both advantages and disadvantages (Jacob & Tennenbaum, 1988; Snyder et al., 1995). Even though members of a couple may attempt to behave in a socially desirable manner in front of a therapist, as they become involved in discussing issues with each other, they commonly become emotionally engaged in the process and reveal at least some natural reactions toward each other (Baucom & Epstein, 1990). However, specific behaviors elicited in the therapist's office in response to instructions to communicate or reach a decision concerning a relationship issue may have limited relevance to the couple's daily interactions (Snyder et al., 1995).

Judicious use of select questionnaires can be an important adjunct to interviews and behavioral assessment. Although they are susceptible to response biases, they can provide a quick overview of areas of strength and concern in a couple's relationship. Because individuals' self-reports concerning their relationship are subjective, two partners' reports may be discrepant, and the therapist can draw such differences to the couple's attention as a way of initiating discussions of the important role that cognition plays in one's relationship.

Given the advantages and disadvantages involved in each approach to assessment, we use a multimethod approach that includes interviews, questionnaires, and behavioral observation (Jacob & Tennenbaum, 1988; Snyder et al., 1995). In the following sections we describe such a multimethod assessment.

We now turn to a description of a typical sequence of assessment procedures.

INITIAL PHONE CONTACT

The partner who makes the first phone contact with the therapist provides initial information about problems that the couple is experiencing; for example, a partner's depression, conflicts about finances, or an affair. Some callers take this opportunity to give a detailed description of their perceptions of the couple's issues. In some cases, the individual merely feels a need to express distress to someone who will listen. In other cases, however, the caller may attempt to establish an alliance with the therapist by portraying the relationship problems as being the partner's fault. It is difficult to assess the motivation of the other partner from the caller's descriptions, so the therapist considers them to be the caller's subjective experience and waits to obtain more direct information from the other person. Because couples therapists need to maintain balance in their relationships with the partners, it is wise to acknowledge that the caller is distressed, note that it is appropriate to seek help for relationship problems, and stress that the therapist looks forward to meeting with the couple to learn more about their relationship.

At times, the therapist needs to decide how to proceed when the caller reports that the partner is unwilling to participate in therapy. We discuss the therapist's options for handling such situations in chapter 8. The remainder of this chapter is based on the assumption that both members of a couple have agreed to attend the assessment sessions.

ADMINISTRATION OF SELF-REPORT QUESTIONNAIRES

When a therapist chooses to administer a set of questionnaires to the members of a couple, they might be mailed to the couple after the initial phone contact, to be completed and returned to the therapist before the first session. This approach allows the therapist to review the findings and incorporate follow-up questions into the interviews. We inform couples that we do not intend to keep their questionnaire responses confidential from their partners and will feel free to share them as seems appropriate in joint sessions. An important exception is the use of scales to screen for physical and psychological abuse occurring in a couple's relationship. We believe it is best to avoid placing individuals at risk for punishment or abuse from a partner for revealing these problems. Consequently, we believe that therapists should administer questionnaires on abuse when each person arrives for an individual interview. One scale that can be used in such circumstances, the revised Conflict Tactics Scale (CTS2; Straus, Hamby, Boney-McCoy, & Sugarman, 1996), is described in the later section on Partners' Individual Histories and Current Functioning.

We now describe some scales that we have found especially useful for assessing particular aspects of couples' relationships, although we do not routinely use any one of them in clinical practice. Therapists who would like to consider a variety of other useful instruments can consult reference volumes on couple and family assessment such as the one edited by Touliatos, Perlmutter, and Straus (1990).

Two measures that survey an *individual's perceptions of the quality of the couple's relationship* in somewhat different ways are the Dyadic Adjustment Scale (DAS; Spanier, 1976) and the Marital Satisfaction Inventory (MSI; Snyder, 1979, 1997; Snyder & Aikman, 1999; Snyder, Wills, & Keiser, 1981). They tap major areas of relationship functioning such as affection, finances, sexual intimacy, leisure time, quality of communication, and so forth. Discrepancies in partners' perceptions can be discussed during the assessment feedback session.

The DAS has been used extensively in research studies on couples' relationships as well as in clinical practice (Busby, Christensen, Crane, & Larson, 1995; Touliatos et al., 1990). Spanier's (1976) original scale construction procedures, including a factor analysis, resulted in a set of 32 items that comprise four subscales: Consensus, Cohesion, Affectional Expression, and Satisfaction. However, the subscales are highly intercorrelated; the total-scale Cronbach's alpha has been found to be .96 (Spanier, 1976), and some investigators' factor analyses have failed to replicate Spanier's original subscales (e.g., Crane, Busby, & Larson, 1991; Sharpley & Cross, 1982; Spanier & Thompson, 1982). Consequently, it generally is recommended that only the total score be used, as an index of global relationship adjustment or satisfaction (Kazak, Jarmas, & Snitzer, 1988). Although there has been controversy as to whether the DAS assesses relationship "adjustment" or "distress," substantial research evidence indicates that the DAS taps partners' overall sentiment or subjective feelings concerning their relationship, which are related to other indexes of relationship quality, such as communication quality and relationship standards (Gordon, Baucom, Rankin, Burnett, & Epstein, 1999; Touliatos et al., 1990). The DAS also reliably differentiates distressed from nondistressed couples (Crane, Allgood, Larson, & Griffin, 1990). Concerning the utility of the DAS, its widespread use has resulted in norms that the therapist may find useful in gauging a couple's satisfaction. In addition, the first 15 DAS items assess the degree to which each partner views the couple as agreeing or disagreeing about major areas of their relationship, such as finances, career decisions, affection, and time spent together. The clinician can use those items to quickly identify particular areas of conflict in a couple's relationship, for further assessment through interviews.

Busby et al. (1995) created a 14-item Revised DAS by deleting DAS items that were heterogeneous (i.e., assessing content that was different from content of any other items). Although the Revised DAS lacks the extensive research evidence of the original DAS, Busby et al. reported good internal consistency and validity evidence for the measure, and its brevity is an advantage in clinical assessment. On the other hand, with only 6 items assessing consensus between partners about key areas of their relationship, the therapist is limited in identifying a couple's areas of conflict.

Snyder (1979) developed the original 280-item MSI to provide a multidimensional measure of relationship quality, with a Global Satisfaction subscale, a Conventionalization (social desirability) subscale, and nine subscales assessing different aspects of couples' interaction (Affective Communication, Problem-Solving Communication, Leisure Time Together, Disagreement About Finances, Sexual Dissatisfaction, Role Orientation, Family of Origin History of Distress, Dissatisfaction With Children, and Conflict Over Childrearing). The original MSI subscales were found to have good internal consistency, test–retest reliability, and ability to differentiate between couples in therapy and those who sought no assistance for relationship problems (Snyder et al., 1981; Touliatos et al., 1990). The Marital Satisfaction Inventory—Revised (MSI–R) was subsequently developed (Snyder, 1997; Snyder & Aikman, 1999) with a more extensive and geographically diverse standardization sample and psychometric evaluations. The new 150-item instrument, which is written at a sixth-grade reading level and in a manner relevant to nonmarried and same-sex couples as well as married heterosexual couples, can be completed in less than 30 min. It includes two validity scales—Inconsistency (in responding to item content) and Conventionalization—a Global Distress scale (the best single MSI–R index of an individual's overall feelings about the relationship), and 10 scales assessing specific areas of relationship distress (the original 9 subscales plus a new one assessing intimidation and physical aggression). Studies on the MSI–R have found scale internal consistency coefficients averaging .82 (excluding the Inconsistency scale), test–retest coefficients averaging .79, and evidence of convergent and discriminant validity in relation to external measures completed by couples and clinical raters (Snyder, 1997; Snyder & Aikman, 1999). The MSI allows the clinician to plot profiles of two partners' scores on the set of subscales, comparing partners' levels of concerns in the various areas of their relationship and identifying how each person's concerns compare with established norms (Snyder & Aikman, 1999), and a computerized interpretive report is available. Thus, the MSI can be useful for identifying significant issues in a couple's relationship, which can be explored further through clinical interviews; however, its utility for this purpose must be weighed against the considerable length of the scale. As with the DAS, there is evidence that individuals' scores on the various MSI scales are influenced by their overall positive versus negative feelings about their relationship (Jacob & Tennenbaum, 1988).

We have described the clinical use of these measures of the global quality of a couple's relationship in more detail elsewhere (Baucom & Epstein, 1990). As just described, their total scores can be used in the initial assessment for judging the degree of distress in a relationship; however, the scales can be even more valuable if the therapist examines both partners' responses to individual items, for identification of specific areas of conflict or dissatisfaction that can be targeted in treatment.

Concerning the assessment of *need fulfillment*, Prager and Buhrmester's (1998) Need Fulfillment Inventory (NFI) focuses on the degrees to which one perceives that one's needs are being met in the relationship. The NFI has 20 subscales assessing human needs within three major groups: (a) *agentic*, corresponding to those needs that we label individually oriented (e.g., autonomy, achievement, power, self-actualization), (b) *communal* (e.g., companionship, nurturance, intimacy, sexual fulfillment), and (c) *survival* (e.g., health, food, physical safety). The 20 needs were identified from cluster analyses of large lists of human needs derived from theoretical and empirical literature. Prager and Buhrmester wrote 5–6 NFI items to assess each of the needs, and the respondent is asked to indicate how important the need is to him or her and the degree to which the need currently is being satisfied. When undergraduate students' responses to the 20 subscales were subjected to a factor analysis, the result was three factors with eigenvalues greater than

1, representing Agentic, Communal, and Survival needs. The Cronbach's alpha coefficients for the 20 subscales ranged from .93 to .73, and those for the items loading highest on the Agentic, Communal and Survival factors were .95, .91 and .58, respectively. Evidence for the validity of the NFI Agentic and Communal factors included positive correlations with measures of life satisfaction, dyadic adjustment, self-esteem, and job satisfaction as well as negative correlations with measures of depression, trait anxiety, and loneliness (Prager & Buhrmester, 1998). Prager and Buhrmester found similar validity results in a second study in which members of couples used a reduced 50-item version of the NFI to describe both their own and their partners' needs.

For assessing the degree to which each partner's *sexual intimacy needs* are being met in the relationship, the therapist can use the Sexual Interaction Inventory (SII; LoPiccolo & Steger, 1974) or the Golombok–Rust Inventory of Sexual Satisfaction (GRISS; Rust & Golombok, 1986a) to screen for sexual satisfaction and dysfunctions. The SII is a 102-item scale that assesses "dissatisfaction with frequency and range of sexual behaviors engaged in, self-acceptance, pleasure obtained from sexual activity, accurate knowledge of partner's preferred sexual activities, and acceptance of partner" (LoPiccolo & Daiss, 1987, p. 200). Using a 6-point Likert scale, the respondent answers 6 questions about each of 17 types of sexual behavior within a heterosexual couple's relationship: 7 concerning the female's actions toward the male, 7 concerning the male's actions toward the female, and 3 regarding mutual interaction. For each type of behavior, the respondent reports its frequency of occurrence as well as each partner's real and ideal levels of satisfaction with that behavior. The 11 scales derived from the SII reveal a variety of aspects of the couple's experience and concerns within their sexual relationship, such as how satisfied each partner is with the frequency of each type of sexual behavior, how much the partners agree regarding the occurrence of particular behaviors, and the degree to which individuals perceive accurately their partner's views and satisfaction with sexual behaviors. LoPiccolo and Steger (1974) reported good internal consistency for the SII subscales, ranging from .85 to .93 as well as adequate 2-week test–retest reliability, ranging from .67 to .90. In addition, the SII discriminates couples who sought therapy for sexual problems from couples who are satisfied with their sexual relationships, and it is sensitive to improvement in sexual functioning due to treatment (Jacob & Tennenbaum, 1988).

The GRISS (Rust & Golombok, 1986a, 1986b) includes 28 items that compose 12 subscales assessing male and female sexual problems and dysfunctions (e.g., premature ejaculation, impotence, vaginismus, female anorgasmia, male avoidance of sex, female avoidance of sex, male dissatisfaction, female dissatisfaction, infrequency, noncommunication about sex). Each member of a couple uses a 5-point Likert scale to indicate how often each item applies to the couple. Rust and Golombok (1986b) reported total-scale split–half reliabilities of .94 and .87 for women and men, respectively, and subscale split–half reliabilities ranging from .61 to .83. The GRISS also discriminates between sex therapy clients and control individuals who have no sexual problems, and GRISS scores are correlated significantly with therapist ratings of client sexual problems as well as with ratings of improvement in therapy.

Inventories such as the SII and GRISS can be very useful in screening for the existence of particular sources of sexual dissatisfaction or dysfunction, but they do not identify the context and meanings that the sexual behaviors have within the couple's relationship. For example, if a person feels that a partner is generally too intrusive, that person might try to distance him- or herself sexually. Such avoidance is different from anxiety regarding or even aversion to sexual behavior, which may have its roots in an individual's past traumatic sexual experiences. To assess such patterns, the therapist must supplement information from the self-report measure with interviews with the couple and individuals. Overall, we do not routinely administer either the SII or the GRISS, but we do inquire about the quality of the couple's sexual relationship during the initial couple interview and, when there is evidence of sexual concerns, these questionnaires can be used to gather more detailed data. Given that many individuals initially are uncomfortable disclosing sexual information to a stranger, questionnaires provide an opportunity for them to let the therapist know about sexual concerns in a less direct way.

H. I. McCubbin and Patterson's (1987) 71-item Family Inventory of Life Events and Changes (FILE) can help partners identify *demands* they have faced. Its items, which compose nine subscales, describe normative and nonnormative events that may occur, including conflict among family members, pregnancy and childbearing, finances and business, changes in work status, work–family role strain, illnesses and caretaking responsibilities, child care, losses through deaths and endings of relationships, transitions of a family member into or out of the home, and legal issues. The FILE can provide a therapist with a quick screening for various stressful experiences that have occurred during the past year within the couple's relationship and within their environment, which can be explored further through interviews for their impact on the individuals and couple. H. I. McCubbin and Patterson (1987) reported a Cronbach's alpha of .81 for the total scale. The subscale alphas range from .72 to .16, but the FILE taps a wide variety of life demands that in many cases seem unlikely to co-occur within a couple's relationship, so internal consistency indices may be an inadequate reflection of this instrument's value in clinical assessment. In contrast, the 4-week test–retest reliabilities are .80 for the total scale and .64–.84 for the subscales. Evidence of the FILE's validity as an index of stressful life events includes its ability to differentiate high-conflict families from low-conflict families and its correlations with other measures of family functioning (H. I. McCubbin & Patterson,

1987). We believe that it is most useful for the therapist to administer the FILE either before or at the beginning of the initial couples assessment interview, scan the partners' responses, and ask them about any items that one or both of them has reported. As with other questionnaires, the therapist needs to explore the impact of each life experience on the members of a couple by interviewing them.

For *self-report measures of behavioral interactions* Weiss, Hops, and Patterson (1973) developed the Areas-of-Change Questionnaire (A-C) to assess marital dissatisfaction in terms of the degree to which members of a couple want each other to make specific types of behavioral changes. The A-C has two parts; the first asks the respondent how much change, on a 7-point scale ranging from +3 (*much more*) to –3 (*much less*), he or she wants the partner to make for each of 34 types of behavior. The content of the items addresses emotional expression, companionship, finances, relatives, friends, sex, child management, housework, leisure time, work habits, and so on. For example, an item states, "I want my partner to participate in decisions about spending money." In the second part of the A-C, the respondent uses the same items to indicate how much change the partner wants him or her to make.

In a review of the A-C, Jacob and Tennenbaum (1988) noted that it has demonstrated good internal consistency, split–half reliability, and test–retest reliability as well as negative correlations (ranging from –.42 to –.70) of its total score with measures of global marital distress. It also reliably differentiates groups of distressed and nondistressed couples and reflects positive changes over the course of couples therapy. Nevertheless, the advantage of the A-C in clinical assessment is in the inspection of both partners' responses to individual items, to identify both the areas of strength in the relationship (in which little or no change is desired) and the areas that can be targeted for change in therapy (Baucom & Epstein, 1990). Moreover, comparison of partners' responses may reveal discrepancies between the behaviors that one person wants a partner to change and the degree to which the partner perceives that the person desires such changes (Margolin, Talovic, & Weinstein, 1983). The breadth of the behaviors surveyed by the A-C makes it a valuable screening measure.

Christensen and his colleagues (Christensen, 1988; Christensen & Heavey, 1990; Christensen & Shenk, 1991) developed the 35-item Communication Patterns Questionnaire (CPQ) to assess partners' perceptions of dyadic patterns in their *communication concerning conflictual areas* in their relationship. Using a 9-point Likert response scale (that ranges from *very unlikely* to *very likely*), each member of a couple reports whether particular dyadic patterns occur at three points: when a relationship problem arises, during a discussion of a problem, and after such a discussion. The CPQ has subscales assessing Mutual Constructive Communication (e.g., mutual discussion of problems and expression of feelings), Demand–Withdraw Communication (man demands–woman withdraws, woman demands–man withdraws, and total demand–withdraw for the couple), and Mutual Avoidance. On a clinical level, a therapist also may use some additional unscored CPQ items to identify mutual verbal and physical aggression. Studies with the CPQ have found adequate subscale internal consistencies; for example, Christensen and Shenk (1991) found subscale Cronbach's alphas with a mean of .71 and a range from .62 to .86. Validity of the CPQ has been demonstrated in its ability to differentiate nondistressed, clinic, and divorcing couples as well as in its correlations with measures of relationship satisfaction. The wording of the CPQ items limits its use to heterosexual couples.

Numerous reliable and valid scales are available for the assessment of *relationship cognitions*, such as the Marital Attitude Survey (MAS; Pretzer, Epstein, & Fleming, 1991), which assesses attributions and expectancies; the Relationship Belief Inventory (RBI; Eidelson & Epstein, 1982); and the Inventory of Specific Relationship Standards (ISRS; Baucom, Epstein, Rankin, & Burnett, 1996). The MAS includes subscales assessing the degree to which an individual attributes relationship problems to his or her own personality, own behavior, the partner's personality, the partner's behavior, the partner's lack of love, and the partner's malicious intent. It also includes subscales assessing expectancies: the degree to which the individual believes the couple has the ability to improve problems in their relationship and the degree to which they will effect such change. The MAS has demonstrated internal consistency coefficients ranging from .93 to .58 and validity in its correlations with indexes of relationship satisfaction and communication quality (Epstein et al., 1987; Pretzer et al., 1991).

The RBI (Eidelson & Epstein, 1982; Epstein & Eidelson, 1981) includes five scales assessing potentially unrealistic beliefs about couple relationships: disagreement is destructive, partners should be able to mind-read each other's thoughts and feelings, partners cannot change their relationship, relationship problems are due to innate differences between men and women, and one must be a perfect sexual partner. Overall, the RBI subscales have demonstrated varying reliability and validity, but the RBI has served well as an overall index of dysfunctional relationship beliefs (Bradbury & Fincham, 1993).

We and our colleagues (Baucom, Epstein, Daiuto, et al., 1996; Baucom, Epstein, Rankin, & Burnett, 1996) developed the 60-item ISRS to assess partners' personal standards concerning the major relationship dimensions of *boundaries* (the degree of togetherness vs. autonomy between partners), *expressive* and *instrumental investment* (time and energy one puts into the relationship), and *power/control* (how decision-making power is distributed between partners). For each of these dimensions the ISRS includes items assessing the individual's standards within 12 different areas of relationship functioning (e.g., household tasks, relationships with friends, sexual interaction, parenting, negative communication, and positive communication). An example of an ISRS item is, "My partner and I should have the same views on religious or philosophical issues." Each item has three sections, asking how much the respondent believes a characteristic should be true of the couple's relationship, whether he or she is satisfied with the way the standard is met in the relationship, and how upset he or she would be if the standard were not met. The ISRS subscales assessing the major dimensions of standards have Cronbach's alphas ranging from .77 to .65 (computed separately for women and men), and their validity has been demonstrated in correlations with measures of relationship satisfaction, communication patterns, and attributions (Baucom, Epstein, Daiuto, et al., 1996; Baucom, Epstein, Rankin, & Burnett, 1996). Although we use these cognitive measures in our research, in clinical practice we primarily assess clients' cognitions through interviews. Nevertheless, clinicians can administer these measures to help ensure a broad assessment or use them as guides for interviews.

JOINT ASSESSMENT SESSION

The major goals of the initial joint interview (one or two sessions, depending on the amount of material that a couple presents) are to:

- Begin to establish a balanced working relationship with the two partners.
- Obtain an initial description from each partner about the reasons for seeking therapy (and the agendas for therapy and the relationship).
- Inform the couple about the general procedures of a cognitive–behavioral approach.
- Establish guidelines for appropriate therapist and client behavior during sessions.
- Obtain a relationship history.
- Assess the current functioning of the relationship.

It is likely that the therapist will obtain information about some aspects of each partner's history and current functioning during the joint assessment session as well.

Beginning to Establish a Balanced Therapeutic Relationship

Given that the therapist usually has spoken with only one member of the couple in setting up the appointment, it is important to convey an interest in hearing equally from the two parties:

Therapist: Marion, I spoke only briefly with John when he called about making an appointment, so I don't know much about why the two of you decided to contact me. During this session, I would like to get both of your views on how your relationship is going, and how I might be of help to you. I also want to let you know how I work with couples. So (looking back and forth between the partners), how did you decide to contact me, and how might I be helpful?

The therapist also demonstrates balance by limiting how long each partner talks. If one individual speaks for a long time, the therapist can say something such as,

Lydia, it's been helpful to get your perspective on that; I'd also like to hear how Jason feels about it. Getting both of your views helps me understand your relationship. So, Jason, what are your thoughts about the ways that the two of you have handled finances?

When partners voice different opinions about events that have occurred between them, it is important for the therapist to communicate respect for each person's views. Furthermore, whenever one person attempts to blame the other for his or her own actions (e.g., a physically abusive individual suggests that the partner incited the abuse; an individual who had an affair states that it was caused by neglect by the partner), the therapist focuses on personal responsibility for one's actions.

Brief Statement of Why the Couple Is Seeking Assistance

We explain to the couple that three to four sessions will likely be required to gain an adequate understanding of the relationship and to devise an appropriate treatment plan. However, if a couple is experiencing a crisis, such as physical violence or the need to make an immediate decision regarding a job opportunity in another location, the circumstances of the crisis become the top priority. Nevertheless, it is important for the therapist to return to a more thorough assessment as soon as possible.

The goal of this inquiry is to obtain an overview of the partners' concerns. In general, couples feel a need to express their concerns, giving the therapist a sense of the issues they are facing. However, the opportunity for distressed partners to express their feelings to an outsider can lead to blaming and create a negative atmosphere in the first session. It is crucial that the therapist intervene to prevent either member of the couple from feeling that coming to therapy sessions is aversive and is to be avoided. The therapist can clarify that sessions are to be a safe place for thinking about and working on problems and that both partners are to present their concerns in a nonblaming way. One way to control adversarial interactions is to request that each partner speak directly to the therapist rather than to the other person.

The initial discussion of the couple's issues is likely to give the therapist information about demands the couple is facing, involving characteristics of the individuals, their dyadic interaction, and their environment. In addition, the therapist might hear about the attributions the partners make about the causes of their problems. Sometimes the partners spontaneously describe their attributions (e.g., "He's spending more time at work because he's tired of being with me"), but at other times the therapist might ask about them (e.g., "Joan, what are your ideas about why Art has been spending more time at work?"). After this brief discussion about the couple's presenting concerns, the therapist shifts to an interview about the history of the couple's relationship, to learn about the developmental context for the current concerns.

Relationship History

Purposes of Taking a Relationship History

Taking a relationship history serves several purposes:

- To understand how a couple's relationship has developed over time.
- To address more positive aspects of the relationship in contrast to the current distress.
- To observe each partner's affective style and current degree of engagement in the relationship as the partners review significant events in their history.

Understanding the relationship's development. Several areas need to be assessed concerning factors that have shaped a couple's relationship over time. What demands have the partners experienced previously, and how did they adapt to them? To what extent have the past demands continued into the present? Do the partners blame each other or themselves for past problems, and are there any unresolved negative feelings about those past events (e.g., anger over an affair)? What individual, couple, and environmental resources were available to the couple for dealing with past demands; which ones were used; how helpful were they; are they still available; and are there any new resources that could be used now? Have the members of the couple failed to use available resources because they considered it inappropriate to do so (e.g., viewing it as a weakness to ask relatives for temporary financial assistance)?

Assessing positive aspects of the relationship. When the therapist asks the partners to describe when and how they met, what attracted them to each other, how they spent time together early in the relationship, and how they started thinking about being together for the long term, even members of distressed couples often recall some positive memories and feelings. This focus on more positive earlier times can help counterbalance the negativism that couples experience when they seek therapy. For some couples, this reminder that they related in satisfying ways in the past can generate some hope that current problems can be overcome.

Some individuals derive little pleasure from recalling past positive events because their current global negative feelings dominate their experience of the relationship. In fact, some people who currently feel very negative about their partners tend to "rewrite history," remembering the courtship period as negative as well. It is important for the therapist to be aware of such a negative bias and deal with it during the therapeutic interventions.

Assessment of partners' emotional responsiveness and engagement in the relationship. The therapist may observe that one or both individuals have difficulty regulating emotions when the other person says something provocative or critical. Some clients censor such responses during the initial sessions and reveal them only after becoming more comfortable with the therapist, but those with significant emotion regulation problems may be unable to control their responses even during the first contact. In contrast to this overreactivity, some other individuals exhibit neutral or flat affect. The therapist needs to determine whether such affect reflects clinical depression in an individual who considers his or her relationship important or whether it indicates that the person has disengaged emotionally from the partner. In chapter 12 we describe interventions for individuals who are emotionally disengaged.

Individuals who have become emotionally disengaged from their partners commonly exhibit no significant positive or negative feelings when asked to recall the early stages of the relationship or to discuss the current state of the relationship. In contrast, a depressed partner is likely to report that the relationship is unfulfilling and the situation seems hopeless. The therapist needs to address a disengaged person's lack of motivation and reach an understanding with the couple concerning the appropriateness of couples therapy. Some disengaged partners resist open-ended therapy because they are unwilling to make such a commitment to the relationship; however, they are willing to experiment with a trial period of therapy. In some cases positive changes produced by these sessions give the person sufficient renewed hope for change in the relationship such that he or she decides to continue with further treatment.

Developmental Structure of the Relationship History

Depending on the length of the couple's relationship, the complexity of their lives, and their verbal skills, the relationship history interview may require a full session. A semistructured format for the history is presented in Exhibit 7.1. For married heterosexual couples the interview is divided into three broad time periods: (a) initial interactions and attractions; (b) serious relationship prior to marriage, that is, courtship and how the individuals decided to form a committed relationship; and (c) the relationship since marriage, including developmental events such as the births of children, new jobs, and deaths of parents. For heterosexual and homosexual couples who are not legally married but are in long-term committed relationships, the second and third stages of the history address the period when the relationship became serious but did not yet include an explicit commitment and

EXHIBIT 7.1
Relationship History Interview Outline

Initial interactions and attractions
- How and where the couple met; other people involved in their meeting
- Each person's positive and negative life circumstances at the time
- Characteristics that attracted each person to the other
- Shared activities and how each person felt about them

Serious relationship prior to marriage or comparable committed relationship
- Amount and quality of the couple's interaction (shared time and activities, affection, arguments, quality of communication and decision making)
- Positive and/or negative thoughts and emotions about forming a committed relationship
- Involvements with each other's families, friends, etc.
- Significant events that had positive or negative effects on the relationship

Relationship since marriage or similar explicit commitment
- Circumstances surrounding the decision to get married or make a similar explicit commitment
- Any differences in the partners' levels of readiness to make the commitment; each person's feelings about life changes that he or she anticipated would result from the commitment
- Degrees to which the partners' initial attracting qualities are still present
- Degree of support for the relationship from each person's significant others
- Significant changes that occurred in the relationship (e.g., one person moving into the other's home, formation of stepfamily relationships, merging of partners' financial assets)
- Major positive and negative events involving characteristics of the individuals, the couple, or the environment that have had impacts on the relationship, and the couple's responses to them
- Signs each person noticed that indicated difficulties in the relationship, actions taken to deal with the problems, and changes in the issues over time

then the period after such an explicit commitment was made. The primary emphasis with all couples is placed on the last two stages.

Initial interactions and attractions. The characteristics that attracted each partner to the other can provide clues about ways that each partner antici-pated the relationship would meet his or her needs. There also may be clues about the quality of each person's individual functioning, which can be pur-sued during the individual interviews. For example, Lorena reported that she had a chronic problem with low self-esteem, and she found Paul's interest in her and his respectful behavior to be very attractive. The therapist noted that Lorena's personal difficulties might have influenced her initial attrac-tion to Paul's low-keyed manner, which she now finds frustrating.

Serious relationship prior to marriage or comparable committed relationship. The transition that the partners made toward a psychologically and behav-iorally committed relationship commonly involves (a) thinking of oneself as committed to a monogamous, long-term relationship, (b) communicating the commitment to the partner, and (c) making the commitment public (e.g., telling relatives and friends, purchasing an engagement ring). For many individuals this experience is primarily positive, but others are ambivalent as they face the prospect of reducing their autonomy and making decisions that can affect the rest of their lives. Potential conflicts between partners' needs may seem more significant at this point.

In addition, this stage commonly involves increased involvement with one's partner's network of family, friends, and coworkers. Those relationships vary in quality and impact on the couple. For example, each person's family of origin might enthusiastically accept his or her commitment to the partner, or they may have mixed or even negative reactions. As the couple's world expands beyond their own interactions to relationships with significant others, their ability to adapt to these more complex relationships is tested.

Relationship since marriage. Whether a couple has a legally sanctioned marriage or a personally sanctioned ritual symbolizing the union, the event has significant psychological consequences for the partners, in addition to practical ones involving obligations and responsibilities. For many couples, a wedding ceremony deepens their sense of intimacy and security. On the other hand, some couples identify their wedding as the point when their problems increased; perhaps one partner began to feel trapped by the legal obligations of marriage. Sometimes one partner was more ready for commitment than the other. In some cases an individual's relatives who have felt ambivalent about the couple's relationship become more accepting after the wedding, but others may reject the person's partner or the couple.

In addition, marriage often leads each person to focus on other life changes that might occur during this stage of life, such as having children and buying a home. The partners may agree on whether and when these events should occur, or there may be differences that can develop into significant conflicts. Thus, the relationship history interview should survey the partners' beliefs about what events should accompany this significant stage of life.

Conducting a Relationship History Interview

Balancing input from the two partners. To obtain information from the perspectives of both partners, the clinician can pose questions to both of them, looking at both partners and allowing either person to respond. It would be laborious to obtain both persons' views on every issue, but the therapist can use nonverbal cues to help evaluate whether the couple agree on one person's expressed opinion. The therapist also can state that he or she realizes the partners may not have the same memories or feelings about all past events, and if one person disagrees with what the other has said, it would be important to express it. It also is important for the therapist to enforce a guideline about taking turns expressing views in sessions, because many partners interrupt each other when they disagree with what the other person is saying.

Managing aversive exchanges between partners.   In general, the therapist structures the initial interview so that each member of the couple speaks to the therapist rather than to the partner. This interaction style decreases the likelihood that the couple will engage in a heated exchange about the relationship, and it helps each person view therapy as a safe setting for addressing issues. However, we do not interfere with all exchanges between partners, and it is useful to observe strengths and weaknesses in a couple's communication.

Assessing partners' cognitions and emotions about historical factors.   The therapist must beware of assuming that he or she knows how partners experienced particular life events. For example, each partner's personal standards for the self and the relationship can influence the degree to which an event is experienced as a demand. As partners describe events that have occurred, the therapist should ask each person to express his or her thoughts and emotions about the event. Thus, Sonja and Rashad described changes that occurred in their family life when her father died and her mother came to live with them. Because Sonja highly valued family loyalty but Rashad placed a premium on independence, she found it easier than he did to tolerate the restrictions that her mother's presence placed on their life as a couple and as parents.

Characteristics of the Individual Partners That Have Affected the Couple

During the relationship history interview the therapist listens for and inquires about characteristics of each individual to which the couple has had to adapt. Some characteristics may have affected them only at a particular time, and others may have been chronic influences. Thus, an individual who is highly motivated to achieve may be preoccupied with thoughts about work, be upset about work problems, and spend long hours on projects. Although the person's investment in work is aimed at achieving goals that can benefit the couple, it may interfere with the couple's harmony. When a partner draws attention to a characteristic of the other person, the therapist should ask both people how it affects them individually and as a couple.

When the therapist asks the partners to describe the characteristics that attracted them to each other, they are likely to list specific types of rewarding behavior (e.g., "He listened to me and communicated respect for my views"), broader personality characteristics and temperament (e.g., "I enjoyed her outgoing personality"), physical appearance, intelligence, shared interests and personal values (e.g., "We both valued family"), and aspects of personal success (e.g., "Her career success told me I could count on her to help create a good lifestyle"). The therapist can request specific information about how these positive characteristics were expressed. It is important to ask the couple about any changes that have occurred in those initially attractive characteristics and whether the changes have been upsetting. Finally, the therapist can inquire about attributions an individual makes about causes of changes in a partner's characteristics. For example, Germaine said, "Ivan stopped exercising, gained weight, and slept more. It was obvious that he didn't care about being physically attractive to me anymore."

Assessment of each partner's positive and negative past behaviors. The therapist can ask about each person's expressive and instrumental behaviors at various points in the relationship's development and how satisfying they were to the other person. Thus, Maija described how she had been attracted by the time and energy that Evan put into his volunteer work at a shelter for homeless families. However, she later became frustrated that he devoted more time to helping in the community than to their relationship. It is important that the therapist ask about the specific types of partner behavior that each individual enjoyed early in the relationship and how their frequencies may have changed.

Although decreases in pleasing behaviors commonly reduce partners' satisfaction, an increase in negative behaviors often accompanies the development of a distressed relationship. Consequently, it is important to identify the circumstances under which the negative behaviors increased and each person's awareness of the negative impacts of his or her own behavior. Even relatively mild negative behaviors may have *cumulative negative impacts* on a relationship because they occur frequently or over a long period. In particular, acts that convey contempt, rejection, or ignoring of the other person tend to decrease the other's feelings of self-worth and mutual caring. It is important to ask each partner if he or she has experienced any particular behavior as distressing, even if it was not a traumatic event.

Clients often respond to this inquiry by recalling *small, repetitive behaviors* that violated their standards for the relationship or were irritating. The therapist should ask whether the partner's behaviors have occurred consistently across various situations, to determine whether they may comprise relatively broad characteristics (e.g., psychopathology, personality styles). The existence of such characteristics can be explored further in the individual interviews.

Negative partner behaviors can have long-term influence on a couple's relationship if they were traumatic to the other person. The most common *traumatic behaviors* include infidelity, other forms of abandonment, substance abuse, and psychological and physical abuse. Even if they occur only once, such behaviors undermine the recipient's self-worth; trust; and perceptions of predictability, safety, and control. Care must be exercised when interviewing couples about past traumatic events in their relationship, because one or both partners may be defensive about their roles in the events. In the case of abuse, the divulging of a perpetrator's past actions might anger the individual and provoke retaliatory abuse toward the disclosing partner. Because a perpetrator may show no negative reaction during the session, the therapist cannot easily determine the risk for retaliation. Consequently, we tend to be particularly cautious in eliciting information about past and current abuse during this joint interview. If an individual chooses to mention abuse by the other person, we shift the focus at this point to an inquiry about precautions that the couple takes at present to avoid further abusive behavior. We state the importance of making the relationship safe and satisfying for both partners and discuss approaches they can use to reduce destructive expressions of conflict (e.g., noticing early cues of anger arousal, agreeing to use a cooling-down period before talking further about issues). The therapist can ask the partners to commit themselves, orally or in writing, to a no-violence contract and a focus on constructive resolution of conflicts. The therapist also can give each member of the couple phone numbers of crisis hotlines and other resources to use if needed. The assessment of past abuse and the risk for current abuse is continued during the individual interviews. Some other types of past traumatic behavior within the couple's relationship may be best explored initially in the individual interviews, because a person might find it embarrassing to discuss in front of the partner the details of behavior such as having an affair.

Partners' cognitions about an individual's past behavior. It also is important to inquire about attributions that a person makes about the causes of a partner's past behavior that he or she experienced as unpleasant. To the extent that an individual attributes a partner's displeasing behavior to negative traits and intentions and blames the partner, he or she is likely to have negative emotional and behavioral responses to the partner.

> Therapist: Jasmine, you described how you were upset with some of Lucas's behavior for a long time before you started your affair with Steve. You stressed how sad and angry you were that he often stayed at the office late, forgot special events such as your birthday, and rarely initiated sexually intimacy. I'm wondering if you remember how you interpreted his behavior at the time—what you thought about why he was behaving like that?
>
> Jasmine: It seemed to me that he'd lost interest in me. I was last on his list. When we first got together, he was interested in talking to me, going out and doing things with me. He stopped wanting to do those things.

It also is important to identify each person's attributions about his or her own past behavior. For example, Craig had an angry outburst toward Laura's mother while at a dinner at his in-laws' home. Although he subsequently apologized to Laura and to her mother, he told Laura, "I couldn't help losing my temper when your mother treated me with so much disrespect." When Laura reported Craig's statement to the therapist, the therapist inquired about it.

> Therapist: Craig, would you explain to me what you meant when you said you couldn't help losing you temper toward Laura's mother that day?

Craig:	When someone makes me that angry, I can't keep it inside. I just blow up.
Therapist:	You said that you can't keep your anger inside when it becomes strong. Does it feel uncontrollable—that no matter what you might try, you can't stop the anger from coming out by yelling or cursing? (The therapist continued the questioning, and identified Craig's attribution that his negative behavior was not his responsibility.)

It also can be helpful to assess the degree to which an individual is aware of the impact that his or her behavior has on a partner; that is, the degree to which the person thinks in terms of relational concepts. Sometimes an individual is surprised to hear that a partner was upset by his or her actions, because the person had no intention of behaving negatively. The therapist can explore a gap between the intent and impact of the person's actions. For example, Patricia expressed her upset feelings over Devon's recent comment that she had not been keeping up with her exercise program. When the therapist asked how she interpreted his remark, she explained that she took the comment as an intentional "dig" and an allusion to her failure to lose weight. Surprised by her angry response, Devon maintained that he only mentioned her not exercising because of a discussion he had with coworkers about the difficulties of exercising regularly. At least in this instance he seemed to have little awareness of how his behavior affected his wife. The therapist then might ask Devon, "What do you think you could do differently so that Patricia won't be upset by your comments?" If his response is some version of "Nothing. She's too sensitive, and I can't control that," the therapist has some suggestion that Devon thinks more in individual than in relational terms.

Assessment of partners' motives that have affected the couple. A couple may describe ways in which they have had to adjust to each other's broader response patterns that seem to reflect particular motives. Some couples reveal issues concerning motives without prompting, but in other cases the therapist elicits this information. The therapist can ask the couple to describe the things that they have looked forward to doing together and as individuals, and why. What has each person found enjoyable and meaningful about the joint or individual behavior? The therapist looks for broad patterns in the behaviors and outcomes that the person finds pleasing. Both members of a couple can be sources of information about each person's types and levels of motivation. An individual's partner often can identify what tends to be important to the person. For example, Hillary stated, "Achievement is very important to Jim; he lives and breathes it." Patterns in the couple's interactions during the interview also may suggest motives about which the therapist can inquire. For example, an individual may repeatedly share his or her feelings with the partner, request that the partner also disclose feelings, and talk about a goal of having a close relationship. The therapist can point out these behaviors and ask the individual about his or her thoughts and emotions concerning intimate sharing.

Whenever one person expresses dissatisfaction with a pattern in the other's behavior, it is important to achieve an interpersonal conceptualization that takes mutual influences between partners into account. When Bruce suggested that Corrine's increased desire for autonomy was creating a problem in their relationship, Corrine noted that Bruce had responded in a possessive, controlling manner to her first attempts to schedule individual activities. She stated that she had felt a need to resist his increased control by standing her ground and arranging activities involving more autonomy. Thus, what at first appeared to be a characteristic of one member of the couple took on new meaning as a dyadic pattern influenced by both partners' needs.

Even when the members of a couple have similar types of motivation, fulfilling those needs places demands on them. When both individuals are motivated to achieve, for instance, the therapist should inquire about the ways that the couple has devised for each person to have achievement opportunities while at the same time attending to the maintenance of their relationship and household. How do they schedule their work time, household tasks, child care time, and leisure time? Does the arrangement seem equitable to both people? How was the decision reached about the present arrangement?

Personality styles and temperament that have affected the couple. The partners may describe how particular personality characteristics of one or both individuals have had positive or negative effects on their relationship. Thus, a conscientious person may benefit the couple by performing well at work and earning a good income. In contrast, a conscientious person may create an unnecessarily complex and confusing accounting system for the couple's personal finances. Some couples have had to adapt to particular types of temperament in a partner, such as high emotional reactivity, which create a stressful environment in the home.

Sometimes the members of a couple spontaneously describe each other's personality characteristics, but in other instances the therapist must ask about them. Lonnie reported that he had been attracted by Anisha's "outgoing, friendly personality." Anisha agreed that she had always been outgoing and had many friends. When the therapist asked the couple whether Lonnie was similarly gregarious, they both stated that he was more reserved and that Anisha's high level of extraversion had created conflict between them as they tried to agree on a level of social activities that was acceptable to both of them. Thus, it is important to ask about specific consequences that partners' personality characteristics have had for the couple's relationship.

Clinical disorders and psychopathology that have affected the couple. During the initial couple interview the therapist can gather information about ways in which both members of the couple have had to adapt to one person's cognitive, affective, and behavioral symptoms of psychopathology. As Greta said, "I spend a lot of time thinking about ways to feel less depressed. It dominates my time." Quentin reported that he made many attempts to help Greta when she was feeling depressed and felt frustrated when his efforts were ineffective.

In some cases, a couple may not spontaneously mention one person's psychopathology, but the therapist notices a clue to the existence of a disorder and needs to ask about it. Thus, when the therapist heard Sheela describing a chronic low mood and difficulty becoming motivated to do anything, she inquired about the types, frequency, and intensity of depressive symptoms. The couple's descriptions suggested that Sheela had experienced moderate depression for at least the past year and that it had indeed affected the couple.

Subclinical dysfunctional characterological traits and long-standing unresolved issues that have influenced the couple. The therapist should be attuned to subclinical levels of relatively stable characteristics and unresolved issues from earlier life experiences that individuals may have brought to their relationships, such as deficits in emotional regulation, insecure attachment, low self-esteem, and sexual aversion. To decide whether there is a need for individual therapy in addition to couples therapy, it is helpful to assess the degree to which these characteristics existed before the current relationship. A developmental history concerning the person's earlier life experiences will be taken in the individual interview, but the therapist is likely to learn some relevant historical information during the conjoint relationship history interview. In fact, an individual's partner may volunteer information about the person's subclinical symptoms and unresolved issues. Thus, Monty told the therapist, "Julia has always been a very dependent person. She lived with her parents until she was 32, and she still calls to ask their advice about most decisions she has to make." Later in the individual interview, the therapist can ask about a timeline for a person's symptoms, including the degree to which the individual has exhibited similar responses with other people in various settings and at prior times. We view characterological traits not as invariant but rather as a person's tendency to respond in particular ways in certain contexts. The significance of identifying relatively stable responses is that we can help the client be aware of his or her "tendencies" and the need to respond intentionally in alternative ways to change one's relationship. When such tendencies are severe and rigid, individual therapy may be needed.

It is important to ask about the conditions under which an individual's characteristics have been expressed during the couple's interactions, and how the characteristics have affected those interactions. Consider Mariana, who described how she brought a low level of trust to her relationship with Carlos, based on having been emotionally abused by her parents as a child and abandoned by her first husband. She was alert for signs that Carlos might be untrustworthy, and whenever he behaved in a way that made her uneasy, she withdrew from him. Carlos reported that Mariana's withdrawal frustrated and angered him, leading to arguments between them. The subsequent individual interview with Mariana provided further evidence that her previous experiences in her family of origin and first marriage were contributing to her mistrust of Carlos.

Individuals' resources and vulnerabilities that have influenced the couple. Even multiproblem couples often have a variety of resources that have helped them survive stressful life experiences. Telling the couple that it is important to identify their strengths can help them broaden their focus beyond the negatives. The therapist should survey each person's resources in the areas of (a) personal characteristics such as intelligence, personality characteristics such as self-esteem and persistence, and physical health; (b) acquired knowledge and skills; and (c) acquired tangible resources, such as financial savings and a social support network.

The therapist can survey each person's resources by asking for details of how they coped with particular concerns in the past. For example, Florence and Charles reported that a year ago Florence had been subjected to sexual harassment by her supervisor at work. When the therapist asked the couple how they reacted to the situation, they responded that even though they both expressed their anger about it in the privacy of their home, Florence kept her anger in check when interacting with the supervisor. She consulted an attorney, read literature on sexual harassment, and presented her case to an upper management supervisor in a calm but firm way. The therapist's inquiry revealed that Florence's intelligence, ability to moderate her emotions under stress, social skills, and problem-solving skills had been effective personal resources.

In some cases, an individual has used particular resources effectively in the past but has failed to recognize their relevance for coping with current demands. In other cases, a person is attempting to use resources that worked well in the past but are not good matches for the demands that exist now. Latasha reported that she often became angry when she perceived that Jonas was trying to dominate their decision making about important issues in their relationship. When the therapist asked Jonas about the history of his approach to decision making in relationships with Latasha and other people, he replied that he probably had always tried to take the lead and that in his first marriage his wife preferred that he act as the leader. He had confidence in his leadership skills and continued to use them even when Latasha did not like it. In contrast, some individuals choose not to use available resources because of their beliefs that it is inappropriate to do so (e.g., a sign of weakness). Consequently, the therapist must differentiate between *potential* resources and those that each person *perceives* as resources.

The members of a couple also may identify characteristics of each person that have been vulnerability factors. Paul described how Kirk's chronic depression not only was a stressor on their relationship (e.g., his self-criticism often dominated their conversations), but it also interfered with his ability to make decisions when he and Paul faced problems.

Characteristics of the Couple That Have Affected the Relationship

Problematic dyadic characteristics. The therapist needs to identify any dyadic characteristics that are problematic for a couple. One major type of dyadic characteristic involves *discrepancies* or *similarities* in the two partners' characteristics, such as differences between their needs for autonomy versus affiliation, or similarities in their personality styles (e.g., both are detail oriented). Many couples also need to cope with negative interaction patterns that they developed in response to unresolved relationship issues and that produce *secondary distress*. Assessment of the first type of dyadic demands involves an inquiry about degrees of similarity or difference between two partners' needs and personality styles, as well as possible difficulties that these characteristics create for the couple. To what extent does a difference in two partners' characteristics result in their behaving in seemingly incompatible ways (e.g., one seeking time together and the other seeking time apart)?

The therapist should inquire whether the discrepancies between partners have been chronic or have resulted from a particular life transition or event. A couple may have always been different on a particular characteristic, but the difference was irrelevant to their daily life until a transition occurred. Thus, Tasha and Kevin reported that she had always had a greater need for intimacy than he did, but that she had met her intimacy needs to a certain degree through her relationships with her parents and sisters. However, when the couple moved to another city for a job opportunity, Tasha began to look to Kevin to meet her intimacy needs more, and the difference in their preferences for intimacy became an issue between them.

In terms of assessing secondary distress resulting from a couple's interactions in response to unresolved relationship issues, it is important to collect information about when the negative interactions began to occur, and under what circumstances. Consider Mia and Leon, who had been very open with each other in the early years of their relationship. However, when they developed financial problems because of poor budgeting, Leon began to withdraw whenever Mia tried to discuss finances, and the more he withdrew, the more she pursued him.

Often, asking questions about the antecedents and consequences of a negative behavior by one person elicits information about a pattern of negative reciprocity between partners.

> Therapist: Fran, you described how frustrating it has been for you when Greg makes critical comments about your ways of disciplining the children, and Greg, you said that you sometimes let Fran know that you disagree with her approach. What have you noticed about a typical sequence of events between the two of you during a conversation about discipline?
>
> Greg: Well, it's hard for me to just stand there and say nothing when I hear Fran telling the kids, "I don't care what your

	father says," and then telling them not to do something that I'd already given them permission to do.
Therapist:	So, you are likely to say something negative about Fran's discipline approach after you have heard her contradicting you in front of the children?
Greg:	That's right.
Fran:	Don't make it sound like it's my fault. I only say something like that to the kids after they've been hounding me, saying that you gave them permission, and you are just standing there rolling your eyes disrespectfully.
Therapist:	So there is a sequence in which each of you gets upset about what comes across as disrespectful behavior from the other person, and you behave negatively in return.

When the therapist has identified a pattern of withdrawal by one or both parties, it is important to differentiate between withdrawal that is self-protective and that which reflects an individual's emotional disengagement from the partner. This distinction generally depends on asking the individual about the thoughts and emotions that he or she typically experiences during exchanges with the partner. Individuals who care about their relationships and withdraw to avoid being hurt are likely to describe feeling upset by confrontations with the partner and desiring to escape the distress. In contrast, individuals who are emotionally disengaged are more likely to express relative indifference about the outcomes of exchanges with their partners.

Past dyadic resources and vulnerabilities. In asking a couple to describe how they have responded to various life demands, the therapist can determine how the couple's interaction patterns have been resources or vulnerabilities. A couple might report a tendency to work as a team to collect information from doctors and books, regarding ways of treating a child's chronic disease, and then systematically decide on the best course of action. Their information gathering and joint problem solving is a dyadic resource. In contrast, another couple may have difficulty coping with a child's chronic illness because they are generally disorganized. Thus, when Clara and Ted described how they were affected by having their son diagnosed with cystic fibrosis, Ted said, "There were so many details to take care of, to arrange for his needs, and our home life is so disorganized as it is." When the therapist asked the couple to describe their home life, they explained that they rarely discussed plans and goals, resulting in little coordination of their efforts. Bills often were paid late, appointments often were missed, and objects were lost in their messy house. This pattern was a vulnerability factor, rendering the couple ineffective in adapting to the complications of their child's illness.

Environmental Factors Affecting the Couple

Environmental demands. As described in chapter 5, the couple is embedded in several layers of their interpersonal environment. The innermost layer includes any children they may have as well as other members of their household. The next layer includes significant others such as in-laws and other extended family as well as close friends. It is important to inquire about whom the couple defines as "family," because it is common (particularly in some ethnic groups) to include individuals who are not blood relatives. The next layer is likely to include nonintimate friends and acquaintances. Beyond these layers, other people who can be sources of demands on an individual or couple include representatives of social institutions, including teachers, clergy, police, or social workers. On a broader societal level, the couple may be influenced by discrimination from strangers on the basis of their race, ethnicity, religion, or sexual orientation. The therapist can ask about relationships with individuals at these various levels and identify stressful interactions that occur.

The therapist also needs to collect information about the couple's physical environment. Earlier we noted how crowded, noisy, and dangerous living conditions might interfere with the couple's relationship. Leonard and Dawn reported that since a neighborhood child was killed accidentally during a drive-by gang shooting, they had walked their children to school and supervised them whenever they played outdoors. The time, energy, and worry placed significant demands on them. Some couples spontaneously report environmental demands, but without systematic inquiries by therapists, this important information can be missed.

It is important to recognize that positive life events can be potential sources of demands on a couple. Receiving a large monetary gift from a relative can be stressful, for example, because the couple must decide among ways of saving or using the funds. Sometimes a couple may fail to report such stressors because they think it is inappropriate to express difficulty in dealing with events that most people would choose to have occur in their lives. Consequently, therapists need to ask couples about their reactions to positive events in their lives.

Data concerning individual, dyadic, and environmental sources of demands typically are collected primarily during the couple and individual interviews. We do not routinely use measures such as H. I. McCubbin and Patterson's (1987) FILE, but we believe they can be helpful in identifying factors that otherwise might be overlooked during an interview. The therapist can have the couple complete a questionnaire prior to the joint interview, can ask them to look over the items during the relationship history interview and say which ones describe their experiences, or can use the scale as a guide for interviewing the couple comprehensively.

Environmental resources. One may assess the environmental resources that a couple has had available and those that they have chosen to use by asking them to describe specifically how they remember dealing with each concern they reported. The therapist could say,

Starting with the moment when the doctor told you your son has cystic fibrosis, how have you coped with the changes that his illness has created for you and your family? What specifically have you done to deal with the situation?

These broad questions can be followed with more specific questions focusing on resources the partners have used, such as social support from friends, consultations with medical experts, and financial help from relatives. The therapist then can cite other possible resources that the partners have not mentioned, ask whether they were aware of such resources, and explore any reasons why the partners have declined to use available resources.

Current Relationship Functioning

In this phase of the initial couple interview, we focus on their current concerns and relationship strengths, including (a) demands that they are experiencing, (b) resources that are available and those that are being used, and (c) any individual and couple characteristics that are reducing the couple's ability to adapt to their circumstances. This phase of the interview is an extension of the relationship history and helps the therapist identify what aspects of past functioning have continued and what changes have occurred.

Therapist: Next I'd like to get back to how you view your relationship as it is now, and get some more details about that. I realize that you two might see things quite differently, and my goal is not to establish some absolute truth. I want to know how each of you perceives things. So if your partner is expressing things differently from how you see them, don't worry. You'll have a chance to share your perspective in a few minutes.

Mary, let's start with you. You mentioned earlier that you have had some concern about the way that the two of you have dealt with free time. To what extent does that still occur? Can you clarify your concerns in this area? (As Mary answers this question, the therapist listens for the specific ways in which the couple interacts concerning their free time and what factors she sees as affecting this area of relationship functioning, such as differences in the partners' desires for sharing time together. The therapist wants to understand Mary's view of how the couple currently deals with this issue behaviorally, her emotional reaction to it, and her cognitions about it.)

Mary: We don't seem to have very much free time, which is frustrating to me. When we do have free time, I want to spend time with John, but he doesn't want to spend it with me.

Therapist: What typically happens between the two of you?

Mary: I think he spends more time at work than he needs to. When he comes home, I'm ready to spend some time talking together, but he's tired and wants quiet time alone. On the weekends, I have trouble getting him to plan things we can do together. He spends hours on his woodworking projects. (The therapist is getting a sense that a difference between the partners' preferences for togetherness might be a key dyadic problem and that John's investment in his work might be an individual characteristic affecting the couple.)

Therapist: Mary, why do you think this pattern of little free time between you is happening?

Mary: Well, I think John is bored with our marriage. I think that is a general pattern for him; he gets into something, but after awhile he loses interest in it. And if he isn't interested in something, he doesn't make an effort at it.

Therapist: So your interpretation is that John isn't interested in spending much time with you because he is bored with the relationship, is that right?

Mary: Exactly.

Therapist: And what are your views about how couples should spend their free time?

Mary: I think people should have some time to themselves, but when you are married, you are part of a couple. You should spend lots of your free time together because you want to. You shouldn't have to force somebody to do it.

Therapist: Generally, what emotions do you feel when you don't spend much time together?

Mary: I feel hurt. It's terrible to know that your partner would rather spend time on woodworking than with you. I need to spend time with my husband.

Therapist: What do you do at this point to encourage John to spend more time with you, or do you make those efforts?

Mary: I still try, but not as much as I used to. You can only be rejected so many times before you stop putting yourself in the position to be hurt. Occasionally I'll ask him if he wants to take a walk or rent a movie. Mostly I try to find things to do by myself.

Therapist: John, Mary has said a lot about the way she perceives differences between the two of you when it comes to spending free time together. I'd like to get your perspective on this concern as well. (The therapist then conducts a similar type of inquiry about John's cognitions, emotions, and behavior regarding the issue.)

Although the assessment of this problem area will require more discussion, and the therapist will view it within a broader relationship context, the therapist already is coming to some understanding of Mary's subjective experience (her cognitions and emotions). The therapist has a sense of her *perception* of the behaviors that do and do not occur with regard to the partners' free time. Some information also has been revealed about Mary's *attributions* for the problem (John is bored with her) and her *standards* for how free time should be spent in a marriage. Mary has described her emotional experience of feeling hurt as being due to her perception that John is rejecting her, her attributions for John's behavior, and her standards for marriage. Regarding *behavior patterns*, the therapist has learned that although Mary makes some effort at engaging John during the week, she primarily tries to find things to do by herself so she will not feel rejected. The therapist also will attempt to determine if the issue of free time together is part of a broader pattern, such as a difference in the partners' intimacy and autonomy needs.

Assessment of Concerns Not Mentioned by the Couple

After discussing the areas of concern that the clients have indicated, we inquire whether other important concerns have not been discussed. If the therapist administered questionnaires prior to the couple interview and gained the partners' consent to reveal their responses during the joint interview, he or she can inquire about issues identified on the forms. For example, Mary indicated on the DAS, but not during the interview, that the couple frequently disagreed about friends. When the therapist mentioned this concern, Mary explained that she was distressed that whenever the couple made a rare plan to go out together, John wanted to include other couples, whereas she preferred to spend the time just with him.

We also consider it important to inquire about certain domains that couples often fail to report spontaneously in interviews or on questionnaires, in particular (a) sexual concerns and level of satisfaction with sexual functioning and (b) estrangements from relatives and other significant people in their lives. Thus, Frieda and Louis did not mention that they had not been on speaking terms with their oldest son for the past 2 years until the therapist asked them whether there were any significant people in their life with whom they had cut off contact. Couples often do not volunteer concerns in these areas because they can be sources of embarrassment. Failure to mention estrangements often reflects individuals' attempts to avoid unpleasant emotions associated with thinking about those people, or their lack of recognition that the "unfinished business" from such relationships can be a continuing source of stress.

Assessment of Self-Monitoring and Relationship-Schematic Processing

As in the relationship history, it is important for the clinician to assess the degree to which each individual has an understanding of his or her own role in the couple's current interaction pattern and whether the person monitors his or her own behavior. This information can affect the strategies that the therapist will choose to use in treatment. Partners who monitor their own behavior and understand their own roles in problematic couple interactions can be counted on to contribute actively to change. Frequently, however, the therapist encounters clients who do not closely monitor their behavior and the ways it affects relationship functioning.

> Therapist: We discussed how the two of you have difficulty bringing the evening to a close together, and that typically one of you goes to bed and the other stays up watching television. What does each of you think you tend to do that contributes to maintaining that pattern night after night?
>
> Husband: I really don't think about it. We just seem to be on different schedules, and I couldn't tell you why.

To assess the degree to which such a response reflects a low level of relational thinking, the clinician can inquire

> You two have described how you have been feeling less intimacy between you, and partly that results from going to bed and getting up at different times. What could you each realistically do personally to reestablish the pattern you previously had of beginning and ending your days together?

The therapist can ask further questions to probe whether each person is aware of choices that he or she makes to behave in particular ways and determine what consequences result from those choices.

Identification of Macrolevel Patterns

A hallmark of cognitive–behavioral couples therapy has been its focus on the specific actions of each partner and the context within which they occur. This microlevel processing has tended to deal with each behavior as a separate area of concern. These specific behaviors commonly compose meaningful macrolevel patterns that are a function of (a) the individual partners' personal characteristics, such as normal personality styles, motives, and/or individual psychopathology, and (b) patterns of couple interaction that developed over the course of the relationship, such as patterns for expressing and listening to each other's thoughts and feelings. Consequently, a therapist can collaborate with a couple in identifying common themes and patterns shared by various specific concerns they raised. For example, the therapist might note that the partners repeatedly were upset about several instances that were all related to a difference in their desire for togetherness versus autonomy. It is important for the therapist to be cautious in making an inference that a macrolevel pattern exists without seeking the couple's input about its validity. Thus, the couple may confirm that one person enjoys shared time with the partner more than any other activity but that the partner greatly enjoys some individual pursuits.

Assessing Positives as Well as Problems

Given that couples typically seek intervention when they are distressed, they commonly have a tendency to focus on negative aspects of their relationship. Similarly, the therapist, in an attempt to understand the distress and be responsive to the couple's concerns, focuses energy on areas about which the couple has concern. If the therapist attempts to balance the assessment by asking about positives in a general way, distressed partners often have little to say. Instead, the therapist might guide the couple to engage in more specific discussions of strengths in their relationship. The therapist might note the areas on self-report measures in which an individual did not express concern or displeasure. Also, the therapist often can find areas of strength alluded to during the relationship history interview (e.g., the couple's ability to support each other when one person is struggling with personal concerns, their ability to coparent effectively). Even if an individual cannot identify areas of strength in the relationship, typically that person can respond to questions regarding which areas of the relationship seem to work better than others.

Behavioral Observation of the Couple's Interactions

Given the potential biases in partners' self-reports about their relationship (through interviews and questionnaires), it is important for the therapist to observe how the two individuals actually behave toward each other. As we described in chapters 2 and 5, the quality of a couple's relationship is influenced both by the *frequencies* of particular types of positive and negative actions (e.g., criticisms, supportive acts) and by certain types of *sequences* of behaviors between the partners (e.g., demand–withdraw). Even though a couple is likely to alter their behavior in the presence of an outsider such as their therapist, the therapist still can create conditions in which the couple may reveal important aspects of their behavioral patterns (Snyder et al., 1995; Weiss & Heyman, 1997).

First, the joint session in which the partners present concerns and describe past and present relationship functioning provides opportunities for the therapist to watch them interact, particularly as each person becomes emotionally engaged with the issues being discussed. When Jorge and Lucienne told their therapist about their ineffective attempts to cope with their 6-year-old son, who had been diagnosed with attention deficit disorder, the therapist noticed that each person interrupted the other, often to disagree with the partner's opinion about the types of parenting behavior that worked best with the child. The couple would then debate each other until the therapist encouraged them to take turns talking with him about the child. These observations led the therapist to hypothesize that the couple's ineffective parenting was influenced by their adversarial interactions and difficulty cooperating with each other.

Second, because the initial couple interview is structured so that each member of the couple speaks primarily with the therapist, it is important to create other opportunities to observe how the partners interact with each other. Creating specific interaction tasks can provide a more systematic sample of the ways that partners behave with each other. There are many kinds of interaction tasks that the therapist can set up. For example, the partners can be asked to discuss a characteristic of the couple (e.g., their difficulty in budgeting and saving money) or of either individual (e.g., one person's unhappiness with his or her job). For either type of focus, the couple can be asked to engage in either an instrumental (e.g., decision making) or an emotionally expressive (e.g., sharing thoughts and feelings) interaction. It is useful to get a sample of the couple's ability to have a constructive interaction of each type, to determine whether they are in need of particular behavioral interventions.

We often include one or more of these brief structured interaction tasks toward the end of the initial couple interview. However, therapists need to exercise caution in asking couples to discuss potentially upsetting or conflictual topics before it is known whether there is a risk of violence between partners. Given that an intimidated, abused individual may not reveal abuse by the partner until the individual interview, the possibility that the assessment interaction tasks might provoke abuse when the couple goes home must be considered. A therapist's decision of whether to conduct the tasks before versus after the individual interviews might be based on a global impression of the partners' responses to each other during the joint interview about their relationship. However, some abusive individuals are adept at presenting themselves as calm, reasonable, and under control during meetings with outsiders such as therapists, so it is best for the therapist to lean in the direction of protecting potential victims. Thus, interaction tasks can be scheduled at the end of the initial couple interview(s) or after the two individual interviews.

Decision-Making Instrumental Interactions Concerning the Couple's Relationship

The therapist might ask the couple to select a moderate-sized issue in their relationship, such as a difference in their preferred amounts of socializing as a couple with their friends, to discuss it for 10 minutes, and to attempt to move toward a resolution within the allotted time. Rarely do couples resolve a moderate-sized issue in 10 minutes, but the therapist can observe how positively or negatively they behave toward each other and how effectively they engage in problem solving. Thus, Jorge and Lucienne's therapist asked them to talk for 10 minutes to attempt to devise a specific plan for keeping their son focused on cleaning up his toys. The therapist told the couple,

> You have told me how you have been frustrated by your inability to think of and apply a plan that will improve your son's cleaning up his toys. It

would help me to get a clear picture of how I might assist you in finding a better solution to that problem if you would let me get a sample of how you communicate with each other about the issue. I'd like to sit back and watch for about ten minutes while the two of you try to agree on a reasonable plan for increasing your son's cleaning up.

As the therapist observed the couple's discussion, he observed a repeated behavioral sequence in which each person occasionally would propose a solution, which would lead the other person to point out the drawbacks of that solution and propose a different solution. The person whose solution was criticized would argue for it and dismiss the partner's points concerning its disadvantages, even those that the therapist thought might have merit. Consequently, the couple failed to stay on one topic for long, and their adversarial approach to decision making was ineffective. At the end of the discussion both partners felt frustrated with their failure and angry at each other. The therapist noted the specific aspects of the couple's interaction pattern that interfered with their ability to coordinate their individual approaches toward solutions to a problem and that increased their mutual anger.

The basic approach to analyzing samples of a couple's behavioral interaction is to identify the frequencies and sequences of particular types of positive and negative acts. As we described in chapter 2, the frequency of negative acts, particularly in proportion to the occurrence of positive acts, has a major impact on a couple's distress. In addition, in chapter 5 we detailed negative effects of certain interaction patterns, such as negative reciprocity or escalating exchanges of negative behavior. Thus, the therapist's task is to conduct a "functional analysis," observing instances of positive and negative acts by each person as well as the other partner's acts that precede and follow them (Floyd, Haynes, & Kelly, 1997). For example, when one person has made a critical remark about the partner, what did the partner do before the criticism (perhaps a negative act that elicited the criticism), and what did the partner do after the criticism (perhaps he or she stopped talking, which was reinforcing to the other person). It is important not to draw general conclusions about a couple's typical patterns from observing single instances of an interaction, so the therapist attempts to observe the couple in a variety of conversations and looks for consistencies in their interactions (Baucom & Epstein, 1990; Weiss & Heyman, 1997).

The therapist's attempts to conduct a functional analysis of a couple's behavioral interactions can be aided by familiarity with the detailed micro-analytic coding systems that researchers have developed for identifying how distressed and nondistressed couples communicate while trying to devise solutions to issues. Among the major coding systems are (a) the Marital Interaction Coding System IV (MICS IV; Heyman, Weiss, & Eddy, 1995); (b) the Kategoriensystem fur Partnerschaftliche Interaktion (KPI;

Hahlweg, Reisner, et al., 1984), which was created in Germany but has been translated into English; and (c) the Couples Interaction Scoring System (CISS; Gottman, 1979; Notarius & Markman, 1981). For example, use of the MICS IV involves observing short segments of couples' interaction (30 s at a time) and then coding each partner's behavior during each segment with a set of 37 categories of positive and negative verbal and nonverbal behavior. The unit for coding is the *speaker turn*, defined as a person's expression of a message involving homogeneous content (i.e., one idea). Speaker turns lasting more than 30 seconds are coded as multiple instances of that code. Examples of positive behavior are approve, accept responsibility, compliance, smile/laugh, and positive physical contact; examples of negative behavior include complain, put-down, interrupt, and deny responsibility. There also are codes for dyadic sequences, such as cross-complaining and mutual distancing. To increase interrater reliability and simplify analyses of MICS IV data, the various individual coding categories usually are combined into summary categories. For example, the codes of disagree, deny responsibility, excuse, interrupt, noncompliance, and turn-off are combined into an *invalidation* category. Furthermore, in research studies the codes are often divided into broad positive and negative behavior summary codes. In research, typically two raters code a videotape of a couple's discussion, so they can replay segments as often as necessary to judge the appropriate coding categories; thus the coding process is elaborate and time consuming. Coders receive extensive training, and in research studies this practice has resulted in good levels of interrater reliability (Jacob & Tennenbaum, 1988).

On the basis of a factor analysis of the MICS (Heyman, Eddy, Weiss, & Vivian, 1995), Heyman and his associates created a Rapid Marital Interaction Coding System, which also uses the speaker turn as the coding unit but includes far fewer categories: psychological abuse, distress maintaining attribution, hostility, dysphoric affect, withdrawal, acceptance, relationship enhancing attribution, self-disclosure, humor, constructive problem discussion/solution, and "other." The Rapid Marital Interaction Coding System has demonstrated good interrater reliability and validity in its associations with couples' levels of aggression and marital satisfaction (Heyman, Brown, Feldbau, & O'Leary, 1999; Vivian & Heyman, 1994).

Although all of these coding systems have been used extensively in research and have contributed to therapists' knowledge of communication in couples' relationships, generally they are not practical for clinical use because of the time and expense required to administer them. However, being familiar with one or more of them can help therapists be aware of various communication behaviors that a couple might exhibit. Snyder et al. (1995) proposed that therapists develop their skills for observing couples' interactions by taping at least one therapy session and using one of the coding systems to analyze the couple's behavior during the session. We (Baucom &

Epstein, 1990) presented a checklist version of the MICS that a therapist could use while observing videotapes of couples' discussions.

Several global or macro-analytic coding systems also can be used in a clinical context. These include the Interactional Dimensions Coding System (IDCS; Julien, Markman, & Lindahl, 1989) and the global version of the MICS (MICS–G; Weiss & Tolman, 1990). After observing an entire couple interaction, an observer makes a single rating for each partner on each of the nine IDCS communication dimensions. The nine dimensions include four involving positive communication behavior (communication skills, support/validation, problem solving, and positive affect) and five tapping negative communication behavior (withdrawal, denial, conflict, dominance, and negative affect). The IDCS also includes dimensions of communication behavior that are rated for the dyad rather than for each individual: (a) positive escalation and (b) negative escalation. Similarly, the MICS–G involves observing several minutes of couple interaction at a time and using a 5-point scale (that ranges from *none* to *very high*) to rate each partner on dimensions derived from the microbehavior categories of the original MICS. The rating dimensions and representative microbehavioral cues are conflict (e.g., complain, criticize), problem solving (e.g., proposing a positive solution, compromise), validation (e.g., agreement, approval of the partner), invalidation (e.g., disagreement, excuse), facilitation (e.g., positive mind-reading, paraphrase), and withdrawal (e.g., no response, increases physical distance). The ratings take into account not only the content of what each partner says but also nonverbal cues of affect, such as voice tone and posture. In the manual for the MICS–G, Tolman and Weiss (1990) provided detailed instructions for using the system to rate couples' interaction, and therapists can gain valuable observational experience by applying the MICS–G to a tape of a couple's discussion.

In addition, clinicians can be attuned to communication behaviors and patterns that have been demonstrated in research as particularly important in current and future couples' functioning. Gottman (1994a) isolated four variables that he referred to as the "four horsemen of the Apocalypse" because of their ability to predict couples' future distress and relationship dissolution: criticism, defensiveness, contempt, and stonewalling (withdrawal). Christensen and his colleagues (e.g., Christensen, 1988; Christensen & Heavey, 1990) also have identified problematic demand–withdraw and mutual-avoidance dyadic communication patterns.

However, clinicians need to be cautious in concluding that patterns such as passivity and avoidance have negative consequences for all couples. For example, a member of a couple may have learned that sometimes it is best to avoid escalating an argument when one's partner expresses negative emotions and that it is wise to remain calm, acknowledging to the partner that he or she has been heard and suggesting to the partner that he or she "cool down" before continuing the conversation. At times it is not easy for the therapist or a person's partner to differentiate efforts to avoid addressing problems versus more positive attempts to de-escalate unproductive interactions. Consequently, after a couple has completed an interaction task, the therapist might process with them key moments of the interaction, clarifying what each member was intending to convey and how it was received by the other person.

Discussions Involving Sharing of Thoughts and Feelings About Issues in the Relationship

During an interaction task, the partners might share their thoughts and feelings with each other about an issue in their relationship without attempting to resolve it. Given that individuals differ in their comfort with and ability to express positive versus negative feelings, asking partners to discuss both positive and negative feelings about a topic can be useful.

In assessing couples' abilities to share their thoughts and feelings about issues, the therapist should note several factors:

- Each person's ability to share his or her thoughts and feelings in a clear manner.
- Whether either person expresses positive or negative emotions (or both) so strongly, or with such little regulation, that it makes the partner uncomfortable or otherwise disrupts the couple's communication.
- How much the listener appears to understand the speaker, conveys empathy for what the person is expressing, and communicates respect for the person's opinions and feelings.

As we described in chapter 3, some people struggle with being able to identify and label their feelings and thus have difficulty expressing those feelings. Other people fail to express emotions because they are emotionally disengaged from the partner. Still others know what they feel but avoid expressing those feelings because they consider it inappropriate or fear the consequences of expressing certain feelings. Thus, if one person does not express his or her feelings clearly, or appears to express certain feelings uncomfortably, the therapist needs to explore the person's thoughts that influence the inhibited expressiveness.

Sometimes one member of a couple expresses feelings in such an unregulated way that it can contribute to a demand–withdraw pattern between the two people. It is common that such a person's partner has learned that it is relatively fruitless to try to calm the person once his or her emotion has escalated, and challenging the individual will only inflame the emotional response. Partners of individuals with emotion regulation difficulties often develop patterns for attempting to escape the intense responses. In the confines of the therapy setting, we have observed some partners responding to emotional outbursts by adopting a defensive physical posture (e.g., head down, arms crossed) and appearing to tune out the upset individual.

When an individual expresses strong emotion, it is important to determine whether it reflects a *dispositional* emotion regulation problem or *situational* emotional upset, which is common among members of distressed couples. Sometimes an individual who generally moderates his or her emotions is so upset with a partner during an early therapy session (including structured communication tasks) that he or she expresses intense anger. We tend to use several criteria in making this distinction. First, even partners who are highly distressed about their relationships typically can reduce their anger expression if the therapist directs them to do so in the interest of clear, constructive communication. In contrast, individuals with general emotion regulation problems commonly have difficulty modulating their anger expression when the therapist intervenes and, in fact, may become even more upset at the suggestion that they do so. Second, when the therapist asks how the individual calms him- or herself when very upset, the person with emotional dysregulation problems commonly describes an inability to do so (e.g., "I'm up all night" or "My whole day is ruined"). Third, the person reports strong emotional responses to other life experiences involving a variety of people and events. If it appears that a member of a couple tends to experience and express emotion in such an unregulated manner, individual therapy in conjunction with the couples therapy and a high level of structuring by the therapist of the couple's interactions during sessions may be called for.

Partners need to have a way to demonstrate that they are listening to each other (e.g., head nods, eye contact, reflections of what they have heard) and respect each other's point of view (acknowledge the other's opinion, e.g., "I know it's upsetting for you when I come home late"). The therapist should observe whether a partner engages in negative behavior while the other person is expressing opinions or feelings, such as interrupting to cut the person off or discounting the other's point of view or feelings (e.g., "You have no right to feel that way").

Conversations About the Individual Partners

It also is important for the therapist to assess a couple's ability to address positive and negative experiences in each individual's life. Consequently, the therapist might ask the partners to try to reach a solution about one person's concerns or to discuss the person's thoughts and feelings about those individual concerns. The therapist can focus on whether the partner is able to listen and keep the focus on the individual who is expressing concerns. It is not atypical for a person to complain, "Whenever I try to talk with you about something that is troubling me, the conversation quickly shifts so that we are talking about things that are bothering *you*."

Similarly, the therapist might ask one person to share with his or her partner a recent success or enjoyable experience. The therapist then observes whether the partner is able to share that joy and excitement empathically. Does the partner encourage the person to talk more about the positive experience, validating the person's strengths, or does the partner put a damper on the person's excitement or accomplishments?

Observing a couple engaging in several types of structured discussions would result in a lengthy assessment procedure and probably is not needed. The therapist can individualize the interaction tasks on the basis of information gathered throughout the assessment, such as one person's complaint that the partner does not listen to him or her. In other cases, if the therapist has had opportunities to sample the couple's interactions during their spontaneous exchanges during the couple interview, there may be no need to engage in structured tasks.

As we discussed in chapter 5, many macrolevel patterns occur over longer periods of time, such as when an individual reciprocates a partner's negative behavior days later. Therefore, it is important to supplement behavioral observations made in the office with client reports of typical patterns in their relationship, including delayed consequences.

PARTNERS' INDIVIDUAL HISTORIES AND CURRENT FUNCTIONING

Although it is possible to collect information about each partner's individual history during conjoint interviews, an individual may not be comfortable revealing to the partner certain aspects of his or her past, such as sexual abuse, treatment for psychopathology, and details of past relationships. It also may be uncomfortable for an individual to describe problematic aspects of current functioning (e.g., a sexual dysfunction) in the presence of the partner. In general, our position is that each person is entitled to privacy. If there is no clear reason to believe that those experiences are affecting the present couple relationship, then they need not be shared with the partner. However, if past and present experiences seem to be influencing how the individual is relating to the partner, then it is important to address the effects of those experiences as part of therapy. Even then, the therapist and individual might decide that such issues would be best treated in individual therapy with a different clinician. The therapist still might emphasize to the individual that revealing particular experiences during couple sessions could be helpful in the couple's work together. For example, Shanna had never told Albert that her father had sexually abused her when she was a child, because she feared that Albert would view her negatively. However, Shanna and the couple's therapist discussed that Albert had been confused about her ambivalent feelings about sexual intimacy and that his lack of insight into her life was interfering with the progress of their therapy. The therapist and Shanna concluded that Albert was a mature and supportive partner who seemed capable of coping with information about the past abuse. The therapist emphasized that the decision regarding disclosure was Shanna's.

Some of the information about each individual, such as personality characteristics and psychopathology, will have been identified during the relationship history interview. However, during the individual interview the therapist asks each partner to provide a developmental picture of his or her life, beginning in childhood and progressing to the present. Areas touched on during the couple interviews that are explored in more detail during the individual interview include (a) past and current demands on the individual that influence the couple and (b) the individual's past and current resources that affect the couple.

In Exhibit 7.2 an outline of the information sought in an individual interview is presented.

Past and Current Demands on the Individual

It is important to fill in details concerning issues that an individual resolved effectively in the past and those that still affect the couple's relationship. An example of the former would be an individual who lost a job and adapted effectively by using it as an opportunity to find a more satisfying job. An example of an unresolved issue would be neglect that a person experienced in his or her family of origin, which contributes to chronic insecure attachment. In particular, the individual interview provides a setting for exploring issues that each person might have felt inhibited discussing during the conjoint interview.

Individual Psychopathology and Substance Abuse

An absence of comments about psychopathology during the couple interview is no guarantee that such problems do not exist. We typically initiate a screening for psychopathology during the individual interviews by asking a few general questions such as, "Over the years, including recently, have you experienced any periods of depression, anxiety, or other symptoms that have concerned you or have affected your life? Have you previously sought any professional help for emotional or psychological difficulties?" We also ask about the person's overall health history, as well as past and present use of prescription medications and use of tobacco, caffeine, alcohol, and drugs. Concerning alcohol and other drug use, we ask each person about usage by the self and by the partner, because individuals often feel more comfortable initially revealing a partner's substance abuse without the partner present, especially if the substance-abusing partner also has been physically violent. If concerns arise based on the initial questions about alcohol and drug use, more detailed assessment is needed.

The clinician seeks to understand how the drinking or drug use fits into the couple's relationship, such as (a) antecedents to the person's substance

EXHIBIT 7.2
Individual Interview Outline

Demographic information
• Age, ethnicity, religious affiliation, country of origin if an immigrant (and immigration history), education, current employment

Family of origin
• Members of family of origin, birth order, members currently alive, where they live
• Quality of relationships among members of family of origin during individual's childhood and currently
• Any notable stressful events affecting family of origin during childhood and subsequently (e.g., illnesses, disabilities, deaths, financial problems, unemployment, estranged relationships, substance abuse problems, criminal and legal problems)

Physical health
• Past and current health problems and physical disabilities; impact on daily functioning (job, interpersonal relationships)
• Treatments, medications (side effects)
• Past and current use of tobacco, caffeine, alcohol, drugs; impact on daily functioning (job, interpersonal relationships)

Developmental history
• Educational history (performance in each level of schooling, any learning disabilities)
• Interests and leisure activities (individual and with other people), special talents
• History of symptoms of psychopathology (e.g., anxiety, depression, behavioral problems), any formal diagnoses and treatments received, association of symptoms with particular life experiences (follow up with more detailed assessment of psychopathology if warranted by screening questions)
• Personality characteristics and motives (screening for consistencies in cognitive, emotional, and behavioral response patterns to life events)
• Job history (types of jobs, performance, job satisfaction, career goals)
• Relationship history (friendships, prior romantic relationships), how relationships tended to begin and end, quality of current relationships
• Past and current demands involving own characteristics, relationships with significant others, and other aspects of the person's environment; past and current traumatic experiences (e.g., physical and sexual abuse, psychological abuse, abandonment)
• Personal, relationship, and environmental resources previously used to adapt to life demands (their degree of effectiveness, the individual's attitudes about using resources)

use (e.g., an argument between the partners), (b) the consequences of drinking or drug use (e.g., a partner who drinks is more outgoing and humorous while drinking vs. withdrawn), (c) both partners' attitudes toward substance use, and (d) the couple's ability as a dyad to address substance abuse in an appropriate manner (McCrady & Epstein, 1995). Moreover, it is important to assess how the individual's substance use pattern fits into the couple's relationship history. Some couples became involved with each other in a substance use context (e.g., at bars), and if one or both partners have significantly reduced or stopped substance use, the couple may have difficulty adjusting to the change. If one member has stopped drinking and is attending Alcoholics Anonymous meetings, for instance, the other member's continued drinking might become a source of conflict between them. Other couples who formed their relationships in a substance use context may feel that they have little in common relating to each other when sober.

If an individual reports symptoms that suggest a clinical disorder or a subclinical pattern that may be affecting the couple's relationship, the therapist can conduct a more extensive clinical interview. That assessment relies on the clinician's expertise in assessing psychopathology, and this book cannot provide extensive guidelines for conducting interviews concerning Axis I and Axis II disorders in the *Diagnostic and Statistical Manual of Mental Disorders* (*DSM–IV*; American Psychiatric Association, 1994) system. Clinicians who wish to use a structured interview to guide their assessment will find the following protocols to be useful: the Structured Clinical Interview for *DSM–IV* (First, Gibbon, Spitzer, & Williams, 1995) and the Anxiety Disorders Interview Schedule for *DSM–IV* (DiNardo, Brown, & Barlow, 1994). The latter focuses on anxiety but also includes sections on depression and substance dependence and abuse. These structured interviews are long, but clinicians can benefit from becoming familiar with them as models for differentiating types of psychopathology.

Sometimes the pattern of an individual's psychopathology over the course of his or her life suggests that the person is vulnerable to developing symptoms at times of stress. In such cases, both the couple's relationship problems and the individual's vulnerability may need therapeutic attention. The literature on psychopathology and substance abuse in the couple relationship context suggests that untreated individual problems can interfere with progress in couples therapy (Craske & Zoellner, 1995; Gotlib & Beach, 1995; McCrady & Epstein, 1995). Consequently, if the therapist observes evidence that an individual's psychopathology symptoms or substance abuse is a major stressor, affecting the couple's interaction patterns and eliciting significant distress, it is likely that the individual will need some individual therapy to treat these problems. If the interference from the psychopathology or substance abuse is severe, then evidence of progress in the individual treatment may be a prerequisite for couples therapy. On the other hand, as we describe in chapter 13, there also is substantial evidence that couples interventions can be very useful in treating one member's symptoms of psychopathology, and partner involvements in treatments for substance abuse have been demonstrated to be effective (O'Farrell & Rotunda, 1997). Furthermore, in other cases, the assessment of an individual's personal history indicates that he or she was resilient and symptom free during past stressful experiences but has responded with symptoms during stress in the current relationship. A developmental perspective can help the therapist and client decide between couples therapy alone and a combination of couples therapy and individual therapy.

Personality Styles and Motives

During the individual interview, the therapist can follow up on information gathered during the couple interview, to see if an individual's problematic behavior in the couple context is a broader ingrained pattern that may be relatively difficult to change. For example, during the couple session, Rona described how she felt constant pressure to make daily life at home with her husband and young children run smoothly. During her individual interview, the therapist determined that Rona was a highly conscientious person who consistently felt self-imposed pressure to be productive. The therapist was able to use this knowledge about her personality style in devising appropriate treatment for the couple.

Environmental Demands on the Individual

In the individual interview, the therapist can gather more information about aspects of various levels of a person's external environment that have affected him or her.

- *Demands from nuclear and extended family relationships* (e.g., characteristics of the person's partner; parenting stresses; child illnesses and disabilities; in-law relationship problems; loss of a family member through death, divorce, physical distance, or estrangements).
- *Demands associated with friends and acquaintances* (e.g., personal conflicts; friends who seek support from the individual; a friend's serious illness; loss of a significant friendship through death, physical distance, or estrangement).
- *Demands associated with work* (e.g., workload stresses, work–family role conflicts, work travel and schedules that disrupt personal and couple routines and intimacy, anxiety and depression resulting from work conditions).
- *Demands from interactions with societal institutions and organizations* (e.g., school personnel concerning a child's problems, law enforcement and legal organizations, religious organizations).
- *Demands at a societal level* (e.g., national economic problems, discrimination on the basis of race, ethnicity, sexual orientation, religion, gender, or age).

During the individual interviews partners often feel more comfortable discussing their responses to characteristics of the other person, such as psychopathology and personality styles. The therapist and individual then can discuss how the person can express these concerns in conjoint sessions in a noncritical manner.

Assessment of Physical and Psychological Abuse

As noted earlier, we initially screen for domestic abuse during the individual interviews to minimize the risk of retaliation from a partner when an individual reveals abuse. A detailed discussion of violence assessment is beyond the scope of this book; however, we briefly describe our screening procedures. More information about the assessment of domestic abuse can be found in publications by Heyman and Neidig (1997); Holtzworth-Munroe, Beatty, and Anglin (1995); and Rosenbaum and O'Leary (1986).

Some individuals hesitate to tell a therapist about the occurrence of abusive behavior unless asked directly about it, and some find it easier to report abuse on a questionnaire than in response to direct interview questions. The revised Conflict Tactice Scale (CTS2; Straus et al., 1996) is a widely used self-report screening instrument therapists can administer at the beginning of the individual interview. We have found that the CTS2 allows us to quickly identify forms of abusive behavior that members of a couple fail to report spontaneously, either because they are fearful of divulging it in the presence of the partner or because they have not even considered certain acts as abusive. The CTS2 includes 39 items that fall into five subscales: (a) Physical Assault, such as kicking, punching, choking, or using a weapon against the partner; (b) Psychological Aggression, including verbal and non-verbal aggressive acts, such as stomping out of the room, threatening to hit the partner, or destroying the partner's possessions; (c) Negotiation, involving positive actions to settle a disagreement through discussion; (d) Physical Injury, such as partner was cut, bruised, or needed medical attention; and (e) Sexual Coercion through insistence, threats, or force. Respondents describe both their own behavior and the partner's behavior during the past year. The therapist still needs to interview the client about the context of the violent acts, including (a) the sequence of events between the partners that led to each violent behavior; (b) the sequence of events during a violent incident; (c) the intentions that an individual had in behaving violently; and (d) the consequences of the violence, such as gaining compliance from the other person (Holtzworth-Munroe et al., 1995). Holtzworth-Munroe et al. (1995) also pointed out that the clinician must learn about the severity of the violence; the risk of lethality to the partner or other persons (e.g., a partner's lover); other forms of psychological abuse; and related problems, such as alcohol and other drug use. Examples of psychological abuse include threats of violence, intrusion into the other person's privacy and autonomous functioning, degrading criticism, and withholding or threats to withhold resources that the other person needs (e.g., money). It also is important for the therapist to assess the possibility that partners are reciprocating each other's violence. Neither person is held responsible for violence committed by the other person (although some violent acts may constitute self-defense), and the emphasis is on holding each person responsible for gaining control over his or her own violent acts.

The therapist tells each partner that any information he or she shares about abuse will not be discussed in front of the other person during joint sessions unless the individual and therapist agree that such a disclosure is safe and useful. The therapist also asks the individual how safe he or she feels living with the partner and participating in therapy sessions with the partner. If one or both individuals reveal ongoing psychological or physical abuse, the therapist stresses this as a high-priority issue during the assessment feedback session and states that it is crucial that the couple quickly institute procedures to control aggressive and physically and emotionally hurtful behavior. The therapist then guides the couple in devising and initiating a "no-abuse contract" that specifies in writing the types of behavior that each partner will avoid, as well as procedures that the couple can use to avoid abusive incidents. For example, the contract is likely to include guidelines for taking a "time out" whenever either person notices early cues of mounting tension and aggressiveness in either party. The procedure involves explicitly stating that it seems important to take a time out so the partners can cool down, and the couple agrees how it will be done (e.g., by going to different rooms, or one might take a walk outside). If both partners exhibit commitment and the ability to adhere to the no-abuse contract, it is reasonable for the therapist to continue conjoint couples therapy, with abuse prevention as a major goal to be addressed at the beginning of treatment. However, when an individual reports danger of personal injury or death due to a partner's violence, the therapist shifts to helping that person take action to seek safety (e.g., going to a shelter), and no joint couples therapy is pursued.

Individual's Past and Current Resources That Affect the Couple

During the individual interview the therapist collects detailed information about each partner's resources involving (a) relatively stable personal characteristics (e.g., intelligence, physical health), (b) acquired knowledge and skills, (c) acquired tangible resources (e.g., money), and (d) social support network. A member of a couple may reveal that the relationship has had negative impacts on the use of his or her personal resources. Nicholas reported that he had often turned to his parents and siblings for emotional support in the past, but since marrying Glenda he had refrained from doing so, because Glenda was jealous of his contacts with his family. In other cases the therapist may learn that an individual avoids asking anyone for help because of embarrassment and, for the same reason, the person tries to present a façade of strength in front of the partner. The therapist's knowledge about these inhibiting cognitions regarding use of resources is important for planning interventions.

Thus, the individual interviews allow the therapist to assemble details about each person's past experiences and current functioning. For some clients the individual interview initially is a more comfortable setting in which to discuss personal characteristics. In such cases the therapist and individual can discuss the value of bringing the characteristics into the joint discussions and, if so, how that can most effectively be accomplished.

INTEGRATION OF ASSESSMENT INFORMATION AND FEEDBACK TO THE COUPLE

Following the two interviews with the individual partners, the therapist meets with the couple to give them feedback about the information that has been collected. If the assessment has been conducted in a clear and collaborative manner, the couple likely will find little surprise in the feedback. However, the clinician helps them put the information together and provides them with a framework to understand their relationship. This conceptualization is the basis for the treatment plan, which the clinician also discusses with the couple. The feedback session is a two-way process in which the therapist asks the couple how well the summary fits their own ideas regarding problems and strengths in their relationship and whether other factors should be considered.

The central task is to present to the couple an informal profile of strengths and concerns regarding their relationship, covering demands, resources, and vulnerabilities associated with the individuals, the couple, and the environment. We also note changes that have occurred in these factors over time. We attempt to help the couple understand the factors that have contributed to the development of their current situation, and then we focus on the implications for therapy. In Exhibit 7.3 the major areas to be included in an assessment summary are listed.

Couple's Presenting Concerns

The therapist should begin the feedback by briefly summarizing the concerns that the partners identified in the questionnaires and interviews. This summary should include characteristics of the individuals, the couple, and their environment that the partners have experienced as problematic. When two partners have reported *different perceptions of their relationship*, the therapist can emphasize that it is common for the members of a couple to have discrepant views of (a) what is problematic, (b) what is causing the problems, and (c) what needs to be done to solve the problems. The therapist can emphasize that identifying differences in their views of their relationship is a crucial step toward devising new ways to address them.

When the assessment has indicated characteristics of one or both individuals that create difficulties for the couple, the therapist needs to describe

EXHIBIT 7.3
Outline for Assessment Feedback to the Couple

The couple's presenting concerns
1. Summarize the major areas of concern presented by each member of the couple.
    *   Focus on macrolevel patterns of behavioral interaction (e.g., demand–withdrawal) and core themes and dimensions of relationship functioning (e.g., differences in desires for intimacy).
    *   Identify characteristics of the individuals, couple, and environment involved in concerns.
2. Note and normalize differences in partners' perceptions and standards regarding areas of concern; emphasize the goal of helping partners resolve their differences.
3. Differentiate between sources of primary distress and the couple's coping patterns that produce secondary distress; emphasize the need for constructive interactions to resolve core relationship concerns.

Developmental perspective on the relationship and development of issues
1. Review factors that attracted partners to each other; note aspects of those characteristics that still exist.
2. Review sequence of challenges and demands that they faced as individuals and as a couple.
    *   Summarize the partners' successful and unsuccessful approaches to coping with past demands; describe their behavioral, cognitive, and affective responses to past demands.
    *   Describe development of coping patterns that produced secondary distress.

Resources used in the past, and the outcomes of their use
1. Describe resources of the individuals, the couple, and their environment that were available and those that were used; identify resources currently available.
2. Summarize partners' cognitions about using resources.

Identification of realistic goals for intervention
1. Differentiate between characteristics of the individuals, couple, and environment that are difficult to change and those for which there is potential for some change.
    *   Review the couple's past attempts to produce change and focus on new strategies.
    *   Reiterate the need to eliminate negative interactions as a prerequisite to resolving core relationship issues such as differences in needs.
    *   Emphasize each partner's role in contributing to new patterns and achieving change.
2. Counteract hopelessness about change and focus on attainable steps toward change.

them in a manner that does not portray either person as the primary cause of relationship problems. It can be stressed that couples commonly are faced with adjusting to various characteristics that the partners bring to the relationship, such as depression or high motivation for achievement. However, if the therapist believes that an individual's characteristic warrants individual therapy in addition to couples therapy, the therapist can note that the person's symptoms seem to make it difficult for him or her to deal effectively with the partner in resolving concerns about their relationship. Individual therapy is presented as a means of helping the person work more effectively in couples therapy.

The partners are likely to feel that the feedback is addressing their basic issues if the therapist identifies macrolevel patterns and themes in their concerns (e.g., a lack of intimacy, escalating arguments) rather than focusing primarily on distressing microlevel behavior. The therapist then focuses on characteristics of the *individuals* (e.g., personality styles, psychopathology), the *couple* (e.g., differences in needs, negative interaction patterns that produce secondary distress), and their *environment* (e.g., extended family, job demands) that have contributed to their basic concerns over the course of their relationship. For example, Jana and Luke's therapist noted that the chronic stress of coping with their families' negative reactions to their interfaith relationship had contributed to the couple's own conflicts over the appropriate religious upbringing for their children.

A Developmental Perspective on the Couple's Concerns

The therapist then can summarize the development of the couple's relationship over time, especially the *challenges or demands* that they faced at particular points and the partners' *responses to those challenges*. Changes in the couple's ability to adapt to their current demands are noted, and the apparent reasons are discussed (e.g., a new type of demand occurred for which they were unprepared). As appropriate, the therapist can point out that the members of the couple have a legitimate concern about an issue, such as different levels of desire for togetherness, but that the ways in which they have coped with that concern have become problematic in themselves (producing secondary distress). Feedback about problematic interaction patterns can cover cognitions (e.g., attributing the other's different intimacy needs to a lack of love), emotions (e.g., anger), and behavior (e.g., mutual criticism). Thus, the therapist begins to set up treatment priorities by giving the couple feedback about processes in their interactions that have created new problems. The couple is told that therapy involves helping them develop more effective and mutually satisfying ways of resolving issues.

Past and Current Resources

The therapist should summarize the couple's individual, dyadic, and environmental resources, noting which ones they have used effectively, which ones seem to be available and untapped, and which ones have been ineffective (e.g., a family member who gave them poor financial advice). As needed, the therapist should point out resources that the partners do not recognize as strengths, such as supportive friends. Sources of partners' resistance to using resources (e.g., a standard that one should be self-reliant) are noted, as are the negative consequences of failing to use them.

For example, the therapist's assessment of Elizabeth and Lorne indicated that they had a variety of resources (e.g., intelligence, secure jobs, mutually supportive and affectionate communication), as well as a history of adapting well to various life demands through active problem solving. However, they were feeling confused and emotionally out of control because Lorne had recently been diagnosed with cancer. The therapist helped Elizabeth and Lorne understand the disconcerting cognitive and emotional symptoms that they were experiencing. Then the therapist reviewed with them the assessment information that indicated that they were a high-functioning couple who were accustomed to solving problems on their own. In fact, the assessment had indicated that they tended to avoid relying on outside sources of support. The therapist suggested to the couple that although they had excellent skills for taking direct action with problems, they were now facing a life-threatening problem over which they felt limited personal control. The therapist noted that their self-reliance might be working against them in this situation and that one goal of couples therapy could be assisting them in becoming comfortable drawing on emotional support from extended family and friends, as well as using community resources, such as support groups for couples facing cancer. In addition, they had been deflecting each other's attempts to talk about their fears of Lorne's illness. The therapist described how the couple's avoidance of each other's emotional distress had left them feeling that the other person was ignoring his or her feelings. The therapist suggested that they might benefit from some work on expressing their feelings about the cancer and providing empathic listening and emotional support for each other. Thus, the assessment feedback for this couple focused on their areas of strength, identified some characteristics that were interfering with their coping with Lorne's cancer, and proposed therapeutic interventions.

Counteracting Hopelessness and Establishing a Collaborative Therapeutic Relationship

Couples who reach the point of seeking therapy usually feel helpless and hopeless about resolving their issues. Consequently, to the degree that it is realistic, the therapist's feedback should give the couple hope that they can achieve at least some of the change that they desire. Problems that they have perceived as unchangeable must be reconceptualized as having potential for improvement whenever possible. As Jacobson and Christensen (1996) emphasized, the couple's concerns can be viewed as a mixture of factors that can be changed to a meaningful degree through focused efforts and factors that are unlikely to be changed and are best accepted as unavoidable. Thus, Chloe and Simon's therapist summarized assessment data suggesting that they had different temperaments, in which she had a high level of energy and activity, and he was more sedate. Noting the unlikelihood that they would become similar in temperament, the therapist suggested that they did have potential to improve the way they addressed their difference. Specifically, the therapist gave them examples from their interviews and problem-solving discussions to illustrate that they frequently digressed to other topics and blamed each other for the behaviors associated with their different temperaments. The therapist noted that the couple's conflict seemed to worsen after the birth of their baby, when Chloe spent much time and energy taking care of the child, while Simon often retreated to reading books and watching television. The therapist emphasized that the couple could work on problem-solving skills for developing mutually acceptable ways of handling child care and other responsibilities, given their different temperaments. The key is to give the couple not only a view of what is not working well but also a sense that there may be other attainable, more satisfying ways of relating. However, while ensuring that couples not overlook the potential for improvement, the therapist does not want to provide false hope for changes that do not appear likely.

The assessment feedback should be presented as an interactive process rather than a monologue from the clinician. The therapist can inquire periodically regarding how the feedback fits with the partners' understanding of their relationship, ask the couple for examples to illustrate particular points (e.g., examples of how their work schedules affect their time together), and inquire about issues that the partners feel have been omitted in the therapist's conceptualization. A conversation similar to the following exchange might take place.

Therapist:	It seems that you were attracted to each other by your similar interests and tendency to have fun together. However, eventually you became frustrated by what appeared to be irreconcilable differences in how you prefer to lead certain aspects of your life together. In particular, you try to find solutions to the issue of how much togetherness and how much separateness the two of you should have, but your discussions seem to go around in circles. The most common way that you cope with your frustration is to withdraw from each other for a while. Does that match what you have noticed?
Brent:	Pretty much.
Therapist:	What's your view of that, Sue?
Sue:	We do seem to give up and go off by ourselves, so we don't have to face the frustration.
Therapist:	My discussions with you and observations of your discussions also suggest that you differ on how much togetherness versus separateness you desire. Sue, you seem to have a strong need to have some autonomy in your life, to do lots of things on your own. Brent, you seem to want a lot of togetherness. Of course, there are times when you really

like togetherness, Sue, and times when you really like doing things independently, Brent. But that overall difference seems to be creating some difficulties for you. Would each of you say that I am describing the difference between you accurately?

(Both partners nod their heads.)

Therapist: Can you describe a recent incident in which that issue arose?

Sue: Last Saturday one of my friends called and asked me to help her shop for a dress for a wedding she's going to attend. I wanted to go, but Brent complained that we should spend weekend time together.

Therapist: Brent, do you agree that Sue's example illustrates the difference between you?

Brent: Yes, it's a good example of our different priorities.

Therapist: The two of you face a challenge that although you were very attracted to each other, there's a difference in how much intimacy and independence you desire. That is hard for a lot of couples to negotiate. Sue, you at times feel smothered, and Brent, when she wants to do things without you, you feel unloved. So you both end up feeling discouraged. Although you generally communicate well, you've tried to resolve that difference, and it isn't working well. You have backed off from each other, at least when it comes to discussing that issue. My impression is that in therapy we should focus on finding a better way of interacting that accommodates your different desires for closeness and autonomy. How does that goal sound to you?

This sample of assessment feedback that leads to the setting of treatment goals would likely be only one component of the feedback that the couple would receive about the factors outlined in Exhibit 7.3. Similar discussions would focus on other factors, such as environmental demands that are overwhelming a couple's coping skills. Thus, the therapist might discuss with Sue and Brent how the demands of parenting their young children have affected the amount of free time and energy each person has available for either joint or autonomous activities. Their relationship history indicated that when they had less demanding schedules there was adequate time to meet both togetherness and autonomy needs. Furthermore, time demands associated with their jobs would be reviewed. This broader view of competing demands on the partners' time could contribute to treatment goals focused on meeting the partners' needs.

After the therapist and couple discuss the assessment feedback, the couple is offered the opportunity to talk with each other outside of the session and decide whether they wish to continue in therapy. This strategy models a joint decision-making approach that the partners will be asked to use in a variety of contexts, that is, asking each partner to decide whether he or she wishes to participate in the intervention and to commit to that effort.

Although the initial assessment is an explicit phase in working with a couple and is important for treatment planning, assessment is an ongoing process. Therefore, as we now turn to a description of interventions in the next chapters, it is important to keep in mind that the therapist will continue to assess the couple throughout treatment. In addition, the couple will be asked to monitor their own progress. Self-monitoring can help minimize the likelihood that the couple will inadvertently drift away from the positive changes they have been making.

SUMMARY

The overall goals of assessment are to clarify the couple's presenting concerns, trace the development of the concerns, identify factors currently contributing to these issues, identify relationship strengths that can be used to resolve difficulties, and identify appropriate intervention strategies. The following are the major strategies and procedures used in the assessment.

- Assessment begins with the initial phone contact and is an ongoing process throughout therapy.
- Questionnaires may be used selectively to help identify areas of strength as well as concerns.
- The therapist sets guidelines for collaborative, nonadversarial behavior during the assessment.
- The relationship history identifies relationship strengths as well as the process through which the couple had difficulty adapting to particular demands concerning characteristics of the individuals, the couple, and their environment.
- The assessment identifies past negative experiences as well as current factors that have residual effects on the couple.
- The therapist assesses individual, couple, and environmental resources that are available as well as partners' cognitions about using them.
- The therapist sets up structured discussions between the partners to observe their expressive, listening, and decision-making skills.
- An individual interview with each person creates a safe context for assessing sensitive topics such as partner abuse, substance abuse, the individual's psychopathology, and past trauma in the individual's life.
- The therapist's feedback to the couple summarizes their presenting concerns in terms of macrolevel patterns, the develop-

ment of those issues, difficulties that the couple experienced in adapting to specific demands, and implications for therapy goals.

- The overall goal of the assessment feedback is that the couple will feel that the therapist has identified the major sources of concern in their relationship, has helped them become aware of strengths, and has the knowledge and ability to help them make progress toward meeting their needs.

8

CONDUCTING COUPLES THERAPY

In this chapter we describe generic aspects of conducting cognitive–behavioral therapy with couples. Beginning with the first phone contact with one partner, the therapist faces numerous clinical decisions. The formation of a collaborative therapeutic alliance with both members of a couple begins during the initial contacts and extends throughout therapy. We describe approaches to building the therapeutic alliance, setting goals with the couple, establishing the roles of the therapist and clients, and setting guidelines for constructive couple behavior within and outside sessions.

As we discussed in chapter 7, a couple begins their involvement in therapy when one of the members contacts the clinician to inquire about a possible appointment. The client is likely to ask about the therapist's schedule and availability and fees, and perhaps his or her theoretical orientation, the average length of treatment, and other aspects of how the therapist conducts the treatment. Some callers are familiar with the therapist's particular theoretical orientation, perhaps from previous therapy experiences or from reading about it, whereas others may have little knowledge about therapy of any type. Sometimes both members of the couple are motivated for therapy, but sometimes only one person (usually, but not always, the caller) wants treatment for the relationship. At times, the caller states a desire to have a few individual sessions and then make a decision about inviting the partner to join the therapy, and in other cases the caller states a firm opinion that the partner would never consider couples therapy. Thus, during this brief conversation the therapist obtains some initial information about the couple's relationship and immediately is faced with several clinical decisions, such as whether it is advisable to hold individual sessions with one member before including the other.

In this chapter we discuss a variety of clinical issues that couples therapists commonly face, beginning with the first phone contact and extending over the course of the therapy. These issues include:

- Whether to hold individual sessions with one partner, either as a prelude to conjoint therapy or as a substitute for it.
- How to build a therapeutic alliance with a couple.
- How to set appropriate treatment goals with a couple.
- What the role of the therapist is in intervening with a couple's relationship.
- How to convey expectations for the couple's conduct during and outside therapy sessions.

Because these generic issues commonly arise regardless of a couple's particular presenting problems, we present them as an introduction to conducting couples therapy, before describing specific types of interventions in subsequent chapters.

INDIVIDUAL SESSIONS WITH ONE MEMBER OF A COUPLE

This book focuses on the conjoint treatment of couples' relationships, and the assessment and intervention procedures that we describe involve both partners. Nevertheless, in clinical practice it is not unusual for couples therapists to have requests for individual therapy from one member of a couple, whose primary agenda is trying to improve the relationship. Given that research has indicated the importance of dyadic interactions in couples' adjustment, it is crucial that the therapist be able to assess and intervene with those interactions as directly as possible. Cognitive–behavioral assessment methods rely heavily on the therapist's ability to sample clients' behaviors, cognitions, and emotional responses as they are occurring (Baucom & Epstein, 1990; Rathus & Sanderson, 1999; Weiss & Heyman, 1997). This maximizes the validity of the data, because the therapist does not have to rely solely on partners' subjective memories of their interactions. In terms of intervention, the therapist can observe a couple's interactions first hand and intervene immediately to block a negative pattern or to coach the couple in trying something new. Therefore, our strong preference is to conduct relationship therapy directly with both members of the couple present.

Nevertheless, Bennun (1997) described methods for one-person couples therapy, and our own clinical experience suggests that in some cases a relationship can benefit from changes initiated by one partner. Principles of systems theory and social learning theory suggest that if one partner who attends therapy sessions changes ways of relating to the nonparticipating partner, it is possible to influence the latter person's responses indirectly. For example, if a couple has a history of mutually attacking each other verbally, and one person significantly reduces his or her side of that negative reciprocity, it may be possible to reduce the other person's verbal attacks. Similarly, if the individual who is attending therapy learns to listen to and communicate more respect for the partner's opinions, the partner may be more open to negotiation.

At present, there is minimal research on the efficacy of conducting one-partner couples therapy (Bennun, 1985a, 1985b), so clinicians must use their judgment in agreeing to work with clients who request that format. For clients whose partners adamantly refuse therapy, working individually versus receiving no assistance for their distressed relationships are the only options. Sometimes the person who initiates therapy prefers individual sessions, even though his or her partner would be willing to participate. At times, the caller portrays the partner as refusing to attend therapy, when in fact it is the caller who wants to avoid joint sessions, perhaps to enlist the support of the therapist, or because he or she tends to be intimidated and inhibited in the partner's presence. It is important for the therapist to inquire about the caller's cognitions and emotions concerning the possibility of joint sessions. For example, the therapist can ask, "For a moment, imagine the two of you sitting together in my office talking with me. What do you picture happening?" If the individual anticipates being intimidated and verbally abused by the partner, the therapist can discuss ways in which the sessions will be structured that will provide a controlled, safe setting for both partners. If this inquiry uncovers a caller's concern about the potential for being psychologically and physically abused by the partner after therapy sessions, it is crucial for the therapist to take this concern seriously and make plans with the individual to maintain safe conditions (Holtzworth-Munroe, Beatty, & Anglin, 1995). In cases of imminent danger, the therapist should shift to crisis intervention procedures, such as helping the individual plan a method of safe escape to a shelter. The therapist should not schedule conjoint sessions if it would place an individual at risk for abuse.

The therapist's relationship with the caller during the initial phone conversation is tenuous at best, so the clinician should consider that any reluctance the caller expresses about joint sessions with the partner may be based on concerns that the caller is not yet ready to reveal. As we mentioned in chapter 7, even when both members of a couple attend therapy we typically conduct individual assessment sessions with each partner, to provide an opportunity for each person to disclose information such as fears of abuse.

Consequently, if a caller seems very reluctant to include a partner in therapy for couple problems, it seems wise to schedule an individual assessment session with that person and inquire more at that time about possible abuse and other issues. Research has indicated that many individuals who seek couples therapy report an absence of domestic violence during their initial contact with a clinic but later reveal abuse during individual interviews (Heyman & Neidig, 1997).

Thus, after exploring a caller's reasons for requesting individual sessions, we do not pressure the individual into approaching a partner about attending therapy sessions together; this issue can be explored further in person. We have found that once the individual's concerns have been addressed in a supportive manner, many individuals become more comfortable with the idea of conjoint treatment and agree to invite the partner. During the individual session(s), the therapist also has an opportunity to describe the advantages of being able to observe and intervene directly when both partners are present.

In other cases, the caller prefers conjoint therapy but does not believe that he or she can convince the partner to participate. At times, this problem is representative of a macrolevel pattern in the couple's relationship, in which there is an imbalance in power and the caller's preferences rarely are taken into account. If so, the therapist immediately has an opportunity to intervene with a significant relationship pattern that is likely to be a continuing focus whether subsequent sessions involve one or both partners. Thus, the therapist can explore with the individual possible approaches that could be used to encourage the partner to attend therapy.

In choosing to work with one member of a couple, the therapist and that individual must anticipate the possible consequences if the absent partner eventually joins the therapy. In the next section we discuss ways of establishing a positive therapeutic alliance with both members of a couple. At times, achieving balance in one's relationships with the two individuals is difficult even with both partners present, and the potential for one or both partners to perceive favoritism by the therapist increases if one member attended sessions alone at first, particularly for more than a few sessions. We state our concerns about this explicitly whenever we begin working with one member of a couple and spend time in sessions planning with that person how to avoid a coalition when the partner joins the therapy. We coach the person who has attended individual sessions in ways of discussing with the absent partner that he or she understands how important it is that the two of them have balanced relationships with the therapist. He or she also is encouraged to explore with the partner what arrangements might increase that person's comfort with joining the therapy. Some options include the absent partner having a phone conversation with the therapist or one or more individual sessions, to build a relationship between the partner and the therapist. We emphasize that we are willing to initiate a phone call to the absent partner to indicate our interest in his or her views of the couple's relationship, to offer the option of conjoint sessions, and to answer any questions that he or she might have about our approach to working with couples. We also state to both partners that we want to have balanced relationships with each of them and thus would like either person to alert us if the relationship feels unbalanced. In our experience, these procedures go a long way toward addressing partners' concerns about the therapist's fairness and objectivity.

When it appears that the individual who initiated individual sessions is concerned about losing the positive relationship that he or she has begun to develop with the therapist, it is important for the therapist to discuss ways in which that relationship can be continued in conjoint couple therapy, even if in a somewhat different form. The therapist can stress that he or she will continue to listen carefully to the individual's thoughts and feelings and to identify ways in which the individual's personal needs can be better met within the couple relationship. It is important to distinguish between *being supportive* of the fulfillment of both individuals' needs versus *siding* with either member of the couple in a manner that neglects the other person. Thus, we emphasize that when we shift from individual to couples therapy the person likely will notice that at times we are focused on helping one person express thoughts and feelings, while the other person receives less attention. However, over time both partners will have many opportunities to express themselves and contribute to solutions to the concerns that brought the couple to therapy.

Nevertheless, at times the therapist may conclude that the individual who initially sought treatment has sufficient need for ongoing individual sessions that it would be deleterious to substitute couple sessions for individual sessions. For example, the individual may have individual characteristics (e.g., psychopathology, unresolved personal trauma, communication or assertiveness deficits, lack of a social support network) that likely would place him or her at a significant disadvantage in couple sessions. In such cases it is prudent to suggest continuing individual sessions with that person and to refer the couple to another therapist for couples therapy.

BUILDING A THERAPEUTIC ALLIANCE IN COUPLES THERAPY

When both members of a couple attend assessment and treatment sessions from the beginning of the process, there still is much to be done in building a balanced alliance with the two individuals. As with any form of therapy, in couples therapy an individual who is initially a total stranger to the couple gradually assumes a role of great significance in their lives, learning about and intervening with the most private aspects of their individual and couple functioning.

The goals of establishing an alliance with the couple are

- To establish the therapist's credibility as a person with the knowledge and skills to be helpful with the couple's problems.
- To instill confidence in both partners that the therapist will behave ethically, be unbiased, and maintain confidentiality.
- To create an atmosphere in which each member of the couple views sessions as a safe place to reveal information and experiment with new ways of relating to the partner.
- To establish a collaborative relationship with the couple in which the therapist actively seeks the involvement and creative efforts of the couple rather than dominating and directing goal setting and intervention.

There are countless ways a therapist can interact with a couple to form a balanced positive alliance. Because there is no formula for building an alliance with a couple, we describe some general strategies that can be helpful. There is no substitute for assessing the personal characteristics of each couple and tailoring one's approach to match the partners' personality styles, needs, and ways of coping with relationship issues.

Therapist Credibility

The clients' perceptions that the therapist understands relationships and knows how to intervene effectively can be influenced by a variety of factors. First, some clients tend to give weight to visible physical characteristics associated with age, gender, grooming, and formality versus informality of personal style. A therapist cannot alter his or her age, extent and variety of life experiences, gender, and other demographic characteristics, but it is possible to dress and behave in a relaxed but professional manner. Some clients are concerned if their therapist is not married or might not have extensive personal experience in couple relationships. We believe that it is important to be honest in responding to inquiries about one's marital status but that this should lead to an exploration of the concerns underlying a client's question. Most often, the client is worried that the therapist might not understand his or her life situation and thus might not realize the consequences of making particular changes. For example, Lucy was concerned that the couple's young female graduate student therapist would not understand her reasons for staying in a relationship in which her husband periodically hit her.

Clients also are likely to equate expertise with the therapist's degree of prior clinical experience. To some extent, it is reasonable for a couple to have such a concern. An inexperienced therapist might not have developed an ability to observe patterns in a couple's interactions well or the ability to tolerate and respond constructively to partners' expressions of intense emotion in sessions. An inexperienced therapist also might be vulnerable to being drawn into a coalition with one member of a couple, possibly leading to bias in the therapist's perceptions of the two individuals.

There is no guarantee that more experience will reduce these potential problems for all therapists, and there also is great potential for relatively inexperienced therapists to quickly develop their abilities to maintain impartiality and be a steadying influence in couples therapy. Some therapists enter training with levels of maturity, interpersonal skills, flexibility, and perceptiveness that allow them to function effectively in challenging therapy situations, whereas others need more supervisory input and experience. We have found that a therapist's learning process is often facilitated by videotaping sessions with clients and receiving supervision on the tapes from an experienced couples therapist who provides detailed feedback on the therapist–couple interactions. In particular, the focus can be on balancing the attention paid to the two partners, responding empathically to each person, validating each person's right to his or her subjective thoughts and emotions, and including each partner's preferences in any decision-making discussions during sessions. These types of behavior are likely to facilitate a therapeutic alliance with both partners, regardless of the experience level of the therapist.

Ethical Practice

Some couples enter therapy with concern that the therapist might behave in an unethical or irresponsible manner that would harm them, perhaps because of the couple's prior negative therapy experience or because of negative media publicity about unethical therapists. Conducting couples therapy involves some special professional issues, beyond those involved in clinical work with individual clients. For example, clear guidelines must be set and followed concerning confidentiality of information that each member of a couple might share with the therapist. In chapter 7 we described some advantages of conducting individual interviews with the members of a couple, to provide each person a relatively comfortable setting for disclosing information about past and present personal experiences that the person finds embarrassing or otherwise threatening to discuss in front of the partner. We stressed that each partner should have such an opportunity to discuss this material with the therapist, with clear guidelines that the therapist would break confidentiality only if the individual indicates that he or she is an imminent danger to the self, partner, or some other identified person. In addition, if an individual's past or current experience does not appear to be having a significant negative impact on the couple's relationship or the course of couples therapy, we do not believe that the therapist should press the person to disclose it to the partner. Even when one person discloses in an individual interview an experience (e.g., an ongoing extramarital affair) that seems to be affecting the couple's relationship negatively, the therapist should maintain confidentiality unless an explicit agreement was reached at the outset of treatment that the therapist would not keep secrets. The therapist can tell an individual with an ongoing affair that continuing couples therapy places the therapist in an ethically untenable position (conducting couples therapy when one partner is deceiving the other and the therapist knows it) and can ask the person to find a way to discontinue the couples therapy. Helpful guidelines for handling these and other ethical and professional issues in couples therapy can be found in publications such as Brock (1994), Huber (1994), and Margolin (1982).

Establishing an Atmosphere of Safety

Although a couples therapist may tend to think of therapy as a safe, constructive setting in which distressed couples can improve their relationships, for many clients the picture can look quite different. In couples therapy partners face the prospect of focusing on their relationship problems in close quarters with the person intimately involved in their unhappiness, along with a stranger who suggests that he or she might be able to help. Consequently, it is imperative that the therapist structure the initial sessions with a couple in ways that counteract the clients' fears that participating in therapy will be more trouble than it is worth. Particular aspects of the therapy setting that often are of concern to members of couples must be addressed.

First, the issue of confidentiality we described earlier should be discussed with the couple as soon as possible so that both partners will feel safe sharing information with the therapist, or at least deciding what information to disclose and under what conditions. Second, attending joint sessions places the partners in close proximity, with fewer options for avoiding or withdrawing from each other than they have in daily life, particularly if the therapist stresses open and direct communication between partners during assessment and therapy sessions. Individuals who conclude that these conditions are too painful or can lead to an increase in abuse at home may drop out of therapy. Thus, to establish a good alliance with the couple, the therapist must find a balance between obtaining a sample of their interaction patterns and imposing control over destructive interactions. The therapist can explain to couples that he or she would like to get a sense of how they communicate but will place clear limits on negative behavior so that they both can feel confident that coming to sessions will be constructive. The therapist emphasizes that therapy is a place where the couple can practice new ways to resolve issues and reduce their distress. It is important to acknowledge that thinking about and discussing relationship issues will at times feel stressful but that the therapist wants both partners to indicate when the discomfort reaches a level at which the person's thoughts are "I don't need this! I don't want to stay in this session or come back." The therapist should respect the fact that some couples use avoidance and withdrawal patterns to serve self-protective functions, and it is wise to allow the partners to do some distancing in sessions when they are feeling significant distress. For example, the therapist and couple can agree that either partner can ask for a temporary "time out," during which the current discussion will be discontinued for an agreed-on amount of time.

When working with a couple who has difficulty regulating high levels of emotion and negative behavior during sessions, the therapist can take strong and concrete steps to discourage harmful interactions. For example, to make the guidelines graphic, the therapist might write specific guidelines on a large sheet of paper, review them with the couple, post them in the office, and interrupt the couple quickly whenever a guideline is violated. Consistency in maintaining the structure and ground rules is crucial, and the therapist must be prepared to interrupt or even end a session in which one or both partners refuse to comply. The therapist may then request separate sessions with the partners, to prepare them to collaborate with each other. This establishes the therapist's control of the therapy process, and it offers an opportunity to help each partner explore personal responses that interfere with his or her ability to moderate emotions and behavior. Even though the members of a couple may feel somewhat frustrated when the therapist imposes structure in such ways, it is our experience that the therapist's stance typically reassures them that therapy will be a safe environment and thus contributes to a positive alliance between the therapist and couple.

In some cases partners will be displeased if the therapist blocks their attempts to punish each other during sessions. It is important that the therapist build an alliance with these individuals by expressing empathy for their dissatisfaction with their relationship and stressing that a key goal of therapy is to make changes in the relationship that will make it more satisfying. The therapist can point out in a sympathetic way that the punitive approach that partners have been using may provide occasional satisfaction, but it has not led to improvements in their concerns, and that the therapist wants to help them find new approaches that work better.

It is traditional in cognitive–behavioral therapy to stress with a couple that much of the work involved in the therapy takes place between the scheduled sessions, as the partners carry out various homework assignments that they and the therapist have devised during sessions (Baucom & Epstein, 1990). Consequently, the structure that the therapist imposes to give the partners a sense of safety must be extended to settings outside the office. Of course, the therapist has much less control over the ways that the partners behave toward each other outside the office, but it is important to make plans with the couple concerning specific things they can do to control aversive or abusive experiences at home. Whenever there has been a tense or conflictual discussion between partners during a session, the therapist can spend time toward the end of the session asking the couple what they can do to prevent their feelings from erupting into negative interactions at home during the hours and days ahead. This planning can even extend to a discussion of how a couple who commutes long distances to therapy will interact with each in the car on the long ride home. Even when a couple tells the therapist that they doubt there will be any problems outside of the session, the therapist can play devil's advocate, suggesting that the couple can never be sure that all will go well. The therapist can challenge the clients to think of specific plans they could use "just in case." This planning helps extend the therapist's influence into the couple's life outside the office and helps build a strong therapeutic alliance.

Establishing a Collaborative Relationship With the Couple

Although the therapist brings expertise concerning couple functioning to the therapeutic relationship, he or she also seeks a great deal of input from the partners at every stage of the assessment and treatment. During the assessment process the clinician emphasizes that each person is the expert on his or her needs, sources of satisfaction, stresses, and so forth. When the therapist gives the couple feedback concerning the patterns identified in the assessment, the partners are periodically asked how well the feedback matches their own impressions of the factors influencing their relationship. Whenever there is a mismatch between the therapist's and partners' perceptions, the therapist inquires about the couple's views, using their input to revise the conceptualization of their relationship problems or clarifying aspects of the therapist's feedback that the couple may have misunderstood.

At times the couple and the therapist might have different perspectives on the couple's relationship, at least for some time period. In particular, the couple might enter therapy feeling hopeless and believing that their relationship is doomed. Although the therapist might not easily convince them that there is significant potential for change, the therapist's role often includes providing hope that positive changes can occur in their relationship. It is inadvisable for a therapist to communicate an unwarranted high level of optimism about the potential for progress in therapy, but it is important to help clients break out of distorted, global negative views of their relationships and to instill some hope for change where appropriate (Baucom & Epstein, 1990; Jacobson & Christensen, 1996). Counteracting clients' hopelessness about improving their relationship must involve more than a general statement that the therapist knows how to help couples solve serious problems. Instead, the therapist needs to listen to the couple's account of their past and current difficulties and to probe for any information about relationship strengths and earlier periods during which the partners were more satisfied with their interactions. Then the therapist's messages regarding hope can focus on specific evidence that the couple has had the ability to relate in more positive ways, as well as on aspects of the therapist's approach that are designed to modify distressing aspects of their interactions and facilitate positive changes.

Furthermore, the therapist needs to monitor and work at maintaining an alliance with both members of a couple throughout the course of assessment and treatment, because specific events that occur at any stage of the therapy can add to or detract from the alliance. For example, Beth and Grant's therapist had established a good alliance with them through consistent collaboration and by balancing the amount of attention paid to each person's issues and goals. However, after several weeks of therapy a disruptive event occurred between sessions. When Beth phoned the therapist to complain about Grant's treatment of her since their last therapy session, the therapist made some suggestions about how she could talk with Grant about his behavior. When the couple arrived at their next session, Grant stated that he was very surprised that the therapist had spent a half hour listening to Beth's side of the story and apparently accepting it as accurate. A therapist cannot anticipate all the idiosyncratic ways that members of a couple might interpret his or her actions as violations of therapeutic alliances. Nevertheless, it is wise to think about ways that each member of the couple might construe any intervention and inquire about each partner's views. Often, the members of a couple will be reassured by the therapist's demonstration of concern about maintaining balance.

GOAL SETTING WITH THE COUPLE

As noted, goal setting is a key point in the development of a therapeutic alliance with a couple. It also is crucial to identifying and intervening with aspects of the couple's relationship that are most likely to increase their satisfaction with the relationship. The therapist begins to get a sense of a couple's goals from the first phone contact, although often the goals stated by the caller reflect that person's perspective more than that of the partner, and they often are only a subset of the goals on which the couple and therapist ultimately focus. The therapist begins to get a more extensive picture of a couple's goals during the first joint assessment interview, during which they are asked to describe their reasons for seeking couples therapy. The therapist often needs to help each person translate concerns and complaints into desires for change.

An important aspect of goal setting is that the therapist and couple explicitly discuss how specific behavioral goals address broader macrolevel goals involving core relationship concerns, such as reconciling partners' apparently conflicting needs. For example, Valerie initially spoke about her unhappiness about what she labeled "Rob's preoccupation with his job, insensitivity to my feelings, and selfishness." Further inquiry by the therapist suggested that Valerie interpreted Rob's behavior as meaning that his work was more important to him than she was. She also identified that her intimacy needs were not being fulfilled sufficiently in their relationship. Thus, Valerie and Rob's therapist began to guide them in identifying a macrolevel therapy goal of finding new ways to achieve a mutually acceptable balance between Valerie's needs for intimacy and Rob's strong motivation to achieve. This macrolevel goal was written down, and the couple then generated a few initial ideas about more specific subgoals for the macrolevel goal (e.g., scheduling one block of time each week that would be devoted to leisure activities together and would be protected against any intrusions from work or other people).

It is helpful to periodically evaluate progress that has been made toward achieving the particular macrolevel goals and subgoals that the therapist and members of the couple have agreed to pursue in therapy. A hallmark of the cognitive–behavioral approach is its reliance on an empirical approach to evaluating the effectiveness of treatment (Baucom & Epstein, 1990; Jacobson & Margolin, 1979). The therapist can ask the couple to review the goals that they have set, to discuss the criteria they are using to assess progress, and to rate the level of progress. Couples often feel encouraged when they can see signs of progress, particularly after a history of feeling frustrated and hopeless about change.

At times a couple may agree that they have enacted their planned changes and have met particular criteria that they had set as goals for therapy, but they still do not feel much more satisfied. It is important for the therapist to caution a couple initially that additional areas needing attention might become apparent later. It is important to think of therapy goals as evolving and developing over time. The therapist's task is to monitor progress toward goals and help the couple become aware of any additional goals that should be pursued.

Helping the couple develop new goals can involve increasing the partners' awareness of their motives or needs, personality styles, and other personal characteristics that influence their relationship. At times the couple and therapist are unaware of these factors when therapy begins, but the therapist might observe important patterns as therapy progresses. In such instances the therapist gives the couple feedback about the patterns that he or she has observed over the course of treatment. From these observations, the therapist shares hypotheses with the clients about what this pattern might suggest or asks the couple what this pattern implies to them. The role of the cognitive–behavioral therapist is to *collaborate with the clients in discovering* what individual, couple, or environmental factors affect the couple's relationship in important ways. The therapist relies heavily on the couple to assess their own responses and gather information about their relationship, which sometimes leads to the setting of new therapy goals.

ROLE OF THE THERAPIST IN COUPLES THERAPY

Didactic Skill-Building and Modification of Macropatterns

Cognitive–behavioral couples therapists traditionally have viewed therapy primarily as a skill-building process. Jacobson and Margolin's (1979) seminal text on behavioral marital therapy emphasized teaching couples communication and problem-solving skills as well as coaching couples in setting up contracts to exchange positive behavior. Similarly, our earlier work has focused on teaching couples skills for producing pleasing behavioral interactions as well as skills for monitoring and testing the validity or appropriateness of their cognitions about their relationships (Baucom & Epstein, 1990; Epstein & Baucom, 1989), and these approaches continue to be used widely (e.g., Rathus & Sanderson, 1999). All of these interventions have been based on an assumption that distressed couples have deficits in the skills that well-adjusted couples use to maintain satisfying interactions and to minimize destructive ones.

As we described earlier, empirical findings indicate that happy couples exhibit fewer negative behaviors and more positive behaviors than distressed couples, and behavioral interventions involving skill-building techniques have produced significant increases in relationship adjustment (see Baucom, Shoham, Mueser, Daiuto, & Stickle, 1998, for a review of outcome research). However, distressed and happy couples do not differ consistently in their daily use of particular communication skills such as reflective listening (Gottman, 1999), and couples who become more satisfied after receiving communication and problem-solving skills training commonly discontinue their use of those skills following therapy. Does this mean that cognitive–behavioral therapists should abandon their roles as teachers of relationship skills?

In chapter 9 we describe how helping distressed couples practice constructive communication and problem-solving skills during therapy sessions and at home serves purposes other than remediation of skill deficits. Although some distressed couples have deficits in such skills, many do not. Members of many distressed couples use these skills with other people in their lives, but they have developed patterns in their couple relationships that are dominated by destructive or ineffective behaviors (Birchler, Weiss, & Vincent, 1975). Consequently, therapists can use communication and problem-solving exercises, as well as guided behavior change exercises, for the purpose of *interrupting a couple's ingrained negative patterns*. The partners then experience a contrast between the way it typically feels when they interact negatively and the way it feels while they are behaving in the alternate manner. Although one or two such experiences are unlikely to counteract overlearned negative responses or partners' global negative feelings toward each other, our experience suggests that over time the constructive behavior often produces changes in automatic negative behavior and global negative sentiment. Many couples have reported to us their relief in having a positive discussion of their feelings or a constructive decision-making conversation and their desire for more of it. Equally significant is that the positive interactions may change partners' global negative perceptions of each other, as each person demonstrates the willingness to cooperate and treat the other in a respectful manner. Regardless of whether the couple continues to use the same constructive patterns over time, the therapist's role is to interrupt distressing behaviors and help the couple see that they can relate to each other in more satisfying ways (Baucom & Epstein, 1990).

This same principle applies to cognitive-restructuring procedures, wherein the therapist does not assume that each person will continue to use particular techniques to test the validity of every distressing cognition that he or she experiences. Rather, the therapist's role in encouraging the individual to practice challenging cognitions in sessions and during homework tasks is valuable because it can produce a macrolevel change in which the individual's overall negative view of the partner has been broadened. For example, once the therapist guides an individual in considering that the partner does not routinely have negative intentions and is trying to behave cooperatively, the probability of having consistently negative automatic thoughts about the partner may decrease. The therapist's role is to structure sessions and homework tasks such that cognitive-restructuring exercises interrupt partners' usual ways of thinking and thus produce different experiences of their relationship. Whether couples apply these techniques routinely as skills is less important than whether the therapist has altered their macrolevel cognitions about their relationship.

Therefore, working with couples on behavioral and cognitive-restructuring skills is still an important aspect of a therapist's role. As we see it, the key is how the therapist conceptualizes the processes through which coaching couples in the use of those patterns influences the couple's functioning. The therapist's role in interrupting negative patterns, altering partners' macrolevel views of their relationship, and initiating new interactions that better meet partners' macrolevel needs enhances the traditional skill-training role in cognitive–behavioral couples therapy (CBCT; Baucom & Epstein, 1990).

For example, a therapist might coach a couple in using expressive and listening skills for the purpose of increasing their experiences of intimacy, thereby addressing one of the couple's macrolevel goals for therapy. Although the therapist hopes to increase the couple's use of communication *skills* for sharing their thoughts and emotions, he or she is equally concerned with increasing the partners' *expectancies* that they have the ability to enhance their intimacy. Once the partners have some confidence in their ability to relate intimately, they may be motivated to find additional intimate ways of interacting.

Degree of Structuring and Direction

To intervene actively to interrupt partners' ingrained negative behavioral, cognitive, and affective responses to each other, and to keep the couple focused on working toward specific goals, the therapist can impose a considerable amount of structure during sessions. It is common for members of distressed couples to wander from one topic to another during a therapy session, particularly when they have several concerns about their relationship. Although the therapist wants the couple to have opportunities to identify concerns and to feel understood by the therapist, a lack of focus during sessions is unlikely to be satisfying to them. Consequently, the therapist needs to help the couple organize the way they use the session time to work toward their goals. This approach may entail setting an agenda with the couple at the beginning of each session, specifying the topics to be covered and the amount of time to be devoted to each one, an approach commonly used in cognitive therapy (A. T. Beck, Rush, Shaw, & Emery, 1979; J. S. Beck, 1995; Leahy, 1996). It also involves interrupting the clients when they are straying to a different topic and noting that the other topic can be discussed later.

The amount of structure and level of direction that the therapist provides are influenced by several factors. First, the nature of the couple's interactions can affect the level of structure needed and how directive the therapist needs to be. Couples who have strong, destructive arguments typified by rapidly escalating negative reciprocity often need a great deal of structure in the session. At times the therapist needs to intervene quickly to minimize such destructive exchanges. Over time, the therapist can decrease his or her quick interventions as the partners assume this role for themselves. Second, couples vary in their ability to self-monitor their own behavior, thoughts, and feelings during the session. Thus, some couples can be given the guidelines for decision making or problem solving and can progress from one step to the next with minimal intervention from the therapist. Other couples need much more assistance from the therapist, who needs to remind them frequently of where they are in the process and what might be helpful next. Third, various partners react differently to structure and directiveness, and the therapist needs to alter his or her behavior in a way that will facilitate progress. Some partners very much want the help of an authority figure who will tell them what to do and how to do it. Other partners seem to rebel against structure and feel patronized when a therapist suggests that the couple have 10 minutes of talk time each evening. In such instances the therapist might function more as a consultant, raising possibilities and guiding the couple in considering alternative ways for making changes in their relationship.

Regardless of how much structure seems appropriate for a given couple, behaving directively does not mean imposing one's values and preferences on a couple. The therapist's role is to structure and direct a couple's interactions in the service of *their* goals. For example, interrupting a couple's hostile interactions is consistent with working toward their goals of feeling more warmth and cooperation in their relationship. We explicitly tell the couple why we are intervening in particular ways and preferably gain their consent that we should do so.

CONVEYING EXPECTATIONS OF THE COUPLE DURING
AND OUTSIDE OF THERAPY SESSIONS

The therapist's ability to carry out his or her role depends on the clients' willingness to carry out their roles as well. It is important that the couple be given information about aspects of both the therapist's role and their own roles that will influence the effectiveness of therapy. This information can be given during the first conjoint session with the couple, but so much material is typically discussed during that session that the therapist might need to occasionally repeat particular expectations for the couple if they seem to be drifting from the guidelines. Giving the couple positive feedback when they have adhered to guidelines for constructive interaction is likely to encourage them to maintain their efforts.

Clients vary in their expectancies about therapy, such as the degree to which the therapist will be active, directive, and authoritative. Consequently, to establish a truly collaborative relationship, the therapist needs to describe the ways in which he or she wants to work as a team with the couple and ask them how they feel about doing so. The therapist can emphasize that they are the ones who know their own responses best, so the therapist will be combining his or her expertise with valuable information that only they can provide. In addition, the therapist stresses that change will occur only when the partners each make active efforts to improve their relationship.

As we described earlier, some couples need more structure and direction during therapy sessions than other couples do. With highly distressed couples who behave in aversive and even abusive ways toward each other, it is likely that the therapist will need to convey specific expectations about acceptable behavior during sessions, such as refraining from interrupting each other, moderating voice volume, and refraining from making derogatory comments about each other. If necessary, the therapist should inform clients that violation of particular ground rules (especially regarding abusive behavior) will lead to the termination of the session. The therapist also discusses similar guidelines for constructive interactions at home, particularly making clear expectations regarding the control of abusive behavior. Whenever appropriate, the therapist engages the couple in devising anger management and safety plans, such as "time outs" from each other that either partner can request when there are cues that the danger of violence is increasing (Holtzworth-Munroe et al., 1995).

We also encourage couples to do their best to maintain an open-minded, flexible approach to resolving the issues that brought them into therapy. This expectation can be operationalized for a couple in terms of specific types of responses, such as being willing to try an exercise suggested by the therapist rather than dismissing it. We emphasize being open to trying new ways of responding to one's partner, to learn about the consequences. For example, if an individual expresses pessimism about the therapist's suggestion that the couple brainstorm about activities that may enhance their sense of intimacy, the therapist can suggest that the individual "try it this week, and see how it turns out."

The empirical try-and-see approach also applies to the therapist's interventions. It is important that the therapist ask the couple for ongoing feedback about the impacts of those interventions (Baucom & Epstein, 1990). Typically, the therapist will ask for feedback about which aspects of therapy sessions the clients have found helpful and which ones did not seem helpful. It may be possible to pre-empt dropouts by setting an expectation that the therapist and couple will discuss the partners' feelings about therapy.

The therapist also conveys the expectation that the couple will collaborate with him or her in devising homework tasks to implement changes and will carry out the homework. The therapist then spends time toward the end of each session discussing an appropriate homework assignment for the coming week and reviews the process and outcome of the assignment early in the next session (Baucom & Epstein, 1990). When clients report that they have failed to complete their homework, the therapist inquires about the events that interfered with it. The therapist then can guide the couple in a problem-solving discussion about ways to remove the impediments, thus underscoring the importance of homework.

EMPIRICAL STATUS OF COUPLES THERAPY

As the reader can see in the preceding recommendations for conducting couples therapy, there are many ongoing clinical decisions that the clinician and the couples must make. Many of these decisions are rooted in basic and applied research findings. More specifically, in developing this enhanced cognitive–behavioral approach to treating relationship distress we draw on basic research and theory as described in Part I of this book. In addition, we incorporate clinical insights from several theoretical approaches, including behavioral couples therapy (BCT), CBCT (which includes an emphasis on cognitions as well as behaviors), insight-oriented couples therapy (IOCT), emotion-focused therapy (EFT), integrative couples therapy (ICT), and systemic approaches to working with couples. It is important to understand the empirical status of these various approaches to assisting distressed couples before we describe the specific interventions in detail. All of these approaches have growing bodies of empirical support that demonstrate their efficacy in assisting distressed couples. Elsewhere we and our colleagues have provided a detailed discussion of the empirical status of each of these approaches (Baucom, Epstein, & Gordon, 2000; Baucom et al., 1998), as well as a clinical comparison of the similarities and differences among major approaches to assisting couples (Baucom et al., 2000). Therefore, in this book we provide a brief overview of the empirical status of the theoretical approaches that serve as the foundation of our clinical approach and refer the reader to other sources for a more detailed review and comparison.

In evaluating the empirical status of couple therapy, Baucom et al. (1998) used the criteria developed by Chambless and Hollon (1998)

> If an intervention has been found to be superior to a wait list control condition in at least two studies conducted by two independent research teams (and the bulk of the findings support these results), it was designated as *efficacious*. If the intervention has been found to be superior to a placebo, nonspecific treatment, or rival interventions in two studies conducted by independent research teams, it was designated as *efficacious and specific*. It is important to recognize that the use of the term *specific* in this instance does not imply that an intervention is the treatment of choice for a given disorder; instead, it might indicate only that a treatment was superior to a placebo condition in two investigations. These two categories ('efficacious' and 'efficacious and specific') are modified with the term *possibly* when all other criteria are met for a designation but only one study has been conducted (or two or more by a single research team). Thus, if a treatment has been found to be superior to a wait list in a single study, it is labeled *possibly efficacious*. If a treatment has been found to be superior to a rival treatment in a single study, it is termed *possibly efficacious and specific*. If a treatment has been found to be superior to a wait list in one study and superior to a rival treatment in another study by another investigative team, it meets criteria for efficacy but is only possibly specific; thus, it is termed *efficacious and possibly specific*. (Baucom et al., 1998, p. 55)

Using these criteria, the empirical status of various approaches to couples therapy are provided in the Appendix. Whereas we use the term *couples therapy* in this volume to be inclusive of couples in committed relationships who are not married, we should note that all of these treatment outcome studies were restricted to heterosexual couples, and almost all couples were legally married.

BCT is efficacious and specific, based on the above-mentioned criteria. As the reader can see in the Appendix, more outcome research has been conducted on BCT than on all other approaches combined. BCT is more efficacious than wait list control groups and nonspecific (placebo) interventions, although it has not been found to be more efficacious than the other theoretical approaches being described. Investigators also have evaluated the clinical significance of BCT (i.e., whether the magnitude of the change has real life implications for couples) and have assessed long-term effects of BCT. Although the results vary among studies, the findings overall suggest that between one third and two thirds of couples receiving BCT are likely to be in the nondistressed range at the end of treatment. Most couples maintain these gains for short time periods (6–12 months), but a proportion of these couples demonstrate relapse 2–4 years following treatment.

Baucom and Lester (1986); Baucom, Sayers, and Sher (1990); and Halford, Sanders, and Behrens (1993) have evaluated the efficacy of CBCT, combining behavioral interventions with cognitive restructuring. All three of these investigations found CBCT to be equivalent to BCT in assisting distressed couples. As with most treatment outcome studies, the sample sizes in these investigations were somewhat small, minimizing the likelihood that differences would be detected between active treatment conditions. Because only one research team (Baucom et al., 1990) included a wait list condition in their design, CBCT is most appropriately viewed as possibly efficacious, with all existing evidence suggesting the same magnitude of effects as BCT.

IOCT also is viewed as possibly efficacious. It has been evaluated in only one treatment outcome study to date, in which it was compared with BCT and a wait list condition (Snyder & Wills, 1989). The findings demonstrated that both active conditions were more efficacious than the wait list condition, and the two active treatments were equivalent at posttest and 6-month follow-up. However, in the longest follow-up to date, after 4 years, significantly more of the BCT couples had experienced divorce relative to IOCT couples (38% vs. 3%, respectively; Snyder, Wills, & Grady-Fletcher, 1991). In addition, at 4-year follow-up IOCT couples demonstrated significantly higher levels of marital adjustment than BCT couples. It is unfortunately unknown whether couples received additional interventions during this follow-up period. The long-term effects of IOCT are impressive in this one investigation, and a replication of this finding is needed to understand whether IOCT consistently has this long-term effect.

There have been several investigations of EFT addressing various issues about its efficacy, and the findings to date indicate that EFT is of significant benefit to distressed couples. As the reader can see in the Appendix, EFT appears to be more efficacious than wait list conditions. In an important investigation, Johnson and Greenberg (1985) assigned 45 maritally distressed couples to EFT, BCT, or a waiting list. It is worth noting that the interventions were restricted to moderately distressed couples, because the investigators were concerned that EFT might not be optimal for extremely distressed couples. The findings demonstrated that even with relatively small sample sizes, EFT was superior to BCT in increasing marital adjustment at posttest. On the basis of the consistent posttest superiority of EFT to wait list across studies involving investigators from more than one research team, EFT should be viewed as an efficacious treatment for assisting maritally distressed couples. Given its superiority to the efficacious BCT treatment in Johnson and Greenberg's (1985) investigation, it also is possibly specific and superior to other forms of efficacious treatment.

Jacobson, Christensen, Prince, Cordova, and Eldridge (2000) recently published results from the first investigation comparing Jacobson and Christensen's (1996) ICT with BCT. The findings are based on a small sample size, so the investigators did not use inferential statistical tests to compare the treatment conditions. Based on descriptive statistics, the results demonstrate that ICT, which integrates acceptance along with behavior change, resulted in changes in marital adjustment that were larger in magnitude than the changes observed in BCT, which focuses only on behavior change and skills training. Whereas these findings from the initial study are encouraging, results from a large, ongoing treatment investigation conducted in two sites comparing ICT with BCT suggest that the immediate effects of the two treatments are equivalent (Atkins, 2000). With data collected on 132 couples across the two sites to date, the findings thus far suggest that, at posttest, the effects of the two treatments are equivalent in altering marital adjustment. The equivalence between treatment conditions at posttest also holds when clinical significance is calculated and when effect sizes are compared.

A consideration of the combined results of these various investigations of couple therapy indicates that several approaches, including behavioral, cognitive–behavioral, insight-oriented, emotion-focused, and integrative couples therapy, are helpful to distressed couples. There is little evidence that any single therapeutic approach is more efficacious in general for assisting distressed couples. What also is evident from the findings is that, for any given therapeutic approach, a significant proportion of couples do not improve. In interpreting this conclusion, it is important to recognize that in all of these investigations the couples were randomly assigned to treatment without matching the couples' needs or issues to treatment condition. Although empirical data are necessary to substantiate this possibility, it is also likely that different couples will respond to different types of interventions. In the chapters that follow, we attempt to clarify how these various interventions, which have been demonstrated to be of assistance to distressed couples in general, can be selected and integrated for assisting specific couples.

SUMMARY

In this chapter we have described a variety of generic clinical issues that arise in conducting couples therapy. The therapist's ability to build an alliance with both partners, socialize them into a cognitive–behavioral approach, and facilitate ongoing collaboration among the therapist and two partners is crucial to the success of treatment.

- Building an alliance with the members of a couple requires that the therapist be credible as a helper, respectful of each partner's views and values, and committed to each person's safety and well-being. Openness to learning about each client's life and perspective can compensate for limited professional and personal life experience in establishing the therapist's credibility. Providing structure and setting limits on partners' negative interactions within and outside of sessions also can contribute to the therapeutic alliance by instilling confidence that therapy is a relatively safe setting for working on relationship problems.

- In a collaborative approach to goal setting, the therapist provides feedback from the assessment and solicits input from the partners to devise mutually acceptable goals. The therapist helps the couple identify macrolevel goals that address core issues such as unmet needs as well as more specific subgoals within each major goal.

- Goal setting is an ongoing process in which the therapist and couple monitor progress and add new goals when appropriate. Clearly stated goals allow the therapist and couple to evaluate progress and shift their approach as needed.

- The role of the therapist within a cognitive–behavioral approach includes a didactic component of teaching couples about relationship dynamics and how to use communication, decision-making, cognitive restructuring, and other skills. Our enhanced model also requires that the therapist work to increase partners' awareness of macropatterns of behavior, cognitions, and emotional responses, so that interventions explicitly address those patterns.

- The therapist attempts to strike a balance between directiveness and collaboration with the couple; for example, imposing structure in sessions to control negative interactions, but explicitly doing so to meet the couple's stated goal of achieving more cooperation. The amount of therapist directiveness needed will depend on the couple's own ability and willingness to exercise self-control over their interactions.

- Just as the therapist explains his or her role to the couple, the expectations that the therapist has for the couple's behavior within and outside of sessions are discussed in detail. These expectations include adhering to ground rules concerning conduct, such as using constructive forms of communication and refraining from abusive behavior. Because cognitive–behavioral therapy depends on the client's active involvement in trying new ways of behaving and thinking, the therapist also conveys expectations that the partners will experiment with new responses, both in sessions and in homework assignments.

In the chapters that follow we describe specific interventions for modifying behavioral, cognitive, and emotional aspects of couples' interactions to attain therapy goals. The principles and strategies we have discussed in this chapter are applied throughout the therapist's use of those cognitive–behavioral interventions, to create a structure within which the clinician can effectively implement the interventions in the therapeutic relationship.

EMPIRICAL STATUS OF COUPLE THERAPY FOR THE
TREATMENT OF MARITAL DISTRESS

Treatment and study	Treatment conditions	Major results
	Efficacious and specific treatments	
Behavioral couples therapy (BCT)		
Azrin et al. (1980)	1. BCT ($n = 28$) 2. Attention/placebo ($n = 27$)	1 > 2
Baucom (1982)	1. BCT ($n = 18$) 2. Communication/problem solving ($n = 18$) 3. Behavioral contracting ($n = 18$) 4. Wait list ($n = 18$)	1 = 2 = 3 > 4
Baucom & Lester (1986)	1. BCT ($n = 8$) 2. BCT + cognitive restructuring ($n = 8$) 3. Wait list ($n = 8$)	1 = 2 > 3
Baucom et al. (1990)	1. BCT + cognitive restructuring for couples + emotional expressiveness training ($n = 12$) 2. BCT ($n = 12$) 3. BCT + cognitive restructuring for couples ($n = 12$) 4. BCT + emotional expressiveness training ($n = 12$) 5. Wait list ($n = 12$)	1 = 2 = 3 = 4 > 5
Bennun (1985a)	1. Conjoint BCT ($n = 19$) 2. Group BCT ($n = 19$) 3. Individual BCT ($n = 19$)	1 = 2 = 3
Boelens et al. (1980)	1. Behavioral contracting ($n = 8$) 2. System therapy ($n = 8$) 3. Wait list ($n = 5$)	1 = 2 > 3
Crowe (1978)	1. BCT ($n = 14$) 2. Group analytic therapy ($n = 14$) 3. Attention/placebo ($n = 14$)	1 = 2 = 3
Emmelkamp et al. (1984)	1. Communication/problem solving + behavioral contracting ($n = 17$) 2. Behavioral contracting + communication/problem solving (n = same 17 couples in cross-over design)	1 = 2
Emmelkamp et al. (1988)	1. BCT ($n = 16$) 2. Cognitive restructuring for couples ($n = 16$)	1 = 2
Ewart (1978)	1. BCT ($n = 18$) 2. Wait list ($n = 6$)	women: 1 > 2 men: 1 = 2
Girodo et al. (1980)	1. BCT ($n = 6$) 2. Minnesota Couples' Communication Program ($n = 12$) 3. Wait list ($n = 6$)	1 = 2 = 3

Appendix continues

Treatment and study	Treatment conditions	Major results
Hahlweg et al. (1982)	1. BCT ($n = 17$) 2. Group BCT ($n = 16$) 3. Emotional expressiveness training ($n = 16$) 4. Group emotional expressiveness training ($n = 19$) 5. Wait list ($n = 17$)	$1 = 2 = 3 > 4 = 5$
Halford et al. (1993)	1. BCT ($n = 13$) 2. BCT + cognitive restructuring + affect exploration + generalization training ($n = 13$)	$1 = 2$
Jacobson (1977)	1. BCT ($n = 5$) 2. Wait list ($n = 5$)	$1 > 2$
Jacobson (1978)	1. BCT + good faith behavioral contracting ($n = 8$) 2. BCT + quid pro quo behavioral contracting ($n = 9$) 3. Attention/placebo ($n = 7$) 4. Wait list ($n = 6$)	$1 = 2 > 3, 4$
Jacobson (1984)	1. BCT ($n = 9$) 2. Communication/problem solving ($n = 9$) 3. Behavior exchange ($n = 9$) 4. Wait list ($n = 9$)	$1 = 2 = 3 > 4$
Johnson & Greenberg (1985)	1. Emotion-focused therapy (EFT; $n = 15$) 2. Communication/problem solving ($n = 15$) 3. Wait list ($n = 15$)	$1 > 2 > 3$
Liberman et al. (1976)	1. BCT ($n = 5$) 2. Attention Placebo ($n = 4$)	$1 > 2$
Snyder & Wills (1989)	1 BCT ($n = 29$) 2. Insight-orient marital therapy ($n = 30$) 3. Wait list ($n = 20$)	$1 = 2 > 3$
Tsoi-Hoshmund (1976)	1. BCT ($n = 10$) 2. Attention/placebo ($n = 6$) 3. Wait list ($n = 4$)	$2 = 3$
Turkewitz & O'Leary (1981)	1. Emotional expressiveness training ($n = 10$) 2. BCT ($n = 10$) 3. Wait list ($n = 10$)	$1 = 2 = 3$
Wilson et al. (1988)	1. Group BCT ($n = 5$) 2. Conjoint BCT ($n = 5$) 3. Wait list ($n = 5$)	$1 = 2 > 3$

Efficacious and Possibly Specific Treatments

Emotion-focused couples therapy (EFT)		
Dandeneau & Johnson (1994)	1. EFT ($n = 12$) 2. Waring cognitive therapy ($n = 12$) 3. Wait list ($n = 12$)	$1 = 2 = 3$

Appendix continues

Treatment and study	Treatment conditions	Major results
Goldman & Greenberg (1992)	1. EFT ($n = 14$) 2. System therapy ($n = 14$) 3. Wait list ($n = 14$)	$1 = 2 > 3$
James (1991)	1. EFT + emotional expressiveness training ($n = 14$) 2. EFT ($n = 14$) 3. Wait list ($n = 14$)	$1 = 2 > 3$
Johnson & Greenberg (1985)	See previous entry under BCT	
Walker et al. (1996)	1. EFT ($n = 16$) 2. Wait list ($n = 16$)	$1 > 2$

Possibly Efficacious Treatments		
Cognitive couples therapy		
Emmelkamp et al. (1988)	See previous entry under BCT	
Huber & Milstein (1985)	1. Cognitive restructuring for couples ($n = 9$) 2. Wait list ($n = 8$)	$1 > 2$
Cognitive–behavioral couple therapy (CBT)		
Baucom & Lester (1986)	See previous entry under BCT	
Baucom et al. (1990)	See previous entry under BCT	
Halford et al. (1993)	See previous entry under BCT	
Insight-oriented couple therapy (IOMT)		
Snyder & Wills (1989)	See previous entry under BCT	
Systemic couples therapy (ST)		
Goldman & Greenberg (1992)	See previous entry under EFT	

Appendix continues

Treatment and study	Treatment conditions	Major results
	Promising treatments	
Integrative couples therapy (ICT)		
Atkins (2000)	1. ICT ($n = 65$) 2. BCT ($n = 67$)	1 = 2 (progress report)
Jacobson et al. (2000)	1. ICT ($n = 10$) 2. BCT ($n = 11$)	Not determined

Note. Treatments are designated by number from the previous column. 1 > 2 indicates that Treatment 1 is statistically superior to Treatment 2 in improving marital adjustment at posttest. Major results include statistically significant differences among treatment conditions at posttest; see text for follow-up results.

9

BEHAVIORAL INTERVENTIONS

Behavioral interventions are useful tools for clinicians when considered in light of our overall enhanced cognitive–behavioral model. To meet both partners' needs, address individual differences or psychopathology, and improve the couple's interaction cycles, partners may find it necessary to develop new ways of behaving or communicating with each other. In this chapter we provide guidelines for making behavior changes and for teaching skills that may both change the overall atmosphere of a relationship and respond to specific problem areas. We also discuss specific steps partners can take to share their thoughts and feelings and make decisions. Throughout the chapter, we consider the appropriateness and function of behavioral interventions in couples therapy.

In this chapter we describe a variety of interventions to help couples make adaptive behavioral changes. It is easy for therapists to latch onto structured, concrete, behavioral intervention strategies, because they provide a sense of direction and focus in the treatment. It is understandable that, given the complexity of couples' difficulties and the sense of being out of control that many couples bring to therapy, such interventions can be very appealing. However, a mechanical, routine application of these interventions runs the risk of falling short of optimal effectiveness as well as the possibility that couples will feel that their specific needs have not been heard or addressed.

As we describe more extensively in subsequent chapters, these interventions should be used selectively, with a given purpose in mind, and adapted to the needs of the particular couple. In this chapter we describe behavioral interventions that have been developed but, before doing so, we present our perspective on behavioral change interventions to lay the groundwork for using these specific strategies.

PERSPECTIVES ON BEHAVIOR CHANGE INTERVENTIONS

Both our clinical experience and the empirical literature (Baucom, Shoham, Mueser, Daiuto, & Stickle, 1998) indicate that many couples benefit significantly from behavioral change strategies. At the same time, several couples and therapists raise thoughtful questions about these interventions. These questions fall into at least three categories.

1. Some couples and therapists question whether these interventions are too structured and artificial because they do not mirror what happens in couples' everyday lives. Consequently, will couples really use these strategies on their own, either outside of the therapy session or after treatment has terminated?

2. At times these interventions can appear to focus on concrete yet trivial matters. They do not seem to address the core issues that are central to the couple's functioning. Are these interventions appropriate for addressing macrolevel or thematic issues, or are they suited primarily for approaching specific, isolated behavioral concerns?

3. Most behavioral couples interventions have a strong dyadic focus, emphasizing sequential communication patterns between the partners, for example. At times, isn't this dyadic emphasis a distortion? Are there not occasions when the behaviors, needs, or pathology of one individual are so extreme that the individual needs to be the focus of treatment?

Are Behavioral Interventions Too Structured and Artificial?

Many behavioral intervention strategies are presented in relatively structured ways. For example, behavioral strategies might involve asking each person to engage in two positive or helpful behaviors toward his or her partner each day. Similarly, decision-making or problem-solving conversations are presented as a series of steps to follow in discussing an area of concern. Such an approach may seem odd, given that happy couples do not appear to resolve problems using a specific set of steps. Likewise, nondistressed partners typically do not make reflective-listening responses to what the other individual has just said. Why, then, would we ask distressed couples to do such things if they do not mirror the typical behavior patterns of nondistressed couples?

We believe that such structured interventions can be of assistance to distressed couples. Part of the confusion in this area arises because many behavioral interventions have been presented as *skills training*. This label implies that we are teaching couples how to behave and that they will continue to behave this way for life. At times this appears to be true; for example, one or both partners might be helped by learning to express anger appropriately. At the same time, however, we believe that another paradigm—a rehabilitative model—is useful for this purpose; that is, individuals who have experienced various diseases or accidents often are asked to engage in a series of therapeutic interventions that do not typify the behavior of people without the dysfunction. After breaking a hip, for instance, most individuals undergo physical therapy for rehabilitation. Few of us would argue that this intervention is ridiculous because healthy people do not undergo physical therapy.

In essence, we are suggesting that asking distressed couples to mirror the behavior of happy couples as an initial step often would be inappropriate and unsuccessful. Instead, distressed couples often need a series of interventions to help them begin to interact with each other in more constructive ways—to break a negative pattern that may have become ingrained. Therefore, we do not assume that they will necessarily continue using all of these behavioral strategies throughout their lives. Instead, it is important to differentiate between interventions that help to achieve some intermediate goals for therapy versus interventions that the couple might use for life. Let us return to the example of teaching couples to reflect back what the other person has said. In the natural world, no one reflects each time another person has spoken. However, if partners are not listening to each other well, do not understand each other, and interrupt each other, then teaching them *initially* to reflect can be of benefit. Reflecting forces the listener to try to understand what the other person is saying. It also slows down a rapid, negative escalation process. Once the couple become effective at no longer interrupting and each person truly listens to what the other person says, then reflecting on a systematic basis may be less important. At that point in the process we offer alternatives that involve other ways of helping the speaker feel affirmed.

Using behavioral strategies that we describe later, the partners might similarly be asked to engage in specific behaviors each day and to record those behaviors. Again, very few people naturally do this in their lives. This strategy, however, can be useful if partners have stopped thinking about how to improve their relationship. Once they have regained that focus and are making an effort to attend to the relationship and the partner, such efforts are maintained through *naturally occurring reinforcers*, or responses that take place without the therapist or couple specifically arranging them. Once natural reinforcers begin to occur, the structured intervention might no longer be needed (e.g., a husband continues initiating conversations with his wife because he finds her ideas to be interesting; they no longer have to agree to have a 15-minute conversation each evening at dinner). In addition, the level of structure in various behavioral assignments can be altered to meet the needs of specific couples or the personalities of specific individuals. Some individuals prefer and benefit from structure; other individuals find structure to be confining and controlling. In such instances, behavioral interventions can be presented in a less structured way.

As suggested earlier, one asset of behavioral interventions is that they provide structure for needed change. Over time, many couples develop habits or behavioral patterns that are not constructive for their relationship. Clear, specific, concrete behavioral interventions can help to maintain a focus and bring attention to needed changes. Structured behavioral strategies not only help maintain a focus on specific domains needing attention, but they also help maintain behavior change when motivation is low. For example, many individuals develop an exercise routine that they carry out at given times during the day. Even though a person might not feel like exercising on a given day, the routine can help to maintain the behavior. Similarly, on a couple level, the partners might decide that Friday night is "date night." Once this activity becomes routine, even if one person comes home from work on Friday evening and is tired, their routine might increase the likelihood that the couple continues to engage in some social activity.

Structured behavioral changes also can result in important cognitive changes. Often individuals enter couples therapy believing that their relationship or the partner cannot change. With the application of behavioral interventions that focus the couple on change, an individual might come to realize that change is possible because it is observable. Therefore, as we discuss in chapter 10, the person's expectancies or predictions about the relationship might change. In addition, rather than attributing relationship difficulties to stable, undesirable individual characteristics of the partner, an individual might come to realize that the partner's behavior can change as a function of changes in the context of the couple's relationship.

Can Behavioral Interventions Address Core Issues?

At times, both couples and therapists report that the behavioral interventions do not appear to address central or core issues that brought the couple to therapy. The couple's concerns have been operationalized into concrete behaviors, and they have made corresponding behavioral changes. However, core issues or central concerns are still present. This experience has led some people to wonder whether behavioral interventions are appropriate for couples who are more severely disturbed, couples whose concerns seem to be more diffuse and global, or couples whose concerns involve a lack of positive emotions. Furthermore, research findings are consistent with some of these concerns. For example, Hahlweg, Schindler, Revenstorf, and Brengelmann (1984) found that the quality of affection in the marriage prior to treatment was their best predictor of response to behavioral interventions. When a couple reported a lack of tenderness between them, and the wife reported a lack of togetherness before treatment began, then the couple were less responsive to behavioral interventions. Similarly, Bennun (1985a, 1985b) has found that behavioral interventions were not as successful for presenting complaints involving a low level of affection and a lack of closeness and togetherness. Behavioral interventions were more successful for instrumental concerns, such as household chores and finances, as well as assisting with communication difficulties.

We agree that behavioral interventions are not maximally effective for all presenting complaints, at least in the way that these interventions have been used in previous treatment studies. More specifically, almost all of the investigations of behavioral couples interventions have addressed couples' concerns from a rather micro-analytic perspective. Couples' concerns were typically addressed one at a time, without an emphasis on themes, needs, or motives. Therefore, using behavioral interventions to address central issues and important themes in the relationship might prove to be more effective than focusing solely on the couple's specific concerns. That is why we have concentrated on these larger, macrothemes in our enhanced cognitive–behavioral marital therapy. For example, some couples complain that their major problem is a lack of connectedness between them. We typically will work with such couples to help them consider various ways in which couples create a sense of connectedness. For some couples, this goal is accomplished through shared leisure activities; for others, it is through frequent self-disclosure; for others, it is volunteering together in the community; for others, it is sharing a spiritual or religious base. We help such couples investigate how they might create this important sense of connectedness. Then we use behavioral interventions to achieve these rather broad goals by altering a variety of specific behaviors that are related to this theme. Through this process, individuals often learn what each person needs and desires on a broader, macrolevel and become responsive to the partner's needs and wishes. Once the couple's life is arranged to become responsive to the two persons' needs, many of these structured strategies can be discontinued. However, if they begin to get off track again they return to using more explicit behavioral strategies.

Second, we believe that behavioral interventions alone will not be of maximum assistance to many couples if the couples' functioning is observed over a long time. We also need to emphasize couples' internal experiences, on both a cognitive and an emotional level. Consistent with the theme of this book, these elements are addressed from the perspective of the individual, the couple, and the environment within a developmental perspective. Behavioral interventions are an important component of a multifaceted treatment to assist couples.

What Is the Individual's Role in Dyadic Change?

To a large degree, cognitive–behavioral couples therapists have emphasized the dyadic nature of relationship distress. The couple and their relationship are identified as the clients, which helps the clinician take a nonjudgmental, nonblaming perspective on the two individuals in the relationship. Also, the robustness of reciprocal influences between the two partners demonstrates that neither individual is behaving unilaterally or in isolation. In general, the therapist shares these perspectives on relationships with the couple to emphasize joint responsibility, develop a collaborative mindset, and counteract many individuals' typical approach of blaming their partners.

Although these are constructive goals, as Halford, Sanders, and Behrens (1994) noted, individual responsibility from both partners is essential for intervention to be successful (Halford, 2001). Each individual has much more control over his or her own behavior than over the partner's behavior. In fact, one of the most effective ways to influence one's partner is to change one's own behavior. At the same time, even this mindset can be destructive on occasion. If an individual changes his or her behavior only with the anticipation that the partner will reciprocate, then the individual might become angry, resentful, or decrease his or her own efforts when the partner does not reciprocate or does not do so immediately. Therefore, it is valuable for each member of a couple to adopt a perspective that it is his or her responsibility to behave individually in a way that can create the best relationship possible, regardless of the other person's behavior. In essence, each individual should behave in a manner that is consistent with his or her own value system or standards for what a partner should be like. That is, the person should ask himself or herself, "Do I like and approve of the way I am behaving? Is this how I want to be in a committed, intimate relationship?" Partners can be encouraged to behave adaptively because that is the kind of individual each person strives to be, rather than merely trying to get his or her partner to change. Consequently, when developing behavioral interventions with couples, the therapist should emphasize and have both partners evaluate whether each person is willing to make the individual changes needed, rather than presenting behavior changes on a dyadic level only. The changes asked of the two individuals might be similar for both, or the two persons might need to change in very different ways. The issue of personal responsibility for one's own actions is especially important when an individual behaves abusively toward a partner.

BEHAVIORAL INTERVENTIONS

Couples therapy frequently involves asking partners to make behavioral changes, either through the teaching of specific behavioral skills or through guiding behavior change without skill training. In this section we examine how behavior change might affect the overall tone of the relationship as well as specific aspects of the relationship. The discussion includes general guidelines for using behavioral interventions as well as specific strategies that will help clinicians in guiding couples to change their behaviors.

Behavioral interventions for couples incorporate an almost limitless range of possibilities. This category of interventions fundamentally involves helping couples behave in ways that will be more gratifying for them as a couple and as individuals. In some form or fashion this effort typically involves increasing a variety of positive behaviors and decreasing a broad range of negative behaviors. As we discussed in chapter 2, these behaviors include both expressive and instrumental behaviors focused on one or both partners as individuals, their relationship, or their environment. These behaviors include both communication behaviors and noncommunication behaviors. Furthermore, a differentiation can be made between two broad categories of behavioral interventions:

1. *Guided behavior change*—this includes interventions that involve behavior changes that do not involve a skill component. At times, guided behavior change has been referred to in the behavioral couples therapy literature as *behavioral exchange* strategies. We avoid this term, because it suggests that the two partners are asked to exchange behaviors in a reciprocal manner. As we noted earlier, often each person is asked to make changes that are different from the partner's changes, and these changes are not created in a quid pro quo exchange format.
2. *Skills-based interventions*—this includes interventions that involve teaching skills to couples or providing them with tools (e.g., communication training).

GUIDED BEHAVIOR CHANGE

In many behavioral interventions the therapist talks with the couple about various domains in their relationship that could benefit from changes in behavior. Such conversations do not involve teaching the couple any new skills; rather, the couple, in collaboration with the therapist, decides on ways to change their behavior, or the therapist proposes specific behavioral changes. These guided behavior change strategies can vary a great deal along two dimensions:

1. *Focus*: the degree to which behavior change is targeted toward specific aspects of the relationship versus being more globally applicable (e.g., a partner might agree to assist with cleaning the dinner dishes in the evening vs. agree to be more thoughtful and helpful around the house).
2. *Structure*: the degree to which the behavior change is described in a very precise way, with specific requests for change, versus in a clear, yet less precise way.

An example of a relatively structured intervention would be

This week, I'm asking that you take responsibility for washing the dishes, putting them away, and putting all the leftovers away each weekday evening, Monday through Friday. I'd like for you to keep a record and bring it with you next week to our session, writing down the date, whether you did each of these things, how Jane responded, and how you felt internally.

The therapist might summarize the same change with much less structure; for example: "How would you feel about doing the dishes and putting away leftovers after dinner on weekdays?" We typically talk with the couple about how much structure is needed to help them make the kinds of changes that they want to make, and we adapt our input according to their preferences and what appears to be successful with them.

Altering the Overall Emotional Tone of the Relationship

Guided behavior changes often are introduced early in the therapy in an attempt to shift the overall emotional atmosphere within the relationship by altering the ratio of positive and negative behaviors occurring between the partners. As we have noted in previous chapters, there is a meaningful difference between primary relationship distress and secondary relationship distress. *Primary distress* often results when one or both persons are not having important needs met in the relationship. In response to this lack of fulfillment, couples often behave in increasingly negative ways with each other; this is accompanied by a concomitant drop in the frequency of positive behaviors toward each other, which creates *secondary distress*. As result, by the time that many couples seek intervention there is a considerable excess of negative behaviors between the two partners, with very little positive interaction. Therefore, the therapist might wish to shift the overall emotional tone in the couple's interaction by increasing the frequency of positive behaviors and decreasing negative behaviors. To alter this unsatisfying environment the couple needs to behave in more thoughtful, caring ways toward each other and to decrease their hurtful behaviors. Such intervention strategies typically focus on secondary distress in the hopes of creating a more positive, constructive environment for the couple without addressing their fundamental problems. Once this change is accomplished, the couple might be more willing and motivated to address more difficult and fundamental issues that often underlie their destructive interaction patterns.

At times, the therapist might need to present the above-mentioned rationale only briefly, noting to the couple the importance of beginning to treat each other in a respectful manner, both increasing the positive interactions and decreasing the hurtful behaviors. Some couples can readily recognize that they have allowed themselves to develop these unproductive interaction patterns and take responsibility for changing the interaction. Our general strategy is to provide the minimal amount of structure needed to promote behavior change. Use of minimal structuring contributes to couples' making attributions that they were the ones who created the constructive changes and are responsible for the improvement themselves. However, when additional structure is needed to promote change, such structure is provided. Some couples understand and respond to suggestions that they begin to treat each other as they would treat a friend or associate, with respect and intent to promote goodwill. As Birchler, Weiss, and Vincent (1975) demonstrated, often members of couples interact with strangers in a more respectful manner than they do with their own partners. Without providing explicit guidelines for behavior change beyond asking the person to be more positive and less negative, the therapist still might ask each partner to be specific about what that behavior change would involve.

> Therapist: Max, if you are going to interact with Jenna in a more positive and respectful way, what would you be changing? What would you do more of, and what would you do less of?
>
> Max: Well, I'm not sure. I guess it would mean that I would do things like speak to her when I first come home at the end of the day. And I guess we might sit and have a meal together in the evening and talk during dinner. Is that the kind of thing you mean?
>
> Therapist: Sure. I really want this to come from you. I would like you to think about different times of the day and evening and consider how you as an individual would behave toward Jenna if you were making an effort to be positive with her. Those sound like some good ideas. Can you also think of some things that you are doing now that you would want to stop doing or decrease?
>
> Max: I guess there are things I would quit doing. I think both of us are really quick to jump on the other one if the other person doesn't understand something we say or if the other person does something that is annoying. I could watch my tongue and give her the benefit of the doubt. It feels like we're in a constant war zone, and I don't like it. I think that's probably the most important thing, just stopping the sarcastic responses.

Although not all partners are as compliant or self-observant as Max in the preceding example, the therapist can devise a wide range of interventions to assist individuals with differing levels of motivation and self-awareness. Behavioral clinicians have developed a variety of strategies to help couples shift the overall frequency of positive behaviors, including "love days" (Weiss, Hops, & Patterson, 1973; Wills, Weiss, & Patterson, 1974) and "caring days" (Stuart, 1980). Often we use these techniques by having partners alternate doing at least one nice thing out of the ordinary for the other individual each day. We typically stress that these are to be small acts that the couple could foresee incorporating into their daily routines. The goal of this type of intervention is to help the couple remember to engage in ongoing, pleasurable behaviors that can be maintained over time. As we discussed in chapter 2, such behaviors might incorporate either (a) instrumental or task-oriented behaviors or (b) more expressive behaviors. We frequently make distinctions between these two categories of behaviors and ask couples during the week to include both types of behaviors, if appropriate. Sometimes partners note that they want such behaviors to occur on their own, without direction from the therapist. We acknowledge that this goal is indeed desirable, but it is important to focus on each person's willingness to make the relationship better and that, at present, increased structure and direction from the therapist are important in accomplishing the couple's goals. In essence, the use of guided behavior change runs the risk of altering the attributions or explanations for the partner's behavior in a way that diminishes its importance. That is why it is important to acknowledge each person's efforts and the willingness to try, even when there is very little goodwill between the partners.

Some individuals who have become preoccupied with other aspects of life have difficulty thinking of what to do during the week to improve the relationship. Similarly, in chapter 3 we noted that some partners do not process information well from a relationship perspective. In both instances one person might need some assistance from the partner in thinking of how to make things better. Using the "cookie jar" technique (Weiss & Birchler, 1978), a husband might write down several ways that his partner could behave or things that she could do to improve the relationship. Each of these ideas is written on a separate piece of paper and placed into a jar. The wife might then select one of these from the jar if she is struggling with thinking of specific ways to change her behavior. This technique can be of assistance in priming one individual; however, it is important that an individual not become dependent on another person to provide ideas for change on a consistent basis. Thus, the cookie jar technique might be used when it is needed and then faded out across time, with the clear message that each person is responsible for seeking ways to improve the relationship.

Altering Specific Aspects of the Relationship

The techniques just described are somewhat generic in that they do not focus on the specific needs of a given couple. Therapists often use guided behavior change to help partners make behavioral changes focal to specific issues in their relationship, such as Jenna's unmet need for greater closeness with Max.

Therapist:	Max, one of Jenna's concerns is that she feels a lack of connectedness with you. Therefore, let's think about how you can focus some of your efforts toward trying to increase a sense of connectedness between the two of you. I know "connectedness" is a broad, somewhat vague term, so we need to be more specific about it. Given your understanding of what Jenna would like, and also considering who you are, what are some things that you can do during this next week that might contribute to a greater sense of connectedness between the two of you? We don't need to get grandiose here. A sense of connectedness usually builds from small, concrete ways that people behave toward each other. What are some of your ideas of what you might do?
Max:	If I knew the answer to that, we probably wouldn't be here. I really don't know what she wants. When she starts these conversations about feeling more connected, I don't know what she's asking for. From my standpoint, things are really pretty good, if she just weren't so unhappy. So if you can explain to me or help Jenna to explain to me what she really wants, I'm willing to consider it.
Therapist:	Jenna, we're going to leave it to Max to make the final decisions about what he does this week. But can you make some suggestions? What are some things that Max might do that would contribute to a sense of connectedness? Both of you might think back to times and situations where you've felt more connected and closer to each other.

In the case of Jenna and Max, the therapist focused behavior change on one of Jenna's strongest motives: her desire for a high level of intimacy with Max. Guided behavior changes can be used in a wide variety of other domains as well. For example, both partners might have developed significant anxiety about their sexual relationship and subsequently have avoided sexual interaction. Widely used behavioral strategies such as sensate focus exercises (Masters & Johnson, 1970) involve a significant psychoeducational discussion about the role of anxiety and avoidance in sexual functioning along with specific behavioral assignments, such as body massages given by the partner. Guided behavior change might be aimed at other couple-level phenomena—for example, assisting the couple with time management and organizational skills if they have chaotic lives and experience the negative effects of it.

Likewise, guided behavior change might be used to assist a couple in treating one person's psychopathology. For example, both partners need to understand how to help an individual whose functioning is compromised by the avoidance involved in agoraphobia. Consequently, after explaining the principles involved in the treatment, the therapist might propose the following guided behavior change strategy.

> Therapist: Nina, I know you want to help Alec get over his agoraphobia. And, as you can see, through the exposure exercises, he is getting better. Still, there will be many times when he feels anxious about going to the grocery store alone. But I think you can now understand that going with him runs the risk of actually increasing his avoidance in the long run. Therefore, let me suggest another way. If he is to go to the grocery store alone and begins to express his anxiety, what I'd like you to do is to sit and have a conversation with him. Allow him to express his anxiety and, using the communication guidelines that we have discussed, let him know that you understand how hard it is for him. Then encourage him to go by himself, and when he returns, talk about how it went. If it is appropriate, let him know how proud you are of the effort he is making. That way, he still knows that you care and are concerned about him, but you are encouraging his autonomous behavior, which is critical for him to maintain to continue his improvement.

This example requires that the therapist have a clear understanding of individual psychopathology and how couples' behavioral interactions can contribute to the improvement or exacerbation of the individual's difficulties.

Summary

As we have described, guided behavior change includes a broad set of techniques for producing a variety of behavior changes from one or both partners. Such techniques can be used to change the overall balance of positive to negative behaviors in the relationship as well as to focus on specific domains, including needs and motives of one or both partners, maladaptive interaction patterns, or psychopathology and long-term unresolved individual issues of one person. The therapist must have a clear conceptualization of the couple, each individual, and how they relate to their environment to develop meaningful and appropriate guided behavior change interventions. It is simplistic to suggest that asking a couple merely to be positive toward each other will have a lasting, meaningful impact on a long-term basis for most distressed couples. However, thoughtfully applied, and within the context of a multifaceted intervention strategy, guided behavioral change interventions are effective in assisting couples.

In all of the above-mentioned intervention strategies, the therapist works collaboratively with the couple while providing educational information and suggestions. In each instance, the therapist provides a framework for and a conceptualization of why the specific changes might be of assistance to the couple. We believe that when the couple understand their relationship and healthy relationship principles, they are in a better position to take long-term control over developing and maintaining a healthy relationship. We recommend that the therapist, whenever possible, provide couples with principles that need to be applied and then have the partners discuss and decide how to use those principles with their particular relationship. Such an approach is likely to lead to a sense of collaboration between the therapist and the couple as well as to give the couple responsibility for change.

COMMUNICATION TRAINING

Many therapists look to communication training as the first step in improving couples' functioning. In this section we provide the rationale behind communication training of two types of couples' communication: (a) *couple discussions*, in which partners share thoughts and feelings and (b) problem-solving—or, more accurately, *decision-making conversations*. We break down these conversations into discrete steps to help partners learn or implement the skills of constructive communication. In this section we also consider the relationship between couple discussions and decision-making conversations and the role of the therapist in facilitating this communication.

Communication difficulties are the most common presenting complaints of couples seeking assistance for relationship distress (Geiss & O'Leary, 1981). By the time that they arrive for treatment, most couples are displeased with certain elements of their communication. These difficulties take a wide variety of forms. Some couples report that they rarely talk to each other. Other couples complain that they are on a different wavelength, that each person speaks but the other really does not understand what the speaker is trying to communicate. Many couples complain of painful arguments involving blaming, attacking, defending, withdrawing, or some combination of these. Some couples report that they rarely argue but that there is no depth to their conversations, leaving them feeling distant and disconnected.

Thus, assisting couples with their communication is a frequent component of behavioral couples therapy. Such intervention is typically viewed as skills training, which suggests that the couple lack certain communication skills and that, once the partners have been taught the skills, they will apply them. At times this does appear to be the case. For example, some individuals report that they have had difficulty throughout their lives sharing their feelings and thoughts with other people. On the other hand, some distressed couples report a history of successful communication earlier within their current relationship. However, when their relationship began to deteriorate, for a variety of reasons, their communication began to break down as well. In such instances, the communication difficulties might not be the origin of the relationship difficulties, but by the time the couple seek treatment the communication problems are obvious and exacerbate other difficulties. It is important to realize that assisting a couple with communication might or might not be sufficient to maximize their relationship functioning. For example, one partner might need a great deal more autonomy in the relationship. Helping the couple to communicate more effectively does not ensure that this need will be met. Even after the couple is communicating more productively, the issue of autonomy within the relationship might require significant attention. Nevertheless, for other couples, improvement in communication might be the major intervention that is needed.

A wide range of specific communication guidelines can be provided to a couple, based on empirical findings concerning types of communication that tend to differentiate happy from distressed couples. However, such a long list is likely to be overwhelming to the couple and is not needed. Instead, the therapist can assist the couple with the specific communication difficulties that he or she observes in the couple's interactions and that they report. We find it helpful to distinguish two major goals of communication between partners. First, one or both partners often wish to share their thoughts and feelings about something—perhaps the partner, the relationship, the day's events, or other issues or topics at hand. The purposes of such conversations are to communicate information, express an opinion, relate an emotional response, feel understood by a significant person in one's life, and understand the other individual (Guerney, 1977). Consequently, this type of communication might include discussing such diverse topics as the merits and limitations of a political candidate or extreme hurt and disappointment after one's partner has forgotten an important anniversary. It also might involve providing emotional support to a partner after that individual has struggled at work. We refer to these types of conversations as *couple discussions*.

The second major reason why couples communicate with each other is to make decisions. These conversations are task oriented, instrumental, or solution focused. Concerning the significance of the topics, such conversations can run the gamut from where to seat a guest at dinner to deciding whether to continue with one's marriage. Within behavioral couples therapy, this type of conversation has typically been referred to as "problem solving." However, we are reluctant to use this term because it connotes problems, which usually are considered as areas of distress or concern. Many conversations that involve a decision are not about problematic aspects of a couple's relationship. A couple might be quite excited about the prospect of deciding where to spend their 25th wedding anniversary, for instance. Therefore, the term *problem-solving* is somewhat restricted. Also, for individuals who are conflict avoidant, such a label might make them less likely to participate in conversations with their partners if presented with the idea, "We need to sit down and problem solve." Consequently, we refer to solution-oriented conversations that might involve either problems or positive aspects of a relationship as *decision-making conversations*.

Couple Discussions

Introducing and Presenting the Guidelines

One goal of therapy for most couples is to become comfortable discussing a wide variety of issues with each other, sharing their thoughts and feelings in an open and respectful manner in which both people listen to each other's perspective. Most of the guidelines for couple discussions were developed with these broad, fundamental goals in mind. We believe that it is important to keep guidelines for couple discussions brief and easy to understand. The difficulty for couples comes in implementing these guidelines, particularly when they are discussing emotionally laden topics. In presenting a set of guidelines to couples we borrow heavily from the work of Guerney (1977), who emphasized classic speaking and listening skills. In Appendix 9.A we present the introduction of communication guidelines for couples. In Appendix 9.B, we present the actual guidelines that we give to couples to assist them in having couple discussions.

When we share these guidelines with the couple for the first time, we read the guidelines with them and elaborate on each one. It is important that this presentation is not a long, didactic lecture from the therapist. If during the assessment the couple has provided examples that apply to a specific guideline, these can be mentioned to personalize and bring the guidelines to life. Also, after the therapist elaborates on a specific guideline, it can be helpful to ask each partner to evaluate how effective he or she currently is with that particular way of communicating messages. Given that many distressed partners have a tendency to focus on the deficits and negative behaviors of the other individual, we usually ask each individual to evaluate his or her own behavior rather than evaluating the partner.

Speaker Guidelines

As can be seen in Appendix 9.B, the discussion guidelines are divided into one set for the speaker and another set for the listener. The following points may need to be emphasized about each of the guidelines.

Speaking subjectively.   The first guideline emphasizes speaking subjectively rather than in absolutes. Some individuals present their opinions to their partners as facts or absolute reality. Such presentations increase the likelihood that the other person will disagree to establish his or her own reality. The goal is for each person to present what he or she thinks and how he or she feels about a situation in terms of a subjective experience. Also as a part of this guideline, each partner is asked to speak for himself or herself and to not tell the other person what the other person thinks. This establishes the mindset that each person has responsibility for speaking for himself or herself and that the partner is to avoid mind-reading. Similarly, the second guideline emphasizes the importance of expressing emotions. Given that many partners are more comfortable expressing their ideas or opinions than they are expressing their feelings, this point is singled out to emphasize the importance of sharing one's own emotions. Emotional responses are an important part of an internal, subjective reality that can clarify one person's experience to the other. Emotional expression is particularly important in attempting to create a sense of intimacy, which is a central facet of committed relationships.

Speaking about the partner and relationship. The third guideline recommends that the speaker describe his or her feelings about the partner in situations involving the partner. For example, it might be more helpful to talk about enjoying being with one's partner rather than stating that they had a pleasant dinner experience. Talking about the other individual is a more personal communication. Of course, at times one partner might not wish to personalize the communication and thus choose not to focus on expressing emotions about the other person. This might be particularly true if one person is feeling negatively about the partner but wishes to defuse the situation for the moment.

Sharing underlying positives. The fourth guideline recommends that the speaker express any positive emotions related to a situation that involves an expression of negative feelings. Many individuals find it easy to express a wide variety of negative or upset feelings. Such a pure expression of negative emotion is hard for the person's partner to hear on an extended basis. Often the partner responds to such a negative expression with counterattacks, holding firmly to his or her own position, or withdrawing. When members of a couple are pushed to think about and express positive emotions related to specific situations or their relationship as a whole, often they can. For example, rather than solely expressing anger that one's partner was late, the speaker might also express that he or she was concerned that something bad had happened to the partner. Likewise, if one person is generally feeling somewhat distant and disconnected from the other person, that individual might express a feeling of loneliness, along with a desire to feel close and intimate, as the couple has felt in the past. Consequently, even when there is little positive in the present situation, the speaker can refer to positive feelings from the past or wishes for more positive experiences with the partner in the future. Such expressions can facilitate couples' discussions of difficult or problematic aspects of their relationship.

Speaking specifically, using tact and timing. The final three guidelines apply to almost all communications. The speaker is encouraged to be specific in his or her communication. For instance, we encourage the speaker, when expressing emotions, to be much more specific than simply saying that he or she felt bad or was upset. Knowing more specifically that the speaker felt sad suggests some sense of loss, which is not clear from a broader expression of "upset." This guideline does not imply that the speaker cannot talk about broad issues; rather, it is intended to suggest that this should be done in as clear and precise a manner as possible. In fact, by describing specific thoughts and emotions the individual increases the probability that the therapist and couple will be able to identify important needs and desires that are associated with the feelings. For example, when an individual expresses a mixture of sadness, loneliness, and anger in situations where the partner has been un-available, the therapist may be able to help both members of the couple identify a theme regarding an unmet need for intimacy. Given that some individuals have difficulty differentiating among various emotions or label-ing their emotional experience, we have a list of "feeling words" that we give to couples who can benefit from them (see Appendix 9.C). The categoriza-tion of emotions is consistent with the typology discussed in chapter 3.

The speaker also is asked to talk in "paragraphs"; that is, he or she is asked to present an idea and elaborate on it briefly. Given that we ask the listener to refrain from interrupting, at times the speaker can "have the floor" and continue to speak for a long time. Many individuals have avoided con-versations because their partners engage in lengthy monologues. In addition, it is difficult for the listener to remember the major points of the speaker's message if multiple points are made without breaks.

Finally, the speaker is asked to use tact and timing in presenting his or her message. At times there might be some ideas and feelings that are better left unstated. As Markman, Stanley, and Blumberg (1994) noted, certain views and feelings should sometimes be edited out of a conversation. Simi-larly, the timing of the conversation is important. Many individuals com-plain that their partners begin a conversation about an important issue when the couple is walking out the door to go to work in the morning, when one individual has just arrived home and is decompressing at the end of a work-day, when the couple is preparing for bed, or at other times when talking interferes with other activities and needs. Given that each person has indi-vidual preferences regarding good and bad situations and times to have con-versations, it is important to have partners clarify their own perspectives on this issue.

Listener Guidelines

Listener guidelines span two major categories. First, there are guide-lines that incorporate the listener's internal mindset and nonverbal behavior while the other person is speaking. Second, there are suggestions and guide-lines for how the listener might respond after the other person has finished speaking.

Demonstrating acceptance. While the speaker is talking, the listener has one primary goal: to listen to what the speaker says and to demonstrate interest in and acceptance of the speaker's message. Often as one person speaks, the other individual prepares a rebuttal, interrupts, or gives other signals that the speaker's message is in some manner invalid. We try to give the listener the following mindset instead:

> Your partner is speaking to you, and I want you to focus all of your attention on trying to understand what that person is saying to you. We have discussed how hurt and frustrated both of you feel when the other person doesn't give you a chance to express yourself and doesn't seem to take your feelings seriously. So these guidelines for listening can help create a more positive atmosphere when you talk with each other.

In this guideline a major distinction is made between *acceptance* and *agreement*. It is critical that the listener understand that he or she is not being asked to agree with the speaker. Sometimes the listener will agree; on other occasions he or she will not agree. However, the listener is asked to adopt the philosophy that the speaker has the right to his or her opinion and feelings so that the listener respects that right and accepts that the other person thinks and feels in a given way. We emphasize that if the listener thinks or feels differently from the speaker, this is a particularly important time to focus on trying to understand how one's partner can see things so differently. Rather than tuning out the speaker or preparing a rebuttal, the listener needs to try especially hard to understand a divergent perspective coming from his or her loved one.

In addition to this internal frame of mind, the listener is asked to demonstrate listening and acceptance in nonverbal ways, including facial expressions that demonstrate acceptance, an open and receptive body posture, and paralinguistic responses such as "um-hum" while giving head nods. Again, it is important to emphasize that these nonverbal responses signify listening and acceptance but not necessarily agreement.

Adopting the speaker's perspective. The second guideline for the listener is intended to assist with this understanding and acceptance. This guideline asks the listener to try to understand the situation from the speaker's point of view. In essence, the listener is asked to engage in empathic perspective taking. As we elaborate on this guideline, we often make comments such as the following:

> One approach that might help you to understand the other person's thoughts and feelings is to look at the situation from that person's perspective. That is, you know how you think and feel about the situation from your own point of view. While you're listening, you are not being asked to evaluate the speaker's message from your perspective. Instead, I would recommend that you try to put yourself in your partner's shoes and see what the situation is like for him or her. That might be totally differ-

ent from your own perspective, but understanding the difference is important if the two of you are to communicate well. I want you to see how your partner thinks and feels, given who that person is and how he or she experiences the world.

Responding empathically and with respect. Once the speaker has finished speaking, the listener is asked to respond in some manner that demonstrates that he or she has heard the speaker and accepts that person's message. One way that this can be done is for the listener to offer a reflection, summarizing the speaker's most important thoughts and feelings. Such a response can feel artificial to the couple for several reasons. During the early stages of communication training, we often ask the listener to reflect each time the speaker finishes speaking. We make it clear to the couple that this is to help each person become comfortable in offering reflections. In the real world, no one reflects every time another person finishes speaking. Consequently, reflecting after each person speaks can seem contrived. However, reflections do have merit. The listener cannot reflect empathically if he or she was not listening to the speaker. Moreover, the reflection clarifies whether the listener did indeed understand the speaker's message. If the reflection misses the speaker's major points, the speaker has an opportunity to repeat the message to clarify the misunderstanding. In addition, if the reflection is given with an appropriate tone and nonverbal cues, it can convey a message of understanding and acceptance, which can be pleasing to partners who have a history of feeling alienated from each other. In contrast, a reflection given in a perfunctory manner with an irritated tone of voice can have a very negative effect.

Second, reflections can seem artificial, given the way that they are phrased. We recommend to couples that they not be formulaic in their approach to offering reflections. We encourage them to avoid beginning every reflection with the wording, "I heard you say…" or "You said . . ." Our hope is that the listener will give a heartfelt message that conveys, "I understand how you think and feel."

A third reason that reflections can seem artificial is that they can destroy the tone of the couple's interaction. In particular, if one person has just offered a tender, affectionate, loving comment to the partner, it is unlikely to be rewarding to that person if the partner reflects, "You are feeling very close to me right now. You believe we've finally gotten things back to where our interaction seems natural and normal." As we discuss later, in such instances the listener might wish to respond in other ways that still demonstrate listening and acceptance.

In summary, reflections can be a valuable response after a speaker has finished talking. However, they should not be viewed as the ultimate criterion of good listening skills. Any response that demonstrates that the listener has attended to what the speaker said and conveys respect for the speaker's ideas and emotions can serve as a valuable response. Therefore, we also provide the couple with some suggestions of when reflections can be particularly useful during a conversation. In addition, we provide some possibilities for alternative responses that convey respect for the speaker. These guidelines and alternatives are listed in Appendix 9.D. There is no ultimate list of acceptable types of responses for the listener; therefore, it can be helpful to have a couple discuss what kinds of responses they value and try to use them after listening to their partner. Such a discussion can sensitize the partners to the importance of listening attentively and showing respect for the other person's communication.

Communication cycles. Regardless of whether the responder uses a reflection or some other type of response to demonstrate listening and respect, we help the couple define a communication cycle as the sequence of one person speaking and the other person demonstrating good listening to and respect for the speaker's communication. After this cycle is completed, the original speaker might speak again, or the listener might become the speaker. At times, partners can become confused about who is in the speaker role and who is in the listener role. For training purposes, the therapist might suggest that the couple use some physical object to clarify their various roles. In the PREP program, Markman et al. (1994) provided the couple with a small square of linoleum to signify "the floor." Whoever is holding the floor is in the speaker role. Such props are viewed as training devices, without any suggestion that the couple use them for all of their conversations. At the same time, one sophisticated, well-educated couple reported to the therapist that they were thoroughly enjoying using their new communication guidelines. While in a restaurant, they began to have an important yet difficult conversation. They passed the placard (which was on the table listing the evening specials) back and forth across the table to help them maintain some structure in roles. If you did not have the placard, you could neither express your thoughts or feelings nor order dinner! Some couples might find this approach ridiculous or embarrassing, but this couple used it to remind them of important communication principles and to inject some humor into the midst of a difficult conversation.

Decision-Making Conversations

Many couples report that they have difficulty when they try to make decisions together, and some complain that they never seem to reach a decision but instead become sidetracked onto other issues. Some couples become stalemated as each person takes a position and is unwilling to compromise, and the conversation becomes a test of wills. Other couples remark that their decision-making conversations "blow up" after one person says something hurtful or sarcastic. Some individuals feel that their partners dominate the decision-making process and that their own preferences are rarely heard or represented in final decisions. As a variant of this latter complaint, some individuals report that, to maintain the status quo, their partners refuse to have conversations about issues on which they disagree. In working with specific couples, the therapist can tailor the decision-making process to the couple's particular needs. At the same time, there are several general guidelines that can be helpful for the couple to follow (Baucom & Epstein, 1990). These guidelines, presented in Appendix 9.E, are intended to help the couple move forward from an initial statement of the area that requires a decision to a final solution that both partners can endorse.

Introduction and Presentation of Decision-Making Guidelines

The role of the therapist in presenting and discussing decision-making guidelines is similar to the role described for the therapist in presenting couple discussion guidelines; that is, the therapist provides a written copy of the guidelines to each partner, briefly reads each guideline to the couple, and elaborates on the meaning of that guideline. Again, it is important that the therapist have a conversation and dialogue with the couple rather than delivering a lengthy, didactic monologue. This dialogue can include using examples from the couple's own relationship as well as asking the couple to evaluate their own individual strengths and relative weaknesses within the decision-making paradigm. A few major points of emphasis about each of these guidelines can help the therapist in presenting the guidelines as well as in planning interventions at later points during the process.

Decision-Making Guidelines

Stating the issue. The first guideline asks the couple to clearly and specifically state the issue about which they wish to make a decision. Although it might seem intuitive that couples would begin by stating or clearly defining the topic or issue, often this is not the case. Many couples begin discussing what to do without clarifying or agreeing on the issue. It is difficult to stay on task if the task has not been defined or if the two people understand it differently.

We also recommend that couples address complex or multifaceted issues by breaking them down into several smaller components. Couples can feel overwhelmed if they try to reach decisions about complex issues by considering all facets at one time. Once a multifaceted issue has been broken down into its components, the couple can decide which component to address first and proceed with decision making on that one component prior to considering other aspects of the issue. For example, the problem area of finances might be broken down into: (a) the use of credit cards, (b) who pays the bills, (c) guidelines for obtaining agreement from the partner before spending, (d) whether and how to plan for retirement and children's education, (e) whether and how to allocate funds for enjoyable activities such as travel versus focusing spending on tangible objects, and (f) whether one or both partners needs to earn additional money.

Furthermore, we recommend that the couple clarify the issue in the context of its current status; that is, what is currently happening or not happening. More specifically, we recommend that couples not propose solutions in the statement of the issue, as this wife did: "I would like to have a conversation about your helping out more with chores around the house. I need you to pull your own weight." The difficulty with proposing a solution in a statement of the issue is that it biases the direction of the conversation and the elements that the solution is likely to incorporate. In the preceding example, the statement implies that the husband will do more around the house; this might or might not become a part of the eventual solution. As a result, the wife might be asked to redefine the above issue as, "I would like to discuss how we have distributed household tasks. I am really unhappy with the amount that I am doing on a day-to-day basis." Couples are asked to agree on a statement of the issue before they continue with the next step in the process. This does not mean that the two partners need to have the same feelings or perspective on the issue. One person might be happy with the way that the couple functions in a given area, whereas the other individual is dissatisfied. The agreement to discuss the issue and look for possible solutions does not imply that the two people see the issue in the same way; neither does it imply that discussing the issue means that behavioral changes are required. Instead, it indicates a willingness to address an area that at least one partner wants to discuss.

Clarifying why the issue is important and what each person needs or desires. The second guideline suggests that each partner clarify why the issue is important to that individual. This information might include the meaning that the person gives to the situation. In addition, the person can clarify what he or she needs in the situation without proposing a specific solution:

> I need to feel respected and see us as equals. Right now, it seems to me that if neither of us wants to do mundane tasks around the house, I get them by default of our not deciding. I don't mind doing them, but I need to feel respected.

This step in the process is important, because it can have a significant impact on the solutions that are proposed and that would be acceptable to both partners. For example, the distribution of household tasks might be important to an individual for various reasons. First, the person might be exhausted by the amount of work that he or she is performing. If so, this could lead to a redistribution of chores between the two partners, or even the possibility of hiring someone to help with certain household responsibilities. However, the wife in the previous example might want a redistribution of chores for a very different reason:

I need to feel that we are equals. I actually have enough time to do all that I do, but it feels disrespectful. You seem to think that either it is women's work or someone should be hired to do it.

In this instance, the husband's proposal that someone be hired to assist with household chores could offend his wife, because the issue was related to important needs, such as equity of power in the couple's relationship. As we discuss later, on many occasions couples benefit from having a more extensive couple discussion about an issue prior to embarking on decision-making conversations. In essence, many issues in intimate relationships have great meaning; they are more than a set of specific behaviors to be changed. Understanding what the various issues mean to both people can be quite helpful in thinking about appropriate solutions.

Proposing and discussing alternatives. The third guideline flows from an understanding of how both people perceive the issue and what is important to each person. In the third step of decision making, the couple is asked to propose alternative solutions to the issue they are considering. In doing so, the couple is encouraged to develop solutions that incorporate both people's needs and desires. This approach is quite different from what many individuals routinely do during the process of trying to resolve an issue. Often one partner will propose a solution that is optimal for that individual. It is not surprising that the other partner responds with a counterproposal that is optimal for him or her. The conversation then takes the form of each person trying to persuade the partner to do it "my" way. If a husband proposes a solution that clearly takes into account his wife's desires, she is more likely not only to find his proposal acceptable but also to feel that she is important to him and that he is interested in and committed to her happiness and satisfaction. Consequently, explicit consideration of such alternatives can be important in altering the emotional tone of the conversation.

During this third step of the conversation, the partners are encouraged to focus on a solution or decision that will satisfy them in the present or in the future. When couples are discussing long-standing problems, they often have a tendency to focus on the past, discussing who was wrong and becoming mired in blaming the other person and defending their own actions. This approach typically derails the decision-making process. It can be helpful for couples to review the past to clarify strategies and solutions that have been unsuccessful. Similarly, looking at the past can help them identify high-risk situations. However, focusing on the past in problematic areas of the relationship is itself a high-risk situation for many couples, and therefore they must do so with great care. At times the couple and the therapist might agree that, in certain domains, the couple are much better off not discussing the past anymore. If they do discuss the past, it should lead to alternatives for how to handle the situation, thus tying the past to the present and future.

Some therapists present brainstorming as a routine part of the decision-making process. Brainstorming involves developing a long list of possible solutions without evaluating the solutions when they are generated. During brainstorming, the partners typically are encouraged to develop creative and perhaps even outlandish possible solutions. The purpose of brainstorming is to help couples become creative and avoid focusing on a narrow range of possible outcomes. After listing the alternatives, the couple can return and evaluate each of them. We do not believe that any absolute position should be taken regarding the routine use of brainstorming in decision-making conversations. Some issues do not require a brainstorming process if available alternatives are relatively clear to both partners. Similarly, some couples who can effectively consider several alternatives that reflect both people's preferences and desires do not need the additional structure of brainstorming. However, other couples tend to become narrowly focused on a limited range of solutions, frequently with each partner adopting one specific proposal. In such cases, brainstorming can be helpful in breaking the deadlock or helping the couple become more creative.

Consequently, brainstorming can be used as a strategy to assist couples with specific dysfunctional decision-making strategies, such as being narrowly focused. The therapist can be creative in developing other strategies to meet a particular couple's pattern of generating solutions. For example, in many couples one partner seems to take the lead in proposing most solutions, regardless of the issue under consideration. In such instances the therapist might alter the decision-making process, pointing out this pattern and requesting that the less assertive member of the couple routinely offer solutions before a final solution is adopted.

Adopting a solution or making a plan. After the couple have generated different solutions or possible outcomes, they decide on a specific solution or plan of action. *Specific* is a relative term; what is important is that the agreed-on solution be clear enough that both people know what they have agreed to do and can carry out the agreement successfully. Sometimes couples return to a subsequent therapy session frustrated because the solution did not work out as planned. In discussing what transpired, at times it becomes clear that the two people had understood the agreement differently. Sometimes it seems that the two individuals had different understandings of the agreement when it was first made. It is not surprising that at times partners' memories of a planned solution change, typically in a manner that is consistent with what each partner desired. Therefore, it can be helpful for some couples to write down their agreements. It is unrealistic to ask couples to write down everything on which they agree on a day-to-day basis. This might be more important for some couples than others, or it might be important to write down certain solutions that are of major significance or that involve complex steps. Given the tendency for partners to understand the solution differently, we advocate that one partner restate their final agreement once both people are satisfied with it, and the two partners see whether they in fact have the same idea.

For many of life's issues, there is no agreement or plan that fully satisfies both partners. In such instances, the couple must decide what to do. Some issues lend themselves to a compromise solution in which both persons have their preferences or needs met to some degree. At times this appears to be the preferable strategy. On other occasions such solutions can leave each person feeling disappointed about the outcome. Likewise, there are some decisions for which a compromise is difficult, if not impossible, such as dichotomous issues: "Do we have another child?" In such instances, the couple will have to decide whose desires to follow.

When we see that the couple is confronted with a dichotomous situation, we try to make the dichotomous nature of the problem explicit. Moreover, when it is apparent that both partners have strong convictions about their preferences, we discuss whether either person is likely to be successful in changing the other person's mind. Often both partners make it clear that it is extremely unlikely that the other person will convince them to desire a different outcome or alter their emotional response. On such occasions we recommend to the couple that they not use their time trying to persuade the other individual but rather trying to understand both partners' desires and feelings and deciding how to handle the situation.

Therapist:	Obviously, this is a very important decision about whether to have another child. Based on what you've said, it sounds as if you both have pretty strong feelings about this. Am I correct, Marissa, that you do not want to have another child, and, Saul, you very much want another child? (Both partners nod affirmatively.) Marissa, do you think there is anything that Saul can say that will change your mind such that you personally will want another child?
Marissa:	Absolutely not. I am more than willing to discuss it with Saul, but I can tell you right now, I will not want another child. I am totally dedicated to Saul and our two children, but I do not want to increase the size of our family.
Therapist:	Saul, how about you? Are you likely to change your mind personally, such that you will not want another child?
Saul:	No, I won't change how I feel. When you want a child, you want a child. It is that simple. It comes from the heart, and no argument or rational discussion will change it.
Therapist:	Therefore, it really isn't going to be very helpful for either of you to try to convince the other person, right? If I understand correctly, you have had several conversations along that line, and you both simply get upset. So, let's agree. You are *not* going to change the other person's mind on this issue. Therefore, the goal is not to persuade the other person but rather to decide how you are going to handle a

very important issue when you have different perspectives. That is our goal: what do we do when we come down at different places on such an important issue?

Here is how I would like to recommend that we proceed. Let's focus on the second step of the decision-making guidelines. That is, I want each of you briefly to discuss with the other person your thoughts and feelings about having another child. Let your partner know why this is important to you and what you need personally in this circumstance. The purpose is not to persuade the other person but to let the other person know honestly and openly what your feelings and thoughts are.

After we do that, I'm going to recommend that we look at the pros and cons of having another child and that we do that in a certain way. Typically, Saul, you have presented the pros, and, Marissa, you have presented the cons. Let's not do that again. Instead I am going to ask *both* of you to discuss what you would see as the positive consequences if you were to have another child, gains for each of you individually, for you as a couple, and for your family. Marissa, when you do this, it does not mean that you have changed your mind. Instead, it means that you are trying to be open and present a balanced perspective on this issue. And, Marissa, I'll probably ask you to go first in discussing the good things about having another child. You've already heard Saul discuss this several times. Then we'll talk about the negative consequences of having another child, and I will ask both of you to discuss the downside of this issue. Saul, I'll ask you to go first at that point. Presenting the negative consequences does not mean that you do not want another child, Saul. In essence, I want you to avoid becoming polarized on this issue; in the past, it sounds as if each of you has described having another child in an extreme way, either positively or negatively.

Finally, you are going to need to decide what to do. After you go through these conversations, which might take us several sessions, one of you is going to need to decide to honor the other person's desires on this issue. I don't want you to do it as a martyr, but sometimes on issues such as this, it means deciding that you will put the other person's desires first. That is difficult on issues as important as this one, but that is likely what we will need to do. That will be much better than if either of you feels coerced or pushed into a decision and perhaps feels resentful about it.

This example points out another guideline in the decision-making process: Partners are encouraged not to adopt a solution or outcome that will result in resentment or other strong negative emotions. Adopting such solutions can undermine carrying out the solution or can have a broader negative impact on the relationship. To the extent possible, it is important to anticipate possible resentment and address it. For example, in the preceding scenario, Marissa might recognize that Saul will be unfulfilled if they do not have another child, and she might agree to have one. The couple should discuss whether this outcome has implications for how they handle child-rearing responsibilities ("Look, you wanted the child, so you get up in the middle of the night and rock her") or how Marissa will feel toward Saul if the child is born with disabilities. Similarly, sometimes one partner will agree to a solution even though he or she does not intend to follow through with it, perhaps because the person feels worn down by the discussion and merely wants to end the conversation. Alternatively, one person perceives that the other individual has used such strong logic in presenting a perspective or has been so convincing that the person feels compelled to go along with it, even though he or she knows that follow-through is very unlikely: "I couldn't say no. I couldn't think of any convincing way to disagree." Even when an individual believes that it is reasonable to go along with the partner's preference, he or she still may have ambivalent feelings that result in inconsistent behavior. In such situations, couples often need some assistance in planning how to cope with ambivalent feelings about a decision.

Many couples demonstrate this pattern. During decision-making conversations, one partner routinely goes along with the other individual's preferences. Then the less expressive partner disregards the agreement and does what he or she wishes. When this pattern is noted, it is important for the therapist to discuss it with the couple. This behavioral pattern can occur for several reasons. At times, one person is not assertive enough or does not think as quickly or as clearly as the other individual. In other circumstances the less vocal individual experiences a lack of control in the relationship and sees this strategy as the only way to get what he or she desires. In yet other couples, such an approach appears to be a passive–aggressive strategy that is one person's indirect expression of anger toward the other person. Coming to a clear understanding of the reasons underlying this maladaptive pattern can steer the clinician and the couple toward altering this unproductive decision-making pattern.

Adopting a trial period and reviewing decisions. Some issues involve solutions that are carried out only one time, such as having another child or going to a specific movie. However, other decisions are reached about issues that occur on a repetitive basis. For example, in response to Ann Marie's need for greater autonomy in their relationship, she and Tony agreed that she would take two evenings a month to be with her female friends. The couple decided to try out this solution for 2 months and then evaluate how both of them felt about it.

We recommend that, whenever possible, the couple adopt a trial period for implementing a decision. At the end of this trial period, they re-evaluate the decision. This strategy can be helpful for several reasons. We have found that, for many couples, a trial period allows them to be more creative and willing to try new solutions. When partners believe that they are committing to a solution forever, they are less willing to compromise or try new solutions. However, if they recognize that they are adopting the solution only for a trial period, that the solution will be re-evaluated, and that the solution can be changed if either person is dissatisfied, then many people are more flexible in adopting new or creative solutions or outcomes. Moreover, couples often cannot anticipate how their decision will work outside of the therapy session. A decision might sound good at the moment, but when the partners attempt to implement the decision in their daily lives they sometimes experience several unforeseen difficulties. We recommend that couples consider the review of their solutions at the end of the trial period as a valuable opportunity to incorporate the new experiences and reactions from the trial period. Couples frequently need to fine tune their decisions after implementing them in their daily lives. It is not unusual for couples to find that they need to develop new solutions after trying out the original solution. We believe that therapists often place great emphasis on the problem-solving process during the session but put less emphasis on the implementation of the solution. Such an approach makes sense if the therapist views his or her role as dealing primarily with the communication process. However, if the therapist believes that the follow-through on solutions is central to meeting important needs or strong preferences of the partners, then the implementation of the solution is an essential part of the therapy.

Relationship Between Couple Discussions and Decision-Making Conversations

Although couple discussions and decision-making conversations can be viewed as two different types of conversations with different goals, they need not always function in this way. Couples often have important issues that they wish to discuss both from the perspective of sharing thoughts and feelings as well as making decisions about some aspect of the issue. We recommend initially differentiating between these two types of conversations to help couples become comfortable and proficient in each type. Once the couple have become good at holding both types of conversations, however, different options are available to them. The couple might decide to begin by having a couple discussion, in which each person shares his or her feelings about the issue. The couple might then smoothly move into a decision-making process. In fact, the second step of the decision-making conversation includes discussing each person's perspective on the issue. This should make it clear that the two types of conversation typically are not conducted totally separately.

What is questionable is whether to have one conversation during which a couple both expresses strong emotions and attempts to reach a decision or solution. For many couples, this is more difficult when the couple is discussing some problematic aspect of their relationship that evokes strong negative emotions. The expression of such strong feelings often makes it difficult for the couple to collaborate in reaching a mutually agreeable decision during the same conversation. Consequently, having a separate couple discussion and decision-making conversation is preferable for many couples if they are addressing an emotionally volatile issue. Having a cooling-off period or break after one partner becomes highly emotionally aroused can be helpful before engaging in a decision-making conversation. The therapist can address this issue with the couple. Some couples move comfortably from sharing their thoughts and feelings to making a decision regarding how to address an issue. Other couples have more difficulty. Some couples find that they can combine these conversations when discussing less volatile issues but are wise to separate the two types of conversations for more difficult issues. Rather than presenting a set of rules for couples to follow while conversing with each other, we present these as guidelines and recommendations that need to be adapted to the needs and styles of the two partners.

Role of the Therapist During Couple Conversations

Once the couple understands the communication guidelines just described for different types of conversations, they typically spend a significant amount of time in therapy using these guidelines, or some variation of them, while discussing issues of importance in their relationship. The issues to be addressed are chosen jointly by the couple and the therapist, consistent with the wide variety of factors described throughout this book. The role of the therapist during a couple's conversation in the session can vary significantly depending on the primary emphasis of the session. More specifically, at least two broad phenomena are occurring whenever the couple has a conversation. First, the two partners are engaging in a communication process, and the therapist typically is attuned to the ways in which the couple is interacting. Second, the couple is discussing some substantive issue, and the therapist notes the content of what each partner expresses. Thus, the therapist typically is attending to both the communication process and the content of what the partners are discussing. The couple also is asked to attend to both of these phenomena.

The role of the therapist and how he or she responds during the couple's conversation often are determined by whether the communication process or the content of the conversation appears to be more salient. Some sessions are clearly designated as communication skills training, during which the couple focuses on learning to communicate with each other effectively, attending to agreed-on communication guidelines. In these instances, the therapist assumes the role of a coach, stopping the couple to reinforce good communication and assisting them where change is needed. With such a focus during the session, the therapist might intervene as follows:

> Let's stop for just a moment to talk about your communication. Jackson, when you were telling Nicole about your reaction to last Saturday evening, you mentioned that you were unhappy that she invited another couple to join you without asking you first. I think it would be helpful if you try to be more specific about the particular emotions that you were experiencing. Think back to Saturday night and give her a better understanding of what it was like for you; what were you feeling emotionally? And, Nicole, I know it is hard to look at someone who is upset with you, but do whatever you can to let him know that you really want to understand how he felt about last Saturday evening. Jackson, let's pick up with your telling Nicole what your emotions were when she mentioned she had invited the other couple.

Many behavioral couples therapists have assumed that their role is to focus almost exclusively on the interaction process, assuming that the couple know best how to address the content of their concerns. As we have pointed out throughout this book, we believe that this is too narrow a perspective on understanding couples' functioning and the role of the therapist. Many important, substantive issues need to be addressed in the treatment. Often the therapist will have some perspective on these issues that can assist the couple. Consequently, we believe that the therapist should assume a broader role and often should comment on the substantive issues being discussed. These comments might include providing the therapist's own perspective on the issue, helping the couple see how a specific concern fits into a broader pattern relevant to communal or individual needs, providing educational or didactic information about the topic, or recommending guided behavioral changes to assist the couple in that domain. Therefore, on many occasions the therapist might decide that the communication process is of secondary importance to the substantive issue that the couple is discussing. In such instances, unless the therapist is concerned that one partner is communicating in such a destructive way that it will derail the process, the therapist might not comment at all on the communication process. The therapist might want to keep the focus on the content of what the couple is discussing.

In particular, stopping a couple's discussion to comment on the communication process often will change the emotional tone of the session. Feedback from the therapist focused on the couple's interaction typically is a rather cognitive, rational discussion. The therapist is commenting on the couple's interaction, relating it to specific communication skills and interaction patterns. Such an intervention often has the effect of de-escalating emotion (unless the therapist intervenes explicitly to heighten the expression of emotion from one partner). Therefore, if the therapist wishes to dampen the emotional tone of the session, intervening to comment on the communication process typically will serve that purpose. In addition, such an intervention deflects the focus from the substantive issues that the couple is discussing, at least momentarily. If the therapist wishes to maintain a focus on the issue being discussed and does not want to interfere with the emotional tone of the interaction, then it often is preferable to refrain from commenting on the communication process or to wait until a later time. As with many other clinical decisions during the therapy, there are no absolutes. The therapist must be clear on the primary focus and goal of a specific intervention and select interventions appropriately.

SUMMARY

Behavioral interventions are almost always necessary to help couples create more rewarding relationships and to alleviate relationship distress. A wide variety of behavioral interventions are available to clinicians. Some of these interventions are well articulated and have been written about and researched in depth. Other appropriate behavioral interventions can be created by a clinician for a given couple, based on sound behavioral principles.

- Rather than disregarding behavioral interventions as too structured, artificial, or specific to be useful, therapists should view them as intermediate steps to enable couples to make difficult behavior changes. Once couples have experienced successful interactions, often they can move toward less structured approaches to maintaining desired behavior changes.
- Guided behavior changes, which do not involve teaching skills to couples, vary according to whether they focus on global or specific behavior change and in the degree of structure imposed by the therapist.
- The two categories of couple communication considered in this chapter are *couple discussions*, in which one or both partners wish to share their thoughts and feelings about something, and *decision-making conversations*, in which couples take a more instrumental, task-oriented, or solution-focused approach to communication to make decisions. Interventions consist of providing guidelines for the couple discussion and breaking decision-making conversations into discrete steps to facilitate the couple's communication.
- For maximum effectiveness, behavioral interventions typically are used in combination with cognitive and emotionally focused interventions that address each partner's needs and motives, personality differences, individual psychopathology, mal-

adaptive couple interactions, and the couple's relationship with their environment.

- In addition to ameliorating relationship distress, these behavioral interventions can be used to further strengthen and enhance already positive couple relationships.

We find that couples typically talk to each other for two major reasons. First, couples talk to each other when they want to share their thoughts and feelings with each other. They aren't trying to make any decisions or resolve anything; they merely want to let the other person know what they are thinking or feeling. Couples have this kind of conversation very often. It might involve talking about how the day went; it could involve discussing your reaction to a movie you have seen together. Or it could involve a variety of conversations about your relationship, such as how much you enjoyed spending time together; similarly, you might want to talk about your hurt and disappointment after a miscommunication that left one of you feeling ignored. So we want to help you learn to express these feelings and thoughts in a productive way, whether you are sharing something positive or negative. You both probably also know how critical it is to know that the other person is listening to you and understands you. So we want to focus on being a good listener, as well as sharing your own thoughts and feelings. Therefore, we'll also provide you with some suggestions for listening. We call this kind of conversation a *couple discussion*, because that really is what you are doing, just discussing some topic or issue. We'll be going over some specific guidelines for this type of conversation, but based on what I've said thus far, how well would you say you as an individual share your thoughts and feelings, and listen to the other person talk? For right now, I want you to focus just on yourself as an individual, not how your partner does these things.

Second, couples have conversations because they need to make decisions. These might involve minor day-to-day decisions, such as what to have for dinner tonight, or they might involve more major decisions about whether to take a new job, move to a new house, and so forth. Some of these decisions might involve problematic aspects of the relationship, such as how to divide household chores, if that were a problem. Also, couples need to make decisions about positive aspects of their relationship, you know, how to spend that million dollars you have just inherited. When couples are having these kinds of conversations, we call them *decision-making conversations*. Again, how do you think you do as an individual in having these decision-making conversations with your partner?

It is important to distinguish between these two types of communication because people can get frustrated with each other if they are having different kinds of conversations. For example, if a wife is trying to express her ideas and her feelings about something that has upset her and the husband tries to propose solutions, they might both get upset with each other. She gets frustrated because he doesn't seem to be focusing on a *discussion* of her feelings, and he gets upset because she doesn't pay any attention to his *deci-*

sion-making ideas for how to make things better. Some partners don't seem to have much trouble picking up what kind of conversation the other person is asking for. For other couples, this is a real issue. How about the two of you? How do each of you feel you do in picking up on what kind of conversation the other person wants to have?

APPENDIX 9.B
GUIDELINES FOR COUPLE DISCUSSIONS

Skills for Sharing Thoughts and Emotions

1. State your views *subjectively*, as *your own* feelings and thoughts, not as absolute truths. Also, speak for yourself, what you think and feel, not what your partner thinks and feels.
2. Express your *emotions or feelings; not just your ideas.*
3. When talking about your partner, state your feelings about your partner, not just about an event or a situation.
4. When expressing negative emotions or concerns, also include any *positive feelings* you have about the person or situation.
5. Make your statement as *specific* as possible, both in terms of specific emotions and thoughts.
6. Speak in "paragraphs"; that is, express one main idea with some elaboration and then allow your partner to respond. Speaking for a long time without a break makes it hard for your partner to listen.
7. Express your feelings and thoughts with *tact* and *timing* so that your partner can listen to what you are saying without becoming defensive.

Skills for Listening to Partner

Ways to respond while your partner is speaking:

1. Show that you *understand* your partner's statements and accept his or her right to have those thoughts and feelings. Demonstrate this *acceptance* through your tone of voice, facial expressions, and posture.
2. Try to put yourself *in your partner's place* and look at the situation from his or her perspective to determine how the other person feels and thinks about the issue.

Ways to respond after your partner finishes speaking:

1. After your partner finishes speaking, *summarize* and restate your partner's most important feelings, desires, conflicts, and thoughts. This is called a *reflection*.
2. While in the listener role, *do not*:
   a. ask questions, except for clarification,
   b. express your own viewpoint or opinion,
   c. interpret or change the meaning of your partner's statements,
   d. offer solutions or attempt to solve a problem if one exists,
   e. make judgments or evaluate what your partner has said.

APPENDIX 9.C
FREQUENTLY USED EMOTION WORDS

Positive moods

Happy/joyful		Close/warm		Energetic/vigorous	
Cheerful	Happy	Loving	Warm	Active	Lively
Excited	Pleased	Devoted	Affectionate	Peppy	Vigorous
Amused	Joyful	Secure	Tender	Energetic	Enthusiastic
Delighted	Thrilled	Sexy		Adventurous	
Glad		Close			
		Friendly			

Relaxed/Calm		Other Positive Moods	
Gentle	Peaceful	Agreeable	Ambitious
Calm	Relaxed	Confident	Inspired
Contented		Lucky	

Negative moods

Depressed/sad		Anxious		Angry	
Sad	Bored	Shaky	Tense	Angry	Frustrated
Blue	Gloomy	Restless	Nervous	Resentful	Enraged
Unhappy	Grim	Anxious	Fearful	Furious	Irritated
Discouraged	Low	Panicky	Insecure	Disgusted	Outraged
Miserable	Dejected	Terrified	Frightened	Annoyed	Mad
	Hurt	Worried	Shy		
		Bashful	Confused		

Contemptuous		Fatigued		Other negative moods	
Critical	Disdainful	Exhausted	Listless	Bewildered	Lonely
Contemptuous	Hostile	Fatigued	Sluggish	Jealous	Guilty
		Weary	Wilted	Ashamed	

APPENDIX 9.D
WHEN TO REFLECT THE SPEAKER'S MESSAGE

- When the speaker believes others have not been listening.
- When the listener wants to show respect for the speaker—particularly if the listener plans to disagree or challenge the speaker.
- When the interaction is moving too quickly.
- When the listener wants to make sure he or she understood the speaker.
- When the listener wants to keep the focus on the speaker.
- When the listener wants to assist the speaker in exploring an issue more deeply.

ALTERNATIVES TO REFLECTING

- Reflect, then reciprocate the types of feeling expressed by the speaker—"You really enjoyed getting away together. So did I. It was so relaxing, and I was delighted to see that we have great fun together when we're not so busy."
- Reciprocate immediately: "I love you, too, sweetheart."
- Affirm or show appreciation for statement: "Thank you for saying that. I really worked hard, and it's nice to know you noticed it."
- Develop a conversation based on the emotion expressed.

APPENDIX 9.E
GUIDELINES FOR DECISION-MAKING CONVERSATIONS

1. *State what the issue is, clearly and specifically.*
   a. Phrase the issue in terms of behaviors that are currently occurring or not occurring or in terms of what needs to be decided.
   b. Break down large, complex problems into several smaller problems, and deal with them one at a time.
   c. Make certain that both people agree on the statement of the problem and are willing to discuss it.
2. *Clarify why the issue is important and what your needs are.*
   a. Clarify why the issue is important to you and provide your understanding of the issues involved.
   b. Explain what your needs are that you would like to see taken into account in the solution; do not offer specific solutions at this time.
3. *Discuss possible solutions.*
   a. Propose concrete, specific solutions that take both people's needs and preferences into account. Do not focus on solutions that meet only your individual needs.
   b. Focus on solutions for the present and the future. Do not dwell on the past or attempt to attribute blame for past difficulties.
   c. If you tend to focus on a single or few alternatives, consider brainstorming (generating a variety of possible solutions in a creative way).
4. *Decide on a solution that is feasible and agreeable to both of you.*
   a. If you cannot find a solution that pleases both partners, suggest a compromise solution. If a compromise is not possible, agree to follow one person's preferences.
   b. State your solution in clear, specific, behavioral terms.
   c. After agreeing on a solution, have one partner restate the solution.
   d. Do not accept a solution if you do not intend to follow through with it.
   e. Do not accept a solution that will make you angry or resentful.
5. *Decide on a trial period to implement the solution, if it is a situation that will occur more than once.*
   a. Allow for several attempts of the new solution.
   b. Review the solution at the end of the trial period.
   c. Revise the solution if needed, taking into account what you have learned thus far.

10

INTERVENTIONS FOR MODIFYING COGNITIONS

In this chapter we focus on approaches to intervening with partners' cognitions, either as an adjunct to interventions targeting behaviors and emotions or as factors directly influencing individuals' satisfaction with their relationships. We begin by addressing several issues that have been raised in the literature concerning the relevance and effectiveness of cognitive restructuring as well as the close link between cognitive assessment and intervention.

PERSPECTIVES ON COGNITIVE CHANGE INTERVENTIONS

Although interventions for modifying cognitions have become a standard component of cognitive–behavioral couples therapy (CBCT), clinicians and researchers have raised several important questions concerning their relevance and effectiveness in improving distressed couples' relationships. Some of these issues apply to cognitive interventions in individual as well as in couples therapy; others are specific to the use of cognitive restructuring in the context of an intimate relationship. In addition, some of these issues concern the close link between cognitive assessment and intervention, because a therapist's ability to address an individual's cognitions at the exact moment when they are occurring depends on a clear identification of them. Consequently, we begin this chapter with a discussion of several issues concerning modification of cognitions:

- Theorists and researchers have noted that some cognitive processes that affect individuals' relationships occur in an "automatic" manner that often is beyond awareness. If this is so, how can therapists identify and modify the cognitions if the person is not aware of them? To what extent do interviews and questionnaires assess what people *believe* they must be thinking, rather than the cognitions that *are* actually occurring?

- Cognitive assessment relies on individuals' reports about their internal experiences. In responding to interview questions or to questionnaire items, there is potential for response biases, such as answering in a socially desirable way. How can a therapist have confidence that partners are revealing the cognitions that they experience?

- Cultural differences in cognitions, such as standards about desirable characteristics of a couple relationship, create the potential for therapists to be biased in their assessment of dysfunction and in their selection of particular cognitions to target for change. How can therapists minimize the imposition of their own relationship standards on their clients?

- Cognitive-restructuring procedures that were developed for individual therapy of problems such as depression and anxiety focus on taking personal responsibility for identifying and modifying one's own thinking. However, members of distressed couples commonly blame each other for relationship problems and may react defensively to a therapist's efforts to have them challenge their own thinking. To what extent is it necessary to modify cognitive-restructuring techniques to make them palatable and effective with individuals who view their partners as the source of relationship problems?

- After cognitive-restructuring interventions reduce partners' negative views of each other, to what extent will new negative actions quickly counteract the cognitive changes? If cognitive changes are susceptible to invalidation by subsequent negative behavior, to what extent are cognitive interventions important, compared to behavioral ones?

- Just as couples commonly stop using behavioral skills such as communication guidelines after they complete therapy, they also commonly stop monitoring and challenging their cognitions. There also is no evidence that happy couples naturally monitor and challenge their distressing thoughts. To what extent does this indicate that cognitive-restructuring interventions have only temporary impacts and that partners' use of cognitive-restructuring skills is irrelevant to a long-term successful relationship?

These issues have contributed to some controversy concerning the use of cognitive-restructuring interventions in couples therapy. Because of this controversy, and what we believe is a common underestimation of the degree of flexibility possible in interventions for cognitions, we now turn to a discussion of each issue.

How Can One Modify Cognitions That Are Difficult to Access?

The literature on cognitive therapy (e.g., A. T. Beck, Rush, Shaw, & Emery, 1979; J. S. Beck, 1995; Leahy, 1997) describes *automatic thoughts* as spontaneous cognitions that often occur in a fleeting manner but are largely conscious and accessible to examination by the individual and a therapist. There is an assumption that even though some individuals are unaccustomed to monitoring their own stream-of-consciousness automatic thoughts, with some practice it is possible to become more attuned to them. Cognitive therapists typically teach clients about automatic thoughts and coach them in identifying these thoughts as they occur during and outside therapy sessions.

The cognitive therapy literature describes how an individual's underlying beliefs or schemas about the self and others often can be identified from his or her conscious automatic thoughts. Starting with an individual's automatic thought, the therapist can ask a series of questions that probe for associations to broader beliefs that the individual holds. For example, a woman might report becoming angry that her husband forgot social plans that they had made. A therapist might ask her, "What would it mean to you if your husband forgets about plans that involve you?" and she might reply, "It would mean that spending time with me isn't important to him." The therapist then might ask, "What would it mean to you if spending time with you wasn't important to him?" and she might reply, "I would have made a big mistake marrying him, because I need to be close to someone and share life together." Further discussion may reveal the client's relationship standards, which include specific ideas about what constitutes adequate sharing between two people.

Thus, cognitive therapy procedures typically focus on cognitions that occur spontaneously but are either immediately conscious or accessible through the client's introspection. In contrast to this view, there is evidence from research on human information processing that some cognition occurs beyond the individual's awareness and may not be accessible through direct introspection. As Fiske and Taylor (1991) summarized, "In both social and nonsocial domains, people acquire and use complex information, without being able to report the basis for doing so, suggesting the power of processing outside awareness" (p. 283). Of course, the concept that individuals may not be aware of at least some of the processes influencing their reactions to life events is not new and has been prominent in psychodynamic theoretical approaches (Sager, 1976; Sander, 1998). Thus, a challenge facing therapists is how to identify the cognitive processes and content that contribute to a couple's problems when the partners may not be aware of them.

At the microlevel of an individual's moment-to-moment cognitions, a therapist can stop a couple's interaction to point out that the individual seems to be having a reaction (based on verbal or nonverbal cues) and can inquire about any conscious cognitions. When the individual's reported cognitions do not seem to match the cues that the therapist has observed, the therapist can point out the discrepancy and ask the individual for further feedback. Given the absence of objective ways of measuring clients' subjective cognitions, therapists need to listen carefully, probe possible cognitions, and be open to disconfirmation of their hypotheses. Identification of an individual's significant cognitions about his or her relationship becomes more reliable and valid when the therapist gathers information across situations. For example, it becomes clearer that an individual is selectively perceiving a partner's negative behavior and "tuning out" the positives when the therapist is able to observe several different instances in which the individual overlooked the partner's positive acts.

How Can Therapists Circumvent Clients' Response Biases in Targeting Problematic Cognitions?

Even when members of a couple are aware of their cognitions, there is potential for them to censor what they reveal to their therapist and partner. For example, individuals who are invested in demonstrating to the therapist that they are the wronged party in their relationship may not mention vindictive thoughts toward the partner that might cast them in a negative light. As we described in chapter 8, a therapist can try to reduce response biases by taking steps to communicate that he or she intends to avoid taking sides in the couple's disputes, and he or she can maintain comparable levels of eye contact and conversation with the two partners.

Conjoint sessions often reveal cognitions that each partner might prefer to hide. It is common that each person's actions tend to trigger negative cognitions in the other person and, as the partners become caught up in the moment, their responses to each other become less censored. They are more likely to spontaneously verbalize negative thoughts about each other or in response to brief therapist probes such as, "So what do you think about what he just said?"

Are Cognitive Interventions Biased by Cultural Factors?

The cultural background of the therapist is likely to shape his or her views of what constitutes healthy or desirable cognitions in client couples. The therapist's cultural background may differ from those of the clients, and there is the potential that the therapist will try to impose values on the couple in the name of "cognitive restructuring." Research demonstrates instances in which clients have been diagnosed and treated inappropriately because their therapists did not understand their cultural traditions (Giordano & Carini-Giordano, 1995). Both individual psychiatric diagnostic systems and models of normal marital and family functioning have been developed primarily within Western cultures, and their core assumptions are based on normative experiences in those cultures. For example, Western cultures commonly place a positive value on autonomous functioning and individual achievement. Consequently, a therapist raised in a Western culture may view a couple or family from a different culture that focuses on family loyalty and discourages individuality as enmeshed and dysfunctional. If the therapist challenges the family's standards about boundaries and tries to encourage more independent behavior, the interventions may be inappropriate for meeting the members' needs.

It is important to consider how different levels of culture can influence how a therapist or the partners think about couple relationships. Cultural norms define desirable behavior, what constitutes a problem, and how the members of a relationship solve problems (McGoldrick, Preto, Hines, & Lee, 1991). At broader levels, culture is defined by one's country of origin, race, religion, ethnicity, and regional community norms. However, it also is important to take into account an idiosyncratic culture that has been passed down from one generation to the next in a particular family. For example, for several generations, children in Bob's family had attended private schools that emphasized academic achievement, and they were raised to carry on a family tradition of "excellence in public service." Bob and Carin's therapist needed to consider the partners' family cultures when intervening with their conflicts over standards regarding the amount of time and energy Bob should invest in his career. If a person's cultural traditions are ignored, he or she is likely to resist therapeutic interventions. It is important to not suggest that either partner's beliefs are right or wrong but rather to examine how well the beliefs contribute to the couple having a mutually satisfying relationship. The therapist can coach the partners in considering modified versions of their standards that allow some flexibility in how they relate to each other.

How Can Therapists Overcome Partners' Reluctance to Take Personal Responsibility for Solving Relationship Problems?

The therapist's role in couples therapy involves engaging partners in a collaborative relationship with the clinician and each other, counteracting their tendency to blame each other for relationship problems (Baucom & Epstein, 1990; Jacobson & Margolin, 1979). Cognitive restructuring involves the willingness to rethink one's perspectives, including being open to the possibility that one's own views and behavior are contributing to relationship problems. However, the format of cognitive restructuring in couples therapy sessions creates potential difficulties for establishing collaboration and self-examination by each partner. In individual therapy, the therapist has no history or personal issues with the client, so the client has no objective reason to doubt the therapist's good intentions. In contrast, in couples therapy each individual is more likely to be defensive in the presence of a partner who may be invested in demonstrating that the individual is the cause of relationship problems. When a therapist asks an individual to consider the possibility that his or her cognitions are distorted or inappropriate, the presence of the partner can decrease the person's openness to thinking about and discussing alternative views. Clinicians using interventions in joint sessions must take this defensiveness into account.

First, as we described in chapter 8, the therapist can create a relatively safe atmosphere by imposing ground rules regarding how the members of a couple can interact during sessions and at home between sessions. Second, the attitude that the therapist conveys during cognitive-restructuring interventions can affect how open or defensive each member of a couple will be. If the therapist explicitly or implicitly conveys a message of "Aha! I caught you in distorted thinking, and I am going to pressure you to admit it and change your views," then it is likely that the individual will experience being placed in a one-down position and losing face in front of both the therapist and partner. Consequently, the therapist should convey empathy to each individual for his or her views and how they developed while still helping that person evaluate whether those cognitions have some negative consequences.

The therapist also should emphasize the difference between *negative* thoughts and *distorted* thoughts. The therapist can note that negative *or* positive thoughts might be reasonable or distorted, and the goal is to identify and modify those that appear to be distorted. Each thought will be examined on the basis of experiences that are consistent or inconsistent with it.

Third, the therapist can demonstrate to both partners that their cognitions are subjective (and susceptible to distortion and idiosyncrasies), emphasizing that this is normal and common. For example, in listening to two partners' accounts of a recent argument, a therapist might become aware of and point out that the argument had been based on a misunderstanding due to insufficient communication between partners concerning their intentions.

Fourth, a person's partner can be a valuable source of new information to broaden the person's views, but this is unlikely to occur if the partner's input is conveyed in a critical, demeaning, or controlling manner. When Lisa expressed her discouragement about the level of intimacy in her relationship with Warren, he responded, "Lisa, I can't believe you didn't notice how I changed my schedule so I'd have more evening time with you!" Lisa then perceived Warren as being critical of her, and she focused more on the criticism than on the information that he had made a concerted effort to meet her desire for more time together. The therapist intervened by first praising Warren for realizing that somehow his attempt to meet Lisa's intimacy needs had not had the impact that he had expected. The therapist then pointed out that Warren's way of expressing his surprise and apparent frustration seemed to be distracting Lisa from focusing on his important feedback about changing his schedule.

On the one hand, the therapist can coach the partner to express feedback in a constructive manner; on the other hand, the therapist also may need to explore factors that interfere with the recipient's ability to positively perceive constructive feedback. In the preceding example, the therapist and Lisa discussed her tendency to discount Warren's behavior changes, because she had been very disappointed by temporary changes that he had made in the past.

Fifth, when an individual appears to be defensive about examining his or her cognitions in the presence of the partner, it can be helpful to schedule one or more individual sessions with each person. Even if the other member of the couple is open to self-examination, holding separate sessions with both partners can help maintain balance in the therapist's alliance with the two individuals. During these individual sessions, the therapist uses the abovementioned strategies to encourage each person to consider other ways of thinking about the partner and relationship.

Can Cognitive Interventions Counteract Negative Behavior?

Gottman (1994a, 1999) has noted that a couple commonly need to exchange several positive behaviors to counteract the distress caused by a negative act. Similarly, in chapter 2 we reviewed research indicating that negative behavior has a greater impact than positive behavior on individuals' relationship satisfaction. In therapy, partners often report that a single negative act "wiped out my good feelings and showed me that we were back to square one."

Thus, a course of therapy focused solely on promoting cognitive change likely would not be optimal for most couples. Most couples need to experience behavioral changes to help them view the relationship in new ways. As we describe later in this chapter, behavioral experiments designed to help couples reassess their cognitions are an important part of treatment. In addition, cognitive interventions can help minimize the impact of isolated negative events in the couple's life. For example, we coach individuals in noticing situational factors that affect each other's negative behavior, so negative acts are not automatically attributed to global, stable traits of the partner that are unlikely to change.

Also, instances of negative behavior might have less impact on the couple's slowly developing positive cognitions if the therapist has prepared the couple for potential lapses. The therapist can discuss with the couple how occasional returns to old negative patterns are common and normal and can help them rehearse ways to cope with such lapses (e.g., coping self-statements, discussing the "slip" and agreeing to return to more positive interaction).

Why Teach Couples Cognitive-Restructuring Skills That They Will Not Continue to Use?

In chapter 9 we discussed the importance of having couples practice communication and decision-making behavioral skills even though many happy couples do not naturally engage in those behaviors in a structured way, and treated couples commonly do not continue to use them after therapy ends. Happy couples also do not routinely evaluate the validity of their cognitions to maintain satisfaction with their relationships. As is the case with behavioral interventions, once cognitive-restructuring techniques have helped a couple change their negative interactions and develop more positive views of each other, the partners can use the cognitive-restructuring skills when they find themselves slipping into their previous problematic patterns.

INTERVENTIONS FOR MODIFYING COGNITIONS

General Goals

The interventions we describe for modifying cognitions have several common goals:

- To increase each person's willingness to take personal responsibility for improving the relationship, by understanding circular causality and examining the impact of his or her cognitions and behavioral responses on the couple's interactions.

- To demonstrate that cognitions tend to be subjective, can be distorted or inappropriate, and can influence a couple's interactions.

- To teach the couple about particular types of cognitions and how they affect the ways that individuals process information about each other.

- To increase and improve each individual's monitoring of his or her cognitions and the associations with behavioral and emotional responses.

- To increase mutual understanding of each other's cognitions.

- To teach specific techniques for evaluating the appropriateness of one's cognitions.

- To modify each person's cognitions in ways that broaden his or her perspective on the relationship, providing alternative views to replace relatively narrow and inflexible ones.

As noted earlier, individuals often process information about events in their relationships in automatic ways and fail to understand how their subjective cognitions influence their emotions and behavior. They tend to experience their appraisals of events as valid and think in unidirectional causal terms, blaming their partners for relationship difficulties. Consequently, CBCT is intended to increase each person's awareness of circular causal processes in the relationship; that is, how one's actions affect one's partner as well as how one's partner affects oneself, as in demand–withdraw cycles. As we described in chapter 3, increasing individuals' tendencies to think in relational terms (e.g., "If I do X, it has Y impact on intimate communication with my partner") can increase relationship satisfaction.

Furthermore, cognitive–behavioral therapy (CBT) is designed to develop each person's ability to identify his or her own cognitions and modify them when information, experiences, or further evaluation suggests that they are inappropriate. It is likely that any effective therapy broadens clients' cognitions regarding their life experiences, whether the interventions focus on behavioral changes, shifts in emotional experiences, or direct changes in cognition.

Distressed partners often describe how they saw each other in more positive ways when they were initially attracted to each other, but through particular experiences they came to see each other in new, more negative ways. Cognitive-restructuring interventions are intended to help individuals differentiate between objectively negative patterns (e.g., a partner is truly trying to dominate decision making) and those that are experienced as negative because of the perceiver's cognitive biases (e.g., *any* disagreement by the partner is interpreted as disrespect). As Jacobson and Christensen (1996) emphasized, even when events or characteristics appear to be objectively negative (e.g., a partner's personal habit that most people would find unpleasant), an individual who wants to maintain the relationship can choose either to try to change them or to accept them. Acceptance involves an internal shift with a cognitive component, for example, in how flexibly the person applies his or her relationship standards.

Formats of Interventions

The formats for modifying cognitions can vary from discrete didactic presentations to spontaneous responses to an individual's cognition at any point in a session. Next we provide some examples of these variations in format.

Didactic Presentations

As part of the assessment feedback to a couple, a therapist may discuss examples of how the partners tend to have particular types of cognitive responses that affect their relationship, such as focusing on each other's negative behavior and overlooking positive acts or attributing each other's negative behavior to unchangeable traits. The therapist discusses the importance of cognitive processes in partners' reactions to each other and notes that in CBT the therapist pays attention not only to how people behave toward each other but also to how they interpret each other's actions. The therapist then may note that he or she will work with them on being attuned to and evaluating thoughts about themselves, each other, and their environment, so that these thoughts do not have negative effects on their relationship. The language that the therapist initially uses can influence the individuals' acceptance of cognitive interventions. Although the therapist will want each person to take responsibility for his or her own cognitions, language that externalizes the problem somewhat, by describing cognitions as potential problems over which people can gain control, can be easier for clients to hear than language that focuses on "your distorted thinking."

The therapist can present a didactic description of a type of problematic cognition, such as attributions, either in a routine way (whether or not attributional problems are evident in the session) or at a specific point when there is evidence that the partners' attributions have contributed to conflict and distress. This didactic module involves telling the couple what is known about types of attributions and their impacts on couples' relationships and coaching the partners in identifying the attributions they make as well as their consequences. As we describe in the next section, the therapist then can use a variety of interventions to modify the problematic attributions. The following is an example of a therapist's didactic presentation after hearing about an incident in which Carla initially was upset with Keith when she thought he intentionally chose not to tell her that he had gotten a traffic ticket. Carla had felt better later when Keith told her that he had intended to tell her but had been distracted by a crisis at his job.

> Therapist: The situation that you described occurs very commonly in relationships between people. When one person observes another person behaving in a particular way, especially an unexpected or a negative way, it is natural to wonder why the person is acting like that. People typically try to answer that "why" question, making interpretations about what caused the other person's behavior. For example, Carla, when you discovered that Keith had not told you about his traffic ticket, you were surprised and wondered why he hadn't said

	anything about it. As you began to think that he was intentionally withholding the information from you, you became angry. Does that seem to describe your reaction?
Carla:	Yes. I couldn't believe he wouldn't tell me about something that important.
Therapist:	When a person observes someone else's behavior and makes an inference about why the person behaved that way, we call it an *attribution*. That is, you attribute the behavior to some cause. Carla, you described how you concluded that Keith failed to tell you about the ticket on purpose, as if he was trying to hide it from you, and you were angry because that seemed like a lack of honesty. Am I correct about how you interpreted it?
Carla:	Yes, that's right.
Therapist:	However, when you discussed the incident later, Keith gave you more information about the work problems that were still the main thing on his mind when he arrived home. When you heard Keith's explanation for his behavior, you were less upset with him because you had a different explanation or attribution for why he didn't say anything about the traffic ticket.
Carla:	His explanation about the crisis at work seemed genuine. Still, if it had been me, I'd have been so upset about getting a ticket that I would have told Keith about it right away.
Therapist:	That's an important point, Carla. Often when we try to understand what causes another person's behavior we think about what would cause ourselves to behave that way in a similar situation. However, people behave differently in the same type of situation. Therefore, our attributions about the causes of another's behavior can be off base at times. It is important to check out whether your attributions are on track.

Thus, the therapist uses a real experience in the couple's relationship as a means to instruct them about types of cognitions, ways in which cognitions may be inappropriate, and strategies for examining the appropriateness of their thoughts. Although didactic presentations have a relatively formal educational quality, it is important that they not be overly intellectualized, lengthy, and "dry." The therapist should convey the information in a conversational manner and avoid language that the couple might interpret as criticism of their rationality and good sense. Soliciting the couple's input and reactions also is important so that the presentation does not become a monologue delivered by the therapist.

Informal Interventions

A less formal format is to identify individuals' cognitions as they occur during a session and use specific interventions to modify them, without giving the couple a didactic presentation about types of cognitions and principles of cognitive restructuring. When an individual makes a negative attribution about a partner's behavior during a session, the therapist can help the person consider alternative explanations, without going into a discussion about the nature of attributions per se. For example, Elizabeth and Peter had worked for several weeks on decreasing their mutual criticism and improving their use of expressive and listening skills. However, Elizabeth arrived at a therapy session quite upset.

Elizabeth: I'm so frustrated; it all seems hopeless. Peter told me my ideas about improving our financial situation were "stupid." It seems that he isn't capable of changing how he communicates with me.

Therapist: (after confirming that Peter remembered using the word "stupid") Is that the first time that one of you didn't follow the communication guidelines that you have been working on and criticized the other during the past few weeks?

Elizabeth: That's the first time either of us said something nasty.

Peter: That's right. That's why I don't see why she's making such a big deal about it.

Therapist: Elizabeth, would you explain to Peter what it means to you that he didn't follow the communication guidelines that time?

Elizabeth: I don't like being called stupid—it's disrespectful—and it made me feel like you can't consistently be nice to me. When we discuss something tough like money, you lose it.

Therapist: Peter, what do you remember was going on with you in that situation?

Peter: I wish I hadn't said it, but I was frustrated by our discussion of finances. Most of her ideas seemed to involve *my* making changes in my spending, and I couldn't see what she thought *she* could do about the problem. She needs to look at her role in this, too.

Therapist: You told me that you did use the word "stupid" to describe Elizabeth's ideas. From what you are saying now, was it that they were stupid, or something else?

Peter: No, they weren't stupid. They made sense, but they were all about me and not about her. That's what made me angry.

Therapist: Elizabeth, if Peter had originally expressed his thoughts and feelings the way he just did, instead of labeling your ideas as "stupid," how do you think you might have reacted?

Elizabeth: I would have been less angry, but I disagree that I expect only him to change.

Therapist: OK. Recently both of you seemed impressed with the efforts the other person was putting into improving your relationship. However, your communication broke down somewhat during the recent discussion. A key issue is whether it really meant "back to square one" or whether you have made meaningful changes that temporarily were disrupted when you began discussing a particularly stressful issue.

The therapist continued to explore the situation specificity of Peter's negative behavior. Both members of the couple were able to see that it had not occurred during conversations that both of them viewed as equitable and that it occurred when Peter was angry with Elizabeth for what he viewed as an unbalanced solution. The therapist also noted that it was not surprising that Elizabeth was uneasy about the possibility of a return to the couple's previous negative interactions. Nevertheless, it was important to distinguish between a "slip" under particular conditions and an unchangeable characteristic. Thus, the intervention was intended to reduce the impact of Peter's negative behavior on the positive cognitive change that had occurred during the past weeks. The intervention also focused on how the partners could return to the behavior that had worked well for them. Principles of cognitive restructuring were never addressed explicitly.

We often make such informal interventions and believe that they can improve partners' views of each other and their relationship. However, we also believe that teaching couples about the principles of monitoring and challenging their own cognitions is an important step toward building their abilities to manage their relationship without the input of an outsider. Consequently, we usually use a combination of brief didactic presentations and spontaneous, informal cognitive interventions.

The following are some guidelines that we use for choosing between formal didactic and informal interventions.

- A formal didactic presentation is useful when a particular type of cognition (e.g., extreme standards) appears to have a prominent role in the couple's problems.
- Formal didactic presentations may be more palatable than informal interventions to partners who actively seek and value educational materials, such as self-help books.
- A formal presentation that concludes with a concise summary in the form of a key statement can set the stage for subsequent informal interventions in which the therapist repeats the statement to draw the couple's attention to a particular type of cognitive distortion that might be operating at the moment.
- A formal didactic presentation can be used to interrupt and de-escalate partners' negative emotions and behavioral interactions.
- Formal presentations can be used more often with individuals who are low in relationship schematic processing, to increase the clients' awareness of interpersonal patterns.

- A formal presentation that focuses on general principles rather than an individual's own responses might be chosen when the individual becomes defensive about the therapist's attention to that person's particular responses.
- An informal intervention often is helpful when the therapist wishes to address an individual's problematic cognition at the moment it occurs within a session, without sidetracking for long from an important topic that was being discussed.
- Informal interventions may be more palatable than formal didactic ones with clients who dislike directive input from therapists and others.
- An informal intervention may be preferable when a couple has made a positive change but has a lapse in a specific situation, to get them back on track.

TYPES OF INTERVENTIONS WITH COGNITIONS

In this section we describe a variety of interventions that are designed to change and broaden partners' cognitions about their relationships. These interventions can be classified according to whether they involve: (a) *cognitive techniques*, which focus on an analysis of the content and process of individuals' cognitions, or (b) *behavioral techniques* and *affective techniques*, which provide behavioral or emotional information concerning the appropriateness of a cognition.

We will describe a variety of interventions that vary in their emphases on cognitive versus behavioral and affective techniques. Exhibit 10.1 lists major types of interventions used to modify partners' cognitions, categorized according to these characteristics. Nevertheless, it is important to note that many interventions used for cognitive restructuring include both cognitive and behavioral–affective elements. In the sections that follow we describe each of these types of interventions for modifying problematic cognitions. First we describe the distinction between cognitive versus behavioral–affective interventions.

Cognitive vs. Behavioral–Affective Techniques

We distinguish between interventions that focus solely on the content or process of a client's cognitions and those that create behavioral or emotional experiences (or both) that can be used as information to influence partners' thinking. Cognitive techniques involve intellectual exchanges between the therapist and couple, such as a discussion of alternative causal explanations for a partner's behavior. In contrast, behavioral techniques involve inducing the clients to behave in particular ways and to observe their

EXHIBIT 10.1
Interventions and Techniques for Modifying Cognitions

Cognitive
- Inquiring about the evidence for, or experiences supporting, a cognition.
- Weighing advantages and disadvantages of a cognition.
- Considering the worst possible outcomes of situations that partners fear.
- The inductive "downward-arrow" method.
- Inductively identifying macrolevel patterns from cross-situational response patterns.
- Identifying macrolevel patterns in prior relationships.
- Psychoeducational mini-lectures, readings, and videotapes.
- Increasing relationship schematic thinking by pointing out repetitive cycles in couple interaction.

Behavioral and affective
- Communication and decision-making exercises to create new experiences.
- Behavioral experiments.
- Having the partners act "as if" they have different views and behavioral patterns.
- Role-taking exercises to increase mutual empathy.
- Increasing the awareness and experience of particular emotions.
- Moderating emotions contributing to sentiment override.

own and their partners' actions. The information gained from these behavioral observations might challenge existing cognitions about the relationship and introduce new views. Affective techniques involve either drawing couples' attention to types and variations in their emotional responses or inducing increases or decreases in the strength of particular emotions. For example, helping an individual notice that he or she feels not only anger toward a partner but also loneliness may change the individual's view of the relationship. Partners' observations of their own and each other's emotional responses may change their cognitions; for example, "I didn't realize how much you care about our relationship until I saw you cry about the possibility of our separating."

Socratic Questioning and Guided-Discovery Interventions

Cognitive therapy is well known for methods in which the therapist acts as a teacher who educates the client about common distortions and limitations in people's perceptions, inferences, and basic beliefs or schemas (A. T. Beck et al., 1979; J. S. Beck, 1995; Leahy, 1997). The therapist who conducts individual cognitive therapy is likely to introduce the idea that individuals with problems such as depression and anxiety disorders typically have some distorted and overly negative thoughts. At times the therapist may be directive, pointing out an apparent distortion, such as, "Jim, you just said that Sophia never tells you what she feels. Did you notice that a minute ago she said she felt angry that you bought a new computer without consulting her?" However, usually cognitive therapists emphasize *collaborative em-*

piricism, in which the therapist and client work together to test the validity and utility of a thought, and to develop more adaptive ways of thinking (J. S. Beck, 1995). As J. S. Beck (1995) noted, the collaboration is essential, because the therapist does not know *a priori* whether an individual's cognition is distorted or inappropriate for his or her life situation.

The *validity of a cognition* refers to how accurately it represents the objective characteristics of the individual's life. In couples therapy, the focus is on how validly a cognition represents the characteristics of the individual, the partner, the couple's interactions, and the couple's environment. For example, when an individual attributes a partner's bad mood to dissatisfaction with their relationship, the therapist can coach him or her in thinking about information that supports or refutes that conclusion or in thinking of other possible causes for the partner's mood. Given that partners' experiences of their relationships are so highly subjective, determining an objective reality often is difficult. However, the therapist can assist the partners in assessing whether each person has developed a reasonable perspective on the relationship, given the information and circumstances available.

The *utility of a cognition* refers to how functional or adaptive it is in the individual's life and the couple's relationship. For example, Brad held a standard that he and Emma should share virtually all the same interests and values. It is not useful to try to evaluate whether a standard is valid, but its utility can be assessed. The couple's therapist coached Brad in listing the advantages and disadvantages of trying to live according to his standard. One clear advantage was that the couple would rarely disagree about how to spend their time, and neither person would have to worry about trying to find ways to please the other. As the therapist asked Brad to think about possible complications of striving toward being the same, Brad noted that neither person would feel free to grow as an individual or develop a new interest. When the therapist asked Brad if only their similarities initially attracted him to Emma, he replied that, to the contrary, he liked her lively personality because it helped him overcome his shyness. Finally, Brad noted that Emma often became angry at him when he tried to restrict her from pursuing interests that were different from his. Thus, it became clear to Brad that although it was fine to value sharing in their relationship, his standard had significant disadvantages.

Socratic questioning methods commonly are used in individual cognitive therapy to challenge the validity of individuals' distorted or inappropriate cognitions (see, e.g., J. S. Beck, 1995). Socratic questioning involves asking the client questions that induce him or her to think about the logic involved in a particular cognition or to consider information that bears on the appropriateness of the cognition. For instance, a husband might report the thought, "My wife doesn't love me because she rarely shows physical affection or tells me that she loves me." A therapist might encourage him to examine the logic in his inference as well as evidence for its validity by asking questions such as:

- What are the ways that a person who loves someone might demonstrate that feeling?
- What other reasons, other than not loving you, might explain your wife's infrequent expression of physical affection?
- You mentioned that you originally were attracted by your wife's quiet, gentle personality. Given that she has that personal style, how can you tell how she feels about experiences in her life, whether they involve her job, her friends, events in the news, or her relationship with you?
- In the early years of your relationship, how could you tell that she loved you? Has she directly told you that her feelings for you have changed? Direct expressions of her love seem to be more important to you than they used to be. What do you think has changed, so that those direct expressions mean more to you now?

If the man acknowledges that his wife may still love him, but he expresses a standard that she should express her feelings in a particular way, the therapist might use a series of questions to guide him in considering the advantages and disadvantages of that standard.

In the context of an empathic, caring relationship between a therapist and individual client, Socratic questioning commonly is effective in helping the client evaluate whether his or her cognitions are inappropriate. However, we have found that such questioning must be used with great care in couples therapy. As we noted earlier, members of distressed couples commonly are accustomed to their partners blaming them for problems and challenging the validity of their thinking. These individuals are likely to respond defensively if they perceive a therapist as also questioning the validity of their perceptions, standards, and so forth, particularly in front of the partner. Therefore, several of the interventions described next involve questioning members of a couple about information concerning the appropriateness of their cognitions, but it is crucial to use them judiciously and tactfully. Other interventions we describe minimize questioning of an individual's existing cognitions or directly suggesting alternative ways of thinking.

These other interventions create conditions in which the members of a couple can gain new information that modifies their cognitions about their relationship. Rather than directly questioning an existing cognition, the therapist's role is to facilitate new experiences, knowledge, and understanding. We refer to these as *guided discovery* interventions[1] because they emphasize the clients' discovery of new perspectives through their new experiences.

---

[1]The term *guided discovery* typically is used in a more restricted way in the cognitive therapy literature (e.g., J. S. Beck, 1995) to refer to the downward-arrow procedure we describe.

Interventions that provide clients with new information can involve cognitive, behavioral, or affective strategies. The role plays, role reversals, communication exercises, "as-if" exercises, explorations of cross-situational consistency in partners' responses, and psychoeducational interventions that we cover in this section provide new information that increases partners' understanding of themselves, each other, and their relationship. The broader perspective achieved through these new experiences often changes the partners' perceptions, attributions, expectancies, assumptions, and standards concerning their relationship. These techniques are especially important in work with distressed partners who need to feel that their therapist has no stake in demonstrating who is right or wrong. We commonly use a combination of direct questioning of cognitions and setting up conditions for new experiences, and several of the techniques described next involve both strategies.

Cognitive Interventions

The interventions in this section use primarily cognitive strategies to address partners' ways of thinking. In other words, they rely on intellectual analyses of the logic, existing evidence, or pros and cons concerning the appropriateness of a person's cognitions. In contrast to the behavioral and affective interventions we describe in the next section, these approaches do not involve inducing the members of a couple to behave or experience their emotions in new ways. However, some of the interventions involve asking partners to make observations of events in their current relationship as well as recall events that took place in past relationships. As we have noted, therapists need to be cautious in using these cognitive interventions, because individuals who are accustomed to having their partners challenge their views may be defensive when a therapist attempts to examine the validity or utility of their perceptions, attributions, expectancies, assumptions, or standards.

Inquiring About the Evidence For, or Experiences Supporting, a Cognition

When a member of a couple expresses a cognition that appears to be contributing to distress and conflict between partners, the therapist can ask a sequence of questions regarding the available evidence that supports or fails to support the cognition (J. S. Beck, 1995). The following is an example of such an intervention:

Adam:	I was really upset yesterday when I got home after a bad day at work. When I tried to talk with Sasha about it, she just kept watching TV and showed no interest in me.
Therapist:	When you tried talking with Sasha about your bad day, she seemed disinterested?
Adam:	Yes. She just quickly said hello and went back to watching the news.

Therapist:	What thoughts do you remember going through your mind at that moment?
Adam:	I was thinking, "I had a lousy day, and all she cares about is watching the news."
Therapist:	You were feeling unimportant to Sasha?
Adam:	You bet!
Therapist:	I can see that if Sasha didn't care about the bad day you had, it would be upsetting. What happened that indicated to you that the news was more important to her than you were?
Adam:	When I walked in and said hello, she slightly looked at me and only said hello, but I could tell that she was just paying attention to the TV.
Therapist:	Was there some way that you were trying to let her know about your bad day, and she wasn't responding to it?
Adam:	Well . . . I think it was obvious that I was in a bad mood . . .
Therapist:	Can you help me understand how you demonstrated that mood, and how you can tell whether Sasha noticed your mood and ignored it?

The therapist continued to help Adam evaluate his attribution that Sasha was not interested in him. Adam focused on how intent Sasha had been on watching the news. The therapist asked Adam to consider the possibility that Sasha's behavior was due to something other than a lack of interest in him. Cognitive therapists often use this *alternative-explanations* approach to challenge an individual's negative attributions (J. S. Beck, 1995). Adam was able to think of alternative reasons why Sasha was focusing on the news, including her great concern about political violence in her country of origin, because she had many relatives living there.

> Therapist: Adam, it is possible that your understanding of Sasha's behavior was right on target, but it also is possible that she behaved that way for different reasons. Understanding the basis of her behavior is important, because it will affect how you respond to Sasha. Now that you have considered the situation more fully, what are your current thoughts and feelings about her focusing on television?

Another form of examining the evidence is to ask the individual to think about *past interactions* with the partner and how information about those interactions might influence the person's thoughts about the current situation. Thus, Adam told the therapist that Sasha often has been an empathic listener when he was upset about things, but sometimes she becomes absorbed in something she is doing. The therapist guided Adam in distinguishing between Sasha's overall interest in him and her behavior in particular situations when she becomes absorbed in something else, as in the reported incident.

A characteristic of conjoint couples therapy that distinguishes it from individual therapy is the presence of each person's partner as an important source of information about the person's cognitions. Of course, the partner may have a vested interest in presenting himself or herself in a positive light. Although members of a couple sometimes discount information or input from their partners, it often either is persuasive or at least makes the individual begin to question his or her negative cognitions. For example, the therapist asked Sasha to describe what she was thinking, feeling, and doing when Adam entered their living room as she was watching the TV news. She said that she was paying close attention to the international news, hoping to hear what was going on in her homeland. She remembered saying hello to Adam, but she did not notice anything suggesting that he was upset and needed her attention. She said she is sorry that he had a bad day and that she believes she would have paid more attention to him if he had told her directly that he wanted to talk. The therapist then asked Adam how Sasha's input influenced his view that she was not interested in his feelings that day. Adam did not experience a major shift in his thoughts about the incident, partly because of his general view that Sasha often becomes too absorbed in other things that interest her. The therapist uncovered through further questioning that Adam held a standard that the couple should share more of each other's life. We describe methods for addressing standards later.

Another option is to follow up the cognitive exploration of evidence for a cognition with a *behavioral intervention* that will produce additional evidence. A therapist can guide a couple in setting up behavioral experiments to gather new information concerning alternative explanations for an individual's cognition. Thus, Adam and Sasha might agree to a plan in which Adam would approach Sasha when she was watching the TV news (speaking in a way that she agreed would be appropriate), and he could see how receptive she was. We describe behavioral experiments in more detail later.

Weighing Advantages and Disadvantages of a Cognition

A therapist can coach the members of a couple in identifying and evaluating the advantages and disadvantages of maintaining a particular cognition (Baucom & Epstein, 1990; J. S. Beck, 1995). This type of intervention addresses the utility or appropriateness of the cognition within the couple's relationship and is particularly helpful when assessing standards. In the case of Brad and Emma, described earlier, the therapist helped Brad examine the advantages and disadvantages of applying his standard that he and Emma should share virtually all the same interests and values. Similarly, Adam and Sasha's therapist noted that Adam believed there were particular ways in which Sasha should demonstrate her interest in and involvement with him. When the therapist inquired about Sasha's standards in this area, she explained that she also valued closeness with Adam, but that she had always been a person who felt a need for some time alone, to think, read, or just relax. When Adam heard her comments, he responded, "Why can't you relax by spending time with me?" The therapist responded as follows:

It seems the two of you have somewhat different standards for how much of your free time you should spend together and the specific ways in which you should demonstrate that you are important to each other. Adam, it seems that when Sasha pays attention to you, you feel that she is demonstrating that you are important to her. Sasha, it seems that you also value closeness and togetherness with Adam, but you have a need for some alone time as well, and this has been true your whole life, not just since you met Adam. Your standard is that the two of you should share time, thoughts, and so forth, but each person should also have a certain amount of private time. What are the impressions that the two of you have had about the similarities and differences in your standards?

The therapist then engaged the couple in identifying how much their standards overlapped, and what specific differences existed. The therapist coached each person in discussing advantages and disadvantages of his or her own standards. Then the therapist invited the partner to add any additional advantages and disadvantages of which he or she was aware. Some therapists ask the couple to write lists of the advantages and disadvantages, so they can present them for review. Individuals often are more receptive to hearing the disadvantages of a standard if the therapist first acknowledges that there are some reasonable advantages to the standard. For example, Adam and Sasha's therapist noted that an advantage of Adam's standards concerning a high degree of togetherness and mutual attention was that in a world of demanding jobs and other stresses it was reassuring and comforting to have a steady source of support from each other. Among the disadvantages of Adam's standard was that Sasha had always needed and enjoyed some private time, and she was resentful of the pressure she felt from him to change a lifelong pattern of having some time to spend by herself.

The therapist balanced this consideration of advantages and disadvantages by coaching Sasha in weighing the advantages and disadvantages of her standards concerning breaks from togetherness and attentiveness. One advantage was that having time apart to think, relax, and pursue one's own interests was helpful for reducing stress, concentrating on solutions to personal problems, and growing as an individual. In addition, time apart gave both people interesting experiences to bring to the relationship. A disadvantage was that she might not be available at particular times when Adam needed her the most. Another disadvantage was that it sometimes might give her an excuse for avoiding spending time working on relationship issues with Adam. Adam added another disadvantage to the list: Sasha's standard about spending time alone resulted in her frequently failing to tell him her plans, which he considered impolite.

Cognitive explorations of advantages and disadvantages can be supplemented by asking the couple to try to recall consequences of behaving according to the existing cognition. Some clients may be convinced more by direct observations of disadvantages associated with a cognition than by an intellectual discussion of them. For example, Adam and Sasha's therapist suggested that for an entire week each partner keep a log of the times that they spent together or apart each day and record the quality of intimacy they felt in their relationship each day, on a scale ranging from *too intimate* to *too distant*. In reviewing the logs, Adam became aware that although he had rated the relationship as more distant than Sasha did overall, he rated more periods as intimate than he had expected. Sasha's ratings indicated that she also felt a lack of intimacy at times. This information led her to consider disadvantages of the degree to which her standard emphasized autonomy and to think about ways to create more opportunities for togetherness.

Thus, the strategy of weighing advantages and disadvantages is used as a step toward developing a revised cognition. Once a couple are aware of the limitations of an existing cognition, they may be motivated to consider a new way of thinking, particularly if the new way has fewer disadvantages and more advantages than the original cognition. Adam and Sasha's therapist led them into a discussion of how they could devise a shared standard regarding appropriate degrees of togetherness and attentiveness that would include the advantages of both partners' personal standards and minimize the disadvantages. The couple agreed on a standard that each person should have opportunities for independence but that they should balance them with shared experiences that both individuals will be able to see as reflections of a mutual commitment to intimacy in their relationship. The therapist guided each partner in thinking of the implications of the proposed changes in his or her personal standard. Then the therapist asked the couple to plan specific ways of behaving according to their revised standard and guided them in translating this cognitive exercise into a behavioral experiment that they would try at home. Adam and Sasha decided that they would inform each other of plans to engage in independent activities, they would schedule some shared time and activities each week, and they would "check in" with each other briefly at least once each week to see how each person was feeling about their degree of intimacy. Such a behavioral intervention provides new information about the advantages and disadvantages of behaving according to the revised standard. The therapist emphasizes that the couple should view any negative consequences as evidence that the new standard, or the ways of enacting it, need some fine-tuning. The therapist and couple examine the difficulties that the couple experienced and problem-solve about ways to revise the standard, or different ways of behaving toward each other. This is another example of how a primarily cognitive intervention can be supplemented with a behavioral intervention.

Thus, the major steps in helping a couple reconcile conflicts between their standards are to:

- Clarify each person's standard.
- List advantages and disadvantages of each person's standard, with input from both partners.
- Search for some overlap in the partners' standards and develop a common standard that both feel comfortable endorsing (taking into account advantages and disadvantages for each person).
- Translate the shared standard into specific behaviors that each person will enact.
- Try behaving according to the new standard for a trial period and then evaluate its impact on each person and the relationship.
- Problem-solve about any difficulties that arise during the trial period, recognizing that shifting long-standing personal standards is likely to be difficult for each individual.
- Modify the new standard and try another trial period, as needed.

Sometimes it is useful, or even necessary, to conduct an analysis of one person's standards during a separate session with that person. The presence of the person's partner might make it too difficult for him or her to consider disadvantages of a personal standard, particularly if the couple has argued over their differences in the past. An individual session can help that person to consider the therapist's questioning without becoming as defensive and to acknowledge that a standard has negative consequences that could be reduced by modifying the standard. The therapist can offer the individual support in describing to the partner the important shifts that the person is making in the original standard, to benefit their relationship. In addition, it is important to discuss with the person that making a decision to modify a long-standing standard is unlikely to result automatically in lasting change in the belief. Thus, when Adam said that he considered it very reasonable to modify his belief in togetherness to accommodate Sasha's need for some autonomy, their therapist discussed with the couple how Adam had held his belief in togetherness virtually for his entire life, so changing it probably would take some time.

Couples need to be prepared to make repeated efforts to challenge their long-standing cognitions and not be discouraged when they find themselves thinking in "the old ways." As Adam and Sasha's therapist noted, "Adam, when you see Sasha taking time for herself, you may find yourself thinking that she should be focusing on togetherness. When that occurs, you may need to remind yourself of the advantages of allowing for some time apart."

In this section we have focused on evaluating the advantages and disadvantages of relationship standards, but it also can be helpful to examine the utility or appropriateness of other types of cognitions. For instance, Nina frequently worried about Carlo's reactions to her behavior, such as expecting he would be bored if she talked about her job. She often told Carlo about her worries and asked him for reassurance. He found this behavior annoying, and his negative response then added to Nina's concern that her behavior displeased him. The couple's therapist guided Nina in identifying the advantages and disadvantages of worrying about the impact of her behavior on Carlo. The therapist discussed the difference between thinking ahead in ways that help a person avoid or solve problems and worrying or engaging in "wheel-spinning" negative expectancies that generate anxiety but no useful solutions. She then coached Nina in thinking about instances in which she had worried about Carlo's opinions of her and whether the worrying had been useful. Nina saw the disadvantages to her worrying and agreed to the therapist's suggestion that she spend some time in individual therapy learning skills for counteracting worry.

Considering the Worst Possible Outcomes

Another form of questioning addresses extreme negative predictions that individuals make about events in their relationships. The therapist typically asks three types of questions:

- What is the worst possible outcome that you think could occur?
- What is the likelihood that the worst outcome will occur?
- How will you cope if it does occur?

Nina and Carlo's therapist asked Nina to think about "the worst thing that could happen if Carlo is uninterested in something you are saying," the likelihood that the worst outcome actually would occur, and how she could cope if it did occur (J. S. Beck, 1995; Leahy, 1996). Nina's worst fear was that Carlo would become so bored and unhappy that he would end their relationship. She initially estimated that it was very likely that he would eventually leave her. The therapist coached Nina in considering available information about how bored or unhappy Carlo was with her daily discussions. She noted that sometimes his nonverbal behavior while she was talking suggested boredom and wandering attention, but he denied being bored. Nina reported that occasionally Carlo would become angry when she asked for reassurance and would leave the room. Carlo stated that he left the room because he was upset about her worrying and asking for reassurance, not because she was boring. In couples therapy we commonly ask the individual's partner for feedback that addresses the person's worst fears, but it also is important to coach the individual in actively seeking evidence. In Nina's case, the therapist coached her in considering information about whether Carlo withdrew from her out of boredom.

The therapist also asked both partners about experiences that suggested the opposite of Nina's negative expectancy, namely, that Carlo was interested in her and valued their relationship. Together they noted that Carlo initiated "dates" in which they went out to dinner or a movie. In addition, Carlo noted that sometimes he was not very interested in a particular topic that Nina was discussing but that he was willing to listen. The therapist and couple identified that Carlo rarely tells Nina what things he does and does not enjoy, leading Nina to mind-read his feelings, often inaccurately. The couple then identified new ways of communicating that they agreed to try during the coming week, which would address Nina's worst-outcome" predictions. Thus, the cognitive intervention was followed by a behavioral intervention that could produce more objective evidence regarding the appropriateness of Nina's cognitions.

It also is important to ask the individual to discuss how he or she would cope if the worst-case negative expectancies came true. The therapist said that even though the evidence suggested that Carlo was not going to leave Nina, Nina might worry less if she had more confidence in her ability to cope with being on her own if that ever did occur. When the therapist asked Nina to think about her social support network and her ability to take care of herself when she was without a partner in the past, Nina noted that she took good care of herself when she was single and that she has many friends. The therapist asked her to consider the difference between "could not live alone" and "do not want to live alone." Nina agreed that the latter was a better description of her, concluding that she has the ability to cope with being alone but greatly prefers having a close couple relationship. The therapist coached her in reminding herself of that distinction when she feels anxiety that the couple's relationship might end.

The "Downward Arrow"

Often when an individual is distressed about an event in his or her relationship, the cognition that he or she reports seems insufficiently significant to elicit such a strong response. The "downward-arrow" technique is used to identify broader beliefs (assumptions and standards) that underlie specific cognitions that an individual experiences in particular situations (J. S. Beck, 1995; Burns, 1980; Leahy, 1996). The goal is to tap underlying meanings of which the couple may have been unaware. For example, Ken became very angry during a therapy session when Brenda disagreed with him about a financial issue. He told the therapist that when he became angry he was thinking, "I know what I'm talking about, but she isn't paying attention." Although Ken's cognition was negative, it did not seem to warrant the intense anger that he experienced. The therapist then asked Ken a series of questions, including, "If it's true that Brenda wasn't paying attention to the opinion you were expressing, what's bad about that in your view?" and "What does that seem to mean about you, Brenda, and your relationship?" Ken revealed a broad attribution—"She has lost all respect for me"—and a standard, "Respect is essential in a marriage." Thus, the downward-arrow questions uncovered beliefs that understandably upset Ken greatly. Once Ken was aware of these underlying beliefs, the therapist could guide him in considering their appropriateness.

We have found that individuals often are more amenable to modifying inappropriate underlying beliefs if the therapist helps them understand their origins. Thus, the therapist asked Ken to describe previous times when he felt concern about whether people in his life respected him, leading to an exploration of his experiences in his family of origin, in which his parents had been demanding and critical of him (see our subsequent description of family-of-origin exploration). Ken and Brenda subsequently experienced his angry responses in a new way, as reflections of an unresolved issue in his life rather than a problem specific to their relationship. Their awareness of this sore point helped them plan ways to cope with and even prevent Ken's anger flare-ups during future disagreements.

Inductively Identifying Macrolevel Cognitions From Cross-Situational Responses

Throughout this book we have noted how members of a couple often are not fully aware of the broader, macrolevel cognitions involved in their responses to particular situations in their lives. This lack of awareness limits their ability to modify macrolevel cognitions that are affecting their relationships in negative ways. Consequently, therapists need techniques for developing clients' understanding of themes that influence their responses to their relationships. In contrast to downward-arrow questioning, which involves deducing one type of cognition from another, we also help individuals to identify *inductively* macrolevel cognitions by examining cross-situational patterns in their responses. For example, Matthew was highly motivated to be in control of events in his life but did not consciously think about that theme in each situation. He usually was highly attuned to cues that another person—in particular, his wife, Abby—seemed to be trying to control him, and he responded automatically in an adversarial, resistant manner. During the initial couple assessment interview, Abby complained about Matthew's argumentative behavior, and during the couple's structured decision-making discussion, Matthew resisted Abby's suggestions. Nevertheless, Matthew did not seem to be aware of how broadly he responded to Abby on a control dimension.

The couple's therapist asked them to keep written logs of arguments that occurred between sessions, including the setting; topic; and how they thought, felt, and behaved. Similarly, when the couple began to argue during sessions, the therapist explored each person's cognitions and emotions and wrote notes about their behavioral patterns. The therapist then reviewed this information with the couple and asked them to look for general patterns. To minimize individuals' defensiveness about noticing and acknowledging their broad patterns and themes, it is important that the therapist guide them in looking for patterns in a nonevaluative way. For example, if Abby remarked in an angry tone, "He's always trying to control me," it is likely that

Matthew would respond defensively. In contrast, the therapist models a caring, nonevaluative approach to "seeing what we can learn about general patterns in the ways you interact with each other" and coaches the couple in using that approach. It is preferable for the partners to identify the patterns and themes themselves, so they will be attuned to doing it on their own, but the therapist assists as much as necessary. When Abby noted, "It seems that when I state an opinion, Matthew usually debates it," the therapist added, "I did notice that when Abby gives an opinion, you usually give yours fairly quickly, Matthew. Are you aware of any particular thoughts and emotions when you hear her telling you what she thinks?" Matthew and Abby became aware that it was important to Matthew to feel in control of his life but that he was overreacting to a variety of situations in which there was minimal threat from Abby. The therapist built on the couple's increased awareness of this issue by guiding them in experimenting with egalitarian decision-making discussions.

Identifying Patterns in Prior Relationships

Although cognitive–behavioral therapists emphasize patterns and themes that are currently occurring in a couple's relationship, the partners' past experiences that have shaped their broader behavioral, cognitive, and affective responses can be important foci for intervention. Sometimes an individual's motivation to work on changing a current way of thinking increases when the person becomes aware of the negative consequences that have resulted from those patterns in past relationships. Using material from the individual history interviews, a therapist can coach an individual in examining how a particular standard has affected his or her past relationships as well as the current one. A review of Matthew's personal history revealed that his parents had been very controlling and that he had developed strong motivation to "fight back." In each of his two significant couple relationships before he met Abby, there had been frequent arguments. Matthew stated, "I seem to get involved with women who appear easygoing at first but turn out to be opinionated and aggressive." When the therapist asked Matthew to give specific examples of opinionated and aggressive behavior that either a former partner or Abby exhibited, he described instances in which a woman firmly disagreed with him, adding, "It's like they don't respect me, and think that things should go their way." Similar to explorations of cross-situational patterns in the couple's current relationship, these discussions can provide new information that broadens the couple's views of the basic factors influencing both partners' behaviors, thoughts, and feelings.

A therapist must be cautious in exploring patterns in an individual's past relationships during joint sessions with the couple. First, the individual might be reluctant to acknowledge ways in which he or she contributed to problems in those relationships, because it might involve losing face in front of the partner. Second, the partner might use the information as ammunition to blame the individual for the couple's problems; for example, "You drove away Susan and Vicky with your criticism, and now you are driving me away." Consequently, the therapist should consider exploring patterns in each person's past relationships in individual sessions, to prepare the partners for subsequent discussions of the material during joint sessions.

Psychoeducational Interventions

Therapists can facilitate cognitive change by presenting couples educational materials concerning intimate relationships (Baucom & Epstein, 1990). Psychoeducational interventions are primarily cognitive in nature, introducing information that may address the appropriateness of individuals' existing cognitions and develop new ways of thinking. Three formats that can be used are (a) didactic mini-lectures, (b) reading materials, and (c) audio- or videotapes. It is beyond the scope of this book to review a variety of specific psychoeducational materials available for use with couples, so we briefly describe some examples.

Didactic mini-lectures. We already have mentioned how we introduce particular interventions to a couple by explaining how they address important aspects of relationships. In addition to teaching couples about processes such as communication patterns and skills, sentiment override, and attributions, a therapist can present didactic material about particular content areas of concern to a couple. Many couples experience stress from their attempts to work together in parenting their children, for instance. Discussions of parenting strategies and ways to work as a team are helpful, particularly if the therapist tailors the information to particular problems a couple is having with their children. These didactic presentations also can include information about normal child development and can modify unrealistic standards that some couples have about the behavior and emotional maturity their children should exhibit (Webster-Stratton & Herbert, 1994). Couples who face special stressors, such as a child or elderly parent with special needs, can be given mini-lectures on ways to cope with the problems as a couple. Other types of valuable information include normal stages of relationship development (e.g., issues that commonly arise when the "honeymoon stage" ends), time management skills, and anger management skills.

Educational material can modify partners' cognitions in several ways. Some individuals have unrealistically romantic standards that the initial high level of emotional and sexual passion in their relationship should continue indefinitely, no matter what the circumstances. Information about normal changes in individuals' feelings over time and in response to life stresses may contribute to the development of more realistic standards. Presentations on stages and forms of love (e.g., common shifts to a less passionate but deeper emotional bond) may produce more benign interpretations of changes that the individuals have experienced (Goldstine, Larner, Zuckerman, & Goldstine, 1993).

Presentations on time management skills can help alter individuals' assumptions that they lack the ability to cope with the competing demands in their lives. When partners believe that they can use particular time management techniques in their own relationship, they may develop more optimistic expectancies that they can run their household and still have time together as a couple. Similarly, psychoeducational presentations on anger management may modify partners' assumption that anger arousal is an automatic process that is beyond their control and responsibility (Heyman & Neidig, 1997). They can develop more positive efficacy expectancies for controlling destructive expression of anger by learning about particular techniques.

Reading materials. Many couples buy self-help books on couple relationships, and these vary considerably in quality. We believe it is important that therapists be prepared to recommend some high-quality books that are consistent with the interventions one is pursuing in therapy. Markman, Stanley, and Blumberg's (1994) *Fighting for Your Marriage*; Notarius and Markman's (1993) *We Can Work It Out*; Fincham, Fernandes, and Humphreys's (1993) *Communicating in Relationships*; and Christensen and Jacobson's (2000) *Reconcilable Differences* are excellent sources on ways to improve communication and conflict resolution. A. T. Beck's (1988) *Love Is Never Enough* presents a cognitive–behavioral approach to understanding and improving couples' relationship problems, and Burns's (1989) *The Feeling Good Handbook* is a detailed self-help approach to cognitive therapy that focuses mostly on individuals' problems but also addresses relationship difficulties. Spring's (1996) *After the Affair* helps couples apply cognitive–behavioral principles to coping with infidelity. When a therapist recommends such texts to couples, it is helpful to "assign" particular chapters for homework and review the material they are reading on a weekly basis.

Readings can provide information that may change the ways that partners think about relationships in general, and their relationship in particular. Books on constructive communication skills, for instance, emphasize the value of collaborating with one's partner and the disadvantages of behaving in an adversarial manner. All of these books emphasize concepts of mutual causation and taking personal responsibility for change, so they can increase partners' relational thinking. Furthermore, they provide a wealth of information about specific types of problematic and constructive communication behaviors, both verbal and nonverbal.

Books on depression, infidelity, domestic abuse, and other problems can increase partners' sense of hope that there are things they can do to improve their individual and couple adjustment. Clients often have limited perspective on their problems, because they have had few opportunities to learn how their experiences compare with those of other couples, what experiences are in the normal range, and what types of interventions are efficacious. Books on clinical problems commonly provide these types of information, such as common reactions that members of couples tend to experience when one person has had an affair and which strategies for coping with infidelity tend to be more constructive than others. For some individuals a popular book may be more persuasive than didactic presentations by a therapist alone.

In addition to books, we commonly give couples handouts that address particular cognitive, affective, and behavioral factors in relationship functioning as well as guidelines for modifying problematic responses. Many of those handouts are included in this book, in the form of exhibits, such as those listing constructive, expressive, listening, and decision-making guidelines (e.g., Appendixes 9.B, 9.C, 9.D, and 9.E). Handouts are invaluable in helping couples generalize their work in sessions to their interactions in daily life. Some couples keep their handouts on communication and decision-making guidelines available when they sit down to talk. Such handouts repeatedly remind each person of new ways of thinking and behaving. For example, even when a couple's therapist has coached them in following egalitarian decision-making guidelines during sessions, they may revert to adversarial discussions at home, where they feel vulnerable with no third party to protect them. However, if at such times each person refers to a handout on the values and guidelines for cooperative decision making, the probability that the couple will have successful interactions might increase. In general, cognitive–behavioral therapists do not assume that effects of the interventions they make during sessions will automatically generalize to the couple's interactions outside sessions. Handouts are a way of exporting therapy interventions to a couple's daily life.

Audiotapes and videotapes. Audiotaped and videotaped materials have become increasingly available, and they can be useful adjuncts to couples therapy. Markman, Stanley, and Blumberg's (1994) *Fighting for Your Marriage* videotapes present didactic material on marital conflict and detailed demonstrations of communication and conflict management skills. Videotaped models of couples demonstrating constructive communication are especially helpful in developing better skills in some couples. Videotapes also can be a vivid means of presenting information that may modify partners' cognitions about their relationship and motivate them to try interacting in new ways. Markman et al.'s films include samples of couples communicating in negative ways, didactic presentations regarding empirical evidence supporting the need for constructive communication, testimonials by couples who have benefited from the communication skills program, and samples of expressive and listening skills modeled by couples. Client couples who view the tapes may increase their expectancies that they can communicate in more satisfying ways and may increase their belief that it is appropriate and important for them to make some behavior changes to improve the relationship.

Methods for Increasing Relational Thinking

As we described in chapters 3 and 7, individuals vary in the degree to which they think in terms of sequences of interactions and patterns of mutual influence in their relationships. Individuals' failure to think in relational terms can contribute to their blaming their partners for relationship problems and failing to be aware of actions they themselves can initiate that may contribute to solving problems or enhancing their relationship. A therapist can increase partners' relational thinking by drawing their attention to repetitive, circular patterns in their interactions. When an individual attributes a partner's negative emotional or behavioral response to characteristics of the partner, the therapist can coach the person in considering alternative causes, including his or her own actions (Baucom & Epstein, 1990). Thus, a therapist may notice that a couple has developed a demand–withdraw pattern in which the individual who pursues fails to consider that this behavior elicits the partner's withdrawal, and vice versa. Repeatedly pointing out cycles in the couple's interactions and discussing the general principle of circular causality can broaden the ways that members of a couple conceptualize their relationship. Alternatively, the therapist can ask what each person thinks might occur if he or she behaved differently toward the partner.

In general, a therapist can help individuals improve their ability to process events in their relationship in terms of relational concepts by frequently asking them what they have learned about their interactions. In addition, the therapist can interrupt a destructive interaction during a session and ask the partners what pattern they observe occurring that they and the therapist have discussed previously. Clients' internalization of relational concepts often is a gradual process, particularly if they have focused on blaming each other for problems.

Behavioral and Affective Interventions

The overall goal of these interventions is to create conditions in which the members of a couple experience their relationship in new ways, a form of guided discovery. The new experiences provide information that can be used to address the validity or utility of the partners' cognitions and to develop new ways of thinking. Sometimes the therapist has introduced behavioral change, such as communication skills training, because there is a need to alter a destructive pattern. When the couple has adopted the constructive behavior change successfully, the therapist has an opportunity to point out the change and thus influence their views of their relationship; for example, "We are able to discuss important issues without abusing each other verbally, so maybe there is hope for us yet!"

Alternatively, a therapist may begin with a cognitive intervention, such as examining the advantages and disadvantages of a standard and guiding the couple in devising a revised standard. Cognitive interventions can be followed by behavioral interventions that introduce information about the validity or utility of the new cognition, such as data about actual consequences of behaving according to a revised standard.

Similarly, people commonly use their emotional experiences to appraise their relationships, and the particular emotions they notice can color their overall views. For example, individuals who feel strong anger toward their partners may fail to notice other, less vivid emotions that they are experiencing, such as sadness and hurt. The anger may contribute to "sentiment override," in which the individual fails to notice or appreciate a partner's positive actions. Consequently, interventions that increase individuals' awareness and expression of the full range of their emotions may broaden the couple's views of their relationship.

Furthermore, some individuals experience emotions that are so intense that they dominate the person's other responses within the couple relationship. Individuals who experience unregulated anger, for instance, may be at risk for abusive behavior toward their partners. This section includes descriptions of some interventions that provide couples with new information about their emotional responses as well as interventions intended to reduce the intensity of emotions that dominate and control individuals' experiences of their relationship. Both types of affective interventions, which we discuss in more detail in chapter 11, can be used to produce cognitive change.

Using Communication and Decision-Making Exercises to Modify Cognitions

As we described in chapter 9, practicing expressive, listening, and decision-making skills accomplishes more than building behavioral skills, and the positive effects can extend well beyond the time when the couple discontinues using the specific skills at home. The communication guidelines embody the basic principles of empathy, congruence, and positive regard that Carl Rogers (1957) described as crucial for a supportive relationship. As members of a couple use these guidelines, they frequently view each other less as adversaries and more as cooperative and even supportive partners. Individuals who initially attribute each other's more positive communication behaviors to guidelines imposed by the therapist observe their partner taking turns; reflecting their feelings; and refraining from the usual frustrating behaviors, such as interrupting. Experiencing the effects of constructive communication may counteract partners' negative views of their relationship. To promote cognitive change, we draw couples' attention to specific contrasts between new, constructive ways that they are behaving and the negative ways that they displayed previously:

Therapist: Shadae and Jahmal, you seemed to be communicating in a more effective and positive way than you have in the past, and it was clear to me that you were following the communication guidelines pretty well. How did it seem to you?

Shadae: It was a lot calmer than usual, and it did seem like we actually communicated.

Jahmal: I wouldn't count on our doing that well at home tonight, but it was nice not to feel like we're battling.

Therapist:	What did you notice that each of you was doing differently, especially yourself?
Shadae:	I think I got to the point more quickly and expressed my feelings in fewer words than I usually do. Jahmal didn't jump in to interrupt me, either.
Jahmal:	I felt like saying something when I didn't agree with her, but I held off.
Therapist:	How difficult was it to do that?
Jahmal:	To be honest, I came close, but I told myself I'd better wait my turn.
Therapist:	Shadae, could you tell that he was struggling a bit not to interrupt you?
Shadae:	He was squirming in his seat, so I thought he was going to say something.
Therapist:	Jahmal, Shadae mentioned that she was keeping her messages briefer than usual. How did it compare to your usual discussions?
Jahmal:	Usually she talks so long that I get frustrated. This was better.

At this point the therapist can ask the couple questions about what they have learned from the contrast between the present communication and their past interactions. The therapist's goals are to use communication skills training to produce two important types of cognitive change:

1. To broaden the couple's views of the range of different ways that they are capable of interacting, so they are more aware of options and choices in each situation.
2. To have the couple become aware of the positive consequences of particular communication behaviors, so they will be motivated to use them.

The therapist's decision about the degree of questioning needed depends on how much the partners are attuned to their interaction processes and notice the new information provided as they use the skills. Individuals who do not tend to think in systemic, relational terms generally need more prompting from the therapist to notice how their typical pattern is problematic and how different ways of behaving are more effective and satisfying.

Behavioral Experiments

Each time a couple is coached in using communication and decision-making behavioral guidelines it serves as an experiment in relating to each other in new ways. The partners have opportunities to develop new cognitions about their relationship, such as more positive expectancies about the outcomes of expressing their feelings and needs to each other. *Behavioral experiments* designed to produce cognitive change (J. S. Beck, 1995) can involve a variety of interventions aside from communication and decision-making skills training. When the therapist has identified a particular cognition in need of modification, he or she can collaborate with the couple in devising a behavioral experiment specifically intended to create a new experience for the couple regarding the cognition.

Consider Rosa and Gloria, who both were socialized with traditional female gender role values emphasizing sensitivity to others' needs and giving of oneself to benefit others. Their mutual emphasis on sensitivity and giving led to a high rate of supportive behavior between the partners. However, Rosa felt trapped and overburdened in their relationship, commenting,

> I care a lot about Gloria, but I feel like I'm on duty all the time. Sometimes I want to go off and do something that is fun for me, but she acts like I'm abandoning her, and I feel guilty. I also wish she would talk to someone else about her problems for a while.

Further discussion revealed that, in spite of Rosa's ambivalence, both she and Gloria believed that caring partners "are there for each other whenever needed." The therapist asked a series of questions to identify the advantages and disadvantages of their shared standard. Rosa and Gloria were able to think of some disadvantages, including the risk that living according to the standard would eventually make one or both of them feel stress from constantly being responsible for each other. Nevertheless, having lived their whole lives according to traditional gender roles for women, they expressed, "Intellectually, we can understand the idea of taking breaks from each other and looking to others for support sometimes, but emotionally it makes us feel uneasy." The therapist validated their unease about making a change that was somewhat inconsistent with their standard and proposed two steps. First, Rosa and Gloria could devise a modified standard about sensitivity and support that would retain the basic principles of their existing standard but would be more flexible concerning opportunities for some independence. Second, when they had agreed on a revised standard, they could try behavioral experiments in which they acted according to the new standard. As the therapist put it,

> You can see how it feels to behave differently, and what effects the changes have on your relationship. If it goes well, you can try some more. If behaving differently results in unpleasant feelings or problems between you, we can explore what didn't work well, and either try again or revise the plan.

Rosa and Gloria modified their standard to

> We should be sensitive to each other's needs and be the primary sources of support for each other, but we each need breaks from that responsibility and opportunities to pursue our independent interests. We will try to be there for each other on a regular basis but will give each other breaks by taking care of ourselves or seeking some support from family and friends.

The therapist then coached them in planning specific ways in which they would not seek support or provide support for each other at particular times. Gloria noted that she typically asks for Rosa's advice about problems with her coworkers. They agreed on an experiment in which the next time a work problem arose Gloria would call a friend or her sister to talk about it. If Rosa noticed this occurring, she would stay out of it. During the next session Rosa and Gloria told the therapist that Gloria had called her sister about a problem at work while Rosa was busy doing something else. The therapist guided their discussion of the ways they had experienced the experiment.

Therapist: The idea of the experiment was to see how each of you felt while trying the new way of behaving, and how it affected your relationship. So, what was it like?

Gloria: I felt a little like I was being secretive, going into the bedroom to call my sister.

Therapist: Once you started the conversation with your sister, how was it then?

Gloria: My sister was surprised that I was calling her about an issue like that, because I rarely do that. I told her that I was feeling stuck and thought she could be helpful because she deals with all kinds of people at her job. She seemed to accept that, and we had a good talk. After a few minutes, I stopped feeling strange and got a lot out of talking with her.

Therapist: Rosa, what was your experience during that time? Were you aware that Gloria had a problem and was calling her sister?

Rosa: I knew something was up, because Gloria acts hyper when something is on her mind. I started thinking that I should ask her if something was wrong, but I remembered the plan and didn't. I was wondering if she'd get angry with me for not asking. Then I noticed that she went into the bedroom and half closed the door. It wasn't subtle, so I figured she was calling someone. I felt a little shut out, maybe even a little jealous, but I decided to focus on what I was doing. After a while, she came out of the bedroom and seemed to be in a good mood. I said hello and she said hello back and gave me a hug. That relieved most of my uneasy feeling. I enjoyed doing my own stuff, although I was distracted by the situation.

Therapist: Did either of you notice any delayed effects of trying this new way of interacting?

Rosa: I felt uncomfortable because I didn't know whether I should ask her what happened or pretend that I didn't notice anything. I don't feel a need to lead separate lives, just to have a break sometimes. It's not clear to me what is doing too much and what is too little.

Gloria:	I agree. I didn't know if I should tell you about my talk with my sister or not. This is confusing.
Therapist:	It sounds like one result of not turning solely to each other for support was that you each experienced some reactions that we had not planned for. That's part of the learning process when you try doing things a new way. It's great that you noticed your reactions, so now you can discuss how you would like to handle the situation in the future. One of the issues that came up was whether the two of you should avoid acknowledging to each other that Gloria was talking to someone else about a job problem. What are the pros and cons of doing that, and what are your preferences?

The therapist emphasized that, regardless of the outcome of the experiment, it was a learning experience, and adjustments can be made. In this case it was important for the therapist to allay Rosa and Gloria's concerns about the awkwardness and confusion they felt during the experiment, so they would not abandon the attempt to modify their standard.

"Acting-As-If" Exercises

Another type of intervention that allows members of a couple to experience their relationship in a different way involves asking them to behave temporarily as if they had different cognitions or emotions concerning their relationship (J. S. Beck, 1995). The therapist emphasizes that the individuals are not committing themselves to continue the new ways of responding and that the only goal is to get a different perspective. The minimal commitment to change involved in "acting-as-if" exercises may appeal to clients who are uncomfortable enacting new behavior or trying to think differently.

For example, Stuart's standard that "a strong male keeps his feelings under control" had frustrated Clara. Stuart generally viewed emotional expression as a weakness and inhibited his expression of feelings in his relationship with Clara. During couples therapy sessions, when Stuart resisted trying expressive and listening skills, the therapist used an as-if intervention.

Therapist: Stuart, I know that using these expressive skills isn't appealing to you, but I also know that Clara has described how she would feel closer to you if she got a chance to hear a little more about your feelings. You both have put time and energy into working with me because you care about your relationship and would like to get along better. However, because the two of you haven't used the expressiveness and listening guidelines, none of us knows what it would be like if you did. It seems to me that if we are going to figure out some ways for you to get along better it would be helpful to see how different patterns might work. What I'd like to suggest is that you try a brief trial period of using these guidelines "as if" you wanted to express your feelings to Clara, even though we all know that it isn't your actual goal. Then you and Clara can experience what it would be like if the two of you were communicating in that way. It doesn't need to change what you will choose to do after the exercise is over—it's just an experiment.

Readers may view this as a type of intervention more commonly used by strategic therapists in that the therapist may seem to have a different intention than what is stated to the couple. We believe that it is crucial to be direct with clients, to foster a collaborative therapeutic relationship. Consequently, the preceding example should reflect the therapist's true appraisal of the two partners' motives and feelings. The therapist judged that Stuart had little motivation to express his feelings to Clara but that he wanted to find a way to have a satisfying relationship with her. The therapist did not know whether the experience during the as-if exercise would give Stuart a more favorable view of expressing himself, but it was clear that the couple was stuck in an unsatisfactory pattern. If Stuart tried expressing himself "as if" he wanted to do so, and if Clara's response were pleasant for him, he might reconsider his belief that he should communicate in a way that maximized his sense of control.

Role Taking

In role-taking interventions the members of a couple also "try on" different perspectives, which can create new experiences of each other and their relationship. Most commonly, the therapist asks the partners to reverse roles, pretending to be each other and carrying out particular types of interactions from those perspectives. The rationale provided for the role reversal is that it will increase their understanding of each other. Stuart and Clara's therapist also asked them to try a role reversal, in which Stuart would role play Clara by talking about sharing feelings more, and Clara would role play Stuart by explaining his ideas about expressing feelings. It is important to tell the partners not to portray an exaggerated version of the other person, because it would not be a realistic interaction, and the other person probably would respond defensively. The therapist's role is to keep the dialogue going, occasionally interjecting a probe such as, "Stuart, can you think of anything else Clara would typically be thinking about, that you could say in your role as her?"

During role plays many individuals focus more on what their partners may be experiencing than they have before, and they gain greater empathy for the partner. This increased empathy often includes a different emotional response as well as cognitive understanding. For example, empathically experiencing a partner's sadness may increase an individual's perception that the partner is vulnerable and elicit his or her desire to take care of the partner. In addition, many individuals have an experience similar to that of Stuart, who was surprised at his reaction when he heard Clara playing his role: "I sound sort of insensitive to Clara. I don't want to come across like I'm indifferent." This response provided an opportunity for the therapist to suggest a behavioral experiment in which Stuart tried low-level disclosures of his feelings to Clara.

Increasing Awareness and Expression of Emotions

In chapter 11 we detail techniques that can be used to increase individuals' awareness of the full range of their emotional responses within their relationships, so their views of the relationships are not biased by especially vivid emotions that overshadow others. Some individuals avoid experiencing particular emotions that they consider inappropriate or threatening; for example, a person may view anxiety and sadness as signs of weakness. Other individuals might view anger as an inappropriately aggressive feeling. Consequently, therapists may need to access such emotions gradually, so the person does not feel overwhelmed. As described in chapters 8 and 11, the therapist creates a safe environment by modeling good listening skills when an individual is expressing feelings, coaching the person's partner in the use of nonjudgmental reflective skills, explicitly stating guidelines for respectful behavior, and intervening quickly to interrupt nonsupportive responses from the partner.

We do not describe details of approaches to amplifying an individual's emotional experience here because they are covered in chapter 11. They include interventions such as (a) asking the person to describe feelings in greater detail, (b) reflecting hints of particular emotions to which the person only alluded, (c) providing a list of labels for different types of emotions, (d) expressing inferences about emotions that are implicit in the client's verbal and nonverbal behavior, and (e) heightening a person's mild emotional response by repeating a vivid phrase that seems to be associated with emotion (e.g., "It's like trying to be heard across the Grand Canyon"). These interventions may facilitate cognitive change when they increase both partners' knowledge of the person's subjective experiences of their relationship.

Increased awareness of the range of emotions that an individual is experiencing can serve as a gateway into the person's cognitions regarding his or her relationship. For example, the therapist helped Jin-Ying become aware that she not only was angry at Xi-Jian concerning his lack of participation with household chores but she also experienced fleeting periods of sadness. The therapist then explored the cognitions associated with each of her emotions. Her anger was associated with thoughts that Xi-Jian was unfairly shirking his share of responsibilities at home. Her sadness reflected two cognitive themes: (a) "Xi-Jian does what he pleases because I am not important to him" and (b) "Between my job and responsibilities at home, all I have to look forward to is a life of drudgery." These themes emphasized losses, both of Xi-Jian's caring and of her personal freedom to enjoy her life. Because Jin-Ying had focused on her angry feelings, neither member of the couple had been aware of these other thoughts that she was having about their marriage.

Uncovering the sadness and associated cognitions identified new issues that the couple needed to address to improve their relationship.

Moderating Emotions That Contribute to Sentiment Override

In contrast to interventions used to enhance the experience of emotions that individuals avoid or fail to notice, other interventions can be used to help individuals reduce their experience and expression of strong negative emotions. These interventions, which we describe fully in chapter 11, can contribute to cognitive change when they reduce sentiment override; that is, they decrease the tendency for a person's negative feelings about the partner to color perceptions and other cognitions about the partner (Weiss, 1980). If an individual's persistent anger toward a partner leads him or her to selectively notice the partner's negative behavior and overlook positive actions, for instance, reduction of the anger may help the individual notice the partner's attempts to collaborate in problem solving.

To avoid making some individuals perceive that their emotions are being invalidated, it is important for the therapist to convey that it is natural for partners to feel negative emotions at times but that persistent, strong negative emotions can interfere with responses necessary to solve relationship problems. In chapter 11 we describe several interventions that can be used to contain strong negative emotions, including (a) scheduling particular times for discussing thoughts and emotions with constructive expressive and listening skills, (b) practicing compartmentalizing the experience of the emotions by writing down the feelings during set times and focusing on other life activities during the rest of the day, (c) expressing the negative emotions to supportive friends, and (d) developing the ability to tolerate emotional distress as a normal aspect of life (e.g., through self-soothing behavior). As the individual's ability to contain strong negative emotions improves, the therapist can use the cognitive and behavioral interventions described in this chapter to modify the negative cognitions that have been associated with the person's negative emotions toward the partner.

SUMMARY

In this chapter we have addressed some issues that have been raised in the literature concerning the utility of interventions focused on modifying couples' cognitions. We also have described a variety of cognitive, behavioral, and affective interventions that can be used to produce change in problematic cognitions.

- Some cognitions occur with little or no awareness on the individual's part, or are censored because of response biases, but they often can be accessed through systematic assessment.

- Therapists must use caution to minimize biases in cognitive assessment and intervention based on cultural differences between therapist and clients.
- Partners' reluctance to take responsibility for subjectivity and possible distortions in their cognitions can be reduced through techniques such as creating a safe atmosphere for self-disclosure by setting ground rules, conveying acceptance for the individual's experiences, and demonstrating that subjectivity and cognitive distortion are normal.
- It is difficult to maintain positive cognitive changes in the face of continued negative behavioral interactions, but the effects of isolated negative actions can be minimized by preparing the couple for potential lapses and by focusing on situational rather than dispositional attributions for negative acts.
- Couples need not routinely use cognitive-restructuring skills to maintain positive cognitive changes.
- Interventions for modifying problematic cognitions are designed to broaden partners' thinking about themselves, each other, their relationship, and how they interact with their environment.
- We have described a variety of interventions that induce individuals to examine the appropriateness or utility of their cognitions and create new information that results in new ways of thinking about their relationship.
- Some cognitive interventions involve formal didactic presentations, whereas others are used informally whenever the couple's ongoing interactions during therapy sessions present opportunities for cognitive restructuring.
- Whenever possible, it is desirable for the couple to "discover" new information on their own, because a major goal is for clients to develop the ability to monitor and modify their own problematic cognitions.
- Our approach involves choosing interventions on the basis of the degree of active guidance the partners appear to need in examining and challenging their ways of thinking, versus needing direction from their therapist.
- Cognitive interventions involve addressing the logic of a cognition, considering information about the appropriateness of a cognition, weighing advantages and disadvantages of a cognition, identifying broad beliefs underlying specific cognitions in particular situations, identifying underlying beliefs from themes in partners' cross-situational response patterns, and identifying how partners' cognitions about each other were shaped by their past significant relationships.

- Behavioral interventions such as communication and decision-making training, behavioral experiments, "acting-as-if" exercises, and role reversals can produce cognitive changes by providing the couple with new information concerning their relationship.
- Affective interventions that increase awareness and expression of emotions or that decrease persistent negative emotional responses can produce cognitive change by providing couples with new information about their relationship and reducing biased perceptions due to sentiment override.
- At present there are no research findings to guide clinicians' selection of the most appropriate and effective interventions for particular types of cognitions.
- It is important for therapists to be flexible and patient in their attempts to modify individuals' cognitions about their relationships, because they commonly have roots in basic macrolevel issues and needs, and in distressed couples they have been reinforced over time by negative behavioral interactions.

11

ADDRESSING EMOTIONS

Interventions targeted solely at emotions might appear to be artificial and impractical after our discussion in chapter 10 noting the reciprocal relationship between cognitions and emotions. However, some partners present in therapy with a particular difficulty in addressing negative emotions, positive emotions, or both. Although cognitive, cultural, or systemic factors can contribute to individuals' problems with emotions, in this chapter we target the emotional experiences themselves. We provide a series of interventions aimed at altering both the experience and expression of emotions. In doing so, the couple can benefit from more constructive discussions of emotions, the confrontation of key relationship issues, and improvements in the emotional tone of their interactions.

As we discussed in chapter 10, emotions and cognitions are integrally related and compose an individual's subjective experience. Consequently, it is almost impossible to intervene with partners' emotions without addressing their cognitions in some manner. In addition, an individual's emotional experience is significantly influenced by his or her own and other people's behavior. Therefore, labeling interventions as focusing on emotions is a relative statement only. Many behavioral and cognitive interventions are designed explicitly to affect emotions as well. For example, many directed behavior changes are intended to create a more positive emotional environment in the relationship. Similarly, many communication guidelines are aimed to decrease the hurtful, destructive impact of certain statements. Within the cognitive domain, helping the individual to understand the couple's interactions differently is intended to alter the person's emotional experience as well. In actuality, we rarely intervene solely with emotions. Instead, we take advantage of the rich interplay among emotions, cognitions, and behavior. This approach allows us to use a variety of interventions to understand, accept, and alter emotions in adaptive ways. In this chapter we discuss strategies that focus on ways to maintain and enhance partners' healthy emotional experience and expression.

As we discussed in chapter 3, the experience and expression of negative emotions per se is not considered maladaptive. However, the frequency and magnitude of experiencing negative emotions as well as the manner in which they are expressed, either can be part of a healthy relationship or can contribute to significant relationship difficulties. Although emotional experience and expression are major aspects of individual psychopathology, we address these individual disorders more specifically in chapter 12.

One major focus of the current chapter is on interventions that help the partners experience emotions that are minimized or avoided. Minimization and avoidance can occur for various reasons. As we discussed previously, some individuals have a generally avoidant coping style in dealing with negative emotions or areas of discomfort. Other individuals are not generally avoidant, but they have had specific experiences in their families of origin, earlier romantic relationships, or earlier in the current relationship that are too painful for them to process internally or discuss with the partner. Furthermore, some individuals have beliefs about emotions that can inhibit their experience of emotions. For example, some people believe that anger is sinful, signifies immaturity, or is equivalent to a lack of control. Therefore, over time the individual has learned to avoid experiencing anger, either blocking an emotional response or focusing on other emotions that are less threatening.

In this chapter we also discuss emotional experiences that are at the other end of the continuum; that is, some individuals focus excessively on distressing feelings or experience them as uncontrollable. These individuals may dwell on the negative feelings caused by relationship problems in their daily lives. Indeed, some individuals report that their relationship distress affects all facets of their lives. They cannot stop thinking about the relationship and feeling upset, even when at work or in settings that typically would be enjoyable. In some instances this extreme focus on negative feelings exhausts the person emotionally and makes it difficult for him or her to enjoy aspects of the relationship that are more positive. This style influences not only the individual but also his or her partner and the relationship. As we discussed in chapter 3, negative mood states typically influence the way that the individual interacts with the partner. In addition, these negative moods can influence a relationship because the individual creates a generally negative atmosphere that affects the partner, even if the two individuals are not frequently discussing the negative feelings. Consequently, at times it becomes important to find ways to contain the experience and expression of negative moods.

The preceding discussion focuses on the frequency and duration of experiencing and expressing negative moods. Some individuals also experience poor affect regulation with regard to the intensity of moods experienced. They have intense emotional responses when most other people would likely have only a mild emotional response to the circumstances. Linehan (1993) described poor affect regulation as a central component of borderline personality disorder; however, many individuals have poor emotion regulation without the other symptoms of borderline personality disorder. These individuals' emotional responses can present a challenge both to the couple and to the therapist. Often, even when apparently minor issues are raised, the individual experiences and expresses extreme negative emotions. As a result, the couple experiences many bouts of extreme upset in their relationship, and the therapist expends significant effort and energy regulating the emotional tone of the therapy sessions. Consequently, in addition to discussing the frequency and duration of negative moods, we give some consideration to circumstances in which one or both members of a couple exhibit limited ability to regulate emotional intensity.

ACCESSING EMOTIONS THAT ARE MINIMIZED AND AVOIDED

The inhibition of emotion not only prevents individuals from confronting their feelings about important relationship issues, but it also can prevent couples from successfully engaging in cognitive and behavioral interventions for those issues. In this section we address ways therapy can assist individuals in accessing their emotions. After considering the process by which people handle their emotions, we discuss strategies for encouraging the expression and amplification of an individual's feelings.

In deciding to help a member of a couple experience and express emotions more fully, the therapist should have some rationale for why this might be helpful to the couple. We do not assume that experiencing deep emotion at all times is inherently valuable to the individual or couple. However, there are instances in which helping a person experience and express emotions more fully can be facilitative. First, understanding one's own feelings can be helpful in recognizing the bases of one's happiness and discontent. Therefore, if one person knows he or she is generally dissatisfied with the relationship but cannot pinpoint what in the relationship brings joy and happiness or anger and disappointment, it can be much more difficult to develop an intervention plan. Second, an individual might act on his or her emotions without clearly understanding what those emotions are or why he or she is feeling that way. Thus, an angry husband might retaliate in subtle ways without having full awareness of his feelings or being aware that he is behaving in a passive–aggressive manner. Becoming aware of his anger can be important in helping him recognize the basis for his behavior and deciding to change it. Third, emotions typically are related to cognitions, and helping a person understand his or her feelings can help to clarify that person's cognitions about a situation as well. Finally, on a communicative level, the expression of emotion carries a great deal of information to the partner. Partners who fail to express emotion may feel more distant, less intimate, and more disengaged from each other. When any of these factors seem to be present and interfering with the couple's relationship, the therapist might consider interventions designed to help one or both partners experience and express their emotions more fully.

A Conceptual Framework

Before using specific interventions to broaden an individual's range of emotional experience, it is important to have a conceptualization of this process. Our belief is that a great deal of psychotherapy, with both couples and individuals, involves helping clients confront aspects of reality that they typically avoid. As we discussed in chapter 4, people avoid certain emotions, memories, circumstances, or interactions because these experiences create discomfort. Consequently, they develop avoidance and escape strategies that are reinforced because they are effective on an immediate basis in alleviating the immediate negative consequences of experiencing uncomfortable emotions. However, often the long-term consequences are detrimental to the couple or the individual because important issues are avoided.

This short-term negative reinforcement can help to explain why many individuals and couples are unsuccessful in carrying out what appear to be reasonable, constructive behavior changes that would benefit their relationships in the long term. To help the individual and the couple confront distressing emotions, the clinician can view the process as a graduated exposure and desensitization procedure; that is, the individual is gradually asked to confront increasingly difficult aspects of emotions, at each stage being accepted and affirmed by the partner, rather than experiencing the anticipated negative consequences for confronting the emotion. Avoiding these negative consequences means that the clinician must be attuned to how the clinician, the partner, and the individual himself or herself responds to difficult emotions. The therapist might have values or emotional reactions to the expression of certain emotion that provide subtle feedback to the individual that his or her expression is unacceptable in some way, for example, that feeling sexually attracted to individuals other than one's partner is immoral or disgusting. Even if the therapist and the individual's partner respond in a supportive manner, the individual can still punish himself or herself for experiencing and expressing certain emotions.

Thus, accessing and uncovering emotions that individuals find difficult can be a slow process. Even if the clinician is successful in rapidly accessing an individual's strong, underlying negative emotions in a short time period, the person might subsequently feel overwhelmed and become concerned that the clinician will proceed too quickly and disrupt a safe environment that had been maintained through avoidance. In response, the individual might withdraw; for example, resisting further affective exploration, canceling sessions, or even terminating treatment if the experience was extremely overwhelming. Consider Leon, who felt dominated by Rosemary but was quite uncomfortable with his negative feelings toward her and frequently rationalized her abusive behavior toward him as helping to keep him focused on the relationship. In an individual session with Leon, the therapist helped him to begin to recognize his deep anger toward Rosemary. In the next couple session, Leon expressed some of this anger at a very mild level. Rosemary actually expressed appreciation to him, because it was one of the few times when he had let her know about something he did not like. From the therapist's perspective, it seemed that the session had been successful, and progress was being made on an important issue. The therapist was then surprised when Leon canceled the next two couple sessions with excuses that seemed implausible. In retrospect, the therapist concluded that Leon had become frightened by his own emotions and consequences that he feared he would receive from Rosemary and had canceled the sessions to avoid further uncomfortable feelings.

In the preceding discussion we pointed out that individuals often deal with unacceptable or discomfiting emotions by avoiding or distorting their experience of these emotions. One major strategy for distorting the experience and expression of these emotions is to focus one's attention on less threatening emotions instead. An individual might feel very hurt by a partner's remarks, for instance. However, experiencing hurt, which increases that person's sense of vulnerability, might be too threatening. The individual might experience anger instead of hurt, focusing on the unfairness and unjustness of the partner's comments. For many individuals anger feels like a stronger and more protective emotion than hurt, fear, or sadness (Christensen, Jacobson, & Babcock, 1995).

Clinicians and theoreticians vary in their explanations of how an individual is able to avoid certain emotions and experience other emotions instead. From a psychodynamic perspective, this phenomenon would be viewed as a defense mechanism in which a threatening feeling is converted intrapsychically into a less threatening emotion. From a behavioral perspective, this mechanism could be understood as latching onto a trace of another emotion that the individual is feeling and amplifying it—a form of selectively attending to certain emotions. Alternatively, perhaps the person's emotional response has become overlearned because it is less threatening than avoided emotions. Regardless of one's understanding of how this psychological process occurs, clinicians often are confronted with partners who avoid or have difficulty experiencing certain emotions.

The tendency of some individuals to protect themselves by experiencing and expressing emotions that provide a sense of strength and power to avoid more vulnerable emotions is behind Jacobson and Christensen's (1996) comment that beneath an individual's expression of "hard" emotions typically are "soft" emotions. Although this hypothesis might at times be true, it is important to recognize that almost any emotion can seem unacceptable to a given individual. An individual might avoid the experience of anger, sadness, anxiety, tenderness, love, joy, or excitement. Depending on the individual's history and temperament, almost any given emotion has the potential to become aversive and therefore avoided.

Consistent with this point of view, Greenberg and Safran (1987) differentiated among functions of emotions. Greenberg and Johnson applied this differentiation of emotions to couples' relationships through their development of emotionally focused therapy (Johnson & Greenberg, 1995). Greenberg and Safran (1987) differentiated among primary and secondary emotions.

> *Primary emotions* are here-and-now direct responses to situations; *secondary emotions* are reactions to, and attempts to cope with, these direct responses, often obscuring awareness of the primary response. For example, angry defensiveness is often expressed in marital conflict, rather than hurt, fear, or some other primary affect. (Johnson, 1996, p. 40)

This covering up of primary emotions can serve two purposes: (a) avoiding an emotion that is uncomfortable or unacceptable to that individual and (b) avoiding communication of the primary emotions to another person for fear of some negative consequence. We agree with Johnson (1996) that the goal is to help the individual move beyond an experience of secondary emotions to be able to experience primary emotions and to express them when appropriate.

Johnson and Greenberg (1995) developed emotionally focused therapy within the context of attachment theory. They view relationship distress as involving some disruption of the attachment bond between the two partners. Consequently, they believe that the primary emotions that need to be uncovered and expressed between partners center around attachment issues. We concur that these issues are important for some couples but, as we have addressed in previous chapters, a multitude of factors can contribute to relationship discord. Therefore, underlying emotions that an individual avoids or minimizes might relate to a wide variety of issues, not only attachment issues. For example, Dana avoided experiencing guilt when she made a poor judgment at work that reflected badly on her entire work team. This avoidance of guilt resulted from discomfort with seeing herself as defective rather than fearing abandonment by or censure from her partner Harry. In this instance, her avoidance of guilt was related to her need to see herself as a competent, achieving individual. Harry could not understand her withdrawal, which she credited to being tired and overworked at the office. Instead, he continued to feel pushed away by Dana and unconvinced by her explanation for her behavior. This avoidance deprived Dana of the opportunity to obtain emotional support from Harry.

Interventions to Access and Heighten Emotional Experience

Several specific interventions can be used to help individuals access and heighten the experience of emotion in a conjoint session. During the sessions, it is important to understand the flow of the interaction between the therapist and each individual as well as between the two partners. Much of the time the therapist is speaking to one of the two individuals, particularly the individual who is having difficulty accessing emotion. This one-on-one interaction between the therapist and one partner is essential, because the therapist must build a safe environment and skillfully lead the individual through a process to access emotions that are threatening or uncomfortable to that person. The other partner typically cannot be expected to assume this role; in fact, his or her attempts to do so in the past may have contributed to the person's inhibition. Therefore, unlike practicing communication guidelines in which the two partners interact directly with each other, much of the focus of uncovering and accessing emotions is between the therapist and one member of the couple. This is not to say that this goal is the sole focus of this type of therapy session. At times, particularly once an individual has greater access to specific emotions or experiences, the therapist will ask the individual to communicate this emotion to the partner. The therapist might also ask the other person to participate, contributing his or her knowledge of the individual and that person's experience within the current relationship as well as previous relationships. Often the other person has observations and insights that can be valuable during the process. Even when the therapist is focused primarily on one individual, the therapist can maintain contact with the other partner through head nods, eye contact, thanking the partner for listening, and so forth.

Creating a Safe Environment for Experiencing and Expressing Emotions

In her discussion of emotionally focused therapy, Johnson (1996) provided an in-depth discussion of the steps and specific interventions for accessing emotions. We believe that her suggestions for accessing emotions are applicable across theoretical orientations, and we draw on them heavily in the discussion that follows. First, the therapist must create a safe environment for a couple within which emotions can be experienced and expressed adaptively. Consequently, when an individual is expressing his or her emotions during the session, it is important that the individual feels heard and validated. To accomplish this goal, the therapist and partner can use the listening skills we described in chapter 9.

After the individual finishes speaking, the therapist provides some type of response to validate the individual's experience, for example, reflecting the individual's important thoughts and feelings. If the therapist believes that the other partner will be able to demonstrate this same level of acceptance and validation, then the therapist might ask the partner to reflect the speaker's feelings instead of the therapist doing so. In addition, given that there are two individuals present, the therapist must be certain to avoid the appearance of taking sides. Consequently, the therapist will frequently ask for the other individual's experience as well, particularly if the emotions are about an interaction that occurred between the partners. To be able to explore further one individual's emotional experience, it is often necessary to limit the couple's direct interaction if it seems likely to escalate negatively. Such interactions create an environment in which individuals typically become defensive and do not feel safe exploring other emotions. At other times the therapist might direct the partners to have a direct interaction, anticipating that they will have strong negative reactions to each other. In essence, this direct interaction can heighten emotional experience for one partner. The therapist needs to recognize that after an angry exchange between partners, one individual might be less likely at that point to explore feelings that are more vulnerable.

Even if the therapist creates a safe environment, often clients enter the session expressing secondary emotions. It is important to accept and validate the legitimacy of these secondary emotions before attempting to access primary emotions. The secondary emotions in fact are quite real and legitimate in the sense that they are what the individual currently is experiencing.

Increasing the Range of Emotional Experience by Accessing Primary Emotions

Using questions to amplify emotional experience. Rather than suggesting to an individual that his or her emotional experience is invalid or not what he or she truly feels, accessing additional emotions should be seen as an extension of the individual's current emotional experience. One way to attempt to increase this experience of emotion is by using questions that ask the individual to describe the emotion(s) and experiences in more detail or with additional clarification. On some occasions the individual spontaneously begins to describe other emotions that have been avoided. Often the individual only briefly alludes to this more unacceptable emotion in response to the therapist's question. The therapist can pose questions in many different ways. Most important, the therapist should avoid questions that seem to suggest that the individual is being dishonest, deceptive, or less than forthcoming. Instead, the questions are intended to allow the individual to say more, take chances, and become more vulnerable.

> Therapist: Chad, you mentioned that you were very angry with Monique for confronting your mother when she came to visit. What was that like for you? Your mother had come to see her new grandchild for the first time and was making suggestions about parenting. What did you experience when Monique disagreed with her?
>
> Chad: I was really upset and angry. We have had a very shaky relationship with my mother. I saw her coming to visit as a true attempt at reconciliation on her part. My mother made one suggestion, and Monique immediately disagreed with her. It was so foolish; it just wasn't needed. I wouldn't be at all surprised if my mother never comes back to visit us again. She's old; it's a long trip; she has lots of these excuses not to return.
>
> Therapist: So it seemed to you that Monique needlessly provoked a confrontation, and that made you angry, is that right? It also sounds like you were a little worried that your mom might not come back; is that a part of it?
>
> Chad: I guess so, I mean, I've had such a mixed relationship with my mother over the years. I hoped that our new child would give us some focus to bring us back together. And now that's not likely to happen. I don't think I'm going to have a mother to interact with, and our child might not have a grandmother who's a part of his life.

In this example the therapist began by asking a question of the essence "Tell me more." In doing so the therapist described the context of the interaction with the mother, hoping that it would allow Chad to re-engage his emotions. The therapist's second statement focused on the sense of worry that Chad's mother might not return. The therapist assumed that this concern was the more uncomfortable emotion for Chad and wanted to amplify it. The question focusing on worry was phrased in a tentative, somewhat low-key manner so that Chad could take the lead in describing the emotion without feeling defensive because of a statement about strong feelings offered by the therapist.

As Johnson (1996) noted, there are several ways one can phrase questions that ask the individual to amplify current emotions and differentiate among various ones.

> Questions such as: What happens to you when . . . How do feel as you listen to . . . or as you say . . . what is it like for you . . . directly ask the client to differentiate his/her experience. The focus here may be on inner experience or on the process of interaction between the partners. (p. 46)

The previous discussion assumes that, with appropriate prompts, an individual can articulate his or her internal emotional experience. Whereas some people do this easily, others struggle. People who avoid emotions or who are not attuned to emotions can have difficulty differentiating among and labeling various specific emotions. They might know only that they feel negatively about something or are upset. Therefore, to assist partners who need help in labeling their specific emotions, we provide them with a list of frequently used emotion words, such as those in Appendix 9C.

Going beyond what is stated: Reflections of "implied feelings" and interpretations. At times the therapist can help the individual expand his or her experience of emotion by going beyond what is explicitly verbalized. The therapist might note from the person's posture, inflection, or glance at the partner, along with accumulated knowledge of the individual, that the person likely is experiencing a certain emotion. If this emotion appears to be important and suggested by nonverbal cues and knowledge of the person, the therapist might choose to label the feeling in a tentative manner. This approach requires knowledge of the individual, anticipation of whether he or she is likely to acknowledge this emotion, and a judgment of whether the timing is right within the context of the session and the overall therapy. Johnson (1996) referred to such responses as "evocative responding," because they go beyond what is explicit and can evoke other emotions.

> Therapist: You said you were really confused by Carmen's response. From the look on your face just now, it seemed that you might also have been feeling a little frightened that she might be telling you it was over. Were you worried or concerned a little when she answered your question that you were finally hearing the answer that you had so dreaded?

Interpretations go even further than eliciting emotions that have been implied in that what has been said is put into another context, thus shifting the meaning in some way. Interpretations suggest to the individual that there might be another way to experience or understand some phenomenon (e.g., providing a different attribution concerning the meaning of a partner's behavior). Although interpretations have been most directly identified with psychodynamic theory, many schools of therapy involve interpretations. Various schools of therapy merely differ on the kind of interpretation that is provided. Thus, a given behavior could be interpreted as resulting from a skill deficit, an unresolved intrapsychic conflict, or a threat to attachment needs, according to various theoretical orientations. There is no single focus for the interpretation in our approach to couple's interventions. Thus far in this book, we have discussed how individual, couple, and environmental factors contribute to relationship distress. In addition, distress involves individuals' responses to both the immediate, proximal context, and results as well from distal factors, including personality, temperament, and experiences in the current relationship and previous relationships. Consequently, the interpretation can focus on any of these factors as appropriate. What is important is that the therapist does not provide an interpretation that is so different from the individual's experience and understanding that the interpretation will be rejected. The interpretation needs to be consistent with an overall understanding and conceptualization of the individual and the relationship that have been developing over the course of therapy. If the interpretation is well timed and fits or expands the individual's understanding, it can help to broaden the person's emotional experience.

> Therapist: Joanna, I can understand that when you found Ned's letter to another woman this week, you decided that you just don't care any more, that your feelings have died. You've worked very hard on the relationship these past months; then you open the desk drawer, and you find this letter. I'm sure that a part of you feels that way; why go on, why bother? But you've also said recently that you can't imagine yourself without Ned, that it would be too painful to be without him. Is there a part of you that still feels that way? I really don't know, but I worry whether a part of your lack of feeling is because it would hurt too much to care at this point. You've moved pretty quickly to discussing divorce, so I want us to take some time before you make such major life decisions. What was it like when you found the letter; what were your feelings at that point?

In the preceding example the therapist offers an interpretation of the wife's reported lack of emotions, phrased as a concern for the wife. The therapist gives a different meaning to the lack of emotions and then attempts to reintroduce emotions by asking Joanna to recount her experience of finding the letter. Although this interpretation focuses on the present and immediate past, the interpretations can draw from a client's more historical experiences. As we discuss in chapter 13, this can be of particular importance when an individual's current emotional responses appear to be related to past traumatic or repeated negative experiences.

Relating emotions to cognitions and behavior. Many of the preceding interventions imply helping the individual relate his or her emotions to cognitions and behaviors and to the external environment (Ellis, 1976). Emotions do not exist in a vacuum but rather are integrally related to thoughts and emotions. Helping the individual to experience these linkages can be quite helpful. Many people may be frightened by experiencing strong emotional reactions without seeing the relationship of these emotions to thoughts or actions. In such an instance, the emotions can feel out of control and as if they are controlling the individual. Instead, the therapist should help the individual to see how emotional responses follow from that individual's thoughts and behaviors as well as influence cognitions and behaviors. The therapist can comment on how these linkages occur both within the individual and between the individuals, using questions such as "What were you feeling in that situation?" Markman, Stanley, and Blumberg (1994) proposed having individuals learn to express their feelings in the form of "XYZ" statements. Although not proposed as a rigid format for speaking, XYZ statements take the following form: "When you do X in situation Y, I feel Z." This format is intended to help the individual relate emotions to behavior that elicits them. Also, questions such as "When you were thinking about what happened, what emotions did you have?" ask the individual to relate emotional experience to his or her thoughts. Helping the individual to see emotions as normal and natural components of experience closely related to one's thoughts and behaviors can help legitimize emotional experience, making it seem less foreign and dangerous.

Heightening Emotional Experiences

The preceding discussion highlights strategies that the therapist might use to broaden the individual's range of emotional experience. Thus, an individual who previously avoided experiencing anger might become more comfortable experiencing it within the relationship. Even after the person begins to experience anger, he or she might limit the experience of anger in other ways. First, the person might limit the depth or magnitude of anger that is experienced or expressed:

> Yes, Roy, I was mildly annoyed when you told my coworkers that I snore so loudly at night that you go to the other room. I'm their new dean, and it isn't easy for a female to get the respect of the senior male faculty. You didn't help very much.

In addition, the individual might limit the experience of anger to situations that involve minor, less threatening issues. For example, after several months in therapy, Anita and Hector seemed to be making little progress. They both agreed that it was time to be honest and talk about the fundamental issues in their relationship, what bothered both of them, and what held them back from making progress. Anita spoke first:

> Well, there are two major things that really upset me. First, you sniff a lot. I've asked you to go to the doctor, and you haven't gone. I don't think I can take it any longer. It drives me crazy, and I'm really angry with you for constantly sniffing.

Anita continued with her second concern, but she failed to describe feelings of anger and resentment that her husband often made fun of her, that he made explicit that he did not enjoy talking with her, and that he generally found her boring. Her unwillingness to process her emotions about these more central aspects of their relationship required significant attention.

The therapist can heighten the intensity of emotional experience and encourage emotional responses to more threatening issues in several ways that supplement the above-mentioned strategies:

- Repeating a phrase at selected moments to heighten the impact of the phrase.
- Using poignant images and metaphors to heighten the experience.
- Altering the therapist's own behavior in a more emotional direction, such as shifting body position or using a volume of speech and inflection that emphasize the emotional experience.
- Asking individuals to express their internal emotional experience to their partners to transform the internal, subjective experience into an interpersonal experience.
- Maintaining a focus on important emotional experiences or "blocking exits" so that the individual and the couple are not derailed from the emotional experience (Johnson, 1996).

Repeating key phrases. People use key phrases in their speech for a variety of reasons. Most repetitive phrases provide a kind of shorthand that carries a particular meaning, often an emotional meaning, either positive or negative. Sportscasters develop key phrases to convey emotion about a team playing poorly or performing well—"Bring in the horses and close the barn door. There's a storm a brewin'!" Similarly, partners give each other pet names, often terms of endearment, or they may develop key phrases that capture negative emotions regarding their relationship. The therapist can capitalize on phrases that have particular meaning to the individual, as a way of heightening the emotional aspect of the experience.

Therapist: Andy, when you brought up the idea to Betsy of having another child, you said it was like "beating your head against a wall." You've mentioned that several times when you become frustrated with Betsy. What is that image like for you—beating your head against a wall?

Andy: Actually, it's a perfect image. The wall doesn't answer back. It just stands there—firm, resolved, but uninvolved. When you beat your head against it, you're the one who walks away with the pain. It doesn't even know that you've been there.

The therapist might capitalize on this discussion later in the therapy. When Andy again expresses his frustration with Betsy for not responding, the therapist might repeat this key phrase again, "It feels like beating your head against the wall, is that right?"

Using metaphors and images. The above example of "beating your head against the wall" also relies on the use of metaphor. Metaphors can be useful because they offer specific, concrete images that typically involve the senses. In this example, it is not difficult to imagine the physical pain that derives from striking one's head against a hard wall. For some individuals, discussions of emotions and cognitions seem abstract and difficult to process and discuss at that level. However, metaphors and similes provide people with a language that evokes a strong experiential component. Not all individuals use metaphors frequently or view them as useful ways to describe their experiences. However, for other individuals these are prime ways to experience and express emotions. Therefore, a therapist can focus on metaphors to the degree that they are consistent with an individual's way of processing and speaking. At the same time, the therapist must be attentive to the impact of a metaphor on the other partner. Often metaphors are expressed in an extreme way to convey a vivid image and associated emotion. This extreme description can seem like an exaggeration or distortion to a person's partner, particularly if it reflects negatively on the partner. In the previous example, Betsy might take great exception to being compared to a wall. Therefore, the therapist can either moderate the use of metaphors or prepare the listening partner to accept that this extreme expression is a useful way of conveying emotion. The therapist can emphasize that the partner does not have to agree with the image portrayed in the metaphor, but it still helps in understanding the other person's internal experience. In addition, as in the next example, the therapist can encourage the individual who uses a metaphor to include a positive image, even if it does not seem to represent current reality.

Cheryl and Gerard had sought couples counseling primarily because Cheryl was furious with Gerard, perceiving him as self-focused. Gerard frequently felt unjustly accused, claiming that Cheryl overreacted and made a "mountain out of a molehill."

> Cheryl: I have just about had it. I'm not sure there is any reason to go on with this relationship. We've been working at this for some time, and as we agreed, Wednesday night is our date night. This past week, we had decided to stay home and have a pleasant, quiet evening with just the two of us. I stopped at the grocery on the way home and got the ingredients for a nice dinner. When Gerard came home, I was finishing the cooking. I poured him a glass of wine and suggested that rather than helping me, he take a few moments to unwind before dinner. Well, he got involved watching a basketball game and didn't want to turn it off. He proposed a compromise that we keep the food warm in the oven and then have a "lovely dinner" during the 20-minute halftime during the game. I was so angry, I could have killed him. I looked at him sitting in the chair, and I could envision us 20 years from now in those exact same positions.
>
> Therapist: That sounds like it was an awful evening for you. You had really looked forward to the evening and were making an effort to make it special. Then Gerard responded in a way that made you feel very unimportant and secondary. Is that what it was like?

Cheryl: Exactly. I felt like I had made all this effort, and he totally blew it off.

Therapist: You said you looked at him and could envision what it would be like 20 years from now. Could you describe that scene in a bit more detail, really put yourself there?

Cheryl: It's awful. I can see myself getting old and being alone with him in the house. Whether it's the television, the computer, or whatever new gadget exists by that point. I get my 20 minutes, which is a filler for Gerard between his activities.

Therapist: Would you describe the emotions that go with that scene? What do you feel in that scene?

Cheryl: Lonely, absolutely lonely, with nothing to look forward to, and it's frightening. This could really happen to me.

Therapist: That sounds very frightening and very lonely. Would you now envision a second scene 20 years into the future, with you and Gerard in that same room. This time, describe what's happening and how you feel if it's the way that you want it to be.

Cheryl: I'll do it if you want me to. But it's painful because it points out what I'll never have. But if it could be what I want, we would both be in the room, probably sitting and both reading books. He might stop for a moment, look at me, and ask to share something that he's reading. It's nothing profound, and we don't have any particular magic moment, but it's a small way that we connect.

Therapist: That feels very different, doesn't it? I want you to tell Gerard about the fear that you currently have and what you want with him in the future. Just the fear and your dreams for the future, the good dreams.

Using therapist nonverbals. In addition to directing the individual's verbalizations as a way of heightening emotional experience, the therapist can use his or her own nonverbal communication to create a more emotional environment. This increased affective environment can facilitate the individual's experience of heightened emotion. Facial expression, body posture, volume of speech, and vocal inflection carry a great deal of affective information. The therapist can alter his or her own nonverbal behavior to create or enhance a specific emotional tone in the therapy session. For example, if the individual is feeling somewhat distant and therefore uncomfortable expressing emotions, the therapist might lean forward in the chair as if reaching out to the individual and decreasing distance. Similarly, the therapist might make eye contact as another way to decrease distance with the individual. If the individual is experiencing sadness, the therapist might speak in a soft tone and low volume to mirror and emphasize the individual's emotional state. The therapist can use nonverbal cues to create a safer environment, thus allowing for an increased experience of emotion, or the therapist can use nonverbal cues to mirror the individual's current emotional state.

Expressing emotions to the partner. In the preceding examples much of the interaction has focused on the therapist and one individual, with the therapist using various strategies to increase the breadth and magnitude of emotional experience. Once these emotions have been accessed, at times their intensity can be increased by asking the individual to express them to the partner. However, asking an individual to express these difficult emotions to a partner does not always have the intended effect. If the therapist is encouraging the individual to express emotions that involve confronting his or her partner with expressions of discontent, the individual might become frightened and actually express less emotional intensity to feel comfortable continuing the interaction. Furthermore, it then becomes important for the person's partner to respond to expressions of primary emotion in a nondefensive way. Phrased more behaviorally, if the individual avoids certain emotions because they feel threatening, then it is important that the person not be punished when he or she expresses these previously avoided emotions.

It is important that the therapist make all possible efforts to ensure that the negative consequences the individual anticipates for experiencing and expressing primary emotions not be confirmed. This aspect is important in making therapy sessions feel safe for both partners. In many instances the person's partner responds appropriately, without assistance from the therapist. However, the therapist cannot assume that all partners will respond sympathetically to each other's emotional expression. In some cases, the other partner feels threatened by the openness of the individual's self-disclosure and responds in a destructive manner. This response is particularly likely when the speaker is not expressing tender, vulnerable emotions but is expressing "harder" emotions, such as anger or frustration.

When the therapist has concerns that the partner might respond in a destructive way, the therapist can provide structure to increase the likelihood that these important moments are successful. It can be helpful for the therapist to clarify to the other partner how hard it is for this individual to express certain feelings. When that person does express those feelings, it is important to convey that the individual needs to feel validated and accepted by the therapist but, more important, by the partner. We emphasize that this acceptance is different from agreeing with the individual. Consequently, if the therapist is concerned about Gerard's possible response to Cheryl in the preceding example, the therapist might proceed as follows.

> Therapist: Gerard, Cheryl is getting ready to tell you something very important, so it is critical that you do your best to understand and accept her feelings, even if you don't agree with her. It might be hard, but remember, that is all you need to do right now, listen and try to understand what it is like for her.

It is important to realize that the therapist might have a variety of reasons for asking one person to express difficult feelings to the partner. It might initiate a decision-making conversation about a very important issue that has long been avoided. Alternatively, the therapist might intend to have both people express their feelings and thoughts about an interaction they have had, in preparation for cognitive restructuring. The therapy session might take a variety of directions once the members of the couple have expressed their emotions.

Avoiding diversions from emotional experience. As an individual begins to experience uncomfortable emotions, often that person has a tendency to try to escape from, or lessen the focus on, emotions. As noted earlier, this escape response can be negatively reinforcing because it lessens or removes the discomfort accompanying negative emotional experience. To help the individual become more comfortable with these emotions, it is important to help him or her maintain a focus on the feelings (a form of exposure and response prevention). As Johnson (1996) noted, it is important for the therapist to "block the exits"; that is, the therapist should be aware of a variety of strategies that the individual or the person's partner might use to divert the focus from current emotions.

In one diversion strategy, the individual can *express confusion* about what he or she feels. In such instances, the therapist can attempt to validate this confusion but not let the individual off the hook; for example, "That's okay. This issue is difficult, and it can be confusing. Just take your time and try to focus in on your emotions. We'll wait for you."

Another strategy individuals use to lessen emotional experience involves shifting to a more cognitive, intellectual focus. Given that our approach to couples therapy includes cognitive restructuring, psychoeducational discussions, and structured behavioral changes, the individual can feel justified making this shift to a more cognitive, rational emphasis. When such a shift occurs, the therapist can be responsive to the individual, but quickly put the individual back on track, focusing on emotions.

> Cheryl: Sure, I'd be glad to tell Gerard what I was feeling. But I was really struck when you asked me to develop a visual image of being with him in a room 20 years from now. I assume you wanted me to experience good feelings, and it actually worked. Is that something that you think we should do more often at home? Sort of practice positive visual imagery— isn't that what psychologists do with athletes these days? Anything that we can do to get a more positive focus would be fine with me.
>
> Therapist: I'm glad that was helpful to you, and before we finish today, let's discuss whether this might be a useful strategy for you to use more generally. But I don't want to take us away from where we were. Try to get yourself back to your feel-

ings. Tell Gerard about the fears that you have and your good dreams for the future.

Alternatively, the individual might attempt to divert the focus from uncomfortable emotions by *provoking the partner* to respond and take them in a different direction. The therapist can quickly interrupt the interaction and attempt to refocus the individual and the couple.

Cheryl: Sure, I'd be glad to tell Gerard about my future dreams. Boy, if I could get him to turn off the television and actually read a book, that itself would be a fantasy. *TV Guide* and the sports pages just about sum up his literary repertoire.

Therapist: Cheryl, let's stop. That's clearly not going to get a very receptive response from Gerard. I wonder what happened just now. I asked you to talk to him about your fears and dreams, and instead you said some pretty derogatory things about him. What did you feel at that moment when I asked you to express your fears and dreams?

This discussion of ways that an individual can escape from a focus on difficult emotions presents examples and is not exhaustive. The therapist needs to be alert to a wide variety of ways that a given individual or partner behaves to divert attention from feeling and talking about uncomfortable emotions. The avoidant individual often is not fully aware of the basis of this behavior. When the therapist becomes aware of customary ways that either person uses to divert his or her focus, it can be helpful to point them out to the couple so they can avoid those responses in the future. To avoid distracting the couple while they are in the midst of an interaction addressing emotions, the therapist's observation can be made later.

Therapist: Cheryl, I noticed something that happened while we were discussing your feelings a few minutes ago. We have talked about how hard it is for you to express negative feelings to Gerard. And, like almost everything else, when something feels somewhat dangerous, it is natural to try to avoid it or back off from it. I'm not sure about this, but one thing you seem to do when the emotions become uncomfortable is to switch from your feelings and start talking about something in a more intellectual way; for example, whether we should use visual imagery for you at home. Does that fit at all for you? Are you aware of doing that—getting more intellectual when you are uncomfortable emotionally?

Conclusions

The preceding discussion addresses several ways that a therapist can assist an individual and a couple in helping one person become more aware of certain emotions and increase the intensity of that emotional experience.

In most instances, we do not see this broadened experiencing of emotions as an end in itself; rather, it can be used to promote the well-being of the individual and the couple. Inhibitions or difficulty in experiencing and expressing emotions can have numerous consequences for a couple, such as contributing to a lack of intimacy between two partners. Moreover, the lack of awareness of emotions can contribute to inhibited sexual desire or lack of sexual arousal. Similarly, a person might still act on an emotion of which he or she is not fully aware. For example, a husband who is uncomfortable with his anger might avoid thinking about the anger and behave toward his wife in a passive–aggressive manner, without being aware of the underlying basis for the behavior.

Because emotions typically are related to cognitions, accessing emotions can be an important bridge to understanding an individual's important expectancies, attributions, and so forth. Consequently, as an individual's emotions become more explicit, the related cognitions can be identified as well. Furthermore, an individual's emotional responses that are based on traumatic experiences from earlier relationships can influence emotional responses to the current partner. Becoming aware of emotions that are related to previous traumas can help the individual separate the past from the present. Consequently, while helping an individual to access emotions, the therapist must have in mind ways to help the individual and the couple use that new awareness. Various approaches to using each person's emotional awareness for individual and couple well-being are discussed in subsequent chapters.

WHEN ONE OR BOTH INDIVIDUALS FOCUS ON EMOTIONS TO AN EXTREME DEGREE

In contrast to the previous problem, some individuals experience upsetting emotions to such an extreme degree that all facets of their lives, including their relationships, are caught in a pervasive negative atmosphere. In this section we explore ways the therapist can help the individual reduce the frequency of negative emotions and increase the occurrence of positive emotions. We outline each goal and describe interventions used to target individuals' excessive focus on negative emotions.

Frequent or prolonged experiences of positive emotions typically will not present a difficulty for a couple. However, it can become quite problematic when one or both individuals experience negative emotions for a long period or with great frequency. The basis for an extended experience of negative emotions varies from one couple to the next. In some instances, an individual appears to have a temperament that involves a high level of emotional reactivity. Other individuals have developed a coping style in which they deal with distress by approaching or focusing on the distress. Consequently, when the couple is having relationship difficulties, the individual who uses this approach strategy frequently experiences distressing emotions about the relationship and the partner. Alternatively, other individuals do not have an overall tendency to focus on negative emotions, but they experience pervasive negative emotions after a major interpersonal trauma occurs within the relationship. For example, in our research with individuals who have experienced an extramarital affair, the injured person often is overwhelmed with negative emotions. These individuals may have shown little tendency to focus on negative emotions in previous day-to-day experiences, but after the trauma they continue to be overwhelmed by extreme negative feelings. Therefore, the basis for experiencing frequent negative emotions varies and has implications for subsequent therapeutic interventions. In the discussion that follows, we focus on general guidelines for helping a couple address frequent and persistent experiences of negative emotion.

Interventions for assisting individuals and couples who are experiencing frequent and persistent negative emotions fall into two broad categories:

1. Interventions that help the individual contain or limit the experience and expression of such emotions to certain times and situations.
2. Interventions intended to alter the balance of positive to negative emotional experience.

Interventions that address containment of emotion and shifting the proportion of positive to negative emotions can be focused on the couple or on the individuals. In this chapter we emphasize couple interventions, while briefly noting individual interventions that can be of assistance as well. Perhaps these interventions can best be viewed as adaptation strategies; that is, often it is impossible to limit the experience of negative emotions and shift the balance of positive to negative emotions to the degree that the individual, couple, and therapist might desire. However, the following strategies can help to diminish the extremity of the responses.

One of the difficulties for both the individual and the couple is that the individual tends to be experiencing negative emotions on a very frequent or almost continuous basis. These negative emotions often are strongly based in reality and therefore cannot be eliminated (i.e., they are responses to actual negative life events), but their frequency and duration can be addressed. Most individuals do not have total voluntary control over their emotions, so they cannot decide to feel bad only on certain occasions or at certain times of the day. However, a couple can alter their way of addressing an individual's negative emotions to decrease their frequency and duration. Several strategies can be of assistance in this regard:

- Scheduling times to discuss emotions and related thoughts with one's partner.
- Practicing "healthy compartmentalization."

- Seeking alternative means to communicate feelings and elicit support.
- Tolerating distressing feelings.

SCHEDULING TIMES TO DISCUSS EMOTIONS AND RELATED THOUGHTS

Negative emotions often are tied to important thoughts. As an individual continues to think about upsetting ideas, the negative emotions continue to be generated and accentuated. Scheduling specific opportunities to discuss the individual's thoughts and feelings can free the individual to address other issues at other times. That is, if a person knows that he or she and the partner are going to have a conversation that evening about what is upsetting, this knowledge can allow the individual to focus current attention on other issues. Otherwise, the individual may continuously dwell on the upsetting thoughts and feelings. In some ways, these strategies overlap with recommendations for the treatment of generalized anxiety disorder, which involves a pervasive sense of worry (T. A. Brown, O'Leary, & Barlow, 1993). T. A. Brown et al. (1993) pointed to the importance of setting aside times for the individual to focus on and address their worries, to prevent intermittent "worry behaviors."

When couples have these scheduled conversations, it is important that the individual feels understood and accepted. These conversations should be long enough that the individual does not feel rushed and that strong emotions can be addressed. Providing a sense of acceptance is a general communication guideline, but it is particularly important when one individual has frequent or protracted negative feelings about something in the relationship. Unfortunately, the person's partner often is tired of hearing about it and becomes less attentive. If the partner tries to move the discussion forward by avoiding, distancing, and not listening to the upset individual, this response typically prolongs the individual's upset feelings. Therefore, couples need to use good listening skills on these occasions, such as those described in chapter 9. The partner also needs to recognize that when an individual has strong negative feelings about an important issue, expressing those feelings once often is not sufficient. Consequently, an individual might need to have several conversations, even if the partner is demonstrating excellent listening skills.

On some occasions, the couple might decide to have additional conversations about one person's upset feelings. However, this repetition can run the risk of alienating the other partner, who over time begins to disengage, avoid, and withdraw. Consequently, it is important that the couple have other strategies for dealing with emotions. If the individual continues to experience emotional upset about the same issues even after they have been well processed, sometimes it is not productive to have additional conversations immediately. In these instances it can be helpful if the distressed individual can clarify that he or she is still upset and can convey the message, "I can handle it for now." For example, the partner might comment that the individual seems distressed and ask, "What's wrong?" Rather than reengaging in a repetitive conversation, the individual might respond, "Nothing new, it's just the same old feelings. It probably isn't helpful for us to talk about it right now; I think I can handle it for now." If this kind of exchange is to be successful, it is important that the individual does not present the comments as an implied criticism and threat: "I'll deal with it!" Similarly, this suggestion is not to be confused with the disingenuous comment, "Nothing's wrong. I'm just fine," that some individuals make while otherwise demonstrating significant distress. Rather, the individual is to acknowledge that he or she is upset but that there is nothing new to say at the moment. The individual will attempt to cope with the issue internally rather than placing the couple in a repetitive conversation.

The preceding guidelines are helpful to individuals who experience negative moods frequently and with great duration. They also are particularly valuable for individuals who have difficulty regulating the intensity of their moods. One key to regulating emotional intensity is to be prepared for situations that elicit affect. Planning ahead for difficult or important conversations, including ways to keep the emotional level moderated, can be valuable for the individual and the partner. Also, it is important for emotionally reactive individuals to have an experience of being heard and validated by others. Otherwise, they are likely to experience frustration and escalate their emotional expressions to be heard.

Practicing "Healthy" Compartmentalization

Individuals vary widely in how helpful they find the approach of setting aside specific times to address issues of concern. Some people are quite adept at compartmentalization, or setting aside distressing thoughts and feelings and leaving them for a later time. For example, some individuals report that they might have an argument with their partner early in the morning. However, once they arrive at work or become involved in their other activities for the day, they set the argument aside and focus on their other activities. They are not inappropriately denying or avoiding relationship issues, but they are able to limit the occasions during which they focus on relationship concerns. This strategy can be an effective adaptation that serves the individual and other people well. Most parents hope that their children's teachers can, for instance, set aside their personal lives while they focus on the students. Other people are not nearly as successful at this "healthy compartmentalization." When an individual has difficulty setting distressing feelings aside, the therapist might suggest developing or improving this skill. In the following example the therapist presents this notion to Molly and Seth, soon after Molly had learned of Seth's infidelity.

> Therapist: Right now, you are in a real crisis; it feels like your world has been turned upside down. We will focus on several things, and one of the immediate issues that we need to address is the extremely upsetting emotions that you have been experiencing, Molly. These feelings are very understandable and typical at a time like this, but as you have mentioned, they feel overwhelming, and at times you don't know if you can go on. If I understand correctly, you are thinking about Seth's affair almost constantly. As you think about it, you experience a whole variety of overwhelming emotions, ranging from fury, to panic, to depression, to confusion. You keep asking yourself, over and over, "Why did he do this? What was he thinking?" Those questions are all extremely important, and we are going to address all of them. However, allowing yourself to focus all day, every day, on these questions and the emotions that they create is indeed overwhelming. Also, am I right that you are spending a great deal of your time together each evening discussing what happened? You mentioned that you might stay up until 2:00 a.m. several nights in a row talking about it. [Couple affirms.]
>
> Let me tell you what I recommend we try to do. Molly, you're going to be upset, you're going to ask these questions, and the two of you need to have many conversations at home and here. But I want you to start to limit those conversations and your focus on what happened. I'm not trying to minimize what has happened; it is important. I simply want you to do this in a way that is going to work for you. Molly, I want to recommend that you write down the most important questions that you have for Seth. And I want you to give those questions to him so that he can be thinking about them. Ask your questions, but don't do it in a hostile way. Then I want the two of you to set aside several discussion times between now and next week to address these issues. Let's not make those marathon conversations. What would be a good amount of time to set aside in an evening? [The couple responds that one hour per conversation would be good.]
>
> Molly, I hope that writing down the questions, giving them to Seth, and knowing that you will have certain times to talk with him about the affair will help you to focus on other aspects of your life as well. I also want you to make a special effort to do that; this will be very important. It will not be easy. It might help if you make certain to keep yourself busy, focus on other things—basically, distract yourself. That does not mean what has happened is unimportant; it is huge. It also is important, though, that you begin to give your life some sense of normality. Molly, how are you in general at being able to set things aside and focus on other issues? What are things that you can do during the day to help you get away from thinking about this for at least some periods of time?

The notion of healthy compartmentalization can be particularly valuable to individuals with poor emotion regulation ability. Linehan (1993) discussed the importance of developing a "wise mind," which involves integrating one's emotions and cognitions in experiencing the world. To accomplish this task, Linehan pointed to the importance of focusing on only one thing at the current moment, focusing attention on that one issue. Linehan's advice is similar to our suggestion that the individual find ways to become engaged and focused on other aspects of life apart from the negative feelings.

Using Alternative Means of Communication and Seeking Support

The goals of setting aside time for communication about frequent negative feelings between the partners are twofold: (a) to limit the individual's focus on upsetting emotions and (b) to limit the couple's potential for unnecessary negative interactions. As discussed earlier, limiting the partners' interactions can limit negative exchanges but might not satisfactorily limit the individual's own experience of negative emotions. When an individual continues to experience negative emotions, two major strategies can be used. First, the individual can seek alternative ways to express his or her feelings. Second, the individual can attempt to tolerate the distress, learning to be more accepting of having negative feelings.

An individual can seek alternative ways to express negative emotions, either in solitude or in interaction with other people. Some people find it helpful to express their feelings in writing, through a journal, which allows the individual to express himself or herself in an honest fashion without being distracted by the partner's responses. This approach works well for some individuals, but other people might benefit more from interpersonal expressions of emotion. They can turn to friends or family members to express their negative feelings (Jacobson & Christensen, 1996). Although expressing these feelings can result in significant social support for the individual, some cautions should be provided. In expressing negative feelings about the partner or relationship to friends or family members, the individual might disclose very negative information about the partner. At the time, the third party in the conversation might provide significant support. However, the individual might later regret having shared this information. If the partner learns that intimate information has been shared with another individual, this awareness might have negative consequences for the couple or for the partner's relationship with that other individual. Also, the other person in the conversation might develop extremely negative feelings and attitudes toward the partner, even after the individual and partner have reconciled. For example, Dina told her mother about Mario's infidelity. In doing so, she provided many details and allowed her mother to see how heartbroken she was. Even though Dina and Mario worked through these problems after many months, Dina's mother's relationship with Mario was permanently damaged. Finally, if the other person in the conversation makes derogatory statements about the partner in an attempt to be supportive, the individual might later resent the negative comments about his or her partner. Therefore, although the short-term benefits of sharing negative feelings about the partner and the relationship with others can be attractive, there also is potential for long-term negative consequences.

Using Distress Tolerance

It is important that individuals who are prone to negative feelings have an ability to tolerate the distress that they experience. In her discussion of interventions to help individuals with borderline personality disorder, Linehan (1993) discussed in detail how to help an individual develop increased distress tolerance. To a large degree, this approach involves a nonjudgmental acceptance of one's emotions as well as the current situation as it is. An important message is that negative emotions are a natural part of life; they provide the individual with important information about how the individual is experiencing the world. Thus, in general, they are neither good nor bad. They are to be valued and accepted.

Consider Gladys, who had grown up in a family in which both parents experienced significant clinical depression and came to view negative emotions as frightening and dangerous, assuming that an individual might not recover from them for months, if at all. Consequently, she became quite anxious anytime Oscar came home from work feeling down or depressed. She believed that it was essential that she and Oscar develop a plan immediately to get him out of his negative mood. In this example, the therapist provides an explanation to Gladys and Oscar about how to address negative emotions that are more normal.

Therapist: Gladys, given the depression that both of your parents experienced, it is understandable why you become concerned about Oscar when he feels down at the end of the day. Rather than trying to get him out of his negative mood immediately, I suggest that you try something different. Emotions, both positive ones and negative ones, are a normal part of life. I think it is important that both of you be allowed to have the emotions that you experience without passing judgment on them. For most people, if they are allowed to experience their emotions and have those emotions accepted by loved ones, the emotions are likely to take a normal course. The person experiences the feelings, processes what they are about, takes action if necessary, and over time moves forward. I think it would be helpful if you can begin to see Oscar's feelings as simply a part of who he is. Allow him to have those emotions; then, if he wants to discuss them with you, great. If there are times when he needs to be quiet and address them by himself, try to accept that. Try to show understanding and empathy for his feelings, rather than rushing to change them. Remember the communication guidelines that we talked about in terms of being a good listener, and try to accept the other person's feelings and thoughts, even if you don't agree with them.

This acceptance can be important in tolerating difficult relationship, personal, and environmental factors that contribute to negative moods. Linehan (1993) discussed several specific strategies that help an individual tolerate distress and that have pertinence to relationship functioning. Several of these strategies are noted elsewhere in our discussion: (a) distracting oneself from the negative feelings and events, as discussed earlier; (b) self-soothing, which involves a range of positive behaviors oriented toward the self, which we discussed in chapter 2; (c) improving the moment by replacing negative events with positive events, as we discuss next; and (d) thinking about the pros and cons of tolerating distress. It is important to assist individuals who have difficulty containing negative emotions, but the therapist must not suggest that experiencing and expressing negative emotions in general are inappropriate.

Using Interventions to Shift the Focus From Negatives

The above-mentioned interventions are designed to help an individual experience and communicate negative emotions in a constructive and contained manner. In addition, at times it is helpful to shift the focus away from the individual's experience of negative emotions and thoughts. This shift can be accomplished in at least two ways. Within the individual, it is helpful to alter the balance of positive versus negative emotional experience. Altering the ratio of positives to negatives is important for many distressed couples and is particularly important for people who generally tend to experience frequent negative emotions. As we described in chapter 3, the experience of negative emotions increases a person's tendency to focus cognitively on negatives as well, including memories of other negative events (Osgarby & Halford, 1995). Therefore, a variety of behavioral and cognitive interventions can be used to shift the experience from negative to positive emotion. These interventions can involve, for example, asking the individual to track positive events in the relationship, discuss with the partner what is positive in their relationship, or express appreciation for the partner's thoughtful behaviors and acts of kindness (Baucom & Epstein, 1990). In addition, guided behavior change and effective communication can alter the ratio of positive to negative experience for the individual.

Furthermore, it can be helpful to maintain some balance in roles between the two partners. Often when one person is highly distressed about the relationship, that individual's concerns become the couple's primary focus. Although this is not always true, in some couples the more distressed person airs his or her complaints while the other person listens. As these roles become more consistent, there is a tendency for them to become more extreme, with the distressed individual becoming a complainer. Being in this negative role can itself increase the individual's focus on negatives. It can be helpful to emphasize to the couple the importance of the other partner's sharing his or her feelings to avoid these polarized roles. Expression of the other partner's emotions and thoughts should include both positive and negative expression, as appropriate. Moreover, some individuals become self-focused and self-absorbed when in a negative mood. Helping the individual shift away from a self-focus by listening to his or her partner instead and focusing on the partner can be helpful in reducing the person's global negative feelings.

Another way that the individual can reduce a self-focus is to direct energy and effort outside of the relationship, perhaps toward the broader community. As we discussed in chapter 2, both instrumental and expressive behaviors focused outside of the couple not only decrease negative self-focus but also can fulfill the individual's own positive needs. Such behaviors might include civic and community involvement, religious activities, and so on. Once a couple becomes highly distressed, a great deal of their energy and attention are focused on the distressed relationship. Some couples are able to break this negative cycle by focusing outward, toward other people. This focus provides the couple with an opportunity to work well as a team, highlighting their shared values in a context that does not emphasize their differences and distress. We have worked with several couples who report that they feel better after they have engaged in volunteer activities together, functioning as a team again.

The activities just described are only suggestions. What is important is for the therapist to understand the principle that negative emotions can generate a self-absorbed state in which they provide the context for more negative emotions. Therefore, containing the experience and expression of these emotions, shifting the individual's negative to positive experience, shifting attention to the other partner's experience, and focusing outside of the couple are all broad strategies to break this negative pattern. The therapist and couple can use this broad principle to develop a wide variety of additional strategies.

SUMMARY

In earlier cognitive–behavioral models of relationship functioning, emotions were relegated to a secondary role. This was based on the assumption that if appropriate cognitive and behavioral changes occurred, then emotional changes would develop correspondingly. As a result, little attention was given to addressing emotions directly. The current chapter emphasizes the importance of addressing emotions directly, along with strategies for altering a variety of concerns regarding partners' emotions.

- Several interventions are available to assist people who have difficulty experiencing and expressing emotions and people who experience emotion frequently, with long durations, and with great intensity. The therapist and couple should gauge the degree to which either person's emotional experience needs to be improved.

- Some individuals avoid expressing their primary emotional responses to situations to protect themselves from uncomfortable emotions and their partners' possible negative reactions to their communication of those emotions. Instead, these individuals express secondary emotions.

- Some interventions for individuals with a lack of or limited emotional experiences include encouraging the partner's acceptance of the individual's experience; using questions, reflections, and interpretations to draw out the individual's primary emotions; describing emotions through metaphors and images; helping individuals express emotions to their partners, and discouraging the individuals' attempts to distract themselves from experiencing emotion.

- Some individuals focus on negative feelings about the partner to such an extent that the frequent discussion and experience of those feelings exacerbate relationship distress.

- One set of interventions to reduce frequent negative emotions attempts to limit the experience and expression of emotion to certain times and situations. These interventions include scheduling times to discuss feelings with the partner, distracting oneself with other activities, increasing one's tolerance for distress, and finding ways to express the negative emotions other than through discussions with one's partner.

- Another set of interventions to prevent individuals from dwelling on negative emotions uses behavioral and cognitive techniques that increase the number of positive emotions and shift the partners' communication roles to draw the individual out of a preoccupation with his or her negative feelings.

- Once the individual experiences and expresses emotions at an adaptive level, the therapist should integrate these emotional gains with cognitive and behavioral interventions to achieve treatment goals.

12

INTERVENTIONS FOR COUPLE
PATTERNS AND INTERACTIONS

In the previous chapters on interventions for modifying behavioral, cognitive, and affective elements of a couple's relationship we have presented the building blocks of cognitive–behavioral therapy. Now we turn to ways these interventions can be used to address concerns about the couple as a dyad, characteristics of the individual partners, and the couple's interactions with their environment. We describe interventions focused on the couple; in chapter 13 we discuss interventions addressing characteristics of individual partners, and in chapter 14 we describe interventions focusing on the couple's physical and interpersonal environment. In these chapters we also consider clinical decisions concerning the sequencing of interventions. Interventions for behavior, cognitions, and emotions typically are combined and integrated within sessions, so we do not attempt to present guidelines for sequencing them. However, we describe the therapist's decision-making process concerning the sequencing of interventions for couples who present with particular patterns of secondary distress and guidelines for deciding when to focus on these patterns before intervening with core relationship issues involved in a couple's primary distress.

As described earlier, dyadic problems can be conceptualized as developing at two levels:

- *Primary distress*: distress resulting when members of a couple are unable to resolve issues associated with degrees of difference or similarity between the two individuals.
- *Secondary distress*: distress resulting when the interaction patterns that a couple have developed to cope with unresolved issues in their relationship become problematic in themselves.

Primary distress can result from a difference between partners' preferences or motives; for example, two people differ in the amount that they like to interact with other people and prefer different kinds of leisure activities. Such differences may become major sources of conflict and dissatisfaction, as the individuals perceive that they are incompatible and are unable to meet their needs within their relationship (Jacobson & Christensen, 1996). Other sources of primary distress may involve ways in which partners are similar. For example, if neither partner is detail oriented, the couple may fail to attend to important aspects of daily life, such as due dates for bills.

Secondary distress develops from the particular ways that members of a couple interact behaviorally in response to issues that are sources of their primary distress. Although many couples find mutually satisfying ways of resolving concerns that derive from differences or similarities in their needs, personality styles, and other characteristics, other couples' responses are ineffective in resolving the issues and become major sources of distress themselves (Markman, Stanley, & Blumberg, 1994). In earlier chapters we have described four major interaction patterns that may be ineffective in resolving primary distress and may create secondary distress:

- *Mutual attack*: Partners engage in reciprocal (and often escalating) aggressive behavior, such as criticism, threats, and in some cases psychological or physical abuse.
- *Demand–withdrawal*: One partner pursues the other, often in an aggressive manner, in an attempt to gain the other's attention and compliance, while the other partner withdraws physically and/or refuses to pay attention.
- *Mutual withdrawal*: Partners engage in reciprocal distancing to escape aversive interactions.
- *Unilateral or mutual disengagement*: One or both partners no longer are invested psychologically and emotionally in the relationship with the other person, so even when he or she is physically present the other's responses have little or no impact.

Many couples enter therapy with their interactions dominated by these types of behavioral patterns, and in many cases they are among the major concerns that partners present to therapists. Even though members of a couple may be aware of their underlying issues, such as unmet needs, a therapist's attempts to address the underlying issues without modifying the distressing coping patterns may be fruitless. For example, June and Reggie initially were uncomfortable about the difference in their needs for intimacy. At first they had long, mutually frustrating discussions about the difference, and increasingly they had arguments marked by mutual criticism. By the time they contacted a therapist they were avoiding each other, the arguments and alienation so unpleasant that they had discussed divorce. At that point June and Reggie were focused on their secondary distress and had lost perspective on their core intimacy issue.

Consequently, in the sequencing of interventions, we believe that the most productive therapeutic strategy often is to improve the overall tone of a couple's relationship by modifying negative interaction patterns associated with secondary distress and then to focus on primary distress associated with core issues that the couple's interaction patterns have failed to resolve.

Thus, this chapter is organized into two major sections: (a) interventions for modifying interaction patterns producing secondary distress and (b) interventions for resolving core dyadic relationship issues.

Because some couples *are* aware of their core issues, it is important that therapists discuss the two levels of intervention with them and provide a clear rationale for focusing on negative interactions patterns first. It is important that couples know that the therapist understands and will help them address their underlying issues. Furthermore, it often is possible to begin intervening with core issues after a brief period, as long as a couple can modify their problematic interactions sufficiently. The couple can practice the *process* of interacting constructively while discussing the *content* of their issues, such as discrepant needs. Thus, in this chapter we present interventions for secondary distress before those for primary distress, but in practice they may be combined.

INTERVENTIONS FOR MODIFYING SECONDARY DISTRESS INTERACTION PATTERNS

In this section we describe a variety of interventions that we use to decrease patterns of mutual attack, demand–withdrawal, mutual withdrawal, and disengagement that are contributing to a couple's secondary distress, and to substitute positive interactions. We also discuss guidelines for deciding on the sequencing of interventions for each interaction pattern. These interventions follow from our conceptual model that identifies behavioral, cognitive, and affective factors that contribute to negative couple interactions. The interventions include

- Increasing relational, circular causal thinking.

- Decreasing overlearned responses from prior relationships.
- Establishing guidelines for couple interactions inside and outside of sessions, including constructive communication skills.
- Decreasing partners' distorted cognitions about each other's behavior.
- Decreasing emotional unresponsiveness or dysregulation.

To the extent possible, we attempt to implement these interventions during conjoint sessions with both members of a couple, because the central goal is to alter dyadic processes contributing to secondary distress. However, sometimes one or both members of a couple are so reactive to their partner's presence that they have difficulty focusing on their own role in negative interactions and decreasing overlearned behavioral, cognitive, and affective responses. In such cases it may be necessary to schedule some individual sessions with each member of the couple to create a less charged atmosphere in which they can practice new responses and prepare to resist the "triggers" they typically experience when interacting with the partner.

In addition, when there is evidence that aspects of a couple's environment are affecting their negative interaction patterns, it is important to intervene quickly to reduce the stress. For example, if the partners' families of origin are actively taking sides in the couple's conflicts, the therapist may need to emphasize to the couple how difficult it is for them to make clear decisions as a couple and resolve basic concerns in their relationship as long as others are involved. Similarly, if demands from jobs and children interfere with a couple's ability to interact in constructive ways and lead to negative patterns, it is important for the therapist to intervene early in therapy to help the couple develop ways to protect themselves more from these intrusions that distract, tire, and upset them.

Interventions for Attack–Attack Patterns

Couples who engage in attack–attack interaction patterns are the stereotype of the angry, conflictual, distressed couple. They present a challenge to the couples therapist because the sessions often are filled with anger, rapid escalation of arguments that lead to stalemates, hurt feelings, and a sense of despair (Gottman, 1999; Weiss & Heyman, 1997). As a result, in terms of sequencing interventions, it is essential that early in treatment the therapist help couples minimize these types of interactions during the therapy sessions and outside of sessions. The therapist commonly needs to modify aspects of these negative interactions, including the couple's negative behavior, their negative cognitions about each other and the relationship, and their negative emotions, to pave the way for interventions that address underlying concerns about core relationship issues. To accomplish this task, a variety of interventions is available.

Providing Ongoing Feedback About Circular, Mutual Impacts

Regardless of the particular interaction pattern that a couple displays, it is essential that the couple become aware of the pattern. Until partners recognize their interaction patterns when they occur, these patterns are difficult, if not impossible, to alter. Therefore, a first step in working with couples engaged in mutual attack is to discuss with them the nature of their interaction and how the partners influence each other. These couples typically know that they argue, but a more detailed understanding of their interaction is necessary. In particular, it is important that each person acknowledge his or her role in the interaction. One way of accomplishing this goal is to discuss the concept of negative reciprocity with couples and point out how negative behavior from one person typically results in negative behavior from the partner (Baucom & Epstein, 1990). We then point out to the couple that it is possible to break this pattern in two ways. First, it is important to not initiate a negative interaction that involves blaming and complaining about the other person in a derogatory or demeaning way. Second, even if one person does make a critical or hurtful comment, it is important for the other individual not to reciprocate and escalate this process. Therefore, we speak to each individual about his or her responsibility for not initiating or maintaining a negative interaction pattern, no matter how tempting it may be to do so when one is upset with one's partner.

After discussing the couple's typical interaction pattern and allowing them to provide details of how the negative interaction escalates, it is important to obtain the partners' commitment to change this pattern. When asked if they wish to change this form of interaction, typically both partners respond affirmatively. After obtaining a commitment from both individuals to change the pattern, it can be helpful to ask each person to address what he or she might do specifically to alter this pattern. The following is a brief excerpt from a therapy session with this goal in mind.

Therapist: It's a positive sign that you both want to change this pattern, but having that desire usually is not enough. You've developed such a strong pattern now that it takes little to set it off. I want each of you to think for a moment about what you can do specifically to help change this way of interacting.

Rebecca: Well, I think for me it would be not to push Sam's buttons. I know when I call him irresponsible it really sets him off, probably because he heard that his entire life growing up.

Therapist: It's great that you are able to pinpoint that specific behavior. What are some other things that you can do to avoid initiating these interactions? Also, if Sam seems to start the argument, what can you do to pull back so that it doesn't escalate, Rebecca?

In spite of these commitments and willingness to change their interaction pattern, such couples often erupt into negative exchanges and a *rapid escalation of negative feelings* during sessions. To counteract this tendency the therapist must be comfortable with and knowledgeable about how to control such sessions. One strategy is to establish an appropriate tone and way of interacting with the couple during sessions. By modeling respect and treating each person with dignity, the therapist creates guidelines for how the couple should interact with each other. In addition, the therapist can slow the pace of the interaction through his or her own tone and volume of voice, rate of speech, and body language. In essence, starting in the first session, the therapist attempts to create a more relaxed, less intense therapy atmosphere.

If the partners are interacting with each other and begin to escalate negative reciprocity, the therapist must intervene quickly, particularly early in treatment. The therapist stops the couple's interaction, comments on the specific behaviors that are contributing to the escalation of negative feelings, and discusses with the couple how they might interact differently. This may involve a discussion of communication guidelines as described in chapter 9. Stopping the couple's interaction quickly accomplishes two goals. First, it interrupts the negative reciprocity that tends to escalate rapidly. Second, the ensuing discussion often is much more cognitive, focusing on specific behaviors in the interaction. This can have the important impact of de-escalating rising emotion (Gottman, 1999). In general, a therapist must know how to decrease the affective intensity of the session when necessary by becoming more cognitive in the session.

Decreasing Overlearned Negative Behavioral Responses Developed in Prior Relationships and Substituting Constructive Behavior

At times, a couple's negative behavioral responses, such as aggression, are overlearned responses developed in prior relationships. When this is the case, it can be helpful not only to point out as soon as possible the pattern in the current relationship but also to note how one or both partners' behaviors developed in previous relationships. Responses such as verbally attacking significant others may have been functional in protecting an individual or meeting the person's needs in prior relationships. The therapist draws on information gathered in the individual and couple history interviews to identify similarities between an individual's current behaviors and responses that were advantageous in his or her family of origin or a prior couple relationship. The therapist can point out ways in which aggressive responses that may have served a function in the past appear to continue automatically in the present relationship, producing negative consequences. If the therapist believes that an individual's automatic negative responses to a partner are associated with a level of individual psychopathology that significantly interferes with his or her ability to take part constructively in couple sessions, a referral for individual therapy may be appropriate at this point. Thus, Katja developed an argumentative style in her competitive family of origin, and it tended to contribute to an attack–attack pattern in her relationship with Tomas. The couple's therapist discussed with them how Katja was "a well-trained debater." The therapist noted that Katja tends to debate in such a persistent manner that Tomas experiences her as coercive rather than collaborative, prompting him to fight back. Katja acknowledged that whereas she had felt compelled to be argumentative to be respected in her family of origin, she did not need to behave this way to gain Tomas's respect. She and the therapist discussed alternative ways to express an opinion that differed from Tomas's. The therapist judged that Katja's argumentative response did not reflect significant psychopathology that might have called for a referral for individual therapy.

When secondary-distress interactions appear to be ingrained automatic responses that occur between partners, we also use techniques described in chapter 10 for increasing partners' relational thinking and awareness of their macrolevel behavioral patterns. The goal is to make the patterns less automatic and to create opportunities for more constructive interactions. Then we use a variety of interventions for guided behavior changes and skills building, to modify specific microlevel behaviors that comprise the macrolevel patterns that have been identified. Thus, a therapist might determine that when one member of a couple seeks support from the other to address unfulfilled achievement needs (e.g., disappointment and frustration with his or her career), the other person feels inept and criticizes the person for complaining. This response may elicit a pattern of mutual criticism. After pointing out this pattern to the couple, the therapist might work to increase mutual social support between the partners by coaching them in expressive and listening skills and devising informal or formal agreements to provide each other with particular types of support that each person desires.

Thus, as with other types of overlearned negative behavioral responses from prior relationships, interventions for automatic mutual-attack responses involve

- Increasing awareness of the pattern.
- Identifying the positive functions that the responses served in the past.
- Emphasizing the pattern's negative impact on the couple's ability to resolve concerns in their relationship.
- Instituting behavior changes involving more positive responses.

Establishing Guidelines for Couples' Interactions

Continuing to interrupt a couple, stop their rapidly escalating arguments, and dampen the negative affect can be an exhausting experience for the therapist and the couple. Consequently, it is important that the couple begin to take responsibility for changing behaviors themselves. This occurs as the partners become more comfortable with following communication guidelines and as other aspects of their relationship improve. In addition, often it is helpful at the beginning of a session to remind the couple of problematic behaviors that they need to strive to avoid and new interactions that they are attempting to establish. Thus, in addition to playing the role of interrupting partners' specific negative interaction sequences, the therapist establishes an overall framework in which a major goal for the couple during each session will be to avoid attacking or counterattacking each other.

> Therapist: We have been working a great deal on trying to change some of the ways that you interact, so let's be particularly attentive to those tonight. More specifically, we have seen that your interactions go much more smoothly when neither of you interrupts the other. Also, we have talked about how each of you tries to prove your point by making the other person's position look foolish or extreme. So, tonight when each of you is discussing your perspective on having another child, it will be important to respect the other person's opinion and not try to make it look foolish by restating it in a more extreme way.

Decreasing Partners' Negative Cognitions That Contribute to Attack–Attack Patterns

At times, focusing on the behavioral aspects of mutual attacks is sufficient to alter such patterns. In other instances individuals' increased awareness of their behavioral contributions to the couple's mutually aggressive interactions is insufficient to stop the negative behavior, and the partners' cognitions about each other may continue to fuel the aggression. Several of the interventions that we described in chapter 10 for modifying cognitions may help decrease partners' mutual attacks and may be necessary early in therapy to facilitate the desired behavior change. As we described in chapters 8 and 10, therapists must be cautious in challenging individuals' cognitions in the presence of their partners, to minimize defensiveness, so we look for opportunities to illustrate the impact of distorted or inappropriate cognitions, using instances that occur during early sessions or that a couple relates about recent interaction at home. For example, a therapist might identify an individual's personal standard that seems to contribute to aggressive exchanges and coach the person in evaluating its advantages and disadvantages. Thus, Sondra was much neater and more organized than Nicholas. She had complained about "the big mess" from his working for several days on a large jigsaw puzzle on the dining room table. Nicholas became very angry when he came home from work the next day and found that Sondra had taken the puzzle apart and put it away. On the basis of his standard that "people who violate your rights deserve to be punished," he proceeded to dump all of Sondra's CDs, which she had carefully arranged in alphabetical order, onto the floor. When Nicholas explained that dumping Sondra's CDs was justified, the therapist asked him to consider the advantages and disadvantages of trying to resolve the couple's differences by retaliating. Nicholas acknowledged that his punitive approach tended to make Sondra less supportive and cooperative rather than open to changing her own approach. The therapist then guided Nicholas in considering a modified standard that emphasized expressing his dissatisfaction with Sondra in a way that would convey the seriousness of the issue but would not involve retaliation.

Decreasing Emotional Dysregulation

Mutual attack between partners also can result when one or both partners have difficulty regulating their emotions. Unregulated emotional reactions are likely to elicit negative coping styles, including attack (Linehan, 1993). In chapter 11 we described two broad categories of interventions to (a) help the individual contain or limit the experience of strong negative emotions to particular times and situations and (b) create a more satisfying balance of positive to negative emotional experiences. The following are examples of ways in which these types of interventions may be used to reduce couples' aggression.

To help each partner contain strong emotions at times when they need to work collaboratively, the therapist can coach the couple in scheduling separate times in which they can use expressive and empathic listening skills to share emotions versus times for cognitively oriented decision-making discussions (Baucom & Epstein, 1990; Fincham, Fernandes, & Humphreys, 1993). Knowing that there will be ample opportunities for expressing emotions helps some individuals adhere to guidelines for decision-making discussions. Because strong emotional responses may have become relatively automatic, the therapist may need to intervene repeatedly to keep each partner focused on noticing emotions but "saving" them for a later time when they can be discussed more thoroughly and will not interfere with finding solutions to relationship issues.

In addition, Linehan's (1993) distress-tolerance approach can be used to help each individual accept that it is natural to feel some anger when one experiences conflict with one's partner. The therapist can stress that it need not be inevitable that an individual becomes distracted from problem solving by strong emotions or must release tension by expressing the anger aggressively. Instead, each person could think of the angry feelings as "signals that my partner and I are dealing with something that is important to me, so I need to take the time to understand each of our needs and see what solutions are possible."

As we described in chapter 11, another approach to reducing pervasive negative emotion is to increase partners' experiences of positive emotions in interactions with each other. For example, if a couple has an unresolved issue regarding a difference in their personality styles, the therapist might encourage them to schedule more activities together that they both tend to enjoy in spite of their differences (Baucom & Epstein, 1990; Fincham et al., 1993; Markman et al., 1994). In future situations when the partners are experiencing strong negative feelings toward each other, they can remind themselves of the positive experiences. The therapist notes that this approach is not intended to invalidate individuals' upset about issues in their relationship; rather, it is to counteract pervasive negative feelings or sentiment override (Weiss, 1980) that fuel aggressive behavior.

> Therapist: Finding ways to deal with the differences in your personalities can be challenging and requires some creativity and effort on both of your parts. If you often have negative feelings about your relationship, it is easy to be motivated to criticize, threaten, or punish each other. That's why I think it is very important to increase opportunities for each of you to experience pleasant emotions in your relationship. Those positive feelings can help you stay motivated to keep working on resolving the issues that concern you.

If the therapist determines that an individual's difficulty in regulating his or her emotions reflects more pervasive psychopathology, it may be appropriate to refer him or her for individual therapy early in treatment; otherwise, untreated severe levels of psychopathology are likely to interfere with progress in couples therapy. Interventions for untreated substance abuse and the existence of severe psychological or physical partner abuse also must be addressed as prerequisites to conducting general couples therapy. If the level of individual psychopathology is lower, the therapist might schedule a few individual sessions with each person, to prepare them to work together more smoothly in joint sessions, and these sessions can be used to help a partner cope better with his or her own and the partner's psychopathology symptoms. In subsequent joint sessions, the therapist could work with the couple to reduce stressful secondary-distress interactions that maintain or exacerbate an individual's psychopathology (see chapter 13).

All of the above intervention strategies can be adapted for use with any of the interaction patterns we describe next. For example, it almost always is appropriate to point out the couple's interaction pattern and note when one or both partners' behaviors were learned in earlier relationships—a pattern of response that is no longer needed in the current relationship. Rather than reiterating how to use each intervention with each interaction pattern, we emphasize interventions that are particularly pertinent to altering a given interaction pattern and note priorities for sequencing interventions.

Interventions for Demand–Withdraw Patterns

Demand–withdraw patterns are one of the most common interaction patterns among distressed couples (Gottman, 1999; Weiss & Heyman, 1997). In this interaction pattern, one person tends to pursue the other in an aggressive or assertive manner while the other person actively withdraws from interaction. This pattern tends to be circular and self-perpetuating, and it often becomes more accentuated over time. The person who is in the demanding role typically wishes to engage the other individual. As the other person withdraws, the first person becomes more demanding, which leads to further withdrawal. At times, the more demanding partner escalates the approach behavior to an extreme level, including yelling or making extremely derogatory comments, in an attempt to force the other person to become engaged in a conversation. This interaction pattern results in a great deal of frustration and exasperation for both persons, yet they frequently have no idea how to alter it. Overall, the therapist attempts to help the couple create a safe environment within which the withdrawing partner can engage without fearing retaliation and the demanding partner has alternative ways to seek engagement without being demanding.

Providing Ongoing Feedback About Circular, Mutual Impacts

Most couples recognize the demand–withdraw pattern when it is described by a therapist. Similarly, they understand how this pattern becomes more extreme and escalates during a conversation as well as over time within the relationship. To change this pattern, it is helpful for the couple and the therapist to develop an understanding early in therapy of why this interaction pattern occurs; once these factors are understood, appropriate interventions can be designed. There is no singular basis for this behavioral pattern, so understanding its roots for a particular couple is essential.

On some occasions, the demand–withdraw pattern reflects differences in the two persons' levels of comfort and desires for intimacy and engagement (Prager, 1995). The person who assumes the approach role often has a greater need for intimacy. The person who withdraws might desire less intimacy, greater autonomy, or both, and the withdrawal is an attempt to decrease intimacy.

In other instances this pattern reflects each person's typical style of dealing with stress, with one person routinely confronting and addressing difficulties directly, and the other withdrawing and distancing himself or herself from the stressor (Lazarus & Folkman, 1984). Alternatively, this pattern can reflect a difference in the two partners' desires to change a given situation. An individual who wants change typically must make that desire known and approach the other person. Some partners withdraw to maintain the status quo, as we described in chapter 5 in our discussion of interactions associated with power. When there is a power differential between the two partners, the less powerful person needs to approach the more powerful individual one to effect change.

On other occasions, the demand–withdraw pattern reflects a difference in the two individuals' comfort in expressing, or ability to express, themselves verbally (Baucom & Epstein, 1990); that is, one partner is more verbally facile then the other. Consequently, when they have a discussion, the more verbal member tends to dominate the interaction, and the less verbal partner feels inadequate or unable to hold his or her own in the conversation. Similarly, some individuals have had the experience that if they express their opinions their partners punish them in some manner. As a result, they avoid or withdraw from these aversive interactions. Once the basis for a particular couple's demand–withdraw pattern is known, the therapist and couple can devise strategies for attempting to alter the pattern.

Establishing Guidelines for Couples' Interactions

During the initial treatment sessions, the therapist can attempt to set guidelines for reducing both demands and withdrawal. It is important to discuss various verbal and nonverbal forms of demands and withdrawal. Among the more obvious are instances of one person following the other around and trying to initiate conversation while the partner leaves a room or the house. More subtle actions include changing the subject of a conversation from a neutral topic to a personal one (demand), or vice versa (withdrawal), and the degree to which each person looks at the partner versus other foci such as a television or passersby. After reviewing the negative consequences of demand–withdrawal patterns, the therapist and couple can develop guidelines for communication and noncommunication behaviors that are neither aggressively demanding nor actively withdrawing. For example, an individual may directly request a break from talking with the partner but should not unilaterally cut off communication unless the partner is behaving abusively. These guidelines then are followed during all subsequent sessions.

Whereas providing general guidelines to avoid the demand–withdraw pattern can be of assistance to couples, understanding why the pattern occurs can suggest additional specific changes that might benefit the couple. If the pattern reflects differences between the partners in level of desired intimacy, then the therapist will discuss with the couple that their different needs, a source of primary distress, should be a major focus in therapy. The interventions for primary distress that are described throughout this book, and especially in the second section of this chapter, can be used as soon as any problematic secondary-distress interaction patterns have been decreased.

If the pattern results because one person's typical style is to address concerns when they arise but the other individual likes to back away from problems before addressing them, then the couple can problem-solve on how to address such differences. For example, the couple might agree that when one person has a concern he or she would like to address, that person will tell the other, and they will decide on a mutually agreeable time to address the issue. Often the person who is in the approach role believes that "If I don't force the issue, we'll never deal with it." Thus, by agreeing on a time to address issues, the partner who wishes to discuss the issue does not need to force discussions prematurely.

Likewise, if the demand–withdraw pattern results from an apparent power differential, the therapist can coach the couple in agreeing to problem-solve on issues of concern to either person. If the individual who has had less power perceives that the couple has a new way of making decisions that allows his or her preferences to be heard and considered, then the need to demand decreases. Similarly, if the partners agree that one person is more verbal and the other person has more difficulty holding his or her own in conversations, the couple can agree that both people will have an opportunity to express their opinions and preferences when problem solving. The more verbal member will do his or her best to avoid overwhelming the other person with superior verbal skills.

In addition to being overwhelmed verbally, one person might withdraw because he or she feels punished in other ways by the partner for speaking or being engaged. For example, the person in the demand role might express emotions at a level of intensity that is aversive to the withdrawing partner, or he or she might consistently criticize the withdrawing partner's ideas. The therapist can identify these specific behaviors that fuel demand–withdraw patterns and then coach the couple in using guidelines for altering them. When such a pattern exists, it is important that the therapist intervene with it quickly, to facilitate the mutual communication that will be needed to resolve core relationship issues.

Modifying Cognitions and Emotions That Elicit Demand Responses to a Partner's Withdrawal

Interventions for the demand component of a demand–withdraw pattern are for the most part the same as those described in the previous section on mutual aggression. However, there are some particular types of cognitive and affective responses that may mediate an individual's tendency to pursue a partner who is withdrawing, and these require intervention early in therapy. Perhaps among the most common are those involving insecurity and anxiety, including insecure attachment responses, which we described in chapter 4. Individuals who feel threatened, anxious, and even angry when they perceive that a partner is physically or emotionally unavailable often pressure the partner for more attention and nurturing behavior. If the partner responds to the demands by withdrawing more, the insecure individual may become even more distressed and escalate the demands. Consequently, couples therapists need to determine the degree to which an individual's demanding behavior in response to a partner's withdrawal is elicited by cognitions and emotions associated with insecurity (Johnson & Greenberg, 1995). In such instances, cognitive-restructuring techniques (see chapter 10) may be used to help the individual examine the belief that the partner is rejecting him or her. Often, if any intervention reduces the person's demanding actions, the partner responds to the decreased pressure by withdrawing less, and the demander's insecure responses decrease. If it appears that an individual's level of insecurity is so high that the therapist cannot pay sufficient attention to it in the context of joint couple sessions, a recommendation for individual therapy may be appropriate.

Modifying Cognitions That Contribute to Withdrawal

Withdrawal behavior often results from beliefs that remaining in close contact with one's partner is dangerous or that it will lead to some negative consequence. An individual who selectively notices ways in which a partner treats him or her poorly may conclude that withdrawal will minimize the costs of being in the relationship. Interventions described in chapter 10 for reducing selective perceptions may counteract such a bias and reduce the person's withdrawal.

Some individuals predict that they or the partner will do something harmful if they allow themselves to express their thoughts and emotions. In some cases the expectancy is based on a memory of a past incident when such negative consequences did occur. Thus, Carla had vivid memories of being ridiculed by her parents any time she expressed her opinions. Interventions that may help modify distorted, negative expectancies include (a) helping the individual understand gradations of expressiveness (counteracting dichotomous thinking), (b) exploring the drawbacks of failing to discuss important topics with one's partner, and (c) enlisting the person's partner to help the person practice constructive expressive skills. We typically integrate these cognitive interventions with behavioral interventions. Coaching the couple in constructive communication also may decrease the person's expectancy that the partner will respond negatively. Thus, Carla had less reason to fear that Trevor would belittle her ideas because he was encouraged to focus on reflective listening.

Decreasing Deficits in Emotional Awareness and Expression That Lead to Withdrawal

Other individuals have difficulty verbalizing their emotions and withdraw from their partner to avoid the discomfort of being in an emotional situation. It is crucial to intervene early in therapy to reduce factors that inhibit an individual's expression of important feelings. In chapter 11 we described several strategies for accessing and heightening emotional experiences. Beginning in the first couple assessment session, the therapist creates a safe atmosphere in which the individual can experience and express emotions by setting guidelines for mutually respectful behavior between partners. Second, the therapist uses empathic listening skills to convey interest in and validation of the individual's feelings. The therapist then can coach the partner in reflecting the person's feelings in a similar manner. Third, by asking the individual to describe feelings in more detail, the therapist may be able to elicit hints of emotions that previously were not expressed. Individuals who have difficulty differentiating among emotions can be given a list of frequently used words for describing positive and negative emotions (see chapter 11 and Appendix 9C). When the therapist has established rapport with an individual, he or she also may be able to present "interpretations" concerning cognitions and emotions that the person did not express but that were suggested by the circumstances.

Interventions for Mutual Withdrawal Patterns

A relationship in which both partners withdraw decreases the likelihood of immediate conflict. Thus, couples evidencing this pattern of interaction often see themselves as "nice people" who do not want to behave negatively or say hurtful things to their partners. Nevertheless, even when members of a couple have a tacit agreement of "Let's not make waves," the pattern is likely to have drawbacks for their relationship (Christensen & Shenk, 1991; Gottman, 1999). On the one hand, the couple's lack of interaction can interfere with their ability to work together to accomplish tasks for the maintenance of their home or family, or to respond to either person's needs that are not being met. In addition, mutual withdrawal can help to avoid immediate conflict, but it also contributes to greater distance between partners, such that they can begin to feel isolated or even detached.

In contrast to a couple with a demand–withdraw pattern, partners who both withdraw are likely to reinforce each other's problematic response because they may view each other's responses as natural and desirable. Consequently, at times the therapist is the primary agent seeking change in the couple's mutual-withdrawal pattern. The following are examples of interventions that are especially relevant for intervening with these couples. Because many of the interventions are similar to those used with withdrawing partners in demand–withdraw patterns, we describe details only of those that vary when used with mutual withdrawal.

Noting Mutual Withdrawal and Establishing Guidelines for Couples' Interactions

When a therapist identifies a mutual-withdrawal pattern in a couple, it is important to bring it to their attention in an early treatment session and set guidelines that encourage greater interaction between partners. The therapist can note that the partners seem to dislike conflict, value politeness, and often are concerned about upsetting the other person. The therapist then can give a brief didactic presentation on the advantages and disadvantages of mutual withdrawal. On the one hand, it creates a relatively serene atmosphere in their home, and neither person needs to worry much about hurting the other's feelings. On the other hand, mutual withdrawal blocks the couple's ability to identify and collaborate on resolving issues that concern either person or their relationship. Furthermore, many couples who engage in mutual withdrawal think dichotomously, that they either must avoid or have destructive arguments. The therapist can clarify that the goal is to help them continue to be "nice people" but individuals who respectfully can present concerns for the well-being of each person and the relationship.

Modifying Cognitions That Contribute to Mutual Withdrawal

In working with mutual withdrawal, the therapist can use the same types of interventions used to address cognitions associated with withdrawal in a demand–withdraw pattern. In addition, the therapist also may need to modify specific types of cognitions that can result from two individuals observing each other's withdrawal. For example, an individual who is overly concerned about the possibility of hurting others' feelings may inaccurately attribute a partner's withdrawal as a sign that the partner is fragile and could not tolerate hearing about the person's views. The therapist must counteract the circular process in which each person is hypervigilant and selectively attends to cues that the other does not want to deal with issues, thus creating a "walking on eggshells" culture in the relationship. The therapist may counteract these negative perceptions and inferences by setting guidelines during initial therapy sessions for constructive interaction, emphasizing the positive values and good manners of both partners and eliciting feedback from each individual that he or she feels capable of tolerating the other's opinions and feelings. Soon after introducing these guidelines, the therapist can coach the couple in the use of expressive and listening skills to discuss topics, beginning with relatively benign ones. The therapist also can help the couple adjust their standards for appropriate expressiveness by stressing that neither person is ever likely to develop a confrontational style but, by increasing their ability to discuss areas of concern, they will be able to adapt to issues that arise from time to time.

Using Strategies to Increase Awareness and Expression of Emotion

The therapist can apply the interventions described above in the *Demand–Withdraw Patterns* section for enhancing two withdrawn individuals' abilities to monitor and express their emotions, beginning in the early sessions. As noted earlier, the primary differences in treating two withdrawing partners simultaneously involve the ways in which they elicit and reinforce each other's avoidance of interaction. The therapist may initially need to be the main source of reflective listening as each person is encouraged to express thoughts and feelings, because neither partner feels comfortable reflecting what the other has expressed. The therapist can coach each person in reflecting, beginning with benign topics. Each person's concerns about how the other will react to the person's expressions may be addressed by encouraging the other person to discuss his or her readiness to listen. Given that the partners may share the same inhibitions against expression, the therapist also can coach them in supporting each other's communication efforts.

Interventions for Disengagement Patterns

Disengagement involves subjective, internal experiences as well as overt behavior. An individual who is psychologically disengaged from a partner has stopped trying to fulfill his or her personal needs within the relationship and has reached a state of acceptance that the partner is not a viable source of gratification. Gottman (1999), in reviewing research on couples' disengagement, concluded that "most marriages end with a whimper, the result of people gradually drifting apart and not feeling liked, loved, and respected" (p. 24). The psychologically disengaged person may interact behaviorally with the partner, or the person may withdraw to invest time and energy elsewhere, but in either case there is minimal interest in the partner. As Paula stated, "I care about Arnold as a person and want him to have a happy life, but I just don't look to him as a part of my life now."

Disengagement is difficult to treat, because a disengaged individual lacks motivation to work on the relationship. Often a disengaged person's partner is more engaged and is pressing him or her to invest time and energy in the relationship. On the surface, this may resemble a demand–withdraw pattern, but it lacks the withdrawing individual's emotional motivation (e.g., fear of rejection by the partner or fear of being hurt by the partner). A disengaged individual's primary motivation for attending couples therapy often is to appease and reduce pressure from the more engaged partner. In other instances, the disengaged partner is seeking the safe environment of a therapy setting to tell the partner that the relationship is over for him or her. Some disengaged partners are engaged in affairs, and the revelation of the infidelity may have been the driving force behind the couple's seeking therapy. In cases of infidelity, as we describe in chapter 13, it is crucial for the therapist to intervene quickly, using a crisis intervention framework, to help the partners absorb the blow of this trauma to each person and the relationship and to eventually work toward a decision of whether they want to stay together.

Although disengaged individuals commonly lack motivation to commit themselves to working toward a goal of saving the relationship, they may accept a role of exploring whether the couple has the potential to relate in more satisfying ways, in spite of being skeptical about the chances for such change. Therefore, after confirming that the individual feels detached, the therapist can note that people cannot simply create feelings that are lacking. However, an individual can choose to invest time and energy in trying to change a relationship and seeing what effect any changes might have on one's feelings about a partner. In spite of a lack of emotional drive to work on one's relationship, a person may do so for particular logical reasons, such as the welfare of the couple's children. The therapist also might comment that it appears that the couple has never before had an opportunity when both individuals decided to invest energy in the relationship at the same time and had a therapist to guide them in doing so. Our experience is that, in many couples, one member gradually disengaged from the relationship while the other was preoccupied with other concerns, such as developing a career. When the latter person finally is more available, he or she is surprised and alarmed to find that the partner is now the one whose time and energy are invested in other aspects of life. The therapist can stress that this development is unfortunate but that they now have an opportunity to focus on their relationship at the same time.

The therapist also can point out the imbalance in the amounts of energy the two partners are investing in their relationship. As long as that pattern continues, the imbalance in their levels of caring about the relationship is likely to persist. The therapist can note that people often come to value things in which they invest time and energy, so the less the disengaged person invests in the relationship the more detached the person will feel. If the more engaged individual is willing to give less, and the disengaged person is willing to give more to the partner for a while, the greater involvement might be rewarding and increase intimacy. It is important that the therapist differentiate between making a commitment to working on the relationship for a fixed amount of time versus making a commitment to being with one's partner indefinitely. The therapist should present such suggestions as experiments in which the disengaged person can invest energy in the relationship and then observe what, if any, impact it has on his or her feelings toward the partner. The therapist needs to acknowledge that the changes may make little or no difference and that after a trial period the couple still needs to decide the best course of action. If the individual still feels disengaged, the couple can consider options such as separating or staying together but redefining their roles in each other's lives. Thus, this process initially involves a cognitive-restructuring intervention intended to reduce the disengaged partner's perception that he or she is being pressured into making insincere promises of commitment to the relationship.

When the therapist suggests such a trial period, sometimes the engaged partner has a response such as, "I don't want her to do all that if she doesn't really feel like it." The therapist can stress that the disengaged partner is willing to make efforts for the sake of the years that the couple has invested in their relationship, for the well-being of their children, or whatever source of motivation is relevant. The therapist may need to coach the engaged partner in refraining from criticizing the disengaged partner for what he or she perceives as halfhearted efforts; the disengaged person's efforts to engage despite a lack of positive feelings should be recognized. The following types of interventions may be helpful in intervening with couples that include a disengaged member.

Establishing Guidelines for Couples' Interactions

If the partners agree to experiment with making changes in their relationship, the therapist can formalize the new pattern by recommending that they follow particular behavioral guidelines, during sessions and at home. The guidelines might include ways in which the engaged partner can reduce his or her investment behavior as well as ways in which the disengaged partner can express investment. Because a disengaged person often has shifted investment to outside people and activities (e.g., friends, a job), the guidelines might include reducing particular ways in which the person invests time with them.

Modifying Cognitions That Reduce Motivation to Work on the Relationship

As we noted earlier, a psychologically disengaged individual typically lacks emotions that might provide motivation to invest time and energy in the relationship. Consequently, in an early session a therapist may need to modify a person's belief that there is no good reason to work on a relationship unless one "feels like it." The therapist might identify other situations in which the person took actions even when there was no emotional drive to do so, based on logical reasons. For example, Jack had taken courses at the local college, not because he felt excited about doing so but because he knew it increased his chances for advancement at his job. The therapist also identified that Jack had enjoyed some of the classes once he became involved in them. These interventions may increase the person's belief that actions can be taken in the absence of positive emotions and in fact may produce positive feelings.

Some disengaged individuals predict that if they put energy into the relationship their partner will erroneously conclude that they have become more engaged and committed. Because this expectancy may be well founded, it is important for the therapist to guide the person in expressing the fear. It is desirable for the engaged partner to state that he or she will resist assuming that the person's efforts reflect increased positive feelings, but the disengaged partner still may be concerned that his or her effort will be misinterpreted. Consequently, the therapist can periodically ask the engaged partner how he or she is interpreting changes in the disengaged person's behavior.

Reducing External Demands on the Disengaged Person

Sometimes an individual's disengagement from a partner results from external demands that drain energy that the person might otherwise invest in the relationship. At times the individual is aware of the dampening effects that the external demands have on his or her feelings toward the partner, but in other cases the person just feels detached and is unsure why, an ambiguous demand of the sort described by Boss (1988). When the person attributes the disengaged feelings to problems in the relationship rather than to the environmental demands, his or her level of motivation to work on the relationship or on reducing those demands may be low. During an initial session, the therapist can describe ways in which environmental demands can affect people's feelings about their relationships and can discuss with the disengaged person the possibility of trying to reduce specific demands and to observe the impact on the feeling of detachment. Thus, if the couple's intimacy needs have been neglected for years because of one or both partners' job demands, the therapist might coach them in using expressive and listening skills to share their thoughts and feelings about the situation. Next, the therapist could guide the couple in decision-making discussions to devise ways to increase intimacy within the time constraints imposed by their jobs.

Increasing Emotional Experience and Expression

Sometimes interventions for facilitating awareness and expression of feelings among actively withdrawn partners also may be successful in increasing a disengaged individual's feelings toward a partner. In addition, if the disengaged individual's failure to be aware of and express emotions has contributed to the other partner's tendency to overlook those feelings, the individual's increased expression of emotions may help the partner become more responsive to the person's needs.

Moreover, in some cases an individual experiences depression that is unrelated to the quality of the couple relationship but that results in a global emotional "flatness" that includes feeling detached from the partner. When the therapist's assessment suggests that a disengaged person is clinically depressed, it is important to have a discussion with the couple during an early session concerning the treatment options described in chapter 13 and to suggest re-evaluating the person's level of attachment to the partner once any dampening effects of depression have lifted.

Interventions for Building Trust and Repairing Effects of Prior Negative Interactions

The preceding sections describe interventions for couples' *ongoing* mutual attack, demand–withdraw, mutual withdrawal, and disengagement patterns that are contributing to secondary distress in their relationships. Reduction of these patterns creates a positive atmosphere in which a couple can work together in resolving basic issues such as differences in their needs. However, partners' memories of *past* negative interactions also may create a global negative atmosphere in which they find it difficult to trust each other and collaborate in addressing core relationship issues. In these cases, there is a need for "repair" or "recovery" from damages from past negative experiences (Gottman, 1999; Wile, 1993). For example, Peter described how he "will never forget the nasty things that Felicia has said to me when we are arguing," and he noted that he has great difficulty trusting her not to abuse him verbally. Even though Felicia adamantly stated that she was committed to their relationship and had stopped attacking Peter verbally, any signs of conflict between the partners revived his memories of her past hurtful behavior and triggered his desire to protect himself by withdrawing. These responses interfered with Peter's ability to discuss any significant issues with Felicia. The couple's therapist helped them see that for them to improve their relationship they needed to recover from the past negative interactions. In this section we describe several approaches therapists can use to help couples rebuild trust and repair effects of negative interactions. Some interventions steer the couple away from ineffective strategies that they have used, whereas others focus on new steps that each person can take. These interventions can be used during initial sessions to overcome partners' reluctance to be engaged in therapy. They also can be used periodically and as the therapist and couple near the end of their work together to reduce the probability that the couple will experience lapses in positive interactions as disheartening relapses (i.e., "we're back to square one").

Focusing Attention on Negative Events That Have Significance for One or Both Individuals

Sometimes individuals who have hurt their partners prefer to move on with daily life and act as if the events never occurred or as if the events should be ignored because they occurred in the past. A drawback to this approach is that the partner who considers the incidents to be significant is likely to view the individual as uncaring, irresponsible, and therefore untrustworthy. For example, when Felicia proposed that Peter should "put the arguments in the past and move on," he concluded that she took no responsibility for abusing him verbally and therefore might do so again in the future. Therefore, a therapist can recommend that both members of a couple explicitly acknowledge that the negative interactions occurred and that they were very upsetting to at least one of them. The therapist also may give a didactic presentation regarding variation in the amounts of time it takes different people to recover from past distressing experiences. Trying to force one's partner to progress faster than is natural for him or her runs the risk of backfiring and increasing the partner's upset, so it generally is best to discuss each person's current feelings and respect them.

Acknowledgement of past negative behavior also can include an agreement between the partners to sit down and discuss a problem again, using more constructive expressive, listening, and decision-making skills. The therapist can guide the couple in noticing how each person demonstrated an ability and willingness to interact positively, a promising sign for the future.

Facilitating Apologies for Negative Behavior

Even though a person who behaved negatively may prefer to put it in the past, it is important for the therapist to encourage the person to acknowledge the behavior and its negative impact on the partner and to express regret that it occurred, if the regret is genuine (Wile, 1993). The therapist should emphasize that apologizing for past negative actions is not equivalent to agreeing that one's partner's ideas and behavior are more valid or correct.

The key is to demonstrate concern for the negative impact that one's actions had on the partner, no matter how benign one believes one's motives were or how negative the partner's own behavior was. When there is a pattern of one person typically being the one to apologize or to try to repair the relationship, the therapist can emphasize the importance of balance, in which both partners demonstrate their willingness to take responsibility for overcoming past negatives.

Planning Noncontingent Positive Acts to Counteract a Pattern of Negative Interaction

A therapist can help a couple devise a plan for each person to behave *noncontingently* in ways that he or she knows the other person would enjoy, to express caring and commitment. Noncontingent positive acts are not based on specific requests from the partner and are not tied to receiving any reinforcement from the partner (Baucom & Epstein, 1990; Jacobson & Margolin, 1979). For example, Frieda decided to take breaks from work to make unplanned phone calls to Peter, just to say hello and share information about each person's day. Some couples benefit from using humor with each other, as long as it involves sharing funny moments rather than either person belittling the other.

When a couple has a history of negative interaction, it is not unusual for each individual to discount the significance of a partner's present positive behavior and to predict that the partner will return to negative behavior at some point. Consequently, increasing positive acts may not reduce secondary distress unless the therapist directly addresses each person's cognitions about the other's behavior. Thus, Peter initially was skeptical of Felicia's motivation ("Maybe she's trying to look good in front of the therapist"). The therapist guided Peter in considering alternative attributions for Felicia's phone calls, and Peter gradually acknowledged that she seemed to be showing some interest in him and in improving their relationship. Nevertheless, noncontingent positive behaviors often must accumulate over time to shift the overall tone of a relationship that was damaged by prior hurtful acts. Therapists must be encouraging and supportive of each person's efforts to behave positively, preparing them for disappointments when the recipient does not appreciate their good intentions. In the early stages of therapy, each person's best sources of reinforcement may be positive feedback from the therapist and self-reinforcement ("I am doing something good for our relationship, even if my partner doesn't realize it yet. I like being this way, even though it is hard when my partner doesn't respond").

Planning and Carrying out Cohesiveness Rituals

Especially after the therapist has helped the couple reduce secondary-distress interactions, he or she can review with the couple types of rituals that have made them feel close in the past as well as new rituals that might enhance a sense of cohesiveness (Gottman, 1999). The couple then schedules times to try these rituals, which may help counteract hurt and alienation from past negative interactions. Thus, Felicia and Peter agreed to meet for lunch once a week, a ritual that they had enjoyed before their busy schedules interfered with it. The therapist cautioned them that their lunches initially might feel contrived and lack the close feelings of the past, so it is best to have modest expectations and make the most of opportunities to share pleasant times.

Conclusions Regarding Interventions for Secondary Distress

When a distressed couple begins therapy, much of the negative interaction that the therapist observes may represent a pattern that the partners developed in the course of trying to resolve basic issues in their relationship. Negative, ineffective ways of coping with concerns such as conflicting needs, personality styles, and life goals may themselves become sources of secondary distress. Patterns such as escalating mutual attacks, demand–withdrawal, and mutual withdrawal may become major factors in partners' distress and even their desire to end the relationship. Other individuals may have become disengaged psychologically from their partners and lack motivation to work on improving their relationships. It is important for a therapist to identify the core underlying issues that remain unresolved in a couple's relationship and help them set goals for addressing those issues. However, the therapist frequently needs to begin by helping the couple reduce interactions that are producing secondary distress to create the more positive, collaborative atmosphere required for work with core issues.

In this section we have described how a therapist can use a variety of interventions detailed in earlier chapters for modifying negative behavior, cognitions, and emotions that comprise attack–attack, demand–withdraw, mutual-withdrawal, and disengagement patterns associated with secondary distress. Among the interventions that may be used are establishing guidelines for the couple's interactions, providing ongoing feedback about their interaction patterns, using techniques for modifying cognitions that contribute to negative affective and behavioral responses to a partner, using methods for either increasing awareness and expression of emotions or for moderating the experience and expression of unregulated emotions, and decreasing automatic negative behavioral responses learned in prior relationships by increasing partners' awareness of their origins and guiding the couple in trying more constructive ways of interacting. The same types of interventions are appropriate for a variety of problematic couples' interactions, but they are adapted according to the particular pattern that the couple exhibits.

Given that patterns producing secondary distress may be ingrained in a couple's interactions, the therapist may need to use these interventions throughout therapy. As the focus shifts to addressing core relationship issues, the therapist and couple need to be aware of the risk that the partners' primary distress concerning unresolved issues may trigger habitual negative coping responses. Thus, at times the therapist will shift back and forth between the interventions for primary distress described in the next section and those for secondary distress.

INTERVENTIONS FOR RESOLVING CORE DYADIC RELATIONSHIP ISSUES

Differences in partners' needs, preferences, and personality styles have the potential to cause conflict and unhappiness. However, the ways that partners experience differences subjectively and interact with each other about them behaviorally are likely to determine whether they influence the relationship negatively. Partners may be able to adapt well to basic differences between them if they have good problem-solving and conflict resolution skills, appraise them as relatively unimportant, or accept them rather than feeling a need to change each other (Jacobson & Christensen, 1996; Notarius & Markman, 1993). The interventions we describe in this section address partners' behaviors, cognitions, and emotions that influence the couple's ability to resolve differences between them.

Other couples experience primary distress resulting from characteristics on which they are *similar*. Their similarities may result in neglect of particular roles that must be enacted to meet the couple's needs, such as two partners who are equally inattentive to details in daily life and frequently miss appointments and let bills go unpaid. Similarly, in some couples both partners are very relationally oriented and might spend an inordinate amount of time trying to understand each person's behavior by having discussions that never seem to end. This shared tendency might make it difficult for the couple to focus on the mundane aspects of life outside of the relationship. Consequently, in this section we also describe strategies for assisting couples whose primary distress results from their similarities rather than their differences.

Major goals of interventions for primary distress are:

- Increasing partners' awareness of each person's needs or motives, personality styles, and temperament, and the degree to which the couple have found ways to be responsive to both people's needs.
- Increasing partners' acceptance of these individual differences as variations in normal aspects of being human.
- Increasing individuals' sense of self-efficacy and range of strategies for making changes in a relationship that can resolve issues regarding differences or similarities in partners' needs, personality styles, and so forth.

As is the case with therapy for secondary distress, approaches to dealing with primary distress draw on the range of interventions for modifying behavior, cognitions, and emotions that we described in earlier chapters. Consequently, we provide brief descriptions of typical interventions and refer the reader to other chapters in which more details are available.

Increasing Awareness of Partners' Unique Styles and Degrees to Which Relationship Patterns Are Compatible With Both Partners' Needs and Preferences

During the initial assessment of the couple (see chapter 7), the therapist identifies normal needs or motives, other personality styles, and aspects of temperament that tend to be characteristic of each partner. Individuals vary in their awareness of consistency in their own and their partners' cognitive, emotional, and behavioral responses across situations and time. Consequently, when differences or similarities in partners' characteristics appear to be contributing to primary distress, one of the therapist's tasks is to be sure that both individuals are adequately aware of each person's relevant needs, preferences, and so forth. However, in drawing attention to consistencies in each person's characteristics, the therapist also needs to counteract tendencies that individuals may have toward attributing relationship problems to invariant traits.

Inductive "Downward-Arrow" Cognitive Approach

As we discussed in chapter 10, the therapist can guide each individual in identifying an underlying need, value, or other personal characteristic by asking a series of questions concerning the association of one type of cognition with another, broader one. For example, Jerome stated that he was upset that Mira opposed his taking a new job that required frequent, brief trips out of town. When the therapist inquired about the thoughts associated with his distress, he reported, "I was thinking that she's going to block my chances of succeeding in my career." The therapist asked Jerome what it meant to him if he were to be blocked in his career, and he replied, "My dreams of getting ahead and really accomplishing a lot won't come true." When the therapist asked him to describe his dreams about his career and his feelings about them, Jerome said,

> I often picture myself as the president of a company, making major decisions that move the company ahead toward success. It's exciting to imagine that, and it keeps me working hard and looking for opportunities to get ahead. I don't think Mira knows how important that is to me, or she doesn't care.

The therapist's sequence of questions helped uncover Jerome's strong motivation to achieve professionally.

Next, the therapist gave Jerome feedback about his apparent strong desire to achieve, and Jerome agreed that this had been true of him since he was a child. The therapist then asked Mira how aware she had been of Jerome's focus on achievement, using a sequence of "downward-arrow" questions to explore her thoughts about Jerome's job opportunity. She clarified that she had a strong desire to be close to Jerome, which she expected would be disrupted if he traveled frequently. Thus, the therapist had identified important, adaptive needs in each person that had become a source of distress for them.

Deducing Macrolevel Patterns From Cross-Situational Response Patterns

Another method of identifying individuals' needs and personality styles involves identifying common types of responses that the person exhibits across various situations (see chapter 10). When Jerome's therapist asked him about other situations in which he felt frustrated in his relationship with Mira or other people, a majority of the situations Jerome identified had a common theme of other people interfering with his goals.

Similarly, when the therapist asked Mira to report other situations in her relationship with Jerome that tended to upset her, she primarily described instances in which chores, extended family members, friends, or Jerome's work interfered with their opportunities to spend time together. Aside from her irritation at such times, she reported sadness at the lack of intimacy. The therapist discussed with the partners the differences in their basic needs, and the couple agreed that their inability to adapt to the differences was detracting from their marital satisfaction. The therapist stressed that it would be important to find various specific (microlevel) behavior changes that might help fulfill each person's general (macrolevel) needs better. This approach is detailed later in this chapter.

Sometimes one person has difficulty understanding the partner's needs, because these needs or preferences are so different from the person's own desires that they seem foreign. For example, Mira enjoyed being successful in her job and other settings, but she had never known anyone for whom achievement was as important as it was to Jerome. Consequently, she had difficulty empathizing with the frustration and sense of hopelessness that Jerome felt when he perceived impediments to his career opportunities. In fact, she considered his strong need for achievement to be abnormal and was not highly motivated to work with him on devising ways to fulfill his needs better. In the next section, we cover interventions to increase partners' understanding and acceptance of differences in their personal characteristics.

Increasing Partners' Acceptance of Each Other's Personal Characteristics

Members of a couple might perceive differences in their characteristics as variations within a normal range, or they may conclude that one of them has normal, desirable qualities and the other does not. In the latter case each person may view the other's characteristics as problematic, or both members might view one of them as dysfunctional. These types of skewed conclusions can have negative impacts on the couple's ability to adapt to their differences.

- An individual who devalues a partner's characteristics may be less satisfied being in the relationship and frustrated with the partner for not being similar to him or her.
- The devalued partner may feel alienated, angry, and unmotivated to resolve the couple's differences.
- The individual who considers his or her own, but not the partner's, characteristics as normal may take little personal responsibility for resolving their differences.
- The couple may develop ineffective and distressing interaction patterns (i.e., secondary distress), such as the devaluing individual aggressively criticizing and the devalued individual defending or withdrawing.

Thus, lack of empathy and acceptance of each other's personality is likely to involve negative cognitions, emotions, and behaviors. As Jacobson and Christensen (1996) stressed, at times the solution to a couple's differences might lie predominantly in accepting the differences, changing how one thinks and feels about them. At other times it may involve negotiating behavioral changes to decrease the degrees of differences or find better ways to integrate them. We believe that members of a couple are more likely to resolve their differences when both individuals view their own and each other's needs and personality styles as legitimate and normal. Consequently, interventions for increasing acceptance of each other's characteristics include approaches for increasing mutual empathy (understanding each other's subjective experiences) and for modifying individuals' extreme standards about what constitutes appropriate ways of thinking, feeling, and behaving.

Psychoeducational Mini-lectures, Readings, and Videotapes

In chapter 10 we described the use of psychoeducational approaches to broaden clients' views of their relationships. Regarding the need to increase partners' empathy and acceptance of each other's normal personal characteristics, the therapist can use formal "mini-lectures," brief readings, and videotapes to demonstrate normal variability in human needs, personality styles, and temperament. In general, the goal is to counteract individuals' tendencies to think in good–bad or normal–abnormal dichotomies, increasing their awareness that many characteristics exist along a normal continuum. For example, Mira and Jerome's therapist discussed the achievement and intimacy needs that had become issues in their relationship:

Therapist: Both of you have been describing ways in which you have different degrees of desire for achievement and for intimacy. Sometimes it has sounded like you view each other as two very different types of people, even opposites. You have also described how the other person's needs seem unfamiliar and even strange to you, sort of like trying to understand a person from another culture. However, there is substantial research evidence that people vary widely in their degrees of motivation for achievement as well as for intimacy. What sometimes is challenging is when two people with different levels of a need form a close relationship and discover that they have to find ways to adapt to their differences, because the differences affect the ways that the two people behave in daily life. It doesn't work well if partners try to pressure each other to be more like themselves, because each person is responding to his or her normal needs. What does seem to work is when both individuals do their best to learn about the other's needs, communicate their understanding and acceptance of the other person's characteristics, and work together to find better ways of living with the differences. You are concerned about your different levels of motivation for achievement and for intimacy, so let's discuss what options you may have for dealing with the normal differences that exist between you.

Books and videotapes such as Markman et al.'s (1994) *Fighting for Your Marriage* normalize gender differences in communication styles, although therapists need to beware of popular literature that tends to dichotomize and stereotype gender differences.

Expressive and Listening Skills

Throughout this book, we have emphasized the value that communication training can have for increasing mutual understanding and validation between partners. Even though it is stressed that empathic reflective listening does not require that a person agree with the ideas and emotions that the partner is expressing, placing oneself in the partner's frame of reference often leads an individual to become more sympathetic toward and accepting of the partner's responses (Guerney, 1977; Jacobson & Christensen, 1996). The structure imposed by the guidelines for expression and listening slow the interaction, allowing some individuals to learn more about a partner's experiences. Often a couple has escalated their arguments so quickly that neither of them has listened well enough to fully understand the other's motivation and values, and each person's criticism and defensiveness gave the other the impression that their differences were insurmountable. Many therapists primarily coach couples in reflecting each other's messages to increase the degree to which they listen to each other. However, the use of expressive and listening skills also may produce cognitive shifts in which each person comes to view the other's personal characteristics as more reasonable and normal, rather than dismissing them as inappropriate. This increased acceptance may increase partners' openness to decision-making discussions with each other, with the goal of finding ways to allow each person to be himself or herself within the relationship.

Role-Taking Exercises

Another approach to increasing partners' acceptance of each other's characteristics is to ask them to engage in role reversals, in which they role play each other while discussing experiences associated with their needs and personality styles. As we described in chapter 10, the therapist can emphasize that role playing the other person often helps one gain a sense of how he or she thinks and feels and that this perspective may make the other person's differences seem less strange or unreasonable. Thus, when Rowena role played Len, describing the great satisfaction that he derived from socializing with other people, she found herself "able to feel a little of the pleasure he must feel when he's hanging around with people he likes, trading stories, and talking about topics like politics." Rowena noted that she could never be as eager to socialize as Len is, but she became somewhat less likely to judge his extraversion as abnormal. The therapist was able to shift the couple's focus away from whose personality was more normal to discussions of how they could adapt to the difference in their affiliation tendencies.

Reattribution Interventions

As we noted earlier, a key goal of psychoeducation, communication skills practice, and role-taking exercises is to modify partners' negative cognitions about each other's characteristics to produce greater empathy and acceptance of differences. Individuals who more fully understand each other's needs, personality styles, and temperament still may prefer that the other person behaved differently but may be less likely to take the other's actions personally. Often a couple's therapist needs to guide each individual in considering the validity of negative attributions that he or she has made about causes of the partner's behavior. For example, because Carl had attributed Noreen's enjoyment of autonomy to her not caring about him, the therapist guided Carl in considering alternative explanations based on the information that Noreen had expressed about her experiences. Because Carl grew up in a close-knit family and had always had a strong desire to affiliate with other people, he automatically made an inference that her choosing of autonomous activities reflected a rejection of others rather than an attraction to the solitary activities. The therapist asked Carl to consider information that Noreen provided about the pleasure she anticipated and experienced when she was able to sit by herself and have no distractions while she read a book, listened to music, or explored the Internet for information about other countries and cultures. Carl noted that

I can see that when she's thinking about doing something alone, she's focused on the fun of doing it, and she's not thinking that it will be great to get away from me. It's less upsetting to think of it that way.

The reattribution process may result in a more benign view of the partner's characteristics and increased motivation to discuss ways to meet the partner's needs as well as one's own. However, the attributional shift may not make it clearer to the two individuals how they could integrate their different characteristics. The couple may need assistance in creatively generating new ways of interacting, so they can perceive that their needs are not mutually exclusive. In a later section we describe procedures for developing new interaction patterns.

Modification of Extreme or Inflexible Standards

An individual who does not accept a partner's characteristics makes a judgment that those characteristics fail to meet his or her personal standards for ways that a partner "should" be. Consequently, one way of increasing one's acceptance of a partner involves redefining the partner's characteristics so they are perceived as fitting into one's existing standards. For example, when Carl no longer attributed Noreen's interest in autonomous activities as stemming from detachment from him, her behavior fit within his standards for the type of emotional bond that should exist between partners. He then was able to view her autonomous behavior as a separate type of characteristic that coexisted with her desire for closeness with him. Thus, he did not need to modify his standard about having a high level of closeness in their relationship.

Another way of increasing acceptance of a partner's characteristics is to broaden the range of one's standards for what is appropriate. Thus, even when Carl made more positive attributions for Noreen's autonomy motivation, he still was uncomfortable with the idea that she enjoyed solitary time, because he strongly believed that a couple's top priority should be sharing time and activities with each other. He believed that she valued closeness with him, but he stated, "There's just so much time in every day, and she can't be close with me and do all those other things at the same time. Each of us has to make some sacrifices."

In chapter 10 we describe how a therapist may be able to "soften" an individual's extreme or rigid standard by guiding him or her in comparing the advantages and disadvantages of living according to the standard. Among the advantages that Carl listed for his standard that Noreen's top priority should be sharing time with him were that he would have frequent concrete reminders of her commitment and would not need to expend any effort to reassure himself about it, and he would have consistent companionship and would not need to find ways to entertain himself. Carl had difficulty identifying disadvantages of his standard until the therapist asked him to think about its impact on Noreen. He could see that at times she might feel deprived of opportunities to do things that were very satisfying for her and might feel obligated to do things with him. When the therapist asked Carl how he might feel if he knew that Noreen felt pressured to choose togetherness each time she thought about doing something by herself, he said he probably would feel "a little selfish and guilty, and I'd always be wondering if she was enjoying our time together." Thus, he could see that imposing his standard on Noreen could detract from the quality of the times that they spent together, because it raised the question of whether she chose togetherness of her own free will. Noreen entered the discussion, agreeing that Carl's standard "feels like he's controlling my choices, and I want to be able to choose to spend time with him because I'm looking forward to it." The therapist coached Carl in thinking of ways to modify his standard such that it retained his basic valuing of togetherness but included acceptance of Noreen's interest in some autonomous activities. Carl suggested that a reasonable standard might be stated as

> In a close relationship, the two people value each other a lot and enjoy being together. They make choices to be together and try not to coerce each other. Noreen and I should show our special bond by taking each other's needs into account. Sometimes Noreen should consider how much I value togetherness and be sure we have a lot of that. However, I also should consider the pleasure she gains from doing some things on her own and show I think she's special by letting her be herself and do those things.

It is important to note that many individuals fail to shift their long-standing standards as easily as this example might suggest. Often a therapist needs to draw an individual's attention to disadvantages of a standard that the person has overlooked or minimized and may need to guide the individual in imagining a scenario concerning the impact of the standard on the couple's relationship over a period of time. For example, the therapist might ask Carl to imagine how he and Noreen would get along if he pressed her to substitute joint activities for most of her individual ones, imagining whether they would become closer or more distant. Therapists should avoid imposing their own standards when challenging an individual's standards about a partner's characteristics. However, we believe that when a therapist perceives potential drawbacks to a person's standard it is appropriate to bring these to the person's attention so that he or she can evaluate the pros and cons of the belief.

Some individuals are uncomfortable thinking that their partners' characteristics can be different from their own, yet both are normal and appropriate ways of thinking, feeling, and behaving. In such cases the therapist may need to use psychoeducational interventions, such as mini-lectures and readings that describe normal differences in male and female gender roles. It is important to emphasize that the differences are "just different ways of relating to others" rather than one being superior to the other. Sometimes it also is helpful to remind the couple that they reported being attracted to each other by some of the characteristics on which they differ and that the difference has become more of an issue over time as the partners have become aware of some of the drawbacks associated with those tendencies. Thus, Helen always knew that Charlie was an organized person, but it was not until they had lived together for a few years that she realized how much he preferred to structure his time, activities, and home. When the therapist asked Helen if she imagined that their relationship would be more satisfying for her if Charlie became less organized, she replied that they might end up in some trouble, because she tends to be relatively disorganized. As she stated, "If one of us wasn't taking charge of keeping our finances and home in order, it could be chaotic."

When a couple is experiencing difficulty because of a characteristic on which they are similar, they still may make negative comparisons with each other concerning their relative degrees of the characteristic. For example, Tia and Allen both were highly motivated to achieve in their work and personal lives. This similarity had attracted them to each other, and each understood and supported their pursuit of excellence. As the couple faced increasing responsibilities from buying a house and having their first child, they began to perceive each other as the person who was too busy pursuing personal goals to do a fair share of the household work. Their therapist helped them see that they still valued similar achievement goals but needed to be creative and flexible in finding new ways to integrate their family responsibilities into the career pattern that had worked well in the past. Because the couple tended to blame each other for the problems, the therapist guided them toward making more external attributions for the source of difficulty; recognizing that their relationship functioned well until the demands of a baby and new house had been added to the mix. The therapist pointed out that both partners had lived according to a standard emphasizing support for one's own and the other person's achievement and that this shared standard predominantly had advantages for them in the past. The therapist coached Tia and Allen in devising a modified standard that emphasized valuing each other's achievement motivation, empathizing with the internal conflict each felt about the costs of neglecting either work or family, and supporting each other's efforts to balance roles.

Some other couples have difficulty considering making changes in a particular shared characteristic that they consider to be a defining characteristic of their relationship. Mike and Dawn were drawn to each other by their shared tendencies to experience and express their emotions in a moderately unregulated way. Their emotional intensity contributed to a feeling of intimacy and a very pleasurable sexual relationship. Consequently, they viewed it as a key aspect of "who we are as a couple." However, their unregulated emotional expression also had led to instances of emotional and physical abuse, such as demeaning criticism, slapping, and shoving. When their therapist suggested that eliminating the abuse might involve increasing their ability to regulate their emotions, the couple initially became defensive, suggesting that they did not want the therapist to try to "make us like some of the couples we know who have boring lives with no excitement." It was important that the therapist avoid being viewed by the couple as devaluing a quality that they valued so highly. Thus, the therapist spent a good deal of time talking with Mike and Dawn about all of the special experiences that they have shared and then emphasized that he had no intention of trying to make changes that might deprive them of similar future experiences. The therapist then introduced the idea of "compartmentalizing" emotional experiences such that the couple can choose to have intense experiences at particular times but also control certain types of emotional expression, such as abusive expressions of anger, at other times. A key was to validate the couple's basic standard concerning their similar characteristic while demonstrating to them that making specific changes to resolve an area of concern need not change the overall ways that the partners relate to each other.

Increasing Skills and Self-Efficacy for Resolving Dyadic Concerns

Although partners' cognitive and emotional changes of greater understanding and acceptance of differences between them are important aspects of resolving relationship concerns, often couples will remain distressed unless they gain confidence that they can effectively reduce or accommodate differences. In the first section of this chapter, we described how a sense of hopelessness about resolving differences often contributes to couples' developing distressing interactions such as mutual attack or a demand–withdraw pattern. Consequently, therapists may be able to help reduce both current and future distress by increasing couples' behavioral skills and sense of efficacy for coping with their concerns. We assume that initially a therapist may be able to use primarily cognitive interventions to boost partners' optimism that they can resolve issues more effectively, but the couple needs to observe some success firsthand through behavioral interventions to maintain that confidence (Baucom & Epstein, 1990; Epstein, 1985; Epstein, Baucom, & Daiuto, 1997). Other couples may not experience any increased sense of efficacy until they see positive results. The following are some interventions that can be used to develop behavioral skills and increased efficacy expectancies.

Psychoeducational Presentations

Just as psychoeducational mini-lectures, videotapes, and readings can be useful in increasing partners' acceptance of each other's characteristics as normal, they may be used to increase expectancies that using particular behavioral skills can help resolve concerns about those characteristics. For example, books for lay readers concerning communication and problem-solving skills, such as Notarius and Markman's (1993) *We Can Work It Out*, Markman et al.'s (1994) *Fighting For Your Marriage*, and Christensen and Jacobson's (2000) *Reconcilable Differences* present constructive, optimistic arguments that with some effort couples should be able to resolve differences and increase satisfaction in their relationships. These books may be especially convincing for some individuals because they cite research evidence that the skills they describe can be effective. In addition, videotapes such as those made to accompany Markman et al.'s (1994) book include couples giving testimonials about the positive impact of the communication skills, as well as numerous samples of couple discussions with versus without use of the skills. There is no guarantee that a couple will respond to these motivational aspects of psychoeducational materials by concluding, "If it works for those couples, it can work for us," but many couples seem to be sufficiently impressed that they are willing to put time and effort into experimenting with the procedures.

Communication and Decision-Making Skills

We will not reiterate the details of expressive, listening, and decision-making skills that we described in chapter 9. However, it is important to note that the main goals in using those interventions to help a couple resolve issues associated with their personal characteristics are

- Achieving mutual understanding of exactly what differences or similarities in the two individuals' characteristics create a demand or concern that requires a new approach.
- Identifying the process through which a difference or similarity has a negative impact (e.g., Mike and Dawn's similar emotional dysregulation produced rapid escalation of anger, with no mechanisms for inhibiting abusive behavior).
- Collaboratively identifying one or more feasible changes that the couple could try to decrease the typical interaction pattern and substitute a potentially constructive one, making sure to accommodate both people's needs in the proposed solution in addressing these core relationship issues.
- Giving the couple repeated opportunities to practice the new behavior, both with coaching from the therapist and at home, and to observe the effects on the targeted issue.

Details regarding the process of *how* a difference or similarity between partners affects them can be "fleshed out" by having the couple use expressive and listening skills to discuss the concern. Thus, at a general level, Nina and Grace had noted that their different desires for autonomy often led to arguments. However, when each person had an opportunity to express more fully how she experienced the difference on a daily basis, some possibilities for changing the pattern became clearer. Nina described how she did not enjoy winter sports as Grace did but felt hurt when Grace chose to go cross-country skiing with friends rather than spending the day with her. Nina stressed that when there is an activity that she likes more than Grace does, she usually chooses to forego it. As Grace reflected back Nina's messages, Nina also expressed jealousy that Grace was spending time with particular female friends and fear that Grace might leave her for someone else with whom she shared more leisure interests. This discussion revealed that the difference posed more than a problem with reconciling the partners' different autonomy needs. For Nina, Grace's activities with her own friends represented a threat to the stability of their relationship, raising issues of their relative levels of commitment and trustworthiness. The therapist guided them in discussing these important issues of commitment and trust as a prerequisite to finding mutually acceptable ways of handling their autonomy issue.

Thus, therapists must be aware that a difference between partners may be a "loaded issue" for one or both of them because of idiosyncratic meanings that each person attaches to the difference. It may be necessary to address the validity of each person's negative cognitions about the difference, using interventions we detailed in chapter 10, to decrease the negative impact that the difference has on each individual. In some cases, modifying the negative cognitions will eliminate the need for the couple to negotiate new ways of interacting regarding a difference in a personal characteristic. Thus, as Nina considered many ways in which Grace had demonstrated commitment to her, she began to be less concerned about Grace's social activities.

The therapist can coach a couple in decision-making discussions to identify new ways to interact regarding a difference or similarity in a personal characteristic. Sometimes members of a couple overestimate the extent of change that is needed, so the therapist can encourage them to think of small adjustments in the ways that they interact that may be sufficient to resolve the issue. For example, when partners who both pay little attention to details of daily life develop problems such as a messy home or overdue bills, they may believe that only a major change in their personality styles will be sufficient to reduce the chaos. With this view, they may feel discouraged when asked to brainstorm possible changes that they could try. Consequently, the therapist may need to guide them in listing smaller changes and being open to initiating and evaluating them on a trial basis. Perhaps the couple will experience relief and an increased sense of efficacy if they list several small but important chores (e.g., removing stacks of accumulated mail from their kitchen table and sorting it) and successfully schedule and carry out one of the tasks together for an hour during the next week. The therapist can emphasize that the couple can make progress toward a broader (macrolevel) change concerning their personal characteristics by focusing on specific (microlevel) actions that contribute to the larger pattern. This approach can help counteract partners' cognitions associated with hopelessness about their relationship, such as, "We're basically very different people, and we can't change who we are. This relationship just won't work." The key is to encourage the couple to experiment with specific, alternative solutions and learn from the results which specific changes are most satisfying and sustainable.

"As-If" Behavioral Experiments

Some individuals are reluctant to try new ways of interacting regarding differences or similarities, because they are concerned that doing so commits them to continuing the changes. The therapist may motivate them to try a new approach by describing it as an opportunity to "see what it is like to be a certain way even when you are not actually that way." The therapist can suggest that reluctant partners act "as if" they were a little more similar or different from each other or had a different way of responding to their similarity or difference. For example, Nina and Grace's therapist addressed their approach to their different degrees of autonomy.

> Therapist: It appears that you see yourselves as very different, almost opposites, in the degree to which you seek out and enjoy separate activities versus togetherness. As long as you believe and act as if you are so different, you may continue to feel hopeless about ever working out your differences. Sometimes it may help to act as if a difference really isn't so great, and that there's a middle ground that feels comfortable to both of you. I'm not suggesting that either of you has to actually commit yourself to becoming less or more independent. What I am suggesting is that we can all learn a lot if during the coming week you would be willing to act as if the two of you are somewhat more similar regarding preferences for separate versus shared activities. (The therapist then asks each person to describe what types of behavior she might exhibit if the partners were more similar. Next, the therapist asks them if they would be willing to try behaving in these ways just for the coming week and then to report about the experience during the next therapy session.)

Conclusions Regarding Interventions for Primary Distress

Usually the first step toward resolving issues involving differences and similarities in partners' needs and preferences is to use interventions designed to increase their awareness of their own and each other's characteristics, such as noting both persons' needs and the degree to which their interaction patterns are compatible with those characteristics. Individuals who lack awareness of their macrolevel characteristics may be assisted in identifying them by means of cognitive interventions such as the downward-arrow approach and deducing patterns from consistencies in the person's responses across situations. Moreover, a therapist may increase partners' awareness of their macrolevel characteristics simply by pointing out the patterns that he or she has observed. As we discussed in chapter 10, the decision whether to use a guided-discovery approach, in which the clients draw their own conclusions from consideration of available information, rather than a didactic approach, may depend on the degree to which the clients appear to prefer thinking independently rather than receiving direction.

Once members of a couple are aware of the types of personal qualities that are the bases of their primary distress, resolution of the issues often requires that they attain greater acceptance of each other's characteristics. Individuals commonly view their own characteristics as more appropriate or normal than those of their partners, so they lack motivation to accommodate or compromise. Even individuals who are similar on a characteristic may criticize the partner for having a relatively higher or lower level of that characteristic, as a means of blaming the partner for their relationship difficulties. Consequently, therapists may use interventions designed to increase each person's acceptance that both individuals' characteristics are within a normal range (if they are indeed within an adaptive range) and are reasonable ways of being. The goal is to guide the couple toward viewing the problem as a challenge of finding better ways of adapting to the combination of their characteristics. Psychoeducational interventions involving mini-lectures by the therapist, readings, and videotapes can be used to convey that both partners' characteristics are normal but that they conflict with each other sufficiently that they need to be reconciled. When individuals lack understanding of and sympathy for each other's characteristics, the therapist may coach them in the use of expressive and listening skills to help them view each other's responses as reasonable rather than foreign and threatening. Mutual empathy also may be enhanced by guiding a couple in role-taking exercises, in which each person attempts to respond in the way they believe the other person typically responds, paying attention to thoughts and feelings while in the role of the partner. Another cognitive intervention that may increase individuals' acceptance of their partners' characteristics involves guiding each person in considering more benign reasons why the other person tends to respond differently than oneself. In addition, a therapist might guide each member of a couple in exploring the advantages and disadvantages of imposing his or her own characteristics as the standards by which the partner should live. Sometimes an individual is able to view a partner's characteristics in a new way, such that they are acceptable within the scope of the person's existing standards. In other cases an individual may be willing to modify his or her standards so that aspects of the partner that once were unacceptable now are considered reasonable and appropriate. These cognitive changes broaden the range of aspects of a partner the individual considers acceptable.

Often, awareness and acceptance of differences or similarities in partners' characteristics are insufficient to resolve an issue in a couple's relationship. When the couple's interactions interfere with the expression of one or both individuals' needs, personality styles, or temperament, the couple are likely to experience primary distress until they develop new patterns that are more consistent with the partners' characteristics. Consequently, therapists may use a number of interventions to increase a couple's skills and sense of efficacy for making changes that resolve their concerns. Psychoeducational presentations, such as therapist mini-lectures, readings, and videotapes, may be used to provide evidence that couples such as themselves have been successful in resolving core relationship concerns. The therapist also can coach the couple in using expressive, listening, and decision-making skills to identify limitations in their current ways of responding to each other's personal characteristics and to devise new approaches. Finally, therapists may overcome some individuals' reluctance to try new ways of interacting with a partner by coaching the person in behaving as if he or she typically responded differently, without making a commitment to maintain such changes. Although many individuals are uneasy or opposed to changing their own responses in the interest of improving their relationship, a combination of the interventions we have described may encourage partners to collaborate in resolving dyadic issues.

SUMMARY

Therapists commonly need to assess and intervene with both *primary distress*, associated with unresolved dyadic issues such as differences between partners' needs or other personal characteristics, and *secondary distress*, associated with ineffective and destructive approaches the partners developed to cope with those unresolved issues. In this chapter we have addressed the following concepts and methods for understanding and modifying both levels of distress-eliciting couple patterns.

- The negative interaction patterns, including mutual attack, demand–withdraw, mutual withdrawal, and disengagement, that couples bring to therapy commonly create secondary distress, and behavioral approaches to couples therapy traditionally have focused on modifying these presenting problems.
- It often is necessary for the therapist to intervene early in therapy to modify interaction patterns associated with secondary distress and create a more positive atmosphere in a relationship before a couple will be willing and able to collaborate in making micro- and macrolevel changes to resolve core relationship issues associated with primary distress.
- Interventions described in earlier chapters for modifying behavior, cognitions, and emotions can be used to modify interactions associated with secondary distress and to produce more effective and satisfying solutions to core issues in the couple's relationship.

13

ADDRESSING INDIVIDUAL PSYCHOPATHOLOGY, UNRESOLVED ISSUES, AND INTERPERSONAL TRAUMAS WITHIN COUPLES THERAPY

In previous chapters we have discussed a range of issues that many couples confront in their relationships, including a variety of external stressors, normal developmental changes for both individuals and the couple, and the interactive patterns that develop while two people live together on a long-term basis. In this chapter we discuss how these relationship issues can become further complicated when one or both individuals demonstrate individual psychopathology, have an undiagnosable yet important unresolved issue from their individual past, or are experiencing continuing negative personal effects from a trauma within the current relationship. Within this context, the therapist must consider whether individual therapy, couples therapy, or both, are appropriate. In addition, the appropriate use of medication must be considered. Finally, the therapist should understand how to use a variety of couple-based interventions to assist in the treatment of individual dysfunction.

We recognize that a discussion of the relationship between individual maladaptive functioning and relationship functioning is a complex and controversial issue. For some clinicians and theoreticians, particularly those who adopt a systems perspective, individual and relationship functioning are almost inseparable. That is because systems theorists understand individual functioning within the context of the broader couple and family system. Therefore, individual symptoms are viewed by some clinicians as manifestations of relationship difficulties or as serving important functions for the relationship, such as stable complementary helper–helpee roles for the partners (Fraenkel, 1997). Our own position is consistent with a stress–diathesis model for understanding psychopathology—various individuals have predispositions or vulnerabilities to experience different types of psychopathology, particularly under stress. This propensity is manifested in various ways, based on the individual's learning history and current context. Extensive research demonstrates that living in a hostile or critical family environment creates major stress and increases the likelihood of relapse or exacerbation of individual psychological symptoms (Butzlaff & Hooley, 1998). Thus, the stress of a distressed marriage can precipitate, maintain, or exacerbate individual psychopathology. In addition, the symptoms of various types of psychopathology create hardships for the couple and likewise can precipitate, maintain, or exacerbate relationship discord, as we discussed in chapter 5. For example, living with an individual who has an obsessive–compulsive disorder and must return home frequently to check the stove to see if it is turned off can become a major source of contention between partners. In addition, some couples might more easily accommodate this checking behavior, and the person's partner might inadvertently reinforce or maintain this troubling behavior. As Rohrbaugh et al. (in press) noted, couples vary in the degree to which there is *symptom–system fit*, that is, the degree to which the symptom is tolerated and becomes incorporated into the couple's relationship. An important task for the clinician is to understand this mutually reciprocal influence between individual and relationship maladaptive functioning. This cause–effect relationship and reciprocal influence will vary from one individual and couple to the next and thus require flexibility in treatment. Consequently, the therapist should be aware of a variety of types of interventions that can address individual issues within a couples' context (Snyder & Whisman, in press).

INDIVIDUAL PSYCHOPATHOLOGY

Symptoms stemming from an individual's psychopathology can create relationship distress, and relationship distress can trigger, exacerbate, or maintain an individual's symptoms of psychopathology. In the following section we present three strategies for addressing this reciprocal relationship between psychopathology and couple difficulties. We describe how the level of partner involvement in treatment of individual psychopathology ranges on a continuum from partner-assisted interventions to disorder-specific couples' interventions to general couples therapy. Our discussion considers how to balance individual and couples' problems; what types of interventions are appropriate in various situations; and how to implement couples interventions in cases where individual psychopathology is present, using panic disorder with agoraphobia as an example.

As we and our colleagues discussed elsewhere (Baucom, Shoham, Mueser, Daiuto, & Stickle, 1998), several efficacious couple- and family-based interventions have been developed for various disorders, including depression, anxiety disorders, bipolar disorder, sexual dysfunction, alcoholism, and schizophrenia. In many instances, these couples-based interventions were developed as treatments for individual psychopathology, without the assumption that a couple was experiencing significant relationship distress. Instead the clinician concluded that the treatment of choice for the individual disorder was a couples- or family-based intervention because it was seen as important to create an environment that would assist with and support changes that the individual needed to make. Consistent with this hypothesis, couples-based interventions have been found to be efficacious in many instances in treating individual psychopathology, regardless of whether relationship distress is present. In this chapter we focus attention on how to assist couples for whom relationship distress and individual psychopathology both are present. Before we discuss the specifics of such interventions, it is helpful to have a conceptual overview of how couples-based interventions have been used in treating individual psychopathology among adults.

There are at least three types of couples-based interventions that couples therapists can use when individual psychopathology is present (Baucom et al., 1998):

- partner-assisted interventions,
- disorder-specific couples' interventions, and
- couples therapy.

The first two approaches can be used regardless of whether the couple is reporting relationship distress. By definition, the third type of intervention is couples therapy for relationship distress. Given that we are focusing solely on circumstances in which both relationship distress and individual psychopathology are present, in this chapter we address how all three approaches can be used within a couple context.

First, some interventions can be viewed as *partner-assisted interventions*, in which the partner is used as a surrogate therapist or coach in assisting the identified patient in addressing the individual problems (in the current discussion we refer to the individual with the diagnosable disorder as the *identified patient*. However, we do not use this term when interacting with couples). Partner-assisted interventions can be used when the identified patient has specific therapy "homework" assignments outside of treatment sessions that address the individual psychopathology. The partner helps and coaches the patient in conducting the homework assignments. For example, a partner might accompany an agoraphobic individual on some exposure outings as a means of offering support of and reinforcement for adherence to the treatment protocol. Alternatively, a partner might attend a social event with a socially anxious individual to encourage that person to confront his or her fears. Within the interventions the couple relationship supports the treatment plan for the individual, but the couple's relationship is not the explicit focus of the intervention. The therapist must understand the individual psychopathology and the changes that the individual needs to make to improve functioning. The partner is merely being asked to assist the individual in making these changes. This goal can be complicated when the couple is experiencing significant relationship distress because working together as an effective team for the well-being of one individual can be difficult for many distressed couples. In addition, the members of a distressed couple may view placing one partner in the "coach" role as altering the balance of power in their relationship, with the coaching partner being "one up." Thus, therapists who use partner-assisted interventions must be cautious about their impacts on partners' roles in their relationship.

A second way of involving a partner in addressing individual psychopathology within a couple context is with a *disorder-specific couples intervention*. Such interventions focus on the relationship, specifically, the ways that a couple's interaction patterns or roles might contribute to the precipitation, exacerbation, or maintenance of individual symptoms. As such, these interventions target the couple's relationship, but only as (a) the relationship appears to influence the individual disorder directly or (b) the individual disorder influences the relationship. For example, a therapist might note how a partner's making excuses for an alcoholic individual helps to maintain the person's drinking. Therefore, the therapist might ask the couple to discuss how they will respond to the outside world when the alcoholic cannot go to work. Similarly, the individual's heavy drinking in the evening might result in very little interaction between the two partners. Therefore, the couple might discuss ways that they can increase their interaction with each other, perhaps structuring time in the evening together that also decreases the likelihood of excessive alcohol use. In contrast, if the individual has difficulties with his or her in-laws, but this issue is unrelated to the drinking problem, then focusing on in-law problems would not be a disorder-specific couples intervention.

As we discussed in chapter 4, we make no assumptions that the partner or the couple is attempting to maintain the individual symptoms through their interaction patterns. In some instances the destructive interaction patterns are a part of the relationship distress and exacerbate individual psychopathology. In other instances a partner might even attempt to be supportive of the individual but inadvertently contribute to symptom maintenance. For example, a partner might try to support a depressed individual by encouraging that person to stay in bed and rest if the person complains of a lack of energy and motivation. Unfortunately, this approach might exacerbate depressive symptoms if it becomes a frequent pattern. Finally, a partner does benefit from the other person's symptoms in some instances. For example, a depressed person might become very dependent on a partner, and the partner experiences an increase in self-esteem, feeling important and needed. Thus, the partner might not want the depressed person to become more self-sufficient.

Couples therapy, as described throughout this volume, is a third type of intervention that can be used when individual disorders are present. Such interventions are based on the logic that the overall functioning of the couple contributes in a broad sense to the development or maintenance of individual symptoms. For example, if an individual is vulnerable to depression, being in a distressed relationship might precipitate or exacerbate such symptoms. This precipitation or exacerbation might be due both to an excess of negative interactions and to the lack of support needed by the individual (I. A. Gotlib & Beach, 1995). As Beach and O'Leary (1992) and Jacobson, Fruzzetti, Dobson, Whisman, and Hops (1993) have demonstrated, cognitive–behavioral couples therapy can be effective in alleviating depression along with relationship distress. Developing a healthy, supportive relationship might be one of the most effective buffers against individual psychopathology. To the degree that couples therapy can contribute to the development and maintenance of such an environment, it can be effective in alleviating individual psychopathology.

Although we have described these three types of interventions as being discrete, in reality they can overlap significantly. For example, if the couple alter their schedules so that the partner can accompany the individual on exposure outings for agoraphobia, this incorporates a partner-assisted component. In addition, if the couple change their interaction pattern to accomplish this task, this might be seen as a disorder-specific couples' intervention. The exact categorization of these interventions is not important; instead, it is important that the therapist understands different types of interventions and develops an effective treatment plan. In addition, a complete treatment plan might incorporate all three types of interventions. Given that we are focusing on individual psychopathology within the context of relationship distress, our emphasis will be on how to target individual psychopathology within couples therapy, incorporating partner-assisted and disorder-specific interventions when appropriate.

DEVELOPING A COLLABORATIVE MINDSET FOR ADDRESSING COUPLE AND INDIVIDUAL PROBLEMS

It is important that the partner with individual psychopathology not feel blamed by the therapist or the other partner for relationship problems or for the person's individual difficulties (e.g., "If he just buckled down, he could come out of that depression"). The manner in which the therapist attempts to integrate relationship distress and individual psychopathology depends partly on how intervention was initiated. In many instances, the couple has requested couples therapy for relationship distress. During the initial assessment, or as intervention proceeds, the therapist might become aware that one or both individuals are experiencing significant individual symptoms, but the person has never been diagnosed with a disorder. In this instance the therapist must find a way to raise the issue of the individual's symptoms without appearing to shift blame for relationship problems to that individual. The therapist's task is easier if during the initial assessment of relationship distress one or both partners acknowledge a history of psychopathology or a current diagnosis. In some cases one person reports previous or current individual psychotherapy, and the therapist provides feedback on how relationship and individual functioning can reciprocally influence each other. During the initial assessment or during intervention, the therapist might conclude that the couple's relationship is contributing to the individual's distress. In this case, the therapist is confronted with the challenge of integrating a focus on the individual into the treatment, without causing that person to feel blamed for the couple's distress. Furthermore, if the therapist has been working with one person in individual therapy prior to initiating couples therapy, then the person's partner might feel like an outsider, assuming that the therapist's primary allegiance is to the individual who has been receiving individual therapy. Next we offer examples of how the therapist might attempt to integrate interventions for couples' and individual functioning.

First, in the case of Wilma and Owen, who had sought couples therapy for a variety of relationship difficulties, the therapist became aware that Owen had a moderate level of obsessive–compulsive disorder that contributed to the couple's difficulties but had never been diagnosed or addressed. Owen engaged in frequent cleaning and checking behaviors that made Wilma feel inadequate. Wilma had primary responsibility for cleaning the kitchen after dinner, but each evening, soon after she completed the cleanup, Owen returned to the kitchen and meticulously cleaned the countertops. Also, Owen would call Wilma frequently from work to see how she was proceeding with her daily "to-do" list of tasks and errands. As the initial assessment continued, it became clear that Owen engaged in other checking behaviors not involving Wilma. During the assessment, Owen was able to tell Wilma for the first time that he felt anxious on an ongoing basis and that his repetitive cleaning and checking behaviors alleviated his anxiety for a brief time. During the feedback session, the therapist first discussed several areas of relationship difficulty that seemed unrelated to Owen's obsessive–compulsiveness. Then the therapist continued as follows.

> Therapist: Another area that you have mentioned is Owen's anxiety and how you two deal with that within your marriage. Owen, I think it is great that you told Wilma about the anxiety that you experience from day to day. It is understandable that you have tried to find some ways to lower your anxiety because it makes you so uncomfortable. If I understand correctly, there are at least two major things that tend to lower your anxiety on a short-term basis. First, you feel less anxious if you check up on things, making certain that everything is on track and being done. You might call Wilma multiple times during the day if you start to feel anxious, checking to see how she is doing with her "to-do list." Although this is to lower your anxiety, it tends to make Wilma feel that you do not have confidence in her ability to do routine tasks. Wilma, although it feels bad, can you understand that Owen's checking is not as much about your competence as it is his finding some way to lower his own anxiety temporarily? [Wilma responds affirmatively.]
> Second, Owen, you also feel less anxious if you clean things, even if someone else has already cleaned them. It sounds like that's another way of making sure that everything is as it should be: clean and spotless. If I understand correctly, the frequent checking and cleaning works for a short time period, but then you start to feel anxious again, and you need to do it all over. Is that right? [Owen responds affirmatively.]
> Here's what I'd like to do. First, Owen, I would like to help you find a better way to deal with the anxiety so that it doesn't return as often. There are some strategies that work for many people, and they might be helpful to you. Wilma, I think you could be helpful with this. I will help you both understand how the anxiety works and how the two of you can work as a team to help Owen lower his anxiety. Wilma, in general, will you help with this? [Wilma responds affirmatively.] Second, Owen, I think the way that you are trying to lower your anxiety is having negative consequences for your relationship with Wilma. Based on what we have discussed today, she might have a better understanding of your checking and cleaning behaviors. However, even if she doesn't take this as your questioning her competency, she still might never like your calling several times a day to ask her about her chores. I think it is contributing to a generally negative environment between the two of you. I have some ideas of how you two might respond differently so that your anxiety doesn't spread into the relationship as much.

In this example the therapist felt that Owen would be open to hearing a discussion about his anxiety and integrating it into an overall understanding of the couple's functioning. At times, an individual might be defensive, particularly during the initial assessment. In that case, the therapist might present the individual symptoms in a more tentative and minor way. Alternatively, the therapist might decide to refrain from initially discussing individual difficulties and wait until a specific pattern of behavior occurs within the context of therapy (e.g., when symptomatic behaviors lead to an argument between partners). Then those specific behaviors can be targeted because of their impact on the relationship. Frequently there is no need for a therapist to apply a specific diagnostic label to an individual, as long as the individual's patterns of behaviors and internal processing are appropriately addressed.

The situation is somewhat different if a person has sought individual psychotherapy and the therapist and client believe that the individual's relationship is contributing to that person's distress and symptoms. In such instances, the therapist must help the person's partner understand why a couples-based intervention might be preferable to individual therapy. In the following example, the therapist explains to Shane why such an intervention could be helpful.

> Therapist: Shane, thank you for coming. As you know, Melanie and I have been meeting for several weeks. She has given me permission to discuss with you much of what she and I have talked about. As you likely have seen and experienced, Melanie has been feeling down and dejected for several months. Sometimes I have found that when one person starts making changes and the person's partner doesn't understand why, it can be confusing and potentially problematic for the couple. I want you to understand what Melanie is going to be working on. Also, I'd like to ask for your help as she attempts to make some of those changes. For example, she has mentioned that it has been hard for her to get out of bed and get going in the mornings. She and I have talked about the possibility of her trying to change her morning routine to get her up and involved in the day's activities. I certainly don't want to make you responsible for getting her out of bed, but it can be very helpful if you two work together to establish a new morning routine. To help with some of these changes that Melanie is going to try to make personally, I think it would be most helpful if the three of us started meeting together. Shane, what are your observations of how Melanie has been doing these past months, and have you found any things that seem to be helpful to her? [Shane responds.]
>
> In addition to discussing how you, Shane, can help Melanie make some individual changes, I also would like to discuss how you both feel about your marriage. Melanie has mentioned to me that she generally feels that you two have become more distant over the last couple of years. In a moment, Shane, I'd like to get your views about your relationship. The reason this is so important is that we know that depression and relationship concerns really influence each other. For example, when one person is feeling down and somewhat depressed, we know it often affects the other person and the relationship. It also works in the other direction. When people start feeling more distant from each other, it can

contribute to making one person feeling sad and dejected. Therefore, it would be nice if we could talk some about your relationship and decide whether you and Melanie want to spend some time working on it as well. Shane, what is your sense of how the two of you are doing as a couple?

Developing a Treatment Plan: Integrating a Focus on Relationship and Individual Concerns

Once both partners have agreed that a couples-based intervention is appropriate, the therapist must decide how to sequence and integrate various individual and relationship concerns within conjoint couples sessions. This sequencing and integration will vary from one couple to the next. If the relationship is not highly distressed, and important elements of individual distress are not due to the relationship, the therapist might begin by focusing on the individual concerns and gradually broaden to focus on the relationship. Later we present an example of an integrated couples-based intervention for panic disorder with agoraphobia and relationship distress that begins with an emphasis on the anxiety symptoms.

Even if relationship issues appear to be a major factor in an individual's symptoms, individual difficulties might still be addressed initially if they create a crisis or dangerous situation for the individual or the couple. For example, if one person appears to be depressed because of relationship problems and has become suicidal, that individual's suicidal concerns require immediate attention. Then, to minimize the likelihood of continued suicidal ideation, the relationship issues must be addressed early in the therapy.

In instances in which an individual's symptoms appear to be due to relationship functioning and there is no immediate crisis, frequently the therapy can focus initially, and sometimes almost exclusively, on the relationship. For example, Beach and O'Leary (1992) found that cognitive–behavioral marital therapy was effective for alleviating both marital distress and depression if the relationship distress appeared to be the cause of the depression. In some instances, as the relationship improves, the individual symptomatology is alleviated without further emphasis on individual functioning. On other occasions the relationship might precipitate or exacerbate individual symptoms, but the individual's symptoms then have generalized to other domains of his or her life. At times, the conditions in these other parts of the person's life have changed and now are maintaining the symptoms; therefore, focusing therapeutic intervention on the relationship would be inadequate. For example, Vanessa developed a significant amount of anxiety, worrying that Darnell might divorce her because of their relationship problems. As her anxiety grew, she also became sensitive to others' evaluations of her at work, and she began to make many catastrophic predictions there as well. Although she had a history of being a valued employee, she now became worried that she would be demoted, her responsibilities curtailed, or perhaps that she would be fired from her position. Her lack of confidence in herself spread to many domains of life, and she began to withdraw from several friends and no longer took initiative at work. Although she and Darnell were making progress on their relationship through their couples therapy, she now had developed a pattern of avoidance in other areas of her life which required additional therapeutic attention.

The preceding examples highlight some broad considerations regarding sequencing and emphasis of interventions within couples therapy when individual psychopathology is present. However, there is rarely a firm distinction between focusing on the relationship versus on the individual. The therapist is unlikely to spend several sessions focusing on an individual's symptoms without devoting attention to how the relationship is affected. Consequently, both within sessions and across sessions, there often is a dual focus on individual and couples' functioning, just as there is when a relationship is composed of two well-adjusted individuals.

Application of Couples-Based Interventions to Specific Disorders

A discussion of how to apply couples-based interventions to a wide variety of specific disorders is beyond the scope of this book. In fact, several articles, book chapters, and volumes have focused on couples-based interventions for particular disorders (Snyder & Whisman, in press), including treatments for depression (Beach, Sandeen, & O'Leary, 1990), anxiety (Barlow, O'Brien, & Last, 1984; Baucom, Stanton, & Epstein, in press), alcohol dependence (O'Farrell, Choquette, Cutter, Brown, & McCourt, 1993), bipolar disorder (Miklowitz & Goldstein, 1997; Simoneau, Miklowitz, Richards, Saleem, & George, 1999), and schizophrenia (Falloon, Boyd, & McGill, 1984; Tarrier et al., 1989). Baucom et al. (1998) reviewed the empirical status of these interventions.

To be effective in working with individual disorders within a couple context, the therapist needs an understanding of the disorder that an individual is experiencing. In addition, the therapist must understand how these individual symptoms are exacerbated or maintained within an intimate relationship, including understanding how the individual psychopathology influences the fulfillment of both persons' needs and motives and the couple's interaction patterns. For example, Joyce explained how Lewis's agoraphobia had interfered with her life. She was quite achievement oriented and committed to advancing in her firm. In the past, she had turned down opportunities with other firms because it meant relocating to another part of the country, which made Lewis extremely anxious. Joyce also was an outgoing, energetic person who enjoyed social contact, both with Lewis present and by herself, with friends. However, Lewis's discomfort with driving more than several miles from home restricted their social life. Furthermore, although Joyce wanted to feel closer to and more intimate with Lewis, her anger at him for the restrictions that the agoraphobia created significantly interfered with their intimacy. The agoraphobia interfered with Lewis's life in numerous ways as well, including his desire to be successful professionally. These issues were an important part of the couples therapy.

To give the reader a sense of how this integration between relationship distress and individual psychopathology can be accomplished, we highlight one disorder: panic disorder with agoraphobia. In designing such an interventions, we have developed a general sequencing that proceeds from partner-assisted interventions (emphasizing exposure), to disorder-specific interventions (altering the couple's relationship to assist in alleviating agoraphobia), to broader couples therapy. Throughout the intervention, the couple's relationship is addressed, even during sessions involving the agoraphobic individual's exposure to feared situations. The importance of mutual support as a couple resource is highlighted, and guidelines for couple discussions and decision-making conversations are introduced, initially focusing on the exposure outings. Consequently, the intervention allows the couple to begin their work with an emphasis on support and on learning important communication guidelines.

This sequencing of interventions can be altered depending on the particular couple. If there is a great deal of anger and animosity between the two partners, for instance, then asking them to work together during exposure outings might be counterproductive. In this case the initial focus might be on decreasing negatives in the couple's interaction, along with creating an overall more positive, collaborative relationship between the two partners.

Axis I Disorders: Focus on Panic Disorder With Agoraphobia

The major empirically supported treatment for panic disorder with agoraphobia involves exposure to feared stimuli, both *interoceptive exposure* (focusing on feared body sensations) and *in vivo exposure* (focusing on fears involving the outside world). The logic underlying these interventions is that individuals with agoraphobia experience certain bodily sensations and external situations as dangerous. Often when the individual experiences bodily sensations related to physiological arousal, such as increased heart rate or sweating, the individual interprets these sensations as indicating that something terrible (e.g., a heart attack) is about to occur. The person's fear of those symptoms exacerbates the arousal, perhaps leading to a panic attack. The individual subsequently engages in various maladaptive escape and avoidance responses in hopes of avoiding further panic attacks; these responses can greatly disrupt the individual's and the couple's life. Exposure interventions, arranged from less threatening to more threatening situations, help the individual confront the feared stimuli and remain in the situation until the anxiety subsides. Over time, the individual learns that escape and avoidance are not necessary, because catastrophic results do not occur. Thus, the individual learns that even if a panic attack occurs, the symptoms, although unpleasant, are not harmful. The details for implementing interoceptive and in vivo exposure are provided elsewhere (Craske & Barlow, 2001). The same interventions that are most frequently used with the individual alone are adapted when an agoraphobic person's partner is included in the process.

Partner-assisted interventions. Within our couples-based approach, agoraphobic individuals' partners are present for all phases of the treatment of agoraphobia. The partner comes to understand the basis for panic attacks and agoraphobic avoidance. This understanding can be helpful in altering the partner's attributions for the individual's avoidance behavior and overdependence on the partner. Rather than seeing the individual as lacking motivation or wanting the partner to assume undue responsibilities, the partner can come to see the individual as using a variety of maladaptive strategies to avoid and lower anxiety. The partner recognizes the importance of the individual's confronting feared bodily sensations or external environmental situations.

The agoraphobic individual's partner is asked to participate during both interoceptive and in vivo exposure. During interoceptive exposure the individual participates in a set of exercises that create a variety of physical sensations similar to those associated with anxiety and panic, such as dizziness from spinning in a swivel chair, lightheadedness from hyperventilation, or increased heart rate from walking up stairs. During this phase of treatment, the partner assumes multiple roles. The partner learns (and personally experiences) the exposure exercises and serves as a coach as the individual practices interoceptive exposure outside of the therapy sessions. The partner also is taught to provide emotional support as the individual proceeds through the exposure process.

In addition to confronting uncomfortable bodily sensations, agoraphobic individuals must confront external environmental situations that elicit anxiety (in vivo exposure). These situations either evoke a sense of being unsafe or out of control, or they present settings in which help is unavailable if the individual should experience a panic attack or some physical disability. Consequently, many agoraphobic individuals are fearful of going far from home, driving in a car, or being inside of buildings away from the exits. In vivo exposure involves confronting these situations one at a time until the anxiety subsides.

In a partner-assisted intervention, the partner is involved in the in vivo exposures as well, although his or her role shifts across time. Agoraphobic individuals have a tendency to rely on *safety signals*—people or objects that indicate to individuals that they are safe from the dangers they believe could occur in the event of anxiety symptoms. These signals might include having tranquilizers available or being in the presence of a loved one, particularly one's partner. Over the course of exposure, it is important to remove the safety signal so the individual recognizes that he or she can confront anxiety-eliciting situations in the world without a "crutch." Therefore, over time the partner is faded from the actual exposure outings, although he or she still maintains a supportive role. Even then, it remains appropriate for the partner to support the individual emotionally, provide encouragement, ask about the exposure after it is completed, and sometimes discuss the individual's exposure before it occurs.

As the preceding discussion indicates, the two individuals interact extensively with each other during the exposure outings. Given the importance of the agoraphobic individual's maintaining a focus on his or her emotions instead of avoiding them, teaching the couple guidelines for expressing emotions and for effective listening can assist them during the exposure as well as at other times when effective communication is important in their relationship. In addition, given that the couple spends time discussing their preparations prior to the exposure outings and troubleshooting once an exposure is completed, they also can benefit significantly from learning the decision-making guidelines described in chapter 9. Consequently, couples are taught these communication guidelines, initially implementing them with exposure outings. Thus, partner-assisted interventions focus on what an individual needs to do to address his or her individual symptoms and psychopathology. In this context, partners assume a role of surrogate therapist, coach, and supporter.

Disorder-specific interventions. If a couple is successful with the exposure exercises, the agoraphobic individual experiences less anxiety, tolerates anxiety better, and is less avoidant of the environment. To help the individual continue to make progress and maintain treatment gains, it is important to examine the couple's relationship. Over time, many couples have altered their roles within the family to accommodate the individual's agoraphobic avoidance. Developing a healthy sense of autonomy is one critical goal in addressing agoraphobia. Therefore, the couple should examine their relationship to explore ways that they can alter their roles to strengthen the individual's sense of autonomy and efficacy (Baucom et al., in press).

Next is an example of how a therapist introduced the notion of supporting Daniel's autonomy and reallocating responsibilities between Daniel and Louise.

> Therapist: We have been focusing on ways that you as a couple can work together to make progress on Daniel's avoidance of certain situations through the exposure outings that you have been having. What we want to do tonight is to start broadening our thinking on how you can work together as a team to make even more progress. Thus, we are going to look beyond the practice exposure sessions that you have been having. When one member of a couple or a family has a problem such as agoraphobia or a medical problem, the whole family is faced with learning ways to adapt to the problem that allow them to keep functioning as well as they know how. However, if you are not careful, it can have some

unintended, negative effects. Let's say that for a husband to get over a medical problem, he needs to get a lot of physical exercise. Well, if the family has taken over his chores while he was sick and continues to do that, then it doesn't encourage him to get the exercise that he now needs.

The same thing can happen when someone develops agoraphobia. The person is very uncomfortable in certain situations and avoids carrying out responsibilities that involve going into those situations. Often the person's partner or other family members take over those responsibilities; for example, a husband might do all the grocery shopping because it makes his wife so uneasy to go to the supermarket. As you are learning, to get over the agoraphobia you have to confront those situations that make you uncomfortable. So one thing that we are going to want to look at in your relationship is how you have learned to adapt or work around the agoraphobia, and how those ways now discourage the exposure that you need to get better.

Can you give me some examples of how you two now divide up responsibilities and roles such that if you continued to operate this way, it probably wouldn't help Daniel get over his agoraphobia? [Couple gives examples.] For the rest of the session, I want you to select an area involving chores and responsibilities that could contribute to Daniel's autonomy if you made appropriate changes in that area. What area would that be?

In addition to addressing the importance of autonomy for agoraphobic individuals, the therapist should consider both partners' communal needs. Many couples have learned to base their ways of meeting their communal needs on their interactions regarding an individual's anxiety and avoidance. For example, the agoraphobic person might be most comfortable walking in a mall while holding hands with his or her partner. Consequently, even physical contact and affection can focus on safety or on soothing the agoraphobic individual, with the couple sharing physical affection infrequently in situations unrelated to agoraphobia. As the therapist encourages increased autonomy, the couple's sense of affiliation and intimacy can be disrupted. Thus, therapeutic progress might threaten the fulfillment of important needs of one or both partners. The therapist and the couple must develop new ways for the partners to affiliate and feel close to each other that are healthy and help to maintain the individual's progress.

Addressing relationship issues unrelated to agoraphobia. Thus far, the interventions described focus primarily on one partner's agoraphobia. In the third stage of therapy, the therapist broadens the focus even further, to a consideration of other relationship issues that do not directly involve the individual's agoraphobia. To the degree that the couple has a discordant relationship, their distress can contribute to the agoraphobic individual's overall level of stress, thus making sustained progress more difficult. Therefore, in the final phase of treatment, the therapist helps the couple address significant relationship issues in ways that would be addressed with any distressed couple. In the following example, the therapist introduces these ideas to Daniel and Louise.

Therapist: Today, I am going to ask you to look at your relationship more fully, beyond just how you two relate to the agoraphobia. I think this is important for several reasons related to the agoraphobia as well as for improving your relationship more generally.

First, as I think you both know, agoraphobia and other aspects of your relationship are not truly independent of each other. Everything fits together to affect your relationship.

Second, as we were discussing last week, as your agoraphobia lessens it gives the two of you all sorts of new opportunities, and as a result your relationship is likely to change in some ways. I hope that those changes will be positive, but I want you to think about those changes and decide what you want rather than having the changes merely happen without your thinking about them. For example, as we celebrate your increasing freedom from the agoraphobia, we want to make sure you both still feel very connected. What are some ways that you (a) have already seen your relationship start to change as a result of treatment, or (b) could anticipate that it might change? [Couple responds].

Third, I have found that it is easier for most couples to work together on the agoraphobia exercises if they are feeling good toward each other in other areas of their relationship. For example, if you have just had an argument about something else in your marriage, you might not be very motivated to go with your partner on an exposure practice for an hour and a half.

Fourth, most people's anxiety symptoms increase during times of high stress, regardless of where the stress is coming from. And for most couples, their relationship is both a major source of support and a source of stress at various times. So, particularly when we think long term about keeping your agoraphobia symptoms to a minimum, we want to make certain that your relationship is a very positive force in your life and not a source of stress.

Finally, you have expressed some concerns about your relationship in general, not focused on panic or agoraphobia. I want to help you develop the most gratifying relationship possible for both of you.

We have presented treatment of relationship distress and agoraphobia in a couple's context at some length. Agoraphobia does not merit special attention relative to other disorders. Rather, we selected this disorder as one example to make clear how relationship distress and individual psychopathology can be considered in an integrated fashion. The principles just described apply to all disorders. It is unrealistic to expect that a couples therapist will have significant expertise in every area of individual psychopathology. However, he or she can develop a general understanding of specific disorders and, using the above principles, can develop a thoughtful approach to integrating the treatment of individual psychopathology and relationship distress.

Axis II Disorders and Extreme Personality Traits

The preceding examples focus primarily on Axis I or symptom-based disorders. In some ways, these disorders are easier to confront within the context of couples therapy, because they commonly involve subjective distress or restrictions in the individual's life. However, when the individual demonstrates an extreme personality or characteristics of a personality disorder, this can be more difficult to address because an individual typically sees his or her personality as part of himself or herself and may be offended by suggestions that aspects of his or her personality are maladaptive. For example, some individuals show little flexibility; they believe that they see the world in the correct manner and that their job is to help other people see the world as they do. Needless to say, this style can be difficult to address when compromise is needed between partners. Extreme characteristics occurring in one partner can be presented as differences between the partners in individual style and thus are addressed in chapter 12.

At times the couple's difficulties appear to result when one individual is extreme on a given dimension. In such instances, we typically comment on how different the two individuals are on this characteristic. In addition, we note in a nonpejorative way that one individual appears to be rather far out on this dimension relative to most adults. We suggest that although it might not be maladaptive personally for the individual to be this way, it does create complications for the couple's relationship. Consequently, we encourage the individual to push himself or herself to make changes on this dimension to a reasonable degree. This change typically is translated into specific behaviors that the individual is willing to try, to accommodate the partner and the relationship. At the same time, the other partner is asked to understand that this dimension might be a relatively stable characteristic of the other individual and that that person will likely be able to make changes only within certain limits. This expectation provides the context for acceptance of one's partner (Christensen, Jacobson, & Babcock, 1995). At times partners can accept characteristics of the other individual that are less than optimal. Yet in other instances, these extreme characteristics serve as the basis for one individual's decision to leave the relationship. It is possible to respect and love an individual yet decide that maintaining a long-term, intimate relationship with that person is not rewarding or requires too much compromise and effort.

UNRESOLVED PERSONAL ISSUES FROM EARLIER RELATIONSHIPS

Everyone approaches current intimate relationships with beliefs influenced by past romantic or familial relationships. For some individuals the unresolved issues from those earlier relationships are so intense that they interfere with individuals' ability to fulfill their needs with their current partner. In this section we explore the ways that past issues can continue to haunt individuals in their current relationships.

Some individuals have experienced earlier relationships, particularly couples' relationships and those within the family of origin, that resulted in unresolved issues for that individual. For example, the person might have grown up in a rejecting environment and developed the belief that he or she is unlovable. Similarly, an individual who grew up in a chaotic, unpredictable environment may hold a belief that other people cannot be counted on to meet one's needs. Individuals who were sexually abused in childhood commonly develop the belief that one should not trust people, particularly loved ones, who will abuse you for their own pleasure.

These extreme beliefs, emotional reactions, and behavioral responses described in this section do not "fit" the individual's current relationship, and they lead the individual to respond inappropriately to his or her partner. In chapter 10 we outlined interventions for dealing with distorted cognitions. Similarly, in chapter 11 we addressed dysfunctional emotional responses. The interventions described in those chapters apply to the current discussion, which involves a set of relatively well-defined distorted cognitions and extreme emotional experiences and responses. The types of relationship schemas that we are describing are more resistant to change than individuals' isolated misunderstandings or misinterpretations of their partners' behaviors, because they have been rehearsed and reinforced for many years and across many situations and relationships. Consequently, addressing these unresolved individual issues is difficult.

In addition, as Young, Beck, and Weinberger (1993) noted, these unresolved issues are resistant to change because the beliefs and emotional responses continue unquestioned. This set of beliefs, or *schemas*, leads the person to categorize, select, and encode information in a way that maintains the beliefs and emotional responses (Epstein & Baucom, 1993). For example, if the individual has developed a strong belief that partners cannot be trusted and will lie, cheat, and manipulate, that person selectively attends to such experiences in his or her current relationship. Alvin felt at a loss in terms of how to address this issue with Jade. Jade had had a prior marriage in which she had felt deceived by her husband, who often lied to her. Their marriage ended when she discovered a long series of extramarital affairs. This painful experience, combined with a childhood experience in which her upper-middle-class family was humiliated after her father was convicted of income tax evasion, had left Jade with a strong distrust of males. In particular, she was sensitized to situations in which another person failed to provide information. Alvin, her current husband, was a rather quiet individual, who offered little information about his day's activities, typically responding, "The day was fine. Nothing of significance happened." When around Alvin's colleagues at social gatherings, Jade inevitably learned more details about Alvin's work. She interpreted this pattern as deceitfulness and withholding on Alvin's part. Over time, Alvin began to feel that Jade was interrogating him each evening when he came home from work. During the therapy sessions, Alvin commented that at times he did share information with Jade but that it seemed to bring her little satisfaction or relief. According to Alvin, Jade was always searching for what was left unsaid, regardless of whether it had significance. As is evident in this example, the individual not only has a strong set of beliefs and accompanying emotional responses but also behaves in a manner consistent with these distorted beliefs. The individual's behavior influences other people, including the partner, to respond in ways that often are consistent with the individual's schema, thus reinforcing the beliefs. In this sense, the beliefs create a self-fulfilling prophecy.

Common Individual, Unresolved Issues That Influence Relationships

These earlier experiences can make an individual vulnerable in certain areas of relationship functioning. There is no comprehensive list of unresolved issues, problematic schemas, or core conflictual areas that may affect relationship functioning. However, researchers, theoreticians, and clinicians from diverse theoretical perspectives acknowledge the importance of such issues for individual and relationship functioning. From a cognitive perspective, Young (1990) proposed a set of 16 specific maladaptive schemas that fit into six domains: (a) instability and disconnection, (b) impaired autonomy, (c) undesirability, (d) restricted self-expression, (e) restricted gratification, and (f) impaired limits. *Instability and disconnection* involve the belief that one's needs for security, safety, and nurturance will not be met within intimate relationships. Thus, individuals might inappropriately be preoccupied with fears of abandonment, abuse, or emotional deprivation. *Impaired autonomy* involves a set of beliefs that cause the individual to struggle in functioning as a separate, competent individual. These schemas involve the belief that one cannot handle everyday responsibilities without significant help from others, that if negative events occur, the individual will be unable to protect himself or herself or cope effectively, and so forth. As we discussed earlier in this chapter, people with agoraphobia often struggle with an impaired sense of autonomy. The third category, *undesirability*, involves the belief that, for one reason or another, an individual will not be desirable to other people, whether it is because of physical attractiveness, social skills, intelligence, or some other reason. Beliefs about undesirability might affect both one's communal needs and his or her individual needs, such as the need for professional achievements. Fourth, *restricted self-expression* involves ignoring one's own emotions and preferences for a variety of reasons. The individual might have learned that such expression results in anger or retaliation from other individuals; similarly, the person might have come to believe that expression of one's own feelings and desires is selfish. In essence, the individual might have developed several highly dysfunctional beliefs about emotions, as we discussed in chapter 10. *Restricted gratification* involves an excessive emphasis on responsibility, work, and meeting excessively high standards to the exclusion of pleasure, fun, and enjoyment. Subsequently, the individual might come to view leisure time as wasteful. Extreme beliefs in this area can influence intimate relationships because the individual may view time with a partner as secondary to, or even interfering with, time devoted to achievement. Finally, Young commented on individuals who have *impaired limits*, believing that they deserve special entitlements, indulging their own personal desires and goals, and showing a lack of respect for the rights of others. More extreme versions of these beliefs can include narcissistic and antisocial characteristics.

Many of the distorted schemas that Young (1990) addressed center on the two broad sets of communal and individually oriented motives and needs that we have discussed extensively. From a psychodynamic perspective, Luborsky and Crits-Christoph (1998) addressed many of the same issues, referring to *core conflictual relationship themes*. As the label suggests, these themes are seen as areas of core conflict that an individual experiences within relationships. Barber, Crits-Christoph, and Luborsky (1998) concluded that these conflictual themes form eight clusters: (a) the desire to be independent and have individuality; (b) the wish to hurt and control others; (c) the wish to be controlled and hurt; (d) the wish to withdraw; (e) the wish to be close; (f) the wish to be loved and understood; (g) the wish to feel good; and (h) the wish to achieve.

Conjoint vs. Individual Intervention to Address Individual, Unresolved Issues

One decision that couples therapists must make is whether these individual issues can best be addressed in couples therapy or individual therapy. It is unfortunate that, at present, there are no empirical findings to guide these important clinical decisions. We believe that three interrelated factors should be considered when making the decisions:

1. The individual's awareness and insight regarding the issue are likely to influence whether the issue can be handled successfully within a couple context.
2. The pervasiveness and severity of the individual's personal issues likely will affect the therapist's treatment decisions concerning conjoint versus individual therapy.
3. The partner's responses to the individual's disclosure of information about personal vulnerabilities influence whether the individual believes conjoint sessions will feel safe.

For example, if a husband can articulate that being abandoned by his alcoholic mother during childhood makes him concerned that his wife will do the same, then this understanding might make it easier to approach these issues in couples therapy. Couples therapy also is more likely to be helpful if the husband appears to be open to learning how the current relationship can be different from his relationship with his mother. However, if the person does not have much understanding of the complex issues involved, or if the partner seems likely to use the individual's disclosures in a hurtful manner, then individual intervention to clarify the issues and deal with painful emotions associated with these early events should be considered.

A clinician might conclude from his or her assessment that one person's schemas produce such pervasive and intense negative responses to the partner that initially these schemas are unlikely to be modified by new types of couples' interactions during conjoint sessions. The clinician may determine that the person needs individual therapy to address these broader thematic issues before he or she will be ready to experiment with new ways of relating in couples therapy. For example, if the clinician concludes that an individual's fear of abandonment is so strong that he or she will not be able to process the new experiences in a different light and learn from couples therapy, then individual intervention is likely to be needed.

Attempting to uncover long-term issues and understand them can create vulnerability in the individual. Exploring threatening individual issues often is difficult when a partner is present, particularly when the relationship is distressed and partners use personal information to hurt each other. However, not all partners are angry and attacking. Many partners are empathic and understanding and sincerely want to be of assistance in improving the relationship and contributing to the other individual's well-being. In such instances, the partner often can be a helpful resource in exploring the other individual's personal issues.

Conjoint Interventions for Individual, Unresolved Issues

If a therapist concludes that it is appropriate to address these long-term, unresolved issues in a couple context, then the intervention involves several steps. First, the nature of each schema or the core conflictual relationship theme needs to be clarified, incorporating information from the initial assessment and conceptualization as well as ongoing assessment during therapy. At times some of these core themes are apparent in the initial assessment. Often the individual or the partner labels the issue: "I just don't think that I can count on you to be there when I really need you." The therapist will typically address this concern within the context of the current relationship, focusing on specific instances that have occurred and addressing attributions for both persons' recent behavior and expectancies for the future. Similarly, the clinician helps the couple make decisions regarding ways to change both people's behavior so that the individual can experience the partner as more dependable and committed. Even after significant therapeutic effort, at times individuals persist in their beliefs, for example, the partner is not viewed as dependable, even in the face of much evidence to the contrary. The persistence of these beliefs can indicate to the therapist that they might relate to experiences that predate the current relationship.

Given the circumstances just described, a second step is to try to understand how previous relationships and experiences have shaped the individual's current beliefs. As Snyder (1999) noted, at times an individual may lack an awareness of important experiences from the past and their relationship to the present. In such instances the therapist might decide to explore the individual's past in more depth to discover important developmental factors that have not been raised in the treatment to date. Snyder (1999) referred to this exploration of earlier developmental factors as *affective reconstruction*. At times, the therapist can use experiences in the couple's current life to initiate discussions about previous intimate relationships, family of origin, and so forth. For example, couples frequently plan trips to visit or have conversations with their families of origin. These interactions and anticipated interactions provide opportunities for conversations between the therapist and clients that allow for exploration of their earlier relationships. In the following example, Wade and Shelby had spent time during the previous week discussing their upcoming holiday schedule and their planned trip to visit Wade's mother. They returned to the session asking the therapist for advice on how to handle Wade's mother. One of Shelby's major presenting concerns about their couple relationship was Wade's difficulty opening up to her, sharing his feelings and opinions with her. They attempted several strategies to assist Wade in becoming more expressive, but he continued to explain that he just was not comfortable opening up to Shelby or anyone else.

Shelby: We need your help. We're at a real impasse. We have a trip coming up to visit Wade's mother, and we're both dreading it. These family visits have never worked well, and it's horrible for both of us.

Therapist: Help me understand what the concerns are. What are the difficulties in interacting with your mother, Wade?

Wade: That woman is so domineering that she could intimidate Godzilla. I had two siblings growing up, and we all handled it in different ways. I avoided her. I was always a good student, so I simply withdrew to my books: "Sorry, Mom. Can't talk now. Have to study."

Therapist: How did that work?

Wade: Well, it worked in keeping me away from her and keeping the conflict down. I didn't end up with much of a mother, but having no mother might be better than Godzilla.

Therapist: What happens now when you go home?

Wade: Well, it's a problem. I've been out of school for 20 years, so
                I can't go up to my room to study history. I'm stuck having
                to be around her and interact with her. In addition, I've
                never found a way to do that. Sometimes I stay relatively
                quiet, let her talk and plan things, and go along with it.
                Other times, I can't take it, and I blow up at her.
Therapist: I don't want to ignore your request to discuss how to handle
                the upcoming trip to visit your mother. But first, let's talk
                about the impact that your relationship with your mom has
                had on who you are today and how it has affected your
                other relationships.

Often the person's partner can be of assistance in this process of understanding how past relationship events are impinging on the current relationship. The two individuals frequently have discussed each person's past, particularly their families of origin. The individual himself or herself at times does not have the distance and perspective needed to make these linkages between the past and the present. However, the partner often can point out issues or patterns that the individual has described previously and that might be pertinent to the current relationship.

Understanding how previous experiences have shaped an individual can be useful to the couple. The first step in the process is for the individual to see the differences between the current relationship and the past and to respond to the current relationship in the present. Making this differentiation of the present from the past assumes some understanding of the past. Often an individual is defensive about viewing reactions and behavior in the current relationship as being distorted because of his or her past experiences. The individual may consider such an acknowledgement to be tantamount to saying that his or her perspective and responses are wrong and that the other person is right. Therefore, it is important that the therapist present the individual's responses to these earlier experiences whenever possible as normal and natural responses to extreme or maladaptive circumstances. In the present, given that the original circumstances no longer are present, this response is no longer needed.

In addition, the partner can benefit from understanding the individual's past and how past experiences have helped to shape the individual's cognitive, emotional, and behavioral responses. It can lead the partner to have increased empathy and compassion for the person, even though the person's behaviors still are unpleasant and unrewarding. Thus, understanding an individual's past experiences and resulting vulnerabilities can alter the partner's attributions for the individual's behavior.

In many instances, a person's cognitive and emotional responses based on a schema appear to be automatic or conditioned, lacking much cognitive processing. Therefore, after such an emotional response occurs, the individual is asked to step back and evaluate whether the type and degree of emotional response are warranted given the current situation, or whether the response seems to be based on his or her experiences in earlier relationships. The earlier negative experiences can be viewed as making the individual vulnerable to responding in ways that might not be relevant in the current relationship.

In addition to internal monitoring to separate the past from the present, the couple is urged to help the vulnerable individual experience new learning within the context of the current relationship. In essence, this new learning is based on planned behavioral changes. More specifically, couples are encouraged to confront the problematic situations and to make an extra effort to handle them in different ways so that the vulnerable individual can experience them differently. It is particularly important to enlist the other partner's cooperation and understanding during this process. Rather than attacking the individual because of his or her vulnerability, we hope that the partner can view this process as a joint task that will help the other individual and their relationship as well. Next is an example of how a therapist introduced differentiating the past from the present and creating a new set of learning experiences for the couple.

Therapist: Sam, it is helpful to understand what it was like for you growing up. Being the youngest child in an intellectually competitive family must have been a challenge. In a situation like that, you do what you can to hold your own and defend yourself. That's a form of psychological survival. When people grow up with that, over time that kind of defensiveness can become an automatic response. You learned to do it as a child to protect yourself and it worked; now it is automatic. In part, that might help to explain why both you and Patti comment on how hard it is for you not to become defensive when she raises some area of concern. Also, when you do become defensive she becomes somewhat attacking, which justifies your being defensive. Let's see if we can't break this pattern.

That's going to involve two steps. First, Sam, it will really be important for you to separate your relationship with Patti from what happened to you in the past. Your defending yourself when you were growing up was adaptive; if you hadn't, you would have been humiliated. But, hopefully, you don't need to do that anymore with Patti. So, when she starts to raise a concern, it will be important for you to realize that you are in a different situation now and do not need to respond to her defensively. You need to find something to say to yourself internally, to slow down this process and realize that defending yourself is not necessary. What could you say to yourself at those times?

Sam: That's the problem. At the time, I'm just responding to what she's saying. It seems to me that she's being unfair, so it's natural to defend myself. I'm not sure what to do.

Therapist:	Something needs to alert you that you are in this high-risk situation before you start responding defensively. This works in different ways for different people. For some people, it is an idea that they have in their head that serves as a trigger for defensiveness. For example, an individual might think, "That's ridiculous; she's being unfair again." Thoughts like that could be a red flag that tells you that you're at risk of becoming defensive. For other people, it's more of an emotional, and perhaps even physical, response. If you find yourself becoming very angry at her, that might alert you that you are at risk for becoming defensive. Perhaps if you feel your muscles tighten or your breathing increasing, that would be the warning sign. What do you notice internally that tells you that you are headed toward defending yourself?
Sam:	I think it's probably a combination of all that. I can feel my fists tighten, my jaw clench, and I'm thinking that she's being unfair or even ridiculous.
Therapist:	When you start to experience those things, can you let that serve as a signal that you need to put on the brakes and not respond defensively?
Sam:	I don't know. It sounds reasonable. But then, what do I do instead?
Therapist:	Well, you might need a variety of options. You might try to use the listening skills that we discussed, realizing that Patti has a right to her opinion, even if you disagree. You could convey respect for her point of view and then explain how you see the issue differently. Or, if after stepping back you think she has a good point, you can agree with it. What are some thoughts that you have about what to do instead of becoming defensive?

In this example the therapist attempted to help Sam see the linkages between his experiences growing up and his current behavior toward Patti. By presenting his responses during childhood as a natural consequence of the circumstances in his family of origin, the therapist minimized Sam's defensiveness about his general tendency to defend himself. It then made sense to Sam that he would need to make an effort to address this overlearned response that had served him well in the past. The discussion of things Sam might do instead of responding defensively could easily have been recommended by the therapist, even if Sam's family of origin had never been discussed. However, Sam's increased understanding of his well-learned response, and his recognition of the importance of overcoming it, motivated him to make this change. Therefore, increasing both partners' insight into the roots of an individual's behavior can help normalize or depathologize it for both of them. Moreover, it can help to set the context for making current behavioral

EXHIBIT 13.1.
Guidelines for Addressing Individual, Unresolved
Issues in a Conjoint Setting

1. Explore individual, unresolved issues in a way that affirms that they result from an attempt to cope with a difficult set of prior circumstances.
2. Clarify how the current relationship with the partner is different from the past, calling for new responses.
3. Help the couple confront these difficult situations together to establish a new internal response for the individual, along with a different set of behaviors toward the partner.
4. Emphasize the need for change from both people to assist the individual.
5. Recognize that long-standing issues create vulnerabilities that might continue to a degree on an ongoing basis.

changes, based on the partners' recognition of how difficult and effortful such change is likely to be.

Although the therapist might use a variety of intervention strategies to clarify what early experiences have significantly influenced an individual and how these relate to the current intimate relationship, several general principles, outlined in Exhibit 13.1, are important in assisting such couples. First, these earlier experiences should be addressed in a way that does not lead to a characterization of the individual as sick or pathological. Instead, this exploration should clarify how the individual's response was adaptive or was an understandable attempt to cope with a difficult set of prior circumstances. This approach will facilitate empathy from the individual's partner and minimize defensiveness from the individual. Second, the exploration of the individual's past must help him or her become aware of how the relationship with the partner is different from the past and therefore no longer necessitates previous cognitions, emotions, and behavioral responses. Third, the individual and the partner must be willing to confront these difficult situations and work together in attempting to create a different behavioral sequence. Numerous trials will be required for individuals to learn different internal and external responses to well-ingrained patterns that developed over many years. Fourth, it is important that the partners develop a team perspective for helping the individual, because a change in the couple's interaction pattern requires changes by both individuals. Finally, in many instances, the couple must recognize that they are dealing with an area of vulnerability for the individual. Despite progress and persistent effort, at times the individual is likely to resort to former patterns of thinking, feeling, and behaving, based on this well-ingrained schema. When this occurs, the couple should not panic or give up but recognize the need to persist.

TRAUMATIC EXPERIENCES IN THE CURRENT RELATIONSHIP

Some partners may enter therapy during or after a crisis, such as an extramarital affair or domestic violence. Others may not point to a particular negative event, but they may complain that their core beliefs about their partners or relationship have been shaken. In these cases the individual often goes through stages resembling responses to traumatic events. In this section we apply the term *interpersonal trauma* to situations that disrupt an individual's assumptions about the relationship. We outline various interventions designed to target each phase in the individual's response to the negative event, which include absorbing the blow of the event and becoming overwhelmed, giving meaning to the event, and moving forward with the relationship.

Almost all couples who seek treatment for relationship distress have a history of interactions in their relationships that continue to evoke negative emotional responses; in fact, such distress is a major focus of this book. In addition, however, there is a class of negative events that are distinct and evoke extreme negative responses. As Gordon and Baucom (1998c) discussed, some extreme negative events are experienced as traumas. From a cognitive perspective, the defining characteristic of traumas is that they disrupt the individual's basic assumptions about the partner, the relationship, or both. If one person has an extramarital affair or physically abuses the other individual, this behavior markedly disrupts the individual's assumptions about safety, security, and the partner's commitment to his or her well-being. When these basic assumptions appear to be disconfirmed, strong negative emotions typically follow. (We refer to the individual who has engaged in the unacceptable, traumatic behavior as the *participating partner* and use the term *injured partner* to refer to the other individual.) When one person has been traumatized in the relationship, it is essential that the therapist respond to the trauma to help the couple move forward, not only in the area focal to the trauma (e.g., infidelity, physical abuse) but also in other aspects of their relationship.

Stages in Response to Relationship Trauma

The response of injured partners to such traumatic events typically unfolds in three stages: (a) absorbing the blow, (b) gaining understanding, and (c) moving forward. Each of these stages involves strong cognitive, emotional, and behavioral reactions that must be addressed. Consequently, a clinician must intervene according to what stage the individual and the couple is experiencing.

Absorbing the Blow

In the initial response to trauma, *absorbing the blow*, the injured partner experiences the traumatic event and is overwhelmed. The participating partner has behaved in some manner that the injured partner cannot comprehend within the context of the existing relationship. Therefore, the individual experiences his or her important assumptions about the partner as being disconfirmed; similarly, the injured person often develops negative expectancies about the partner's future behavior and the relationship. When the assumptions are shattered, the individual's life can seem quite unpredictable, and the person experiences extreme emotional lability, including anger, fear, sadness, confusion, or some combination of these. Behaviorally speaking, the injured person often retreats to maintain a sense of safety because the relationship now seems unpredictable, and the participating partner has demonstrated a willingness to hurt the injured person. The injured person also might retaliate, engaging in destructive acts of vengeance.

Several strategies are appropriate to address these strong responses. First, it is important that neither individual create further harm during this extremely emotional state. For example, the injured partner must not seek retribution in destructive ways, such as harming the third party in an extramarital affair. Second, it is important to create as much safety for the injured person and the couple's relationship as possible. Often, appropriate boundaries need to be created for the individual or couple. In the case of infidelity, it might involve limiting interaction between the participating partner and the third party. If physical abuse between the two partners is involved, appropriate boundaries might involve separating the individuals. Such boundaries contribute to a sense of safety and predictability and thus can decrease extreme emotional volatility.

Giving Meaning

To place the trauma into some understandable context, the partners need to discuss what occurred and try to obtain some understanding of the event(s). Processing what has occurred introduces the second stage, *giving meaning*. To help the injured partner and couple move forward, the injured party must develop a new conceptualization of the partner and their relationship. Perhaps the injured person had never considered infidelity to be a realistic possibility in the couple's relationship; now the injured person must develop a new understanding of his or her partner. This attempt at new understanding often comes in the form of repetitive questioning: "How could you do this? What were you thinking? You're not the person I thought I knew." Developing this new view of the partner involves coming to an understanding of the various factors that contributed to the participating partner's decision to engage in unacceptable behavior. As Gordon and Baucom (1998c) discussed, this process involves a significant amount of cognitive restructuring. In particular, the members of the couple try to understand how individual characteristics of the participating partner, the injured partner, the relationship, and the environment contributed to the context within which the participating partner chose to behave in that way. The goal is not to blame the victim but rather to understand the context for the participating person's behavior. The participating partner is held responsible for his or her decision to respond to this context in an inappropriate way. As the injured partner develops a more realistic set of attributions for the behavior, realistic expectancies for the participating partner's future behavior also evolve. This increased understanding and predictability often help the injured party to experience less extreme emotions toward the partner and what has occurred.

Next we offer an example of how a therapist worked with Robert and Amelia regarding the affair that Robert had had with a coworker, Cassie. The affair was particularly devastating to Amelia because both she and Robert reported that they loved each other and had a very good marriage. (Although many individuals assume that an extramarital affair implies significant marital discord prior to the affair, Glass and Wright [1985] found that more than 50% of men in a community sample who had had extramarital affairs reported that they were happy in their marriages.) As part of a work team, Robert and Cassie had numerous meetings together and occasionally traveled together on business. Neither Robert nor Cassie had ever had an affair, and he reported that neither of them had this kind of relationship in mind as their relationship developed. Instead, they gradually got to know each other, communicated easily with each other, and Robert gradually lowered his guard, because he had not even considered the possibility of becoming involved with Cassie. In the following excerpt, the therapist discusses Robert's family of origin and how his development might have put him at risk for the recent affair. In other sessions, the therapist explored Robert's functioning at the time of the affair as well as other factors that contributed to the context.

> Therapist: Robert, you mentioned earlier that you are the youngest of three children, with two older sisters. Can you tell me what it was like growing up with them and with your parents?
>
> Robert: Well, it was really very good. My parents loved each other and got along well. My sisters and I actually got along well and really cared about each other. I spent a lot of time with them. We grew up in a rural area, and there were not many kids in the neighborhood. But they often had their female friends around, so I grew up around older females.
>
> Therapist: Did you enjoy being with them? How did you relate to them?
>
> Robert: I enjoyed it a lot. I've always liked females, and I'm comfortable with them, maybe because of my sisters. Generally, I think I'm a good friend, and most females seem to trust me as a person. It's not sexual or flirtatious; I just get along with them as people.
>
> Therapist: And has that been true as an adult as well?
>
> Robert: I think so. Maybe Amelia has a better sense of that. But generally, I'm very comfortable being around females, and I enjoy talking with them and joking with them.

Therapist:	Amelia, what are your observations from watching Robert interact with females?
Amelia:	I think they love him, just as I did. He's a handsome man, bright, articulate, and very open. Robert relates beautifully with females, and they really respond. Although I don't think he is particularly flirty, I don't think he picks up on it when other females are sexually attracted to him. At some of his office parties, I think some of the females are pretty inappropriate with him, even with me standing there. I think that these females often think he is interested because he doesn' back them off when they flirt with him.
Therapist:	Robert, what is your sense of what Amelia is describing?
Robert:	Well, if I don't notice it, I don't notice it. I didn't grow up relating to females in a sexual way. Maybe I'm not good at understanding if they're flirting with me.
Therapist:	OK, let's try to make sense of what we've talked about so far. Let's think about some ways that this might have put you at risk or contributed to your relationship with Cassie. Amelia, what do you understand about what Robert has said and how it might have contributed to creating a high-risk situation with Cassie?
Amelia:	I knew all that about his growing up and his sisters, but I never thought about it from the standpoint of his relationship with Cassie. To be honest, what I hear sort of frightens me. I think Robert is being honest with me, that he wasn't setting out to have an affair. I think he grew up around females, and he really does understand them, almost instinctively. He is open and kind, and he really doesn't relate to females in a particularly sexual way. I think that makes them feel safe, and they open up around him. Then when they become romantically interested and start flirting with him, he doesn't notice.
Therapist:	Robert, would you think about what Amelia is saying?
Robert:	I think it makes sense, and I think that probably is what happened with Cassie. I wasn't looking for any kind of involvement with Cassie. She was a friend and a coworker. At some point, I just seemed to go down a slippery slope, and once I was there, it was too late to do anything about it.
Amelia:	I guess what worries me is that he didn't see it coming when it started. If he knew what he might be getting into, hopefully he could reform and commit not to do it again. But I believe him; I don't think he knew it was developing at this level early on.
Therapist:	At this point, I think you both are developing a good understanding of *one* factor that might have put Robert at risk. We'll continue to try to understand a variety of factors

and how they fit together to create this circumstance that you were in. Amelia, I know it seems frightening that it could happen again. We will continue to try to understand the various factors that contributed to this recent situation, and then we will explore if there are changes we can make to decrease the chances of it happening again in the future.

This example describes how one factor in Robert's developmental history helped to put him at risk for certain types of extramarital relationships. The therapist continued with a discussion of other factors from the past, along with a consideration of what was happening with Robert in the period leading up to and during the development of his relationship with Cassie. Further discussion of other factors, such as external stresses, the quality of the relationship between Robert and Amelia, and how Amelia was functioning individually, all contributed to providing a realistic perspective on the context within which Robert decided to have an extramarital affair.

Many times these discussions can lead to understanding and sometimes even compassion on the part of the injured person. Attempting to understand how the infidelity developed sets the stage for the next phase of treatment. As Amelia alluded to, the couple and therapist will spend considerable time addressing whether future extramarital relationships seem likely and what changes are needed to minimize this risk if the couple decides to stay together. These considerations, with an increased focus on the present and future, mark the transition into the third stage of treatment.

Moving Forward

Finally, the couple enter the third stage of the process, *moving forward*. Having developed a realistic understanding of why the unacceptable behavior occurred, the couple are able to evaluate their current relationship. They can assess what changes would be needed on the individual, couple, and environmental levels to decrease the likelihood that this inappropriate behavior will occur again. At this point some couples decide to remain together and work on their relationship and individual issues, as needed. On the basis of a realistic assessment, other couples decide to move forward while terminating their relationship. In either case, one would hope the injured person will give up the right to ongoing retribution, demands for restitution, anger, and hostility that currently dominate the relationship.

Our experience is that treating relationship traumas is different from addressing a wide variety of other negative experiences in a couple's relationship. In most cases, after relationship traumas, the injured individual is not able to move forward—either individually or as part of a couple—without addressing the trauma. In fact, Gordon and Baucom (1998b) found that individuals who said that they had forgiven their partners but had not gone through the psychological process just described were more likely to have distressed relationships, compared to individuals who been through this three-stage process. Thus, the clinician is unlikely to be successful in asking the couple to focus on the present and the future if previous relationship traumas have not been addressed. The ongoing negative feelings and disruption of assumptions frequently interfere with the couple's progress.

It is not always clear when current negative feelings are based on previous traumas within the current relationship. The therapist should consider this possibility when individuals' current emotional responses appear to be extreme or inappropriate, based on the current interactions between the partners. Similarly, if one partner makes consistent efforts to improve the relationship and the other partner continues to respond with anger, hurt, or fear, then one possibility is that this continuing emotional response is the result of unresolved prior traumatic experiences in the relationship. For example, although Marvin and Wanda had been in therapy for some time, Marvin continued to express hostility and anger toward Wanda for what appeared to be minor transgressions. Only after considerable time could he clarify that he had not been able to "get over" the ways that she had behaved four years previously. At that time she had experienced an "identity crisis," had become quite self-absorbed, and had significantly changed her role in the family without having any discussions and reaching agreements with Marvin that she would shift roles. She no longer was available to transport the children and frequently failed to prepare evening meals, a responsibility that she had accepted for many years. Marvin felt abandoned and angry that Wanda would "desert" him in this way without discussing such major changes. The therapist concluded that this change had been a traumatic event for Marvin and that the couple needed to address it before he would let go of his anger. As Marvin stated,

> How can I trust her? I trusted her before and she deserted me. I have to keep my guard up; I will never let that happen to me again. If it means I need to stay angry, I will stay angry.

Finally, even when a couple appears to be progressing well in processing traumatic events, disruptive negative emotions resurface and can be extremely confusing to one or both members of the couple who felt they were making progress. These extreme emotional responses have a flashback or reexperiencing quality about them, similar to what is experienced in posttraumatic stress disorder. In most instances, these responses are triggered by an external or internal stimulus that is associated with the original trauma. For example, Laura and Cliff had been in therapy for several months, processing the aftermath of an affair that Cliff had the previous year. They both were pleased that they were coming to a clearer understanding of the factors that contributed to Cliff's decision to become involved with another woman. They were committed to their marriage and felt that their relationship was becoming stronger than it had ever been. Then one day Laura unexpectedly became very upset when she saw some of Cliff's underwear on the floor. Laura described crying for hours, and it ruined her day. When Cliff came home he could not understand, because the affair had ended a year earlier, and he and Laura had been making significant progress in their relationship. In working with couples who have experienced a relationship trauma, it is beneficial to prepare them for these flashback-type phenomena with the attendant emotional distress. We explain these experiences to couples as conditioned or learned emotional responses that are evoked by some stimulus or aspect of the environment that originally was related to the trauma. We then provide the couple with suggestions of how to respond. It is important to determine whether the individual is distressed because factors in the current relationship are upsetting; for example, a wife is spending little time with her husband, which is important to him. If so, then the present interaction patterns in the relationship become the focus of the intervention. If it appears that the emotional response is a conditioned reaction to a stimulus from the past, it is important to label it as such. This labeling does not invalidate the emotional response but instead clarifies the basis for it. The couple then should respond to the needs of the injured partner. On such occasions, some injured partners need significant reassurance, whether these are verbal statements of love and commitment or some form of physical comfort. Other individuals need distance and time away from the participating partner to recover from the emotional response. A key feature is labeling the basis for the emotion so that the participating partner does not misinterpret the interaction and can be responsive to the injured person's needs. In addition, the emotional responses of the participating partner must be considered. At times, the participating partner is truly remorseful for the behavior and attempts to put it in the past. The participating partner can feel quite discouraged and frustrated when the injured partner has repeated flashback experiences, thus bringing the traumatic event back into focus in their current lives. The participating partner consequently also needs opportunities to express his or her feelings about the difficulty of living with the past and possible feelings of continuing shame, guilt, and frustration.

In the preceding discussion, we have addressed how to process a traumatic relationship event, such as an affair. As we also noted, the third stage of treatment involves shifting the emphasis to the present and the future. In this stage there is considerable focus on how to change the relationship to decrease the likelihood of affairs in the future. Moreover, the extramarital activities occurred within the context of a broader couple relationship that needs to be discussed. Several factors in the relationship unrelated to the affair might need to be addressed as well. In most instances, it is appropriate to integrate a discussion of the traumatic event, as suggested earlier, with helping the couple address other problematic aspects of their relationship. In some instances, couples are motivated to begin creating a more positive, loving relationship from the beginning of treatment. For other couples, however, the injured person is emotionally distraught or feels unsafe with the partner. In these instances, focusing on tender feelings and becoming vulnerable to the partner must be undertaken gradually as the traumatic event is processed.

SUMMARY

Couples therapy can become increasingly challenging when one or both partners is experiencing significant individual difficulties, because the individual issues can influence the couple's relationship functioning, or relationship functioning can precipitate, maintain, or exacerbate an individual partner's distress. In this chapter we have described a variety of ways to incorporate a focus on individual psychopathology into couples therapy, as described below.

- Successfully incorporating these individual issues into couples therapy requires a breadth of knowledge and treatment interventions on the part of the therapist, which may call for collaboration with other mental health service providers.
- Therapists can include partners in the treatment of individuals' clinical disorders or subclinical phenomena through *partner-assisted interventions*, which use the partner as a coach; *disorder-specific couples interventions*, which target symptom-maintaining behaviors in the relationship; or *couples therapy*, as described throughout this book, which improves individual symptoms by increasing relationship satisfaction.
- Long-term unresolved issues extending beyond the current relationship can interfere with the fulfillment of individuals' communal and individually oriented needs and relationship quality. The therapist should determine whether to use individual or couples' interventions to address the impact of one person's core interpersonal beliefs on the current relationship.
- Relationship traumas are negative events in the current relationship that disrupt an individual's assumptions about the partner or relationship. Interventions for traumas such as affairs or domestic violence target each stage experienced by the injured partner after the negative event: (a) *absorbing the blow* of the traumatic event, (b) *giving meaning* to the event and developing a new conceptualization of the partner and relationship, and (c) *moving forward* by evaluating the current relationship.
- We have provided several interventions that require the therapist to sequence and integrate strategies aimed at both individuals and the couple's relationship.

14

INTERVENTIONS FOR
ENVIRONMENTAL DEMANDS

In this chapter we describe methods for increasing partners' awareness of how their physical and interpersonal environment influence their relationship as well as ways that their environment can benefit them. We discuss interventions for decreasing residual effects of past negative experiences and effects of present environmental demands; we also describe ways of facilitating couples' positive involvements in their environment.

As we described in chapter 5, couples face a variety of demands associated with their physical and interpersonal environments. The literature on cognitive–behavioral couples therapy has primarily addressed environmental factors as issues to which couples need to apply problem-solving skills. The generic *process* of finding solutions to demands that a couple faces has been emphasized, but little attention has been paid to the *content* of particular types of environmental demands. Although generic problem-solving skills are crucial to successful coping with environmental demands, it also is important to consider particular characteristics of the demands as well as the couple's coping resources and strategies, in designing appropriate interventions. Consequently, we begin this chapter with a brief overview of several major dimensions on which environmental demands can vary and implications that different types of demands may have for intervention. Next we discuss the importance of considering the resources that are available to couples for coping with environmental demands as well as the attitudes that the partners have about using those resources. We then describe goals and specific strategies for intervention. Throughout this book we have described how couples must adapt to residual effects of past experiences that they had as individuals or as a couple as well as to present conditions. Consequently, the interventions in this chapter are organized into separate sections focused on past and current environmental demands. Although some interventions for past and current experiences overlap, this organization highlights special issues that must be addressed in each area. All of the other characteristics of environmental demands described in this section can be equally true of past and current demands, so they are addressed whenever appropriate in both sections on intervention strategies.

TYPES OF ENVIRONMENTAL DEMANDS
AND IMPLICATIONS FOR INTERVENTION

- Some environmental demands involve the partners' *past experiences* with their physical or interpersonal environment that still affect the couple, even though the original source of the stress may no longer be present, whereas others involve *current experiences.*

Members of a couple are influenced not only by their current environment but also by residual effects of experiences that they had with their past physical and interpersonal environments. For example, an individual who grew up in a cramped, dirty household may have little tolerance for disorder in the couple's current home. Similarly, a person who experienced emotional and physical abuse as a child may experience anxiety whenever a partner expresses any anger, even in a benign way. Identifying the degree to which partners are responding to past rather than current experiences has important implications for treatment. First, members of couples enter therapy with varying levels of awareness and attitudes concerning lasting impacts of prior life experiences. Some individuals believe that people's past experiences inevitably shape their present responses, whereas others believe that the impacts of past events, particularly from childhood, fade and become inconsequential. When a therapist has identified past environmental events that appear to be influencing a couple's present interactions, the intervention may need to address the couple's beliefs about the relevance of past experiences.

Second, often the aspects of a couple's past environmental demands that still affect them are no longer accessible for direct intervention. For example, an individual's earlier experiences with an abusive parent or severe job stresses may have changed significantly or ended, so there is no opportunity or need to help the person cope with the original source of stress. Instead, therapists must help the individual cope with his or her residual responses, such as automatic cognitive, emotional, and behavioral responses. Thus, an individual who grew up with an abusive parent may automatically become anxious and withdraw whenever conflict arises with his or her partner. If the individual still has a stressful relationship with that parent, helping the person interact with the parent more effectively may reduce stress on the individual and couple. In other cases, the abusive parent may be deceased. Consequently, the most realistic approach to intervention may involve reducing the individual's automatic anxiety response and tendency to withdraw from verbal conflict with the partner. Some of the interventions we describe in this chapter for dealing with past environmental demands focus on reducing such automatic responses.

- Some environmental demands have *indirect effects* on the couple, through their impact on one member, whereas others have *direct effects* on the couple's dyadic interactions.

As we discussed in chapter 5, an environmental demand may have an indirect impact on a couple by means of its effect on one member's functioning, or it may directly influence the couple's interactions. As an example of an indirect effect, one person may become so anxious and preoccupied because of job demands that his or her participation in the couple's relationship decreases. In contrast, financial demands may directly affect a couple's interactions by dominating their daily conversations and decreasing intimacy in their relationship.

This distinction has important implications for treatment. When the pathway is primarily through one person, the therapist needs to devise interventions that (a) help the person cope with the external demand, (b) decrease the couple's negative responses to the individual's poor coping pattern (e.g., mutual avoidance when the individual becomes anxious), and (c) increase the partner's social support of the stressed individual. It is important to emphasize that anything affecting either person negatively is likely to affect both of them and that therapy is intended to help them work as a team to cope with stressful individual or shared experiences.

- Demands involve "layers" of the couple's interpersonal and physical environments.

A couple's relationship is embedded in several layers of their physical and interpersonal environments (Carter & McGoldrick, 1999). The most proximal layer involves the physical characteristics and conditions of their home as well as the couple's interpersonal relationships with children and other adults who live there. Broader layers of the physical environment include characteristics of the neighborhood, workplace, wider community, state, and nation (e.g., congestion, noise, pollution, commuting distance to work, employment and economic conditions). Similarly, broader layers of the interpersonal environment involve relationships with extended family, friends, neighbors, coworkers, school personnel, helping professionals, and members of other social institutions (e.g., social service agencies), and broader social influences (e.g., societal discrimination on the basis of race).

An important implication of this multilayer view of environmental demands is that couples therapists often need to help their clients devise strategies to address factors that extend well beyond the confines of their dyadic interactions and home life. Effective intervention often requires the therapist to be familiar with the workings of schools, local child protective services agencies, religious organizations, and other aspects of the larger social system that create demands on the couple or provide potential resources for them (Carter & McGoldrick, 1999). Sometimes interventions are limited to coaching a couple in problem solving about more effective ways of coping with difficulties from a particular aspect of their physical or interpersonal environment; at other times the therapist may intervene more actively to reduce demands on a couple or to increase their access to helpful resources. For example, a therapist might initiate a meeting involving the couple, therapist, and school officials, to resolve an impasse between the couple and school concerning an appropriate educational program for their learning-disabled child.

- Demands vary along dimensions of chronic versus acute, volitional versus nonvolitional, ambiguous versus unambiguous, normative versus nonnormative, and isolated versus cumulative.

In chapter 6 we described each of these dimensions along which demands can vary. These characteristics often affect the ways that members of a couple perceive the demands, as well as the couple's experience and skills for adapting to them. For example, a couple may become habituated to a chronic demand and experience minimal stress from it; however, the onset of an acute demand may be disconcerting and anxiety provoking. In contrast, other individuals may experience a sense of helplessness and hopelessness from unremitting chronic stressors, but they may perceive the onset of a new demand as a potentially solvable challenge. Furthermore, some individuals take a relatively passive stance toward situations that they have chosen to experience, such as a more demanding job, believing that they should accept any unpleasant consequences of their choices. In addition, although cumulative demands have the potential to overwhelm a couple's coping ability, success in coping with past difficulties may increase the partners' confidence and coping skills (M. A. McCubbin & McCubbin, 1989). Knowledge of ways in which couples interpret the types of demands they face and the impacts that these appraisals have on their coping efforts can help the therapist plan interventions.

Successful coping is affected not only by the nature of the demands but also by the resources that the couple have available. In the next section we describe factors that therapists need to consider in maximizing couples' use of individual, couple, and environmental resources.

IMPACT OF AVAILABLE AND PERCEIVED RESOURCES ON INTERVENTIONS FOR ENVIRONMENTAL DEMANDS

A couple's ability to adapt to aspects of their environment depends on their coping resources. Therapeutic interventions must take into account:

- The individual, couple, and environmental resources available to the couple.
- The partners' awareness of the available resources.
- Each individual's attitudes about using those resources.

A major type of resources involves the partners' typical patterns of coping with demanding life events, such as active problem solving or avoidance (described in chapter 6). Sometimes two partners' coping styles are consistent with each other (e.g., mutual avoidance of dealing with concerns), and sometimes they are at odds with each other (e.g., one partner prefers active problem solving but the other prefers avoidance). Interventions must take into account both the degree of compatibility between two partners' coping styles and their effectiveness. For example, a couple may be comfortable with each other's similar tendency to avoid thinking about areas of concern, but the result may be that no one takes the actions needed to counteract the couple's financial problems. Therapists need to guide couples in identifying how well their coping styles help them solve problems and in considering other approaches when necessary.

As we described previously, couples may be unaware of some resources that are available to them, such as community services and support groups for particular problems such as coping with a family member's chronic illness. Therefore, one of the therapist's roles is to increase the couple's knowledge of potential resources and to determine whether the partners have favorable attitudes toward using these options. When partners choose not to use potentially useful approaches, the therapist needs to address their negative attitudes about using the resources.

In addition, a couple's ability to use available resources can be impeded by the existence of negative, ineffective interaction patterns between the partners. A couple who engage in a pattern of mutual attack, demand–withdrawal, mutual withdrawal, or disengagement are unlikely to work well together as a team in coping with environmental demands. Methods for reducing interactions that interfere with the couple's collaborative efforts were described in chapter 12.

Although this chapter emphasizes interventions to assist couples who are having difficulty adapting to environmental demands, in earlier chapters we also have noted ways in which a couple's involvement with their environment is an important source of positive experiences. Many couples become involved with their environment to meet important communally oriented and individually oriented needs. For example, many couples have meaningful experiences investing time and energy together in working for a social cause. Consequently, sometimes the focus of therapy is on improving the quality of a couple's relationship by helping them increase mutually rewarding relations with their environment. This chapter includes a section on interventions that may facilitate couples' positive involvements with their environment.

INTERVENTIONS FOR PAST ENVIRONMENTAL DEMANDS THAT AFFECT CURRENT FUNCTIONING

The histories of the couple and of each individual may reveal past experiences with their environment that continue to affect them in significant ways. A member of the couple may have residual effects of physical, emotional, or sexual abuse in his or her family of origin, for instance. Posttraumatic stress symptoms, lack of trust in others, and sexual aversion and other sexual dysfunctions commonly affect the individual and the couple's current interactions (McKenry & Price, 2000). Other stressful past interpersonal experiences, such as deaths of relatives and close friends, loss of an important job, and estrangements from significant others, can have lasting effects on an individual's self-esteem and sense of security as well as the couple's relationship. Past negative experiences with aspects of the physical environment similarly can affect an individual's current functioning. An individual who grew up with poverty and deprivation, for instance, may focus on creating an attractive home with expensive furnishings to a degree that is upsetting to his or her partner.

Sometimes couples are aware of residual impacts of past environmental events, but at other times they do not see the connection. In some cases, one member of a couple understands the link between past experiences and current problems, but the person's partner has little understanding or sympathy. Even when a couple is aware of effects of past events, they may not know adequate ways to reduce them. Consequently, the major goals of intervention are to:

- increase couples' awareness and realistic appraisal of current effects of past environmental events;

- decrease overlearned cognitive, emotional, and behavioral responses based on past experiences; and
- reduce the impact of past experiences by changing current conditions.

Increasing Awareness and Realistic Appraisal of Responses to Past Environmental Events

Members of a couple may underestimate or overestimate the association between past events and present distress. On the one hand, in recent years popular media and some self-help books have portrayed patterns in which individuals who had stressful childhood experiences (e.g., an alcoholic parent) inevitably have adult adjustment and relationship problems (Searles & Windle, 1990). These popular portrayals may contribute to some individuals' impressions that negative impacts of stressful childhood experiences are normative and chronic. Although many people function well in spite of their stressful childhoods (Searles & Windle, 1990; Walsh, 1998), some individuals enter couples therapy having been exposed to messages in the popular media and assume that their current relationship problems were caused by earlier life experiences that were beyond their control. On the other hand, some individuals discount their own or their partners' prior life experiences as influences on current relationship problems. We have worked with couples in which there was substantial evidence that one member's physical or sexual abuse in childhood affected his or her responses to the partner. However, the person's partner's expressed a belief such as, "That happened 20 years ago. It should have worn off by now." Some other partners find it hard to comprehend the lasting effects of a person's past experience, because the event was not something that he or she personally considers traumatic or repulsive. Thus, Sun Kum had little empathy when Jae discussed his chronic anxiety about his work performance and tied it to the trauma he experienced when he lost his job 2 years before they met. Her initial response was, "It was just a job. You got another one." Jae explained that losing the job had been a major blow to his self-esteem, because he had largely defined himself in terms of his work. Because Sun Kum valued work but based her identity on a variety of other aspects of her life, she attributed Jae's persistent worry, and its effects on their daily life, to "his personality problems."

Some people have difficulty feeling sympathetic about their own or a partner's negative past experiences that are normative. They believe that people should expect these things to occur in their lives and accept them in a philosophical manner. Thus, Victor said to Faye, "You're not the only one who's ever been left by someone they loved. It happens every day!"

Finally, members of a couple may underestimate cumulative effects from a series of environmental demands that an individual experienced in the past

(M. A. McCubbin & McCubbin, 1989). Thus, it may not seem logical to a couple that a person's past depressive episodes were triggered by events such as criticism from a boss and an argument with an acquaintance. However, the therapist's assessment may have revealed that those events were preceded by a series of events that the person experienced as failures, so the individual attached great significance to the final triggering events as "further proof that I'm a loser." Other individuals experience a wearing down of their usual resilience when several demands accumulate; eventually they are too fatigued and distracted to cope effectively with the latest issue.

When members of a couple overestimate or underestimate the residual effects of past environmental events, several types of interventions can be useful in addressing these cognitions.

- Didactic presentations about effects of past experiences on present functioning.
- Feedback from individual and couple assessments, illustrating residual effects.
- Use of expressive and listening skills to increase partners' empathy about lasting effects of each other's past experiences.
- Role-reversal exercises to facilitate mutual empathy.

First, the therapist can give a *didactic presentation* about empirical knowledge concerning the effects that prior life stresses can have on people's current functioning. On the one hand, people who are skeptical about lasting effects of past experiences can be informed about evidence of the potential for such lasting influences despite individuals' desires to move beyond them. On the other hand, individuals who overestimate effects of past experiences and believe they or their partners have been inevitably and permanently affected by past events can be given brief didactic presentations on factors that commonly contribute to resilience among individuals exposed to life stresses. The therapist can cite relevant research findings such as those indicating that a large percentage of adult children of alcoholics are free of psychopathology, interpersonal problems, and substance abuse (Easley & Epstein, 1991).

A second type of intervention involves using *feedback from the individual and couple assessments* to provide the couple a different perspective on the impact of past demands. For example, the therapist can point out evidence that an individual exhibits a response pattern that is similar to responses that he or she learned in the family of origin or other earlier relationships. Thus, Margaret and Tom's therapist described how Margaret's tendency to withdraw when the couple began to argue seemed to be a broad pattern in her close relationships, with parallels to the experiences that she had described in which her "best defense" against her verbally abusive parents was to say as little as possible.

Therapist:	Margaret, I noticed that you reacted to Tom just now. What emotion were you feeling, and what seemed to trigger the feelings?
Margaret:	I felt anxious when Tom raised his voice and started to speak so forcefully.
Therapist:	Does this usually happen when Tom debates with you?
Margaret:	Yes. I often want to get up and leave the room.
Therapist:	Did this situation remind you of any others you experienced earlier in your life?
Margaret:	It reminded me of living with my parents. If I have to live like that again, I don't think I can stand it.
Tom:	But that was many years ago, and I'm not your father!
Therapist:	Tom, you're right; you aren't Margaret's father. The two of you have made it clear to me that you are different from him in many ways. However, one of the tricky things about painful past experiences is that they are stored in people's memories and are easily triggered by situations that are similar in some way. Sometimes all it takes is one aspect of how someone else is behaving to set off the association in a person's mind. Margaret, there seems to be something about Tom's behavior when he is disagreeing with you that you associate with your father, and your self-protective reaction happens very quickly. It is important for both of you to be aware of how you respond in those situations, so you can develop your ability to deal with Margaret's automatic sensitivity to Tom's style. We can discuss several options for changing the pattern. Tom, since you know Margaret reacts quickly when you raise your voice and speak forcefully, perhaps you could work on expressing your views in a different style. Margaret, the more you can catch yourself responding automatically to Tom's style, the more you may be able to view it as different from your father's style and behave differently in return. Let's discuss some options for changing your pattern.

Third, the therapist can coach the couple in using *expressive and empathic listening skills* to discuss an individual's past and present experiences, to increase the couple's awareness of residual effects of the past events. Thus, Margaret and Tom's therapist asked Margaret to describe her family-of-origin experiences to Tom as well as the automatic responses she has to his debating style, and Tom was asked to respond with empathic listening skills. In turn, Tom had an opportunity to express what it was like for him when Margaret withdrew, and Margaret practiced empathic listening and reflecting.

Fourth, a therapist can ask a couple to engage in a *role-reversal exercise*, in which they role play each other. Thus, Tom was asked to pretend that he was Margaret and describe her family-of-origin experiences as well as her present responses to conflict, while Margaret played the role of Tom and discussed what it is like to talk with a partner who becomes anxious and withdraws. Tom developed a greater appreciation of the degree to which Margaret's vivid memories of her parents' verbal abuse could be triggered by his forceful debating style, and Margaret better understood Tom's frustration with her withdrawal.

When members of a couple more fully appreciate the impacts of each other's past experiences, it may reduce the degree to which they blame each other for particular types of negative responses (Guerney, 1977). Instead, they may be more sympathetic about each other's vulnerabilities and relatively automatic ways of protecting themselves, and the therapist can assist them in problem solving about more supportive ways of behaving with each other.

Reducing the Impact of Past Experiences by Decreasing Individuals' Overlearned Automatic Cognitive, Emotional, and Behavioral Responses

One of the ways in which past environmental experiences continue to influence a couple's relationship is through overlearned automatic cognitive, emotional, and behavioral responses (see chapter 12). An individual who has developed a belief that one cannot rely on significant others for consistent emotional support, for example, may automatically interpret any inconsistent behavior by a partner as a sign that the partner is generally unreliable (Johnson & Greenberg, 1994a). When asked to consider that interpretation in light of other experiences with the partner, the individual may understand the distortion in his or her automatic thoughts. Nevertheless, the person's basic schema is likely to persist and influence more interpretations of the partner's behavior. Consequently, a therapist can coach the individual in noticing instances in which he or she is interpreting a partner's behavior negatively, in considering the degree to which the interpretation is another instance of a macrolevel view based on past experiences, and in thinking about the degree to which the negative interpretation actually fits the current circumstances with the partner. Other techniques for helping couples challenge such ingrained schemas were described in chapter 10.

Furthermore, a partner's action can trigger an individual's strong emotional and behavioral responses without the individual having any conscious thoughts about it. For example, while having sexual relations with Todd, Melissa occasionally and unexpectedly became very anxious and pushed him away. If he continued to touch her or tried to talk to her, she became angry and stormed away. Later, Melissa felt bad about the incident tried to explain to Todd that he was not doing anything wrong. She was in individual therapy to deal with continuing distress from the sexual abuse she experienced from her father during childhood, but her strong emotional and behavioral responses during sexual intimacy continued. The couple's therapist also worked with them on how they could cope with Melissa's responses whenever they occurred (Maltz, 1988; McCarthy, 1997). The therapist asked Melissa to identify the specific types of circumstances in which she reacted strongly, and she was able to narrow it down to times when she felt restricted physically. The therapist suggested that the couple experiment with positions that would maximize Melissa's sense of physical freedom. The therapist also coached both members of the couple in using self-instruction or self-statements to reduce both partners' emotional arousal, Melissa's behavioral withdrawal, and Todd's pursuit of her. Melissa composed a self-statement: "Relax and enjoy the close feelings with Todd. He loves me, and this is a safe relationship." Detailed procedures for conducting self-instructional training can be found in Meichenbaum's (1985) book. We described other emotional regulation techniques in chapter 11.

Modifying the Individual's Responses to Chronic Negative Life Experiences

Some past environmental experiences still affect an individual because the person continues to be exposed to them and has not developed new ways of responding to them. The concepts and methods used by intergenerational family therapists (e.g., Carter & McGoldrick, 1999) can address partners' tendencies to respond to significant others just as they did in earlier times. If an adult continues to relate to his or her parents in the manner that was established during childhood, this relationship may interfere with the person's ability to develop new patterns with a partner. Thus, the therapist discussed with Margaret how she had never tried behaving differently toward her parents, so their relationships currently were essentially the same as when she was a child. When Margaret and Tom visited her parents, she was reserved and withdrew if her parents criticized her. This behavior often led to an argument between Margaret and Tom during their drive home from the visit, typically when Tom commented, "Why in the world do you just sit there and let them treat you that way?"

The therapist used several types of interventions to alter Margaret's typical responses to her parents. The first involved *addressing Margaret's macrolevel schema* regarding her relationship with her parents. The therapist discussed with Margaret how she appears to think about interactions with her parents from the perspective of the child who had little power, even though she is now an adult who has more sophisticated social skills and does not depend on her parents for her survival (Young, 1990; Young & Klosko, 1993). Margaret agreed that when she visits her parents she feels "like I'm 10 years old again." The therapist suggested that Margaret might feel more comfortable and in control if she caught herself responding as the 10-year-old and experimented with a new pattern.

A second type of cognitive intervention involves *coaching the individual in considering the validity of long-standing cognitions* that have interfered with his or her ability to cope better with a chronic negative life experience. For example, Margaret avoided asserting herself with her parents in part because she viewed them as self-confident and strong. The therapist helped Margaret examine her attribution that her parents behave aggressively because they are self-confident and secure. Margaret was guided in considering the possibility that their behavior reflected defensiveness and insecurity and that if she behaved assertively they might back down from their aggressive stance once they realized that they could not intimidate her.

Third, the therapist used *behavioral interventions to provide the client new experiences* concerning her ability to relate to her parents differently. During therapy sessions, Margaret was asked to practice acting "as if" she were assertive and confident with her parents. Engaging a person's partner in helping him or her experiment with behaving in new ways can enhance the couple's ability to deal with chronic difficulties in the individual's life. The therapist asked Tom to role play one of Margaret's parents, to help her rehearse assertive responses. As Margaret observed herself behaving assertively, she began to believe she could be assertive with her parents. When she felt ready, she behaved in this as-if manner during a visit with them. Tom's role was to lend support through subtle cues, such as a wink when she was asserting herself or a quiet reassuring comment such as, "Remember, they no longer have power over you."

Finally, interventions described in chapter 11 can be used to *modify emotional responses* that an individual continues to have in family-of-origin and other ongoing significant relationships. Margaret's anxiety in the presence of her parents might be decreased by helping her to identify a hierarchy of stressful types of interactions with her parents and to reduce her emotional reactivity to those situations by using strategies such as positive self-talk or muscle relaxation. The calming effect of such interventions can make it easier for the individual to engage in positive self-talk and effective behavioral responses when he or she is exposed to the chronic negative demands. By altering the individual's cognitive, behavioral, and affective responses to those situations, the therapist may empower the person to respond more effectively to chronic demands. Engaging the person's partner in a supportive role counteracts negative impacts of the demands on the couple's relationship.

INTERVENTIONS FOR CURRENT ENVIRONMENTAL DEMANDS

In this section we describe interventions for increasing a couple's ability to adapt to positive and negative demands that have developed within their current physical and interpersonal environments. The major goals of interventions with current environmental demands overlap considerably with those of interventions for helping individuals cope with their past experiences.

- Increase partners' awareness of current demands on the individual and couple.
- Maximize realistic appraisals of demands and the use of effective coping strategies.
- Facilitate the couple's communication and problem-solving skills for using resources.
- Assist the couple in using appropriate strategies for particular common positive and negative environmental demands.

Increasing Awareness of the Impacts of Current Demands on the Individuals and the Couple

Members of a couple often underestimate the ways in which particular environmental demands affect their relationship. A couple may complain to a therapist about their hectic schedules and competing demands on their time from their family and work roles, failing to understand how these demands are interfering with intimacy in their relationship and are increasing their bickering. Some couples may not realize how aspects of their physical environment (e.g., chronic noise or clutter) affect their relationship. In such cases, interventions are needed to increase partners' awareness of impacts of their environment and changes that may be beneficial. Although it is important for a couple to realize how powerful environmental influences can be, actually experimenting with different ways of coping may demonstrate to the couple that they have more ability to control their environment than they thought possible.

The therapist can briefly describe how the couple have provided information about environmental conditions that appear to interfere with their functioning, even though the couple may have become accustomed to their presence to some degree. Often clients equate chronicity of circumstances with inevitability: "If it has been this way for so long, that must mean it is destined to be this way." Ken and Emily believed that their demanding life left them virtually helpless to have a life as a couple. They remarked that their life had been that way for so long that they had lost control over it. Their therapist acknowledged how busy and stressful the couple's lives were and reflected the feelings of frustration and disappointment that they had expressed. The therapist then guided the couple in thinking about whether having no time together was inevitable.

Therapist: Your busy schedules interfere with having opportunities to relate to each other in intimate ways as you did in the past. After your life has been that way for so long, it seems difficult to imagine finding ways to change it. I wonder if you have become so discouraged that you might even overlook small opportunities for some couple time. I heard how you used to enjoy time together, so it would be unfortunate if even small opportunities were lost. Can we review what typical days and evenings are like, during the week and on the weekends, to see if there's something that you have overlooked?

Some individuals hold an assumption that intimate, loving feelings are solely the result of chemistry between two people and are not affected by environmental events. A therapist can challenge this assumption by presenting a didactic description of common stages in couple relationships, beginning with the initial "honeymoon" or "sparkle" stage (Goldstine, Larner, Zuckerman, & Goldstine, 1993), in which the partners focus on each other's positive qualities and feel close, versus subsequent stages when life stresses and areas of incompatibility become more obvious and ambivalent feelings emerge. The therapist also can inquire about instances in which temporary stressful or distracting circumstances led the partners to feel less intimate for a while even during the early stages of their relationship, as well as instances when they experienced even small doses of more intimate feelings in recent times. If partners understand how variations in situational conditions influence their intimacy feelings, they may consider ways in which they can manipulate situations in their daily lives to increase positive feelings. It is useful to explore Prager's (1995) distinction between a broader (macrolevel) intimate relationship and specific, situational intimate interactions as they apply to the couple's experience.

It is important for a therapist to set realistic expectancies when designing experiments to test whether changing the environment will help the couple. Because a small, temporary change in a couple's environment is unlikely to result in their feeling very differently, we emphasize the idea of looking for "hints" that changing the environment has potential to improve subjective feelings. The next step is to problem-solve about ways to build in more of those changes whenever it is realistic to do so. In the next section we describe ways of guiding a couple in identifying potential changes in their environment.

As we described earlier, demands may originate from levels of the couple's environment that range from their nuclear family to broad societal influences, such as racial discrimination. A couple may be aware of some levels of demands, but the therapist may need to point out others and be sure that interventions target all relevant levels. Thus, Connie and Joanne described stresses from their jobs but said nothing about environmental stresses associated with living as a lesbian couple. When their therapist asked them if being a lesbian couple affected how they dealt with any aspects of their world, they noted that they kept the nature of their relationship private at their jobs because of fear of discrimination, and they were self-conscious about how they expressed affection to each other in public. Although they seemed resigned to "the way it is in our society," the therapist explored the degree to which the societal stressors were detracting from the quality of the couple's relationship (L. S. Brown, 1995). Because Connie and Joanne had a limited support network because of their unease about "coming out" to many people, the therapist engaged them in problem solving to identify ways of expanding their support system.

Thus, a major goal of these cognitive and behavioral interventions is to increase the couple's awareness that environmental circumstances influence their subjective feelings about their relationship. A second important goal is to demonstrate to the couple that systematic efforts to change their environmental circumstances can produce more positive feelings. These goals can be addressed by (a) making brief didactic presentations, (b) asking the couple to think about experiences in which their environment influenced them, and (c) setting up behavioral experiments involving manipulation of their environment.

Maximizing Realistic Appraisals and the Use of Effective Coping Strategies

The preceding interventions focus on helping couples recognize how their environment influences their relationship. Moreover, couples commonly need assistance in developing strategies for influencing those environmental events. The primary form of intervention is decision making or problem solving, in which the therapist guides the couple in defining a concern, identifying a feasible solution, and implementing it. In some cases, a couple may have taken little action because they have underestimated the potential for improving their environment. Other couples overestimated their ability to change aspects of their environment and became demoralized when their efforts fell short of their expectations. In either case a therapist must help the couple overcome their sense of helplessness and hopelessness, distinguishing between aspects of their environment that can be changed and those that are very difficult or even impossible to change.

Realistic appraisal of the potential for changing an environmental demand involves

- identifying the specific changes that would be required;
- identifying the resources needed to produce the required changes, and ways to use them; and
- determining whether the relevant resources are available and whether the members of the couple are willing to use them.

For example, Ken and Emily's therapist coached them in identifying aspects of their work and home environments that were interfering with their intimate experiences. They agreed that interruptions from the children interfered with them sharing their ideas and feelings the way they had done in the past, that the extensive time they spent on work projects and chores depleted their energy and time for each other, and that the marked decrease in their shared leisure activities made their relationship feel neutral at best. The couple noted specific changes that would be required to improve the situation, including fewer interruptions of their conversations by their children, more time together during some evenings, more rest, and opportunities to go out together socially. The necessary resources they identified were effective parenting skills, time management skills, and reliable babysitters. The therapist then coached Ken and Emily in decision-making discussions to identify specific actions that they could take to implement change.

It is important that a therapist help a couple review a variety of personal, couple, and environmental resources that are already available or potentially available. Often people repeatedly use the resources that are most familiar to them and fail to search for new ones. Sometimes the partners can think of new resources on their own during brainstorming discussions, but at other times input from the therapist is needed. Katerina and Bob's therapist told them about low-cost money management counseling services available in their community, and Kendra and Noah's therapist gave them information about parenting classes. At times a couple may be aware of appropriate resources but have not made sufficient, consistent use of them. Thus, Kendra and Noah initially responded that they had already taken a parenting class at the local elementary school, but it had not been helpful. However, when their therapist asked for details about the class and how the couple implemented the methods that were taught, it became clear that the class provided mostly general principles and limited opportunities for participants to practice interventions for their particular parenting challenges. The therapist praised Kendra and Noah for the efforts they had made to improve their parenting skills but noted the limitations of the class they had taken and proposed that they may have better results if they try an alternative class that other couples had found useful.

Modifying Resistance to Using Available Resources

When one or both members of a couple are reluctant to use environmental resources because they hold standards that it is inappropriate to do so, the therapist needs to decide whether it may be appropriate to challenge the standards. As we discussed previously, it is important to respect cultural differences in people's values and standards, including strong beliefs in self-sufficiency. Sometimes it is a matter of identifying whether an individual has developed an extreme version of a commonly shared cultural standard. Some individuals hold a standard that turning to others for *any* help is a sign of weakness, immaturity, or other personal deficiencies. Other people view help seeking as appropriate if one's difficulties were nonvolitional and external but believe that if they were due to conscious choices, "You made your bed, so go lie in it." As Monique and Allen told their therapist, "We chose to move from a small town to a big city for a job opportunity, so we just have to learn to live with the noise, congestion, crazy drivers, and back-biting at the office."

When such cognitions block a couple's use of available resources, the therapist can use a variety of cognitive-restructuring interventions. When a couple views reliance on external resources as unacceptable because they chose their circumstances, we typically begin by asking how they made the decision that placed them in that situation and what advantages and disadvantages they had considered. The therapist might point out disadvantages that the couple had overlooked or underestimated during their decision making and ask them how much their standard requires that they refuse assistance even if they had misjudged some of the problems that they would encounter. The couple are guided in distinguishing between demands that one realistically appraised and chose versus those that were not truly accepted and chosen. If the therapist also identifies that an individual is refusing help as a means of punishing himself or herself for making a "bad choice," the appropriateness and utility of the standard concerning punishing oneself for mistakes need to be challenged.

Thus, Monique and Allen expressed anger toward themselves for moving to a big city environment that they experienced as oppressive, and Allen even remarked that, "Maybe if we suffer here we'll learn never to make a mistake like that again." The therapist addressed the advantages and disadvantages of the couple punishing themselves for their decision. One advantage was that they would remember the experience vividly and would be especially cautious when faced with future decisions. Disadvantages included the emotional distress and demoralization the couple felt when they thought of themselves as deserving punishment and the fact that their approach led them to avoid turning to potential resources in their environment that might decrease their environmental stress. The therapist also challenged the couple's belief that they should have been able to anticipate all of the problems that they were encountering. When the therapist asked them how they would have known about problems such as politics at their jobs, they reported that there were no clues during their job interviews. When the therapist asked Monique and Allen whether in hindsight their decision regarding the positive and negative aspects of the city environment seemed reasonable, they replied that theoretically it seemed reasonable, but so far the negatives were outweighing the positives. They noted that the stresses at their jobs interfered with the time and energy they had for enjoying the advantages of city life. The therapist then guided the couple in thinking of ways to restore the balance, reducing negative demands when possible and increasing positive experiences. For example, the couple devised plans for setting limits on the hours they were willing to spend on work projects when they were at home and scheduling time to develop new friendships and enjoy the cultural opportunities in the city together. This plan included joining a local church that had an active program of social activities for couples their age. The therapist asked Monique and Allen to compare the advantages and disadvantages of this problem-solving approach to using available resources with those of the self-punishment they had been using, and the contrast motivated them to work toward meeting their needs rather than denying themselves.

Cognitive interventions often will have limited impact on a couple's resistance to using available resources unless the partners experience positive outcomes when they actually try using the resources. After the couple devises strategies for using particular environmental resources, it is important for the therapist to coach them in implementing the plans. For example, Monique and Allen's therapist guided them in setting up and carrying out a plan to join the church social group and to schedule some time for leisure activities for the coming week.

Promoting Acceptance of Environmental Factors That Are Difficult to Change

Some negative aspects of a couple's environment are unlikely to be changed through their efforts, because no adequate personal or external resources are available. It is important for the couple and therapist to appraise when attempts to change the circumstances are likely to benefit the couple and when the costs of attempting to implement change are too great. When it appears that engagement strategies are unlikely to improve the situation, deciding to take no action and to accept the existing conditions as satisfactory may be the wisest approach, similar to Jacobson and Christensen's (1996) focus on helping partners reach acceptance of each other's characteristics that are relatively unchangeable.

Consider Jesse, who was emotionally abused by his parents throughout his childhood and adolescence and had maintained minimal contact with them since he left home to go to college. When he and Heidi decided to get married, he began to think about trying to reconcile with his parents so that his wife and any children they might have could know his parents. Although Heidi did not want Jesse to be hurt more, she understood his motivation and agreed that they should try some contact with his parents. The couple sought therapy to help them make decisions about relating to Jesse's parents. The therapist guided them in considering various degrees of involvement with Jesse's parents, ranging from brief phone calls to inviting them to the wedding. Jesse initially phoned his parents' home and spoke with his mother, who was cordial and seemed genuinely pleased to hear from him. However, during a second call, his father grilled him about his life and told him he thought Jesse would have a better job by now. Subsequently, the therapist and couple rehearsed ways of responding assertively if the parents became verbally abusive. When Jesse and Heidi met his parents for lunch at a restaurant, both parents were rude to Heidi, stating that their living together was "immoral, cheap sex." During therapy, the couple again weighed the pros and cons of different levels of contact with Jesse's parents, and they concluded that the likelihood of his parents becoming less abusive, even if confronted about it, was low. They decided to keep future contact to a minimum, and the therapist addressed Jesse's grief over once again losing the hope of having a good relationship with his parents.

ADAPTATION STRATEGIES FOR COMMON POSITIVE AND NEGATIVE ENVIRONMENTAL DEMANDS

In this section we describe typical issues that arise with certain types of environmental demands. Given the great variety of demands that couples experience, a comprehensive review is impossible, but the following examples illustrate ways that environmental demands affect individual and couple functioning and strategies that are relevant for reducing their negative impacts. Along with brief examples, we provide citations of literature that clinicians might find helpful.

Remarriage and Stepfamily Issues

When an individual who has lost a mate through death or divorce remarries, integrating children and extended family members from the "old" family with the new partner and his or her children and extended family can be challenging. Visher and Visher (1988) described difficulties that remarried couples commonly experience regarding conflicting loyalties to original and new family members, conflicts over a stepparent's degree of legitimate power with the stepchildren, unrealistic expectations that love and respect will develop quickly among stepfamily members, and boundary issues concerning who are "insiders" and "outsiders" in the family. The newly married couple has no "honeymoon" period, without children present, during which to build intimacy in their relationship, and they commonly have to deal with environmental stressors involving children, ex-spouses, and extended family members. Many stepfamilies also experience financial stresses due in part to child support and alimony payments that one or both partners may be making. These couples often need assistance with developing realistic standards for their own, their children's, and each other's performance in their stepfamily roles, as well as with effective communication and decision making.

A variety of cognitive–behavioral interventions are well suited to the needs of couples in stepfamilies (Leslie & Epstein, 1988). A therapist can make brief didactic presentations about the issues that stepfamilies commonly experience, to increase partners' awareness of these demands, convey that the issues are normal, and introduce decision-making conversations to devise ways to address the difficulties. Excellent publications are available (e.g., C. Berman, 1986; Papernow, 1992; Stuart & Jacobson, 1985; Visher & Visher, 1982) to supplement information provided by the therapist. In addition, the therapist can ask each member of the couple to describe how he or she had envisioned life in the stepfamily and how the realities compare to those expectancies. This discussion may uncover potentially unrealistic standards, such as a belief that stepchildren should automatically like and respect their stepparent (Visher & Visher, 1988). The therapist might address such beliefs by discussing with the individual how automatic liking and respect would be highly desirable but that he or she still is in many ways a stranger to the children and that close relationships generally develop gradually as people get to know each other. Couples who pressure children into accepting a stepparent as a substitute for an absent biological parent also may need input from the therapist about the loyalty conflicts that this demand may create for the children. Concerning the stepparent's role as an authority figure, it often is helpful to have the couple problem-solve about ways to gradually include the stepparent in monitoring, directing, and disciplining the children. It is important for the parent and stepparent to realize that children are likely to view the stepparent as an "insider" who has a right to discipline them if he or she has bonded with them emotionally, by demonstrating interest in their lives or providing social support. Once the couple have agreed on ways in which the stepparent will be involved with the stepchildren, the therapist might invite them to bring the children to a session, during which the couple can present a united front in describing the plan to the children. This intervention establishes the couple as a significant unit in the family and potentially reduces loyalty conflicts among the adults and children.

Concerning the logistic and financial complexities of stepfamily life, the couple may benefit from sessions on how to mediate conflicts between stepsiblings, ways to communicate constructively with hostile former spouses concerning the children, and decision making concerning money management. Referrals to community resources such as budgeting and credit counseling services and stepfamily support groups also may be useful.

Losses of Significant Relationships

It is inevitable that, at some time, one or both members of a couple will experience the loss of a relationship with a significant relative or friend through death, a long-distance move, or estrangement. The couples therapist needs to identify the subjective meaning of the loss for each partner, as well as how the loss has disrupted each person's life and the functioning of the couple (C. I. Murray, 2000; Neimeyer, 1998; Walsh, 1998). The therapist can ask each individual about these aspects of the loss and can encourage the partners to use reflecting skills to communicate to each other their understanding of the subjective experiences. In some cases the lost individual played a significant role in meeting needs of one or both partners, and they must compensate for the loss. When Jill's mother died of cancer, Jill felt strong grief, because she and her mother had been very close. As Jill explained, "We were the best of friends as well as mother and daughter." Even though Jill and Eric had a mutually satisfying level of intimacy in their relationship, Jill had continued to seek a healthy level of emotional support from her mother periodically. When her mother died, it was unclear whether she would now turn to Eric at times when she would have sought support from her mother. Thus, the couple needed to renegotiate their roles with each other. Coaching partners in the use of expressive and listening skills in discussing each other's ways of experiencing and coping with loss may increase mutual empathy and support.

Another issue that commonly arises is that two partners may have different ways of grieving the loss of a significant person (Neimeyer, 1998). Some individuals prefer to express strong emotions openly; others prefer to retreat into private contemplation. Similarly, some people focus on moving toward psychological detachment from a deceased significant other, whereas others maintain a psychological relationship with the deceased; for example, sensing the person's "presence" or feeling that aspects of the deceased are incorporated within oneself (Klass, Silverman, & Nickman, 1996). Conflicts can arise if the members of a couple do not understand or support each other's style of grieving and even criticize or pressure the other person to respond differently (C. I. Murray, 2000; Walsh, 1998). A therapist can help such couples by addressing the individuals' different standards about how people "should" grieve. The therapist can ask each person about various ways that he or she has observed other people grieving over a loss and what ways seem most sensible and comfortable for him or her. If an individual expresses a narrow standard about grieving, the therapist might introduce didactic information concerning wide variations among people in normal grief responses. The interventions we described in chapter 11 for dealing with basic differences in partners' individual characteristics all are relevant to addressing standards concerning coping with losses. Given that the professional literature has included widely varying theoretical views of what constitutes "normal" grieving (C. I. Murray, 2000), it is important for the therapist to avoid imposing his or her own personal standards concerning grief on the members of a couple.

The therapist also may need to modify negative attributions, such as one person's inference that the partner must not have cared enough for a deceased person because the partner showed little emotion. As we described in chapter 10, the therapist can use a variety of interventions for encouraging an individual to consider alternative explanations for a partner's behavior, such as coaching the individual in brainstorming possible causes or asking the partner for feedback about the thoughts and emotions associated with the controversial behavior. Some couples also benefit from role-reversal role plays, in which each individual may be able to experience how the other is responding to the loss of the significant person. These explorations of causes for the partner's behavior are also likely to involve discussion of standards concerning styles of coping with loss, as described earlier in this chapter.

Walsh (1998) provided an excellent description of additional risk factors for poor adjustment to the death of a significant other (e.g., sudden, unexpected deaths that give survivors no opportunity to resolve unfinished business in relationships with the deceased), as well as interventions that can help grieving couples and families.

Sometimes a member of a couple has lost a significant relationship through estrangement, such as when a longtime friend or family member becomes angry and cuts off contact, or physical and psychological distance develop as the parties' interests and daily lives increasingly move in different directions (Jerrome, 1994). At such times, the partner may not understand the person's ambivalent feelings toward the lost relationship and may respond in what the individual experiences as an unsupportive manner. For example, an individual who had been a close friend of Glenn's since childhood abruptly ended their relationship after an argument. Although Glenn was resentful and angry, he also felt great pain at the loss. Glenn's wife, Evelyn, had negative feelings toward his friend "for treating him shabbily." Evelyn's anger made it difficult for her to empathize when Glenn spoke of missing his friend, and she would criticize Glenn for not being more indignant. The couple's therapist addressed Evelyn's attempt to impose her standard that "you should totally reject people who treat you poorly." Her standard made it difficult for her to understand how Glenn could be both angry and sad at the loss of his friendship. In turn, Glenn had difficulty understanding Evelyn's "all-or-nothing" standard about accepting or rejecting people, because he held a standard that one should look for the good in a person. The therapist guided the couple in using expressive and listening skills to understand and communicate respect for differences in their beliefs. As with losses through death, it is important to assist partners in understanding and accepting individual differences in responses to loss through estrangement.

A special case of loss involves a couple's experience with infertility. Although diagnostic and treatment methods for infertility have improved considerably in recent years, many couples who seek assistance ultimately are unsuccessful in conceiving a child. In addition, the high cost of the medical procedures is often a major stressor, and some couples remain in limbo without a clear diagnosis. Mikesell and Stohner (1995) noted common responses among both women and men who are diagnosed as infertile, including emotional distress, a sense of loss, role failure, stigmatization, and lowered self-esteem. Women are more likely than men to experience depression and a sense of loss even when the partner is the one identified as infertile. Some fertile men feel anger toward their infertile female partners, perceiving them as obstacles to having children who will carry on the family name. The attributions that individuals make for the cause of the inability to conceive, and the degree to which they assign blame, can significantly influence the couple's relationship distress. Many infertile couples face the difficult situation of trying to provide the other person emotional support at a time when each individual feels a great need for support himself or herself. Instead of providing the couple support, some extended family members and friends increase stress by questioning them about when they will have a baby. Consequently, therapists can help infertile couples by (a) identifying and modifying distress-producing cognitions, such as rigid gender role standards (particularly that a "normal" woman or man becomes a parent) and self-criticism; (b) helping each partner cope with the losses and grief that he or she is experiencing; (c) improving the couple's expressive and listening skills to foster mutual emotional support; and (d) enhancing the couple's decision making to deal with intrusive family and friends and medical treatments that make the couple's sexual relationship regimented (Mikesell & Stohner, 1995).

The therapist can attempt to soften rigid standards that one should be a parent, enabling the partners to view it as a strong preference rather than a requirement to have a satisfying life. The therapist might discuss with the couple whether they would judge other childless couples to be inferior, what other sources of meaning they have in their lives, and whether they would consider other means of becoming parents, such as adoption. Didactic presentations on positive ways that couples cope with infertility also may be helpful. The couple may benefit from decision-making discussions and role-play exercises focused on preparing them to respond effectively to family members and other individuals who ask them uncomfortable questions or otherwise pressure them about their childless status. Expressive and listening skills can be used to enhance empathy with each other's thoughts and emotions concerning infertility.

Parenting Children With Special Needs

Parenting involves a variety of challenges under the best of conditions, but many couples have children with special needs, such as physical and intellectual disabilities, chronic illnesses, or psychopathology, which place additional demands on the couple (Barkley, 2000; Nicholson, 1998; Wood, 1995). For example, Wendy and Barry's 4-year-old daughter was born with physical and mental disabilities that required frequent diagnostic and treatment appointments with a variety of professionals who sometimes gave the couple conflicting evaluations and recommendations. In addition to the substantial daily demands of caring for their child's special needs, the couple were faced with making difficult decisions about the most appropriate treatments and preschool setting. When Wendy and Barry felt overwhelmed by these stresses, they tended to engage in escalating arguments, which created secondary distress. The therapist "caught" the couple engaging in an escalating argument during a therapy session on a day when they had already been to a doctor's appointment and a physical therapy appointment with their daughter. The therapist interrupted the argument, noting that it seemed to be focused on each person's perception that the other did not appreciate the personal sacrifices he or she was making in caring for their child. The therapist commented that the couple behaved in an adversarial manner at times when both appeared to need support, thereby adding secondary distress to the difficulties they already faced with their child. Next, the therapist guided the partners in using expressive and listening skills to communicate with each other about the stresses they had experienced during the day and the types of support they might find helpful from the other. The therapist also coached the couple in decision making about ways to use their professional resources effectively and protect some time for leisure.

Wendy and Barry's therapist also helped them develop techniques for reducing their anxiety, such as muscle relaxation exercises, giving each other massages, and planning ways to have breaks from dealing with their daughter's problems. Inducing the couple to value breaks involved challenging their standard that responsible parents should always put their child's needs first. The therapist asked the couple to list the advantages and disadvantages of neglecting one's own needs to take care of another person. Wendy and Barry were able to see the danger of "burnout," in which neglecting one's own well-being might compromise one's ability to be a good caretaker for another person (Felder, 1990).

When a couple has difficulty dealing with a child's behavior problems, as is common in cases of attention deficit hyperactivity disorder, sessions devoted to helping them plan new behavior management techniques might be followed by sessions that include the child (Barkley, 1998). During the family sessions, the therapist can coach and support the couple in using the parenting skills. The therapist might ask the parents and child to play a board game together, for example, coaching the parents in managing the child's disruptive and off-task behavior during the game.

The "Sandwich Generation"

More and more couples comprise what has been called the "sandwich generation," raising their children at the same time that they are caring for frail or disabled elderly parents (Walsh, 1999). This double duty often is combined with demands of one or both partners' jobs, producing role strain on the couple. Members of these couples commonly experience internal conflict concerning several demands that compete for their time and energy. If an individual sets high standards for his or her performance in all of these roles, the level of stress can be overwhelming. Moreover, members of a couple may be in conflict regarding each other's priorities. Although Tina was fond of Joe's parents, she perceived him as devoting too much time to helping his mother care for his father, who had Alzheimer's disease, and too little time sharing the responsibilities related to their three young children. In turn, Joe was resentful that Tina seemed insensitive to his exhaustion when he returned from his parents' home.

Couples who are trying to balance caring for their parents and children often need assistance with (a) resolving internal and couple conflicts over standards for appropriate performance of roles, (b) communicating constructively about their needs and feelings, (c) increasing mutual empathy and support, (d) making decisions about ways to manage their limited time and to set priorities among the tasks they face, and (e) identifying and using resources that can lighten their load. Concerning an individual's personal standards about meeting competing roles, a therapist might ask an individual such as Joe to describe all of the responsibilities he feels toward his wife, children, and parents and then list the advantages and disadvantages of trying to do it all. Felder's (1990) book for family caretakers provides an excellent description of the risks for burnout and strategies that individuals can use to take care of their own needs as well as those of significant others. The therapist should validate Joe's good intentions to be supportive to all the significant people in his life and engage Tina in acknowledging Joe's good intentions. Then the therapist could guide Joe in exploring how he has been risking burnout and upsetting Tina by trying to do so much for so many people. If Joe has difficulty assertively asking his siblings to share more of the responsibilities, the therapist might work with him on the assertiveness deficit.

If Tina has made an attribution that Joe's parents are more important to him than she and the children are, the therapist might guide her in considering alternative explanations; for example, that the problem is primarily Joe's pushing himself to do too much and his inefficient use of environmental resources. The therapist would coach the couple in using expressive and listening skills to discuss each other's motives and intentions and in using decision-making skills to devise new ways that Joe can fulfill his roles. The partners also could discuss new ways to reserve time for themselves as a couple so that their relationship will no longer be neglected.

Work Demands

We previously described situations in which a couple was affected by work demands experienced by one or both partners. Work can encroach on time that the couple could otherwise spend together. Sometimes the intrusion involves hours at the office, but it also can involve "taking the job home," either through actually doing paperwork or making phone calls or through intrusive thoughts and emotions about work when the partners are together. Work demands can create boundary and investment conflicts between partners (Haddock, Zimmerman, Ziemba, & Current, 2001). The members of a couple may have different standards about the degree to which work should be performed or even thought about at home as well as the relative time and energy that partners should invest in work versus in their couple and parent–child relationships. Often when an individual believes that a partner works too much, the individual attributes it to the partner's lack of caring about their relationship.

Therapists can help partners examine differences in their standards concerning boundaries and investment associated with work and evaluate the advantages and disadvantages of living according to those standards. When Carrie complained that Matt "often drifts off to thinking about work when I'm talking with him," their therapist guided them in comparing their different standards about the degree to which an individual should devote time and attention to work while at home. The therapist asked them to use expressive and listening skills to communicate about their standards. As the couple discussed the advantages and disadvantages of Carrie's view that "work should be left at the office," she was able to see that there were times when it was virtually impossible for an individual to succeed at certain assignments within standard work hours. In turn, Matt saw that if he set no clear boundaries for the times and places in which he would think about work projects his personal life would suffer, and ironically the conflict in his marriage would decrease his ability to perform his work well. Therapists often need to guide a couple in decision-making discussions, to share power in reconciling differences in their standards about work and family roles (Haddock et al., 2001).

A second intervention involves helping the members of a couple examine the validity of negative attributions they make about each other's work and family role behavior. Carrie interpreted Matt's becoming lost in thought about work as being due to his caring more about his job than about her. The therapist coached Carrie in considering alternative explanations for his behavior, such as "Matt feels responsible for contributing to our having a comfortable lifestyle, so he experiences pressure to please his boss and succeed in his job."

A third type of intervention involves helping the couple develop better skills for setting limits with work intrusions, such as handling phone calls from the boss during family time (Haddock et al., 2001). The therapist may need to explore reasons why partners are reluctant to try particular limit-setting strategies, such as fear that not answering the phone during dinnertime might incur a boss's wrath or result in a missed business opportunity. Often when individuals are willing to experiment with such strategies for a few days they discover that their fears were unfounded.

Some individuals manage work time poorly because they are perfectionists and feel inadequate if they need to assign certain tasks a lower priority and delay work on them. As a result, they often feel overburdened by multiple tasks and rarely feel comfortable taking breaks. Therapists may be helpful to these individuals by guiding them in identifying some tasks for which a delay would likely result in no negative consequences. In addition, some individuals have difficulty scheduling their time effectively (Goldenberg & Goldenberg, 1994). For example, Becky commonly underestimated the time required to complete tasks at her job as well as those involving household chores, so she often was significantly behind schedule. This tendency was especially problematic because it disrupted plans that she and Howard made to work on particular chores together or to spend leisure time together. Their therapist coached them in discussions focused on scheduling times for Becky's projects from her job, times for chores, and times for leisure. These discussions included a review and possible revisions of Becky's initial time estimates. The therapist and couple established behavioral experiments to check the accuracy of Becky's new estimates for completing tasks.

Finally, some individuals need interventions for reducing intrusive thoughts and unregulated emotions associated with work, especially anxiety. Many of the interventions we described in chapter 11 for use with emotional dysregulation are appropriate for work-related distress that interferes with the individual's ability to focus on the couple's relationship. Individuals whose work-related anxiety is associated with generalized anxiety disorder may require individual therapy in addition to couples therapy.

The assessment of each couple is likely to reveal other types of environmental demands, as well as personal and environmental resources that the therapist can guide the couple in using. Although this discussion has focused on helping couples cope better with environmental factors that *detract* from the quality of their relationships, a couple's environment also can provide opportunities for meeting the partners' needs and *strengthening* their relationship. In the following section we describe ways in which a couple can use their interactions with their environment to benefit their relationship.

USING THE ENVIRONMENT TO MEET PARTNERS' NEEDS

As we described earlier, couples sometimes can satisfy their communally oriented and individually oriented needs by participating in outside activities together. Some couples experience closeness by participating together in groups such as bridge clubs, bowling leagues, or bicycling clubs. The shared activities reinforce the couple's sense of "who we are." The partners consider these activities not only enjoyable ways of socializing with each other and defining their bond but also as a means of making friends and sometimes fulfilling individual needs for achievement. Some couples meet their altruistic needs by working together for a social cause or an organization that serves disadvantaged people. Furthermore, each person may fulfill individually oriented needs by participating in some outside activities individually, rather than looking to the relationship to meet all of his or her needs. To make good use of available opportunities in their environment, a couple may need assistance with:

- increasing awareness of opportunities for involvement with their environment,

- increasing realistic decisions regarding types of involvement with the environment, and
- overcoming individual and couple impediments to involvement in the environment.

Increasing Awareness of Opportunities for Involvement With the Environment

Although members of some couples are aware of satisfying ways to become involved in their environment together or individually, other couples can benefit from guidance in identifying and experimenting with such opportunities. We have worked with couples whose complaint about feeling "blah" about their relationship and their daily personal lives appeared to be caused at least partly by the restricted life they led. When the therapist guided them in reviewing times when they had felt better, and the types of activities that brought meaning and enjoyment to their lives, the partners often became motivated to create some changes in their routines. Discussions of potential changes must be realistic in terms of the couple's time, resources, and constraints. The therapist can coach the couple in decision making about feasible and interesting activities they could pursue in their environment.

For example, in the early years of Deirdre and Lou's relationship, the couple had devoted a large amount of their free time to outdoor activities such as hiking, camping, and nature photography. They also invested considerable time, energy, and money into environmental organizations such as the Audubon Society. However, the births of their children and increasing demands from their jobs drastically reduced their abilities to be involved in these outside activities. They felt helpless to change their new routines and were resigned to dreaming of a time in the future when they could resume the outside involvements that they had enjoyed so much and that had defined them as a couple.

Their therapist asked them to specify the aspects of each activity that had special meaning to them. Deirdre had especially enjoyed it when she and Lou represented the local chapter of the Audubon Society in lobbying their state legislature. She had felt proud of them as a couple for their commitment to a worthy cause and for their skills as a lobbying team. When the therapist asked what current activities gave her any of the same feelings about their relationship, she said that they seem to work well together as parents, but the lack of opportunities to be "the dynamic duo" felt like a major loss. Lou expressed similar feelings about the change in their life together. The therapist then coached the couple in thinking of ways in which they could become involved in outside activities that might produce the feeling of "making a difference in the world."

Increasing Realistic Decision-Making Regarding Appropriate Types of Involvement

Once a couple are aware of opportunities for fulfilling their needs either individually or as a couple, they must determine which options are the most appropriate for them. Some options might meet one person's individual needs but detract from the couple's relationship, or other options might benefit the couple relationship at the expense of one or both individuals. In addition, any new activity that involves more time and energy than the partners can afford is likely to increase stress. Consequently, Deirdre and Lou's therapist suggested that they consider the pros and cons of the ideas they had generated about ways to be involved in the outside world. Any new activities would have to be more limited than their previous involvements, because of their other responsibilities at work and at home. Sometimes a therapist must guide a couple in considering how more modest involvements still can be meaningful. Deirdre and Lou identified an activity with the local Audubon Society that they both considered attractive and feasible within their time constraints. They made plans to initiate the activity during the next week.

Overcoming Individual and Couple Impediments to Involvement in the Environment

Efforts to help a couple increase fulfilling involvements in their environment also must recognize characteristics of the individuals or couple that might interfere with their participation. Sometimes members of a couple have rarely "ventured into the world" much during their lives, because of limited social skills; a personality style such as introversion; or a clinical disorder such as social anxiety, agoraphobia, or depression. At the couple level, some partners lack skills for coordinating their efforts and organizing their time well enough to carry out activities together in the outside world. Some couples have difficulty resolving differences in the degrees to which a particular type of involvement in the environment is attractive to them. Consequently, it is important to consider characteristics of the individual partners and the couple as a dyad when discussing ways of increasing a couple's involvement with the outside world.

Although in some cases individual therapy may be needed, many individual characteristics that interfere with external involvements may be treated in the couple context. Thus, in chapter 13 we described partner-assisted treatment of panic disorder with agoraphobia that severely restricts involvements in the outside world. Similarly, some couples may be limited by one person's social anxiety. Seema complained that her life was restricted to her part-time job and taking care of the couple's home and young children. However, the therapist's assessment revealed that Seema suffered from social anxiety. She was very self-conscious when with people other than her few close friends, because she usually was concerned that others would find her uninteresting and awkward. Her husband Ron's attempts to reassure her about her personal characteristics and to encourage her to go out socially, individually or as a couple, usually were unsuccessful. The therapist talked with the couple about ways that Seema's anxiety in social situations was limiting her ability to engage in outside activities with or without Ron. Ron was coached in reflective listening as Seema described her anxiety symptoms so she would feel more understood by him. The therapist then discussed ways in which Ron could be helpful in a partner-assisted approach to reducing Seema's social anxiety.

Sometimes a *difference* between two partners' personal characteristics (e.g., a difference in extraversion or in novelty seeking) interferes with the couple's ability to take advantage of opportunities in their environment. As we described in chapter 12, the major interventions for such discrepancies focus on helping a couple develop mutually acceptable standards for types and degrees of outside involvements and increase their ability to negotiate ways of translating the standards into actions. A couple needs to reach agreement on *how much* they should be involved outside their relationship, individually or together, and *what behaviors* are acceptable ways of being involved in their environment. This chapter cannot cover the range of individual and dyadic characteristics that may limit a couple's involvements in their environment, or the variety of possible interventions. However, all of the interventions described in chapters 12 (for couples' patterns and interactions) and 13 (for individual psychopathology, unresolved personal issues, and interpersonal traumas) can be used to address these factors.

SUMMARY

Cognitive–behavioral couples therapists traditionally have focused on couples' here-and-now interactions and have mainly addressed aspects of the environment as problems that a couple can learn to handle better through problem-solving skills training. Although the skills approach is still an important aspect of our work with couples who are dealing with environmental demands, it is by no means the only focus. Our enhanced cognitive–behavioral approach takes a broadened ecological perspective in which the couple is embedded in layers of social systems as well as the physical environment. Not only does the couple's environment present demands on their relationship, but it also provides resources that can help them adapt to problems and fulfill their individually and communally oriented needs.

A key implication of this view is that therapists need to be prepared to use interventions targeting different levels of the couple's interactions with their environment, such as parenting skill training and interventions designed to change the couple's relationships with extended family, friends, and coworkers. The interventions may sometimes involve including significant others in sessions, such as family sessions in which a couple practices parenting skills with their children. Depending on their areas of expertise, couples therapists may refer their clients to family therapists and other professionals to address particular types of environmental factors. Nevertheless, this model requires that the couples therapist always keep in mind the "big picture" of the various environmental influences on the couple. Key concepts in this approach include the following:

- Therapists must attend to both past and current experiences that at present affect a couple's functioning. Sometimes a therapist needs to increase partners' understanding that past traumatic experiences may be contributing to current relationship problems. Alternatively, a therapist may need to counteract individuals' beliefs that their past traumatic experiences have doomed them to have personal and relationship problems forever.
- Couples commonly need increased awareness of environmental factors that influence their relationship and of how those factors affect fulfillment of their needs.
- Interventions are needed to decrease overlearned cognitive, emotional, and behavioral responses to environmental events.
- Past negative experiences that have continued into the present may be counteracted by developing new ways for individuals to relate to them.
- Couples often need assistance in recognizing and accessing available resources.
- Gaining access to environmental resources and sources of fulfillment depends on reducing effects of individual and couple characteristics that impede contacts with the environment.

15

CONCLUDING REMARKS

Working with distressed couples can be a complex, demanding, yet potentially rewarding process both for the couple and for the therapist. The treatment outcome research to date indicates that we and our colleagues are of assistance to the majority of couples seeking intervention for distressed marriages, and approximately 50% of them are in the nondistressed range of functioning at the end of therapy (Baucom, Shoham, Mueser, Daiuto, & Stickle, 1998). These findings are based on rather limited, skills-based approaches to couples therapy stemming from a cognitive–behavioral perspective. In an attempt to broaden our conceptualizations of relationship functioning and to increase the range of interventions available to couples therapists, we have presented an enhanced cognitive–behavioral perspective on relationship functioning in this book. Our hope is that a skilled therapist using this variety of interventions can assist couples in obtaining the optimal functioning that is possible for them as a unique couple. Given that individuals' satisfaction with their intimate relationships is one of the most important factors in overall quality of life for many people, continuing to improve our interventions is of utmost importance.

FACTORS TO CONSIDER IN WORKING WITH COUPLES

In the first section of this book we presented a broadened, cognitive–behavioral perspective on relationship functioning. We attempted to elucidate many factors for the therapist to consider in understanding the couple and in developing treatment plans for that couple.

Individual, Couple, and Environment

First, the therapist should recognize the unique individuality of each partner, that individual's learning history, needs, preferences, and typical interaction style. Relationship satisfaction and distress both are greatly influenced by individual differences and similarities between the two partners, characteristics of the individuals that often lie within the normal, adaptive range. These individual characteristics include both partners' communal and individual needs, along with a variety of other personality characteristics. These similarities and differences between partners do not lead to inevitable distress or satisfaction, but partners' understanding of these differences and similarities, along with adaptive ways to address them behaviorally, is essential for healthy relationship functioning.

Moreover, individual psychopathology and/or long-term unresolved issues for one or both individuals are important to consider in relationship functioning. Relationship distress can serve as a broad-based, chronic stressor on an individual who is susceptible to developing psychological symptoms. Thus, relationship distress can precipitate, exacerbate, and greatly affect the course of individual psychopathology for one or both partners. In addition, individual psychological distress can serve as a major stressor on relationships in a variety of ways, ranging from creating a more negative emotional tone in the relationship, to creating a distribution of relationship roles that is unsatisfying for one or both partners, and so forth. Understanding and integrating individual psychopathology and vulnerabilities into relationship functioning is important in helping couples resolve concern in both realms.

Although understanding the two partners as individuals is essential, the couple relationship is more than the sum of these two persons. In addition, couples tend to develop a unique way of interacting with each other that is responsive to the needs of both persons, their characteristics as a dyad, and the environment within which they live. Many couples develop effective ways to address the needs and desires of the partners, both through their ways of communicating and through other behavioral interactions. However, other couples struggle in these efforts, and over time they become distressed about their relationship. Often, interaction patterns such as mutual attack, demand–withdraw, mutual withdrawal, and disengagement not only fail to meet the partners' needs but also commonly become sources of distress in themselves. Thus, a second important level for therapists to understand is the couple's functioning as a unit, as they attempt to be responsive to the demands presented by the characteristics of the individuals, the couple as a dyad, and their environment.

Third, the couple experience their relationship within the context of an ongoing environment that both places demands on them and supplies resources for their relationship. These environmental factors range from the impact of immediate family members, extended family, and local community, to a broader culture that either validates and encourages the couple or creates additional stressors for them. This broader environment serves not only as a source of stress and/or support for the couple, but the couple's own functioning can be greatly enhanced by integration into broader communities. Many individuals express that they enjoy their partners when they are interacting as a couple with other individuals. Similarly, giving back to the community as a couple can contribute to a sense of intimacy and purpose as the couple reaffirm their values and commitments beyond themselves.

Patterns Across Time and Domains of Relationship Functioning

All of these factors—the individual, the couple, and the environment—need to be considered within a developmental perspective as the couple proceed through various stages of the couple and family life cycle. These stages often place demands on the couple and the individuals to adapt and change. Thus, strategies that were adaptive in earlier phases of the relationship often must be augmented or replaced as couples face new demands. Many of these changes in demands are normative, such as responding to the birth of children or shifting from the startup phase of careers to maintaining a long-term professional position. Understanding these developmental factors can help to clarify why a couple is experiencing difficulties at present although they prospered at earlier points in their relationship. In addition, some changes that occur over time are not normative and result from forces both outside and within the couple. Thus, major changes in a society's economic well-being can significantly influence the day-to-day life of a couple. On the other hand, traumas from within the relationship, such as infidelity or domestic abuse, can send couples into a tailspin, disrupting their typical way of functioning and relating to each other.

As we have noted throughout this book, a thoughtful understanding of couple functioning involves developing a perspective on broader, thematic macrolevel issues that cut across a variety of relationship domains. At the same time, these broader themes are played out in more specific, microlevel behaviors in day-to-day interactions. It is important that couples therapists understand the "bigger picture" issues and the specific ways they are exhibited.

Likewise, the competent couples therapist is attentive to the level, types, and magnitude of both negative and positive aspects of the couple's relationship functioning. Many couples who seek intervention initially exhibit a high level of destructive, aversive behavior that must be addressed. Given the salience of these negative, behaviors it is easy for both the therapist and the couple to focus on these aspects of the relationship as the primary domains for intervention. Although this is critical, often it is not enough. A variety of empirical investigations demonstrate that alleviation of negatives does not necessarily result in an increase in positive behaviors within a relationship. This traditional emphasis on decreasing negative behaviors likely is one factor that has contributed to the broad set of findings that many couples are less distressed at the end of couples therapy, but they are not in the happy or optimal range of functioning (Baucom et al., 1998). To help couples reach their full potential, an increased emphasis on positive behaviors that are central to meeting the couple's needs and preferences is essential.

Cognitions, Emotions, and Behaviors in Relationship Functioning

In examining the variety of factors that are central to relationship functioning, therapists must assess and understand the various domains of psychological functioning for each individual. Each person has internal experiences that include both his or her cognitions and emotional responses concerning the two partners, the relationship, and the environment. This cognitive–affective constellation is a very subjective experience for each person, and understanding each individual's thoughts and emotional experiences regarding the relationship is of great importance. This internal, subjective experience both influences the individual's behavior and is responsive to the partner's behavior. It is unfortunate that, among distressed couples, the relationship between each person's external behaviors and the other individual's internal, subjective experience often goes awry. As members of a couple begin to solidify negative attitudes and sentiments toward each other and the relationship, negative behaviors from the partner are emphasized, and positive behaviors and attempts to improve the relationship often are minimized or ignored. Thus, understanding and addressing this cognitive–affective–behavioral complex is a significant part of effective conceptualization and treatment planning.

Our elucidation of these factors in Part I might lead therapists to feel overwhelmed by the task of taking all of these factors into account in understanding a couple. Although it is important for therapists to keep this wide variety of factors in mind while assessing a given couple, not all of these factors will need to be addressed in working with a particular couple. Instead, as the couple and therapist develop a conceptualization of the couple's functioning, often two or three major factors or themes emerge and become the bases for treatment planning. To address all of these factors systematically with each couple would be overwhelming, unnecessary, and constitute poor treatment planning. Throughout this book we have described guidelines that clinicians can use in deciding how to prioritize and sequence interventions, based on the degrees of primary and secondary distress that a couple exhibits as well as the major patterns and themes in their concerns.

Behavioral, Cognitive, and Emotionally Oriented Interventions

In addressing all these domains of concern, the therapist has available a wide variety of behavioral, cognitive, and emotionally oriented interventions to address individual, couple, and environmental factors. These interventions should not be used in a routine, mechanized manner but rather selected specifically for a given couple and adapted to be responsive to that couple's needs. Thus, the therapist can create a wide variety of guided behavior changes either to alter the overall relationship environment or to influence a specific domain of relationship functioning. In addition, the therapist can help the couple develop appropriate communication skills or help them return to their previous level of adaptive communication by providing suggestions and guidelines for couple discussions and decision-making or problem-solving interactions.

A wide variety of cognitive interventions also is available to couples therapists. This broad range of interventions falls into two sets of strategies: Socratic questioning and guided discovery. Socratic questioning involves a series of questions to help the individual re-evaluate his or her perspective on some area of concern within the relationship and might involve addressing the individual's selective attention, attributions, expectancies, assumptions, and relationship standards. Socratic questioning can be used effectively when applied judiciously; however, the presence of the individual's partner can make Socratic questioning more complicated to use than in individual therapy, because having one's thoughts and cognitions challenged in the presence of an adversarial partner can be threatening. Frequently, the partner has already suggested that the individual's perspective is distorted and unreasonable; therefore, the therapist must be cautious not to contribute further to this mindset. Guided-discovery strategies, in which either individual or the couple come to view the relationship in a different way, not through questioning but through a new set of experiences, also can be used. For example, if a husband clarifies that he withdrew from his wife because she is very important to him and he felt ashamed of his recent behavior, this might have a significant impact on his wife, who previously interpreted his withdrawal as reflecting a lack of love for her.

Previous formulations of cognitive–behavioral interventions have de-emphasized the role of emotion in relationship functioning. This de-emphasis of emotion within intimate relationships seems odd, given that the affective component of relationships is so salient to partners themselves. In all likelihood, the de-emphasis does not suggest that theoreticians, researchers, and clinicians consider emotions unimportant in intimate relationships but rather that direct intervention with emotions is complex and challenging. We have proposed several ways for intervening directly with couples' emotions. On one end of the continuum are couples in which one or both partners experience difficulty experiencing or expressing emotions. On the other end of the continuum are individuals who have significant difficulty regulating his or her emotions; such individuals present a challenge to clinicians. Poor affect regulation in the presence of relationship discord means that the couple often experiences relationship crises, and any sustained effort at addressing specific concerns is difficult when either person is overwhelmed by negative feelings. Thus, helping some partners become more comfortable experiencing and expressing emotions and attending to other partners' difficulties in regulating emotions are important aspects of cognitive–behavioral couples therapy.

In considering cognitive, affective, and behavioral interventions for addressing individual, couple, and environmental factors, therapists must be cautious in applying their own definitions of healthy relationship functioning. There likely are multiple ways to have successful relationships, and a great deal of our theory and empirical research is based on work with middle-class, White couples. Therefore, therapists must be certain that their own standards for healthy relationships do not inappropriately influence the treatment plan. If certain aspects of a couple's relationship appear to be of central importance in their distress, then these factors must be addressed. However, if the couple's relationship deviates from the therapist's own value system but these deviations do not seem to be contributing to the couple's current relationship discord, these aspects of the relationship should not become foci of intervention.

INTERVENING TO ASSIST DISTRESSED COUPLES

Addressing Primary and Secondary Distress

Considering the above-mentioned factors, the therapist and couple develop a common understanding of the most salient factors contributing to their relationship distress. On the basis of this conceptualization, the therapist and couple evolve a treatment plan both to alleviate distress and to optimize the couple's relationship functioning. We have recommended that this treatment plan be developed to address the core thematic concerns of the couple—what we have termed *primary distress*. This primary distress might involve the couple's difficulty in responding to each person's important needs, such as desired level of intimacy, an inability to respond to one individual's psychopathology, poor communication skills resulting in frequent hurt feelings, or difficulty adapting to overwhelming environmental stressors.

Although all couples face demands, distressed couples typically have difficulties adapting to these demands and often respond in maladaptive ways that further complicate relationship discord—what we have termed *secondary distress*. For example, two partners might differ in their desire for intimacy. As the partner who desires greater intimacy engages in a variety of approach behaviors, the individual desiring less closeness backs away, creating greater distance. Over time, these attempts to find a way to balance differing desires for intimacy can become accentuated into an extreme demand–withdraw pattern as one person feels hurt and ignored while the other person feels encroached on or engulfed. These destructive interaction patterns often are self-maintaining, and by the time the couple seek therapy the patterns often have become problems themselves.

Thus, therapists must be attentive both to destructive interactive processes that have developed as well as to important substantive concerns, such as desires for closeness, being nurtured by the partner, autonomy, and individual achievement. Simultaneous attention to both the process of the couple's interactions and the substance of their concerns places the therapist in an optimal position to assist them. Attending only to interactive processes or the substance of concerns without attending to the other is likely to lead to limited and temporary improvement.

In addressing both interactive processes and substantive concerns, therapists often need to decide on the sequence in which various issues will be addressed. At present, there are no research findings or cogent theoretical arguments to guide the therapist in making these relatively complex decisions. Any single algorithm for sequencing treatment interventions is likely to result in a simplistic, mechanized approach to working with couples who present an ever-changing picture for themselves and the therapist. In some instances, treatment can begin with a focus on the most central areas of concern. This approach is easiest perhaps with partners who do not experience a great deal of anger, hostility, and hurtful behaviors toward each other. These negative and hurtful behaviors are so salient and destructive that they typically require immediate attention. Thus, for the mutually attacking couple, stopping or significantly decreasing the destructive interactions often is necessary before one can address other substantive issues. Many of these central issues, such as feeling unloved, involve a sense of vulnerability and hurt feelings that are difficult for partners to express in an openly hostile environment. Thus, decreasing a high rate of negativity is helpful in allowing partners to explore their vulnerabilities both internally and with the other person.

On the other hand, if there is not a high level of negativity, and the partners are able to listen to each other in a constructive fashion, then central areas of concern between the two partners can be addressed early in treatment. Furthermore, at times one individual's psychopathology is so destructive to the couple's relationship functioning that it must receive immediate attention through individual therapy. In other instances, when either individual's distress is the result of marital discord or the partner is receptive to helping the individual, individual psychopathology can be addressed in a couple's context.

Using A Cogent Yet Flexible Approach to Assisting Couples

We also believe that the field of couples research and therapy has reached a point at which lengthy theoretical debates no longer serve us well. The empirical literature demonstrates that a variety of theoretical orientations are of assistance to distressed couples, including cognitive–behavioral, psychodynamic, and emotion-focused therapies, and that no one orientation is the treatment of choice for all couples (Baucom et al., 1998). Insight-oriented perspectives can be helpful to cognitive–behavioral therapists exploring how current behavior patterns, cognitions, and emotional responses have developed on a long-term basis, prior to the current relationship. These factors can be quite important in developing and implementing effective treatment strategies. Emotion-focused therapy has similarly brought much-needed attention to the essential role of emotional functioning in intimate relationships. Although some other major theoretical approaches to couples therapy have not as yet been tested empirically, it seems likely that future research will reveal that their interventions provide additional valuable approaches for particular types of relationship problems. Different theoretical perspectives have differentially emphasized certain variables of importance in relationship functioning. Our belief is that the variables articulated by a given theoretical approach are likely to be particularly salient for some couples but not for others. Our hope is that the broadened cognitive–behavioral perspective outlined herein provides a strategy for attending to these theoretically diverse factors in a meaningful way.

In addition to remaining theoretically diverse and flexible in understanding a variety of couples, therapists must maintain a sense of flexibility while intervening with a given couple. Conceptualizations of the couple change as the treatment continues. When couples are responsive to interventions, a cascading effect often occurs in which areas of initial concern to the partners no longer appear to be problematic. Often, specific aspects of the relationship are distressing or viewed as problematic within the context of the partners' overall views of their relationship. As one domain in the couple's relationship improves, other aspects may improve as well, given the interrelatedness of various aspects of relationship functioning. Furthermore, both normative and unexpected changes occur in the relationship during treatment, ranging from changing child care needs as children mature to the disclosure of infidelity. As a result, the therapist's conceptualization and treatment plan must be flexible and attentive to changes occurring at a variety of levels over the course of treatment.

Finally, we recommend that couples therapists broaden their perspective of their roles to see themselves as relationship consultants who can be available to a couple on an ongoing basis. Early cognitive–behavioral conceptualizations emphasized the importance of skill building so that couples could become self-sufficient and not need a therapist in the future. We certainly wish to enhance the skills, understanding, and efficacy of couples long term. By attending to the individual, the couple, and their interaction with their environment, along with promoting changes outside of the therapy session, maintenance of adaptive functioning is built into the intervention approach we have adopted. In addition, prior to terminating treatment the couple and therapist typically discuss strategies for ongoing self-monitoring, such as periodic conversations about the "state of the union," yearly retreats to focus on the relationship, and so forth. Even with these strategies in place, many couples continue to value and benefit from periodic contact with a couples therapist at various times in their relationship. Rather than being an indication of treatment failure, a couple's return to see their therapist can be viewed as the couple's judicious use of a significant resource in their environment. Many couples can benefit from meeting periodically with a relationship specialist who is committed to their well-being as they continue to experience the complex yet potentially vastly rewarding world of committed, intimate relationships.

REFERENCES

Alberti, R. E., & Emmons, M. L. (1986). *Your perfect right: A guide to assertive living.* San Luis Obispo, CA: Impact.

Allen, E. A., Baucom, D. H., Burnett, C. K., Epstein, N., & Rankin-Esquer, L. A. (1996, November). *Autonomy, egalitarianism, and communication among married spouses versus first married spouses.* Paper presented at the annual meeting of the Association for the Advancement of Behavior Therapy, New York.

American Psychiatric Association. (1994). *Diagnostic and statistical manual of mental disorders* (4th ed.). Washington, DC: Author.

Anderson, C. M., Dimidjian, S., & Miller, A. (1995). Redefining the past, present, and future: Therapy with long-term marriages at midlife. In N. S. Jacobson & A. S. Gurman (Eds.), *Clinical handbook of couple therapy* (pp. 247–260). New York: Guilford Press.

Arkowitz, H., Holliday, S., & Hutter, M. (1982, November). *Depressed women and their husbands: A study of marital interaction and adjustment.* Paper presented at the annual meeting of the Association for Advancement of Behavior Therapy, Los Angeles.

Atkins, D. C. (2000, November). *Research design and procedures of the Multi-Site Couple Therapy Study.* Paper presented at the annual meeting of the Association for the Advancement of Behavior Therapy, New Orleans, LA.

Azrin, N. H., Besalel, V. A., Betchel, R., Michalicek, A., Mancera, M., Carroll, D., Shuford, D., & Cox, J. (1980). Comparison of reciprocity and discussion-type counseling for marital problems. *American Journal of Family Therapy, 8,* 21–28.

Azrin, N. H., Naster, B. J., & Jones, R. (1973). A rapid learning-based procedure for marital counseling. *Behavior Research and Therapy, 11,* 365–382.

Bakan, D. (1966). *The duality of human existence.* Boston: Beacon Press.

Baldwin, M. W. (1992). Relational schemas and the processing of social information. *Psychological Bulletin, 112,* 461–484.

Baldwin, M. W., Carrell, S. E., & Lopez, D. F. (1990). Priming relationship schemas: My advisor and the Pope are watching me from the back of my mind. *Journal of Experimental Psychology, 26,* 435–454.

Bandura, A. (1977). *Social learning theory.* Englewood Cliffs, NJ: Prentice Hall.

Barber, J. P., Crits-Christoph, P., & Luborsky, L. (1998). A guide to the CCRT standard categories and their classification. In L. Luborsky & P. Crits-Christoph (Eds.), *Understanding transference: The core conflict relationship theme method* (pp. 43–54). Washington, DC: American Psychological Association.

Barkley, R. A. (1998). *Attention-deficit hyperactivity disorder: A handbook for diagnosis and treatment* (2nd ed.). New York: Guilford Press.

Barkley, R. A. (2000). *Taking charge of ADHD: The complete, authoritative guide for parents.* New York: Guilford Press.

Barling, J. (1990). Employment and marital functioning. In F. D. Fincham & T. N. Bradbury (Eds.), *The psychology of marriage: Basic issues and applications* (pp. 201–225). New York: Guilford Press.

Barlow, D. H. (1988). *Anxiety and its disorders: The nature and treatment of anxiety and panic.* New York: Guilford Press.

Barlow, D. H., O'Brien, G. T., & Last, C. G. (1984). Couples treatment of agoraphobia. *Behavior Therapy, 15,* 41–58.

Barnett, L. R., & Nietzel, M. T. (1979). Relationship of instrumental and affective behaviours and self-esteem to marital satisfaction in distressed and nondistressed couples. *Journal of Consulting and Clinical Psychology, 47,* 946–957.

Batson, C. D. (1987). Prosocial motivation: Is it ever truly altruistic? In L. Berkowitz (Ed.), *Advances in experimental social psychology* (Vol. 20, pp. 65–122). San Diego, CA: Academic Press.

Batson, C. D. (1991). *The altruistic question: Toward a social-psychological answer.* Hillsdale, NJ: Erlbaum.

Baucom, D. H. (1982). A comparison of behavioral contracting and problem-solving/communications training in behavioral marital therapy. *Behavior Therapy, 13,* 162–174.

Baucom, D. H. (1999, November). *Therapeutic implications of gender differences in cognitive processing in marital relationships.* Paper presented at the annual meeting of the Association for the Advancement of Behavior Therapy, Toronto, Ontario, Canada.

Baucom, D. H., & Epstein, N. (1990). *Cognitive–behavioral marital therapy.* New York: Brunner/Mazel.

Baucom, D. H., Epstein, N., Daiuto, A. D., Carels, R. A., Rankin, L., & Burnett, C. K. (1996). Cognitions in marriage: The relationship between standards and attributions. *Journal of Family Psychology, 10,* 209–222.

Baucom, D. H., Epstein, N., & Gordon, K. C. (2000). Marital therapy: Theory, practice, and empirical status. In C. R. Snyder & R. E. Ingram (Eds.), *Handbook of psychological change: Psychotherapy processes and practices for the 21st century* (pp. 280–308). New York: Wiley.

Baucom, D. H., Epstein, N., Rankin, L. A., & Burnett, C. K. (1996). Assessing relationship standards: The Inventory of Specific Relationship Standards. *Journal of Family Psychology, 10,* 72–88.

Baucom, D. H., Epstein, N., Sayers, S. L., & Sher, T. G. (1989). The role of cognitions in marital relationships: Definitional, methodological, and conceptual issues. *Journal of Consulting and Clinical Psychology, 57,* 31–38.

Baucom, D. H., & Lester, G. W. (1986). The usefulness of cognitive restructuring as an adjunct to behavioral marital therapy. *Behavior Therapy, 17,* 385–403.

Baucom, D. H., & Mehlman, S. K. (1984). Predicting marital status following behavioral marital therapy: A comparison of models of marital relationships. In K. Hahlweg & N. S. Jacobson (Eds.), *Marital interaction: Analysis and modification* (pp. 89–104). New York: Guilford Press.

Baucom, D. H., & Ragland, L. (1998, July). *Predicting and preventing marital distress: The results of a longitudinal prevention program.* Paper presented at the World Congress of Behavioral and Cognitive Therapies, Acapulco, Mexico.

Baucom, D. H., Sayers, S. L., & Duhe, A. (1989). Attributional style and attributional patterns among married couples. *Journal of Personality and Social Psychology, 56,* 596–607.

Baucom, D. H., Sayers, S. L., & Sher, T. G. (1990). Supplementing behavioral marital therapy with cognitive restructuring and emotional expressiveness training: An outcome investigation. *Journal of Consulting and Clinical Psychology, 58,* 636–645.

Baucom, D. H., Shoham, V., Mueser, K. T., Daiuto, A. D., & Stickle, T. R. (1998). Empirically supported couples and family therapies for adult problems. *Journal of Consulting and Clinical Psychology, 66,* 53–88.

Baucom, D. H., Stanton, S., & Epstein, N. (in press). Anxiety. In D. K. Snyder & M. A. Whisman (Eds.), *Treating difficult couples.* New York: Guilford Press.

Baumeister, R. F., & Leary, M. R. (1995). The need to belong: Desire for interpersonal attachments as a fundamental human motivation. *Psychological Bulletin, 117,* 497–529.

Beach, S. R. H. (Ed.). (2000). *Marital and family processes in depression: A scientific foundation for clinical practice.* Washington, DC: American Psychological Association.

Beach, S. R. H., & Fincham, F. D. (1994). Toward an integrated model of negative affectivity in marriage. In S. M. Johnson & L. S. Greenberg (Eds.), *The heart of the matter: Perspectives on emotion in marital therapy* (pp. 227–255). New York: Brunner/Mazel.

Beach, S. R. H., Fincham, F. D., Katz, J., & Bradbury, T. N. (1996). Social support in marriage: A cognitive perspective. In G. R. Pierce, B. R. Sarason, & I. G. Sarason (Eds.), *Handbook of social support and the family* (pp. 43–65). New York: Plenum.

Beach, S. R. H., & O'Leary, K. D. (1992). Treating depression in the context of marital discord: Outcome and predictors of response of marital therapy versus cognitive therapy. *Behavior Therapy, 23,* 507–528.

Beach, S. R. H., Sandeen, E. E., & O'Leary, K. D. (1990). *Depression in marriage: A model for etiology and treatment.* New York: Guilford Press.

Beach, S. R. H., & Tesser, A. (1993). Decision making power and marital satisfaction: A self-evaluation maintenance perspective. *Journal of Social and Clinical Psychology, 12,* 471–494.

Beach, S. R. H., Whisman, M. A., & O'Leary, K. D. (1994). Marital therapy for depression: Theoretical foundation, current status, and future directions. *Behavior Therapy, 25,* 345–371.

Beck, A. T. (1988). *Love is never enough.* New York: Harper & Row.

Beck, A. T., Rush, A. J., Shaw, B. F., & Emery, G. (1979). *Cognitive therapy of depression.* New York: Guilford Press.

Beck, J. S. (1995). *Cognitive therapy: Basics and beyond.* New York: Guilford Press.

Belsky, J. (1990). Children and marriage. In F. D. Fincham & T. N. Bradbury (Eds.), *The psychology of marriage: Basic issues and applications* (pp. 172–200). New York: Guilford Press.

Belsky, J., & Kelly, J. (1994). *The transition to parenthood: How a first child changes a marriage: Why some couples grow closer and others apart.* New York: Delacorte.

Bennett, L. A., & Wolin, S. J. (1990). Family culture and alcoholism transmission. In R. L. Collins, K. E. Leonard, & J. S. Searles (Eds.), *Alcohol and the family: Research and clinical perspectives* (pp. 194–219). New York: Guilford Press.

Bennun, I. (1985a). Behavioural marital therapy: An outcome evaluation of conjoint, group and one spouse treatment. *Scandinavian Journal of Behaviour Therapy, 14,* 157–168.

Bennun, I. (1985b). Prediction and responsiveness in behavioural marital therapy. *Behavioural Psychotherapy, 13,* 186–201.

Bennun, I. (1997). Relationship interventions with one partner. In W. K. Halford & H. J. Markman (Eds.), *Clinical handbook of marriage and couples interventions* (pp. 451–470). Chichester, England: Wiley.

Berman, C. (1986). *Making it as a stepparent: New roles/new rules.* New York: Harper & Row.

Berman, W. H., Marcus, L., & Berman, E. R. (1994). Attachment in marital relations. In M. B. Sperling & W. H. Berman (Eds.), *Attachment in adults: Clinical and developmental perspectives* (pp. 204–231). New York: Guilford Press.

Bielby, W. T., & Bielby, L. D. (1989). Family ties: Balancing commitments to work and family in dual earner households. *American Sociological Review, 4,* 776–789.

Biglan, A., Hops, H., Sherman, L., Friedman, L. S., Arthur, J., & Osteen, V. (1985). Problem solving interactions of depressed women and their spouses. *Behavior Therapy, 16,* 431–451.

Billingsley, A. (1992). *Climbing Jacob's ladder: The enduring legacy of African American families.* New York: Simon & Schuster.

Birchler, G. R., Clopton, J. R., & Adams, N. L. (1984). Marital conflict resolution: Factors influencing concordance between partners and trained coders. *American Journal of Family Therapy, 12,* 15–28.

Birchler, G. R., Weiss, R. L., & Vincent, J. P. (1975). Multimethod analysis of social reinforcement exchange between maritally distressed and nondistressed spouse and stranger dyads. *Journal of Personality and Social Psychology, 31*, 349–360.

Blacker, L. (1999). The launching phase of the life cycle. In B. Carter & M. McGoldrick (Eds.), *The expanded family life cycle: Individual, family, and social perspectives* (3rd ed., pp. 287–306). Boston: Allyn & Bacon.

Blaney, P. (1986). Affect and memory: A review. *Psychological Bulletin, 99*, 229–246.

Bless, H., Hamilton, D. L., & Mackie, D. M. (1992). Mood effects on the organization of person information. *European Journal of Social Psychology, 22*, 497–509.

Bless, H., Mackie, D. M., & Schwarz, N. (1992). Mood effects on attitude judgments: Independent effects of mood before and after message elaboration. *Journal of Personality and Social Psychology, 63*, 585–595.

Boelens, W., Emmelkamp, P., MacGillavry, D., & Markvoort, M. (1980). A clinical evaluation of marital treatment: Reciprocity counseling vs. system-theoretic counseling. *Behavior Analysis and Modification, 4*, 85–96.

Bond, M. H. (Ed.). (1996). *The handbook of Chinese psychology.* Oxford, England: Oxford University Press.

Boss, P. (1988). *Family stress management.* Newbury Park, CA: Sage.

Bowlby, J. (1988). *A secure base.* New York: Basic Books.

Bowlby, J. (1989). The role of attachment in personality development and psychopathology. In S. Greenspan & G. Pollock (Eds.), *The course of life: Infancy* (Vol. 1, pp. 229–270). Madison, CT: International Universities Press.

Bradbury, T. N., & Fincham, F. D. (1990). Attributions in marriage: Review and critique. *Psychological Bulletin, 107*, 3–33.

Bradbury, T. N., & Fincham, F. D. (1992). Attributions and behavior in marital interaction. *Journal of Personality and Social Psychology, 63*, 613–628.

Bradbury, T. N., & Fincham, F. D. (1993). Assessing dysfunctional cognition in marriage: A reconsideration of the Relationship Belief Inventory. *Psychological Assessment, 5*, 92–101.

Bradbury, T. N., & Karney, B. R. (1993). Longitudinal study of marital interaction and dysfunction: Review and analysis. *Clinical Psychology Review, 13*, 15–27.

Braithwaite, R. L. (1981). Interpersonal relations between Black males and Black females. In L. E. Gary (Ed.), *Black men* (pp. 83–97). Beverly Hills, CA: Sage.

Brehm, S. S. (1992). *Intimate relationships* (2nd ed.). New York: McGraw-Hill.

Brock, G. W. (Ed.). (1994). *American Association for Marriage and Family Therapy: Ethics casebook.* Washington, DC: American Association for Marriage and Family Therapy.

Broderick, J. E., & O'Leary, K. D. (1986). Contributions of affect, attitudes, and behavior to marital satisfaction. *Journal of Consulting and Clinical Psychology, 54*, 514–517.

Brown, L. S. (1995). Therapy with same-sex couples: An introduction. In N. S. Jacobson & A. S. Gurman (Eds.), *Clinical handbook of couple therapy* (pp. 274–291). New York: Guilford Press.

Brown, T. A., O'Leary, T. A., & Barlow, D. H. (1993). Generalized anxiety disorder. In D. H. Barlow (Ed.), *Clinical handbook of psychological disorders: A step-by-step treatment manual* (2nd ed., pp. 137–188). New York: Guilford Press.

Burns, D. D. (1980). *Feeling good: The new mood therapy.* New York: Morrow.

Burns, D. D. (1989). *The feeling good handbook: Using the new mood therapy in everyday life.* New York: Morrow.

Busby, D. M., Christensen, C., Crane, D. R., & Larson, J. H. (1995). A revision of the Dyadic Adjustment Scale for use with distressed and nondistressed couples: Construct hierarchy and multidimensional scales. *Journal of Marital and Family Therapy, 21,* 289–308.

Buss, A. H. (1995). *Personality: Temperament, social behavior, and the self.* Boston: Allyn & Bacon.

Butzlaff, R. L., & Hooley, J. M. (1998). Expressed emotion and psychiatric relapse: A meta-analysis. *Archives of General Psychiatry, 55,* 547–552.

Cacioppo, J. T., Petty, R. E., Feinstein, J. A., & Jarvis, W. B. G. (1996). Dispositional differences in cognitive motivation: The life and times of individuals varying in need for cognition. *Psychological Bulletin, 119,* 197–253.

Calhoun, K. S., & Resick, P. A. (1993). Post-traumatic stress disorder. In D. H. Barlow (Ed.), *Clinical handbook of psychological disorders* (2nd ed., pp. 48–98). New York: Guilford Press.

Carels, R. A., & Baucom, D. H. (1999). Support in marriage: Factors associated with online perceptions of support helpfulness. *Journal of Family Psychology, 13,* 131–144.

Carlo, G., Eisenberg, N., Troyer, D., Switzer, G., & Speer, A. L. (1991). The altruistic personality: In what contexts is it apparent? *Journal of Personality and Social Psychology, 61,* 450–458.

Carter, B., & McGoldrick, M. (Eds.). (1999). *The expanded family life cycle: Individual, family, and social perspectives* (3rd ed.). Boston: Allyn & Bacon.

Cattell, R. B. (1957). *Personality and motivation: Structure and measurement.* Yonkers, NY: Word Book.

Cazenave, N. A. (1983). Black male–female relationships: The perceptions of 155 middle class Black men. *Family Relations, 32,* 341–350.

Chambless, D. L., & Hollon, S. (1998). Defining empirically supported therapies. *Journal of Consulting and Clinical Psychology, 66,* 7–18.

Cherlin, A. J. (1992). *Marriage, divorce, and remarriage* (Rev. ed.). Cambridge, MA: Harvard University Press.

Christensen, A. (1987). Detection of conflict patterns in couples. In K. Hahlweg & M. J. Goldstein (Eds.), *Understanding major mental disorder: The contribution of family interaction research* (pp. 250–265). New York: Family Process.

Christensen, A. (1988). Dysfunctional interaction patterns in couples. In P. Noller & M. A. Fitzpatrick (Eds.), *Perspectives on marital interaction. Monographs in social psychology of language* (No. 1, pp. 31–52). Clevedon, England: Multilingual Matters.

Christensen, A., & Heavey, C. L. (1990). Gender and social structure in the demand/withdraw pattern of marital conflict. *Journal of Personality and Social Psychology, 59,* 73–81.

Christensen, A., & Heavey, C. L. (1993). Gender differences in marital conflict: The demand/withdraw interaction pattern. In S. Oskamp & M. Costanzo (Eds.), *Gender issues in contemporary society: Claremont Symposium on Applied Social Psychology* (Vol. 6, pp. 113–141). Newbury Park, CA: Sage.

Christensen, A., & Jacobson, N. S. (2000). *Reconcilable differences.* New York: Guilford Press.

Christensen, A., Jacobson, N. S., & Babcock, J. C. (1995). Integrative behavioral couple therapy. In N. S. Jacobson & A. S. Gurman (Eds.), *Clinical handbook of couple therapy* (pp. 31–64). New York: Guilford Press.

Christensen, A., & Nies, D. C. (1980). The Spouse Observation Checklist: Empirical analysis and critique. *American Journal of Family Therapy, 8,* 69–79.

Christensen, A., & Shenk, J. L. (1991). Communication, conflict, and psychological distance in nondistressed, clinic, and divorcing couples. *Journal of Consulting and Clinical Psychology, 59,* 458–463.

Christensen, A., & Sullaway, M. (1984). *Communication Patterns Questionnaire.* Unpublished questionnaire, University of California, Los Angeles.

Clark, L. A., & Watson, D. (1991). General affective dispositions in physical and psychological health. In C. R. Snyder & D. R. Forsyth (Eds.), *Handbook of social and clinical psychology* (pp. 221–245). Tarrytown, NY: Pergamon.

Clayton, D. C., & Baucom, D. H. (1998, November). *Relationship standards as mediators of marital quality.* Paper presented at the annual meeting of the Association for the Advancement of Behavior Therapy, Washington, DC.

Coleman, D. H., & Straus, M. A. (1986). Marital power, conflict, and violence in a nationally representative sample of American couples. *Violence and Victims, 1,* 141–157.

Cook, J., Tyson, R., White, J., Rushe, R., Gottman, J. M., & Murray, J. (1995). The mathematics of marital conflict: Qualitative dynamic mathematical modeling of marital interaction. *Journal of Family Psychology, 9,* 110–130.

Costa, P. T., & McCrae, R. R. (1992). *Revised NEO Personality Inventory and NEO Five-Factor Inventory professional manual.* Odessa, FL: Psychological Assessment Resources.

Cowan, P. A., Cowan, C. P., & Schulz, M. S. (1996). Thinking about risk and resilience in families. In E. M. Hetherington & E. A. Blechman (Eds.), *Stress, coping, and resiliency in children and families* (pp. 1–38). Mahwah, NJ: Erlbaum.

Coyne, J. C. (1976). Depression and the response of others. *Journal of Abnormal Psychology, 85,* 186–193.

Crane, D. R., Allgood, S. M., Larson, J. H., & Griffin, W. (1990). Assessing marital quality with distressed and nondistressed couples: A comparison and equivalency table for three frequently used measures. *Journal of Marriage and the Family, 52,* 87–93.

Crane, D. R., Busby, D. M., & Larson, J. H. (1991). A factor analysis of the Dyadic Adjustment Scale with distressed and non-distressed couples. *American Journal of Family Therapy, 19,* 60–66.

Craske, M. G., & Barlow, D. H. (2001). Panic disorder and agoraphobia. In D. H. Barlow (Ed.), *Clinical handbook of psychological disorders: A step-by-step treatment manual* (3rd ed., pp. 1–59). New York: Guilford Press.

Craske, M. G., & Zoellner, L. A. (1995). Anxiety disorders: The role of marital therapy. In N. S. Jacobson & A. S. Gurman (Eds.), *Clinical handbook of couple therapy* (pp. 394–410). New York: Guilford Press.

Cummings, E. M., Davies, P. T., & Campbell, S. B. (2000). *Developmental psychopathology and family process: Theory, research, and clinical implications.* New York: Guilford Press.

Cutrona, C. E. (1996a). Social support as a determinant of marital quality: The interplay of negative and supportive behaviors. In G. R. Pierce, B. R. Sarason, & I. G. Sarason (Eds.), *Handbook of social support and the family* (pp. 173–194). New York: Plenum.

Cutrona, C. E. (1996b). *Social support in couples: Marriage as a resource in times of stress.* Thousand Oaks, CA: Sage.

Cutrona, C. E., Cohen, B., & Igram, S. (1990). Contextual determinants of the perceived supportiveness of helping behaviors. *Journal of Social and Personal Relationships, 7,* 553–562.

Cutrona, C. E., Hessling, R. M., & Suhr, J. A. (1997). The influence of husband and wife personality on marital social support interactions. *Personal Relations, 4,* 379–393.

Cutrona, C. E., & Suhr, J. A. (1992). Controllability of stressful events and satisfaction with spouse support behaviors. *Communication Research, 19,* 154–174.

Cutrona, C. E., & Suhr, J. A. (1994). Social support communication in the context of marriage: An analysis of couples' supportive interactions. In B. Burleson, T. Albrecht, & I. Sarason (Eds.), *The communication of social support: Messages, interactions, relationships, and community* (pp. 113–125). Newbury Park, CA: Sage.

Cutrona, C. E., Suhr, J. A., & MacFarlane, R. (1990). Interpersonal transactions and the psychological sense of support. In S. Duck & R. Silver (Eds.), *Personal relationships and social support* (pp. 30–45). London: Sage

Daiuto, A. D., Baucom, D. H., Epstein, N., & Dutton, S. S. (1998). The application of cognitive–behavioral marital therapy to the assessment and treatment of agoraphobia: Implications of empirical research. *Clinical Psychology Review, 18,* 663–687.

Dandeneau, M. L., & Johnson, S. M. (1994). Facilitating intimacy: Interventions and effects. *Journal of Marital and Family Therapy, 20,* 17–33.

Davila, J., & Bradbury, T. N. (1996, November). *Attachment stability in the early years of marriage.* Paper presented at the annual meeting of the Association for Advancement of Behavior Therapy, New York.

Davila, J., Burge, D., & Hammen, C. (1997). Why does attachment style change? *Journal of Personality and Social Psychology, 73,* 826–838.

Deffenbacher, J. L. (1996). Cognitive–behavioral approaches to anger reduction. In K. S. Dobson & K. D. Craig (Eds.), *Advances in cognitive–behavioral therapy* (pp. 31–62). Thousand Oaks, CA: Sage.

Digman, J. M. (1989). Five robust trait dimensions: Development, stability, and utility. *Journal of Personality, 57*, 195–214.

DiNardo, P. A., Brown, T. A., & Barlow, D. H. (1994). *Anxiety Disorders Interview Schedule for DSM–IV: Lifetime Version (ADIS–IV–L)*. Albany, NY: Graywind.

Dryden, W., & Ellis, A. (1988). Rational–emotive therapy. In K. S. Dobson (Ed.), *Handbook of cognitive–behavioral therapies* (pp. 214–272). New York: Guilford Press.

D'Zurilla, T. J. (1988). Problem-solving therapies. In K. S. Dobson (Ed.), *Handbook of cognitive–behavioral therapies* (pp. 85–135). New York: Guilford Press.

Easley, M., & Epstein, N. (1991). Coping with stress in a family with an alcoholic parent. *Family Relations, 40*, 218–224.

Eidelson, R. J., & Epstein, N. (1982). Cognition and relationship maladjustment: Development of a measure of dysfunctional relationship beliefs. *Journal of Consulting and Clinical Psychology, 50*, 715–720.

Ellis, A. (1976). Techniques of handling anger in marriage. *Journal of Marriage and Family Counseling, 2*, 305–315.

Ellis, A. (1986). Rational–emotive therapy applied to relationship therapy. *Journal of Rational–Emotive Therapy, 4*(1), 4–21.

Emmelkamp, P., van der Helm, M., MacGillavry, D., & van Zanten, B. (1984). Marital therapy with clinically distressed couples: A comparative evaluation of system-theoretic, contingency contracting, and communication skills approaches. In K. Hahlweg and N.S. Jacobson (Eds.), *Marital interaction: Analysis and modification* (pp. 36–52). New York: Guilford Press.

Emmelkamp, P. M. G., van Linden van den Heuvell, C., Ruphan, M., Sanderman, R., Scholing, A., & Stroink, F. (1988). Cognitive and behavioral interventions: A comparative evaluation with clinically distressed couples. *Journal of Family Psychology, 1*, 365–377.

Epstein, N. (1982). Cognitive therapy with couples. *American Journal of Family Therapy, 10*, 5–16.

Epstein, N. (1985). Depression and marital dysfunction: Cognitive and behavioral linkages. *International Journal of Mental Health, 13*, 86–104.

Epstein, N., & Baucom, D. H. (1989). Cognitive–behavioral marital therapy. In A. Freeman, K. M. Simon, L. E. Beutler, H. Arkowitz (Eds.), *Comprehensive handbook of cognitive therapy* (pp. 491–513). New York: Plenum.

Epstein, N., & Baucom, D. H. (1993). Cognitive factors in marital disturbance. In K. S. Dobson & P. C. Kendall (Eds.), *Psychopathology and cognition* (pp. 351–385). San Diego, CA: Academic Press.

Epstein, N., Baucom, D. H., & Daiuto, A. D. (1997). Cognitive–behavioral couples therapy. In W. K. Halford & H. J. Markman (Eds.), *Clinical handbook of marriage and couples interventions* (pp. 415–449). Chichester, England: Wiley.

Epstein, N., Baucom, D. H., & Rankin, L. A. (1993). Treatment of marital conflict: A cognitive–behavioral approach. *Clinical Psychology Review, 13*, 45–57.

Epstein, N., & Eidelson, R. J. (1981). Unrealistic beliefs of clinical couples: Their relationship to expectations, goals and satisfaction. *American Journal of Family Therapy, 9*, 13–22.

Epstein, N., Pretzer, J. L., & Fleming, B. (1987). The role of cognitive appraisal in self-reports of marital communication. *Behavior Therapy, 18*, 51–69.

Epstein, N., & Schlesinger, S. E. (1994). Couples problems. In F. M. Dattilio & A. M. Freeman (Eds.), *Cognitive–behavioral strategies in crisis intervention* (pp. 258–277). New York: Guilford Press.

Ewart, C. K. (1978, August). *Behavior contracts in couple therapy: An experimental evaluation of quid pro quo and good faith models.* Paper presented at the annual meeting of the Association for Advancement of Behavior Therapy, Toronto.

Falloon, I. R. H., Boyd, J. L., & McGill, C. W. (1984). *Family care of schizophrenia: A problem-solving approach to the treatment of mental illness.* New York: Guilford Press.

Felder, L. (1990). *When a loved one is ill: How to take better care of your loved one, your family, and yourself.* New York: New American Library.

Figley, C. R. (1983). Catastrophes: An overview of family reactions. In C. R. Figley & H. I. McCubbin (Eds.), *Stress and the family: Vol. II. Coping with catastrophe* (pp. 3–20). New York: Brunner/Mazel.

Fincham, F. D., Beach, S. R., & Nelson, G. (1987). Attribution processes in distressed and nondistressed couples: III. Causal and responsibility attributions for spouse behavior. *Cognitive Therapy and Research, 11*, 71–86.

Fincham, F. D., & Bradbury, T. N. (1989). The impact of attributions in marriage: An individual difference analysis. *Journal of Social and Personal Relationships, 6*, 69–85.

Fincham, F. D., Bradbury, T. N., & Scott, C. K. (1990). Cognition in marriage. In F. D. Fincham & T. N. Bradbury (Eds.), *The psychology of marriage: Basic issues and applications* (pp. 118–149). New York: Guilford Press.

Fincham, F. D., Fernandes, L. O. L., & Humphreys, K. (1993). *Communicating in relationships: A guide for couples and professionals.* Champaign, IL: Research Press.

Fincham, F. D., Garnier, P. C., Gano-Phillips, S., & Osborne, L. N. (1995). Preinteraction expectations, marital satisfaction, and accessibility: A new look at sentiment override. *Journal of Family Psychology, 9*, 3–14.

First, M. B., Gibbon, M., Spitzer, R. L., & Williams, J. B. W. (1995). *User's guide for the Structured Clinical Interview for DSM–IV Axis I disorders.* New York: Biometrics Research.

Fiske, S. T., & Taylor, S. E. (1991). *Social cognition.* New York: McGraw-Hill.

Fitzpatrick, M. A. (1988). Approaches to marital interaction. In P. Noller & M. A. Fitzpatrick (Eds.), *Monographs in social psychology of language: Vol. 1. Perspectives on marital interaction* (pp. 1–28). Clevedon, England: Multilingual Matters.

Floyd, F. J., Haynes, S. N., & Kelly, S. (1997). Marital assessment: A dynamic functional–analytic approach. In W. K. Halford & H. J. Markman (Eds.), *Clinical handbook of marriage and couples interventions* (pp. 349–377). Chichester, England: Wiley.

Fraenkel, P. (1997). Systems approaches to couple therapy. In W. K. Halford & H. J. Markman (Eds.), *Clinical handbook of marriage and couples intervention* (pp. 379–413). Chichester, England: Wiley.

Freeman, A., & Dattilio, F. M. (1994). Introduction. In F. M. Dattilio & A. Freeman (Eds.), *Cognitive–behavioral strategies in crisis intervention* (pp. 1–22). New York: Guilford Press.

Frieze, I. H., & McHugh, M. C. (1992). Power and influence strategies in violent and nonviolent marriages. *Psychology of Women Quarterly, 16,* 449–465.

Furstenberg, F., & Spanier, G. B. (1984). *Recycling the family.* Beverly Hills, CA: Sage.

Geiss, S. K., & O'Leary, K. D. (1981). Therapist ratings of frequency and severity of marital problems: Implications for research. *Journal of Marital and Family Therapy, 7,* 515–520.

Giordano, J., & Carini-Giordano, M. A. (1995). Ethnic dimensions in family treatment. In R. H. Mikesell, D. D. Lusterman, & S. H. McDaniel (Eds.), *Integrating family therapy: Handbook of family psychology and systems theory* (pp. 347–356). Washington, DC: American Psychological Association.

Girodo, M., Stein, S. J., & Dotzenroth, S. E. (1980). The effects of communication skills training and contracting on marital relations. *Behavioral Engineering, 6,* 61–76.

Glass, S. P., & Wright, T. L. (1985). Sex differences in type of extramarital involvement and marital dissatisfaction. *Sex Roles, 12,* 1101–1119.

Glass, S. P., & Wright, T. L. (1997). Reconstructing marriages after the trauma of infidelity. In W. K. Halford & H. J. Markman (Eds.), *Clinical handbook of marriage and couples interventions* (pp. 471–507). Chichester, England: Wiley.

Glick, S. (1996). *Examining the relationship between perceived emotional expressiveness and marital adjustment.* Unpublished doctoral dissertation, University of North Carolina at Chapel Hill.

Goldenberg, H., & Goldenberg, I. (1994). *Counseling today's families* (2nd ed.). Pacific Grove, CA: Brooks/Cole.

Goldman, A., & Greenberg, L. (1992). Comparison of integrated systemic and emotionally focused approaches to couples therapy. *Journal of Consulting and Clinical Psychology, 60,* 962–969.

Goldstein, A. J., & Chambless, D. L. (1978). A reanalysis of agoraphobia. *Behavior Therapy, 9,* 47–59.

Goldstein, A. P., & Michaels, G. Y. (1985). *Empathy: Development, training, and consequences.* Hillsdale, NJ: Erlbaum.

Goldstine, D., Larner, K., Zuckerman, S., & Goldstine, H. (1993). The three stages of love. In A. Arkoff (Ed.), *Psychology and personal growth* (4th ed., pp. 350–356). Boston: Allyn & Bacon.

Gordon, K. C., & Baucom, D. H. (1998a, November). *Addressing infidelity: Preliminary results for a forgiveness-based marital intervention.* Paper presented at the annual meeting of the Association for the Advancement of Behavior Therapy, Washington, DC.

Gordon, K. C., & Baucom, D. H. (1998b, November). *"True" forgiveness versus "false" forgiveness: Further validation of a cognitive–behavioral stage model of forgiveness.* Paper presented at the annual meeting of the Association for the Advancement of Behavior Therapy, Washington, DC.

Gordon, K. C., & Baucom, D. H. (1998c). Understanding betrayals in marriage: A synthesized model of forgiveness. *Family Process, 37,* 425–449.

Gordon, K. C., & Baucom, D. H. (1999). A forgiveness-based intervention for addressing extramarital affairs. *Clinical Psychology: Science and Practice, 6,* 382–399.

Gordon, K. C., Baucom, D. H., Rankin, L., Burnett, C. K., & Epstein, N. (1999). The interaction between marital standards and communication patterns: How does it contribute to marital adjustment? *Journal of Marital and Family Therapy, 25,* 211–223.

Gordon, K. C., Baucom, D. H., & Snyder, D. K. (2000). The use of forgiveness in marital therapy. In M. E. McCullough, K. Pargament, & C. Thorsen (Eds.), *Forgiveness: Theory, research, and practice* (pp. 203–227). New York: Guilford Press.

Gotlib, I. H., & Beach, S. R. H. (1995). A marital/family discord model of depression: Implications for therapeutic intervention. In N. S. Jacobson & A. S. Gurman (Eds.), *Clinical handbook of couple therapy* (pp. 411–436). New York: Guilford Press.

Gotlib, I. H., & Robinson, L. A. (1982). Responses to depressed individuals: Discrepancies between self-report and observer-rated behaviour. *Journal of Abnormal Psychology, 91,* 231–240.

Gottman, J. M. (1979). *Marital interaction: Experimental investigations.* New York: Academic Press.

Gottman, J. M. (1994a). *What predicts divorce?* Hillsdale, NJ: Erlbaum.

Gottman, J. M. (1994b). *Why marriages succeed or fail.* New York: Simon & Schuster.

Gottman, J. M. (1999). *The marriage clinic: A scientifically-based marital therapy.* New York: Norton.

Gottman, J. M., & Krokoff, L. J. (1989). Marital interaction and satisfaction: A longitudinal view. *Journal of Consulting and Clinical Psychology, 57,* 47–52.

Gottman, J. M., & Levenson, R. W. (1988). The social psychophysiology of marriage. In P. Noller & M. A. Fitzpatrick (Eds.), *Perspectives on marital interaction. Monographs in social psychology of language* (No. 1, pp. 182–200). Clevedon, England: Multilingual Matters.

Gottman, J. M., & Levenson, R. W. (1992). Marital processes predictive of later dissolution: Behavior, physiology, and health. *Journal of Personality and Social Psychology, 63,* 221–233.

Gottman, J. M., Markman, H. J., & Notarius, C. I. (1977). The topography of marital conflict: A sequential analysis of verbal and nonverbal behavior. *Journal of Marriage and the Family, 39,* 461–477.

Gottman, J. M., & Notarius, C. I. (2000). Decade review: Observing marital interaction. *Journal of Marriage and the Family, 62,* 927–947.

Gray-Little, B. (1982). Marital quality and power processes among Black couples. *Journal of Marriage and the Family, 44,* 633–646.

Gray-Little, B., Baucom, D. H., & Hamby, S. L. (1996). Marital power, marital adjustment, and therapy outcome. *Journal of Family Psychology, 10,* 292–303.

Gray-Little, B., & Burks, N. (1983). Power and satisfaction in marriage: A review and critique. *Psychological Bulletin, 93,* 513–538.

Greenberg, L. S., & Johnson, S. M. (1988). *Emotionally focused therapy for couples.* New York: Guilford Press.

Greenberg, L. S., & Safran, J. D. (1987). *Emotion in psychotherapy: Affect, cognition, and the process of change.* New York: Guilford Press.

Greenstone, J. L., & Leviton, S. C. (1993). *Elements of crisis intervention: Crises and how to respond to them.* Pacific Grove, CA: Brooks/Cole.

Gudykunst, W. B., & Ting-Toomey, S. (1988). *Culture and interpersonal communication.* Newbury Park, CA: Sage.

Guerney, B. G., Jr. (1977). *Relationship enhancement.* San Francisco: Jossey-Bass.

Haddock, S. A., Zimmerman, T. S., Ziemba, S., & Current, L. R. (2001). Ten adaptive strategies for family and work balance: Advice from successful families. *Journal of Marital and Family Therapy, 27,* 445–458.

Hahlweg, K., Reisner, L., Kohli, G., Vollmer, M., Schindler, L., & Revenstorf, D. (1984). Development and validity of a new system to analyze interpersonal communication (KPI: Kategoriensystem fur partnerschaftliche Interaktion). In K. Hahlweg & N. S. Jacobson (Eds.), *Marital interaction: Analysis and modification* (pp. 182–198). New York: Guilford Press.

Hahlweg, K., Revenstorf, D., & Schindler, L. (1982). Treatment of marital distress: Comparing formats and modalities. *Advances in Behavior Research and Therapy, 4,* 57–74.

Hahlweg, K., Schindler, L., Revenstorf, D., & Brengelmann, J. C. (1984). The Munich Marital Therapy Study. In K. Hahlweg & N. S. Jacobson (Eds.), *Marital interaction: Analysis and modification* (pp. 3–26). New York: Guilford Press.

Halford, W. K. (2001). *Brief therapy for couples: Helping partners help themselves.* New York: Guilford Press.

Halford, W. K., & Bouma, R. (1997). Individual psychopathology and marital distress. In W. K. Halford & H. J. Markman (Eds.), *Clinical handbook of marriage and couples interventions* (pp. 291–321). Chichester, England: Wiley.

Halford, W. K., Hahlweg, K., & Dunne, M. (1990). Cross-cultural consistency of marital communication associated with marital distress. *Journal of Marriage and the Family, 52,* 487–500.

Halford, W. K., Kelly, A., & Markman, H. J. (1997). The concept of a healthy marriage. In W. K. Halford & H. J. Markman (Eds.), *Clinical handbook of marriage and couples interventions* (pp. 3–12). Chichester, England: Wiley.

Halford, W. K., & Sanders, M. R. (1988). Dyadic behaviours and requests for change in Australian maritally distressed and non-distressed couples. *Australian Journal of Psychology, 40,* 45–52.

Halford, W. K., Sanders, M. R., & Behrens, B. C. (1993). A comparison of the generalization of behavioral marital therapy and enhanced behavioral marital therapy. *Journal of Consulting and Clinical Psychology, 61,* 51–60.

Halford, W. K., Sanders, M. R., & Behrens, B. C. (1994). Self-regulation in behavioral couples' therapy. *Behavior Therapy, 25,* 431–452.

Hetherington, E. M. (1972). Effects of parental absence on personality development in adolescent daughters. *Developmental Psychology, 7,* 313–326.

Heyman, R. E., Brown, P. D., Feldbau, S. R., & O'Leary, K. D. (1999). Couples' communication variables as predictors of dropout and treatment response in wife abuse treatment programs. *Behavior Therapy, 30,* 165–190.

Heyman, R. E., Eddy, J. M., Weiss, R. L., & Vivian, D. (1995). Factor analysis of the Marital Interaction Coding System (MICS). *Journal of Family Psychology, 9,* 209–215.

Heyman, R. E., & Neidig, P. H. (1997). Physical aggression couples treatment. In W. K. Halford & H. J. Markman (Eds.), *Clinical handbook of marriage and couples intervention* (pp. 589–617). Chichester, England: Wiley.

Heyman, R. E., Weiss, R. L., & Eddy, J. M. (1995). Marital Interaction Coding System: Revision and empirical evaluation. *Behaviour Research and Therapy, 33,* 737–746.

Hill, R. (1949). *Families under stress.* New York: Harper & Row.

Hill, R. (1958). Generic features of families under stress. *Social Casework, 49,* 139–150.

Hines, P. M. (1999). The family life cycle of African American families living in poverty. In B. Carter & M. McGoldrick (Eds.), *The expanded family life cycle: Individual, family, and social perspectives* (3rd ed., pp. 327–345). Boston: Allyn & Bacon.

Hines, P. M., Preto, N. G., McGoldrick, M., Almeida, R., & Weltman, S. (1999). Culture and the family life cycle. In B. Carter & M. McGoldrick (Eds.), *The expanded family life cycle: Individual, family, and social perspectives* (3rd ed., pp. 69–87). Boston: Allyn & Bacon.

Holtzworth-Munroe, A., Beatty, S. B., & Anglin, K. (1995). The assessment and treatment of marital violence: An introduction for the marital therapist. In N. S. Jacobson & A. S. Gurman (Eds.), *Clinical handbook of couple therapy* (pp. 317–349). New York: Guilford Press.

Holtzworth-Munroe, A., & Jacobson, N. S. (1985). Causal attributions of married couples: When do they search for causes? What do they conclude when they do? *Journal of Personality and Social Psychology, 48,* 1398–1412.

Hooley, J. M., & Teasdale, J. D. (1989). Predictors of relapse in unipolar depressives: Expressed emotion, marital distress, and perceived criticism. *Journal of Abnormal Psychology, 98,* 229–237.

Horowitz, M. J. (1989). Relationship schema formulation: Role-relationship models and intrapsychic conflict. *Psychiatry, 52*, 260–274.

Howes, M. J., & Hokanson, J. E. (1979). Conversational and social responses to depressive interpersonal behavior. *Journal of Abnormal Psychology, 88*, 625–634.

Hsu, J. (1985). The Chinese family: Relations, problems, and therapy. In W. Tseng & D. Y. H. Wu (Eds.), *Chinese culture and mental health* (pp. 95–112). Orlando, FL: Academic Press.

Huber, C. H. (1994). *Ethical, legal and professional issues in the practice of marriage and family therapy* (2nd ed.). New York: Macmillan.

Huber, C. H., & Milstein, B. (1985). Cognitive restructuring and a collaborative set in couples' work. *American Journal of Family Therapy, 13* (2), 17–27.

Hull, C. L. (1943). *Principles of behavior.* New York: Appleton-Century-Crofts.

Huston, T. L. (1983). Power. In H. H. Kelley, E. Berscheid, A. Christensen, J. H. Harvey, T. L. Huston, G. Levinger, E. McClintock, L. A. Peplau, & D. R. Peterson (Eds.), *Close relationships* (pp. 169–219). New York: Freeman.

Huston, T. L., Robins, E., Atkinson, H., & McHale, S. M. (1987). Surveying the landscape of marital behaviours: A behavioural self-report approach to studying marriage. *Applied Social Psychology Annual, 7*, 45–72.

Imber-Black, E. (1999). Creating meaningful rituals for new life cycle transitions. In B. Carter & M. McGoldrick (Eds.), *The expanded family life cycle: Individual, family, and social perspectives* (3rd ed., pp. 202–214). Boston: Allyn & Bacon.

Isen, A. M. (1987). Positive affect, cognitive processes, and social behavior. In L. Berkowitz (Ed.), *Advances in experimental social psychology* (Vol. 20, pp. 203–253). San Diego, CA: Academic Press.

Iverson, A., & Baucom, D. H. (1990). Behavioral marital therapy outcomes: Alternate interpretations of the data. *Behavior Therapy, 21*, 129–138.

Izard, C. (1977). *Human emotions.* New York: Plenum.

Jacob, T., & Tennenbaum, D. L. (1988). *Family assessment: Rationale, methods, and future directions.* New York: Plenum.

Jacobson, N. S. (1977). Problem-solving and contingency contracting in the treatment of marital discord. *Journal of Consulting and Clinical Psychology, 45*, 92–100.

Jacobson, N. S. (1978). Specific and nonspecific factors in the effectiveness of a behavioral approach to the treatment of marital discord. *Journal of Consulting and Clinical Psychology, 46*, 442–452.

Jacobson, N. S. (1983). Beyond empiricism: The politics of marital therapy. *American Journal of Family Therapy, 11*, 11–24.

Jacobson, N. S. (1984). A component analysis of behavioral marital therapy: The relative effectiveness of behavior exchange and communication/problem-solving training. *Journal of Consulting and Clinical Psychology, 52*, 295–305.

Jacobson, N. S., & Christensen, A. (1996). *Integrative couple therapy: Promoting acceptance and change.* New York: Norton.

Jacobson, N. S., Christensen, A., Prince, S. E., Cordova, J., & Eldridge, K. A. (2000). Integrative behavioral couple therapy: An acceptance-based, promising new treatment for couple discord. *Journal of Consulting and Clinical Psychology, 68,* 351–355.

Jacobson, N. S., Dobson, K. S., Fruzzetti, A. E., Schmaling, K. B., & Salusky, S. (1991). Marital therapy as a treatment for depression. *Journal of Consulting and Clinical Psychology, 59,* 547–557.

Jacobson, N. S., Follette, W. C., & McDonald, D. W. (1982). Reactivity to positive and negative behavior in distressed and nondistressed married couples. *Journal of Consulting and Clinical Psychology, 50,* 706–714.

Jacobson, N. S., Follette, W. C., Revenstorf, D., Baucom, D. H., Hahlweg, K., & Margolin, G. (1984). Variability in outcome and clinical significance of behavioral marital therapy: A reanalysis of outcome data. *Journal of Consulting and Clinical Psychology, 52,* 497–504.

Jacobson, N. S., Fruzzetti, A. E., Dobson, K. S., Whisman, M., & Hops, H. (1993). Couple therapy as a treatment for depression: II. The effects of relationship quality and therapy on depressive relapse. *Journal of Consulting and Clinical Psychology, 61,* 516–519.

Jacobson, N. S., & Margolin, G. (1979). *Marital therapy: Strategies based on social learning and behavior exchange principles.* New York: Brunner/Mazel.

Jacobson, N. S., & Moore, D. (1981). Spouses as observers of the events in their relationship. *Journal of Consulting and Clinical Psychology, 49,* 269–277.

Jacobson, N. S., Waldron, H., & Moore, D. (1980). Toward a behavioral profile of marital distress. *Journal of Consulting and Clinical Psychology, 48,* 696–703.

James, P. S. (1991). Effects of a communication training component added to an emotionally focused couples therapy. *Journal of Marital and Family Therapy, 17,* 263–275.

Jarvis, W. B. G., & Petty, R. E. (1996). The need to evaluate. *Journal of Personality and Social Psychology, 70,* 172–194.

Jerrome, D. (1994). Family estrangement: Parents and children who "lose touch." *Journal of Family Therapy, 16,* 241–258.

Jocklin, V., McGue, M., & Lykken, D. T. (1996). Personality and divorce: A genetic analysis. *Journal of Personality and Social Psychology, 71,* 288–299.

John, O. P., & Srivastava, S. (1999). The Big Five trait taxonomy: History, measurement, and theoretical perspectives. In L. A. Pervin & O. P. John (Eds.), *Handbook of personality: Theory and research* (pp. 102–138). New York: Guilford Press.

Johnson, S. M. (1996). *The practice of emotionally focused marital therapy.* New York: Brunner/Mazel.

Johnson, S. M., & Greenberg, L. S. (1985). Emotionally focused couples therapy: An outcome study. *Journal of Marital and Family Therapy, 11,* 313–317.

Johnson, S. M., & Greenberg, L. S. (1992). Emotionally focused therapy: Restructuring attachment. In S. H. Budman, M. F. Hoyt, & S. Friedman (Eds.), *The first session in brief therapy* (pp. 204–224). New York: Guilford Press.

Johnson, S. M., & Greenberg, L. S. (1994a). Emotion in intimate relationships: Theory and implications for therapy. In S. M. Johnson & L. S. Greenberg (Eds.), *The heart of the matter: Perspectives on emotion in marital therapy* (pp. 3–22). New York: Brunner/Mazel.

Johnson, S. M., & Greenberg, L. S. (Eds.). (1994b). *The heart of the matter: Perspectives on emotion in marital therapy.* New York: Brunner/Mazel.

Johnson, S. M., & Greenberg, L. S. (1995). The emotionally focused approach to problems in adult attachment. In N. S. Jacobson & A. S. Gurman (Eds.), *Clinical handbook of couple therapy* (pp. 121–141). New York: Guilford Press.

Joseph, G. I., & Lewis, J. (1981). *Common differences: Conflicts in Black and White feminist perspectives.* Boston: South End.

Jouriles, E. N., & Farris, A. M. (1992). Effects of marital conflict on subsequent parent–son interactions. *Behavior Therapy, 23,* 355–374.

Julien, D., Arellano, C., & Turgeon, L. (1997). Gender issues in heterosexual, gay and lesbian couples. In W. K. Halford & H. J. Markman (Eds.), *Clinical handbook of marriage and couples interventions* (pp. 107–128). Chichester, England: Wiley.

Julien, D., & Markman, H. J. (1991). Social support and social networks as determinants of individual and marital outcomes. *Journal of Social and Personal Relationships, 8,* 549–568.

Julien, D., Markman, H. J., & Lindahl, K. M. (1989). A comparison of a global and a microanalytic coding system: Implications for future trends in studying interactions. *Behavioral Assessment, 11,* 81–100.

Kagan, J. (1994). *Galen's prophecy: Temperament in human nature.* New York: Basic Books.

Kaplan, H. S. (Ed.). (1983). *The evaluation of sexual disorders: Psychological and medical aspects.* New York: Brunner/Mazel.

Kaplan, H. S. (1995). *The sexual desire disorders: Dysfunctional regulation of sexual motivation.* New York: Brunner/Mazel.

Karney, B. R., & Bradbury, T. N. (1995). The longitudinal course of marital quality and stability: A review of theory, methods, and research. *Psychological Bulletin, 118,* 3–34.

Karney, B. R., & Bradbury, T. N. (1997). Neuroticism, marital interaction, and the trajectory of marital satisfaction. *Journal of Personality and Social Psychology, 72,* 1075–1092.

Karney, B. R., Bradbury, T. N., Fincham, F. D., & Sullivan, K. T. (1994). The role of negative affectivity in the association between attributions and marital satisfaction. *Journal of Personality and Social Psychology, 66,* 413–424.

Kazak, A. E., Jarmas, A., & Snitzer, L. (1988). The assessment of marital satisfaction: An evaluation of the Dyadic Adjustment Scale. *Journal of Family Psychology, 2,* 82–91.

Kirkpatrick, L. A. (1998). Evolution, pair-bonding, and reproductive strategies: A reconceptualization of adult attachment. In J. A. Simpson & W. S. Rholes (Eds.), *Attachment theory and close relationships* (pp. 353–393). New York: Guilford Press.

Klass, D., Silverman, P., & Nickman, S. (Eds.). (1996). *Continuing bonds: New understandings of grief.* Washington, DC: Taylor & Francis.

Kobak, R., Ruckdeschel, K., & Hazan, C. (1994). From symptom to signal: An attachment view of emotion in marital therapy. In S. M. Johnson & L. S. Greenberg (Eds.), *The heart of the matter: Perspectives on emotion in marital therapy* (pp. 46–71). New York: Brunner/Mazel.

Kuhl, J. (1994). A theory of action and state orientations. In J. Kuhl & J. Beckmann (Eds.), *Volition and personality: Action versus state orientation* (pp. 9–46). Seattle, WA: Hogrefe & Huber.

Larsen, R. J., & Ketelaar, T. (1991). Personality and susceptibility to positive and negative emotional states. *Journal of Personality and Social Psychology, 61,* 132–140.

Larson, J. H., & Holman, T. B. (1994). Premarital predictors of marital quality and stability. *Family Relations, 43,* 228–237.

Lawrence, E., Eldridge, K. A., & Christensen, A. (1998). The enhancement of traditional behavioral couples therapy: Consideration of individual factors and dyadic development. *Clinical Psychology Review, 18,* 745–764.

Lazarus, R. S. (1991). *Emotion and adaption.* New York: Oxford University Press.

Lazarus, R. S., & Folkman, S. (1984). *Stress, appraisal and coping.* New York: Springer.

Leahy, R. (1996). *Cognitive therapy: Basic principles and applications.* Northvale, NJ: Jason Aronson.

Leahy, R. (Ed.). (1997). *Practicing cognitive therapy: A guide to interventions.* Northvale, NJ: Jason Aronson.

Leslie, L. A., Anderson, E. A., & Branson, M. P. (1991). Responsibility for children: The role of gender and employment. *Journal of Family Issues, 12,* 197–210.

Leslie, L. A., & Epstein, N. (1988). Cognitive–behavioral treatment of remarried families. In N. Epstein, S. E. Schlesinger, & W. Dryden (Eds.), *Cognitive–behavioral therapy with families* (pp. 151–182). New York: Brunner/Mazel.

Levenson, R. W., & Gottman, J. M. (1985). Physiological and affective predictors of change in relationship satisfaction. *Journal of Personality and Social Psychology, 49,* 85–94.

Liberman, R., Levine, J., Wheeler, E., Sanders, N., & Wallace, C. J. (1976). Marital therapy in groups: A comparative evaluation of behavioral and interaction formats. *Acta Psychiatrica Scandinavica, 266,* 1–34.

Lindahl, K. M., Malik, N. M., & Bradbury, T. N. (1997). The developmental course of couples' relationships. In W. K. Halford & H. J. Markman (Eds.), *Clinical handbook of marriage and couples interventions* (pp. 203–223). Chichester, England: Wiley.

Linehan, M. M. (1993). *Cognitive–behavioral treatment of borderline personality disorder.* New York: Guilford Press.

LoPiccolo, J., & Daiss, S. (1987). Assessment of sexual dysfunction. In K. D. O'Leary (Ed.), *Assessment of marital discord: An integration of research and clinical practice* (pp. 183–221). Hillsdale, NJ: Erlbaum.

LoPiccolo, J., & Steger, J. C. (1974). The Sexual Interaction Inventory: A new instrument for assessment of sexual dysfunction. *Archives of Sexual Behavior, 3,* 585–595.

Luborsky, L., & Crits-Christoph, P. (Eds.). (1998). *Understanding transference: The core conflict relationship method.* Washington, DC: American Psychological Association.

Madanes, C. (1991). Strategic family therapy. In A. S. Gurman & D. P. Kniskern (Eds.), *Handbook of family therapy* (pp. 396–416). New York: Brunner/Mazel.

Maltz, W. (1988). Identifying and treating the sexual repercussions of incest: A couples therapy approach. *Journal of Sex and Marital Therapy, 14,* 142–170.

Margolin, G. (1981). Behavior exchange in happy and unhappy marriages: A family cycle perspective. *Behavior Therapy, 12,* 329–343.

Margolin, G. (1982). Ethical and legal considerations in marital and family therapy. *American Psychologist, 37,* 788–802.

Margolin, G., Talovic, S., & Weinstein, C. D. (1983). Areas of Change Questionnaire: A practical approach to marital assessment. *Journal of Consulting and Clinical Psychology, 51,* 944–955.

Margolin, G., & Wampold, B. E. (1981). Sequential analysis of conflict and accord in distressed and nondistressed marital partners. *Journal of Consulting and Clinical Psychology, 49,* 554–567.

Markman, H. J., & Notarius, C. I. (1987). Coding marital and family interaction: Current status. In T. Jacob (Ed.), *Family interaction and psychopathology: Theories, methods, and findings. Applied clinical psychology* (pp. 329–390). New York: Plenum.

Markman, H. J., Stanley, S. M., & Blumberg, S. L. (1994). *Fighting for your marriage: Positive steps for preventing divorce and preserving a lasting love.* San Francisco: Jossey-Bass.

Maslow, A. (1954). *Motivation and personality.* New York: Harper & Row.

Masters, W. H., & Johnson, V. E. (1970). *Human sexual inadequacy.* Boston: Little, Brown.

McAdams, D. P. (1980). A thematic coding system for the intimacy motive. *Journal of Research in Personality, 14,* 413–432.

McAdams, D. P. (1984). Human motives and personal relationships. In V. Derlega (Ed.), *Communication, intimacy, and close relationships* (pp. 41–70). New York: Academic Press.

McAdams, D. P. (1985). *Power, intimacy, and the life story: Personological inquiries into identity.* New York: Guilford Press.

McAdams, D. P. (1988). Personal needs and personal relationships. In S. W. Duck (Ed.), *Handbook of personal relationships* (pp. 7–22). London: Wiley.

McAdams, D. P., Hoffman, B. J., Mansfield, E. D., & Day, R. (1996). Themes of agency and communication in significant autobiographical scenes. *Journal of Personality, 64,* 339–377.

McAdams, D. P., & Powers, J. (1981). Themes of intimacy in behavior and thought. *Journal of Personality and Social Psychology, 40,* 573–587.

McCarter, L. M., & Levenson, R. W. (1996, October). *Sex differences in physiological reactivity to the acoustic startle.* Paper presented at the Society for Psychophysiological Research, Vancouver, British Columbia, Canada.

McCarthy, B. W. (1997). Therapeutic and iatrogenic interventions with adults who were sexually abused as children. *Journal of Sex and Marital Therapy, 23,* 118–125.

McClelland, D. C. (1987). *Human motivation.* Cambridge, England: Cambridge University Press.

McClelland, D. C., Davis, W. B., Kalin, R., & Wanner, E. (1972). *The drinking man: Alcohol and human motivation.* New York: Free Press.

McCrady, B. S., & Epstein, E. E. (1995). Marital therapy in the treatment of alcohol problems. In N. S. Jacobson & A. S. Gurman (Eds.), *Clinical handbook of couple therapy* (pp. 369–393). New York: Guilford Press.

McCubbin, H. I., & Patterson, J. M. (1983). Family transitions: Adaptation to stress. In H. I. McCubbin & C. R. Figley (Eds.), *Stress and the family: Vol. I. Coping with normative transitions* (pp. 5–25). New York: Brunner/Mazel.

McCubbin, H. I., & Patterson, J. M. (1987). FILE: Family Inventory of Life Events and Changes. In H. I. McCubbin & A. I. Thompson (Eds.), *Family assessment inventories for research and practice* (pp. 81–98). Madison: University of Wisconsin, Family Stress Coping and Health Project.

McCubbin, M. A., & McCubbin, H. I. (1989). Theoretical orientation to family stress and coping. In C. R. Figley (Ed.), *Treating stress in families* (pp. 3–43). New York: Brunner/Mazel.

McGoldrick, M., Preto, N. G., Hines, P. M., & Lee, E. (1991). Ethnicity and family therapy. In A. S. Gurman & D. P. Kniskern (Eds.), *Handbook of family therapy* (Vol. 2, pp. 546–582). New York: Brunner/Mazel.

McKenry, P. C., & Price, S. J. (Eds.). (2000). *Families and change: Coping with stressful events and transitions.* Thousand Oaks, CA: Sage.

Mehrabian, A. (1994). Evidence bearing on the Affiliative Tendency (MAFF) and Sensitivity to Rejection (MSR) Scales. *Current Psychology: Developmental, Learning, Personality, Social, 13,* 97–117.

Meichenbaum, D. (1985). *Stress inoculation training.* New York: Pergamon Press.

Metz, M. E., & Epstein, N. (2002). Assessing the role of relationship conflict in sexual dysfunction. *Journal of Sex and Marital Therapy, 28,* 139–164.

Mikesell, S. G., & Stohner, M. (1995). Infertility and pregnancy loss: The role of the family consultant. In R. H. Mikesell, D. D. Lusterman, & S. H. McDaniel (Eds.), *Integrating family therapy: Handbook of family psychology and systems theory* (pp. 421–436). Washington, DC: American Psychological Association.

Miklowitz, D. J. (1995). The evolution of family-based psychopathology. In R. H. Mikesell, D. D. Lusterman, & S. H. McDaniel (Eds.), *Integrating family therapy:*

Handbook of family psychology and systems theory (pp. 183–198). Washington, DC: American Psychological Association.

Miklowitz, D. J., & Goldstein, M. J. (1997). *Bipolar disorder: A family-focused treatment approach.* New York: Guilford Press.

Miller, G. E., & Bradbury, T. N. (1995). Refining the association between attributions and behavior in marital interaction. *Journal of Family Psychology, 9,* 196–208.

Miller, N., & Dollard, J. (1941). *Social learning and imitation.* New Haven, CT: Yale University Press.

Minuchin, S. (1974). *Families and family therapy.* Cambridge, MA: Harvard University Press.

Murray, C. I. (2000). Coping with death, dying, and grief in families. In P. C. McKenry & S. J. Price (Eds.), *Families and change: Coping with stressful events and transitions* (2nd ed., pp. 120–153). Thousand Oaks, CA: Sage.

Murray, H. A. (1938). *Explorations in personality.* New York: Oxford University Press.

Murstein, B. I., Cerreto, M., & MacDonald, M. G. (1977). A theory and investigation of the effect of exchange-orientation on marriage and friendship. *Journal of Marriage and the Family, 39,* 543–548.

Napier, A. Y. (1988). *The fragile bond.* New York: Harper & Row.

Neimeyer, R. (1998). *Lessons of loss: A guide to coping.* New York: McGraw-Hill.

Nelson, G. M., & Beach, S. R. H. (1990). Sequential interaction in depression: Effects of depressive behavior on spousal aggression. *Behavior Therapy, 21,* 167–182.

Nichols, M. P., & Schwartz, R. C. (2001). *Family therapy: Concepts and methods.* Boston: Allyn & Bacon.

Nicholson, I. R. (1998). Schizophrenia and the family. In L. L'Abate (Ed.), *Family psychopathology: The relational roots of dysfunctional behavior* (pp. 280–310). New York: Guilford Press.

Nickols, S. Y. (1994). Work/family stresses. In P. C. McKenry & S. J. Price (Eds.), *Families and change: Coping with stressful events* (pp. 66–87). Thousand Oaks, CA: Sage.

Notarius, C. I., Benson, P. R., Sloane, D., & Vanzetti, N. A. (1989). Exploring the interface between perception and behavior: An analysis of marital interaction in distressed and nondistressed couples. *Behavioral Assessment, 11,* 39–64.

Notarius, C. I., & Markman, H. J. (1981). The Couples Interaction Scoring System. In E. E. Filsinger & R. A. Lewis (Eds.), *Assessing marriage: New behavioral approaches* (pp. 112–127). Beverly Hills, CA: Sage.

Notarius, C. L., & Markman, H. J. (1993). *We can work it out: Making sense of marital conflict.* New York: Putnam.

O'Farrell, T. J., Choquette, K. A., Cutter, H. S. G., Brown, E. D., & McCourt, W. F. (1993). Behavioral marital therapy with and without additional couples relapse prevention sessions for alcoholics and their wives. *Journal of Studies on Alcohol, 54,* 652–666.

O'Farrell, T. J., & Rotunda, R. (1997). Couples interventions and alcohol abuse. In W. K. Halford & H. J. Markman (Eds.), *Clinical handbook of marriage and couples interventions* (pp. 555–588). Chichester, England: Wiley.

Osgarby, S. M. (1998). Memory and positive exhange in marital satisfaction. Unpublished Doctoral Dissertation, School of Applied Psychology, Griffith University, Australia.

Osgarby, S. M., & Halford, W. K. (1995). *Do you remember? Couple's access and recall of information about their partners and their relationship interactions.* Unpublished manuscript, School of Applied Psychology, Griffith University, Australia.

Palmer, C. A., & Baucom, D. H. (1998, November). *How our marriages lasted: Couples' reflections on staying together.* Paper presented at the annual meeting of the Association for the Advancement of Behavior Therapy, Washington, DC.

Papernow, P. L. (1992). *Becoming a stepfamily: Patterns of development in remarried families.* New York: Gardner.

Pasch, L. A., & Bradbury, T. N. (1998). Social support, conflict, and the development of marital dysfunction. *Journal of Consulting and Clinical Psychology, 66,* 219–230.

Pasch, L. A., Bradbury, T. N., & Davila, J. (1997). Gender, negative affectivity, and observed social support behavior in marital interaction. *Personal Relationships, 4,* 361–378.

Pasch, L. A., Bradbury, T. N., & Sullivan, K. T. (1997). Social support in marriage: An analysis of intraindividual and interpersonal components. In G. R. Pierce, B. Lakey, I. G. Sarason, & B. R. Sarason (Eds.), *Sourcebook of theory and research on social support and personality* (pp. 229–256). New York: Plenum.

Paunonen, S. V. (1998). Hierarchical organization of personality and prediction of behavior. *Journal of Personality and Social Psychology, 74,* 538–556.

Penner, L. A., & Finkelstein, M. A. (1998). Dispositional and structural determinants of volunteerism. *Journal of Personality and Social Psychology, 74,* 525–537.

Prager, K. J. (1995). *The psychology of intimacy.* New York: Guilford Press.

Prager, K. J., & Buhrmester, D. (1998). Intimacy and need fulfillment in couple relationships. *Journal of Social and Personal Relationships, 15,* 435–469.

Pretzer, J., Epstein, N., & Fleming, B. (1991). Marital Attitude Survey: A measure of dysfunctional attributions and expectancies. *Journal of Cognitive Psychotherapy: An International Quarterly, 5,* 131–148.

Rankin-Esquer, L. A., Baucom, D. H., Clayton, D. C., Tomcik, N., & Mullens, J. A. (1999). *Cognitive processing in intimate relationships: Relationship schemas and individual schemas.* Manuscript in preparation.

Rankin-Esquer, L. A., Burnett, C. K., Baucom, D. H., & Epstein, N. (1997). Autonomy and relatedness in marital functioning. *Journal of Marital and Family Therapy, 23,* 175–190.

Rathus, J. H., & Sanderson, W. C. (1999). *Marital distress: Cognitive behavioral interventions for couples.* Northvale, NJ: Jason Aronson.

Raush, H. L., Barry, W. A., Hertel, R. K., & Swain, M. A. (1974). *Communication, conflict and marriage*. San Francisco: Jossey-Bass.

Reis, H. T., Senchak, M., & Solomon, B. (1985). Sex differences in the intimacy of social interaction: Further examination of potential explanations. *Journal of Personality and Social Psychology, 48*, 1204–1217.

Reiss, S., & Havercamp, S. M. (1998). Toward a comprehensive assessment of fundamental motivation: Factor structure of the Reiss Profiles. *Psychological Assessment, 10*, 97–106.

Revenstorf, D., Hahlweg, K., Schindler, L., & Vogel, B. (1984). Interaction analysis of marital conflict. In K. Hahlweg & N. S. Jacobson (Eds.), *Marital interaction: Analysis and modification* (pp. 159–181). New York: Guilford Press.

Rodgers, W. L., & Thornton, A. (1985). Changing patterns of first marriage in the United States. *Demography, 22*, 265–279.

Rogers, C. R. (1957). The necessary and sufficient conditions of therapeutic personality change. *Journal of Consulting Psychology, 21*, 95–103.

Rohrbaugh, M. J., Shoham, V., Trost, S., Muramoto, M., Cate, R., & Leischow, S. (2001). Couple-dynamics of change resistant smoking: Toward a family-consultation model. *Family Process, 40*, 15–31.

Rolls, E. (1987). Information representation, processing and storage in the brain: Analysis at the single neuron level. In J. P. Changeux & M. Konishi (Eds.), *The neural and molecular bases of learning* (pp. 503–540). Chichester, England: Wiley.

Rolls, E. (1989). The representation and storage of information in neuronal networks in the primate cerebral cortex and hippocampus. In R. Durbin, C. Miall, & G. Mitchison (Eds.), *The computing neuron* (pp. 125–159). Wokingham, England: Addison-Wesley.

Rolls, E. (1990). A theory of emotion, and its application to understanding the neural basis of emotion. *Cognition & Emotion, 4*, 161–190.

Rook, K., & Pietromonaco, P. (1987). Close relationships: Ties that heal or ties that bind. *Advances in Personal Relationships, 1*, 1–35.

Root, M. P. P. (1995). Conceptualization and treatment of eating disorders in couples. In N. S. Jacobson & A. S. Gurman (Eds.), *Clinical handbook of couple therapy* (pp. 437–457). New York: Guilford Press.

Rosenbaum, A., & O'Leary, K. D. (1986). Treatment of marital violence. In N. S. Jacobson & A. S. Gurman (Eds.), *Clinical handbook of marital therapy* (pp. 385–405). New York: Guilford Press.

Rothbard, J. C., & Shaver, P. R. (1994). Continuity of attachment across the life span. In M. B. Sperling & W. H. Berman (Eds.), *Attachment in adults: Clinical and developmental perspectives* (pp. 31–72). New York: Guilford Press.

Rust, J., & Golombok, S. (1986a). *The Golombok–Rust Inventory of Sexual Satisfaction*. London: NFER—Nelson.

Rust, J., & Golombok, S. (1986b). The GRISS: A psychometric instrument for the assessment of sexual dysfunction. *Archives of Sexual Behavior, 15*, 153–161.

Sager, C. J. (1976). *Marriage contracts and couple therapy: Hidden forces in intimate relationships*. New York: Brunner/Mazel.

Sander, F. M. (1998). Psychoanalytic couple therapy. In F. M. Dattilio (Ed.), *Case studies in couple and family therapy: Systemic and cognitive perspectives* (pp. 427–449). New York: Guilford Press.

Schaap, C. P. D. R. (1984). Conflict resolution and marital satisfaction. *Nederlands Tijdschrift voor de Psychologie en Haar Grensgebieden, 39*, 396–403.

Schaller, M., Boyd, C., Yohannes, J., & O'Brien, M. (1995). The prejudiced personality revisited: Personal need for structure and formation of erroneous group stereotypes. *Journal of Personality and Social Psychology, 68*, 544–555.

Schaller, M., & Cialdini, R. B. (1990). Happiness, sadness, and helping: A motivational integration. In E. T. Higgins & R. M. Sorrentino (Eds.), *Handbook of motivation and cognition: Foundations of social behavior* (Vol. 2, pp. 527–561). New York: Guilford Press.

Schilling, E. A., Baucom, D. H., Burnett, C. K., Allen, E. A., & Ragland, L. (2000). *Altering the course of marriage: The effect of PREP communication skills acquisition on couples' risk of becoming maritally distressed*. Manuscript submitted for publication.

Schmaling, K. B., & Jacobson, N. S. (1990). Marital interaction and depression. *Journal of Abnormal Psychology, 99*, 229–236.

Schuerger, J. M., Zarrella, K. L., & Hotz, A. S. (1989). Factors that influence the temporal stability of personality by questionnaire. *Journal of Personality and Social Psychology, 56*, 777–783.

Schwarz, N., Bless, H., & Bohner, G. (1991). Mood and persuasion: Affective states influence the processing of persuasive communications. In M. Zanna (Ed.), *Advances in experimental social psychology* (Vol. 24, pp. 161–199). San Diego, CA: Academic Press.

Searles, J. S., & Windle, M. (1990). Introduction and overview: Salient issues in the children of alcoholics literature. In M. Windle & J. S. Searles (Eds.), *Children of alcoholics: Critical perspectives* (pp. 1–8). New York: Guilford Press.

Sharpley, C. F., & Cross, D. G. (1982). A psychometric evaluation of the Spanier Dyadic Adjustment Scale. *Journal of Marriage and the Family, 44*, 739–741.

Simoneau, T. L., Miklowitz, D. J., Richards, J. A., Saleem, R., & George, E. L. (1999). Bipolar disorder and family communication: Effects of a psychoeducational treatment program. *Journal of Abnormal Psychology, 108*, 588–597.

Simpson, J. A., & Rholes, W. S. (Eds.). (1998). *Attachment theory and close relationships*. New York: Guilford Press.

Snyder, D. K. (1979). Multidimensional assessment of marital satisfaction. *Journal of Marriage and the Family, 41*, 813–823.

Snyder, D. K. (1997). *Manual for the Marital Satisfaction Inventory*. Los Angeles: Western Psychological Services.

Snyder, D. K. (1999). Affective reconstruction in the context of a pluralistic approach to couples therapy. *Clinical Psychology: Science and Practice, 6*, 348–365.

Snyder, D. K., & Aikman, G. G. (1999). The Marital Satisfaction Inventory—Revised. In M. E. Maruish (Ed.), *Use of psychological testing for treatment planning and outcomes assessment* (pp. 1173–1210). Mahwah, NJ: Erlbaum.

Snyder, D. K., Cavell, T. A., Heffer, R. W., & Mangrum, L. F. (1995). Marital and family assessment: A multifaceted, multilevel approach. In R. H. Mikesell, D. D. Lusterman, & S. H. McDaniel (Eds.), *Integrating family therapy: Handbook of family psychology and systems theory* (pp. 163–182). Washington, DC: American Psychological Association.

Snyder, D. K., & Regts, J. M. (1982). Factor scales for assessing marital disharmony and disaffection. *Journal of Consulting and Clinical Psychology, 50*, 736–743.

Snyder, D. K., & Whisman, M. A. (Eds.). (in press). *Treating difficult couples.* New York: Guilford Press.

Snyder, D. K., & Wills, R. M. (1989). Behavioral versus insight-oriented marital therapy: Effects on individual and interspousal functioning. *Journal of Consulting and Clinical Psychology, 57*, 39–46.

Snyder, D. K., Wills, R. M., & Grady-Fletcher, A. (1991). Long-term effectiveness of behavioral versus insight-oriented marital therapy: A 4-year follow-up study. *Journal of Consulting and Clinical Psychology, 59*, 138–141.

Snyder, D. K., Wills, R. M., & Keiser, T. W. (1981). Empirical validation of the Marital Satisfaction Inventory: An actuarial approach. *Journal of Consulting and Clinical Psychology, 49*, 262–268.

Spanier, G. B. (1976). Measuring dyadic adjustment: New scales for assessing the quality of marriage and similar dyads. *Journal of Marriage and the Family, 38*, 15–28.

Spanier, G. B., & Thompson, L. (1982). A confirmatory analysis of the Dyadic Adjustment Scale. *Journal of Marriage and the Family, 44*, 731–738.

Spielberger, C. D. (1985). Anxiety, cognition, and affect: A state–trait perspective. In A. H. Tuma & J. Maser (Eds.), *Anxiety and the anxiety disorders.* Hillsdale, NJ: Erlbaum.

Spring, J. A. (1996). *After the affair.* New York: HarperCollins.

Stevenson, H. W., Chen, C., & Lee, S. (1992). Chinese families. In J. L. Roopnarine & D. B. Carter (Eds.), *Parent–child socialization in diverse cultures* (pp. 17–33). Norwood, NJ: Ablex.

Stewart, A. J., & Rubin, Z. (1976). Power motivation in the dating couple. *Journal of Personality and Social Psychology, 34*, 305–309.

Straus, M. A., Hamby, S. L., Boney-McCoy, S., & Sugarman, D. B. (1996). The Revised Conflict Tactics Scales (CTS2): Development and preliminary psychometric data. *Journal of Family Issues, 17*, 283–316.

Strelau, J. (1985). Diversity of personality dimensions based on arousal theories: Need for integration. In J. T. Spence & C. E. Izard (Eds.), *Motivation, emotion, and personality* (pp. 147–166). Amsterdam: North-Holland.

Stuart, R. B. (1969). Operant interpersonal treatment for marital discord. *Journal of Consulting and Clinical Psychology, 33*, 675–682.

Stuart, R. B. (1980). *Helping couples change: A social learning approach to marital therapy.* New York: Guilford Press.

Stuart, R. B., & Jacobson, B. (1985). *Second marriage: Make it happy, make it last!* New York: Norton.

Suhr, J. A. (1990). *The development of the Social Support Behavior Code.* Unpublished master's thesis, University of Iowa, Iowa City.

Sullivan, L. J. (1999, November). *Observational measurement of relationship schemas.* Paper presented at the annual meeting of the Association for Advancement of Behavior Therapy, Toronto, Ontario, Canada.

Sullivan, L. J., & Baucom, D. H. (2000). *Relationship Schematic Processing Coding manual.* Unpublished materials, University of North Carolina at Chapel Hill.

Tarrier, N., Barrowclough, C., Vaughn, C., Bamrah, J., Porceddu, K., Watts, S., & Freeman, H. (1989). Community management of schizophrenia: A two-year follow-up of a behavioral intervention with families. *British Journal of Psychiatry, 154,* 625–628.

Tesser, A. (1988). Toward a self-evaluation maintenance model of social behavior. In L. Berkowitz (Ed.), *Advances in experimental psychology* (Vol. 21, pp. 181–227). New York: Academic Press.

Thibaut, J. W., & Kelley, H. H. (1959). *The social psychology of groups.* New York: Wiley.

Thorndike, E. L. (1911). *Animal intelligence.* New York: Macmillan.

Todd, T. (1986). Structural–strategic marital therapy. In N. S. Jacobson & A. S. Gurman (Eds.), *Clinical handbook of marital therapy* (pp. 71–105). New York: Guilford Press.

Tolman, A. O., & Weiss, R. L. (1990). *Marital Interaction Coding System—Global (MICS–G): Training manual for observers.* Eugene: Oregon Marital Studies Program, University of Oregon.

Touliatos, J., Perlmutter, B. F., & Straus, M. A. (Eds.). (1990). *Handbook of family measurement techniques.* Newbury Park, CA: Sage.

Tsoi-Hoshmand, L. (1976). Marital therapy: An integrated behavioral–learning approach. *Journal of Marriage and Family Counseling, 2,* 179–191.

Turkewitz, H., & O'Leary, K. D. (1981). A comparative outcome study of behavioral marital therapy and communication therapy. *Journal of Marital and Family Therapy, 7,* 159–169.

Turner, B. F., & Turner, C. B. (1974). Evaluations of women and men among Black and White college students. *Sociological Quarterly, 15,* 442–456.

Van Widenfelt, B., Markman, H. J., Guerney, B., Behrens, B. C., & Hosman, C. (1997). Prevention of relationship problems. In W. K. Halford & H. J. Markman (Eds.), *Clinical handbook of marriage and couples interventions* (pp. 651–675). Chichester, England: Wiley.

Vanzetti, N. A., Notarius, C. I., & NeeSmith, D. (1992). Specific and generalized expectancies in marital interaction. *Journal of Family Psychology, 6,* 171–183.

Visher, E. B., & Visher, J. S. (1982). *How to win as a stepfamily.* New York: Dembner Books.

Visher, E. B., & Visher, J. S. (1988). *Old loyalties, new ties: Therapeutic strategies with stepfamilies*. New York: Brunner/Mazel.

Vivian, D. (1991, May). *Gender sensitivity in couples' communication: A preliminary proposal for a global multilevel coding system*. Paper presented at the Indiana University Conference for Research on Clinical Problems—Marital Violence: Theoretical and Empirical Perspectives, Bloomington.

Vivian, D., & Heyman, R. (1994, November). *Aggression against wives: Mutual verbal combat "in context."* Paper presented at the annual meeting of the Association for Advancement of Behavior Therapy, San Diego, CA.

Walker, J. G., Johnson, S., Manion, I., & Cloutier, P. (1996). Emotionally focused marital intervention for couples with chronically ill children. *Journal of Consulting and Clinical Psychology, 64,* 1029–1036.

Walsh, F. (1998). *Strengthening family resilience*. New York: Guilford Press.

Walsh, F. (1999). Families in later life: Challenges and opportunities. In B. Carter & M. McGoldrick (Eds.), *The expanded family life cycle: Individual, family, and social perspectives* (3rd ed., pp. 307–326). Boston: Allyn & Bacon.

Watson, D., & Tellegen, A. (1985). Toward the structure of affect. *Psychological Bulletin, 98,* 219–235.

Watzlawick, P., Beavin, J. H., & Jackson, D. (1967). *Pragmatics of human communication*. New York: Norton.

Webster-Stratton, C., & Herbert, M. (1994). *Troubled families—Problem children: Working with parents: A collaborative process*. Chichester, England: Wiley.

Weiss, R. L. (1980). Strategic behavioral marital therapy: Toward a model for assessment and intervention. In J. P. Vincent (Ed.), *Advances in family intervention, assessment and theory* (Vol. 1, pp. 229–271). Greenwich, CT: JAI Press.

Weiss, R. L., & Birchler, G. R. (1978). Adults with marital dysfunction. In M. Hersen & A. S. Bellack (Eds.), *Behavior therapy in the psychiatric setting* (pp. 331–364). Baltimore: Williams & Wilkins.

Weiss, R. L., & Heyman, R. E. (1990a). Marital distress. In A. S. Bellack, M. Hersen, & A. E. Kazdin (Eds.), *International handbook of behavior modification and therapy* (2nd ed., pp. 475–501). New York: Plenum.

Weiss, R. L., & Heyman, R. E. (1990b). Observation of marital interaction. In F. D. Fincham & T. N. Bradbury (Eds.), *The psychology of marriage: Basic issues and applications* (pp. 87–117). New York: Guilford Press.

Weiss, R. L., & Heyman, R. E. (1997). A clinical–research overview of couples interactions. In W. K. Halford & H. J. Markman (Eds.), *Clinical handbook of marriage and couples interventions* (pp. 39–41). Chichester, England: Wiley.

Weiss, R. L., Hops, H., & Patterson, G. R. (1973). A framework for conceptualizing marital conflict, a technology for altering it, some data for evaluating it. In M. Hersen & A. S. Bellack (Eds.), *Behavior change: Methodology, concepts and practice* (pp. 309–342). Champaign, IL: Research Press.

Weiss, R. L., & Tolman, A. O. (1990). The Marital Interaction Coding System—Global (MICS–G): A global companion to the MICS. *Behavioral Assessment, 12,* 271–294.

White, L., & Edwards, J. N. (1993). Emptying the nest and parental well-being: An analysis of national panel data. *American Sociological Review, 55,* 235–242.

Wile, D. B. (1993). *After the fight: A night in the life of a couple.* New York: Guilford Press.

Willis, J. T. (1990). Some destructive elements of African American male–female relationships. *Family Therapy, 17,* 139–147.

Wills, T. A., Blechman, E. A., & McNamara, G. (1996). Family support, coping, and competence. In E. M. Hetherington & E. A. Blechman (Eds.), *Stress, coping, and resiliency in children and families* (pp. 107–133). Mahwah, NJ: Erlbaum.

Wills, T. A., Weiss, R. L., & Patterson, G. R. (1974). A behavioral analysis of the determinants of marital satisfaction. *Journal of Consulting and Clinical Psychology, 42,* 802–811.

Wilson, G. L., Bornstein, P. H., & Wilson, L. J. (1988). Treatment of relationship dysfunction: An empirical evaluation of group and conjoint behavioral marital therapy. *Journal of Consulting and Clinical Psychology, 56,* 929–931.

Winter, D. G. (1973). *The power motive.* New York: Free Press.

Winter, D. G., McClelland, D. C., & Stewart, A. J. (1982). *A new defense of the liberal arts.* San Francisco: Jossey-Bass.

Winter, D. G., Stewart, A. J., & McClelland, D. C. (1977). Husband's motives and wife's career level. *Journal of Personality and Social Psychology, 35,* 159–166.

Wood, B. L. (1995). A developmental biopsychosocial approach to the treatment of chronic illness in children and adolescents. In R. H. Mikesell, D. D. Lusterman, & S. H. McDaniel (Eds.), *Integrating family therapy: Handbook of family psychology and systems theory* (pp. 437–455). Washington, DC: American Psychological Association.

Wright, D. W., Nelson, B. S., & Georgen, K. E. (1994). Marital problems. In P. C. McKenry & S. J. Price (Eds.), *Families and change: Coping with stressful events* (pp. 40–65). Thousand Oaks, CA: Sage.

Young, J. E. (1990). *Cognitive therapy for personality disorders: A schema-focused approach.* Sarasota, FL: Professional Resource Exchange.

Young, J. E., Beck, A. T., & Weinberger, A. (1993). Depression. In D. H. Barlow (Ed.), *Clinical handbook of psychological disorders: A step-by-step treatment manual* (2nd ed., pp. 240–277). New York: Guilford Press.

Young, J. E., & Klosko, J. S. (1993). *Reinventing your life: How to break free from negative life patterns.* New York: Dutton.

AUTHOR INDEX

Feinstein, J. A., 112
Feldbau, S. R., 250
Felder, L., 498, 499
Fernandes, L. O. L., 361, 411
Figley, C. R., 189, 193
Fincham, F. D., 68, 69, 75, 76, 82, 96, 107, 157, 200, 226, 361, 411, 412
Finkelstein, M. A., 114
First, M. B., 257
Fiske, S. T., 148, 336
Fitzpatrick, M. A., 92
Fleming, B., 69, 162, 218, 226
Floyd, F. J., 249
Folkman, S., 175, 195, 203, 413
Follette, W. C., 29
Fraenkel, P., 442
Freeman, A., 196
Frieze, I. H., 118
Fruzzetti, A. E., 134, 445
Furstenberg, F., 46

Gano-Phillips, S., 76
Garnier, P. C., 76
Geiss, S. K., 50, 307
George, E. L., 450
Georgen, K. E., 170
Gibbon, M., 257
Giordano, J., 337
Girodo, M., 290
Glass, S. P., 141, 202, 468
Glick, S., 92
Goldenberg, H., 500
Goldenberg, I., 500
Goldman, A., 292
Goldstein, A. J., 138
Goldstein, A. P. 114
Goldstein, M. J., 134, 135, 450
Goldstine, D., 126, 360, 488
Goldstine, H., 126, 360, 488
Golombok, S., 223
Gordon, K. C., 14, 53, 71, 140, 141, 202, 221, 285, 466, 467, 470

Gotlib, I. H., 17, 52, 136, 184, 257, 445
Gottman, J. M., 27, 30, 38, 43, 52, 54, 59, 60, 80, 83, 84, 87, 88, 89, 95, 98, 100, 102, 107, 118, 135, 146, 147, 152, 202, 250, 251, 281, 339, 406, 408, 412, 417, 419, 422, 425
Grady-Fletcher, A., 287
Gray-Little, B., 39, 118

Greenberg, L. S., 11, 17, 55, 86, 89, 91, 141, 142, 154, 200, 287, 291, 292, 380, 415, 484
Greenstone, J. L., 196, 205
Griffin, W., 221
Gudykunst, W. B., 46

Guerney, B. G., Jr., 183, 308, 309, 430, 484

Haddock, S. A., 499, 500
Hahlweg, K., 29, 45, 92, 147, 202, 250, 291, 299
Halford, W. K., 14, 19, 27, 29, 45, 48, 49, 51, 75, 76, 92, 96, 133, 140, 287, 291, 292, 300, 400
Hamby, S. L., 39, 118, 220
Hamilton, D., 94, 95
Hammen, C., 115
Havercamp, S. M., 112, 114, 121
Haynes, S. N., 249
Hazan, C., 114, 115, 163, 200
Heavey, C. L., 13, 39, 54, 129, 135, 225, 251
Heffer, R. W., 217
Herbert, M., 360
Hertel, R. K., 196
Hessling, R. M., 19, 32
Hetherington, E. M., 86
Heyman, R. E., 14, 27, 28, 47, 94, 109, 146, 163, 165, 202, 247, 249, 250, 259, 270, 272, 361, 406, 412
Hill, R., 185, 186, 187, 199
Hines, P. M., 92, 116, 177, 189, 337
Hoffman, B. J., 112
Hokanson, J. E., 52
Holliday, S., 135
Hollon, S., 286
Holman, T. B., 182, 199, 200, 201
Holtzworth-Munroe, A., 68, 95, 201, 259, 271, 284
Hooley, J. M., 52, 134, 44
Hops, H., 165, 225, 304, 445
Horowitz, M. J., 77
Hosman, C., 183
Hotz, A. S., 82
Howes, M. J., 52
Hsu, J., 37
Huber, C. H., 276, 292
Hull, C. L., 108
Humphreys, K., 361, 411
Hutter, M., 135
Huston, T. L., 40, 117

SUBJECT INDEX

adaptation to, 494–496
grief response, 495
"Love days," 304

Macropatterns, 146–168
behavioral analyses neglect of, 146
behavioral coding system, 251
behavioral intervention, 299
and boundary permeability, 153–156
changes in, 165–168
communally-oriented need fulfillment, 151–165
couple teamwork versus individual initiative, 160–163
cross-sectional identification, 358–359
environmental demands interaction, 147, 170
individually-oriented need fulfillment, 151–165
in interpersonal demands, 188
joint interview assessment, 246
microlevel processes integration, 165–168
power need behaviors, 163–165
in primary distress, 428
and relationship themes, overview, 12–14, 146–147
subjectivity in identification of, 148–149
therapists' bias in identification of, 149
Marital Attitude Survey, 226
Marital Interaction Coding System, 249–251
Marital Satisfaction Inventory, 220–222
Marital Satisfaction Inventory-Revised, 221–222
Marital standards. See Standards, marital
Memory, emotions impact on, 95–96
Metaphors, emotional experience amplification, 387–389
Microbehaviors, 146–168
behavioral analysis focus, 146
changes in, 165–168
environmental demands interactions, 147, 169–170, 188
macrolevel processes integration, 165–168
overview, 12–14, 146–147
and power needs, 163–165
in problem solving, 162
Midlife stage, and motivational conflict, 127
"Mini-lectures"

and acceptance of partner, 429–430
gender role issues, 433
Mood states, and cognition, 95–97
Motives, 107–129
characteristics, 107–111
cognition in, 111
communally-oriented, 112–116, 120–129
definition, 15, 108
developmental factors, 126–128
emotion in, 110–111
and expectancies, 111
individual differences, 16–17
individual interview assessment, 257
individually-oriented, 112–129
in intimate relationships, 15–17, 107–129
joint interview assessment, 236–237
needs distinction, 108
overview, 15–17
parental influences, 109
and tailored interventions, 109
Mutual attack pattern. See also Negative reciprocity
definition, 404
interventions, 406–412
Mutual withdrawal pattern
definition, 404
interventions, 417–418

Need Fulfillment Inventory, 222–223
Needs, 107–129
individual differences, 16–17
and instrumental behavior, 36–37
in intimate relationships, 15–17, 107–129
and motives, 108
Negative affectivity, 82–84
couple relationship effects, 83–84, 98
individual differences, 82–83
longitudinal research, 17
stability, 82
as vulnerability factor, 200
Negative attribution, 68–69
Negative behavior, 47–63
apologies for, 423–424
coding systems, 249, 511
cognitive interventions, 339–340
couple relationship effects, 56–68
didactic skill-building approach, 280–282
editing response, 54–55

individual interview assessment, 258
joint interview assessment, 237
and subclinical dysfunction, 139–142
as vulnerability factor, 200
Physical abuse
individual interview assessment, 259–260
interpersonal traumatic effect, 52–53
joint interview assessment, 234–235
Positive affectivity, 82–83
Positive behavior, 28–47
coding systems, 249–251
cultural and contextual factors, 45–47
expressive aspects, 31–34, 44
focus of, 30
gender differences, 59–61
guided reinforcement, 304–306
instrumental form of, 34–40, 44
joint interview assessment, 234, 247
negative behavior balancing, 59–61
noncontingency benefits, 424
observational approach, 249–251
patterns of, 27–28
and reciprocity, 30–31
selective attention, 68
skill-building of, 280–282
social support function of, 32
stage perspective, 40–42
Positive emotions
categories of, 79–80, 330
couple discussion guidelines, 310
empirical investigations, 19
family contagion of, 101–102
and goal attainment, 110–111
impact on behavior, 99–102
impact on cognition, 94–97
maximization of, 11–12, 18–20
motives and needs link, 19–20
negative emotions relationship, 102–103
shifting balance of, 400–401
Positive reciprocity, 30–31, 99–102
Posttraumatic stress disorder, 471. See also Traumatic events
Power motive
behavioral patterns, 163–165
central goal of, 117
couples' relationship theme implications, 128–129
cultural factors, 118
in demand-withdraw pattern, 415
gender differences, 123

intervention issues, 163–165
intimacy needs balancing, 126
inventory assessment, 226–227
macropattern identification, biases, 148–149
and relationship expectancies, 111
withdrawal as manifestation of, 117–118
Premarital Relationship Enhancement Program (PREP), 60, 314
Primary appraisal, 203
Primary distress
causes of, 402
cross-situational patterns, 428
definition, 185, 404
guided behavior change, 302
inductive "downward-arrow" approach, 427–428
interventions, 426–440, 512–513
sequencing of, 513
macrolevel patterns, 428
Primary emotions, 89–90
accessibility, 379–380
functions, 378
therapeutic implications, 89–90, 328
Problem solving. See also Decision-making conversations
behavioral observations, 248–251
feedback to couple 265
as coping resource, 197–198
couple teamwork versus individual initiative, 160–163
factors in effectiveness of, 39
task-oriented concerns, 38–39
Psychoeducational interventions, 360–362
and acceptance of partner, 429–430
gender role issues, 433–434
and increased efficacy expectancies, 435–436
overview, 360–362
Psychological abuse, 259–260
Psychopathology, 133–139, 441–456. See also Depression
couples' relationship influences, 133–139, 442–445
overview, 17–18
couples therapy, 445
disorder-specific couples intervention, 444–445
guided behavior change, 306
individual interview assessment, 255–257

ABOUT THE AUTHORS

Norman B. Epstein is professor in the Department of Family Studies at the University of Maryland, College Park. He received his doctorate in clinical psychology from the University of California at Los Angeles in 1974. His teaching, research, and professional publications have been focused on understanding and treating dysfunction in couple and family relationships as well as on the relationship between individual psychopathology and relationship functioning. He has developed and evaluated cognitive–behavioral assessment and treatment procedures for distressed couples. In addition, he has conducted empirical studies of depression and anxiety within the family context, parent–child communication patterns, family stress and coping, and cognitive factors in marital and family dysfunction. Throughout his career, he has maintained a part-time clinical practice with individuals, couples, and families. He is a clinical member and an approved supervisor of the American Association for Marriage and Family Therapy, with 26 years of experience in training and supervising couples and family therapists. He is a Fellow of the American Psychological Association, a Diplomate of the American Board of Assessment Psychology, and a Founding Fellow of the Academy of Cognitive Therapy. Since the early 1980s, he and Donald H. Baucom have had a very productive collaboration and good friendship as they have worked to advance theory, research, and clinical practice in the area of couple relationships.

Donald H. Baucom is professor and director of clinical psychology in the Department of Psychology at The University of North Carolina at Chapel Hill. He received his doctorate in clinical psychology from that university in 1976. Since that time, he has pursued research on couples with a variety of emphases. He has conducted several investigations evaluating the efficacy of cognitive–behavioral couples therapy. He also conducts intervention research to prevent marital distress among newlyweds, as well as couple-based interventions for couples experiencing health problems. He has won several teaching awards, and he has held an endowed chair at the University of North Carolina. He is a member of the American Psychological Association, a Diplomate of the American Board of Assessment Psychology, and a Founding Fellow of the Academy of Cognitive Therapy. In addition to teaching graduate and undergraduate students, he presents frequent workshops and lectures to professional and lay audiences. He has been an active clinician throughout his career, working with both couples and individual adults. He and Norman B. Epstein began their research and writing collaboration in the early 1980s and have enjoyed decades of collaborative contributions to the empirical, theoretical, and clinical literatures, along with a valued friendship.